Seventeen Famous

OPERAS

SEVENTEEN

Famous Operas

BY

ERNEST NEWMAN

1955

ALFRED A. KNOPF

NEW YORK

782
N552SE

L. C. CATALOG CARD NUMBER: 54–7209

© ERNEST NEWMAN, 1954

THIS IS A BORZOI BOOK,
PUBLISHED BY ALFRED A. KNOPF, INC.

FIRST AMERICAN EDITION

TO

VERA

Prelude

THE GENERAL purpose of this book has been fully set forth in the "Overtures" to the two preceding volumes of the series of which it is a part, and there is no need to go over the ground again. I have mingled, however, rather more criticism with exposition in the present book, the justification for that procedure lying in the nature of some of the subjects. But in the main the general intention has been the same as before—to assist the reader to get more value out of his listening to the opera discussed, in particular the wireless listener, who often needs to be helped to visualise the stage action. I have constantly been astonished, when talking to seasoned opera-goers, to realise how little they really know of the drama of a given work.

I have forborne to add English translations to the first lines of the vocal themes I have quoted, preferring to give the reader a summary of them in the text. It is seldom that the first line of an English translation happens to correspond exactly with that of the original German, French or Italian text; for the translator has had to think not merely of the opening words of the melody but of the sense of the whole passage, and so he re-casts the opening line to suit his general scheme.

I hope no one will regard the various spellings of the same name—Basile and Basilio, Anna and Ana, Rodolphe and Rodolfo, and so on—as due to either lack of care or weakness of intellect on my part. My general principle has been to spell a character's name as it appears in the novel, play or opera under discussion at the moment.

I have to thank Messrs. Boosey and Hawkes for their permission to quote from the score of *Salome*, and Messrs. Ricordi and Company for a similar permission in the matter of the Puccini operas.

E. N.

Contents

Seventeen Famous

OPERAS

Salome

RICHARD STRAUSS [1864–1949]

PRINCIPAL CHARACTERS

HEROD	*Tenor*
HERODIAS	*Mezzo-soprano*
SALOME [1]	*Soprano*
JOCHANAAN (JOHN THE BAPTIST)	*Baritone*
NARRABOTH	*Tenor*
HERODIAS' PAGE	*Contralto*

1

HE SALOME story is told in substantially the same way in the 14th chapter of St. Matthew and the 6th of St. Mark. The Tetrarch had married Herodias, "his brother Philip's wife." Herodias, furious at John the Baptist's denunciation of the union, would have had him put to death; but Herod shrank from doing so for the reason, among others, that he "feared the multitude," which "counted him as a prophet"; so John was put in prison. On the Tetrarch's birthday the daughter of Herodias by her former marriage so pleased Herod with her dancing that he swore an oath that he would give her whatever she might ask of him, "even unto the half of my kingdom." At the prompting of Herodias she demanded the head of the Baptist on a charger; and when she received it "the damsel gave it to her mother." In the Gospels there is no mention of "Salome" by name; she is simply "the daughter of Herodias."

The story, with its rich dramatic and psychological possibilities, had been a favourite with artists from at least the time of Rubens. In the 1870's Flaubert made it the theme of a short story, extend-

[1] The accent is on the second of the four syllables of "Jochanaan." "Salome" is accented on the first syllable.

ing the range of the characters and developing the interest of the milieu. Oscar Wilde became interested in the subject in the mid-eighties, probably through some pictures by Gustave Moreau, for whom the story had long had a curious fascination, and the discussion of these in Huysmans' novel *À Rebours* (1884). In Flaubert the instigator of the execution of the Baptist was still Herodias. In Wilde's play the central dramatic action and the psychological motives are a reversal of those in the Gospel story. It is Salome herself who paves the way for her dance, playing cunningly on the Tetrarch's crazy passion for her; and Herodias, far from willing or wishing her to dance for him, for a while does all she can to deter her. All this and more will become clearer to the reader in our analysis of the opera.

Wilde, who was equally at home in French and English, wrote his play, in 1884, in the former tongue; and good as the English version by Lord Alfred Douglas mostly is it lacks much of the special quality of the original. In June 1892 the play got as far as rehearsal in London, only to have a licence for its production refused by the Lord Chamberlain's office. A German production in Breslau in the winter of 1901 was followed by others in several German towns. The drama soon attracted the attention of Richard Strauss, and when, at a performance of the work in Max Rein-hardt's Kleines Theater in Berlin, a friend remarked to him "This is a subject for you, Strauss," the composer could assure him that he was already engaged on the music for it. A Viennese poet, Anton Lindner, had sent him a copy of the play and offered to turn it into a "libretto" for him. But the specimens of his versification that Lindner sent him turned Strauss for a moment against the scheme; till one day the idea struck him, "Why not set Wilde's [prose] text very much as it stands?" As soon as he began to do so he realised how greatly superior, even as an opera text, Wilde's original was to anything in the conventional "libretto" line that Lindner or any other stage carpenter could fashion out of it. The subject took complete possession of him; and the score was finished on the 20th June 1905. A remark made by Strauss towards the end of his life seems to justify the surmise that he began by composing the Dance of the Seven Veils and the long closing scene, in which he follows the Wilde text practically word for word, whereas in the rest of the opera there are many excisions.

The Dance was certainly composed with an eye to separate publication and performance in the concert room, perhaps in the event of the opera never being completed or not proving a success. It is an obvious "inset" in the score, bearing a different plate mark from the latter. In the opera Strauss employed the usual numbers to indicate the bar groups for ease of identification in rehearsal. By the time the Dance was reached he had got as far as 247, and 248 does not appear until the Dance is over and the general stage action is resumed. The divisions in the Dance itself are indicated not by numbers but by letters.

2

Dresden was to undertake the first performance of the opera,[1] under Kapellmeister Ernst von Schuch, who had already been the first to give Strauss's *Feuersnot* and was later to have the credit of the premières of *Elektra* and *Der Rosenkavalier*. With the first piano rehearsal trouble began: singer after singer declared his or her part to be unsingable and wished to withdraw, until they were shamed into second thoughts on the matter by the declaration of the Herod (Burian) that he already knew his rôle by heart. Further difficulties arose in the course of rehearsals, the Salome (Frau Wittich) being so shocked by some of the producer's instructions that she cried out, "That I *won't* do; I am a respectable woman." But in spite of everything the opera was produced on the 9th December 1905, and though the wiseacres were confident that it would have a short life, as only one or two of the leading theatres could afford to produce a work calling for so large an orchestra and so many rehearsals, it quickly established itself in the German opera houses, notwithstanding the outcry of the puritans and the bigots everywhere. The clergy were loud in their denunciations of it; and as late as 1918 a proposed production in the Vienna Staatsoper had to be abandoned because of the opposition of an influential Austrian prelate who bore the perhaps not inapposite name of Archbishop Piffl. In New York the work was withdrawn after one performance at the instigation of "a certain Mr Morgan," as Strauss called him.[2]

[1] 9th December 1905.
[2] Strauss has given us an entertaining account of the early vicissitudes of the opera in his *Betrachtungen und Erinnerungen* (Zürich, 1949). The

5

The German operatic version of Wilde's text was made by Hedwig Lachmann, Strauss, we may take it for granted, indicating the cuts he desired. For the most part these are rational enough, consisting as they do merely of a condensation of Wilde's expansive and luxuriant imagery. This was necessary. For one thing, music generally moves at a more leisurely pace than speech; for another, the cumulative intensification achieved by the poet by a presentation of the same poetic image in varied forms can be done by music in a few pregnant bars; and for a third, the opera, like the play, had to be in one act, and there are limits to the concentration of which either singers or players or listeners are capable.

But the condensation, we feel, has occasionally been carried a little too far. Thus after one of the many attempts of the Page, in the opening scene, to bring reason into the Salome-infatuated mind of the young Syrian Narraboth, there comes, in Wilde, a fairly long discussion, by the two soldiers, "the Nubian" and "the Cappadocian," of the Tetrarch, Herodias, and the gods of various countries. The Nubian tells of the insatiable blood lust of the gods of his people; "twice in the year we sacrifice to them fifty young men and a hundred maidens; but I am afraid that we never give them quite enough, for they are very harsh to us." The Cappadocian fears that in his country there are no gods left: the Romans must have driven them out; the people seek for them in the mountains but cannot find them; they call them by name but they do not come. The soldiers say that the Jews "worship a God that one cannot see . . . in fact, they only believe in things that one cannot see. . . . That seems to me altogether ridiculous." It is *then* that the voice of Jokanaan is heard from the cistern, prophesying the coming of one mightier than himself: "when he cometh the solitary places shall be glad: they shall blossom as the rose. . . ." In the opera the appositeness of this cry from the

Kaiser sanctioned a production in Berlin only after the Intendant, his Excellency Georg Hülsen-Haeseler, had had the bright idea of bringing the star of Bethlehem into the sky at the finish, to signify the coming of the three Magi. Strauss has told us that the only opera of his ever attended by the Kaiser was *Der Rosenkavalier*, which the Crown Prince persuaded him to hear—once. The verdict of the royal and imperial mountebank on the work was, "Det is keene Musik für mich."

depths is weakened by the elimination of the preceding conversation between the soldiers, the Nubian and the Cappadocian; Jokanaan's annunciation of *the* new religion comes in quite unmotivated after the Page's despairing appeal to Narraboth, "You must not look at her: you look too much at her."

3

The strange thing is that a dramatist whose mind had no roots in music, and who had not the smallest notion of calling in music's co-operation when writing his play, should have constructed it on lines so very accommodating to music as was the case with Wilde and his *Salome*. He himself, in the *De Profundis* of his last years, made the curious observation that the "recurring *motifs*" of his *Salome* made the play "like a piece of music" and "bound it together as a ballad." By "*motifs*," of course, he does not mean what musicians do by that word; but in a way this remark of his goes to the heart of the matter; his method of insistent repetition not only of dramatic points but also of key phrases has been of cardinal assistance to Strauss in the designing of his musical pattern. Again, the lay-out of the play gave the composer all he could have desired in the way of tensions, relaxations and climaxes. There are three gradual ascents to a climax, each of these latter striking a more stunning blow than its predecessor. The first occurs when Salome conceives her morbid passion for the body of Jokanaan; in her great scena (as our fathers would have called it), for the first time in the opera music is given its head. The second occurs when Jokanaan, after his last opprobrious denunciation of Salome, goes down again into the cistern; this, following on the suicide of Narraboth, is, we instinctively sense, a turning-point of the drama. The third climax comes with the slow crescendo of horror that extends from Salome's cunningly engineered dance to the snapping of the last link of sanity in her brain. All this is of the very stuff that music needs for its own purposes; in each successive climax the composer unleashes more and more of the harmonic and orchestral resources of the art. He seizes unerringly on the smallest opportunity for this deployment of modern musical effect. In the section of Wilde's play that corresponds to the second of the two climaxes just mentioned, all we get is this:

Salome: I will kiss thy mouth, Jokanaan.
Jokanaan: I will not look at thee. Thou art accursed, Salome, thou art
    accursed. (*He goes down into the cistern.*)
Salome: I will kiss thy mouth, Jokanaan, I will kiss thy mouth.

There follow a few lines of everyday comment by the Soldiers
and a short lament of the little Page for his dear dead Narraboth;
then Herod and the others come up to the terrace from the
banqueting hall.

Our first feeling, on comparing the prose play with the opera
at this point, is one of regret that Strauss should have cut out the
pathetic little threnody of the Page over the body of Narraboth.
This lament is the last fine strand in a delicate minor motif that
has been weaving in and out of the tissue of the action from the
beginning; and we feel that music could have done so much with
it! Nevertheless Strauss was on the whole wise in keeping the
Narraboth-Page motif rather in the background throughout, and
more especially in denying himself the obvious opportunity for a
lament, in music's poignant vein, at the finish of it. Wilde's
laconic "He goes down into the cistern" becomes in the opera
the legitimate pretext for a purely orchestral interlude in which
Strauss plays, first furiously, then in a spirit of sinister foreboding,
upon the main motifs of Salome and Jochanaan, for nearly thirteen
pages of the score. At the end of it Herod and Herodias come upon
the scene, and the drama becomes vocal and visible again.

The outcry against *Salome* on the ground of its "morbidity,"
"perversity," "immorality" and what not came from people con-
stitutionally unable to distinguish between art and life. The
artistically minded man has no more fear as to the possible effects
of this "perversity" upon the everyday life of the ordinary citizen
than he has of an epidemic of lying and treachery after an evening
with Iago or a rise in the domestic murder statistics after a few
hours of Othello. Other poets before Oscar Wilde had shown us
what happens when the female mind, prone at times to perver-
sities of sexual emotion and hysteria, escapes for a while from the
ordinary restraints upon conduct imposed by social convention:
we have notable examples of the genre in *The Bacchae* of Eu-
ripides and the *Penthesilea* of Kleist. The poets have always been
ahead of the ordinary run of mankind in their intuitions, and in
the case of *Salome* all that Wilde did was to anticipate some of the

darker pages of the case books of the psychiatrists. He himself, in *The Critic as Artist* (1890), had rightly claimed the liberty of the modern artist to probe the darkest and socially most distasteful recesses of the human mind. ". . . There is still much to be done in the sphere of introspection," he makes his mouthpiece Gilbert say in the dialogue. "People sometimes say that fiction is getting too morbid. As far as psychology is concerned, it has never been morbid enough. We have merely touched the surface of the soul, that is all. In one single ivory cell of the brain there are stored away things more marvellous and more terrible than even they have dreamed of who, like the author of *Le Rouge et Le Noir*, have sought to track the soul into its most secret places, and to make life confess its dearest sins."

<h2 style="text-align:center">4</h2>

In most of the creations of art that really matter it is not so much a case of the great artist suddenly finding his subject as that of the subject finding him, and that at the right moment. His rôle, at first, has been passive rather than active: forces are at work within him of which he himself is unconscious at the time, or only vaguely conscious. It was so with Wagner when in 1857 he felt an irresistible inner compulsion to lay aside *Siegfried* and embark upon *Tristan*. The ultimate determining cause of this resolution was a vast fund of musical emotion that had been silently accumulating within him for a long time, and for which the saga-world of the *Ring* provided no psychological outlet. He himself has told us again and again that the conception of each of his works was primarily a musical one; the Wagnerian "text" which is still regarded by the generality as a "setting" of a "libretto" was only the objectivation of this vaguely *musical* mood in speech and stage action. By routes less clearly traceable many another musical work has similarly come into being, the subconscious musical urge preceding the reaching out into the world of the concrete. Strauss himself has told us how some of his songs, and those the best, came into being—not through the sudden impact of a poem that struck him as good raw material for a "setting," but through the chance falling into his hands one day of some poem or other that instantaneously crystallised a vague musical mood that had long been stirring dimly within him. He described the psychological process in a communication to Friedrich von Hausegger in 1903, *à propos* of his songs in general. For some time, he said, he would be without any impulse to compose. Then, one evening, he would be turning over the leaves of a volume of poetry; a poem would arrest his attention, he would read it through, it would chime with the mood he was in, and at once the music would fit itself to the words. He had been in an indefinite musical mood, and all that had hitherto been lacking to him for the creation of a song was a poem that would give this mood verbal definition. When this process was in ideal working order a good song resulted: when the process was reversed, or when the poem turned out to be not wholly consubstantial with the mood, he had to call consciously upon the devices of his craft as a substitute for the subconscious urge, and then the results were less good: the song, he himself knew, was made, not born. There are other routes, of course, by which this composer or that may reach the point at which the musical and the verbal impulses within him become fused into one. But the route here outlined is one made familiar to us by all the great modern musicians: the whole, however dimly sensed at first, has preceded the parts. In Pascal's memorable phrase, "You would not have sought me had you not already found me."

Strauss has told us, *à propos* of the genesis of *Salome*, that for a long time he had been dissatisfied with the current operas on Jewish or Oriental subjects, feeling that they were lacking in true eastern colour and fire. In the case of *Salome*, he said, sheer necessity imposed an exotic harmony on him, finding expression more particularly in strange cadences resembling shot silk; at the same time the need for sharp distinctions in character-painting led him to bi-tonality, for it was impossible for him to be satisfied with the simple rhythmical characterisation with which Mozart had achieved such wonders. He recognized, however, that a work like *Salome* was a once-for-all experiment, generated and determined by a particular subject and consequently not to be recommended for imitation by either himself or any one else. He himself was just ripe for such an experiment in 1905. Between 1888 and 1898 he had produced the majority of the orchestral works on which his reputation in this field now reposes—*Don*

Juan, Macbeth, Till Eulenspiegel's Merry Pranks, Also sprach Zarathustra, Don Quixote and *Ein Heldenleben.* (The *Symphonia Domestica* of 1903 already marked a decline in inspiration.) In these remarkable works, and especially in *Don Quixote* and *Ein Heldenleben*, he had endowed the symphonic poem with a new vision and a new language. With opera he had not been so successful. There is a great deal in the high-minded *Guntram* of 1892–1893—written when he was about twenty-eight—that will always command the respect of the thoughtful; but spiritually and musically the work floated mostly in the Wagnerian waters. The *Feuersnot* of 1900–1901 showed him still not in full command of his powers in opera. It was in *Salome* that for the first time he could utilise for dramatic purposes the riches he had mined for himself in the great series of orchestral works, and, indeed, add to them. He was still not wholly at his ease: he could not quite transport himself into such a character as Jochanaan or bring a Herod always to musical life; [1] but Salome herself is a unique creation, and the orchestra performs miracles of characterisation and pictorial suggestion throughout.

5

The opera is scored for a very large orchestra, that includes six horns, four trumpets, four trombones and bass tuba, five kettledrums, an E flat clarinet, a bass clarinet, a celesta, a heckelphone,[2] an organ, a harmonium and a large array of percussion

---

[1] Strauss as a musical psychologist was most at home with characters either emotionally complex or super-charged—such as Salome, Elektra, the Marschallin, Don Juan—or with a bizarre kink in them, such as Till Eulenspiegel, Don Quixote and Sancho Panza. With characters on a normal plane he was less at ease; his Chrysothemis is a good example of this. He could respect his Jochanaan, but could not depict him with perfect understanding or perhaps with complete sympathy. He had a similar difficulty with the virtuous hero of *The Legend of Joseph.* "*Joseph* is not getting on as quickly as I thought it would," he wrote plaintively to his librettist Hofmannsthal in September 1912. "The chaste Joseph himself is hardly in my line, and I find it difficult to write music for a character that bores me; a God-fearing Joseph like this I find infernally hard to tackle. However, I may yet find lurking in some queer ancestral corner of my nature some pious melody that will do for our good Joseph."

[2] A baritone oboe, sounding an octave lower than written, invented by the

instruments. The string specification is for sixteen first violins, sixteen seconds, ten or twelve violas, ten violoncellos and eight double basses. Strauss, however, did not always insist on this huge apparatus, and he tells us of a good performance he heard of the work in Innsbruck with an orchestra of no more than fifty-six.

Singers and producers would do well to ponder what the composer has to say about the right way to perform *Salome*. He disliked the over-emphasis in which most players of the part of Salome think it the correct thing to indulge: what he had seen and heard in the way of Salome writhings and mouthings in a misguided effort to be "exotic" filled him with disgust. "Anyone who has been in the East," he said, "and observed the decency of the women there, will realise that the part of Salome, a chaste maiden, an oriental princess, should be played with gestures of the simplest, most distinguished kind. . . . Her shipwreck on her first contact with the marvellous external world should stir us to pity, not merely to horror and terror." Our Salomes might take this admonition to heart; the Dance of the Seven Veils in particular should not suggest to us, as it too often does, merely the Dance of the Seven Dials. Producers and stage designers and costumiers too should give up the notion that the opera is there simply as an exhibition ground for their own vulgarities and inanities of "effect." All that is required in the way of fury, pathological passion, perversity and madness, Strauss contended, is in the orchestra. It is quite unnecessary, even if it were at all possible, to duplicate all this on the stage. "The acting of the characters should aim at *the utmost simplicity*," he said; the player of the neurasthenic Herod in particular should bear in mind that even in his moments of wildest aberration the oriental parvenu in him makes him try, before his Roman guests, to copy the dignified bearing of great Caesar in Rome. "To rage and rave simultaneously on the stage and in front of the stage is really too much! The orchestra does all that is necessary in that respect!"

There are many recurrent themes in the opera, but they are not used as motifs in the Wagnerian sense of that term; they do not

German instrument maker Heckel in the late 1880's. It has not succeeded in establishing itself in the ordinary orchestra. Strauss must have been one of the first composers to employ it.

change with the changing psychology and experiences of the characters, but remain essentially the same throughout. Each of them, of course, is characteristic of this person or that, and some of them manifestly have a particular psychological application; but it is frequently impossible for us to say whether a given motif used on a particular occasion refers to, say, Salome, or Jochanaan, or Jochanaan seen just then through the eyes of Salome, or Salome seen just then through the eyes of Jochanaan. Broadly speaking, Strauss employs whichever of his many motifs will best suit his general musical purpose at this moment or that. Quotation on the small scale possible in a book like this is difficult; it would often mean not only an elaborate exposition of the complex harmonies but citation in full score, showing the effects produced by the disposition of the orchestral colours. The most the analyst can do is to provide the reader with a few of the more characteristic motifs to keep in his mind as he listens to a performance; but he must remember that none of the passages quoted here have anything like the same sound or the same psychological nuance on his piano as they have in Strauss's orchestra. These quotations have about the same relation to the total tone-complex as a bone or two of a skeleton has to the living man.

6

As in the case of *Elektra,* there is no overture to the opera. There is merely a swift upward run in a clarinet:

No. 1

which at A takes a shape associated in various ways with Salome later; and the curtain rises disclosing a broad terrace in Herod's palace. On the right there is a great staircase, and towards the background, somewhat to the left, an old cistern encased in green bronze. Some soldiers are leaning over the balcony of the terrace. This latter is supposed to be set above the banqueting hall, where, as we shall learn shortly, the upstart Herod Antipas, Tetrarch of

13

Judaea, is entertaining at dinner some envoys of the mighty Roman Caesar with whom he is anxious to ingratiate himself. In the company also are a number of Jewish zealots who from time to time quarrel violently over sectarian points of doctrine. It is night. Over the terrace the moon shines very brightly.

In the foreground stands a young Syrian, Narraboth, whom Herod has only lately appointed captain of the guard, and a little Page of Herodias, who has a dog-like affection for him. Narraboth's gaze is fixed on the banqueting hall, for he is in love with Salome. "How beautiful is the Princess Salome tonight!" he says: and we hear in the 'cellos a motif characterising his longing:

No. 2

molto espressivo

Towards the end of it (bars three and four of our quotation) the bass clarinet strikes in with sombre foreboding. The Page senses something eerie in the air: "Look at the moon's disc," he says; "how strange it looks! It is like a dead woman rising from a tomb." For the infatuated Narraboth it carries a different suggestion: "It is indeed strange: it is like a little princess who has white doves for feet: one might fancy she was dancing." In his enraptured eyes the white moon and the exquisite maidenhood of the little Salome are always one.[1]

7

Suddenly, as the tempo quickens, a horrid orchestral dissonance rends the air, while from the banqueting hall comes a confused uproar; the Jews have lost their tempers and the rival sects are

[1] The character of Salome becomes utterly nonsensical when it is played by a buxom, hard-bitten soprano in the prime of life. The composer, of course, has asked, as composers so often do, for the impossible—"a sixteen-years-old princess with an Isolde voice," as Strauss has expressed it, that can cut through or soar above the heaviest orchestration. But the spectator should try, in spite of all optical discouragements, to see the daughter of Herodias as little more than a child, as yet ignorant of the complex realities of the world.

trying to shout each other down. Oboes and strings snarl and snap at one another:

No. 3

The double bassoon angrily lays down the law, while the double basses insist on their own doctrine:

No. 4

Strauss's direction for the double bass figure (bar 2) each time it recurs is "howling." So the snapping and bellowing and screeching goes on all over the orchestra; we shall hear more of it at a later stage of the drama. The soldiers comment on it all with cynical detachment: "What a din! Who are these howling wild beasts? . . . It's the Jews; they are always like this, quarrelling over their religion. . . . I think it is ridiculous to wrangle about such things." [1]

Regardless of the tumult within, the infatuated Narraboth, who has never taken his eyes off Salome, breaks into a lyrical strain in praise of her beauty:

No. 5

The Page's fears of what is in the air are rising; to a phrase that is often repeated:

[1] Wilde's text specifies the main doctrinal point at issue: "The Pharisees say that there are angels, and the Sadducees declare that angels do not exist."

No. 6

Du siehst sie im—mer an

he warns the Syrian that it is dangerous to look at Salome so much. But Narraboth merely continues his rhapsody: never has he seen her so pale, he says; she is like the shadow of a white rose in a silver mirror; and once more the anxious little Page warns him that no good can come of this infatuation of his. Meanwhile the Soldiers discuss Herod. He is gloomy tonight, they say; his eyes are fixed on someone, but they cannot see whom. No. 1 in the smooth tones of the clarinet tells us who it is.

As the Page again (No. 6) expresses his anxiety about Narraboth the mood of the music suddenly softens and broadens, and from the cistern the grave voice of Jochanaan is heard, calmly prophesying the coming of One mightier than himself, the latchet of whose shoes he is unworthy to unloose; when He comes the desert places shall be glad and blossom like the rose, the eyes of the blind shall see, the ears of the deaf shall hear. As we have seen, Strauss and his librettist go straight to this point, omitting the discussion by the soldiers, a Nubian and a Cappadocian, of the gods of this country and that. Various themes are allotted to Jochanaan, such as:

No. 7

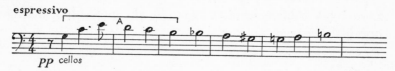

which often broadens out into the following and cognate forms:

No. 8

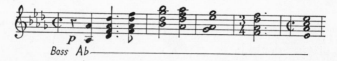

Other themes associated with him will be referred to later. They are not motifs in the fullest sense of the word, for such modifica-

16

tions as they are subjected to from time to time are not dictated
by any inner change in him, any new reaction to his environment.
He is a static character—a personality indeed, but one playing
only a passive part in the dramatic action that envelops him. He is
ultimately of importance not so much in himself as in the medley
of emotions he arouses in the soul of Salome.

One of the Soldiers is for silencing him, for he is weary of this
railing fanatic. But the other has a tender feeling for him: he is a
Prophet named Jochanaan, he explains, a gentle being, who thanks
the Soldier each day when he takes him his food. He comes from
the desert, where he was clothed in camels' hair, fed on locusts
and wild honey, and had a band of disciples: the Soldier confesses, however, that no one can understand the things he says.[1]
The Tetrarch will allow no one to see him. (It is Salome's insistence on seeing him—the insistence of a spoiled child—that
generates the whole tragic action of the play and of the opera.)

8

Since the entry of the voice of Jochanaan the music has been
subdued in tone and colour. It now suddenly flares up again as
the clarinets give out No. 1 once more, and Narraboth, whose
eyes have never left the banqueting hall, cries out that the Princess
has risen from her seat at the table: she is very agitated; now she
is coming out, looking like a dove that has strayed. (Always the
poet's imagery insists on her whiteness, her fragility, the suggestion she conveys of belonging to another and less crudely material
world.) No. 1 sings out yet again in an expanded form in oboes
and violins:

No. 9

[1] In the play we learn much more about the matter from the conversation
of the Soldiers and an enquiring Cappadocian at this point. In this very
cistern the Tetrarch's elder brother, the first husband of Herodias, had been
imprisoned for twelve years: then Herod sent the death ring to the executioner—a gigantic negro, Naaman, standing on one side of the stage—who
strangled the prisoner. No doubt Strauss, for reasons of time-economy, had

as Salome enters hurriedly. When she begins to speak she is not addressing the people on the terrace but communing with herself. She could no longer endure the banquet, she says. Why does the Tetrarch, her mother's husband, keep looking at her so strangely with those little eyes of his that are like a mole's eyes under their twitching lids? How sweet the air is out here! Here she can breathe! and the violins, doubled by the silvery tones of the celesta, give out a suave melody that will become of great importance later:

No. 10

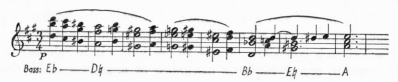

She can stand no more of those Jews from Jerusalem, who tear each other to pieces over their ridiculous observances—here the cackling No. 3 is heard again in the orchestra—or the silent, subtle Egyptians, or the brutal, boorish Romans with their uncouth speech. "How I hate these Romans! How good it is to gaze into the moon, that is like a silver flower, cold and chaste, beautiful as a virgin unspotted!" At one point in her monologue the Page once more addresses an anxious admonition to the Syrian—"Why do you look at her so? Something terrible will happen!"

With a sudden change of key and a slowing of the tempo the deep voice of Jochanaan rings out again from the cistern: "Behold the Lord hath come. The Son of Man is at hand." It rouses Salome from her brooding. "Who was that who cried out?" she asks. "The Prophet," the second Soldier tells her. "Ah!" she says, "he of whom the Tetrarch goes in fear." Narraboth steps forward and asks if he may send for her litter, for the night is fair in the garden. She does not hear him. "He says terrible things about my mother, does he not?" she asks. The Soldier answers evasively;

---

to omit all this, but it is not only of importance to our understanding of the action but has a peculiar significance later, when the dazed Tetrarch, yielding to the importunities of Salome, passively allows Herodias to draw the death ring from his finger and transmit it to the executioner.

and just then a slave enters with a command to her from Herod to return to the banquet. She brushes him aside with a blunt refusal, then asks the Soldier, "Is this Prophet an old man?" Narraboth, sensing evil in the air, urgently begs her to allow him to conduct her back to the hall; but she ignores him, and with a rise of tone asks once more if this Prophet is an old man. No, she is told, he is quite young. Once more the grave voice is heard from the cistern, bidding the land of Palestine not to rejoice because the rod of him who smote it is broken; for from the seed of the serpent will come a basilisk, and its brood will devour the birds.

9

The strangeness of the voice and the enigma of its message impress Salome: she would speak with this man, she says. The second Soldier, in great agitation, tells her that the Tetrarch has commanded that no one, not even the High Priest, shall speak with him. Her only reply is, "I will speak with him! Bring this Prophet forth!" The slave who had brought the message from Herod returns to the hall. The embarrassed Soldiers try to turn Salome from her purpose, but she is inflexible. She goes over to the cistern and peers down into its recesses. The orchestra depicts for us, in a way that no words can do, the horror of what she sees. A prolonged unison tremolo on E flat in the strings, playing *sul ponticello,* is full of grisly suggestion; underneath it some chords in the lower brass suggest the very depths of darkness, and a sombre phrase projects itself serpent-wise in the bass clarinet as Salome says to herself, "How black it is down there! It must be terrible to live in so black a hole! It is like a tomb!" Then she turns upon the Soldiers, and, with mounting anger at being frustrated, again commands them to bring the Prophet out that she may look at him. They dare not, they tell her. In Wilde's play they add a significant line and there is a stage direction both of which Strauss and his librettist unaccountably ignore: "and indeed," they say, "it is not of us that you should ask this thing," whereupon Salome, ejaculating "Ah!", looks meaningly at the young Syrian, of whose infatuation with her she is evidently aware. The little Page, acutely sensitive to what is coming, moans "Oh! what is going to happen? I know that something terrible will happen!" It is a pity that throughout this opening scene of the opera this motive of the Page's love for the Syrian and his apprehensiveness on his account go for practically nothing with the average audience, whereas it should all contribute to the gradual building up of the horror that has been stealing over the action from the commencement.

To the accompaniment of No. 9 Salome now approaches Narraboth and begins to weave her spells about him. He will do this for her, she tells him in cajoling tones, for she has always been kind to him. She wants nothing more than just to see this Prophet of whom she has heard so much, among others from the Tetrarch, who appears to be afraid of him. With increasing distress Narraboth protests that the Tetrarch has forbidden that anyone shall raise the cover of the cistern, and he dare not disobey. With the artfulness of a spoilt child she plays on what she has divined to be his weakness: if he will do just this one thing for her now, tomorrow when she passes him in her litter she will throw him a little flower and smile at him through her muslin veils. "Look at me, Narraboth. Thou knowest that thou wilt do this that I ask of thee."

At last his resolution breaks down: he makes a sign to the soldiers and gives the curt command—"Let the Prophet come forth. The Princess Salome desires to see him." There is a terrifying crescendo and diminuendo in the orchestra, and a triumphant cry of "Ah!" from Salome.

10

The third Soldier goes down into the cistern, and necessarily there has to follow now a brief interval in the stage action before Jochanaan appears, an interval that should contain something that will make it clear to us that the first decisive moment of the drama has arrived, and that it is pregnant with disaster. The poet and the musician achieve this in different ways. Wilde does it through the Page, the young Syrian—and the moon. This last is almost a character in the work, certainly a symbol, and the ordinary opera producer does not sufficiently avail himself of the opportunities with which it provides him; perhaps he has never comprehended them. The aspect of the moon changes with the psychological changes in the drama. As we have seen, it figures at the opening as the symbol of super-terrestrial whiteness and purity, an aspect of it which both Narraboth and the Page instinctively associate with the young Salome they have so far known. But now, when the action takes on a definitely darker tinge, the face of the moon changes, and the Page and Narraboth are nervously sensitive to it. "How strange the moon looks!" says the former; "like the hand of a dead woman who is seeking to cover herself with a shroud." "She has a strange aspect," Narraboth agrees, with his dazed mind still running on Salome: "she is like a little princess whose eyes are of amber. Through the clouds of muslin she is smiling like a little princess." Then the Prophet comes out of the cistern. All this in only a matter of a minute or two in the play.

But the musician has other and far greater resources at his disposal for a situation of this kind than the poet. He can rack our nerves with orchestral effects that are beyond the capacity of words; and music, by its reiterations of motifs and metamorphoses of them, can set our imagination looking before and after in a way that spoken drama cannot do, though the great Greek tragedians —notably Aeschylus in the *Agamemnon*—divined something of the secret of this technique of reminiscence and foreboding in drama, and made fine use of it.[1] To fill in the time and space between the departure of the Soldier and the appearance of Jochanaan, Strauss writes an orchestral interlude, the characters on the stage being immobilised for a while in tense expectancy. The sinister depths of the cistern are once more brought almost visibly before us. One of the Jochanaan motifs (No. 7A) appears in a relatively new form:

[1] They were helped, of course, by the fact that their drama dealt with myths and legends the details of which were known to their audiences, so that a seemingly-casual remark made by a character in the earlier stages of a play would instantly flash upon the spectator's mind the tragic dénouement of the story, and vice versa. The opening speech of the Watchman in the *Agamemnon* is a case in point. Half in hope, half in dim fear, he is waiting, as he has done for a year, for the beacon light that will announce the fall of Troy and the home-coming of Agamemnon. The Greek audience, knowing the tragic end of the great King, would fill with a more definite and more tragic meaning that vague suggestion of fear in the Watchman.

No. 11

Salome too has a new theme that will play a large part in the later stages of the opera:

No. 12

and as Jochanaan at last comes up into view we hear over a string tremolo a new motif in oboes, cor anglais, heckelphone and flutes in octaves, expressive of his sense of the dignity of his mission:

No. 13

11

Salome recoils at the sight of him. He comes slowly forward to the melody first suggested in our No. 7, with which the dignified No. 13 soon becomes interlocked. With a new vehemence he denounces both Herod and Herodias, especially the latter, whose abominations cry out to heaven for chastisement. It gradually dawns on Salome that it is her mother of whom he is speaking. "He is terrible, he is truly terrible!" she murmurs, while the clarinets and a solo violin sing softly a melody that will figure largely in the score henceforth:

No. 14

It suggests the curious interest already inspired in her by this Prophet of retribution, the strange fascination he is beginning to exercise over her. His fanatical eyes are especially terrible; to Salome they look like "the black caverns that are the lair of dragons, black lakes played upon fantastically by the light of the moon." And how emaciated and blanched he is! Her thoughts begin to take on a pathologically sensual tinge: "He is like an ivory statue. Surely he is as chaste as the moon! His flesh must be very cold, cold as ivory! I would look closer at him!"

She pays no heed to the young Syrian's despairing entreaties that she will come away. Jochanaan's attention now becomes fixed on her. Who is this woman, he asks, with golden eyes under gilded eyelids? He does not know who she is. He will not know who she is. Let her begone. "I am Salome, daughter of Herodias, Princess of Judaea," she tells him, to the accompaniment of the motif shown in No. 9. To his renewed objurgations of her mother she merely replies, "Speak again, Jochanaan! Thy voice is as music in mine ear. Tell me what it is I must do." He bids her veil her face and scatter ashes on her head and go into the desert seeking the Son of Man. The meaning of his words evades her. "Who is this Son of Man?" she asks him; "is he as beautiful as thou art?" Again he warns her that he can hear within the palace the beating of the wings of the angel of death.[1]

But Salome is now completely dominated by her perverse passion. For the first time in the opera music is given its full wing; Strauss launches Salome upon a long lyrical scena in which she indulges herself in every variety of sensual image in praise of this strange wasted figure: "Thy body is as white as lilies in a field the mower has never mowed, white as the snows on the mountains of Judaea, whiter than the roses in the garden of the Queen of Arabia, than the feet of the dawn on the leaves, than the breast of the moon reposing on the sea. Suffer me to touch thy body!"

Salome sings the opening words of her long monologue—"Jochanaan, I am amorous of thy body"—to the accompaniment of the ingratiating No. 14 in a solo violin and clarinet: it merges, at the words "Thy body is as white as the snows on the mountains

[1] "Though the day of him [Herod] who shall die in a robe of silver has not yet come," the play adds. Strauss does not set this line.

of Judaea," into a motif which had better be quoted here in the more extended form it will assume towards the end of the opera:

No. 15

At "Suffer me to touch thy body" we come upon one of those many motifs of the precise application of which we cannot be sure. Obviously derived, in part, from our No. 7, it now steals softly upwards (the marking is "espressivo") in the bassoons and 'cellos:

No. 16

Strauss uses it indifferently to accompany now Salome now Jochanaan.

He repulses her with contumely: through woman came evil into the world: he will not listen to her: he will hearken only to the voice of his God. (Here No. 8 rises majestically in the orchestra.) In an instant her mood changes; now she sees him only as foul and abhorrent. His body is hideous, she declares, as hideous as the body of a leper: it is like a plastered wall in which scorpions have made their nest, like a whited sepulchre full of loathsome things. Graphically suggestive of the transition in her from fascination to repulsion is a harmonic and colouristic transformation of the insinuating No. 14 A:

No. 17

The motif is given to the violins playing "col legno,"[1] while the muted violas slither down eerily in two-part harmonies—"like a smear" is Strauss's prescription in the score.

Salome's mood softens again. It is his hair of which she is enamoured, she declares, to the accompaniment of No. 9. It is like clusters of black grapes on the vine-trees of Edom, like the great cedars of Lebanon in whose shade the lions lie and robbers hide; the long dark nights when the moon hides her face are not so black as his hair, nor the forest silence, nor anything in the world. This rhapsody she sings to the motif shown in our No. 10.

Jochanaan, to a combination of one of Salome's motifs (No. 1 A) and one of his own (No. 7 A), bids this "daughter of Sodom" leave him and not profane the temple of his God. This provokes another revulsion in her. His hair is now horrible to her, a mass of dust and mire, like a crown of thorns on his head, a knot of serpents round his neck. With mounting frenzy she tells him, to the accompaniment of a new motif:

No. 18

that it is his mouth she desires, his mouth that is like a scarlet band on a tower of ivory, a pomegranate cut in twain with an ivory knife, and so on, pouring out a flood of images each more

[1] I.e. with the wood, not the hair, of the bow striking the strings. The effect is necessarily peculiar.

corruptly rapturous than the others, while the music lashes itself into a tempest of passion. "Nothing in the world," she concludes, "is as red as thy mouth. Suffer me to kiss thy mouth!"

Again he repulses and objurgates this "daughter of lewdness," but is impotent to check the torrent. The distracted Narraboth, who has been watching her with horror, also tries to recall her to reason, but him too she ignores. At last, tragically aware of the consequences of having disobeyed the orders of the Tetrarch, he can bear it no more: he stabs himself and falls dead between Salome and Jochanaan.[1] The latter exhorts Salome to turn to Him who alone can save her: He is to be found in a boat on the Sea of Galilee, talking with His disciples; she is to kneel at His feet and ask for remission of her sins.

12

The final stage of Salome's great scena is marked by repetition after repetition, with ever-increasing frenzy, of the words "I will kiss thy mouth, Jochanaan!" to a motif that will dominate the last moments of the drama:

No. 19

Hurling a final curse at Salome and her mother, Jochanaan goes down again into the cistern to the accompaniment of the majestic

---

[1] In the play, as we have seen, there follows here a passionate lament by the Page for his dead friend. Strauss omitted this, no doubt for the reasons, among others, that it would have meant the addition of another leading singer to the cast, and too long an interruption of the main stage action: it would certainly have been difficult for the composer to chain the fury of his music at this point and then, after the lapse of some minutes, unleash it again. But Wilde, from the dramatist's no less than from the poet's point of view, was right. The audience should be made to realise, as in the play, that the death of Narraboth signalises the beginning of the catastrophe that has been overhanging the action from the commencement. In the opera the suicide goes for practically nothing; it is doubtful, indeed, whether the average spectator so much as notices it, for his attention is likely to be concentrated just then on Salome and her final frantic cry of "Suffer me to kiss thy mouth, Jochanaan!"

No. 13; and Strauss seizes the opportunity, before the entry of the other characters on the scene, to give his orchestra its head once more, the stage action being immobilized for a few minutes. This incandescent interlude is built up of repetitions and contrapuntal combinations of several motifs now familiar to us, in particular Nos. 8, 11, 13, 14, 15 and 19. At last the music dies down into a long shuddering tremolando in the strings, which leads in time into a sudden outburst of the cackling, snarling No. 3 in the wood wind and violins; for now Herod and Herodias and their company have come upon the scene—including the Jews, who are straining at the leash for an excuse for resuming their cantankerous religious debate. That excuse will soon come, owing to an injudicious remark let fall by the Tetrarch.

Herod is a neurasthenic, beset by fears of all kinds, and just now flown with wine: his indecision is curiously suggested by a succession of slithering whole-tone progressions in one instrument after another, including even the bass tuba:

No. 20

He has come primarily to look for Salome. Where is she? he asks; why did she not return to the banquet as he had commanded? He catches sight of her, but immediately forgets her, for now he is out under the night sky he is neurotically conscious of something sinister in the air. The moon, he finds, has a strange look, "like a naked mad woman seeking everywhere for lovers." Herodias, drily, contemptuously, informs him that the moon is as it always is, just the moon. She would have him go back to the banqueting hall; she particularly resents his looking at Salome as he does. But he orders torches to be brought out, and tables of jasper and tables of ivory; he will drink again in honour of Caesar's ambassadors. He stumbles, finds he has slipped on blood—"an ill omen" —and sees the body of the captain of the guard. How did this happen? he asks querulously; "I gave no orders that he should be slain." The Soldiers tell him of Narraboth's suicide, and he orders the body to be taken away. Suddenly he feels cold; there is a great wind blowing, he insists—as indeed there is in the orchestra—and he hears the beating of mighty wings, a remark to which a fateful significance is given by a quiet upsurge of the Prophet's motif (No. 13) in horns, cor anglais and heckelphone.

He denies that he is sick, as Herodias says: it is her daughter who is sick to death; never has he seen her look so pale. Now his whole thought becomes concentrated on Salome. So far the music allotted to him has been of the declamatory kind, the orchestra supplying the atmosphere of the scene; in general, indeed, the part calls for a great actor rather than an accomplished singer. But now, his wine-cup having been replenished, he becomes for a while fluently lyrical after his fashion as he urges Salome to drink with him:

No. 21

Sa — lo-me, komm, trink Wein — mit mir.

"I am not thirsty, Tetrarch," she mutters in low, sombre tones. He tempts her with fruit; he would like to see her little white teeth biting into it; and a curious figure:

No. 22

glides in and out in the violins (in octaves) and wood wind. (It will take on a horrible suggestiveness towards the end of the opera, where Salome, with the severed head before her, gloats over the idea of at last kissing the mouth of Jochanaan as if she were "biting into a ripe fruit.") "I am not hungry, Tetrarch," she replies quietly. He renews his entreaties; she must sit beside him; he will place her on her mother's throne. "I am not tired, Tetrarch," is her only reply.

13

From the depths of the cistern comes the voice of the Prophet, announcing that the day he had foretold is at last at hand. Hero-

dias angrily asks Herod to silence this scurrilous fanatic: why
does he not hand him over to the Jews, who for months have been
clamouring to have him thrown to them? Herod refuses, for this,
he says, "is a holy man; he is a man who has seen God." This
rouses a tempest among the Jews. No one has seen God since
Elias, shouts one. Perhaps, another replies, Elias did not really
see God, but only His shadow. In a moment the rival sects and
zealots are at each other's throats again, with No. 3 in the forefront of the fray. Strauss builds up a long ensemble that is an
astonishing musical *tour de force*. Dogma is flung in the teeth of
dogma, tempers rise, and when the voice of Jochanaan adds fuel
to the fire by proclaiming that he hears upon the mountains the
feet of Him who shall be the Saviour of the world, and a Roman
opines that this must mean Caesar, and some Nazarenes contend
that it means "Messias, who hath come" and who has performed
miracles in Galilee and is now in Samaria, and the Jews protest
that if He is in Samaria He cannot be Messias, for it is not to the
accursed Samaritans that Messias shall come, the theological pot
boils over.

The turmoil is gradually dominated by the voice of Jochanaan
heaping fresh curses from the cistern on Herodias and prophesying a fearful end for her. Herodias, whose demeanour since the
beginning of the scene has been for the most part one of dry
detachment, for she feels an equal contempt for this drunken
husband of hers who was once a camel-driver, for the Romans,
and for the Jews, now begins to lose her self-control under this
stream of abuse. When the time arrives to act it will find her
ready, and it is drawing inexorably nearer. Herod is now obsessed
by the desire to have Salome dance for him: if she will, he will
give her whatever she may ask of him. Hitherto she has been so
sunk in her morbid broodings over Jochanaan that she has hardly
noticed Herod; now for the first time she becomes interested in
him and his importunities. Herodias, who has all along been irritated by the Tetrarch's unnatural interest in her daughter, urges
her not to listen to him. But Salome, now beginning to see her
way clear before her, plays cunningly upon the drunken neurotic.
She requires him to confirm his promise with an oath. He does so;
but in the middle of his feverish appeal to her he shivers, for once
more a great chill wind seems to him to sweep across the scene;

"it is as if a huge black bird were hovering over the terrace," he says with a shudder; and once more we hear the threatening Jochanaan motif (No. 13), this time in a suitable and sinister metamorphosis. "Why cannot I see it, this bird?" he asks, "this beating of wings is terrible!" Then suddenly his chill changes to a fever. He calls for water to be poured on his hands and for his mantle to be loosened; he tears from his head the wreath of roses that seems to be pressing on his temples like a band of fire.

At last he can breathe again. Once more he begs Salome to dance for him, and despite her mother's urgent appeal to her she promises to do so, whereupon slaves bring unguents and the Seven Veils and remove her sandals.[1] From the cistern comes the Voice again, asking prophetically who is this [Herod] that cometh from Edom, puffed up with pride in his greatness, but whose gorgeous raiment is stained with scarlet. The now terrified Herodias begs the Tetrarch to go indoors; she will not have her daughter dance, she cries, with the maddening sound of this accusing voice in her ears, and with her husband looking at Salome as he is doing. But nothing now can turn him from his purpose that Salome shall dance for him.

14

The musicians strike up a wild prelude, then, at a sign from Salome, break into a softer strain, and the exotic Dance of the Seven Veils begins:

No. 23

The lulling, insinuating melody is sung by a solo viola. It merges into a sinuous strain in the oboe:

[1] This scene is handled with much greater wealth of words by Wilde. The musician has no need of this verbal elaboration, and does right in pressing on swiftly to the climax.

No. 24

the cadence of which is formed from our No. 1 A, while in the
further course of the melody we hear a suggestion (in the minor)
of No. 14 A in the clarinet. For a while after this the music is
mostly luxuriant arabesque, supported at times by the rhythmi-
cally and harmonically striking No. 23. Then a quiet suggestion
of the opening of No. 15 steals in, followed by one of No. 19,
and this again by a fresh hint of No. 15. The mood and speed of
the music change when a broad new theme sings out in the upper
strings, lower wood wind and a solo horn:

No. 25

soaring slowly into a great crescendo. Next No. 14 comes into
prominence, followed by No. 15 in much the same luxuriant form
as it will assume in Salome's closing monologue. Then No. 25,
with a new upper counterpoint, steps into the foreground, followed by No. 10 and hints of No. 14.

At this point, according to the directions in the score, "Salome
seems for a moment to tire, then collects herself and continues
with renewed strength." The music of the final stage of the dance
narrows down once more to the semi-barbaric wildness of the
commencement. Then comes a last passionate enunciation of
No. 15 at breakneck speed, followed by an eerie prolonged shake
on a high A in piccolo, clarinet, celesta and violins, with just a
hint underneath it of No. 14 A in the flutes, as Salome, according
to the score, "pauses for a moment by the cistern like a visionary,"
her thoughts concentrated on Jochanaan. Then, as the orchestra
makes a final convulsive gesture, she rushes forward and throws
herself at Herod's feet.

Herod turns triumphantly to Herodias—"You see, your daughter
has danced for me!"—and he renews his promise to Salome to

grant her whatever she may ask of him. There comes another of those long trills—this time on a note high up in the small E flat clarinet, where the tone is particularly cutting—which Strauss so often employs to create an effect of nervous tension; and underneath it we hear a suggestion of the insinuating No. 14 A as Salome, honeying her voice, asks to be given, on a silver charger . . . The eager Herod takes the words out of her mouth: "on a silver charger, assuredly; but what, O sweet and fair Salome, fairest of all the daughters of Judaea? Whatever it may be, were it the whole of my treasure, thou shalt have it." Rising to her feet she says with a smile, "The head of Jochanaan!" Herod recoils, but the revenge-lusting Herodias now commends her daughter's choice. When Salome repeats her demand she insists that her mother's wish counts for nothing with her in the matter: the decision is her own, and she reminds the Tetrarch of his oath. The horrified Herod tries to turn her from her purpose; let her ask of him anything else, even unto the half of his kingdom, but not this. In cruelly hardened biting tones she repeats her demand, once more reminding him of the oath he had sworn before them all. Herodias, now a raging fiend, sees in Salome's demand a proof of her daughter's love for her; she will avenge her mother on the Jewish fanatic who has loaded her with insults. Herod appeals to whatever affection Salome may feel for him, reminding her of his many kindnesses to her, and offering her his most prized possessions, his great emerald, his hundred white peacocks, priceless jewels which even his wife has never seen, a magic crystal in which it is not lawful for a woman to look, the mantle of the High Priest himself, even the veil of the temple sanctuary; [1] but let her not require of him the head of this man, who is a holy man, one who has been touched by the finger of God, and whose death may bring evil on them all.

15

Salome's only reply is a furious "Give me the head of Jochanaan!" "Truly she is her mother's child," Herod mutters helplessly; "let her be given what she asks." Herodias draws the ring of death from his nerveless hand and gives it to the First Soldier: he takes it to the executioner, who goes down into the cistern.

[1] At this there is an outcry of horror from the Jews.

Herod observes that his ring has gone, and wearily asks who has taken it, and who has drunk the wine that had been in his cup: "Surely some evil will befall someone!" Herodias gives a savage cry of "My daughter has done well!"

Salome is now leaning over the cistern, listening intently. For a few tense moments nothing is heard in the orchestra but an insistent dull throbbing deep down in the double basses and bass drum—except for a single high B flat in a solo double bass, repeated sforzando at intervals in the following bars. This extraordinarily grisly effect provoked much head-shaking in critical circles in the early days of the opera. Most people regarded these four notes—if "notes" be a correct description of the sound emitted—as representing the groans of Jochanaan under the blows of the executioner; but in his *Betrachtungen und Erinnerungen* Strauss makes it finally clear that they are intended to suggest the animal half-moans, half-sighs of the crazed Salome athirst for her prey.[1]

To the persistent throbbing of a low E flat Salome asks impatiently why the executioner is so long about his business: if anyone sought to kill her she would cry out, she would struggle, not endure in silence; and a series of pounding blows in horns and kettledrums gives point to her words. At last her straining ears catch the sound of something falling. "The executioner has dropped his sword," she cries: "he dares not kill him; he is a coward, this slave. Send soldiers down there!" She beckons the Page to her and addresses him: "You were the friend of him who died, were you not? Well, there are not enough dead men here. Go to the soldiers and tell them to descend and bring me the thing I desire, the thing the Tetrarch promised me, the thing that is mine!" As the Page recoils she turns in a delirium to the soldiers, bidding them do what she desires.

The tension that has been increasing in the orchestra ends in a great pounding in the bass drum alone as the huge black arm

---

[1] In a footnote to the orchestral score at this point the composer tells us that the string of the instrument is not to be pressed down upon the fingerboard in the normal way, but pinched firmly between the player's thumb and forefinger, while the bow is drawn across the string in short sharp strokes, "thus producing a sound resembling the choked groaning and sighing of a woman."

of the executioner rises from the cistern, bearing the head of Jochanaan on a silver shield. There is a terrific orchestral outburst as Salome seizes the head. "Herod hides his face with his cloak. Herodias smiles and fans herself. The Nazarenes fall on their knees and begin to pray." These are the stage directions in the play; they are not reproduced in the score, but the observance of them is essential in the opera as in the drama.

16

There comes an immense emotional release in Salome, a strange catharsis of the spirit; and she launches the superb scene that is to occupy the remainder of the score, the recurrent psychological theme of which is her ecstatic cry of "Thou wouldst not suffer me to kiss thy mouth, Jochanaan. Well, I will kiss it now!" The complex musical tissue is woven entirely out of motifs by this time familiar to the reader and which it would be futile to try to specify bar by bar. When she speaks of biting the desired mouth as one bites into a ripe fruit we hear a reminder in the orchestra of the figure (No. 22) that had accompanied the expression of Herod's desire to see her "little white teeth" bite into the fruit he was offering her.[1] Salome's recurrent cry of "I will kiss thy mouth, Jochanaan" is always sung, with mounting passion, to

[1] But we shall hear it again a little later, when Salome says "And thy tongue, that was like a red viper that spat its poison at me—why does it move no more now? It is strange, is it not?"

The more one studies the score the more one is inclined to believe that the final scene was conceived first. Strauss, I imagine, would already have in his mind most of the main motifs of the work, but, as yet, principally as constituents of this superb piece of writing, which is, in essence, a closely and organically knit symphonic poem with a vocal solo. The later allocations of the motifs to this or that passage in the earlier part of the opera was seemingly a matter with him of the suggestion of the moment; thus Strauss's mind, in the episode in which Herod invites Salome to bite into the fruit, would spontaneously revert to the parallel passage in the final monologue. I find this hypothesis more credible than the reverse one—that he *first* invented the "teeth" theme in the episode with Herod and *afterwards* spatchcocked it into the finale; for if the motif were specifically associated in his mind with the idea of "biting into a ripe fruit" why should he employ it a few minutes later, in the closing scene, in the irrelevant context of quite another image—that of the viper's tongue? The true significance of the theme, as we have it in *both* passages in the final monologue, is simply as a

our No. 19, which takes on more and more luxuriant harmonic and orchestral forms.

As has been said already, in this final long monologue Strauss follows Wilde's text virtually word for word, and as it is impossible to quote, or indeed summarise, it all, one can only refer the reader to the play or the score. In the same breath Salome gloats over her fallen enemy and rhapsodises over his fascination for her. He had flung insults at her; now he is dead and she is alive, and his head is hers to do with it what she will, throw it to the dogs or the birds of the air. He had desired only to see his God: "Well, thou hast seen thy God, but me thou didst never see; if thou hadst, thou wouldst have loved me." What shall she do now? She had been chaste, and he had roused her and filled her veins with fire; and "the mystery of Love," she concludes sombrely, "is greater than the mystery of Death."

As she pauses for a while, exhausted, sunk in brooding, Herod mutters, "She is a monster, this daughter of thine!" Herodias tells him that she is well pleased with her daughter, and she will not leave the terrace now. But the quaking Herod insists on her going within. He calls on the slaves to extinguish the torches: he wants neither moon nor stars to look down on him: [he will hide himself in the palace. The torches are put out, the stars disappear; the moon is hidden by a great cloud. The stage is quite dark as the Tetrarch begins to climb the staircase.] [1]

17

Salome now comes into the foreground of the action again. There is a long, nerve-racking shake on a high A natural in the flutes (and, an octave lower, in a clarinet), interspaced with sombre pianissimo chords in the depths of the orchestra and ejaculations of No. 14 A in the oboe and piccolo. Salome finds speech once more, for the last time. "I have kissed thy mouth, Jochanaan:

---

characterisation of Salome's venomous gloating over her vanquished enemy. As such it is mightily effective.

The upshot of it all is that, as I have said, we shall often go far astray if we regard the themes of the opera as "motifs," each with a definite and fixed connotation, in the Wagnerian sense of the term.

[1] The passage here inclosed in brackets does not appear in the score, but it is essential to the staging of the opera.

thy lips had a bitter taste. Was it of blood? No, perchance of love, for they say that love has a bitter taste. . . . But what matters? I have kissed thy mouth, Jochanaan, I have kissed thy mouth." In a final ecstasy of perversity her mind cracks; and Strauss brings in his long-delayed psychological climax in a way possible only to music among the arts. After Salome's final cry the orchestra seems to be preparing to launch another passionate statement of No. 15; but before it has completed its second bar there is an orchestral upheaval that seems to rend the tonal tissue in twain, the upper and lower portions of the harmony asserting themselves in conflicting keys: [1]

No. 26

The spasm is too intense to last more than a moment: the broken Salome has now passed into a strangely mystical sphere in which our everyday concepts of sanity and insanity, the normal and the perverse, cease to have any real meaning. The moon—at the end of the opera, as at the beginning, the silent participator in the action and the silent reflector of the minds of the characters—emerges from the clouds and illuminates her. Herod, on his way out, turns round, and in a spasm of fear and horror cries, "Kill that woman!" "The soldiers rush forward and crush beneath their shields Salome, Daughter of Herodias, Princess of Judaea"; and the curtain falls.

[1] Our quotation shows the passage in merely skeletonised harmonic form. No one who has not heard the opera can have any idea of the shattering force of this clash of keys in the huge orchestra at the point marked with an asterisk.

La Bohème

PUCCINI [1858–1924]

PRINCIPAL CHARACTERS

RODOLFO	*Tenor*
SCHAUNARD	*Baritone*
BENOIT	*Bass*
MIMI	*Soprano*
PARPIGNOL	*Tenor*
MARCELLO	*Baritone*
COLLINE	*Bass*
ALCINDORO	*Bass*
MUSETTA	*Soprano*
A CUSTOM HOUSE SERGEANT	*Bass*

1

THE FIRST thing to note in connection with *La Bohème* is that neither in its original nor its operatic form has it a real "dramatic action": there is no strictly logical sequence of events from one scene to another, no evolution of character under the impact of circumstance; all we have in the opera is four cameos of bohemian life in Paris. This peculiarity of structure, indeed, told a little against Puccini's work at first in some quarters.

The *Scènes de la Vie de Bohème* of Henry Murger (1822–1861), from which the material for Puccini's opera was drawn, is not a continuous novel but a series of sketches of Murger himself and some of the other bohemians and the grisettes among whom his short life was spent, and the adventures, partly authentic, partly fictitious, that befell them.[1] Some of the characters figure in the book in different surroundings, and at times under different names; and the Italian librettists further linked and fused them in a way of their own for the purposes of the opera. For instance, the pathetic little episode of Mimi's muff in the last act of the opera belongs not to Murger's Mimi but to one Francine, whose lover is not the author Rodolphe, but a sculptor, Jacques D. . . . In Murger it is the four men only who always stand for the same types; Rodolphe is always the man of letters, Marcel the painter, Schaunard the musician, and Colline the bookworm and philosopher.

About Schaunard we know, by good luck, more than Murger has told us. In real life he was Alexandre Schanne, who published his memoirs in 1887 under the title of *Souvenirs de Schaunard.* From him we learn that the original of Rodolphe was Murger himself; Colline was an amalgam of a philosopher named Jean Wallon and one Trapadoux, and Marcel a fusion of a Marcel Lazare and a certain Tabar. Schanne's immense nose earned for him among the bohemians of his youth the nickname of Marshal Nez. In some of the early sketches of bohemian life in *Le Corsaire* Murger had slightly disguised him as Schannard: by a printer's error this became Schaunard: and as nobody troubled to correct it, it remained Schaunard ever after. He was born in December 1823; his father was a maker of toys and woolly animals; his mother had a shop in the Passage des Panorames, round the corner from what became later the rue Vivienne. He himself followed painting as a profession, but took up music as a hobby and earned a few francs occasionally by singing in the chorus at small theatres; later he became proficient enough on the viola to play that instrument in the orchestra of the Théâtre-Lyrique. He seems to have had some skill also on the trombone. Between 1850 and 1860 he did various journalistic jobs and wrote a couple of one-act plays; the Paris bohemians of that epoch had to be versatile and agile to

---

[1] The sketches began in the Paris journal *Le Corsaire* in 1848. In November of the following year Murger collaborated with Théodore Barrière in a play, *La Vie de Bohème,* that was produced with great success at the Variétés Theatre and ran for some years: Rodophe, Marcel, Schaunard and Colline all appear in it. The play still makes good reading for opera-goers who wish to construct for themselves the bohemian milieu of Puccini's opera.

keep body and soul together. "Prosperity," for Schanne, meant two meals a day; if he earned as much in a year as a minor book-keeper—say 4,000 francs (about £160 at that time)—he thought himself well off. In 1850 he managed to get a picture exhibited in the Salon, and he published a song or two now and then; but in his last years he was still making toys like his father before him.

2

Puccini's Schaunard, of course, is basically that of Murger. There he is a bit of a painter as well as a musician, but chiefly the latter; he has composed a number of symphonies, including one with the intriguing title *On the Influence of Blue in the Arts*. One of his few lucrative engagements is with a rich Englishman bearing the not quite credible name of Mr. Birn'n, whose sleeping and waking hours are made a misery by a parrot that keeps on reciting speeches from classical tragedies in the best Dramatic Academy style of elocution. The bird belongs to an actress in the apartment below the Englishman; by listening to her rehearsing her rôles it had learned them so thoroughly that it could have deputised for her, if necessary, in the theatre. Several of the inhabitants of the building had terminated their tenancies in despair; but the Englishman was made of sterner stuff. First he tried to buy the bird, with the intention of wringing its neck; but the actress would not part with it. Then Mr. Birn'n had the bright idea of using the piano as a counter-irritant; "the most disagreeable of instruments might be strong enough to contend against the most disagreeable of winged animals," he thought. So he engages Schaunard to play a single scale on the piano from five in the morning until the evening at a fee of two hundred francs a month, rejecting the musician's suggestion that he shall poison the bird with parsley, which the chemists agree in declaring to be "the prussic acid of these animals"; let the Englishman just scatter some bits of parsley on his carpet, says Schaunard, and Coco will meet his death as surely as if he had been dining with Pope Alexander VI (the father of Cesare and Lucrezia Borgia). This episode of the parrot makes a fleeting appearance in the opera, though most spectators miss the point of it.

In Puccini neither Schaunard nor Colline has any feminine encumbrance, the composer and his librettists no doubt feeling

that they had enough love interest on their hands already with
the Rodolfo-Mimi Marcello-Musetta pairs. In Murger, Schaunard
has for mistress a certain Phémie, whom he used to correct, when
necessary, with a cane; but discovering one day that one of her
knees did not quite match the other his artist's sense of symmetry
was outraged and he was compelled to discharge her; however,
he generously presented her with the cane as a souvenir of his
affection.

Schanne tells us that the authentic Tabar had begun to paint a
picture of the Red Sea which he could not complete because of
the cost of models, costumes and so on; so he converted it into
a less expensive "Niobe and her children slain by the arrows of
Apollo and Diana," which was exhibited in the Salon of 1842.
This gave Murger his cue for the marvellous history of that picture of *his* Marcel the acquaintance of which we make again in
the opera. For five or six years Marcel had been working at a
great picture of "The Passage of the Red Sea by the Israelites,"
which was refused so often by the Salon jury that in the end it
knew the way to the Louvre by heart, and could have found its
way there alone if put on wheels. But Marcel never lost faith in
his own genius or in what he was sure was his masterpiece. He
began by altering it a little and sending it in to the Salon again as
"The Crossing of the Rubicon"; but the jury was sharp enough
to see that Caesar was only Pharaoh painted over. The next year
he put a lot of snow in the picture, planted a fir-tree in one corner,
transformed an Egyptian into a grenadier of the Napoleonic
Guard, and renamed the picture "The Passage of the Beresina."
Once more it is recognised and rejected. He now plans to make
it the "Passage des Panorames" (a street in Paris). Before he can
carry out his design a Jewish art dealer, Salomon, offers him the
miserable sum of 150 francs for the picture, in spite of Marcel's
anguished protest that the cobalt in Pharaoh's robe alone had cost
him more than that. In the end he lets it go for that amount plus
a dinner for the four bohemians. Salomon had flatteringly assured
him that he was buying the picture for a rich connoisseur who
proposed to tour Europe with an exhibition of masterpieces. But
a week later, joining a crowd in the Faubourg St. Honoré that is
admiring the sign over a provision dealer's shop, Marcel finds that
the attraction is none other than his "Passage of the Red Sea"; a

boat has been added by another hand, and it is now entitled "The Port of Marseilles." Going away with the enthusiastic comments of the crowd ringing in his ears, Marcel murmurs "Vox populi, vox dei."

3

In Murger both Marcel and Rodolphe fight their way out of bohemia in the end. Marcel gets two pictures into the Salon, one of them being bought by a rich Englishman who had been one of Musette's lovers; with the proceeds the painter pays off some of his debts and treats himself to a real studio. Rodolphe's success was with a book that interested the critics for as long as a month; and even Schaunard had scored a hit with an album of songs. But at the time when we first meet with Rodolphe in bohemia he is starving like the others, though, again like them, he is always gay. At one period his night address is the Avenue de Saint-Cloud, fifth branch of the third tree on the left as you come out of the Bois de Boulogne. His play *Le Vengeur* has been refused by every theatre in Paris. This is the masterpiece we find him burning in the first act of the opera to keep his fingers warm on a winter's day. There is a great deal of manuscript, for it has been copied and re-copied many a time: in Murger he keeps only the latest copy. "I always knew I would manage to place you somewhere some day," he says as the huge manuscript goes into the stove; "but if I'd known what use it was going to be put to I would have added a prologue." When we first meet with him he is ekeing out a living of sorts by editing two fashion magazines, *L'Écharpe d'Iris* and *Le Castor*. Like all the young romantics of the epoch he was Shakespeare-mad. One day Colline met him on the boulevard carrying a rope ladder and a bird-cage with a pigeon in it. It appears that having acquired a new love whose name was Juliet, he had as a matter of course to transform himself into Romeo; he would be obliged, indeed, if Colline would address him only by the name now on his cards—Romeo Montague. One of his first duties will be to kill some Tybalt or other. His Juliet having informed him that there was a balcony outside her apartment, he needs the ladder he is carrying to surmount this. He has done his best also to procure a nightingale to sing when he would have to quit his lady at dawn, with Juliet murmuring

Wilt thou be gone? It is not yet near day:
It was the nightingale, and not the lark,
That pierced the fearful hollow of thine ear;

. . . .

Believe me, love, it was the nightingale.

In his passion for fidelity to the original he had gone so far as to try to obtain a Nurse for his Juliet. His explanation of the pigeon to Colline is that this was the best the bird-seller could do for him, he being out of nightingales at the moment: but pigeons, he had assured Rodolphe-Romeo, also burst into song at dawn. When he calls on Juliet that night complete with ladder and cage, he finds, to his annoyance, that the ladder is superfluous; she had omitted to tell him that her balcony was on the ground level, so that all Romeo had to do to ascend was to throw his leg over it. The pseudo-nightingale wakes them up at an inconveniently early hour the next morning. Juliet, who is as poor as a church mouse, can find nothing for their breakfast but some onions and a bit of bacon, bread and butter. Romeo looks at Juliet: Juliet looks at Romeo; then both look at the pigeon, which is "singing optimistically on its perch." "He was very tender," Romeo remarks appreciatively an hour later: "he had a nice voice," says Juliet. It always heightens our enjoyment of the first act of the opera if we can see each of the four bohemians imaginatively against the Murger background of poverty and gaiety.

4

Colline, in Murger, was the scientist and philosopher of the brotherhood; he was good at mathematics, scholastics, botanics and anything else ending in "ics." Though not of an amorous disposition he had as *amante* a tailoress who spent her days and nights copying out his philosophical works. By the time the book comes to an end we find him inheriting money, marrying well, and giving "evenings," with music and cakes.

Puccini's male characters, then, correspond closely to those of Murger. It is a different matter when we come to the women: Puccini's Mimi and Musetta are composite figures.

In the first act of the opera, when Rodolfo asks his new acquaintance her name, she replies, "They call me Mimi, but my name is Lucia." This is completely meaningless to the audience. It has found its way into the libretto only because one of Murger's sketches tells the story of Rodolphe and a certain Lucille, who went in the bohemian quarter by the name of Mimi. Rodolphe had taken her over as a going concern from one of his friends and fallen madly in love with her. She, however, was an incurable coquette and gold-digger, like virtually all the ladies who figure in the *Scènes de la Vie de Bohème*; she deceived him right and left, only returning to him when it suited her purpose. Schanne tells us that she was a combination of "profound egoism and immense sensibility," "without a vestige of moral sense." Nothing less like the modest, shrinking little Mimi of the first act of the opera could well be imagined.[1] The charming episode of the loss of Mimi's door-key and the artful strategic concealment of it by Rodolfo is taken from another of Murger's stories, that of a certain Francine, a poor little consumptive seamstress who had run away from home to escape the malice of a stepmother and found six months of happiness with the sculptor Jacques D . . . (Puccini transfers her cough to his Mimi of the third act.) It was Murger's Francine, not Rodolphe's Mimi, who had come to Jacques' room one night to light her candle, and, when the last match had gone out, dropped her key and could not find it, because Jacques had had the presence of mind to kick it under a piece of furniture. Both she and her lover come to a horrible end. Puccini further transferred from Francine to Mimi the pathetic episode of the tiny muff brought to warm her hands when she is dying. From another story, *Epilogue des Amours de Rodolphe et de Mademoiselle Mimi*, he took the moving little motive of the broken Mimi, now at death's door, seeking refuge with Marcel, and Colline selling his books and Schaunard his scanty wardrobe

[1] We learn from Schanne that in Murger's Mimi there is something also of a cousin of his named Angèle, a good bourgeoise who married respectably, and of a friend of hers named Marie, who, though married, had a soft spot in her heart for Murger. She seems, like so many of the Frenchwomen of that period in and out of Murger's pages, to have had the poor health that made the type so attractive to poets of *l'école poitrinaire*. The younger Dumas' Marguerite Gautier (Verdi's Violetta) is a later representative of the type.

to buy a few comforts for her before she is taken to the hospital, where she dies in misery.[1]

In Murger, as in Puccini, Musette is Marcel's mistress. It was he who had given her the name of Musette, because she was always singing; her notes were clear, we are told, but not always in tune; some of the Musettas we hear in the theatre imitate her all too conscientiously in this latter respect. She was intelligent, but an incurable man-hunter and gold-digger, reckless, spendthrift, self-indulgent, preferring silks to cottons, driving about in her carriage one week and taking the omnibus the next, according to the state of the purse of her lover of the moment. As in the opera, her barefaced infidelities are a perpetual exasperation to Marcel. In Murger she ends by settling down as the wife of a respectable postmaster, the guardian of a former lover of hers. "She is going to marry," Marcel tells Rodolphe one day. "Contre qui?" asks the latter. From Schanne we learn that Marcel's "singing Musette" was derived from a certain Mme. Pierre Dupont.[2] Schanne describes the real Musette in terms that confirm Murger's delineation of her. She was always "on the make," and always perfectly frank about it. She did very well, till one day in 1863 she set out in the "Atlas" from Marseilles for Algiers, taking with her 40,000 francs, and was drowned.

5

By the time that Puccini's *Manon Lescaut* was off his hands and on the stage, in February 1893, he was in hot pursuit of another subject. According to his friend Fraccaroli he had virtually decided in that same February on Murger's *Scènes de la Vie de Bohème*. But soon there arose that complication with Leoncavallo—

[1] According to Schanne, the Teinturière Phémie with whom Murger endowed Schaunard was one Louisette, who worked in an artificial flower factory and also did some dyeing—hence the "Teinturière." After an illness of three months she lamented that she had no frock to go out in on New Year's Day, and so worked on Schaunard's emotions that to buy her one he sold his new overcoat for thirty francs. She went out gaily in it and never returned to him. This is probably the authentic source of the moving episode of the sale of the coat in Murger and in the opera.

[2] As we have seen, a painting by Schanne was exhibited in the Salon in 1850. It bore the title "Portrait of Mme. Pierre." This was no doubt the Mme. Pierre Dupont who sang. It would be interesting if that picture of the "singing Musette" could be found today.

whose *Pagliacci* had appeared in May 1892—the details of which are still rather obscure, though the main facts are not in dispute. At a chance meeting of the two composers, who were acquaintances rather than friends, they began to discuss their future plans. Puccini happened to say that he had the Murger book in his mind for his next opera; whereupon Leoncavallo leaped from his seat, shouting, "But that is the subject *I* have chosen!" After that, neither of them let the grass grow under his feet. The next morning *Il Secolo,* which belonged to Leoncavallo's publisher Sonzogno, announced that the composer of *Pagliacci* was now engaged on an opera based on Murger's famous work; the same afternoon Ricordi's paper *Il Corriere della Sera* informed the world that Puccini had a *Bohème* in hand. Leoncavallo's *La Bohème* was produced in Venice in 1897, with considerable initial success; but by that time Puccini's work had become well established, and Leoncavallo's proved less and less able to stand up to the competition.

The music of *La Bohème* occupied Puccini all in all, allowing for interruptions, for no more than about eight months, from some time in 1894 to November 1895; but hammering out the libretto had meant two years of hard labour on his part and that of his librettists, Luigi Illica and Giuseppe Giacosa. As usual, Puccini, who was rarely in the least doubt as to what he wanted as dramatist, drove his collaborators to near suicide with his demands for fresh reconstruction, modification and condensation. Giulio Ricordi, who was a fourth in some of the discussions, has left us a lively description of the sorrows of the two devoted librettists, and of the frenzied Puccini gnawing his nails down to the flesh, so that after each conference he had to pay a visit to his manicurist. We will deal with some of the constructional difficulties of the trio as occasion arises in our analysis of the opera.

La Bohème was given for the first time at the Teatro Regio, Turin, under Toscanini, on the 1st February 1896. It had a cool reception from most of the critics, who lamented what one of them called the "degradation" the composer had inflicted on his Muse; but the public warmed to it more and more at each performance, and at Palermo, in April of the same year, it scored a complete success, in spite of the superstitious conviction of Mugnone, the conductor, that no good would come of a production on the 13th of the month, and a Friday at that. For a while, indeed, it seemed that his forebodings would be realised, especially when the oboist did not turn up until half-past nine. The final curtain did not fall until one in the morning, but the audience, instead of leaving, clamoured for more. It ended with the last act being repeated from the entry of Mimi, with as many of the orchestra as had not gone home by then, a Rodolfo without his wig, and a Mimi whisked from her dressing room and pushed on to the stage with her hair down.

The biographers have been at pains to recall that Puccini himself and his fellow-students at the Milan Conservatoire had lived a life of gay poverty closely resembling that of Murger's characters, and have opined that the bohemian scenes of *La Bohème* are so excellent because here the composer was "drawing upon his personal experiences." That assumption is somewhat unnecessary. Shakespeare surely did not have to liquidate Anne Hathaway with a bolster to realise just how Othello felt after the murder of Desdemona. Wagner did not need to have trodden the actual meadows of Monsalvat one Good Friday morning to write the Good Friday music of *Parsifal,* nor to have suffered the worst pangs of conscience, aggravated by a painful wound in the groin, before he could find the right accents of anguish for his maddened Amfortas. Puccini himself had had no first-hand experience of police third-degree methods when he wrote the music for the torture scene in *Tosca,* nor had any female relative of his been deserted by an American naval officer before he could limn his broken-hearted Butterfly. No creative artist worthy of the name is very much dependent upon "personal experiences" in order to place himself inside the skin of a character and speak with the veritable tongue of that character; all he needs is an imagination protean enough to assume for a moment any one of a hundred forms, and a faculty of expression on a par with his imagination. So we need not jump to the innocent conclusion, as more than one biographer has done, that Puccini, thanks to his youthful experiences in Milan, is himself Rodolfo, Marcello, Colline and Schaunard rolled into one; any more than we need suppose that Strauss could never have written his orchestral masterpiece unless he himself had been as crazy as Don Quixote at some time or other.

6

Puccini was fully aware that his characters called for a little explanation on his part; so to each of his four acts he prefixed a few lines taken from Murger's book. The preamble to the first act runs thus: "Mimi was a charming girl of a type that made a peculiar appeal to Rodolphe's plastic and poetic susceptibilities. She was twenty-two, slight, dainty, roguish. Her face suggested a sketch for some aristocratic beauty; her features, the last word in refinement, were softly lit up, as it were, by her limpid blue eyes; [*but in moments of boredom or ill-humor they gave a hint of an almost savage brutality, which a psychologist would probably have read as the sign of a profound egoism or utter insensibility. As a rule, however, her face was charming, with its fresh young smile, its air now tender, now imperiously coquettish*]. The warm lively blood of youth coursed in her veins, giving her complexion a rosy tint underneath its camellia-like whiteness and transparency. This sickly beauty had a great attraction for Rodolphe. . . . But what made him most madly in love with Mimi were her hands, which, despite her domestic duties, she managed to keep whiter than the hands of the Goddess of Idleness." The passage in italics in this quotation was omitted by Puccini: the Mimi he wanted us to take to our hearts in his first act was to have no darker side to her character; she was to be all innocence, aspiration, fragility, patience and pathos.

Puccini thought it further necessary to reproduce the gist of Murger's description of bohemia and its inhabitants. The type, said the French novelist, has appeared in one form or another in all ages, with Villon as one of its supreme representatives: but it is only in Paris that bohemia now exists or can exist. Your genuine bohemian believes in art for art's sake; according to his lights he obeys the imperious call of art, indifferent to failure, poverty, suffering or ridicule. Few even of the best of them win recognition until it is too late; many of them die young. There is a particularly tragic fringe of them, young bohemians who, in addition to being duped by the world, are their own self-dupes: "they mistake a fancy for a vocation . . . and die either the victims of perpetual accesses of pride or the idolators of a chimera." There is another sub-species—the weaker ones who give up the fight against hardship and privation, return to the comfortable paternal fireside, marry their cousins, become small-town notaries, and in their well-fed middle age tell and re-tell with supreme complacency the story of their one-time sacrifices and sufferings for art.

For Murger the bohemians *pur sang* are those of his own type, the young fellows with something in them who, given a bit of luck, will one day make good. "Rain or dust," begins the passage from the *Scènes de la Vie de Bohème* which Puccini has chosen as introduction to his score, "sun or shadow, nothing can stop these bold adventurers. . . . If need be, they will practice abstinence with all the rigor of an anchorite; but let a tiny bit of fortune come their way and they will ride a cock-horse on the most ruinous fantasies, falling in love with the youngest and fairest women, drinking the best and oldest wines, and never finding windows enough to fling their money out of. Then, when their last crown is dead and buried, they start dining again at the table d'hôte of chance, where their cover is always laid, and go marauding in all the industries that have any connection with art, hunting from morn till eve the wild animal known as the five-franc piece. . . . Bohemians speak among themselves a dialect of their own, the product of the studios, the stage and the editorial office. . . . This vocabulary is the hell of rhetoric and the paradise of neologism. . . . A delightful life, and a terrible one. . . ."

This, then, is the milieu, these the character types, that Puccini would have us keep in mind during his first act.

7

The curtain rises on the bohemians' attic in the Latin Quarter of Paris. The scanty furniture consists of a table, a cupboard, a small book-case, four chairs, and an easel. On the right is a stove that shows no sign of giving out any heat. A few books lie about, for Rodolfo and Colline are men of letters; some packs of cards suggest occasional lighter interests. Through a great window we get a side glimpse of roofs and chimneys covered with snow, for it is Christmas eve.

Rodolfo is not working—he is too cold and hungry for the ideas to flow—but staring moodily out of the window. Marcello is at the easel, making an heroic effort with his frozen fingers to add a touch or two to his painting "The Passage of the Red Sea." The motifs given out by the orchestra, such as:

No. 1

and

No. 2

are those which will always characterize the bohemians in their collective aspect.[1] "This Red Sea Passage takes it out of me," Marcello grumbles; "it chills me to the bone." He steps back a little to get a better view of his work, ejaculates "By way of revenge a Pharaoh I will drown," and puts in a few vicious strokes at the canvas.[2] What is Rodolfo doing? he asks over his shoulder. The poet has been lost in depressed contemplation of the view from the window: he sees chimneys pouring out their smoke by the thousand, he says, but this lazy old fraud of a stove

[1] In 1883, towards the end of his three years' course at the Milan Conservatoire, Puccini wrote a *Capriccio Sinfonico* for orchestra which was performed with considerable success at a Conservatoire concert in the July of that year. The full score has never been published, but there exists a contemporary arrangement of it for piano duet by one Giuseppe Frugatta. Puccini not only used two of the themes of this early work for his *Edgar* of 1889 but fashioned out of the main theme of the central allegro section of it the opening bars of *La Bohème*, transposing it a major fourth down, and altering the outline of it at some points. In the *Capriccio* it runs thus:

Readers who possess a score of the opera will find it interesting to compare the two versions. It will be seen that in bar 12 of the above quotation we have a pendant to the theme that reappears in bars 12–19 of *La Bohème*.
[2] Whenever Marcel felt inspired and energetic, Murger tells us, he would engulf another Egyptian.

of theirs does no work—just takes its ease like a gentleman of leisure: [1]

No. 3

Nei cie-li bi-gi guar-do fu-mar dai mil-le co—mi-gno-li Pa-ri-gi

Marcel makes excuse for the delinquent; after all, he admits, it is their fault, for they never feed him, never pay his dues. "And those imbecile forests, what are they all doing underneath the snow?" asks Rodolfo. "Let me communicate a profound thought that has just occurred to me," rejoins Marcello: "I am cold to the marrow"; and he blows on his fingers again. "Nor will I conceal from you," says Rodolfo, "that I no longer believe in the sweat of my brow"; and No. 1 pounds out with humorous impatience in the orchestra. "My fingers are as frozen," continues Marcello, "as if they were embedded in that big block of ice, Musetta's heart," and with a sigh for his lost illusions he puts palette and brushes aside. Rodolfo, as befits a man of letters, becomes philosophical and metaphorical: "Ah, love's a stove that consumes too much fuel." ("And too quickly," interjects Marcello); and the fellow-sufferers from love go on each capping the other's imagery: "where the man is the faggot"—"and the woman does the blowing"—"as the one burns down and out"—"the other stands and looks on." "But meanwhile here we are freezing"—"and what's more, dying of hunger." "Something must be done about it"— "Let's sacrifice a chair"—and Marcello seizes one of them and begins to break it up.

Rodolfo restrains him: he has a better idea. "Eureka!" he cries, taking a bulky manuscript from the table. "Genius will tell: ideas flame forth!" he continues to the strain of No. 3. "Shall we burn

[1] Our No. 3, to which Rodolfo sings of the "grey sky" and smoking chimneys of Paris, is of a gaiety quite unexpected in the circumstances. The fact is that it was originally written in praise of the blue sky of Sicily and the smoking Mount Aetna. Puccini had originally intended it, in 1894, for an opera with a Sicilian setting, La Lupa (based on a play by Giovanni Verga), the plan for which he had soon dropped. He had gone to Sicily, however, to get local colour, and this melody was one of the fruits of his stay there.

the Red Sea?" asks Marcello. "No," says Rodolfo, "think how
the paint will smell! My drama, my ardent drama, shall give
us heat." "You are not going to read it?" protests Marcello in
mock terror; "I'd prefer to freeze!" "No, let the paper burn to
ashes, and the poet's inspiration ascend to the heavens whence it
came. The age will suffer an irreparable literary loss, but Rome
is in peril! Here goes the first act!" Charmingly descriptive music
accompanies the tearing up of the first act of the play, the lighting
of a candle by flint and steel, and the commission to the stove of
the sheets of the dramatic masterpiece that has been refused by
every theatre in Paris.

With No. 3 pursuing its eager course in the orchestra—for even
cold and hunger cannot quench the spirits of our young bohemians—poet and painter draw up their chairs to the stove and
joyously warm their hands. They are in this attitude when the
door at the back is flung violently open and the clumsy bookworm
Colline steps in:

No. 4

and furiously throws a bundle of books on to the table. He is in
a very bad temper: what has happened to the world, he asks
angrily, when the pawnbrokers won't make a man a bit of an
advance on Christmas eve?; and No. 1 gives a comically peevish
point to his grievance. The unaccustomed sight of a fire in the
stove, however, cheers him up a little. This drama of Rodolfo's
is really scintillating, he assures the author; its only fault is that
it is too short. "Brevity is the soul of wit," Rodolfo assures him
complacently. Claiming the right to a complimentary seat at this
unexpected first performance of the play Colline takes Rodolfo's
chair from him and warms his hands at the stove. Marcello
grumbles about the excessive length of the entr'actes, for these
yield no warmth; like a true dramatic critic he clamours for more
action, so Rodolfo bundles the second act into the stove, the
orchestra suggesting a fresh gust of flame. Colline congratulates
him on the profundity of thought displayed in the drama; and
Rodolfo, while lamenting so sad an end to his great love scene,

heroically sends the remaining three acts after the first two. But the flames soon die down and finally sputter out, and then, like critics at the first performance of a play, Marcello and Colline rush at him crying "Down with the author!"

Before they can hurl him too into the stove a joyous new theme to be associated with Schaunard is heard in the orchestra:

No. 5

and their attention is drawn to two shop boys who enter from the back, one bearing provisions, wine and cigars, the other a faggot of wood. The three bohemians delightedly take possession of these unexpected reinforcements, Colline carrying the wood to the stove, Marcello giving an exultant shout of "Bordeaux!" as he examines the label on a bottle of wine. Now they can celebrate Christmas in proper fashion! But why these generous gifts of the gods? The mystery is solved by the exuberant entrance of Schaunard, scattering gold coins on the floor and singing to the melody of No. 5, "All the wealth of the Bank of France is yours!" The others stare incredulously at the money. "Pieces of tin?" suggests Marcello. Schaunard shouts at him to take a closer look at the coins: whose image and superscription do they show? "King Louis Philippe's!" says the awed Rodolfo; and he makes a profound obeisance to his beneficent Majesty.

8

Schaunard explains how he discovered this El Dorado. An English gentleman—he may even have been a Milord—had engaged him on the strength of his reputation as a musician; when Schaunard asked when the lessons were to begin he was told "At once." Pointing to a parrot in a cage outside the first floor of the building, the Englishman had instructed him to keep on playing the piano until the bird dropped dead. After enduring this outrage on his dignity as an artist for three long days, says Schaunard, he turned his famous charm on the servant girl, fascinated her, wheedled some parsley out of her, and gave it to

Lorito, who at once fell dead. The other bohemians take no notice
at all of his long tale, for the one thought in their minds is food.
Rodolfo lights another candle; the faggot is flung into the stove;
Colline's books are swept off the table and a copy of the "Con-
stitutional" spread on it by way of a tablecloth—"a splendid
paper; one can eat and devour the supplement at the same time";
the viands are laid out—a fine pie, cold roast beef, etc.; and the
four chairs are drawn up. Schaunard, still unable to get a hearing
for his story, at last loses his temper; he snatches away the pie the
others have started on, removes the other eatables, puts them in
the cupboard, and tells them that all this must be stored up for
leaner days that are sure to come. This is Christmas eve, when no
one in the Latin Quarter with any sense dines at home. Puccini
builds it all up into an enchanting vocal quartet, the main threads
of which are No. 5 and another joyous theme:

No. 6

Out there in the street, Schaunard continues, there· is the
savoury odour of fritters:

No. 7

girls are singing with their lovers; religion itself demands that
though they may drink at home on Christmas eve they must eat
outside. His enthusiasm infects the others. They lock the doors
and are opening a bottle of wine when a knock is heard: they
know only too well who it is—the landlord, old Benoit, come for
his rent. At first they are for pretending that they are not at home,
but in the end they decide they will have to admit him. He comes
in with an ingratiating smile and hands Marcello his bill. They
greet him with the most effusive cordiality, insist politely on his

joining them at table, pour him out a glass of wine, and drink his health, to the accompaniment of a charming new motive:

No. 8

They keep pressing wine on him, but after each potation he returns like a homing pigeon to the point he started from—the quarter's rent is due, and he looks to Marcello to redeem his promise to pay it. The others nearly faint when the painter draws Benoit's attention to the gold coins spread out on the table. They think he must have taken leave of his senses; but Marcello knows what he is about. The money is convincing proof of their solvency; but he asks the landlord to put aside all thoughts of mere mammon for a few minutes and be one of their festive company.

9

In another delightful ensemble they play artfully on the old man's vanity. They refuse to believe that he is older than they: did not Marcello see him the other evening at the Bal Mabille with a pretty young blonde? "Old rascal!" says one approvingly. "Seducer!" says another; "the man's an oak-tree, a cannon"; the maiden's ardour had been nothing to his. Benoit, who by now has been made to swallow more wine than he can carry, melts into a mood of senile self-satisfaction. He may be getting on, he tells them, but he is still robust. In his youth he had been timid with women, but now he's the very devil among them. Complacently he describes his feminine ideal: he likes them neither as big as a whale or a map of the world and with a face like a full moon, nor on the skinny side, for the lean ones are often very trying, too full of grievances, "like my wife, for example."

The bohemians are scandalised. In a lively quartet they express their horror of this elderly Casanova polluting the chaste atmosphere of their attic; the place must be decontaminated forthwith. Marcello rises to his full physical and moral height; the others follow him, and the bewildered Benoit is hustled to the door and thrown out on to the landing, with their best wishes for a happy Christmas eve.[1]

That little matter of the quarter's rent having been thus satisfactorily settled, the bohemians, to the tune of No. 7, turn to the more important question of where to spend the evening. The voting is in favour of the Momus, the famous café in the Latin Quarter where all the bright young spirits of Paris used to foregather to wrangle about literature and art and politics and set the world in general to rights. (Schanne tells us that it was located at No. 15 in the rue des Prêtres-Saint-Germain l'Auxerrois; it had a great vogue between about 1843 and 1848, numbering notabilities like Baudelaire and Gérard de Nerval among its patrons.) The bohemians divide the money on the table among them, and Colline, on Marcello's advice, promises to make himself more presentable by having a hair-cut and a shave.

As the Rodolfo theme (No. 3) steals out softly in the orchestra the conscientious man of letters announces his intention of staying behind for a little while to order to finish the leading article for one of his papers, the "Beaver," a matter of a mere few minutes for a practised hand like his. So the other three leave him, Schaunard giving him a final playful exhortation to "cut short the Beaver's tail."

Blowing out one of the candles, Rodolfo clears a space on the table and sits down to write. But the ideas will not come; he tears up what he has written and throws down his pen. Just then a timid knock is heard at the door: the Mimi theme, breathed softly by the orchestra:

No. 9

tells us who is without. Rodolfo opens the door for her; in her hand she has a candle and a key. The candle having gone out, she

---

[1] The episode of the bamboozling of the landlord who has called, full of optimism, for his rent is condensed from a similar one in Murger.

has come to get a light from this neighbour of hers. No sooner
has she entered the room than she is seized with a fit of coughing—
the ascent of the stairs has been too much for the fragile, underfed
creature. Rodolfo solicitously places her in a chair, where she
swoons, dropping key and candlestick as she does so. He revives
her by sprinkling water on her face,[1] which gives him an opportunity to observe—and to inform the audience—that while very
beautiful she is also very pale. She apologises for being so troublesome; but he manages to persuade her to sit nearer the fire and
take a sip of wine.

He lights her candle, gives it to her without speaking, and
accompanies her to the door; but just as they are bidding each
other good evening she finds, to her dismay, that she has lost her
key:

No. 10

As the draught from the open door has extinguished her candle
again he relights it from his; but that too fails, and the room is now
in darkness. He manages to locate her by the polite apologies she
is making for all the trouble she is giving; and now the attention
of both of them centres on the lost key. Rodolfo gropes for it
on the floor and at last finds it, but checks the impulse to give it
to Mimi and slips it into his pocket. The music to this little cameo
has been throughout the perfection of quiet simplicity and natu-
ralness; now it is time for Puccini to brace himself for the big
lyrical close to his first act.

10

As they still grope in the darkness Rodolfo's hand touches
Mimi's, and he is shocked by the coolness of it: "How very cold
your little hand is," he says: "let me warm it":

---

[1] There is a charming bit of realism in the orchestra at this point; the
trouble is that the sprinkling by Rodolfo and the sprinkling in the orchestra
rarely coincide in performance.

No. 11

What is the use of searching for the key? he asks. They will never find it in the dark, but soon the moon will be up, and then they will have better luck. To reassure her as she timidly tries to withdraw her hand he begins to tell her all about himself, who and what he is and how he lives. He is a poet. What does he do? He writes. Is that a living? Hardly. Anyhow he lives; and though he is poor he is as happy as any grand seigneur, he declares to a reminiscence of No. 3, writing hymns to love, luxuriating in his dreams, building castles in the air, a pauper in the flesh but in soul a millionaire. Sometimes, though, his coffers are raided by two thieves—two beautiful eyes such as hers; yet he does not regret his loss:

No. 12

Hope is springing to life in his breast again, he assures her. And now that he has told her his story, will she not tell him hers?

To the simple strain of No. 9 she replies, "They call me Mimi, but my name is Lucia." Little has she to tell him about herself. At home or in a shop she embroiders on cloth or silk, and after her simple fashion she is happy, for into the fabrics she weaves the roses and lilies of her dreams: "these things are full of enchantment for me, for they speak of love and spring":

No. 13

and her simple confession ends with a phrase, sung to the words "All this is poetry. Do you understand me?":

No. 14

of which Puccini will make fine use later. "They call me Mimi," she repeats, "but I know not why." She leads a very lonely life in a tiny chamber that looks out over the housetops; but when spring comes it gets the sun's first kiss, she assures him to a melody at once passionate and pathetic, that is the emotional high light of the score thus far:

No. 15

She loves the scent of flowers, but those she makes, alas, are odourless. "More than this I cannot tell you about myself," she concludes with a touch of naïveté, dropping from melody into simple speech; "I am just a neighbour of yours who comes to bother you at an inopportune moment."

Just then, to Rodolfo's annoyance, Marcello, Colline and Schaunard call to him from the street below, urging the sluggard to hurry up with his article and join them. Opening the window and thus admitting the first rays of moonlight into the gloomy room, he assures them that he has only another three lines to write, and then he will be with them at the Momus; nor is he, as they assume, alone. Turning to Mimi, whom now, at last, he really sees as she stands bathed in the moonlight, he sings, to the melody of No. 12, an ecstatic hymn in praise of her beauty: she answers with equal ardour, and for the first time their voices blend in harmony. He kisses her; she would fain disengage herself and send him out to join his companions, but, thinking better of it, shyly asks whether she may come with him. He tries to get her to see that they would be much cosier all by themselves in the attic; but her reply suggests that she will be not unwilling to return there with him after the festivities. And so, to the whispered strains of No. 11, she gives him her arm and they go out together, as befits an operatic hero and heroine, on a C *in alt.*

11

The second act is staged in the heart of the Latin Quarter, where Paris is enjoying itself on Christmas eve. The third act takes place at the Barrière d'Enfer—the toll-gate at which the custom-house officers deal with the provisions brought in from the country; and nothing could be more indicative of the lack of real dramatic evolution in the structure of *La Bohème* than the fact that for a long time Puccini intended his Barrière scene to constitute his *second* act and the Latin Quarter scene his third. (About the fourth act there could never be any doubt; it would obviously have to centre in the death of Mimi.) How the composer and his librettists proposed to handle their original plan for the second and third acts with any appearance at all of dramatic probability is beyond our understanding; but it evidently took Puccini a long time to decide on the present order. His correspondence shows him insisting, as against Illica's wishes, that there must be a Latin Quarter scene that would include the Musetta episode, which latter, he claims, was *his* idea. By what process of reasoning, and exactly at what time, he decided on the present order for acts 2 and 3 we do not know; but we may congratulate ourselves that, as usual, his excellent sense of the theatre pointed out the right course to him in the end.

In his prose preface to the second act he condenses for our benefit some passages from Murger that describe the inseparable attachment to each other of the four bohemians—to whom the Café Momus had given the name of the Four Musketeers—and supply us with the background for an understanding of the new character soon to be introduced—Musetta. She was a fine girl of twenty, we read, coquettish and egoistic, very ambitious but wholly illiterate, taking the revolutions of fortune's wheel philosophically, one day flaunting it in her carriage in the rue Bréda, on the next content with an omnibus in the Latin Quarter.

It is now later in the evening: there has been time for Colline to get groomed for a public appearance, and for Rodolfo and Mimi to join the other three for the great celebration at the Café Momus, which we see, when the curtain rises, on the right-hand side of a square formed by the convergence of various streets. A few citizens are seated at tables outside the café, which is illuminated by a huge lantern. Shopkeepers are touting for the patronage of the miscellaneous crowd circulating in the streets—boys, girls, children, soldiers, servant girls, working girls, gendarmes and so on. Rodolfo and Mimi are strolling up and down arm in arm, obviously preferring each other's company to that of anyone else in the world. Colline stands near a rag shop; Schaunard is bargaining for a pipe and a horn that have taken his fancy in a tinsmith's shop; Marcello is making his way with some difficulty through the milling crowd.

12

The general atmosphere of gaiety is established by a few bars of the Momus theme (No. 7) in the orchestra (the strain to which, in the first act, Schaunard had sung the praises of the odour of fritters and the gay crowd in the street outside the attic). It is upon this theme and one first allotted to the hawkers:

No. 16

that the lively opening chorus is constructed. Everyone is bawling at once, the hawkers trying to sell their various wares, the townsfolk and the street arabs commenting on the uproar, the people outside the café clamouring for service. Schaunard is still bargaining for the tinsmith's horn; the D is out of tune, he declares, and to prove it he blows some D flats that are alien to the E flat scale in which No. 16 is now heard. While Colline is confabulating with a clothes dealer about a coat—"It's rather worn," he says, "but still quite good and cheap"—Rodolfo and Mimi come well into view, to the accompaniment of a tender phrase in the orchestra:

No. 17

They disappear into a milliner's shop, for Mimi has seen a bonnet in the window that takes her fancy. Marcello, jostled by the girls, is doing his best to enjoy himself despite his recent desertion by Musetta: but he is quite unable to share Colline's enthusiasm over an almost unique copy of a Runic grammar which the philosopher has just picked up on a stall.

When Mimi reappears she is wearing the new bonnet, and Rodolfo is telling her how wonderfully its rose trimming suits her complexion; and a little phrase wells up in the orchestra:

No. 18

that will acquire a strange poignancy in the last act. But the appetite of the innocent Mimi whom we have seen in the first act is evidently beginning to grow with what it feeds on: she draws Rodolfo's attention to a pretty coral necklace. By now, perhaps, he is beginning to appreciate the wisdom of Ovid's advice to the young lover—"Don't call on her on her birthday; you'll find it too expensive"; but he manages to side-track her by telling her he has an old uncle who is a millionaire, and if it should please God to take the old gentleman to a better world he will buy her a much finer necklace than this. For a few moments they are lost once more in the crowd at the back of the stage; and when we see them again an exchange of glances between Mimi and some students calls for a little mild comment on Rodolfo's part. The fleeting episode is apt to go unnoticed by the spectator. He should be aware of it, however, for here Puccini is quietly preparing us for the main psychological motive of the third act—the proneness of Rodolfo to accesses of jealousy.

The happy pair light upon the other bohemians just after Marcello, Colline and Schaunard have come out of the café carrying a table, for although it is the depth of winter they are determined to dine out of doors; some worthy citizens seated near by resent the intrusion of these noisy newcomers and move away in a huff.

Having introduced Mimi to his friends, Rodolfo becomes poetical in praise of her charms, and the others chaff the poet for being so high-falutin. But before the feast can begin and the tempestuous Musetta enter to change the whole face of things, Puccini and his librettists, finding themselves with a little space on their hands, insert a delightful interlude in which the children besiege one Parpignol—a toy-seller who enters with his barrow from the rue Dauphin—and pester their mothers to buy them something. Marcello, Colline and Schaunard, after studying the menu, have to shout their orders—turkey, lobster, wine, etc.— to make themselves heard by the waiters. Schaunard puts on considerable dog to impress the latter; Mimi having timidly suggested that she would like some custard, Schaunard, with an air of tremendous importance, bids the waiter bring "The best you have! For a lady!"

13

Parpignol having left the scene, drawing after him, like another Pied Piper, all the children, Mimi tells Marcello of the pretty pink bonnet Rodolfo has bought her, to a theme:

No. 19

Un-a cuf-fiet-taa piz-zi, tut-ta   ro—sa,   ri—ca—ma—ta

out of which, in conjunction with another given to Marcello ("Oh beautiful age of illusions and utopias, when the heart still believes and hopes!"):

No. 20

O bel-la e-tà d'in-gan-ni e du-to-pi — e!

Puccini proceeds, as usual, to make a charming vignette, musically self-contained and self-sufficing yet fitting neatly into the general frame.

Rodolfo's and Mimi's rhapsodies on love begin to get on the nerves of Marcello, who becomes more and more pessimistic as he thinks of his faithless Musetta. But just as the bohemians are about to drink a toast there is a diversion that gives the act a totally new turn. From the rue Mazarin there bursts on the scene like a tornado the rip-roaring Musetta herself:

No. 21

having in tow her latest protector, a rich, pompous, fussy, over-dressed old beau of the name of Alcindoro, whom, however, she addresses by the pet-dog name of Lulu. She is very pretty, very coquettish, very artful, knowing all the tricks of the trade. Poor Alcindoro is already near the end of his patience with her tyran-nical caprices. He wants to dine unobtrusively inside the café; but Musetta, having at once recognised her bohemian friends, insists on having the table lately vacated by the little group of townsfolk. "The naughty Elder," says Colline, looking critically at Lulu. "With the chaste Susanna!" Marcello adds contemptuously. "What fine clothes she wears!" says Mimi enviously; to which Rodolfo rejoins sententiously, "The angels go naked." Before Rodolfo can reply to her query "Who is she?" Marcello supplies the information: "I'll tell you. Her name is Musetta: her surname is temptation: as for her vocation, she is like a magnetic needle, so often does she change her direction in love [1]: she is a screech-

[1] The English version of the text—"as to her vocation, like a rose in the breezes she changes her lover for lovers without number"—is based on a

owl, that most bloodthirsty of birds, whose favourite morsel is the heart. For my part, I've no heart left, so pass me the ragout."

While the others are chattering together, Musetta, to a motive as expressive of her restless vitality as No. 21:

No. 22

goes on railing at everyone and everything. (Perhaps No. 21 is Musetta herself, No. 22 Musetta as seen through Marcello's eyes.) She is furious because Marcello so pointedly ignores her and Schaunard laughs at her tantrums; and she has no one to back her up, she complains, but this old pelican of a Lulu! She could scratch everyone's eyes out. She complains to the waiter that the plate he has put before her smells of onions; and before he can remove it she dashes it on the ground. Some working-girls who are crossing the stage point her out to each other and laugh: she is evidently well known in the Quarter. Poor old Alcindoro tries in vain to pacify her: "Manners! Manners!" he keeps ejaculating; "Try to behave! What will all the people say?"

14

"Now the fun is at its height!" says Schaunard, during another of those miniature ensembles of which Puccini is so fond in *La Bohème*. Colline agrees. Rodolfo gives Mimi a quiet hint that he would never forgive her if *she* were to behave as Musetta has done; she protests that she loves him too much for the question of forgiveness ever to arise between them. Marcello, though he still refuses to take the smallest notice of Musetta, is visibly weakening, and she changes her strategy accordingly. For the benefit of them all, but mainly of Marcello, she launches, in what is virtually an aria in waltz time, into a flattering description of herself:

---

misunderstanding of the Italian words, "Per sua vocazione fa la rosa dei venti; gira e muta soventi d'amanti e d'amore." "La rosa dei venti" is literally "the rose of the winds," but its idiomatic meaning is the card beneath the magnetic needle, showing the points of the mariner's compass.

No. 23

Wherever she goes, she assures them, all masculine eyes are drawn to her. ("Tie me to my chair!" Marcello implores his friends.) She is conscious of her power, and simply *must* exercise it over men. "Why do you"—she addresses Marcello directly, "you who were once in love with me, try so stupidly to fly from me now? I know you don't want to speak your grief; but I know also that you are dying of it." [1] While she pauses for a moment for breath Rodolfo explains to Mimi that Musetta was once Marcello's love, but the fickle creature had deserted him for a more luxurious life with another. Mimi understands it all at last, and her sympathies seem to be with poor Musetta, for in her opinion great love means in the end great sorrow. Alcindoro manages to get in an occasional "Softly! Softly! Manners!" Colline and Schaunard philosophise aside on the sad case of Musetta and Marcello; the former finds the girl not unattractive, but finally, much in the spirit of Kipling's "A woman is only a woman, but a good cigar is a smoke," he decides that for his part he'd rather have his pipe and a Greek text.

Musetta, now sure of her triumph, approaches Marcello, who is too hypnotised to take flight as he would obviously like to do. She sees that in order to play her last card she must get rid of Lulu, which she does by howling that she is suffering agonies from a tight shoe and packing him off with it to a neighbouring shop to get her another pair. Marcello is quite melted now; his heart is not dead, he assures her, and is hers any time she likes to come for it. At the height of the big ensemble she throws herself into his arms to a thunderous outburst of No. 23 in the orchestra.

[1] Musetta's song was originally a piano piece the idea of which had come to Puccini one day when he was being gently rocked in a boat on the waters of a lake. Later he was asked, along with Mancinelli and Franchetti, to write something for the launching of an Italian battleship at Genoa; and his contribution was this waltz-melody! Thinking it too good to be wasted, he decided later to put it into the mouth of Musetta; and his correspondence shows him demanding from Giocosa a text that would go with the rhythm of it.

The enthusiasm of the bohemians wanes as the waiter approaches them with their bill; each turns it over to the other for settlement, and each finds, to his dismay, that he has no money in his pockets; even Schaunard's purse has mysteriously disappeared. Fortunately for them a diversion now occurs. In the distance a tattoo is heard, and the populace pours upon the stage to welcome the military band that soon arrives, headed by a gigantic drum-major.[1] Puccini builds up a big finale in the simplest way imaginable: he introduces just one new melody—Musetta's ironic goodbye to the still absent Alcindoro:

No. 24

but for the rest he merely fastens, in the orchestra, one familiar tune to the tail of another—the tattoo, No. 5, No. 16, No. 21, etc.—without any conceivable rhyme or reason, and on top of the orchestra brings the whole of the vocal resources of the company into play. It is a brazen evasion of the problem of dramatic composition, but somehow the dodge works to perfection. While this hullabaloo is going on Musetta places the bohemians' bill and that of Alcindoro on the latter's plate before she and her friends decamp in the rear of the departing tattoo and the crowd, Musetta, unable to walk in only one shoe, being carried out by Marcello and Colline to the cheers of the multitude, Rodolfo and Mimi following arm in arm, and Schaunard, blowing his horn, at the tail of the procession. The stage is completely empty by the time Lulu returns with a carefully wrapped up pair of new shoes for Musetta. The waiters make a combined rush at him: and as he realises that he has not only lost his mistress but has a double bill to pay he collapses in a chair.[2]

[1] The fanfare is a French one, dating from the time of Louis Philippe. It was found for Puccini by his publisher Giulio Ricordi.
[2] This seems to be Puccini's final version of the scene just before the fall of the curtain. There are at least two vocal scores of *La Bohème*, differing from each other in some small respects, as in the present instance.

15

When next we meet the bohemians it is towards the end of February. Much has happened since the joyous racketing at the Café Momus. Rodolfo, we are asked to believe, is now insanely jealous without the virtuous Mimi having given him much justification for being so; she has also developed consumption. Musetta has been at her old tricks again, and her relations with Marcello are once more those of cat and dog.

Conscious that he is not evolving his action dramatically but only depicting a series of isolated episodes that follow each other in no inevitable sequence, Puccini prefixes to his third act a few sentences taken from Murger's account of the ups and downs of the love of Rodolfo and Mimi, the breaking of Rodolfo's heart, the brief periods of reconciliation during which their love for each other was as ardent as ever. We are given also a thumbnail sketch of Musetta—her genius for elegance, her love of luxury, her invincible egoism, her slavery to her caprices.

The scene of the third act is at the Barrière d'Enfer, on an outer boulevard. On the left is a small open space with a tavern facing the closed toll-gate, on the right a road leading from the rue d'Enfer to the Latin Quarter. Over the tavern hangs a sign-board, Marcello's masterpiece "The Passage of the Red Sea" (now bearing the inscription "The Port of Marseilles"), which the painter has had to sell in order to pay for his and Musetta's board and lodging. On either side of the door of the tavern are bold frescoes of a Turk and a Zouave—further commercial products of Marcello's art. Lights are showing in the lower room of the inn; every now and then we hear shouts, roars of laughter, and the clinking of glasses. Round a brazier is seated a group of sleepy custom-house officials; another comes out of the tavern with wine. Gaunt plane trees, with marble benches between them, stretch out towards the boulevards. It is early morning, cold and dreary, of a day near the end of February; snow is falling steadily.

Over a shuddering open fifth in the 'cellos that persists as a ground bass for more than a hundred bars we hear, as the curtain rises, a succession of hollow fifths in flutes and harp:

No. 25

that match the bleak desolation of the place and the hour. Now
and then there comes from inside the tavern a song, in thirds and
sixths, which is no doubt intended to be that of joyous topers
toasting their lasses, but actually does no more than add an extra
touch to the melancholy mood invoked by No. 25:

No. 26

Even a fragment of a song from Musetta, to the tune of No. 23,
does nothing to dispel the prevailing gloom.[1] Outside the gates
the scavengers, stamping their feet and blowing on their fingers,
are clamouring to be admitted, but it is a little while before one
of the officials opens the gate to allow them to pass through to
the rue d'Enfer.

16

Later a sergeant, coming out from the guard-house, gives the
sign for the toll-gate to be opened, and as the first faint streaks
of daylight appear and the snow ceases to fall the people waiting
outside pour through—milk-women, peasant women with their
butter, cheese and eggs, and so on. When they have all moved
away, Mimi enters furtively, as if unsure of her direction, from
the rue d'Enfer, to the soft accompaniment of No. 9 in the orchestra. She is seized with a fit of coughing: Puccini is determined at
the outset to secure our sympathies with her in her latest metamorphosis. She asks the sergeant where she can find an inn in
which a painter is working: he points it out to her. Then she

[1] It was Ricordi's suggestion, gladly adopted by Puccini, that Musetta
should sing this fragment from her song of the second act. It is an excellent
way of letting us know that she is in the tavern with Marcello, and that her
frivolous, inconstant character remains unchanged. She does not appear in
person until much later in the present act.

accosts a servant girl who has come out of the tavern, asking her in broken accents if she can find for her a painter named Marcello and tell him that Mimi is waiting outside. The girl goes back into the inn, and soon Marcello emerges. Day has now dawned, drear and murky; the bell of the Hospice Sainte Thérèse rings softly for matins; and—quite unnecessarily, one cannot help thinking— Nos. 1 and 2 are repeated a few times in the orchestra.

Marcello, running to Mimi, explains, for our benefit more than hers, that he and Musetta have been located in the inn for a month or so, he keeping the pot boiling by painting the figures of the Turk and the Zouave on the façade, Musetta contributing something to their finances by giving singing lessons to the frequenters of the place. Mimi learns that Rodolfo is in the tavern, but she refuses to enter. In despairing accents:

No. 27

she pours out her woes to Marcello: Rodolfo, madly jealous, avoids her though he still loves her. This little episode makes one of those self-contained and entirely convincing musical wholes in which Puccini is seen at his best. The psychology of the situation, however, is not so convincing, partly because the librettists and the composer feel that at all costs, in view of the impending fourth act, we must be entirely on Mimi's side. She implores Marcello's help. He points out to her, like a sensible man of the world, that when two people feel about each other as she and Rodolfo now do and are only making each other wretched, the best thing they can do is to part. She agrees in theory, but pleads rather inconsequently that without the aid of Marcello a solution of the problem is impossible; for she and Rodolfo have often tried to separate, but in vain. "I get on with Musetta, and she with me," Marcello assures her, "because we love gaily: song and laughter, that is the secret of love that does not change"; and once more Mimi agrees with him.

"Well, well," says Marcello, "I will waken him," for it now appears that Rodolfo had arrived at the tavern an hour before dawn and fallen into a sleep of utter exhaustion; and Marcello invites Mimi to look through the window and see for herself. After another spasm of coughing she explains that she has done nothing but cough since the time last night when Rodolfo left her, saying that all was over between them. At daybreak she had hurried here in the hope of finding him. "He's awake now; he has risen and is looking for me," says Marcello; "come with me."

But she only ejaculates "He must not see me": she is too well aware that the big scene is coming that must be played not inside the tavern but in view of the audience. Marcello sensibly suggests that she shall return home and not make a scene there; but apparently she makes at once for the cover of one of the plane-trees. One says "apparently" because the earlier and the later editions of the score differ from each other at this point. In the former, after Mimi's "He must not see me," Marcello says "In that case hide yourself over there," and he points to the tree. She does so as quickly as she can, the orchestra giving out half-a-dozen bars of quiet reminiscence of Nos. 1 and 2 that are obviously intended to give her time to scuttle across the stage before Rodolfo, according to the stage directions, "comes out of the tavern and hastens to Marcello." But in the later score Marcello's reply to her "He must not see me here" is "For mercy's sake, Mimi, return home; don't make a scene here." Nothing is said about her hiding herself. The orchestra merely plays softly for eight bars on a contrapuntal combination of No. 12 and No. 3, which are followed by the five or six bars of the bohemians' music referred to above. Then Rodolfo enters from the tavern.

The librettists obviously did not quite know how to manage the situation, what words to put into the characters' mouths. Marcello's "Hide yourself over there," with the stage direction "pointing to the plane-trees," makes sense in itself, as does the later direction, "Mimi cautiously approaches [from the cover of the trees] to listen" to the dialogue between the two men; but in the later edition the first and only hint of Mimi having withdrawn to the trees, and of the reason for this, is a direction later on, "Mimi cautiously approaches to listen": from where she listens we are not told just then, though we read further on that she "comes closer and closer, under cover of the trees."

No. 28

The whole thing is a piece of bad stage construction. Without a moment's warning to us, without a moment's hesitation on his part, the Rodolfo who only a minute or two before has been sleeping the sleep of the exhausted is suddenly awake in full possession of his faculties and "comes out and hastens towards Marcello," crying, "Ah, Marcello, at last [I've found you]." The "At last" implies, surely, that he has been looking for Marcello for some time. The orchestra—rather inconsequently, but then Puccini rarely pauses to ask himself whether the circumstances in which he now wants to revive an old tune have any relevance to the circumstances in which it is now to appear—accompanies the remark with No. 10, the melody to which Mimi, in the first act, had sung "How stupid I am! Where can I have left the key of my room?" Then Rodolfo gets to the point with extraordinary abruptness: "No one can hear us here; I want a separation from Mimi";[1]

[1] This is perhaps the feeblest piece of construction in the whole work. "Finalmente" may be taken as meaning either "At last I've found you"—which is the translation given in the English edition—or "At last we can talk without being overheard." The episode is equally ridiculous whichever way we take it. My conjecture is that there had been a change of mind on the part of the librettists and the composer at this point. Mimi and Rodolfo having had their crucial quarrel the night before, naturally the librettists had sent the poet off in the early hours of the morning in search of his old boon-companion Marcello. If we imagine him, at the point of the drama now in question, rushing in *from the town* and conveniently lighting on Marcello at the tavern, the words put into his mouth are quite plausible: he bursts out at once with the thought that has been uppermost in his mind for hours. But no doubt the librettists and Puccini realised at this point that all this would simply be a duplication of the entry of Mimi; so to avoid that they hit on the device of making Rodolfo arrive at the tavern *before* the scene opens. But then a new problem arose—how to get him on to the stage in time for Mimi to overhear his conversation with Marcello; and it was here that their invention broke down. It is asking too much of us to believe that the fuming, desperate Rodolfo, after finding his friend an hour before dawn, had said nothing at all to him then about the reason for his visit, but had flung himself on to a bench ("sopra una panca," Marcello tells Mimi),

71

and he launches into a story of how he had thought his love for her was dead, but her blue eyes had revived it.

17

This interests the eavesdropping Mimi, who approaches warily to listen to what may follow. Marcello takes a common-sense line with his friend—why try to bring the dead past back to life again? If love does not laugh and sparkle it is nothing but weariness. "The trouble is that you are jealous, choleric, fantastic, chockfull of prejudices, tiresome, pig-headed." Nothing we have so far seen of Rodolfo in the opera has given us any suspicion of these elements in his make-up, apart from the almost imperceptible hint to which reference has been made on page 62; but since Puccini will have it so for the pathetic purposes of the present act and the next, the poor fellow pleads guilty to at any rate the first item of the indictment. But he insists that his jealousy is justified. "With bitter irony," as the stage direction puts it, he tells Marcello that Mimi is a coquette who flirts with everyone:

No. 29

let any miserable little puppy of a Vicomte make eyes at her and she does all she can to lure him into her toils—which is true enough to Murger but not at all congruous with the opera as we have seen it evolving thus far—if the word "evolving" is at all suitable to the series of episodes that is La Bohème.

Marcello doubts whether all this is true, and Rodolfo agrees with him. "In vain I try to hide my torment: I love her above all things in the world. But I live in fear," he concludes—and Mimi, still in the cover of the trees, creeps a little nearer to hear what is coming. Mimi, he says, to the accompaniment of some sombre chords in the orchestra that are like a presage of funeral bells:

and slept the sleep of the utterly exhausted for a couple of hours; and now, a mere twenty-three bars after Marcello, looking through the window, has seen him stretching himself, he rushes into the open, shouting "I want a separation from Mimi!"

No. 30

"Mimi is sickly; every day she grows weaker; the poor little creature, I fear, is doomed. Every day she is racked with coughing,
and her cheeks betray her malady." And the only shelter he can
offer her is a squalid fireless garret through which the north wind
blows cruelly. Yet she smiles and sings, while he is consumed
with remorse. "She is a hothouse flower; poverty has wasted her,
and to bring her back to life more is required than love." We may
feel that Rodolfo's self-indictment is psychologically a trifle over-
done for the purposes of the situation, but there can be no doubt
as to the power of Puccini's musical handling of it, especially
when he launches a melodic and harmonic complex:

No. 31

that keeps reiterating itself, in the best Puccini fashion, throughout the description of Mimi's malady. The artist in Puccini, as
we all know, delighted in scenes of suffering, with a touch of
torture in them for preference; and there being no opportunity
for anything of that kind anywhere else in *La Bohème* he makes
one here, Rodolfo abandoning himself to the very luxury of self-
torture as he thinks of all that Mimi has suffered and is now suffering, and Mimi, lost in self-pity, coughing and sobbing "Ah!
I must die!" from the cover of the plane-tree. It is her coughing
that in the end reveals her presence. The repentant Rodolfo runs
to her—the orchestra giving out a tender reminiscence of No. 9
—and embraces her affectionately. He would take her into the
warmth of the tavern, but the poor creature, mindful as ever that
the big scene must be played out to the end in full view of the

audience, refuses the invitation, declaring that the odour of the place would stifle her.

18

It is now time the lovers were left alone for a while; so the librettists give Marcello a pretext for leaving the stage. And here we come upon another of the sundry little discrepancies between the two vocal scores of the work. The frivolous No. 12 flares out in the orchestra, and Musetta's brazen laugh is heard from within the tavern. "That's Musetta laughing," Marcello cries, looking through the window; "with whom? Ah, the coquette! I will find out!" Having said which, in the earlier score he runs in a frenzy into the tavern, leaving the stage to Rodolfo and Mimi. But in the later score there is no mention of his going into the tavern, though later we find him speaking "from within," and later still we find him on the stage again.

Mimi, now alone with Rodolfo, would bid him a last farewell; she will return to the room of her own which she had left in the first act at the call of love, there to embroider as of old and die. In pathetic accents she makes her last request to him: her few clothes and trinkets and the prayer-book Rodolfo had given her— if he will wrap them up in an apron she will send the porter for them: the final point is given to her appeal by the motive (No. 14) associated in the first act with her dreams of simple happiness. Under her pillow, she continues, he will find her little rose-pink bonnet; perhaps he would like to keep it in remembrance of her. "Farewell!" she sings:

No. 32

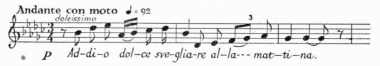

"Farewell the sweet awakenings in the morning; farewell rebukes and jealousy, farewell the anguish of suspicion." [1] Rodolfo takes

[1] This is another case of Puccini's "lifting" from an earlier work. The music of Mimi's "Addio dolce svegliare alla mattina" ("Farewell the sweet awakenings in the morning") and of the quartet that follows is taken bodily from a song, "Sole e amore," written by Puccini in 1887. The librettists, of course, had to provide the old music with new words.

up the strain: "Farewell the life of dreams in your smiles, the kisses of the true poet"; and their voices unite in a despairing final cry of "To be alone together in the winter is death—but when spring comes, with it comes the sun."

But apparently all this, while serious enough as far as the music is concerned, is not to be taken quite at its face value, for according to the stage directions Mimi's "Farewell rebukes and jealousy" is spoken "playfully." The act might well end here, with the reconciliation of the lovers; but Puccini has now to provide us with the key to the situation in the fourth act, where we find Marcello once more abandoned by the volatile Musetta. From the tavern comes the sound of smashing plates and glasses; a little later the pair emerge and break out into a spate of recriminations. Marcello accuses Musetta of flirting with one of the men in the tavern, and threatens to teach her better manners. She replies that as they are not married he has no husband's rights over her, and swears she will do as she likes whenever and wherever she likes. It ends with her saying she is going away, to which Marcello replies "Good riddance!"; and with a final exchange of diplomatic courtesies—"Viper! Witch!" "Shop painter! Toad!" —they part once more, Musetta going off into the town, Marcello returning to the tavern.

All this while Rodolfo and Mimi have been tranquilly colloguing on their own account about lilies and roses and the twittering of the birds in their nests. They have now arrived at the stage of assuring each other that they will not part until the spring comes again with its flowers, and so, "Would that winter might last for ever!"; and they move away hand in hand as the curtain falls. These last words of theirs seem to be an attempt on the librettists' part to work in a reminiscence of one of the most charming episodes in Murger, in which Marcel presents Musette with some flowers. She promises to be faithful to him as long as the flowers last. "But they will be withered in a couple of days," he protests; "if I had known I would have bought immortelles."

19

We have seen Puccini, in the preamble to the first act, suppressing a passage in Murger that showed a less likeable side to the character of Mimi. In the third act of the opera she is still all

innocence, sweetness, pathos; if she has been unhappy with
Rodolfo that is because he is insanely and unjustifiably jealous.
But now in the fourth act we have a Mimi who is obviously of the
same type as Musetta; yet Puccini gives us no light at all on what
has presumably happened between the third act and the fourth;
his paraphrase of Murger in his preface to the last act merely tells
us that for some months the poet and the painter have been living
miserably alone, having had no word for a long time of Mimi
and Musette.

The librettists based their last act on the final chapter but one
of the *Scènes de la Vie de Bohème,* rejecting, however, the grue-
some ending to that. In Murger, Marcel is still mourning over the
desertion of Musette, while Mimi has left Rodolphe for a certain
Vicomte Paul. Painter and poet now occupy two rooms in the
same building. It is Christmas eve once more. The two friends,
sobered by experience, discuss their past, present and future; they
realise it is time they ceased brooding nostalgically over the past
and made an effort to give some conscious direction to their lives.
They will begin by burning all the little souvenirs of their lost
loves—ribbons, letters, faded flowers and so forth. But Marcel
cannot find it in his heart to destroy an old bouquet that Musette
had once worn. So he thrusts it furtively into his waistcoat, and,
happening to turn round at that moment, finds that Rodolphe is
similarly saving from destruction a little night-cap that had once
been Mimi's. "He's as weak as I am," Marcel murmurs to himself.

Just then the door opens and Mimi enters. She has been abandoned, we learn, by the Vicomte, who has even sold the furniture
and trinkets he had given her. In the last stages of hunger and
exhaustion, and knowing she has not long to live, she begs a
night's shelter from the two friends. The next day Colline and
Schaunard call on them, the latter in a summer overcoat, for
having heard that Mimi is ill he had sold his winter clothes and
given the money to Rodolphe. Colline, for his part, has sold his
dearly-beloved books. A doctor is called in, who sends Mimi to
a hospital, where the friends visit her. One day Rodolphe gets a
letter from a friend, a student in the hospital, informing him that
No. 8—Mimi—is dead. Rodolphe is plunged into the depths of
despair. A week later the pair meet by chance, and the student
informs Rodolphe that he had been in error. It appears that when

he wrote his letter he had been away from the hospital for a couple of days, during which Mimi, unknown to him, had been removed to another ward; in No. 8 another woman had been placed, who had died; Mimi was still alive yesterday, neither better nor worse but very unhappy, thinking that Rodolphe must be ill because he had not come to see her. The two men go at once to the hospital, where they learn that Mimi had died at four o'clock that morning. "She is there," says the student, pointing to a great cart in the courtyard: poor friendless Mimi is on her way to the common grave reserved for corpses that no one has claimed.

Puccini, of course, could not let *his* Mimi come to so miserable an end as this; at least she would die surrounded by her bohemian friends. For the rest, however, he keeps fairly closely to the lines of Murger's story, and puts to a new and dexterous use the episode of Colline's sale of his coat. Apart from the little song the philosopher sings on that occasion there is comparatively little that is new in the music of the fourth act: this roused the resentment of some of the Italian audiences in the early days of the opera's appearance; they felt they had been cheated—they had paid for four acts of music and had been fobbed off with not much more than three. It took them some time to realize that the fourth act of *La Bohème* is one of Puccini's most exquisite creations.

20

The curtain having risen again, to the strains of No. 1, we see the attic once more as in the first act, with Marcello at his easel and Rodolfo at his writing-table, each trying to give the impression that he is hard at work, whereas what really interests them is the conversation in which they have evidently been engaged for some time. At the point where we are allowed to eavesdrop Rodolfo is telling his friend that he has just met Musetta, riding in a carriage and pair, with servants in livery, as irresponsibly gay as No. 21 in the orchestra would lead us to expect. He had enquired about the state of her heart, and had been informed that she was blissfully unconscious of its activities, thanks to the velvet that covered it. Marcello, professing to be delighted at the news, slams the paint vigorously on the canvas, not hearing Rodolfo's aside—"Rubbish! You're laughing, but on the wrong side of your face!" But the painter, in turn, has some news for the poet. He has seen Mimi; and now it is Rodolfo's turn to stop writing, bite his lip, and do his best to look unconcerned. Strange as it may seem to us, the virtuous Mimi of our second and third acts was also riding in her carriage, dressed like a queen. "Splendid!" says Rodolfo; "I'm enchanted to hear it"; and now it is Marcello's turn to comment, aside, "You liar, you're eating your heart out for love." They try to work, but it is useless. Rodolfo puts down his pen, Marcello flings away his paint-brush; the latter takes a bunch of ribbons from his pocket and kisses it; later, Rodolfo brings out from a drawer an old bonnet of Mimi's; and each of them lets his memory play, half sweetly, half sadly, on the days that are no more. Their brief duet, which begins with Rodolfo's lament over the lost white hands and fragrant tresses of Mimi:

No. 33

is one of those exquisite vignettes, musically complete and shapely in itself yet blood of the blood of the surrounding dramatic tissue, bone of its bone, a procedure of which the secret is Puccini's. Marcello, brooding upon the dark eyes and saucy lips of Musetta, answers with a countertheme; then their voices blend to the strain of No. 33, Marcello calling to Musetta, Rodolfo pressing to his heart the little rose-pink bonnet which Mimi had left under her pillow when she forsook him. It is a pity that this tender, quiet episode should always be ruined in performance by the necessity the tenor feels himself under to shout the baritone down, and vice versa: what was intended to be a duet degenerates into something like a vocal duel.[1]

[1] It seems to have escaped the notice of everyone concerned that Puccini has enclosed the whole vocal line of this longish episode (four whole pages of the score) within brackets. Manifestly he intended it to be presented to us as a sort of psychological parenthesis: Rodolfo and Marcello, momentarily abstracted from outward crude reality, are lost in their individual nostalgic memories of the happy vanished past. The prolonged pause in voices and orchestra that precedes it is itself significant. The singing of the episode should convey unmistakably this sense of temporary inward abstraction—

As No. 33, the voices having ceased, sings itself out quietly in the upper reaches of the orchestra, the two bohemians make another attempt at a show of indifference. "What time is it?" asks Rodolfo. "Time for our yesterday's dinner," replies Marcello. "Hasn't Schaunard returned yet?" Rodolfo enquires; and No. 5 in the orchestra prepares for the exuberant entry of the musician, flourishing four rolls of bread; he is accompanied by Colline, who carries a paper bag from which he extracts a herring—"a dish worthy of Demosthenes," he assures them.

21

The four seat themselves at the table and profess to be dining like Lucullus. "Now the champagne goes on the ice," says Schaunard, putting a water-bottle into Colline's hat. Addressing Marcello with old-world courtesy as "Baron," and offering him a slice of bread, Rodolfo asks him whether he prefers trout or salmon; another slice, when offered to Duke Schaunard, becomes that great delicacy a parrot's tongue. The Duke politely declines it—"I dare not; I shall be dancing this evening." Colline, having devoured his roll, rises solemnly and begs them to excuse him: he is a Minister of the King, who requires his attendance; he has also to see Guizot. They all bow respectfully to him. Schaunard, feeling he is being neglected, declares that the muse has taken possession of him; but the others shout him down. His suggestion of "something in the choregraphic line," however, is received with enthusiasm—"a dance to vocal music."

They clear away the table and chairs and prepare for the dance. Colline is for a gavotte, Marcello for a minuet, Rodolfo for a pavanella; but Schaunard insists on a fandango, and the orchestra backs him up. In the end they decide on quadrilles. Schaunard, as the musician of the party, gives the beat with an air of professional importance. Rodolfo, approaching Marcello in gallant fashion, bows deeply and addresses him as "Fair Lady": Marcello, putting on a female falsetto, begs the bold man to respect his modesty. Soon they become critical of their partners: Schaunard accuses Colline of dancing like a lackey, which the philosopher regards as an insult that can be wiped out only in blood. They fight a fero-

but it never does. The brackets are even omitted from the first English edition of the score.

cious duel, one armed with the poker, the other with the tongs. Schaunard exhorts Rodolfo and Marcello to bring a stretcher for Colline; the latter, more liberal in his ideas, orders a cemetery for Schaunard. Behind and around them Rodolfo and Marcello dance a rigadoon.

The gaiety is at its height when the door is flung open, to the accompaniment of a crashing chord succeeded by an almost inaudible drum-roll, and Musetta enters in great agitation with the news that Mimi is following her, so ill that she has hardly the strength to climb the stairs. Rodolfo catches sight of his former love seated on the top stair and rushes towards her, followed by Marcello. The lovers fall into each other's arms with cries of "O my Rodolfo! You will have me here with you?" and "My Mimi, for ever!" To the accompaniment of the typical Mimi theme (No. 9), now with darker harmonies, the bohemians lay her gently on the bed, draw the coverlet over her, and adjust the pillow under her head. Musetta hurriedly explains that having chanced to hear that Mimi had left her Vicomte she had sought her far and wide and at last found her, dragging herself along with difficulty, knowing she was dying, but longing to see Rodolfo once more. The orchestra dwells mournfully on No. 13, lingering with profound pathos on the original cadence to this (No. 14), as Mimi tells them how happy she is now, feeling that she may still live, never to be parted from Rodolfo again. But all are painfully aware that she is cold and hungry, and that there is no food in the room, no warmth for her poor little body. "In half an hour she'll be dead," Schaunard whispers to Colline. "I feel so cold," Mimi complains. "If only I had a muff! I feel that my hands will never be warm again!" she stammers feebly, the orchestra still pouring out Nos. 13 and 14 in wave on wave. Rodolfo takes her hand in his. She calls the bohemians to her side by their names, one by one: to Marcello she says, "Listen, Marcello; Musetta is a good soul"; and he murmurs "I know, I know."

22

Schaunard and Colline drift helplessly away: the musician sits at the table, burying his face in his hands; Colline is lost in thought; Musetta takes off her ear-rings, gives them to Marcello to sell, and bids him bring some cordials and a doctor for Mimi, who has now become drowsy. Rodolfo still sits beside her, holding her hand. "You will not leave me?" she murmurs: "No," he assures her, and the orchestra dwells with infinite poignancy on the theme—No. 18—associated with their hour of happiness at the Café Momus.

Musetta declares that she will go in search of a muff, to gratify what may be Mimi's last request; Marcello accompanies her. Meanwhile Colline prepares to make his own great sacrifice for Mimi's sake. He takes off his overcoat, the old comrade that has shared good times and bad with him:

No. 34

"never have you bent your shabby back to rich man or mighty; in your pockets philosophers and poets have found a tranquil refuge. Now that our joyous days together are over I bid you farewell, faithful old friend; farewell, farewell!" Slowly and sadly he folds the coat up and is about to go, but seeing Schaunard sunk in misery he approaches him, pats him on the shoulder and tells him there are two, and only two, acts of kindness it is now in their power to do: "this is mine"—pointing to the coat he is going to sell—"the other, to leave these two together." Schaunard mournfully agrees with the philosopher: as pretext for his departure he takes up the water-bottle. The pair go out, gently closing the door behind them, to the accompaniment, for the last time, of Schaunard's No. 5, its old ebullience now modulated to an expressive andante.

The lovers are now alone. The melody of No. 5 merges imperceptibly into that of No. 12—Rodolfo's outpouring of love to Mimi in the first act. She opens her eyes, sees that the others have left, and lays her hand on Rodolfo's, who kisses it affectionately. She has only been feigning sleep, she says quietly, because she wanted to be alone with him:

No. 35

There are many things she wants to tell him, but one in particular, something vast and profound as the sea—that he is her love and her life. Her arms go round his neck for a moment, then fall weakly again, and with a last pathetic touch of coquetry the wasted creature asks him, "Am I still pretty?" "Lovely as the dawn," he assures her. But she cuts him short: his comparison is wrong—he should have said "as the sunset"; and the sombre No. 30 strikes in with its sinister suggestion of death. Her mind wanders back into the past: "They call me Mimi," she murmurs, "but I know not why." He compares her to a swallow returning to its nest, and shows her the bonnet. She hails it with childlike delight, and motions to him to place it on her head. "Do you remember," she asks him to the melody of No. 10, "the day when first I came to your room?"; and they remind each other of everything that had happened then—how frightened she was, the mislaying of the key, the search for it in the darkness, how Rodolfo, guided by Fate, as he now assures her, had found it, how her blushes were invisible in the gloom, and how he had clasped her hand and found it so cold that he had to warm it into life.

Just then a spasm seizes her and her head falls back. Schaunard enters and hastens to the side of the alarmed Rodolfo, and, with the orchestra giving out No. 9, they lower her gently, she assuring them that she feels better now. Musetta and Marcello steal in, the one bearing a muff, the other a phial. As Mimi appears to be sleeping they converse in low tones that add to the gradually increasing tension of the scene. The doctor is on his way, says Marcello; meanwhile here is a cordial. Mimi opens her eyes, sees the muff, and fastens on it with childlike glee: "how soft and warm it is," she says; "now my hands won't be white with cold"; and the orchestra gives out in the merest whisper, but with a new poignancy of harmony and colour, a phrase that had accompanied Rodolfo's first touch of Mimi's frozen hand in the first act:

No. 36

She thanks him as the supposed donor of the muff. "Here for ever with you, dear," she murmurs: "my hands are warm now, and I shall sleep." Her head falls back, and indeed she appears to be sleeping. Musetta, warming the cordial over a spirit-lamp, breathes a prayer to the Madonna for her. The others move away from the bed and talk in low tones, Rodolfo now and then going back on tip-toe to look at the silent figure, hopeful that it is only sleeping. But Schaunard, in a hoarse whisper, suddenly says, "Marcello, she is dead!"—at the very moment when Colline returns and gives Musetta the money that is now useless. Rodolfo has not heard Schaunard's ejaculation: he is at the side of the room, stretching Musetta's cloak across the window to shut out a shaft of sunlight which he thinks may incommode Mimi. "How is she?" Colline asks him. "You can see," he replies; "quite tranquil." But as he turns round he sees something in the faces of Marcello and Schaunard that frightens him. "What is the meaning of this coming and going?" he asks them, "and why do you look at me like this?" Marcello can only embrace him and murmur "Courage!" Rodolfo raises Mimi, takes her hand in his, and then, realising what has happened, falls sobbing on the bed, while the orchestra seizes upon the simple melody (No. 35) to which, earlier in the scene, Mimi had assured Rodolfo that she had only been feigning sleep, and converts it into a passionate threnody that gradually dies out in silence as the curtain falls:

No. 37

The Barber of Seville

ROSSINI [1792–1868]

PRINCIPAL CHARACTERS

COUNT ALMAVIVA	*Tenor*
FIGARO	*Baritone*
ROSINA	*Mezzo-soprano*
DOCTOR BARTOLO	*Bass*
FIORELLO	*Tenor*
AMBROSIO	*Bass*
BERTA	*Soprano*

1

HE CARON DE BEAUMARCHAIS to whom we owe *The Barber of Seville* and *The Marriage of Figaro* began life in a humble way in January 1732 as Pierre Augustin Caron, the son of a Paris clockmaker. The boy was trained in his father's profession, and at twenty invented a new watch escapement. His idea was stolen by a rival: a lawsuit followed: the young Caron saw to it that the affair received plenty of publicity, and it all ended very much in his favour. The incident was symbolic and prophetic: all his long life he was at variance with someone or other, and practically always victor by virtue of his superior adroitness and his satiric tongue and pen.

By now he had attracted the attention of the Court. He was appointed clockmaker to Louis XV, and before long we find him, rather surprisingly, teaching the guitar and harp to his Majesty's daughters and organising the Court musical entertainments and ballets. In 1755 he married a rich widow, eleven years his senior, who died after some eighteen months of wedlock. Much of the money he inherited from her was lost in lawsuits with her relations. There remained in his hands, however, a small landed property of hers that carried with it the title of de Beaumarchais, by which he chose to be known for the rest of his life. In 1768 he married another widow, who also died within a couple of years.

A born adventurer, cool, audacious, infinitely resourceful and none too scrupulous, for the next thirty years or so he was ready to try his hand at anything that looked like turning out profitably and at the same time attracted him by a spice of difficulty and danger in it. He was equally happy gun-running for the American insurgents (or, during the Terror, for the Dutch), acting as a royalist spy and purloiner of secret documents in London, or insinuating his plays into the Paris theatres and fighting the actors for his author's fees. (Literary men should remember him with gratitude as the founder of the Société des auteurs dramatiques, the prime object of which was to see that the actors at the Comédie Française did not bamboozle playwrights out of their royalties.) He was a man who would have come to the front in any age and any milieu: today he would no doubt be equally notorious, equally successful, as a dealer in armaments, a secret service agent, a Hollywood magnate, a playwright and a smuggler of Swiss watches, nylons or foreign currency.

His excursions into serious drama were not a success; sentimentality did not sit well on him. His literary fame rests today almost entirely on three works—the two immortal Figaro comedies and the *Mémoires*; [1] and the last is as great in its way as the two stage works by which he is mostly known now. In his late thirties he had become closely associated with one of the big financiers of the day, a certain Pâris-Duverney, who had no doubt found him very useful in some of his business transactions and was appropriately grateful. Beaumarchais soon found himself sufficiently in funds to buy for 50,000 livres an appointment as royal secretary that carried with it a title to nobility: when detractors ventured to throw doubts on his claim to be one of the aristocracy he would reply, with a frankness rare among recipients of titles, "If you don't believe me I'll show you the receipt." On the 1st April 1770 he and Pâris-Duverney had a final settlement of

---

[1] Not "mémoires" in the autobiographical sense of the term, but "documents relating to . . ."; the full description of the work in question is *Mémoires dans l'affaire Goezman*.

accounts, the financier acknowledging in writing that he owed Beaumarchais 15,000 livres. Four months later Pâris-Duverney died. His nephew and general heir, Count de la Blache, reluctant to let this ripe plum slip out of his hands, accused Beaumarchais of having falsified the books, and alleged him to be indebted to the estate to the tune of 139,000 livres. The case was decided legally first against Beaumarchais, then in his favour; but he had been imprudent enough just then to incur the hostility of the powerful Duke de Chaulnes by filching the latter's mistress from him, and there was a quarrel that ended in both the Duke and Beaumarchais being placed under arrest.

This gave La Blache an opportunity to reopen his case. When, in the second act of *The Barber*, Bartholo hints at getting Count Almaviva out of the way by attacking him in a night ambuscade, the wily Basile cries "Fie!" on him for the crudity of his technique. Basile knows a better way of ruining the Count's chances with Rosine—by means of calumny, a subject on which he grows eloquent. "Calumny, monsieur! You do wrong to despise it. I have seen the most respectable men pretty well annihilated by it. Take my word for it, there is no stupid vileness, no horror, no absurdity that you can't get the loungers of a big town to believe; —and here in Madrid we have some real experts in that line!" La Blache, with his adversary temporarily out of the way, renewed the battle for the precious livres, and found calumny his best weapon. Forged letters from and to Beaumarchais were put into circulation, and he was accused of having got rid of both his wives by poison. The upshot of it all was that La Blache won his case on a re-trial, and Beaumarchais, at the age of forty-one, was wellnigh ruined.

2

But, as usual, disaster and conflict brought out all that was best in him; his genius needed rough friction to develop all its latent light and heat. The climax in the Pâris-Duverney dispute had come in April 1773. A legal councillor named Goezman had been entrusted with the preparation of a report on the case, which was to come before the tribunal on the fifth of that month. On the first, Beaumarchais, who was, of course, seriously hampered in both defence and attack by the circumstances of his imprisonment, obtained permission to leave the jail on each of the next few mornings on the conditions that he would be accompanied everywhere by a certain M. Santerre, that he would not occupy himself in his free time with anything but the coming lawsuit, and that he would return to the prison each day at nightfall. The person who mattered most to him was of course Goezman, who, he feared, was not as well acquainted with the financial details of the Pâris-Duverney matter as he would have liked him to be; so Beaumarchais's first, indeed only, care was to have a little confidential talk with this influential gentleman.

Friends had told him that his judge Goezman's young wife took an interest of her own occasionally in the cases that came before her husband: as Beaumarchais puts it ironically in his first *Mémoire*, she had assured his chief informant that if a litigant's nature was generous and his cause just, and he asked of her nothing that was inconsistent with her honesty, she would not resent the offer of a little private gift as an outrage on her delicacy. The friend who was acting for Beaumarchais learned that Mme Goezman was so anxious to do all a poor weak woman could do to further the interests of justice that for a trifle of a hundred louis d'or she would arrange for her husband to grant Beaumarchais an audience before the case came on. On the 3rd April the latter did indeed manage to see the judge, but only for a few minutes before the great man's supper. A promise of a longer talk the next day was made, but not kept. Thereupon Mme Goezman guaranteed him an interview on the following morning—the 5th April —in return for a further disinterested transfer of a hundred louis; but as Beaumarchais did not possess that sum she was content with a watch set with diamonds—plus fifteen louis, intended, so she said, for her husband's secretary. But again Beaumarchais was refused the door, making the ninth time in all; the case was heard on that fateful fifth, and, after an all-day sitting of the court, judgment was given against him.

His adversaries were sure he was for ever down and out: but little did they know their man. It had been one of the conditions of the understanding with Mme Goezman that if the promised interview with her husband did not materialise and Beaumarchais lost his case she would return the gifts. This she did, so far as the hundred louis and the watch were concerned, but not as regards

8 7

the fifteen louis for the secretary—which the latter denied ever having been offered him. Thereupon Beaumarchais began to make trouble. The details of the affair having become public property—Beaumarchais had seen to that—Goezman was forced to come into the open with a charge that the litigant, having tried to suborn one of his judges and failed, was now calumniating the latter's innocent wife. The old intrigues, machinations and chicaneries began all over again, but now on a much larger scale, more and more people being dragged into the affair. Beaumarchais took bold aggressive action: since the courts would not give him justice as he conceived it he would appeal to the public. This he did in four *Mémoires*, masterpieces of wit, humour, gay argument and urbane malice that were the delight of a town always appreciative of good rapier play. The full story of his own conduct in the affair was told with irresistible vivacity. Mme Goezman cut a sorry figure in court under his relentless examination. He had turned her inside out, made her contradict herself—in a moment of flurry she was indiscreet enough to deny that she had ever received the fifteen louis—showed her up in all her feminine silliness, disarmed her at times with flattery—gallantly declining to believe that a women who looked, as he assured her, no more than eighteen could possibly be thirty, as she said—goaded her into threatening him with personal violence, worked her up at one moment into a wild-cat fury and the next baffled her by his imperturbable politeness, so that on one occasion, after a particularly devastating handling of her, she smilingly accepted his arm as they left the court. Beaumarchais had everyone on his side: Voltaire, no mean controversialist himself, was enchanted with the *Mémoires*: "Don't tell me," he chuckled, "that this man poisoned his wives; he's much too gay and amusing for that."

3

Everyone on his side—except his judges, who had lost their heads completely. Their verdict, delivered on the 26th February 1774 after an all-day sitting, was worthy of one of his own comedies. The *Mémoires* were condemned to be burned by the public executioner as defamatory, scandalous, and heaven knows what else; Mme Goezman was censured and ordered to refund the fifteen louis; Goezman, an awkward episode in whose private life Beaumarchais had unkindly dragged into the open, was so discredited that he had to give up his post; and both Beaumarchais and Mme Goezman were ordered to appear before the tribunal and beg its pardon on their knees.[1] Beaumarchais must have enjoyed the whole thing immensely; he had become overnight the most popular man in Paris, for every one of his opponents and judges was hated for some reason or other by some one or other from the King down to the man in the street,[2] so that the butchery gave general satisfaction. But the King, who thought the scandal had gone far enough for public safety, had a hint conveyed to Beaumarchais that he did not wish him to develop it any further: meanwhile, till a new trial of the case could be ordered, he was entrusted with a confidential mission in London.[3] *L'affaire Goezman* is of particular importance to us today because so much of the actual Beaumarchais went straight into the making of the immortal Figaro, and something of the acid fun he had poked at French administrators of justice finds its echo in the scene in the third act of *The Marriage of Figaro*, in which the breach of promise case of Marceline v. Figaro, Bartholo intervening, is solemnly tried by that moral pillar of society, Count Almaviva.

Le Barbier de Séville had been written in 1772: it was then an opéra-comique, that is to say a mixture of spoken play and music, which accounts for the relatively large proportion of the latter still surviving in the present form of the work. The play was intended for the Comédie-Italienne, but was refused there because the actor who was to play the barber Figaro jibbed at the part, he having been at one time a barber's apprentice. Recast as an ordinary play, *Le Barbier* was accepted by the Comédie-Française and actually put into rehearsal; but the theatre closed down on it when Beaumarchais was committed to prison at the same time as the Duc de Chaulnes. In 1774, when the Comédie-Française was willing to take it up again, the police forbade a production, for

[1] Beaumarchais was spared this ignominy, however.
[2] The King's favourite, Mme Dubarry, had the episode of Beaumarchais's public tussle with Mme Goezman dramatised and staged at the Court.
[3] We cannot follow the remainder of his busy and varied life in detail here. He got into trouble with the French revolutionaries in 1792, but somehow survived the Terror. After three years in Holland, still active in the business of gun supplies, he returned in 1796 to Paris, really ruined at last, and died on the 18th May 1799.

the Goezman affair was then in full swing and it was rumoured that the comedy contained attacks on the magistrature. It was not until February 1775 that *Le Barbier de Séville, ou la Précaution Inutile*, in five acts, appeared on the stage. It failed decisively on the first night. Beaumarchais, always the realist, saw where he had gone wrong and at once proceeded to put things right. He cut a large quantity of dead wood out of the overgrown tree, suppressed a whole act that had been added to the original opéra-comique, and shortened the action and the speeches at several points. The second performance was a complete success; and when he printed the play he added a long and brilliant "Letter" to his critics in which he anticipated the publicity technique of Bernard Shaw.

4

Figaro, as the author introduces him to us in the opening act of the play, was essentially Beaumarchais himself. Like the latter, he had tried his hand at everything. In Madrid he had been in the service of the rich young grandee Count Almaviva, who, while admiring his remarkable talents, obviously would not trust him any further than he could see him: the Count's first words on recognising him at dead of night outside Rosine's house in Seville are "Why, it's that rogue Figaro!" The latter gives him an account of his vicissitudes since the pair had last met. Almaviva had recommended him for government employment: he had been given a medical job, not, however, in the hospitals, as he had expected, but in the Andalusian stables, where, he now claims, by dosing human beings with the medicines intended for the horses he had not only put money in his pocket but effected some remarkable cures: if occasionally his human patients had died, well, as he philosophically remarks, "there's no universal remedy." He had been dismissed, according to his own account, from sheer jealousy and stupidity on the part of the Minister concerned, who held that literary ambitions were incompatible with a talent for business—for Figaro, it appears, had been writing madrigals and contributing to the papers. But he had taken his dismissal philosophically, maintaining—and here it is the actual Beaumarchais who is speaking from experience—that an exalted personage is doing a poor man like him all the good he can when he refrains from doing him any harm. When the Count smilingly remarks that he remembers quite well what Figaro was when in his service—a bit of a rascal, a good-for-nothing, lazy, disorderly—he gets the biting riposte, "Ah, Monseigneur, with your high ideal of the virtues necessary to a servant, how many masters, would you say, are fit to be valets?" a fencing pass that wins the admiration of the broadminded young grandee.

Figaro, on the occasion of that meeting, resumes the story of his life. He had gone back to Madrid, where he had attempted dramatic authorship. In this he had failed, though he could not understand why, for, as he admits, he had done everything possible to ensure success, employing all the arts of the paid claque and getting himself and his piece talked about in advance in the cafés. But the cabals had beaten him; his play had been hissed, and if ever he sees a chance to get his own back—! The Count interrupts him: "Don't you know that in the law courts one has only twenty-four hours in which to call down curses on his judges?", to which Figaro replies grimly, "In the theatre one has twenty-four years."

Having found it impossible to make any headway in Madrid against the butting animals and stinging insects that everywhere made the literary man's life a burden to him, and being out of funds and very much in debt, he had decided that the honourable emoluments of the razor were preferable to the empty honours of the pen; so he had travelled across Spain, practising his new profession of barber, "made much of in one town, jailed in another, but always superior to events . . . laughing at the fools, defying the rascals, taking my poverty light-heartedly and shaving all and sundry." At last he had come to Seville, where he still is, ready to do anything that Count Almaviva may demand of him. His gay philosophy of life, he assures the Count, is the product of his misfortunes: he forces himself to laugh at everything to keep himself from weeping. He is at every point Beaumarchais himself to the life.

There let us leave him and Beaumarchais for a moment and turn to Rossini.

5

He was in his twenty-fourth year when he wrote *Il Barbiere di Siviglia*. Young as he was he already had several operas to his credit. To some of these, in whole or in part, the Rossini lover still turns with delight, particularly *La Cambiale di Matrimonio* (*Marriage by Bill of Exchange*, 1810), *La Pietra del Paragone* (*The Touchstone*, 1812), *Il Signor Bruschino* (1812), *Tancredi* (1813) and *L'Italiana in Algerì* (*The Italian Girl in Algiers*, 1813); while the sparkling overture to *La Scala di Seta* (*The Silk Ladder*, 1812) has won for itself a secure place in our concert rooms. With the Barber of Seville subject he had had more than one predecessor: in addition to the well-known work of Paisiello (1782) there had been at least four French or German treatments of the theme. Morlacchi, the Italian director of the Dresden Opera from 1810 to 1841, had produced a *Barbiere di Siviglia* there in 1814.

Rossini had been commissioned in December 1815 by Duke Francesco Sforza-Cesarini, the director of the Argentina Theatre in Rome, to provide an opera buffa in which a notable Spanish tenor, Garcia, was to "star." The libretto having been found unsatisfactory, Rossini himself, it is conjectured, suggested the Beaumarchais comedy to his librettist Sterbini, who made a very good job of it. (It is astonishing how naturally and easily both *The Barber* and *The Marriage of Figaro* adapt themselves to the purposes of the musical stage.) As Paisiello still had his fanatical admirers, Sterbini and Rossini thought it diplomatic to call their own work, in the first place, not *The Barber of Seville* but *Almaviva, or the Vain Precaution,* and to make it known that they did so out of deference to the older composer. But their own precaution proved to be in vain; the partisans of Paisiello, joining forces with the personal enemies of the impresario, saw to it that the first performance, on the 20th February 1816, failed miserably. Presumably these gentry, satisfied with their victory, did not turn up on the second night, when the general Roman public, left to itself, welcomed the new work warmly. The Figaro was Zamboni, the Almaviva Manuel del Popolo Garcia,[1] who, on the opening night

[1] He had been born, appropriately enough, in Seville. His daughter Maria was the famous Malibran; another, Pauline, was the still more famous Mme Viardot. His son Manuel Patricio Garcia began as a bass singer but

(though not afterwards) was allowed to substitute for Rossini's music for the serenade to Rosina some arrangements of his own of Spanish folk-melodies, which, he had no doubt thought, supplied a local colour that was lacking in the score.

According to the legends, Rossini dashed off the music of the opera in anything from eight days to a fortnight; his own account of the affair in later years varied from twelve days to thirteen. The score was certainly completed within about three weeks at the most. Verdi's summing up of the matter in one of his letters says the sensible thing—Rossini had certainly lived with the characters for some time previously, and they must have taken musical shape in his mind before ever he put pen to paper. Donizetti's dry comment when he was told that the score had been completed in thirteen days was "Yes, but then Rossini always was a lazy fellow."

The nineteenth century German and English writers on music managed to persuade themselves, and did their best to persuade the world, that Mozart, in his *Marriage of Figaro*, had raised what had been in Beaumarchais a mere "sordid comedy of intrigue" to a loftier ethical sphere—a signal example of the moral sense, as Oscar Wilde put it, intruding where it is not wanted. But whatever we may think of the Beaumarchais-Mozart case there can be no doubt that the one and only *Barber of Seville* in music is and always will be Rossini's. The subject had gone, so far as the music was concerned, to the right man at the right time; Rossini alone had the sprightliness of spirit, the combination of lightness and certainty of touch, and the southern vivacity appropriate to the mercurial Figaro; and the *Barber*, as Verdi said, with its copiousness of genuine musical ideas, its comic verve and its veracity of declamation, remains to this day the best of all Italian opere buffe. It was a young man's work, something that even its creator could achieve to the same degree only once in his life. Weber rightly pointed out that in *The Seraglio* was incarnated "what every man's joyous youthful years are to him, the bloom of which he will never recapture": as Mozart grew in experience of life he was bound to write a *Figaro* and a *Don Giovanni*, "but with the best will in the world he could never have written another *Se-*

---

ultimately settled down to teaching. He died in London in July 1906 at the age of 101. He was the inventor of the laryngoscope.

raglio." Rossini still had a rich comic vein to explore, but a *Barber* he would never accomplish again; there is in it an enjoyment of the absurd comedy of the world, a delight in a coltish kicking up of the heels, that comes to an artist only once in life, and that when he is young and the sap of life in him rich and abundant.

<h1 style="text-align:center">6</h1>

The overture to *The Barber of Seville* is a pleasant enough piece of work, but has no particular bearing on the opera: it could hardly be expected to, seeing that it had begun life as the overture to *Aureliano in Palmira* in 1813, and had been used again in 1815 to introduce *Elisabetta, Regina d'Inghilterra*. It opens with a short andante sostenuto section, not without distinction, the most salient feature of which is a melody in the violins:

No. 1

that would be in place in almost any Rossini overture. With a change of tempo to allegro the strings give out quietly a typical Rossini theme:

No. 2

which, after a brief development, runs on into a second theme in the oboe:

No. 3

Repetitions of these two main themes, together with the first example in the work of a favourite device of Rossini—a long crescendo gradually working up from pianissimo to fortissimo:

94

No. 4

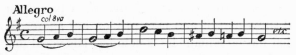

suffice to keep the overture on its feet until the curtain rises.

The scene is a square in Seville, the time, very early morning. On the left is the house of Doctor Bartolo, the windows of which are barred and the blinds closed. Fiorello, a servant of Count Almaviva, steals in cautiously, shepherding a number of musicians with their instruments: they are shortly joined by the Count himself, wrapped in a cloak.[1] He is about to serenade old Bartolo's ward, the fair and young Rosina. They all congratulate themselves, quietly, it is true, but none the less audibly, on the complete silence that reigns in the square, a silence highly propitious to their purpose. Telling each other that they must not speak a word, they keep on speaking, for there is nobody about, Fiorello remarks sagely, whom their performance can disturb, and presumably when the playing and singing begins they will be heard by no one in the adjacent houses but the young person for whose ears the music is intended. We accept the operatic convention, and note with approval the skill with which the composer conveys a suggestion of secrecy and caution: "Keep silence, all; piano, piano, let no one speak," the Count, imitating Fiorello, enjoins on them.

The musicians, having tuned their instruments, preludise for a minute or two on the theme of the coming aria of the amorous Count, which he then launches in full:

No. 5

Ec-co ri-den-te in cie —————— lo Spun-ta la bel-la au-ro——ra

[1] Beaumarchais, who had been in Spain, specifies in detail the costumes he desired for his characters. For Almaviva, in the first act, a large brown Spanish cloak with cape; a turned-down black hat with a coloured ribbon round the crown. For Figaro, the general get-up of a Spanish *majo*; a snood on his head; a white hat with a coloured ribbon round the crown; round his neck a loose kerchief; satin waistcoat and breeches, with silver-mounted buttons and silver-fringed button holes; a broad silk sash; garters with tassels; a coat of brilliant colour, with large facings of the same colour as the waistcoat; white stockings; grey shoes.

Behold, the dawn is breaking, he informs the sleeping world, yet his fair one is still wrapped in slumber; and he implores her to awake and show herself and take pity on her adorer; "Oh happy moment that has no equal!" he concludes. His vocal line becomes more and more exuberant and technically difficult as it proceeds, drawing more and more on the resources of early nineteenth century coloratura, and the aria concludes with a rousing fortissimo flourish on the part of the orchestra.

7

To his chagrin there is no response from the house, and after a brief colloquy with Fiorello, who draws his attention to the rapid oncoming of the morning light, he dismisses the musicians with thanks and a cash donation so liberal that Fiorello can hardly get the grateful creatures to leave. They crowd round the Count, kissing his hands and the hem of his cloak, and it is a long time before Fiorello, getting more and more annoyed with them, can induce them to terminate a chorus of thanksgiving that threatens to be interminable and depart. If they hadn't stopped their noisy chatter, Fiorello remarks acutely, they might have awakened the whole neighbourhood. He retires into the background, where he will await his master's further orders. The Count is disappointed that his fair one had not yet appeared at the window, for she is generally visible on the balcony about this time, inhaling the morning air. He will wait a little longer, for he is so deeply in love that he, a grandee of Spain, is actually prepared to make the lady his Countess, though as yet he does not know her station, or even her name.

His musings—in recitative—are broken in upon by a hearty voice off-stage trilling a gay "La, la, la." The Count decides to see who the newcomer is without himself being seen; so he conceals himself beneath the portico, thus leaving the ground clear for Figaro and his immortal aria. The mental key of this is set in the racy orchestral prelude:

No. 6

and its pendant:

No. 7

The prelude having run its course Figaro enters, with a guitar suspended from his neck. He is in the highest spirits: dawn has come, and he is off to his shop to start the serious business of the day—for apparently Seville cannot really get going till the great Figaro is at his post, ready for action. Is there any better life conceivable, he asks, than that of a barber of quality? "Bravo, Figaro, bravissimo, fortunatissimo!" He is prepared for anything, by night or by day:

No. 8

Pron-to a far tut-to, la notte, il gior-no, sem-pre d'in-tor-no in gi-ro sta.

There is no better profession in the world than his for a man like him; what can't he do with his razors, his combs, his lancets, his shears? He is equally indispensable to ladies and cavaliers, old and young. He is rushed off his feet with orders or appeals—here a cry for a wig, there a demand to be shaved; this client wants bleeding, another sends him off somewhere with a billet-doux; the air is thick with impatient cries of "Figaro! Figaro! Figaro! Figaro!" In vain does he appeal, for heaven's sake, for one call at a time upon his services; it's "Figaro here!", "Figaro there!", "Figaro everywhere!" He has to move like lightning, for he is the factotum of all the town. The aria ends with a breathless apostrophe of himself as the best and most fortunate of mortals:

No. 9

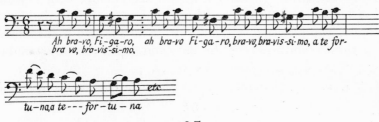

Ah bra-vo, Fi-ga-ro, ah bra-vo Fi-ga-ro, bra-vo, bra-vis-si-mo, a te for-
bra vo, bra-vis-si-mo,

tu—na, a te --- for—tu—na

For energy and gusto the aria has not its equal in all comic opera; for anything to compare with it we have to go to the racy tarantella of Rossini's later years—*La Danza*—which here and there still defeats the technique and the breath control of the best singers, Caruso not excepted.

Figaro continues his catalogue of his own virtues and of the delights of his profession in a recitative. Truly a fine life! Little to do, plenty of fun, and always a doubloon or two in his pocket. Does a Seville girl want to marry and settle down? She sends for Figaro. Is a nice little widow anxious to find another husband? She calls for Figaro. With his comb he can go anywhere by day, with his guitar everywhere by night; the great things are tact and discretion, and Figaro can always be counted on for these. Once more he congratulates himself on his choice of a profession, and his profession on possessing such an ornament to it as the incomparable Figaro. He will have still more reason to be pleased with himself before the opera is over, for henceforth the whole action springs from and depends on him. The others are puppets whose wires he jerks this way and that for his own amusement and profit, for he has more brains, more audacity than the whole of them put together. He is, in fact, Beaumarchais.

8

As Figaro is going off Almaviva emerges from his concealment, and the pair recognise each other. The scene that follows is carried on in recitative. The Count is surprised, and at first none too pleased, to find here in Seville the rapscallion of a Figaro who had been in his service in Madrid, and he asks him a few questions. Figaro assures him that he has not been in any particular trouble with the magistrates, and accounts for his looking so plump and well to his poverty. The Count in his turn explains why *he* is in Seville, of all places. It appears that on the Prado in Madrid [1] he had seen and instantly fallen head over heels in love with a beautiful girl, the daughter, he had been told, of some old doddering Doctor.[2] The pair had left Madrid for Seville. He had followed them thither, and had spent his days and nights recently parading

[1] According to Beaumarchais, six months ago.
[2] In Beaumarchais, Almaviva assumes Rosina to be the Doctor's young wife.

up and down in front of the balcony which he points out to
Figaro.

The barber congratulates him on his extraordinary good luck
—as he puts it in his own idiom, the cheese has fallen straight on
to the macaroni.[1] For in that very house he, Figaro, happens to
be *persona grata,* barber, wig-maker, surgeon, herbalist, apothecary, veterinary, and general handy-man. The young lady in
question is not the old Doctor's daughter, as the Count imagines,
but only his ward. But before he can get any further with his
explanation Rosina and Bartolo appear on the balcony, and Figaro
retires into the background.[2] Rosina is wondering why her unknown admirer has not put in an appearance as usual. She has
brought with her a letter intended for him, but does not know
how to convey it. Bartolo asks what the paper is she is holding
in her hand; she blandly assures him that it is simply the words
of an aria in the new opera, *The Vain Precaution,* that has just
appeared with such great success in Seville. The Count is delighted with her feminine artfulness: "the vain precaution!" he repeats with a chuckle. Figaro too is pleased; he recognises a fel-

[1] The opera libretto does not in general preserve the fine distinction between the manners and the speech of the two characters, an indication of
their different social standing, that Beaumarchais had done: perhaps by 1816
the sense of these distinctions had been lost. We know, however, that they
were very real in the 1770's, and that more than one cool observer foresaw
the social dangers implicit in the two Beaumarchais dramas, in which the
lackey of low degree is so obviously the superior of his aristocratic master
in intelligence, wit and resource. In *The Barber* Beaumarchais seems to have
been at pains to emphasise the difference between the social milieu of the
two chief characters. He puts low-class expressions and idioms into the
barber's mouth of which the Count would have disapproved as severely as
Lord Chesterfield would have done. When Figaro, having persuaded Almaviva to get access to Bartolo's house in the guise of a tipsy soldier, is coaching him for the part, he criticises the Count's acting of it. He would like
a little more realism, especially in the legs; and his own demonstration of
how *he* would play the part draws from the Count the disgusted comment,
"Faugh! that's the drunkenness of the people!" But to these and many other
skilful touches in the plays the modern opera audience is of course quite
insensitive.

[2] Beaumarchais's description of Bartolo is "a doctor; Rosina's guardian;
short black coat, buttoned up; a large wig; a black sash; for out-of-doors, a
long scarlet cloak."

low-craftsman in this innocent-looking young Rosina. Bartolo pours out his scorn on operas in general—long-winded, melancholy, tiresome things, suited only to the barbarous taste of a civilisation run to seed.

9

Rosina lets the paper fall, apparently by accident, and sends the grumbling Bartolo out to retrieve it; and when he has left the balcony she tells the Count, *sotto voce,* to pick the letter up quickly. Just as he does so Bartolo appears in the square. He has his doubts as to Rosina's suggestion that the wind must have carried the paper away, and begins to suspect that he is being fooled. He roughly orders her back into the house and swears that he will have the balcony walled up. At the Count's bidding Figaro reads out the letter: "Your assiduous attentions have piqued my curiosity. My guardian is just going out; as soon as he does so, find some ingenious method of letting me know your name, your condition, and your intentions. It will be impossible for me to come out on the balcony again without my tyrant accompanying me; but rest assured that everything will be done to break her chains that can be done by the unfortunate ROSINA." [1]

"She'll break them all right!" the Count remarks to Figaro; "but tell me, what sort of a fellow is this guardian of hers?" "An old man who seems to have the devil in him," is the reply, "a miser, suspicious, an inveterate grumbler, about a hundred years old but ambitious to play the gallant, who wants to marry Rosina to get her money." Bartolo, as he quits the stage, barks his final instructions at the invisible Rosina; until he returns she is not to admit anyone except Don Basilio, who is to be detained until Bartolo returns. The best thing he himself can do, he mutters as

[1] All this had been managed rather better by Beaumarchais: Rosina's letter is written on the *music* of a song from *The Vain Precaution,* to which Rosina bids Almaviva improvise words that will inform her who he is, etc. He is to sing it in a "casual" sort of way, the implication being that the tune is so well known that anyone might be warbling it at that or any other hour in Seville, and therefore it will not attract any particular attention. This, when the time comes for the song, leads to an amusing episode in which Figaro forces his guitar on the Count, in spite of the latter's protests that he is at best an indifferent performer on that instrument, and coaches him in his stanzas.

he goes off, is to speed up the arrangements already in progress for the marriage.

His parting words have been overheard by the Count, who asks again who is this dotard who proposes to marry Rosina, and who is this Don Basilio? "A solemn fellow," is the answer, "who manages to have a finger in every matrimonial pie, a hypocrite, a veritable down-and-out, with never a farthing in his pocket— and Rosina's music teacher." (Beaumarchais adds another touch that bears on the future—"a poor creature whom it will be easy to twist round our fingers.")

Almaviva explains to Figaro that he wants to woo Rosina without her knowing his name and rank, to make sure that she loves him solely for himself. While they are discussing this matter Figaro gets a glimpse of Rosina behind the shutters, and urges the Count to get to work at once. Almaviva does so, in a little song with guitar and pizzicati strings accompaniment:

No. 10

Se il mio no-me sa-per voi bra-ma———————— te

in which he manages to inform her that his name is Lindoro:

No. 11

Io son Lin-do-ro, che fi-do v'a -do -ro, Che spo-sa vi bra-mo,

and that he is madly in love with her. Encouraged by Figaro's approval of his musical technique he embarks on a second stanza, in which he confesses, with regret, that he is not rich, but assures her of the constancy of his passion. She begins a reply of equal ardour, but after a few notes breaks off suddenly in the middle of the word "Lindoro" and disappears from the watchers outside, who surmise that someone must have entered the room. The distracted Almaviva swears he must somehow get into the house that very day, and calls vehemently on Figaro to provide a means. The shrewd barber exacts an assurance that all the money required will be forthcoming, and then breaks into a lively song in praise of gold, the very thought of which stimulates his mental faculties, he says.

10

Then the dialogue, starting with a carefree melody in the orchestra:

No. 12

drops into the vivacious conversational tone that Italian opera buffa always had at its command as Figaro reveals the brilliant plan of campaign that has occurred to him. This very day a regiment is arriving in the town the colonel of which happens to be a friend of Almaviva's. The Count is to impersonate a soldier who has been billeted on Doctor Bartolo. To the accompaniment of the jolly No. 12, Figaro, whose invention has been tuned to the highest pitch by the thought of easy money, suggests an attractive nuance in this technique. The supposed soldier shall be half-drunk; and the versatile barber gives the Count an imitation of the thick speech and awkward movements of such a one. The conspirators bubble over with joy at the ingenious idea, which will certainly take the Doctor in. (Unfortunately the libretto omits the best reason of all, which had been supplied by Beaumarchais, for Bartolo's being duped by the stratagem; as Figaro points out, the Doctor will argue that a drunken soldier will be more anxious to go off somewhere to sleep off his potations than to meddle in the urgent affairs of the household.)

The pair are about to separate, in the highest glee, when they remember that Figaro has not told the Count where he can find him. This affords the barber a pretext for a patter song over a lively tune in the orchestra:

No. 13

in which he explains where his shop is—just round the corner,
number fifteen on the left, four steps up, the shop with the white
front, with five wigs and some pots of pomade in the window,
and so on: the Count can't mistake it. They can hardly bear to
bring the scene to a close, so full are they of the rich humours and
the possibilities of the coming intrigue, Almaviva, to the melody
of No. 13, singing with exuberant coloratura of his love for Rosina, and Figaro already hearing in imagination the tinkle of the
gold that will pour into his pockets soon. At last, after much repetition of their respective sentiments, they manage to tear themselves away; Figaro goes into Bartolo's house; Almaviva hurries
away to obtain a soldier's uniform. One naturally expects the curtain to fall here; but before this can happen, Rossini and his librettist, for no discoverable reason, bethink themselves of Fiorello,
whose existence we had forgotten. Suddenly coming to life, he
indulges, Leporello-like, in a short recitative grumble about this
master of his, who keeps him glued to the same spot for two long
hours while *he* indulges himself in amorous adventures. He can
put up with this sort of life no longer, he vows. As we are incapable, however, of feeling any interest now in Fiorello's little problems we raise no objection if the producer omits the trifling
episode.

Sterbini and Rossini chose to regard all that has happened until
now as constituting only the first scene of the first act of their
opera, but today we feel justified in following Beaumarchais and
taking it as the first act; the cards have been laid on the table, and
now the game is ready to begin.

11

A certain parallelism runs through the comedy. It extends
further than the simple fact that Almaviva and Bartolo have
concentrated on the pursuit of the same object. Each of them
relies on the brains of a clever hireling to pull him through, and
each of them has to make it worth the hireling's while to co-
operate; "money," Figaro tells the Count, "c'est le nerf de
l'intrigue," while the musician Basilio warns Bartolo not to be
niggardly where he is concerned, for the dissonances to be expected in any business partnership "are best prepared and resolved by the perfect consonance of gold." The next stage of the

action is a matter less of a struggle between the two main forces than of one between the two instruments. Beaumarchais could handle all this in much livelier fashion, not merely because he was a Beaumarchais and Sterbini merely a Sterbini, but because spoken drama can move more swiftly than opera and therefore find room for more of the complexities of intrigue and the agile give-and-take of dialogue; though it must be conceded that Sterbini has been dexterous in general in his condensation of the French original.

It is now a matter of trickster against trickster, ruse against ruse, rogue Figaro against rogue Basilio. In the end, of course, the ruses of the barber will prove superior to those of the pimping music master, though here and there even Figaro can trip up and the race look for a moment like going to his and Almaviva's opponents. Figaro's immediate problem is how to get himself and Almaviva into a strategic position in the Bartolo household, in face of the Doctor's orders to the servants that no one but Basilio is to be admitted while he is out. Beaumarchais shows in humorous detail how this problem has been solved. Bartolo is Figaro's landlord; as the barber explains to the Count, his business premises are the property of the Doctor, who allows him the use of them *gratis*, while he, for his part, shows his gratitude by a promise to Bartolo of ten gold pistoles per annum, also *gratis*. One of his ways of covering his rent is to act not merely as the Doctor's barber but as apothecary, consultant and surgeon to the household. In Beaumarchais' second act we see how he has just applied his medical science—derived from his veterinary practice—to the problem of making all clear for the intrusion of Almaviva into the house: having persuaded one of the servants, humorously named L'Éveillé, that he is ill, he has given him a sedative so potent that he is incapable of anything but yawning for the next few hours. To another, a tottering old fellow with the equally humorous name of La Jeunesse, he has administered a sternutatory that keeps him perpetually on the sneeze; so that, Figaro having thoughtfully left the front door open, there will be nobody there to keep the pseudo-soldier out when he arrives.

Bartolo, whatever his faults may be, is no fool. He is, of course, a stock figure of the comedy of the period, the elderly guardian who wants to marry his rich and pretty young ward. But in brains he is superior to the average of his stage type, as he could hardly help being, seeing that his creator is Beaumarchais. We learn casually that he had become aware in Madrid that a gallant of the name of Count Almaviva had been trying to make Rosina's acquaintance. The incident of the sheet of paper containing an extract from *The Vain Precaution*, which had so mysteriously disappeared after it had fallen into an apparently empty square, has made him very suspicious, though it does not occur to him to associate it in any way with the Count, whom as yet he does not know to be in Seville. His strategy is now determined by recent events. There is no time to be lost; during the day that has now opened he must make arrangements for his marriage to Rosina on the morrow. At this very moment his tool Basilio is engaged in making those arrangements—which is why Bartolo has told his servants that if Don Basilio calls while he is out he is to stay there till he returns.

12

In the next stage of the opera the action has to be condensed and the talk curtailed because of the necessity of giving the characters scope to demonstrate their musical talents. Rosina is the first to do so. The setting is a room in Bartolo's house; we observe that the Venetian blinds have been closed. Rosina, taking advantage of her guardian's absence, has been writing a letter, which she now holds in her hand, to Lindoro.[1] Her great display aria, "Una voce poco fa," [2] so beloved of coloratura sopranos in the concert room as well as in the theatre, begins seriously enough with a declaration of her resolve to be Lindoro's, no matter what her guardian may say or do. Then, quickening her tempo a little, she embarks, like her parallel Norina in a similar situation in *Don Pasquale*, upon a eulogy of her own good qualities. She is a thoroughly good girl, she assures us, respectful, obedient, sweet-natured, affectionate:

[1] Beaumarchais's specification for the costuming of Rosina is simply "a young lady of noble descent, dressed in Spanish fashion."

[2] The listener with no Italian who knows nothing more of the words than these four manages fairly well with "Una voce" but is gravelled by the "poco fa." This is simply an Italian idiom for "a little while ago." What Rosina is saying in her opening words is that a little while ago a voice had resounded in her heart with electrifying effect: it was Lindoro's serenade.

No. 14

Io so—— no—— do-ci-le, son ri — spet —to —— sa

easy to lead and to govern:

No. 15

Mi la-scio reg-ge-re,mi la-scio reg-ge-re, mi fo gui-

dar, mi — fo —— gui—— dar

(Note the pert little stresses on "reggere"; these continue to be
a feature of the melody.) But if anyone thinks he can take advantage of these amiable weaknesses of hers, she continues, let him
look out; in defence of her rights she can be a little devil, a viper,
the mistress of a hundred wiles. Poor Doctor Bartolo will discover
before long what she is capable of in the way of feminine artfulness, especially with the ingenious, unscrupulous Figaro to back
her up.

After the lively aria the action is carried on for some time in
recitative. Having sealed her letter Rosina regrets she has no
trusty messenger, watched as she is by Bartolo, to send it by. Then
she remembers that when she had caught a glimpse of Lindoro
in the square he had been accompanied by the barber, and this
Figaro is a good sort of fellow who might be on her side. At this
point Figaro himself enters, and she bewails her sad situation to
him; sealed up within four walls as she is she might as well be in
a tomb! He is about to tell her something it will do her good to
hear when Bartolo is heard approaching; so the barber conceals
himself where he can get a view of whatever may happen, while
Rosina retires into the background.

Bartolo, muttering to himself, is full of grievances—that cursed
rascal of a barber, for some reason the Doctor cannot fathom, has
turned the house into a hospital with his bleedings, doses of
laudanum and what not: when Bartolo calls in the servants Berta
and Ambrosio to ask them if Figaro has been there talking to

Rosina the one can only sneeze, the other only yawn. Rosina, however, has boldly admitted that she has seen Figaro and has found him very sympathetic. While Bartolo is cursing the barber, Basilio enters.[1] He is invariably smooth, unctuous, deferential towards his employer, and obviously a bit of a knave. He has important news for Bartolo—he has discovered that Count Almaviva is in Seville; and now the Doctor divines who the unknown is who has been hanging about his house lately. The first thing to do, Basilio assures him, is to invent some story about the Count that will put him in bad odour in the town and force him to leave it. The Basilio way of getting rid of an enemy, he explains, is a technique of his own invention that never fails. He launches his famous aria: "Calumny! There's nothing to beat it!" The orchestra is hushed to a *sotto voce* as he begins. Calumny, he says, starts as a gentle breeze, that imperceptibly grows in force as the slander passes from mouth to mouth, from ear to ear, what was no more than an almost inaudible hiss in the first place becoming in time a horrifying roar that rends the air like the firing of a cannon, till the wretched victim finds himself crushed under the weight of public opprobrium and hatred. To depict the gradual swelling of the calumny from a breath to a gale, Rossini employs effectively a device that was always a favourite of his (though not his invention), a slow crescendo beginning almost inaudibly in the strings:

No. 16

and piling up to a fortissimo; but at the words "The miserable wretch, calumniated, bespattered, collapses under the public scourging" the orchestra drops to a pianissimo again as a sinister phrase makes a chromatic descent in the strings and bassoon: [2]

[1] Beaumarchais's description of him is "an organist, Rosina's singing teacher; wears a black turned-down hat, a cassock, and a long cloak without frills or ruffles."

[2] Beaumarchais, of course, took his cue for his description of calumny, either at first or fifty-first hand, from Vergil's famous description, in the fourth book of the *Aeneid,* of the gradual spread of Rumour in Dido's

No. 17

Bartolo agrees with Basilio in principle, but as time is pressing he prefers his own plan—to push on with the marriage; once Rosina is his wife he will put a stop to her amorous escapades; and Basilio says under his breath that to him it's all one so long as there is money in it for him. The pair go into an inner room to talk about the marriage contract, whereupon Figaro emerges cautiously from his hiding-place. Now he understands exactly what is afoot, and he has his plan to help Rosina. When she comes into view again he tells her what he has just overheard—a scheme for a wedding on the morrow. She replies grimly that they will have to reckon with her before that happens! She artfully turns the conversation to the subject of the young man whom she had seen with Figaro under her balcony early that morning—a cousin of his, he assures her, a fine young fellow who has come to Seville to complete his studies and make his fortune if he can. He has only one fault—he is in love. Rosina's eager enquiries elicit the teasing information that the object of this love is a beautiful young creature remarkably like Rosina in appearance, and, in fact, bearing the same name. She breaks into a cascade of coloratura at the welcome news, and Figaro takes up the gay strain. To a delightful chattering melody in the orchestra they discuss their future plan of action. First of all, says Figaro, Rosina is to write a letter to Lindoro. She protests that maidenly modesty would not let her go as far as that—and then, greatly to the barber's admiration, produces the already written letter. Then they unite their voices in a duet, Rosina congratulating herself on the way things have turned out for her—for she has been promised a meeting soon with her Lindoro—Figaro marvelling quietly at the unsuspected depths of artfulness in women in general and this pretty little kitten of a Rosina in particular.

Carthage—Fama, surpassed in swiftness by nothing else that is evil, enlarging herself and gathering strength by her own motion, etc.

13

Figaro having left—presumably to re-establish connections with the Count—Bartolo re-enters. He tackles Rosina boldly on the subject of "the vain precaution," and succeeds in throwing her into some confusion. He demands to know what she and the barber had been talking about. She lies fluently—it was only this trifle and that, the Paris fashions, Figaro's sick little daughter Marcellina, and what not. Not believing a word she says, for she is not yet sufficient of an expert to lie without blushing, Bartolo goes straight to the point. Did Figaro bring her a reply to the letter she had let fall from the balcony? How is it that there are ink-stains on her finger? She can parry that one; she had burnt her finger, and had always been told that ink was the remedy for burns. There were six sheets of paper on the desk when he left, Bartolo continues, for he had counted them; and now there are only five. What has become of the other? Rosina explains that she had used it to wrap up some sweetmeats she had sent to Marcellina. But why the newly cut quill? continues the inexorable Bartolo. Her reply is that she had needed it to design a flower for her embroidery.

He loses patience and seeks relief for his feelings in a pompous aria, in which he asks her whether she really thinks she can impose on a man like him with such feeble tarradiddles, and recommends her to try to improve her technique; the vocal part is very difficult —giving us, as several other arias in Rossini's comic operas do, an idea of the agility expected of the basses in those days—while the orchestral chatter is rich in pointed characterisation. He ends by assuring her that the next time he goes out she will be locked up so effectually that not so much as a breath of air will be able to steal into the room. The aria would be excessively long were it not for the pounding pace at which it goes. Its very length and repetitiousness is the comic stroke; poor old Bartolo is too angry and at the same time too distracted to be able to pull up.

At last, however, quite out of breath, he storms out of the room, whereupon Rosina assures herself and us that the worse he behaves, and the more difficult her situation, the more reserves of feminine guile she has to draw upon. After this brief recitative she too goes out, and the maidservant Berta enters. She has heard knocking without, and, sneezing as she goes, she shuffles off to open the door to the Count. He is now disguised as a soldier and accompanied by a mock-martial motif in the orchestra:

No. 18

Pretending to be tipsy he begins to throw his military weight about: why is there no one in the house to attend to a man of his importance? When Bartolo re-enters the soldier fumbles in his pocket for his billeting paper. (He exasperates Bartolo by never getting his name right—it is now Doctor Balordo, now Barbaro, now Somaro (mule).) He is delighted to hear that the man on whom he has been quartered is a doctor, for that, he explains, constitutes a professional bond between them, he himself being the regimental farrier. A pungently comic duet follows, Bartolo spluttering with rage, the Count puzzling him with his inane behaviour, a mixture of ironic patronage and camaraderie. Almaviva is really playing for time; his purpose is to see Rosina and convey a letter into her hands.

When she enters she is at first taken aback at seeing a soldier there, and stops in her tracks, for Figaro had not disclosed this part of his plan of campaign to her. The duet now becomes a lively trio, the Count frantically endeavouring to give her some idea of what is afoot, Rosina unable as yet to make head or tail of it all, and Bartolo fuming away without the others paying any attention to him. When Rosina comes forward he roughly orders her back to her chamber. Almaviva, who by this time has managed to whisper to her "I am Lindoro," suggests going with her to view his new quarters. This goads Bartolo beyond endurance. He plays his trump card: there will be no quarters for him or anyone like him in this house, for Bartolo happens to possess an official order exempting him from having soldiers billeted on him. This is something the Count had not expected, and for the moment he is completely thrown out of his stride. Still, when the Doctor goes to his desk to hunt for the exemption order Lindoro manages to get in a confidential word or two with Rosina.

Bartolo, having found and read out the order, flourishes it triumphantly in the Count's face, who contemptuously tosses the document in the air. When the Doctor threatens to throw him out the pseudo-soldier affects to take this as a challenge to mortal combat; and fighting, of course, is his trade, as he explains to the accompaniment of the martial No. 18. Pretending to make some preliminary passes with his sword he surreptitiously drops a letter and tells Rosina *sotto voce* to let her handkerchief fall on it, which she does. But as Bartolo has seen all this the Count's invention is once more strained to the utmost. He himself picks up the letter, which is no doubt, he informs Bartolo, a medical prescription. No, he is wrong; it is a letter, obviously the property of the young lady here; and he picks it up and hands it to her along with her handkerchief.

14

The fun becomes fast and furious, Bartolo angrily demanding to see the letter—which Rosina blandly assures him is only the laundry list—and the Count still trying to keep up the bluff. At the height of the imbroglio Berta enters to announce that Figaro and some other people have arrived. With her is Basilio. Bartolo is very glad to see him, for Rosina has stumped him again, the document she has dexterously fobbed off on him having really turned out to be just a laundry list. The Count is delighted with her cleverness; now, as he puts it, they have Bartolo in the bag. Basilio, not having as yet got the hang of it all, remembers that he is a music master and limits his part in the ensemble to a simple trolling of "Sol, Do, Re, Fa, Re, Sol" and so forth; for a big buffo finale of this kind is a sort of Christmas pudding into which anything can go.

Rosina, making the most of the tactical victory she has won with the laundry list, now thinks the time has come to turn on the tears: this she does as the mode of the music changes from major to minor, with a new motif in the oboe that is punctuated by sham sobs; the general tempo, however, remains unchanged:

No. 19

(This short minor inset is admirably designed to obtain a little variety before the main current of the huge finale is resumed, as it will be at the entrance of Figaro.)

Bartolo, completely bluffed, is all contrition now: he apologises abjectly to his dear Rosina, while the Count draws his sword again and threatens him with bodily violence. The tension is broken by the arrival of Figaro with a barber's basin under his arm. What is the matter? he asks; for the hullabaloo is audible in the square, where a large crowd has now gathered. He whispers a word of caution to the Count, and, pushing his basin between him and Bartolo, orders the pseudo-soldier to have better manners. But still the shindy goes on, till at last there comes a knocking at the door that freezes them all into silence. It is the town guard, come to see what the uproar is about. Bartolo explains that this drunken lout of a soldier has threatened and maltreated him; and Basilio confirms the story. Figaro protests that he has come in merely to pour oil on the troubled waters. The Count blusters that he is in a rage only because this rascal of a Doctor has refused to obey a billeting order. Rosina apologises for the too demonstrative soldier, attributing his exuberance to too much wine.

The officer of the guard orders his men to arrest the soldier and take him away; but the Count takes him aside and shows him a document that evidently astounds him, for at once he bids the guards stand back. Rosina, Bartolo and Basilio (not knowing who the "soldier" is) cannot understand this sudden display of respect; but Figaro, who knows well enough that it is due to the Count having disclosed his rank, chuckles quietly over Bartolo's discomfiture, his ironic ejaculations of "Poor Doctor Bartolo!" always standing out clearly from the vocal texture. A big sextet is now built up by a series of imitations between the various vocal parts, in which all profess verbally their inability to understand the new turn that events have taken.[1]

When at last Bartolo and Basilio are able to make their expostulations audible to the guard they are roughly told to be quiet. Finally the six characters express once more, in a massive unison:

[1] There is no *dramatic* reason at all for Berta being on the stage in the finale; she has been brought there only to add an extra female voice to the predominantly male ensemble.

No. 20

Mi——par d'es——ser col——la tes——ta

their complete incapacity to make head or tail of what is going on, so confused are they all by the noise the others are making; and after another thirty pages or so in the score, in which they repeat themselves *ad infinitum*—for Rossini has only about a fortnight in which to write his opera—the act comes at last to a rumbustious end.

15

When the curtain rises again we see the library in the Doctor's house; among the furniture is a clavecin on which stands some music. It is now evening; the tumult and the shouting have died, and Bartolo, in the grateful quiet of his room, is thinking things over. Though he has got rid of the blusterous and inconvenient soldier he is still worried. He has had enquiries made in the town about that soldier, and discovered that the regiment concerned knows no such person. A light breaks upon him—the fellow had probably been sent by Count Almaviva to get information about Rosina. No man is safe in these days, he muses, even within his own four walls.

Almaviva and Figaro, though the first round has gone against them, have still not given up the fight. A knocking is heard at the house door, and soon the Count turns up again, this time disguised as a music teacher, and accompanied by an insinuating, hypocritical tune in the violins:

No. 21

The newcomer is all deference and unction. He calls down on Bartolo and his household peace and joy for the next thousand years. The Doctor has a dim feeling that he has seen this face somewhere or other already, but he keeps his thoughts to himself; Almaviva, for his part, is hoping that his present ruse will have more success than his first. The Doctor keeps begging the new-comer to make an end of compliments and declare his business, but to no effect, the sly, oily No. 21 twining itself endlessly round the conversation of the pair. The duet is Rossini and opera buffa at their best.

At last Bartolo manages to persuade his visitor to come down to earth, introduce himself, and explain his presence there. From the dialogue that follows (in recitative) we learn that this is Don Alonso, a teacher of music, studying with Don Basilio, who, having been suddenly taken ill, has sent his pupil in his stead. Alonso has some difficulty in dissuading the Doctor from rushing off at once to see the sick Basilio, who is of so much importance to him just now. Pretending to be angry, and raising his voice in the hope that Rosina may hear him, the intruder tells Bartolo that, happening to be lodged where Count Almaviva is staying, he had that morning lighted on a letter from the Doctor's ward to his lordship. Don Basilio knows nothing of this letter, but he, Alonso, had brought it with him believing that it would make it easier for him to gain access to the young lady in order to give her her lesson. A glance at the letter makes it clear to Bartolo that the handwriting is really Rosina's. (It is, as a matter of fact, the missive we saw her writing in an earlier scene.) The Count, not having Figaro to back him up, becomes more and more confused both inwardly and outwardly as he gabbles on; but he wins the complete confidence of the Doctor when he argues that if he is given access to the ward he can easily persuade her that the letter had been given to him by another of the naughty Count's lady-loves, thus proving him to have been merely playing with the affections of Rosina. "Bravo!" Bartolo chuckles. "Calumny! Now I recognise you for a worthy pupil of Don Basilio!" He thanks Alonso effusively, embraces him, assures him that he himself will see that the letter gets into his ward's hands, and shuffles off into the inner room. Left to himself the Count realises that this plan of his, which had been devised by him on the spur of the moment, is not as clever as he had thought; still, it was the only way he could think of to prevent Bartolo from turning him out of the house as an irresponsible fool. However, when he gets an opportunity to speak to his Rosina he will be able to explain it all to her satisfaction.[1]

16

Bartolo returns with Rosina, to whom he introduces this Don Alonso who has come to give her her music lesson. At the unexpected sight of Lindoro she is staggered for a moment, but accounts for her choked cry of alarm by alleging a spasm of cramp in her foot. Lindoro assures her, with a grave professional air, that the best cure for a thing of that sort will be the music lesson he is going to give her in the place of Don Basilio. She quite agrees, and artfully elects to sing the rondo from *The Vain Precaution*. Bartolo breaks out with "What is this 'Vain Precaution' that she is always talking about lately?", and she patiently explains once more that it is the title of the new opera that is the rage of the town. The Count (who now seems to have developed a musical accomplishment the possession of which he had disclaimed in a previous talk with Figaro), seats himself at the clavecin to play the accompaniment, while Bartolo settles himself in a chair to listen. The subject of the aria is the powerlessness of any tyrant to influence the heart that is feeling its first love; and of course it is to "Lindoro" that the reassuring confession is made, and "Lindoro" to whom she appeals for help. The "lesson," therefore, containing as it does responses in which Lindoro assures her that he will not fail her, plays, or should do, a vital dramatic part in the intrigue; but all this goes for nothing in a modern production, where the "singing lesson" consists merely of whatever showpiece the prima donna and the producer may elect to insert in the score.

Bartolo does not think much of the aria from *The Vain Precaution*: in *his* young days music was music, not the fiddle-faddle modern stuff served up to them nowadays; and the old donkey

[1] Some points in the rather tangled intrigue are made clearer in Beaumarchais than in the opera; for instance, in the former Bartolo thinks it will be all the easier to get Rosina to take her music lesson from Alonso because she has already told her guardian that she will take no more music lessons from Don Basilio now she knows him to be acting as Bartolo's matrimonial agent. On the other hand, mere words could never achieve and sustain such finesses of ironic comedy as we get in the duet that commences with our No. 21.

proceeds to show them how Cafferelli, according to him, used to sing a gallant little ditty to one Giovanna, a name which, he explains, he is altering to Rosina to suit the present company. While this grotesque exhibition is going on Figaro enters with his basin under his arm, stands behind Bartolo, and mimics him. When the Doctor turns on him he explains that he has come to shave him. Bartolo is for putting this off until tomorrow; but Figaro, producing a doubtfully authentic notebook from his pocket, protests that this is impossible, so many pressing engagements has he the next day—all the regimental officers to be shaved, the Marchioness Andronica's wig to be fitted, Count Bombe's toupet to be fixed, the lawyer Bernadone's dyspepsia to be dosed, and so on: tomorrow is quite out of the question. His whole morning had been wasted, he complains, for when he had come there expressly to shave the Doctor he had found the house in an uproar; now the man wants to put it off again! Does he think Figaro is just a country barber? If so, let him choose another artist, for *he* has had about as much as he can stand; and he takes up his basin as though he were going to throw up his part and walk out of the show.

The bluff works. Bartolo, handing him his bunch of keys, tells him to go into his private room and bring the necessary towels and things, then immediately changes his mind and decides to go himself. This gives Figaro the opportunity to tell Rosina that if only he can get those keys in his hands the game will be won, for among them is the vital key to the balcony. But the suspicious Bartolo is back again in a moment, feeling that it is not wise to leave his rebellious ward with "that devil of a barber." He sends Figaro out with the keys, telling him where he will find everything—"straight down the corridor, above the cupboard, and see that you don't touch anything else." "The trick is won!" Figaro whispers exultantly to Rosina as he goes off, Bartolo explaining complacently why he can't trust this rogue of a barber any further then he can see him, for it was he who had carried Rosina's letter to Count Almaviva, and he, Doctor Bartolo, is too wise an old bird to be caught twice in the same snare.

17

But just then a fearful clatter is heard from within. Bartolo rushes out and returns with Figaro, wailing that all his dishes, eight wine-glasses and a bowl have been smashed to atoms. The barber turns the tables on him by pointing out that it is his own fault for keeping the place in darkness as he does: it was only by the mercy of Providence that he had escaped having his head smashed against the wall; and at the same time he gleefully shows the Count the key of the balcony, which he has detached from the bunch. All now seems to them for the best in the best of all possible worlds as Bartolo seats himself in the chair and orders the barber to begin. But Beaumarchais still has some cards up his sleeve, some as yet unforeseen hurdles for the conspirators to get over.

Almost before Figaro can get to work the recitative in which the foregoing scene has been carried on comes to an abrupt end with a crashing E flat chord in the orchestra as, to everyone's amazement, Don Basilio appears in the doorway: it is one of the most effective entrances in all opera. "Don Basilio!" ejaculates Rosina. "What on earth is this?" asks the Count. Figaro mutters (in effect) "That's torn it!" Bartolo can only babble "What, you here?" To a characteristically unctuous Basilian motif in the orchestra:

No. 22

the unsuspecting Basilio greets the company: "Your servant, good people one and all." He is frankly astounded when the Doctor enquires anxiously about his health, and still more flabbergasted by the next question, "And the court?" [1] The first concern of the conspirators now is to prevent Basilio from expressing more surprise and asking any questions. The Count takes charge. "I have told Doctor Bartolo," he assures the music master, "that everything is now settled"; and Bartolo confirms this. The pseudo-

[1] i.e. the legal body concerned with the marriage.

117

Alonso keeps gabbling on to Basilio, at the same time urging
Bartolo to get rid of the man before he can blurt out something
indiscreet: "He knows nothing of the letter," he reminds the
Doctor, whereupon the latter orders Basilio to take himself off
at once. Figaro backs him up; the worthy man shouldn't be out
of his bed with such a fever on him. So it goes on, in a delightful
give-and-take of talk that is held together musically by the oily
No. 22. But the more the others explain, the less Basilio compre-
hends. Alonso assures him that he is as yellow as a corpse; Figaro,
feeling his pulse, is horrified at its irregularity and diagnoses
scarlatina. The Count is more practical; while also advising the
bewildered Basilio to go home and take some medicine he slips
a purse into his hand. The cumulative weight of testimony as to
his being mortally ill had already begun to impress him: the purse
brings final conviction. The richly comic scene ends with a "Good
night!" from all in turn as they manœuvre him out of the room,
Almaviva leading off with a charming melody:

No. 23

that is worked up into a grand quintet.

With Basilio out of the way Figaro can get on at last with the
lathering of Bartolo, managing it in such a way that he obscures
the Doctor's view of the lovers. While Rosina appears to be
absorbed in the study of the music, Almaviva, to the accompaniment of a new motif in the orchestra:

No. 24

contrives to tell her hurriedly that all is going nicely: now that
Figaro has the balcony key they will be there at the stroke of
midnight to carry her off. She promises to be ready. Figaro does
his best to help them by pretending to have got something in his
eye and asking Bartolo to examine it. But the Doctor chances to

overhear Almaviva trying to account to Rosina for the use of
that letter of hers and for his present disguise; and now he realises
how he has been duped. Leaping angrily from his chair he turns
on Figaro and "Alonso" and orders the latter out of the house. To
a new tune in the orchestra: [1]

No. 25

the others affect to regard him as half-demented and exhort him
to calm himself, while he keeps cursing and threatening them.
The lively quartet ends with Rosina, Figaro and the Count quit-
ting the scene, leaving Bartolo still fuming. He rings for his
servants. Ambrosio he orders to go at once to Don Basilio's house
over the way and bid him to come to him at once. Not trusting
to Berta to guard the door he rushes out to attend to it himself,
thereby leaving the stage clear for what, dramatically considered,
is the weakest episode in the opera—an aria in which Berta complains at great length about the trials of being in service in a
house like this, and enlarges on the absurdity of crack-brained
old men falling in love. Yet the complaint, she admits, is universal,
she herself, mature as she is, not being immune from it. The long
aria is unnecessary; the only functions it can be said to perform
are to give the second soprano an opportunity to distinguish herself and to fill up the interval of time and space between this scene
and the next.

18

On the rising of the curtain we see the Doctor's room again as
in the first act, with the Venetian blinds closed as before. The
time is later the same evening. Bartolo and Basilio are in earnest
confabulation in recitative; Basilio has disclaimed all knowledge
of "Alonso," whom Bartolo now suspects to be an agent of Count
Almaviva, though the shrewder Basilio believes him, on the
evidence of the purse, to be none other than the Count himself.
If that be so, Bartolo rejoins, the need is all the more pressing to

[1] As is so often the case in Italian opera buffa the main musical line in the
Barber is frequently entrusted to the orchestra, the voices confining themselves to a rapid patter that is sometimes hardly more than a monotone.

have the marriage business concluded today; he himself will hurry off to the notary and have the contract drawn up. Basilio pours cold water on this idea: for one thing, it's raining cats and dogs; for another, the notary won't be available that evening because he has already been engaged by Figaro for the marriage of the latter's niece. "But the barber has no nieces!" says Bartolo; "I smell a rat! The scoundrel means to play some trick on me tonight!" Giving Basilio the key to the outer door he sends him off with orders to bring the notary to him at once.

Left alone, the worried Doctor thinks things over: by hook or by crook, by love or by compulsion, Rosina must be made to yield, and quickly. An idea strikes him. That fool of an Alonso has unintentionally put in his hands the ideal weapon for his purpose—Rosina's letter to her lover. She comes in just then, and he unmasks his battery. She has put her innocent trust, he tells her, in a pair of rogues (Figaro and Alonso) who are conspiring to throw her into the arms of Count Almaviva, in proof of which he shows her her own letter to her supposed lover, which has providentially come into his hands. (The spectator must always bear in mind that Rosina still does not know that the humble "Lindoro" to whom she had given her heart is the great Count Almaviva.)

Naturally believing she has been befooled, and being a girl of spirit, she decides to wreak vengeance on the faithless Lindoro. She not only assures Bartolo that she will marry him out of hand but tells him of the Lindoro-Figaro plan to carry her away that night. Bartolo is going off at once to bar the door; but Rosina tells him this will be useless, as they will enter by the window, they having got possession of the key of the balcony. Bartolo is afraid the ruffians may be armed; so he advises Rosina to lock herself up in her room while he runs off to inform the police that according to information received two thieves are going to break into his house. Bewailing her sad fate, she decides to do as he has told her.

Basilio's passing allusion to the bad weather has not been without its dramatic significance. A storm has evidently been brewing, and now it breaks over the house.[1] Rossini throws himself with

---

[1] For this storm music Rossini drew upon an earlier opera, *La Pietra del Paragone* (1812).

delight into the painting of an orchestral picture of a tempest, beginning with a far-off rumble of thunder in the lower strings, hints of lightning flashes in the flute, and the staccato pattering of the first raindrops. Soon the storm is in full fury; then it subsides and gradually dies away in the distance, and we see Figaro and Almaviva stealthily entering from the balcony. Their conversation is carried on in recitative. As Figaro strikes a light Rosina becomes visible. The Count would take her in his arms, but she repulses him with indignant reproaches; she has discovered, she tells him, that he is only a perfidious deceiver, merely feigning love for her in order to get her into the clutches of the vile Count Almaviva. That little misunderstanding is soon cleared up, the Count being delighted to find that she really had loved him as "Lindoro," in ignorance of his rank and name. Opening his cloak and throwing himself at her feet he discloses himself as not Lindoro but Count Almaviva, Grandee of Spain.

19

This happy dénouement brings on, of course, a severe attack of coloratura that racks Rosina for quite a while, the Count kindly aiding and abetting her; and once again we get some idea of the vocal technique expected in those days of male as well as female singers. Figaro has for some time been trying to persuade the happy pair to limit their transports and fix their minds on the business before them, but in vain. At last he manages to make an impression on them; in agitated tones he tells them that he sees two people outside with a lantern. This sobers them, if not to the extent of making them take action, at any rate to that of singing about the necessity of doing so. The Count begins with an exhortation to silence and flight:

No. 26

the theme of which is taken up in turns by the others in characteristically Rossini fashion.[1] Frenziedly, at great length, they entreat
each other to lose no time but fly while the flying's good, remaining all the while, as is the operatic way, glued to their respective
spots. When at last they decide to move they find, to their dismay,
that the ladder by which they had hoped to escape is no longer
there and that someone is stealing in on them. They retire into the
background, Almaviva wrapping his cloak round him once more
and exhorting Rosina to have courage.

Basilio comes in stealthily, with another man whom Figaro
soon recognises, to his delight, as the notary. So he comes forward and reminds the lawyer that he had been engaged to draw
up the marriage deed between his (Figaro's) niece and one Count
Almaviva. Here the couple are, he continues, pointing to the
lovers; and the man of law produces the necessary document. The
bewildered Basilio asks where on earth Doctor Bartolo can be; but
the Count, drawing a ring from his finger with one hand and a
pistol from his pocket with the other, gives the music master his
choice between a bribe and a couple of bullets in his head. Basilio,
always open to reason, has no difficulty in making his choice;
more than that, he signs as one of the witnesses to the marriage,
the other being Figaro.

As the barber locks the music master in a derisive embrace
Bartolo enters with a military patrol. He orders the officer to
arrest Figaro and his accomplice as criminals, but the Count once
more easily settles the matter by revealing his identity and
rank. In a vigorous aria he imperiously puts Bartolo in his
place, and the Doctor, unable to bear up against such a combination of moral indignation and tenor coloratura, soon gives up the
fight.

Almaviva's joy is so overwhelming that it sweeps him off for a
moment into a key signature of five flats as he turns to congratulate Rosina on her escape from the clutches of her tyrant:

[1] The writer of the article on Rossini in *Grove's Dictionary* informs us that
"the eight opening bars of the trio 'Zitti, zitti' are notoriously taken note by
note from Simon's air in Haydn's *Seasons*." This is not strictly true, however,
as the reader can discover for himself by the simple process of comparing
the two melodies.

No. 27

tu in - fe - li - ce   vit - ti — ma

But the key of B flat is soon restored, with the soldiers—who have come in most opportunely for the musical purposes of the composer—adding their felicitations in chorus. The Count continues to pour out the happiness of his heart:

No. 28

Ah il più lie -to, il più fe — li—ce e il mio cor de' co—ri a—man-ti,

the chorus still joining in from time to time, and the solo part proliferating into increasingly difficult coloratura.

By this time Bartolo has recovered his breath, and he uses it in the first place to round on Basilio for going over to the enemy; but Basilio blandly points out that he has merely followed the dictates of reason, Count Almaviva having produced arguments that were really irresistible. Then the Doctor turns to cursing himself for his stupidity in removing the ladder, thus facilitating the marriage. This gives Figaro the opportunity for a suave reminder of the vanity of precautions, whereupon Bartolo retires to his last line of defence; it is quite impossible, he protests, for him to pay Rosina her dowry. The Count cuts him short: he would not in any case accept anything of that sort with his bride; which provokes the cynical comment from Figaro that rogues have the best of it in this world. So everyone has won something and is satisfied. Figaro extinguishes his lantern, as a symbolic way of indicating that all's well that has ended well:

No. 29

Di si fe -li—ce in -ne ——————— sto,

a sentiment taken up by Berta, Bartolo, Basilio and the chorus, followed eventually by the rest of the company. The vista before the lovers, they all declare, is one of pure and endless affection and felicity. If they could foresee the future they would realise that they were being over-optimistic; but the sequel to *The Barber of Seville, or The Vain Precaution* was probably unthought of at this time even by Beaumarchais.

The Marriage of Figaro

MOZART [1756–1791]

PRINCIPAL CHARACTERS

FIGARO	*Bass*
COUNT ALMAVIVA	*Baritone*
COUNTESS ALMAVIVA	*Soprano*
SUSANNA	*Soprano*
CHERUBINO	*Soprano*
DOCTOR BARTOLO	*Bass*
MARCELLINA	*Soprano*
DON CURZIO	*Tenor*
DON BASILIO	*Tenor*
ANTONIO	*Bass*
BARBARINA	*Mezzo-soprano*

1

FOR some years after the production of *The Seraglio* (in July 1782) Mozart, so far as opera was concerned, could make no headway in Vienna. The Austrian empire of those days was a far-spread conglomerate of states and races, and Vienna was the meeting place of them all, the one town in which fame could be won and money made. The taste of the Court and most of the public being mainly for the facile, sparkling Italian opera, the town was overrun by Italian adventurers of all sorts. Mozart himself, though he would have preferred to do something in the German opera line, had in the end to swim with the current or go under. "Every nation has its own opera," he wrote to his father on the 5th February 1783; "why then should we Germans not have ours? Is not the German language as singable as the French or the English, and more so than the Russian? I am engaged now on a German opera on my own account.[1] I have chosen a comedy by Goldoni, *Il Servitore di Due Padroni*, and the text of the first act has already been translated by Baron Binder. All this is a secret, however, for the present."

But this plan came to nothing, and the struggling German opera in Vienna steadily went from bad to worse: not only were the native composers mostly second-raters but the Italian performances had a skill and a polish with which the Germans could hardly compete. In March of that same year the German company was disbanded, the best of the singers being absorbed into the Italian troupe that had been formed by command of the Emperor. Mozart was reduced to composing "numbers" for insertion in works by composers such as Anfossi and Bianchi to keep himself before the operatic public. By the spring of 1783, being bent on writing an Italian opera, he asked his father to get in touch with the Salzburg Abbé Varesco—who had made the *Idomeneo* text for him in 1780—and find out if he could be induced to co-operate with him again. He would like a libretto with seven characters, he said, among them two soprano parts of equal importance, the one "seria," the other "mezzo carattere"; a third soprano and, if necessary, all the men, were to be "entirely buffa."

In June 1783 he was in Salzburg, where he found that Varesco had prepared for him an involved and rather ponderously humorous libretto entitled *L'Oca del Cairo*, in which a goose with a human being concealed inside it played an important part. Mozart's views on libretto writing in general and his present collaborator in particular are expressed in a letter to his father of the 21st June. Varesco seems to have been attributing an exaggerated importance to his own share in the work, and Mozart had to tell him very frankly, through Leopold, that in an opera it is not the text but the music that mostly decides success or failure. Moreover Varesco would have to make whatever and as many alterations as he, Mozart, might demand, for the Abbé's own stage sense could not be trusted. Mozart got as far as writing eight musical numbers for the first act of the Varesco text, but eventually lost interest in it and let the plan drop. He still kept edging himself into the Vienna theatre whenever he got the chance by means of ad-

[1] i.e. without a commission from any theatre.

ditions to other composers' operas. But he was evidently getting rather desperate: "I have looked through a good hundred libretti, and probably more," he had written to Leopold on the 17th May 1783, "and have come upon hardly one that appeals to me." They would have to be altered a good deal, and no doubt the poet who would consent to do this would find it easier to write an entirely new text. Then he mentions "a certain Abbé Da Ponte" who seems to be coming to the fore in Viennese operatic circles. At the moment he is writing a libretto (*Il Ricco d'un Giorno*) for Salieri; this will take him about two months, and then he will do something for Mozart. But Wolfgang does not put much faith in the Abbé's promises: "you know as well as I do how pleasant these Italians can be to your face," he says. It is probable, however, that the shrewd Da Ponte was already quite as much interested in Mozart as the latter was in him.

2

This "Abbé Da Ponte" was an Italian Jew, originally of the name of Emanuele Conegliano, who had come into the world on the 10th March 1749 at Ceneda, a small town near Venice. His quickness of apprehension as a boy attracted the attention of a certain Bishop Lorenzo Da Ponte, who not only provided for his education and baptised him but permitted him to assume his own name. Having been admitted into the lower priestly order the young man became the Abbé Da Ponte, by which engaging title he chose to be known for the remainder of his life. After various wanderings he settled in Vienna in 1781, where he became the protégé of Salieri, and, through him, of the Emperor Joseph II. He was less in favour with Joseph's brother, who succeeded him, as Leopold II, in 1790, and soon his wanderings began again. He ended his days on the 17th August 1838 in the United States. His *Memoirs*, in which, with characteristic self-esteem, he tells us rather too much about himself and far too little about Mozart, had appeared in New York in 1823.

In Vienna he had soon wormed his way into influential circles, having all the qualities of self-assertion and capacity for intrigue that were necessary to keep one's head above water in the turbulent sea of Italian literary and musical life in the capital at that time. But he had also certain qualifications as a librettist which his competitors did not possess in anything like the same degree —comparatively little originality of invention, it is true, but a decided gift for adapting the work of more creative minds than his own to dramatic and musical ends, and a verbal dexterity that generally improved, for practical operatic purposes, on whatever he had appropriated. Mozart certainly owed a good deal to him in the long run.

In the summer and autumn of 1783 Mozart had worked for a time at an opera buffa with the title of *Lo Sposo Deluso*, of which he finished or sketched only the overture, a quartet, a trio, and a couple of arias. In July of the preceding year he had written to his father that an Italian librettist had shown him a text which he might accept if it were altered to his liking. It is conjectured that this librettist was Da Ponte and the work *Lo Sposo Deluso;* and though proof of this is lacking, it seems probable. There is evidence in plenty that he was merciless in his demands on his poets. His letters to his father are highly illuminative on this point: we seem to be reading the story of Puccini and his poets again when we see how imperiously Mozart insisted on dictating the handling of an action and the details of a text; his sense of the stage was evidently keener than that of the majority of opera composers. There must have been times when Varesco in particular felt like a toad under the harrow; and we may take it for granted that Mozart was equally exacting with Da Ponte, though contemporary records of their collaboration are necessarily lacking, as the pair did not correspond but simply talked together.

In all these years the only commission Mozart received was for a "festival" in honour of the Governor-General of the Netherlands. To a text by Stephanie the Younger (who had provided the libretto of *The Seraglio*) he wrote the short *Der Schauspieldirektor* (*The Impresario*), which was produced in the orangery at Schönbrunn on the 7th February 1786 and repeated on the 18th and 25th.

3

Meanwhile, however, he and Da Ponte had been drawing closer together. The latter's recent works had not all been successful, which naturally led to recriminations between him and his composers, each laying the blame on the other. It ended with his quarrelling with Salieri—without, however, losing the support of the Emperor, which was much more important. By this time Mozart, for all his longing to write a German opera, had realised that the only passport to the patronage of the Court and the favour of the public was an Italian opera buffa; Da Ponte, for his part, seems to have been well aware that as a composer Mozart stood head and shoulders above his competitors. A collaboration, therefore, would be to their mutual advantage; as to a new production, Da Ponte thought he would have influence enough with the Emperor for that.

The idea of an opera based on Beaumarchais's *Le Mariage de Figaro* seems to have been in the first place Mozart's; but Da Ponte must have seen at once the scope it offered for the display of his own talents. Beaumarchais alleged that his second Figaro comedy was written not long after the first, but that statement is not taken too seriously by his biographers. Certainly it was not produced in Paris until some nine years after *The Barber of Seville* —on the 27th April 1784. It is one of the commonplaces of literary history that the new work played a not inconsiderable part in producing the ferment of ideas that culminated in the Revolution of some five years later. Certainly the unfortunate Louis XVI was quick to perceive the danger to the old régime inherent in this unflattering picture of a grandee with none of the virtues and all the vices of his order being persistently put in the wrong dialectically and outmanœuvred by the superior intelligence of his lackey; and for a whole four years the French King had refused to licence a performance of the play. Not that there was anything really "revolutionary" in it. As André Hallays has pointed out, there was nothing of the revolutionary in Beaumarchais's make-up. He did no specific thinking about governments and constitutions, put forward no doctrinaire solutions of the political and social problems of the time. He had not the slightest *a priori* objection to things being as they were, and as bad as they were; all he wanted was a wider field for the exercise of his own talents and a larger share of the pickings. He disliked the aristocracy not because it was privileged but because it made too energetic use of its privileges to keep cleverer but less well-born people like himself in their place; and his objection to the French legal system was not the basic one that it was sometimes corrupt and unjust but the more opportunist one that *he* frequently had difficulty in achieving his own ends through it.

As Hallays says, it was not that the *Barber* and the *Marriage* were revolutionary in themselves but that a Parisian public in whom revolutionary ideas had long been germinating read what it wanted into the two plays: "the author proposes, the public disposes." What was really under fire, in the *Marriage* particularly, was not the monarchy or the political and social set-up in general but the arrogance and insolence of the aristocracy; and the audiences revelled in the spectacle of their being duped and outwitted by a barber-valet who had more brains in his little finger than they had in their little noddles. The aristocracy, more appreciative of finesse and wit in the author than apprehensive as to their own security, laughed as heartily as the man in the street at Beaumarchais's audacious sallies.[1] It was only a few of the more intelligent among them who could look ahead and imagine what all this was likely to end in. One of them, Baroness d'Oberkirch, noted that "the *grands seigneurs* laughed at their own expense, and, what was worse, made others laugh. *They will be sorry for it one day.*" She was right.

The impact of the work on European public opinion in general can be gauged by the fact that no fewer than twelve translations of it soon appeared in Germany alone; and it was performed in several German theatres. It was read and quoted with the keenest delight in advanced Viennese circles; and its dangerous tendency was sensed by the Emperor Joseph II, who vetoed its production in the National Theatre. It occurred to the shrewd Da Ponte, however, that an opera on the subject might succeed in sidestepping the censorship.

4

Various reasons probably operated to make Mozart prefer the *Marriage* comedy to that of the *Barber*. For one thing, Paisiello's

---

[1] We have already seen Figaro, in the *Barber*, asking Count Almaviva with cool insolence, "Ah, Monseigneur, with your high ideal of the virtues necessary to a servant, how many masters, would you say, are fit to be valets?" In the *Marriage* he caps this with a stinging rejoinder to the Count's irritated query, "How is it that the servants in this house take longer to dress than their masters?"—"It's because they have no valets to help them."

opera on the latter subject had been given in Vienna in August 1783, and there would be little point in Mozart entering into almost immediate competition with that, even if he could have found a librettist of the quality he desired. For another, the *Barber* could hardly have fitted in with his general notions of a full operatic ensemble; it lacked, for one thing, a second soprano part of any importance. A mere glance at the dramatis personae of the *Marriage* would show him that the new comedy had the number and diversity of characters suitable to his own lively genius, that loved movement for its own precious sake. He would be as well aware as Da Ponte or anyone else of what in these days we would call the publicity value of the Figaro subject; moreover, he himself had suffered so many humiliations at the hands of those in power that it was bound to be a joy to him to write a work in which a typical representative of the ruling class was continually being outwitted and frustrated by his valet. But Mozart looked at the theme through eyes of his own. He saw it as a series of opportunities for the display of his own surpassing genius as a composer; but in order to permit of that display the characters had to be transmuted out of Beaumarchais into Mozart. His Figaro is a masterpiece of musical characterisation, but it is not the Figaro of Beaumarchais as Rossini was to paint him later; the Italian genius had more of what we may call, for convenience' sake, the Latin volatility and gay insouciance of the French original. Mozart's Figaro has more of Germanic seriousness in his make-up. The character of the Countess, again, Mozart deepens in his own way; she feels the pathos of her situation more profoundly than Rossini would have shown her doing. We may sum it all up, perhaps, by saying that while in the Rossini opera we feel that we are always in the company of Beaumarchais, in *The Marriage of Figaro* it is more of Mozart that we are kept thinking than of the French dramatist.

What Mozart does, in fact, is to give a more serious turn to each of the characters. His Countess becomes one of the great wronged characters of opera, a woman who has felt deeply and been deeply hurt. His Susanna has moments of romantic ardour that are not in the pert Susanna of Beaumarchais. Above all, there broods over the whole of the opera a sensuousness that is indeed latent in the original play but is found in nothing like the same profusion there. Consciously or unconsciously love and sex are everywhere present to some degree in the original drama. Figaro and his Susanna are sincerely, though not very romantically, in love with each other. The Count is shown as an inveterate pursuer of women. The Countess, we are subtly made to feel, has a more-than-motherly interest in the little Cherubino. And the page himself is a unique piece of characterisation; this boy somewhere between naïve puberty and artful adolescence in the creation of whom Beaumarchais, as we know, had drawn upon his memories of a precocious romantic adventure of his own at the age of thirteen. As Taine has pointed out, sex in some form or other is everywhere present in *Le Mariage*; even Marceline, approaching middle age, still feels something of its urge, while in Fanchette,[1] the little daughter of the gardener, we have a delicately drawn feminine foil to the not yet fully masculine "Cherubino d'amore." And at every point Mozart has graved more deeply the lines of Beaumarchais and given them a warmer infusion of colour.

5

The first problem that confronted the librettist and the composer was how to overcome the objection of the Emperor to the comedy appearing on the stage at all, in any form. Although Da Ponte's account of the affair was not committed to paper until nearly half a century later we may probably regard it as substantially accurate. The Emperor, to begin with, was inclined to doubt the operatic sufficiency of Mozart, who, he said, though admittedly good at instrumental music, had written only one opera and that not a particularly good one.[2] Da Ponte countered with a skilful piece of flattery: "without your Majesty's gracious protection *I* would have written only one drama for Vienna." Reverting to *The Marriage of Figaro*, the Emperor reminded Da Ponte that he had already refused his German actors permission to perform that work. To this Da Ponte replied that in converting the spoken play into an opera he had omitted several scenes and

[1] Barbarina in the opera.
[2] He was referring to the *Seraglio* of 1782. *Idomeneo* (1781) had been produced in Munich and was as yet unknown in Vienna. Of Mozart's earlier operas the Emperor would of course know nothing.

curtailed others, his virtuous intention throughout having been to eliminate everything that might offend against decency and good taste. He was sure he had created out of the original play a work that would not be unworthy of a theatre honoured by his Majesty's protection. As for the music, in his humble opinion it was masterly. Thereupon the Emperor graciously assured him he would rely on his suppliant's taste and discretion. When Mozart took a copy of the score, or as much of it as he had completed, to the palace, he was allowed to play some selections from it that earned the imperial approval: what they were we are not informed, but no doubt the composer saw to it that they were adapted to his and the librettist's artful strategic purpose. According to Da Ponte Mozart worked at the music step by step with him and finished the opera in six weeks. The overture was written last; it was entered by him in the Catalogue of his works on the 29th April 1786. It may be noted, however, that a letter of Leopold Mozart's of the 11th November 1785 to his daughter indicates that the composition was already well in hand even at that time. (In a letter eight days earlier he had casually mentioned that Wolfgang had "said something [in a recent letter] about a new opera.") On the 11th we get more detailed news: "At last, on the 2nd of this month, I had a letter of no more than a dozen lines from your brother, in which he asks for indulgence as he is up to his eyes in work at his new opera, *Le Nozze di Figaro*. . . . I know the original piece; it is very difficult, and to make it effective as an opera it must have been a good deal altered in translation. God grant that it comes out well dramatically; as regards the music I have no fears. He is in for a lot of trotting about and disputation before he gets the libretto exactly to his liking. . . ."

"On the 28th," Leopold writes again to his daughter on the 18th April 1786, "the *Nozze di Figaro* will have its first performance. A success will mean something, as I know that it will have terrific cabals to contend against: Salieri and his whole gang will once more set heaven and earth in motion. Duschek told me recently that your brother has so many cabals against him because he is so highly esteemed for his exceptional talent and skill." As a matter of fact the first performance did not take place until the 1st May. Perhaps, as the date of the entry in Mozart's Catalogue suggests, the overture was not quite ready by the 28th April.

The new work was highly successful; Leopold, who had gone to Vienna to hear it, told his daughter on the 18th May that at the second performance five numbers, and at the third seven, had to be repeated; and we know now that the Emperor—to the annoyance of the singers—had to forbid encores on the ground that they made the performance excessively long. The work was given nine times in Vienna during the year 1786; after that it dropped out of the local repertory, and did not reappear there until the 29th August 1789. In this revival Adriana Ferrarese del Bene, who was afterwards the first Fiordiligi in *Così fan tutte*, replaced Anna Storace as Susanna, and there was a new Countess—Caterina Cavalieri, who had been the Constanze in *The Seraglio* and the Mademoiselle Silberklang in the *Schauspieldirektor*, and in 1787 became the first Elvira in *Don Giovanni*. For the Ferrarese Mozart wrote in July 1789 a rondo, "Al desio di chi t'adora," to take the place of "Deh vieni, non tardar," and another new aria for Susanna, "Un moto di gioia mi sento." Neither of these numbers is sufficiently interesting to deserve a place in modern performances.

In a letter to his father of the 7th May 1785, in which he told him of the opening of a new and brilliant Italian season in Vienna, Mozart had singled out for special commendation the principal bass-baritone buffo singer, Francesco Benucci. Him he now chose to play Figaro.[1] Stefano Mandini was the Almaviva, Signora Laschi the Countess, Nancy (Anna Selina) Storace—a London-born girl of Italian parentage who had a great vogue just then as a singer of soubrette parts—was the Susanna, and Nannina Gottlieb (in later years the Pamina of the *Magic Flute*) the Barbarina. The parts of Bartolo and Antonio were doubled by Bassani, whose wife played Cherubino. The Marcellina was Signora Mandini. There is no first-rank tenor part in *The Marriage of Figaro*; the two minor rôles for that voice, Basilio and Don Curzio, were taken by the Irish singer Michael Kelly, to whose *Reminiscences* of forty years later (written by Theodore Hook) we owe some interesting sidelights on Mozart, the *Marriage*, and

[1] A contemporary engraving of him shows him as a man of spare build, with a face expressive of shrewdness and a decidedly sardonic humour. He looks the sort of man of whom Beaumarchais himself would have approved as the mercurial, ironic, resourceful Figaro.

the period. In the Catalogue of his own works Mozart enters him as "Occhely," which is explained by the fact that the Irishman was known in Italian operatic circles as O'Kelly. In December 1786 the opera was given in Prague with a success so tremendous that Mozart was commissioned to write a new opera for the local theatre. Thus it was that *Don Giovanni* came into being.

6

Ostensibly Beaumarchais's *Marriage of Figaro* is a sequel to his *Barber of Seville*, but to read the later play immediately after the earlier one is to find ourselves asking a few questions and not getting satisfactory replies to any of them. The setting of the *Marriage* is Count Almaviva's château of Aguas-Frescas, a few miles from Seville, where he had obviously settled down as a feudal grandee after his union with Rosina. But how soon or how late after? It is impossible to say. The interval has obviously been long enough for the Count to have got a little tired of his Rosina and taken to the pursuit of other women, while she, on her part, has had time enough to lose all kittenish high spirits and develop into a dignified *grande dame* with a knowledge of the world that is tinged with the melancholy of lost illusions. We learn, too, that the King of Spain has recently appointed Almaviva his ambassador in London—which suggests that he is no longer the irresponsible young harum-scarum of the *Barber* but a man who counts for something in the larger world.

On the other hand, there are indications that the period of the first act of the second comedy is not much later than the last act of the first. Basile is still Rosina's music teacher, domiciled in the château, where the Count finds his talent for intrigue useful to him. Doctor Bartolo is still practising his profession in Seville, and in his dialogue with Figaro in the second scene of the first act there are unmistakeable signs that his defeat in the *Barber* was so recent as still to be rankling in him. Although he is obviously the accredited physician of the household—one gathers that his summons to Aguas-Frescas is due to the Count having had an accident or the Countess being ill—it is clear that he knows little or nothing of what has been going on in the château recently; it is even news to him that Almaviva has been neglecting his own lady and running after other people's. When Marceline mentions Basile's name Bartolo ejaculates, "What! that other rascal also lives here? The place is a rogues' den! What does he do here?", which suggests that no appreciable interval of time has elapsed between the end of the first play and the beginning of the second. Figaro, again, chaffs Bartolo about the failure of his scheme to marry his ward, in terms which suggest that the incident had been recent enough for the subject to be still a sore one with the Doctor. Figaro's ironic enquiry about the health of Bartolo's mule—which unfortunate animal had had a cataplasm put on its eyes by the barber in the course of his gay medical experiments on the Doctor's household—again seems to indicate that not much time has elapsed between the two plays. The general impression given us by this second scene of the *Marriage* is that Bartolo and Figaro are now meeting for the first, or near-first, time since the last act of the *Barber*; and it is difficult for us to reconcile this time-table with the impression derived from other quarters that a fairly considerable time must be supposed to have elapsed between the two comedies.

7

The Marceline of the *Mariage* is a quite new character, now the housekeeper at Aguas-Frescas, but at some time or other in the distant past, we are given to understand, a flame of Bartolo's more passionate youth, by whom she had a son who had mysteriously disappeared in childhood—a motif that becomes of decisive importance later in the play and in the opera. For the purposes of the imbroglio Beaumarchais has to show Figaro pledged either to marry this housekeeper—who, of course, cannot be in her first youth now—or to pay back some money he had borrowed from her. The motif is really the nodal one of the *Mariage:* it is upon this dilemma of Figaro's that the Count is relying in his machinations to bend Susanna to his will, for Figaro can pay his debt only by the financial assistance of his master, who will come to his rescue only on his own terms. The knot, so awkward for Figaro and Susanna, is cut by a bold stroke on the dramatist's part: it turns out that Figaro is the long-lost child of Bartolo and Marceline. There is comedy of the richest kind in the flabbergasted Doctor's discovery that the young ne'er-do-well who had cheated him out of Rosina and on whom he had hoped to revenge himself by marrying him off to his former mistress, is actually his own son.

At this point a word must be said about the current English misconception of Marcellina as "Dr. Bartolo's housekeeper," an error arising, perhaps, from her being so described in the list of dramatis personae prefixed to the best-known English vocal score of the opera. Nothing could be clearer, one would have thought, than that she is not Bartolo's but Almaviva's housekeeper. Beaumarchais designates her "femme de charge" at the château. In the Italian imprint of the libretto she is called "governante," which has two meanings, that of "preceptress," and that of "housekeeper"; and Marcellina happens to be both of these at Aguas-Frescas. The German commentators have not fallen into the English error in their analyses of the French play and the opera. Hermann Abert, for example, describes her as Rosina's duenna, whom, together with Figaro and Basilio, the Count had taken into his service when he married Rosina: Schurig speaks of her as Dr. Bartolo's "former housekeeper."

All this is as clear as daylight to anyone who has read Beaumarchais with any care. Though there is no acting character of the name of Marcellina in the *Barber*, there are some references there to someone of that name in Bartolo's household. We are told of a Marcellina whom Figaro has put out of action along with the other servants, by bleeding her foot. Towards the end of the *Barber* Doctor Bartolo, to make sure that none of the conspirators shall gain access to Rosina, orders her to go to Marcellina's room and lock and bolt the door. This invisible Marcellina, in fact, is in the *Barber* Bartolo's housekeeper and the young Rosina's governess.

It is obviously in Almaviva's household, not Bartolo's, that Marcellina figures in the *Marriage* as housekeeper and preceptress to the still young Countess. She is not an occasional visitor to the château but a resident there; she moves about freely in it. At the time when the play opens she has sent to Seville for Doctor Bartolo, to whom she explains the whole complicated situation in the château as regards Almaviva, Susanna, Figaro and herself.

137

The Doctor does not even know that Basilio is also located there until Marcellina tells him; and his impatient comment after hearing her story is, "Do I understand, then, that it was to listen to rubbish of this sort that you summoned me from Seville?"

It is unnecessary to pile up any further the evidence that Marcellina is domiciled in the château, not in Seville with Bartolo. Da Ponte follows the French play in all essentials. It is quite clear in the first act of the opera that she knows everything that goes on in the house above and below stairs, while he knows nothing: "Tell me everything," he says. That she has the run of the château is manifest: she walks in and out of Susanna's bedroom as a matter of course, and in the imbroglio in the second act the Count, playing for time, keeps hoping for her appearance. It is made perfectly evident that she was at one time Rosina's governess in Bartolo's household and is now her preceptress and *femme de charge* in Almaviva's. Susanna's parting shot at her after she has left the stage after the quarrel scene is, in Beaumarchais, this: "Goodbye, madame, you pedant! . . . This ancient sibyl! Just because she has a bit of learning and made the Countess's life a burden to her when she was a child she wants now to run the whole château." In the opera we get the same idea in a slightly different phrasing. "Decrepit sibyl!" is how Susanna describes her to her face; and after she has left the scene of combat Susanna calls after her, "Take yourself off, you old pedant, you arrogant Doctoress. You think that because you have read a book or two and plagued the life out of her ladyship when she was young" . . . which is as near Beaumarchais as makes no matter.

Marcellina, then, is *not* Dr. Bartolo's housekeeper but Almaviva's and Rosina's, a point which both audiences and producers would do well to bear in mind.

8

But let us now turn to the opera.

The overture is in no sense "programmatic": the full title of the original play had been *La Folle Journée, ou Le Mariage de Figaro*, and it is upon the "folle journée" in general, rather than the individuals or the incidents of the drama, that Mozart wisely concentrates. Gaiety reigns throughout the overture, from the racy opening theme:

No. 1

through its fanfare-like supplement:

No. 2

and their developments, to the contrasting second subject and beyond:

No. 3

Mozart appears to have coquetted for a moment with the idea of delaying the final return of the opening theme (No. 1) in order to insert an andante con moto section in 6/8 time, based on a lilting melody in the oboe with an accompaniment of plucked strings, the general procedure thus being analogous to that in the overture to *The Seraglio*. The autograph score shows, however, that the page that presumably followed the first bare suggestion of this slower section has been torn out. We feel that Mozart's instinct was sound: it was best to keep the merry atmosphere of the "folle journée" one and indivisible in the overture from sudden start to quick finish.

The time of the commencement of the opera is the morning of the day on which Figaro, who is now the Count's factotum, and Susanna, the Countess's maid, hope to be married. The setting of the first scene is a relatively unfurnished room in the château, the only notable object in it, indeed, being an armchair in the centre; Figaro and Susanna, we cannot help commenting, seem to have delayed for an unconscionable time the full furnishing of what is obviously to be the nuptial chamber. Figaro is busy with a footrule, measuring the length and breadth and height of the room and calling out the figures; while Susanna, looking at herself in a mirror, is wholly absorbed in the ecstasy of trying on a new hat which apparently she has at last shaped and adorned to her satisfaction. It is some little time before the busy Figaro can be induced to take any interest in this masterpiece, but when he does so it meets with his approval.

After a delightful duet the pair discuss the situation in recitative. Figaro explains that he has been busy trying to decide on the best place for the handsome bed the Count has given them. Susanna makes it clear at once that her fiancé's choice of a bedroom is not hers, but she mysteriously refuses for a time to explain her objection to it. It is the most convenient room in the whole château, he tells her, for all concerned, master and mistress, valet and maid:

No. 4

On one side of them is the Countess; if she wants Susanna in the night, all she has to do is to ring, and the maid will be with her in a trice. With equal celerity Figaro can answer the call of the Count, whose bedroom happens to be on the other side. Figaro is obviously not as quick-witted as we would have expected him to be after his exploits in the *Barber*, and the more wideawake Susanna has to teach him some of the facts of life. Suppose all this bell-ringing on the one part and prompt service on the other should turn out to be not quite so simple a routine matter as Figaro, in his innocence, imagines? Suppose the Count rings one night for his valet and sends him off three miles away on some errand or other, and—well, it is only a skip and a jump from the Count's bedroom to Susanna's. Exacting a promise from him that he will not entertain any suspicions on her account, she lays the whole situation before him in recitative. The Count, it appears, wearying a little of amorous hunts in the fashionable world, is now turning his attention to the home coverts; and the game he is planning to bring down is no other than Figaro's Susanna. How

140

can her lover have been so blind as not to see for himself how things have been shaping for some time in the château? The nice dowry the Count has promised her and the fine bedroom he has placed at their disposal have not been disinterested benevolences on his part, as Figaro naïvely imagines, but have been designed to pave the way for the exercise of the feudal *droit du seigneur*. "But," Figaro protests, "he has renounced that right in his domains." No doubt, replies Susanna; but now he repents having done so and proposes to exercise the right where Susanna is concerned, and the insidious Basilio, the Count's crafty tool, whenever he gives her a singing lesson never fails to remind her of her duty to her feudal lord.

At first Figaro is inclined to be incredulous, but in the end he sees that Susanna is right. Now he understands why his master the Count intends to promote him to the rank of courier in the London embassy, for the better pursuit of his designs on Susanna. So far Figaro has undoubtedly been a little obtuse; but now that he sees everything clearly the old spirit of combat and intrigue revives in him. Susanna having run off to answer the Countess's bell, he declares, in the famous cavatina "Se vuol ballare, signor Contino":

No. 5

Allegretto

Se vuol bal - la —— re, Si-gnor Con -ti - no,

his intention to beat his master at his own game: "Do you want to dance, my little Count? Very well; but it shall be to my guitar. Join my school and I will teach you your capers." From now onwards the Count shall be involved in a net of counter-intrigues in which he will be helpless: he, Figaro, the master tactician, who had twisted Bartolo round his little finger in the *Barber*, is going into action.

9

Full of the joy of combat and confident of success he goes out, and as he does so Doctor Bartolo and Marcellina enter, the latter holding a document in her hand which turns out to be Figaro's

contract to marry her. Bartolo asks her testily why she had forborne to consult him on this matter until the very morning of the
valet's union with Susanna. She opines that it is still not too late
to frustrate the marriage; her plan is to confirm Susanna in her
refusal of the Count, who, in his anger, will then insist on Figaro
carrying out his contract either to wed Marcellina or pay off his
debt to her, which the valet cannot do without his lordship's
assistance. Bartolo, having read the contract, promises to do all
he can to help her: it will certainly be a good joke, he says, to get
the cunning rascal who cheated him out of Rosina married to his
old servant! He launches into a vigorous aria in praise of vengeance. Fools and slaves, he says, accept insults and humiliations;
the man of spirit avenges them. And in an affair of this kind,
which calls for secrecy and craft, no one can surpass Doctor
Bartolo, whose talents all Seville knows: so let this rogue of an
ex-barber beware! This time he will lose the game! The character
and the situation are stock ones in opera buffa, and there existed
for it a stock musical apparatus which Mozart employs with his
usual mastery. But, as so often happens with him, he puts so much
of himself and of the resources of music into the aria that much of
it could figure equally well in an episode as serious as the present
one is humorous. We have had much the same experience once
or twice with the Osmin of *The Seraglio.*

Bartolo leaves the stage, rather inconclusively, at the end of
his aria, for no better reason than that Da Ponte has no further
use for him at the moment.[1] Susanna now enters, carrying one
of her mistress's dresses, a cap and a ribbon; and there follows a
bantering duet between her and Marcellina in which, with youth
and a nimbler wit to help her, Susanna finally has the advantage
in the exchange of double-edged compliments. The older lady
felicitates the younger one on being a bride who has the good luck

[1] It is all managed much better in Beaumarchais, where the audience is
placed in possession of more of the essential facts leading up to the imbroglio,
and Bartolo remains on the stage, an amused spectator of the battle of wits
that follows between Marcellina and Susanna. In a performance of the opera
in Paris in 1793 the dialogue of Beaumarchais was substituted for the Da
Ponte recitatives throughout the opera. There is a good deal to be said both
for and against a procedure of this sort: Da Ponte has rejected or condensed
much that we would prefer to be set forth in more detail.

to be the apple of her master's eye: Susanna counters with an ironic tribute to her antagonist's years, which have earned her the respect of all Spain. So it goes on, in true feminine bargee fashion, until Marcellina, compelled to admit defeat, flounces off in a towering rage.

10

Susanna has only just time to preen her feathers and rejoice in her victory over the "sibilla decrepita," the "dottoressa arrogante," the "vecchia pedante" who, because she had a smattering of education, had managed to become Rosina's governess,[1] when the page Cherubino enters. The sensitive little fellow is bursting with self-pity: yesterday the Count, having caught him alone with the gardener's little daughter Barbarina, had dismissed him from his service; and had not the Countess, his kind godmother, interceded for him he would by now be on his travels with never a hope of seeing his dear Susanna again! This last touch amuses her vastly; she had understood, she tells him, that it was the Countess to whom he had secretly given his heart. Ah, the Countess! he sighs: how he envies Susanna, who can see her whenever she likes, who dresses her in the morning and disrobes her at night, pins and unpins her, and adjusts her lace. Learning that the ribbon in Susanna's hand is from the Countess's nightwear he snatches the sanctified object from her and refuses to give it up, swearing he would not surrender it to save his life. In Beaumarchais he indulges at this point in a significant piece of auto-psychoanalysis: he does not know why it is, but for some time the mere sight of a woman is enough to set his heart beating wildly; the words "love" and "pleasure" tremble constantly on his lips, and he roams the park murmuring "I love you!" to the trees, the clouds, the winds, his noble mistress, Susanna and Fanchette; even Marcellina—who, after all, as he explains, is a woman and therefore "interesting"—sets his too susceptible heart on fire. And little Fanchette is kinder to him than the ironic, worldly-wise Susanna, for at least the child listens seriously to the important things he has to say. In the opera Da Ponte gives him an aria to sing that is a skilful rendering of all this in verse:

[1] This was obviously when Rosina was Bartolo's ward and Marcellina his innamorata; but there is no mention of it in the *Barber*.

No. 6

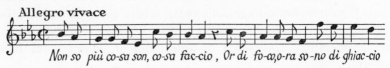

Allegro vivace

Non so più co-sa son, co-sa fac-cio , Or di fo-co,o-ra so-no di ghiac-cio

and Mozart has turned it all into music that is the very soul of juvenile love, ardent, troubled, self-doubting yet ineffably happy. (In the opera the immediate pretext for the aria is that Cherubino has written a canzone which Susanna can sing to the Countess, to herself, to Barbarina, to Marcellina, to every woman in the château; for it is a confession that all womankind ought to hear. This masterpiece he will give to Susanna in return for the ribbon. Mozart postpones the singing of the canzone to the second act of the opera).

Someone is heard approaching from outside; presumably it is the Count, and Cherubino, scared out of his wits, crouches down behind the big armchair, in which the Count, very much at his ease, seats himself when he enters. He has come to take the first decisive step in the siege of the Susanna fortress. He explains the situation in a long scene in recitative. The King has appointed him his ambassador in London, and he proposes to take Figaro —and of course Susanna—there with him. She must know already how much he loves her, for his agent Basilio will have told her all that. What he wants at the moment is that she shall give him an assignation at dusk this evening in the garden. Susanna, doubly embarrassed—by the suggestion, that is virtually a command, and by the awkward problem set her by the presence of Cherubino— can only stammer out a request to be left in peace. But while the Count is assuring her that in return for such a favour he will pay Figaro's debt to Marcellina the voice of Basilio is heard without. Having no desire for the music master's company just then and there the Count tells Susanna to get rid of him quickly, and makes to hide behind the chair. By standing between the pair for a moment Susanna gives the page, who is certainly not lacking in resource, time to slip unobserved into the chair, where she covers him with the dress she had brought with her on her entry. The situation is not without its attraction for the Count, who looks forward now to overhearing, unseen, how his hireling will plead his cause for him. Basilio begins by telling Susanna how foolish she is to reject the advances of an admirer so rich and influential as the Count Almaviva and accept those of a mere page, "Cherubino d'amore," who has been seen hanging round the place that very morning. And that canzone, continues Basilio—who seems to know everything that goes on in and around the château—for whom was that composed, for the Countess's maid or the great lady herself? Anyhow, Susanna will be doing the page a service to warn him not to look so amorously at the Countess when he is serving her at table, for if the Count gets wind of it he will be furious, and Susanna knows what he can be capable of when roused.

11

She turns on him angrily, but he tells her smoothly there is nothing he knows about all this that is not already the talk of the whole château. This is too much for the Count, who now reveals himself, and, in a towering temper, orders Basilio to see that the seducer, as he calls the page, is expelled from the house at once. Mozart now has his actors well set for a fine trio in which, as usual with him, each of the personages speaks true to character while all combine into an enchanting musical whole. The Count storms and threatens; Susanna can only wail confusedly. Only the practised intriguer Basilio remains calm, enjoying himself immensely: this is a situation after his own malicious heart. He addresses the Count in a phrase that is a masterpiece of oily hypocrisy—"I seem to have arrived here at an unfortunate moment; pardon me, my lord":

No. 7

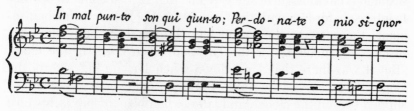

In mal pun-to son qui giun-to; Per-do-na-te o mio si-gnor

At last Susanna's nerves give way; and as she seems to be about to faint the two men gallantly come to her assistance. Solicitously they lead her towards the armchair; this restores her like magic, and she violently repulses them both.

145

Basilio, once more to the unctuous strain of No. 7, protests that what he had said about the page was mere suspicion on his part; but the Count will not hear a word in excuse of Cherubino, who is to be expelled from the château immediately. The precocious boy is manifestly a menace to the morals of the estate; only yesterday, it appears, the Count, having occasion to speak to little Barbarina, the gardener's daughter and Susanna's cousin, had found the door of the cottage locked. At last it had been opened by the girl, who seemed somewhat embarrassed. Looking round for a possible reason for her confusion, the Count—turning for a moment Basilio's sly No. 7 to his own ironic purposes—had perceived the table-cloth; dexterously raising this, whom should he find cowering beneath it but the young Cherubino! He illustrates the situation graphically by lifting the dress from the armchair, thus disclosing the trembling page. He turns on Susanna: now, he says sarcastically, he understands everything. She loses her nerve completely; Basilio alone, as hitherto, is maliciously delighted with the latest turn of events. "Better and better" he ejaculates; "women are all alike," he assures the Count, "they always run true to form." What he had said about the page, he again remarks sardonically, was of course no more than mere suspicion. In the face of all the evidence against her poor Susanna can only raise her hands and implore the protection of heaven.

The delightful trio over, the working out of the drama is resumed in recitative. The Count orders Basilio to bring Figaro before him at once, so that his valet may see for himself the sort of creature his Susanna is. This rouses her to action. Asked by Almaviva to account for the page being there under such highly suspicious circumstances she explains that he had come to beg her to intercede for him with the Countess in the matter of his banishment: the entry of the Count had thrown them both into confusion, and in his terror the boy had taken cover in the chair. "But it was there that I sat down when I came in," retorts the Count. "Yes," says Cherubino timidly, "but when you did so I slipped behind the chair"; and later, when his lordship in his turn had retreated behind it for concealment, he had popped into it once more. The Count is now uncomfortably conscious that the page must have heard the whole of his compromising conversation with Susanna. This deflates him; he finds it difficult now to play the stern moralist, and he is not at all placated by Cherubino's innocent-artful assurance that he had done his best *not* to hear anything that was said.

12

Calling him a viper, Almaviva yanks him out of the chair [1] as a confused noise is heard without and Figaro enters, bearing a bridal veil in his hand, and accompanied by a number of servants and peasants, arrayed in white, who strew flowers before the Count. All this is Figaro's first crafty shot in his campaign against his master: he aims to embarrass him by an organised tribute on the part of his vassals to his benevolence and virtue. The Count, however, is on the alert. "What is the meaning of this comedy?", he asks. Figaro whispers to Susanna, "Now the dance begins; play up to me, my treasure!", to which she replies—rather despairingly after all she has recently gone through—"There's no hope for us!" Turning obsequiously to the Count, Figaro begs him to accept this tribute to the regard he has shown for virtue by abolishing the detested *droit du seigneur*. Almaviva loftily brushes that theme aside: what is it that the valet really wants? Figaro's answer is that he is anxious to be the first to benefit by his lordship's magnanimity: this is why he has arranged his marriage for today, and he asks the Count to make an impressive gesture by placing the white bridal wreath, the symbol of purity, on the head of the bride. "Diabolical cunning!" the Count mutters under his breath: "but I shall be a match for them." He confirms the abolition of the *droit*, modestly disclaiming any special virtue on his part in doing so. "Oh, what goodness!" exclaims Susanna admiringly; "oh, what justice!" echoes Figaro; and the vassals shout "Long life to our lord!" He will perform the ceremony, he

[1] Da Ponte's handling of this scene is one of many arguments in favour of the use of Beaumarchais's original text whenever possible in the recitatives of the opera. In the play the Count's fury with both Susanna and Cherubino and his resolve to frustrate Figaro's marriage are more fully and effectively brought out; and when he is checkmated by the page's artful hint that he had heard every word of Almaviva's attempted seduction of Susanna he whispers in her ear, "Perfidious one! Now you shall not marry Figaro!" This declaration gives the necessary point to the scene that follows; the Count may be baffled for the moment, but for all that the battle of wits is now joined between him and his valet.

assures them, at the first convenient moment, but suggests post-poning it a little while till he can do so on a more imposing scale; and under his breath he invokes Marcellina. The vassals repeat their chorus of praise, and he dismisses them.

The principal characters now have the stage to themselves. Figaro, Susanna and Basilio pay a final compliment to their gracious overlord, but Cherubino is silent, grieving, as Susanna explains to Figaro, over his banishment from the château. The Count at first disregards their appeal to his clemency; but when the page throws out another hint about his lips being sealed Almaviva sees the wisdom of temporising. He will do more than pardon Cherubino, he says; there is a commission vacant in his regiment and this he grants him—on condition that he leaves at once. The Count and Basilio go out, and Figaro, by way of consoling the boy for not seeing Susanna again for some time, sings the famous "Non più andrai":

No. 8

Allegro

Non più an-drai, far-fal-lo-ne a-mo-ro-so, Not-te e gior-no d'in-tor-no gi-ran-do,

The young amorist must say goodbye to all this love-making and turn his attention to the stern realities of the barrack-room and the battlefield, sacrifice his flowing locks and plumed hats; "Narcissus-Adonis" must play a new part as a true son of Mars, sport long moustaches, shoulder a gun and rattle a sabre; dance no more fandangos but march in mud and snow over the hills and through the valleys to the music of trumpets and fifes and cannon. The chaff is all in good part, and it ends with them all marching off in formation to the strains of a military march. So ends the first act of the opera.

From the dramatic point of view Da Ponte's handling of this final scene leaves something to be desired. He does not bring out in his recitatives as Beaumarchais does in his dialogue the fact that already the Count and Figaro are at daggers drawn, the former being piqued beyond endurance by his frustration with Susanna and his suspicions of Cherubino and the Countess, the valet, quite sure of himself now that the talent for intrigue on which he prides himself can have free play, indulging in all sorts of polite insolences to his master. Secondly, Beaumarchais makes it clear that Bartolo and Marcellina have been seen making their way to the town—obviously to take legal action in the matter of Figaro's bond: the Count realises at once the importance of this to his own strategy, for it is through Marcellina that he has been hoping all along to put a spoke in Figaro's wheel. Thirdly, in Beaumarchais, after the Count has departed, Figaro tells Cherubino not to take his banishment too literally: he is to pretend to be resigned to it, put on his travelling clothes, ride away in presence of everyone, gallop as far as the farm, and then return to the château on foot by another route; after that, all he will have to do is to keep out of sight of the Count and trust to Figaro to arrange everything in his favour after that night's fête. Clearly Figaro's grand scheme for fooling and trapping the Count is already fully formed in his mind—which accounts for his self-assured gaiety and hardly veiled insolence throughout the scene. Fourthly, Beaumarchais brings the Countess on in the final moments of the scene, where her motherly—is it entirely motherly, though?—solicitude for poor little Cherubino fans the rising flame of Almaviva's suspicious jealousy of the page. As regards the omission of the Countess from the episode, however, there is something to be said operatically for Da Ponte: he would have weakened the effect of our first introduction to her in the next act had he brought her on for a few minutes at the end of the first. As often happens in opera, he is paying the penalty for being a librettist in the first place and a dramatist only in the second. The music always has a first mortgage on his purely dramatic interests: and to find time and space for the musical expansions insisted on by the composer he has often to omit something that is of the very essence of the action. We shall see a signal instance of this eternal liability of the librettist when we come to examine the structure of the first act of Puccini's *Tosca*.[1]

[1] Da Ponte himself was evidently well aware of the problem. A copy of the *Figaro* text has survived in a foreword to which he accounts for the length of the work by "the multiplicity and variety of the musical numbers" he had to introduce, which "had to be worked in (a) so as not to leave the actors immobilised, (b) to remedy the tedium of the long recitatives, (c) to give a more lively colour to the passions sometimes indicated there . . ." We

13

In the second act we see Figaro putting into operation a plan of campaign that is superb in its audacity. He is evidently one of those who believe that the best defence is attack; to paraphrase his own words, the best way to keep a man from interfering with other people's property is to make him doubtful about the security of his own. The Count has designs on his valet's wife. Very well, the valet will put it into his head that some one has designs on the Countess and is about to proceed to action; this suspicion should keep Almaviva too busy to have much time to devote to Figaro's matrimonial affairs. Furthermore, he hopes to manœuvre his lordship into a compromising situation in which he will be the biter bit, the would-be seducer become the victim of his own wiles. To bring all this about Figaro means to make a quite impudent use of his noble lady; but the strength of his personality and his reputation for skill in intrigue should be enough to overcome her feeble objections. Besides, he knows that the Countess has *her* vulnerable spot—her tenderness for the pretty, amorous page; and on this weakness of hers he works artfully, as we shall see.

The curtain rises on a handsome room in the château.[1] On the left is a window giving on the garden, on the right a door leading to a dressing-room; further left, towards the back of the stage, is an entrance door, while quite at the back is another door leading to the service quarters. The Countess, a noble, dignified figure— one of Mozart's rarest creations—sits musing sadly upon her unhappy lot as a loving wife whose husband, out of sheer frivolity, has begun to neglect her. The key to her elegiac mood is given us in a short orchestral introduction in which Mozart makes liberal use of the twining thirds which he oftens draws upon for moments of great tenderness:

---

shall probably not go far wrong in seeing in this the constant pressure put on him by Mozart to keep the action always filled with musical interest. There is also a long passage in Da Ponte's *Memoirs* in which he speaks feelingly of the difficulties the poor poet often has in providing all the verbal matter the composer needs for the elaborate musical structure of a finale.

[1] In Beaumarchais a bedroom.

No. 9

Later there comes another orchestral passage:

No. 10

in which sighing thirds again play their significant part: the phrase has a marked family resemblance to the lovely strain in Donna Anna's final aria, "Non mi dir," in *Don Giovanni*, in which, before the words "Calma, calma il tuo tormento," she pours out the vials of her tenderness and compassion upon Don Ottavio. The burden of the present exquisite aria is the Countess's grief over lost illusions: "Oh love, bring some comfort to my suffering heart: restore to me my lover, or let me die!"

At the conclusion of it Susanna enters, and, at the Countess's bidding, finishes (in recitative) the story she has been telling her of Almaviva's attempted seduction—or rather purchase, as she puts it—of her. While the Countess is once more lamenting the loss of her husband's affection Figaro enters in the highest spirits, trilling a gay "La, la, la." He tells his lady of the Count's desire to resume his ancient feudal right where Susanna is concerned, of the plan to attach him to the London embassy, and of the Count's resolve, after his frustration, to espouse the cause of Marcellina. The others are astonished that with such a load of care on him Figaro can be so gay. But he is gay, he explains to them, because of the certain success of the grand scheme he has already set on foot for the discomfiture of his lordship. He has sent the Count, through Basilio, an anonymous letter warning him that an admirer of the Countess has made an assignation with her at that night's festivities. The Countess is horrified at the audacity of this; surely Figaro knows what his master is capable of under the spur of jealousy? The angrier the Count gets, Figaro rejoins, the more blunders he will make in his strategy: the valet's plan is to give him so much to think about during the next few hours that he will have no time to bother about Figaro's marriage, which will then come about by itself, as it were.

14

But what about Marcellina? asks Susanna. They need not worry about her, replies Figaro: the Count is their target. Susanna is to grant Almaviva an assignation for that evening, at which she will be impersonated by little Cherubino, whom he has already taken the precaution to retain in the château; the Count and the supposed Susanna will be surprised at the right moment by the Countess, who will then have her husband in the hollow of her hand and will be able to dictate her own terms of peace. Rosina begins to like the idea; perhaps the prospect of seeing the charming page again has some influence on her judgment. The Count, Figaro explains, has gone hunting; so they have ample time in which to dress Cherubino up in Susanna's clothes and coach him in his part. Figaro goes off mightily pleased with himself, singing a gay snatch from his little aria in the first act—"If you are bent on dancing, my little Count, well and good; but it will be to my guitar accompaniment."

The Countess and Susanna resume their conversation. The former regrets that the page had been listening during the attempted seduction in the first act. But why has he not come to sing her the canzone he has written for her? The words are hardly out of her mouth when Cherubino enters, full of sighs and tears, as usual, at the thought of leaving his adored mistress. The incident is rather weakly handled by both Beaumarchais and Da Ponte: the former's prime object was plainly to provide a pre-determined charming stage picture of Cherubino singing his romance to Susanna's accompaniment, with the Countess following the words from the manuscript [1]; for Da Ponte the incident is simply useful as providing Mozart with a "cue for song." The result is the delightful "Voi che sapete"—"Ye ladies who know what love is,

[1] In a footnote in the play Beaumarchais lays it down that the tableau is to be a copy of Vanloo's engraving of *La Conversation espagnole*.

behold the turmoil of my heart, possessed with a desire that is now a delight, now a torment. I freeze and burn by turns: I am in quest of something, but I know not quite what it is. There is no peace for me night or day, yet even my torment is delight"; and so on:

No. 11

Andante con moto

Voi che sa - pe - te che co - sa è a - mor

Da Ponte is always a particularly dexterous artist in words in set situations of this kind, and Mozart finds by instinct the right musical vein for the little song, an atmosphere curiously compounded of naïveté and ardour.

The song and the singer having been duly praised by the two listeners they address themselves to the business of robing Cherubino for the girl part he is to play in the comedy ahead of them. Fortunately he is of the same height and build as Susanna, so that her clothes should fit him to a nicety. For a moment the Countess has her doubts and fears about the wisdom of all this disrobing: what if someone were to come in? Susanna settles that matter by locking the main door. The page's short hair is a bit of a problem, which the Countess solves by sending Susanna into the adjoining cabinet in search of one of her caps. Cherubino's military commission now comes to light—it had been handed him by Basilio, he says—and the Countess observes that in their indecent hurry to get the youngster out of the château they had forgotten to seal it. Then, to the accompaniment of a light-hearted aria, Susanna proceeds with the dismantling and reconstruction of the page, finding a little difficulty in doing so now and then because his head keeps turning in the direction of the Countess; and in any case he remains too much of a boy to make a credible girl without a good deal of coaching.

15

The critical eye of the Countess detects a flaw in his costume: his sleeves should be rolled up further above the elbow if he is to pass as a girl of Susanna's station. As the maid raises the sleeve the stolen ribbon comes to light. It has a spot of blood on it, which the page, in great confusion, explains by his having had a slight accident that morning. Sending Susanna off for some sticking-plaster the Countess takes possession of the ribbon, despite the poor boy's tearful plea that no plaster in the world could have anything like the same healing property. This moves the Countess deeply; but while she is gently reproving him for his infatuation they are startled by a knocking at the door, and the Count's voice is heard asking impatiently why it is locked.

The Countess loses her head: what will this quick-tempered husband of hers, already absurdly jealous of the page, say and do when he discovers him there in partial deshabille—and this after the Count has presumably received a "letter from a friend" palmed off on him by Figaro? Cherubino runs in terror into the adjoining cabinet; the Countess turns the key of it and hides it on her person, after which she unlocks the door to admit the Count. Her evident embarrassment, and her lame explanation that she had been trying on some dresses with Susanna, who had just gone to her own room, make him more suspicious than ever. He produces the letter and invites her to read it; but before she can do so his attention is distracted by a noise in the other room, where the agitated Cherubino has apparently overturned a chair. Almost fainting with fright, the Countess keeps making matters worse for herself by her attempted explanations. The person within, she stammers, is Susanna; whereupon Almaviva reminds her that a minute ago she had told him that Susanna had gone to her own room.

While he is insisting that the dressing-room be opened at once Susanna appears at the door by which she had gone out; catching sight of the Count, who luckily has his back towards her, she slips into an alcove and awaits further developments. A lively trio follows, in which Almaviva, now in a towering rage, demands that the cabinet door shall be opened, the Countess insists that it shall not, and Susanna, guessing from the absence of the page what has happened, wonders how they are to escape now the consequences of Figaro's faith in the perfection of his strategy. In a short ensuing recitative Almaviva declares that he will summon the servants to break the door down; but Rosina dissuades him from doing what will make them both the talk of the whole château.

He decides to do the breaking down himself, and goes off to fetch
the necessary implements; but to make sure that there will be no
trickery behind his back he makes her accompany him; he locks
the door leading to Susanna's quarters and then makes his exit
with the Countess by the main door, which we hear him locking
behind him.

This makes the quick-witted Susanna mistress of the situation.
Emerging from the alcove she runs to the door of the dressing-
room and calls on the terrified Cherubino to open it:

No. 12

What are they to do? If the Count finds the boy there on his return he will kill him; yet all the exits from the room are now
locked. The only way out is by the window on the left: it is a
perilous jump, but the page makes it, and Susanna is relieved to
find that he has landed safely in the garden and is now running
away like a hare. There being no more danger from that quarter
her further course of action is clear: she slips into the dressing-
room and closes the door behind her just as the Count and his lady
return, the former armed with the necessary implements for forcing the door. By now the Countess's nerve has given way completely. She surrenders unconditionally. The occupant of the
room, she confesses, is not her maid but someone of whom it is
really absurd of her husband to harbour any suspicions; they had
merely been engaged in arranging an innocent little joke.

16

The more she pleads for mercy for the page, the more convinced is the Count of her guilt: now he understands why she
had been so moved that morning when he had banished the boy
from the château, and why she had assured him earlier in the
present scene—a telling point in the play, of which, however,
Da Ponte makes no use—that she intended to spend the whole
afternoon and evening in her own apartment. She only adds fuel
to the flames by protesting how innocent was the little masquerade

she had planned, in which they had been so suddenly interrupted that at the present moment the boy is in the dressing-room only half-clothed. She is willing now to give up the key to the Count, but her last-minute plea for mercy for Cherubino, in the name of the love her husband had once felt for her, is the final faggot on the flames. Blind with rage he takes the key and rushes to the door. The whole scene is dramatically more tense in Beaumarchais and moves more swiftly there to its conclusion; but the opera has the advantage over the play of a final duet in which Mozart hits off admirably the agitation of the Countess and the implacable fury of Almaviva.

But his triumph is a short-lived one: his swift deflation is depicted in a single phrase given out by the orchestra as he opens the door of the dressing-room and draws his avenging sword: as will be seen, the phrase comes in like a lion and goes out like a lamb:

No. 13

It is followed by a dazed ejaculation of "Susanna!" by the Count as he sees in the doorway the smiling maid, not the quaking Cherubino he had expected. She at once takes command of the situation: to a demure little phrase in the orchestra:

No. 14

she expresses ironic sympathy with the Count in the little mistake that has turned out so unfortunately for him. The Count and the Countess are equally dismayed: and never in opera has a comic situation been better painted in music of mock-gravity than in the short andante trio that follows.

The Countess, who has been near fainting, is the first of the pair to recover something of her poise, though she is well aware that

her difficulties are by no means over yet. She takes advantage of
the momentary absence of her husband—who has gone into the
dressing-room to investigate for himself—to appeal in agitated
tones:

No. 15

to Susanna for moral support: the orchestral figure that accompanies the maid's assurance that the page is safely away:

No. 16

bubbles over with gay confidence. It is mainly to this strain that
the pair proceed to bait the unfortunate Count on his return. He
is now abjectly penitent, full of apologies for his behaviour and
prayers for forgiveness. The Countess plays magnificently up to
her new rôle of the loving wife unjustly suspected by her jealous
husband, and yields only gradually to Susanna's hypocritical pleas
to her to forgive and forget. But there is still a tiny remnant of
fight left in the Count. He is bound to believe that it was not
Cherubino who had been in the cabinet, and he confesses he had
been misled by the Countess's air of anxiety under his recent
interrogation, which she now makes him believe was only a clever
bit of acting on her part. But what about the letter? he asks.
Thinking there is no more necessity for concealment, the women
tell him that Figaro was the writer of it, and that he had fobbed it
off on the Count *via* Basilio. In his first flush of anger at this news
he launches into new threats of vengeance on his impudent valet;
but in the end he yields to their sly argument that he who wants
to be forgiven should be the first to set others an example of
forgiveness.

17

Everything appears now to be happily settled; and the lively
ensemble ends with a fermata that cannot be too scrupulously

observed in performance; the longer the silence after so much tension the more effective is the unexpected appearance of Figaro, brimful, as usual, of gay assurance. He has news for his lordship, whom he tells (allegro con spirito) that the vassals and the musicians are all ready and straining at the leash to celebrate his marriage. He takes Susanna by the hand and is whirling her off when the Count intervenes. He is not to be rushed like this: there is a little point, he says, that is troubling him, as regards which perhaps the valet can give him some information. The three conspirators at once scent danger; for of course Figaro does not know that they have already revealed him to the Count as the writer of the letter. A new and more dangerous imbroglio is now blowing up, in which the reins of direction seem to be passing again into Almaviva's hands. Dramatically and musically this is the greatest scene in the opera: from now until the end of the act, indeed, we are in the presence of one of the miracles of operatic music. The moods and the motives of the characters change from moment to moment: for each of them Mozart finds the perfect expression, while the texture is a single piece of smooth weaving from start to finish.

Figaro soon finds himself in difficulties. To a melody that is a masterpiece of polite irony:

No. 17

Co-no-sce-te, Si-gnor Fi-ga-ro, que-sto fo-glio chi ver-gò?

the Count shows him the letter and wonders if he can tell him who wrote it. Unaware of the recent run of the scenario, the master intriguer makes a cardinal blunder: after pretending to examine the letter critically he denies all knowledge of it or of the writer. From now onwards his better-informed fellow-conspirators have to keep prompting him. Susanna leads off. "Why," she asks him, with an air of merely reminding him of a little thing that has escaped his memory for the moment, "wasn't it you who gave it to Basilio?" "To take it—," the Countess adds; but before she can complete the sentence the Count interposes a curt "Well, what about it?" Susanna resumes the rôle of prompter: "Don't

you remember? the little dandy?". . . . "Who was to be in the
garden this evening?" supplements the Countess; and once more
the Count asks him sternly if his memory is any better now.
When the puzzled Figaro still denies all knowledge of the letter
the Count tells him bluntly and rudely that he can see in his ugly
face that he is lying. In repartee Figaro is always at home: he
counters with "It is my face that is lying, then, not I," to a delightful snatch of melody:

No. 18

upon which Mozart proceeds to ring, in conjunction with No. 17,
the most exquisite serio-comic changes in one voice after another.

The women try desperately to get command of the situation
again. They tell the floundering Figaro to cease his stupid denials,
for they are no longer necessary, the harmless little comedy he
had intended having come to its natural end. Particularly delightful is the little snatch of counterpoint to No. 18 in which, while
Figaro repeats his assurance that "It is my face that is lying, then,
not I," Susanna and the Countess try to knock it into him that
there is no need for him to keep up the pretence any longer, as
they have already told the Count all about the mysterious letter:

No. 19

To gain time he suggests that his prompt marriage to Susanna
will clear everything up to everyone's satisfaction. The women
renew their entreaties to the Count to let the matter drop and
bring about the happy ending: but he shakes them off and wildly
calls for Marcellina to come to his rescue; for it is she, he feels, who
holds the winning card.

18

Suddenly the tempo whips up as a new personage appears on the scene; it is the half-tipsy gardener Antonio—another stock comic figure into whom Mozart breathes a new life of his own. Antonio has in his hand a pot of dilapidated carnations, and is in the homicidal mood that takes possession of every professional gardener when his flowers have been maltreated. He had become resigned, he gabbles, to all sorts of rubbish being flung every day from the balcony of this room; but when it comes to throwing human beings out on to his frames—well, that's more than he can be expected to put up with. The Count at once pricks up his ears and asks for further details; but Antonio can add nothing more to his story than that a man had been thrown from the balcony, had picked himself up, and had made off with the speed of the wind.

Susanna, as usual, is the first to reassemble her wits. "It was the page!" she manages to say *sotto voce* to Figaro, who, not quite knowing as yet what line to take, plays for time by bursting into fits of helpless laughter, to the great annoyance of both the Count and the gardener. This lout of an Antonio, says Figaro, is in his usual condition—pickled [1] from morning to night; and Susanna and the Countess repeat the indictment. But Almaviva is not to be so easily hoodwinked. He again tells the gardener to get on with his story; whereupon Figaro, having realised that the flying man had got away too quickly for Antonio to be able to identify him, now brazenly declares that it was he. The orchestra seems to comment ironically on this audacious tarradiddle. Susanna and the Countess remark in admiring undertones, "What a brain! What ingenuity!" But the Count is not convinced, while Antonio puts what looks like a poser to Figaro: "Then how have you managed to grow so much taller since then?" Figaro's bland explanation that a man always crouches during a jump makes no impression on the stolid gardener. "It looked to me more like the page," he says; and a wild cry of "Cherubino!" comes from the Count. "Of course!" says Figaro ironically, "having galloped from Seville."

[1] In the libretto "cotto"—"cooked," or, as we would say in the vernacular, "stewed."

The gardener's naïve assurance that the man who had descended from the balcony wasn't on horseback tries the Count's patience severely. He tells the valet to get on with his story. It was really he who had jumped, Figaro explains blithely. He had been in the service quarters, waiting for his adored Susanna, when he heard the Count's voice raised in anger: remembering the anonymous letter he had been scared out of his wits and had taken a flying leap through the window, spraining his ankle in the process; and to prove it he puts on a most convincing limp. "If it was you," continues Antonio, "then I ought to give you this paper that fell from your jacket when you landed." Here is the beginning of a fresh imbroglio: new despair on the part of the Countess and Susanna, a new attempt by the baffled Figaro to gain time until his fellow-conspirators can come to his rescue again.

19

The next section of the ensemble is dominated by a demure little figure in the orchestra:

No. 20

to which everything that the characters have to say accommodates itself. The Count takes possession of the document, reads it, and folds it up again: then he blandly invites Figaro to tell him what is in it. Antonio suggests sarcastically that it may be a list of the valet's debts, a remark that results in his being summarily shooed off the stage. He goes away muttering, to the strain of No. 20, threats of what he will do to Figaro if ever he catches him at his tricks again. The others now address themselves to the question of the mysterious paper. The Count, having glanced at it once more, again asks the valet what he has to say on the subject. Figaro is grounded; but the Countess, who has managed to get a closer glimpse of it, recognises it as the page's regimental commission. Bit by bit she and Susanna manage to relay the information to Figaro, who at last explains to the Count that it is the page's commission, which the latter had left with him. "Why?" is the next awkward question. More *sotto voce* relaying enables Figaro to reply "Because it hadn't been sealed"; whereupon the Count, losing his temper, tears the document up, and the four characters express their various reactions to this new turn of events to the ever-present strain of No. 20.

The action takes yet another turn with the entry of Marcellina, Bartolo and Basilio. The tempo of the music quickens as the foundations are laid for the regulation final ensemble. Everybody has his say, and what they say individually is fused into a perfect musical unity. Marcellina and her friends excitedly demand that the Count, as the law incarnate, shall see that justice is done her. She states her own case—this bankrupt valet is under contract to marry her, and he must do so forthwith: Bartolo is there as her legal representative, Basilio as the most respectable of witnesses.[1] They chatter on and on to the great annoyance of the Count, who from time to time tries to impose silence on them, protesting that he is there expressly to judge the case according to law:

No. 21

The strife of opinions and voices culminates in a lively buffo septet; and when the curtain falls everything is precisely as it was at the beginning, the Count no wiser, the conspirators no further.

20

Figaro, as we have said, is always Beaumarchais, Beaumarchais always Figaro. The impudent, adroit, resourceful, none too scrupulous or truthful adventurer that was Beaumarchais is drawn to the life in the Figaro who plans the intrigue and fights his way through the unexpected difficulties attendant on this in the second act, becoming the more dangerous, the more indomitable, the harder he is pressed. In the third act of the French play we

[1] In Beaumarchais he himself aspires to Marcellina's hand.

see the other Beaumarchais, the practised litigant, the gay derider of the portentous farce of "justice." A room in the château is fitted out faithfully as a court of law, with desks or seats for the judge, the counsel, the witnesses, the lawyers, the ushers, the reporters and the spectators; and the case of Marcellina *versus* Figaro is tried by the Count in gravely ironic style. But we have now arrived at the point in the play where the mass of detail and the intricacies of the intrigue become more than the librettist can cope with, compelled as he is to set aside so much space for musical numbers. As always happens when he loses the support, or much of the support, of his predecessor, Da Ponte's dramatic structure becomes loose and occasionally incoherent, so much has he to omit or to condense. From this point onward, then, the play is transformed into opera pure and simple; and it is to the opera that we now have to address ourselves again.

We are to understand that between the second and the third acts it has been settled between the Countess and Susanna that the latter is to give the Count an assignation in the garden that night, but with an amendment, suggested by the Countess, of Figaro's original plan—she will herself go disguised as the maid and impersonate her. By this means she will be able to test the extent of her husband's fidelity, and if she can catch him *in flagrante delicto* she can not only consolidate her own domestic position with him but impose her own terms in the matter of Susanna's marriage to Figaro.

The setting of the third act is a large salon in the château. The Count is soliloquising (in recitative) on the perplexities that envelop him. He runs over the events that have roused his suspicions: an anonymous letter; Susanna hiding in the dressing-room; the Countess's obvious embarrassment; a man seen jumping from the balcony into the garden, and Figaro impudently claiming that it was he. It may be that one of his lordship's vassals is amusing himself at his expense, for the rabble is inclined to get a bit above itself nowadays; but the serious character of the Countess makes him reluctant to suspect her. And yet—are not all women fundamentally alike? The more he turns it all over in his mind the less sense is he able to make of it, and the more uneasy he is about it. He has sent Basilio off to Seville to discover if the page is really there, and he should be back with his report before the time for the wedding in the evening. Susanna is a further perplexity to him. Has she betrayed his secret to the Countess? If so, he will see to it that Figaro marries Marcellina.

He has been partly overheard by Susanna and the Countess, and the latter having slipped away the maid comes forward to play the next card in the risky game. Ostensibly she has intruded on Almaviva because she wants the Countess's vinaigrette, her ladyship having an attack of the vapours; but this, it becomes evident later, was only a pretext. He is a little surly with her at first, but soon becomes his former ardent self. A bride who loses her groom at the last moment, he hints meaningly, may herself be glad of such feminine consolation as smelling salts can afford. "But I can pay off Marcellina with the dowry you promised me," she objects. "When did I promise a dowry?" he asks. "That was what I understood," Susanna continues; to which his dry reply is, "Yes, but that was when I thought you had made up your mind to understand *me*." Demurely she hints that at last she has seen the light; her duty to his lordship and her own inclinations now draw her in the same direction.

This sets him off on an ardent declaration of his passion: "Cruel one! why all this time have you been kindling my hopes only to extinguish them?":

No. 22

She plays coquettishly with him, simulating an ardour equal to his own. She promises him that she will meet him in the garden when night falls; and the Count expresses his contentment in a lovely phrase into which he evidently puts all his amorous heart:

No. 23

They pursue the delightful subject in a duet that is one of Mozart's little masterpieces, each speaking strictly in character, the Count being all passion, Susanna obviously only flirting with him, but with a serious background to her coquetry when she thinks of her Figaro.

She is departing without the vinaigrette. When the Count reminds her of it she archly confesses that she had invented her ladyship's indisposition as a pretext for a little private talk with him; this pleases him beyond measure. As she goes out he says to himself delightedly, "She's mine now, beyond a doubt!" But Susanna has a final little aside of her own: his lordship may think himself clever, but he will find out his mistake before long. Then, as usual, Beaumarchais springs a new complication on his characters and on us. In the doorway Susanna runs into Figaro, to whom she whispers excitedly, "Don't speak! I have won our cause without a lawyer!"

21

The pair go off exultantly. But the Count has overheard Susanna's incautious remark, and now the fat is all in the fire again. Not only has his passion been frustrated but his pride as a grand seigneur has been outraged by the discovery that his audacious vassals have been playing with him all this time. In an angry accompanied recitative he declares that he will punish Susanna for her treachery. The decision in the lawsuit still rests with him. True, but what if Figaro pays off the debt? Yet how can he? And there is in reserve the half-witted Antonio, who, with proper handling, can be persuaded to refuse his niece to this valet about whom he knows nothing and whom he does not like. Revenge will be sweet: the die is cast; and the Count launches his great aria, the burden of which is that he will not submit to seeing the object of his desire pass into the hands of his valet, that "vile creature," as he calls him. No; the lackey shall not triumph over the grandee; and the thought of his coming revenge fills him with joy. The vigorous aria is one of Mozart's finest; as always in circumstances of this kind, he takes his character for the time being out of the buffo atmosphere in which the drama as a whole is set: Almaviva is here as serious a character as any in the most serious of operas.

But we are soon back to comedy pure and simple. Marcellina, Bartolo and Figaro enter along with Don Curzio, a lawyer, who, by some process of operatic legerdemain which we try in vain to understand—for there has been nothing in the action to suggest that a trial has taken place—announces the decision of the court [1] —either Figaro must pay off his debt to Marcellina or marry her. She is in the seventh heaven of happiness, for she adores the sprightly young valet; while he is in the depths of despair. He appeals to the angry Count, who refuses to upset the judgment: Figaro must either pay up or marry; and he pointedly compliments Don Curzio on his verdict. So does Bartolo, on the grounds that now he too is revenged on his old enemy the barber. But Figaro is still the crafty fox with a thousand twists and turns. He now staggers them all by pleading that he is a gentleman by birth, and this being so he cannot marry without the consent of his noble parents. The Count, vastly amused, asks him who these notabilities may be and where they are. Figaro unfortunately does not know: he has been seeking them in vain, it appears, for the last ten years. He was not a foundling, as Bartolo had sarcastically suggested; he had been stolen by brigands when an infant, for the jewels and the gold and the richly embroidered clothes his exalted parents had lavished on him. And if all these do not constitute a proof of his illustrious origin, he says, what about the mysterious figure impressed on his arm?

"Not a spatula on your right arm?" Marcellina interjects excitedly; and learning that it is just that, she becomes quite incoherent with joy, for who can this be but her long-lost little Raffaello. "Behold your mother!" says Bartolo. "Do you mean my wet-nurse?" asks the incredulous Figaro. "No, your mother." "Behold your father!" says Marcellina, pointing to Bartolo; and the great recognition scene is complete. While Bartolo and Marcellina are embracing their offspring Susanna rushes in with a purse; she has received from the Countess the money to ransom her Figaro, and she appeals to the Count to reverse the verdict of the court. There comes a cloud over her sky for a moment when she sees Figaro embracing Marcellina; but after she has boxed his ears the necessary explanations are given her, Marcellina leading

[1] In Beaumarchais, as we have seen, there is a long trial scene. Mahler evidently felt that there was a lacuna in the opera at the point we have now reached, for in his Vienna performances he inserted Beaumarchais's trial scene, with recitatives of his own composition.

off by introducing herself in a delightful little phrase as her new mother-to-be:

No. 24

Sua ma-dre ab-brac-cia —— te che or vo —— stra sa – rà.

which Figaro caps with a melody still more charming:

No. 25

E quel-lo è mio pa-dre che a te lo di-rò, che a te lo di —rò.

as he presents Susanna formally to his long-lost father. The whole lively action is enclosed within the frame of a sextet, in which the only jarring note is that of the Count, who cannot conceal his mortification at this latest unexpected blow to his plans.

At the end of the ensemble the Count and Curzio quit the stage. Among the others all is gas and gaiters. Bartolo nobly decides to marry Marcellina forthwith. She, in her turn, makes Figaro a present of his promissory note for a thousand pieces of silver, by way of a dowry. Susanna gives him the money she had intended for his ransom; even Bartolo adds a cash contribution of his own. Figaro feels like an Israelite in the desert who has unexpectedly received several extra rations of manna; but while he is hinting that if anyone has anything more to contribute to his privy purse he will not hurt their feelings by refusing it, the happy Susanna hurries him off with her to take the good news to the Countess and her uncle Antonio. The recitative ends with the two happy couples declaring in a brief passage in four-part harmony that if the Count should now feel like bursting that will be all right so far as they are concerned. Then they leave the stage arm in arm.

22

One of the most engaging features of this opera is the free-and-easy way in which everyone seems to stroll into other people's quarters; so we are not unduly surprised to find Cherubino and little Barbarina now coming into the drawing-room, this being the most likely place on the Almaviva estate, apparently, for the gardener's daughter to tell the page that it has been arranged for him that he shall attend Figaro's wedding festivity disguised as a girl! He dreads, he protests, the anger of the Count, who believes him to be in Seville—which apprehension on his part makes it still more difficult for us to believe that he is now strolling about the château. However, there was no other place or time in the libretto in which Da Ponte could make us acquainted with this little piece of stage carpentry, which will become a vital part of the final dénouement; so here it had to come.

The little couple having left the stage after their very brief dialogue in recitative the Countess comes into the salon. In a recitativo accompagnato she tells us that she is anxiously awaiting news from Susanna as to the Count's reception of the promise of an assignation in the garden, of the wisdom of which she has her doubts. Still, she muses, there is nothing very wrong about her impersonating Susanna, and *vice versa;* and anyhow she has been drawn into all this by the frivolous conduct of her husband, who, by all appearances, no longer loves her; and she breaks into a pensive aria in which, for the second time in the opera—for Mozart manifestly has a special fondness for her—she pours out her sorrow over the days that are no more:

No. 26

In the allegro section that follows, however, she indulges herself in the hope that her own constancy will have its reward in the return of the Count's affection.

As she leaves the stage Almaviva and Antonio enter. The gardener has some news that his master finds rather upsetting: the page supposed to be in Seville is in hiding somewhere on the estate; in proof of which he produces Cherubino's hat, which, with his clothes, the boy had left at the gardener's cottage. A minute or so suffices to convey this information to the Count and to us: then the pair go out and the Countess returns, accompanied by Susanna. The maid, it appears, has told her mistress by now of the Count's acceptance of the assignation at nightfall; the only thing necessary now is to fix up the details of the affair. This is done by the maid taking down from the Countess's dictation a canzonetta the opening words of which allude vaguely to the evening zephyrs playing about the pine-wood: as the Countess remarks after the charming little duet has run its course, the Count will be able to infer the rest. A pin from the Countess's dress has to be used to "seal" the letter, to which a postscript is added asking the recipient of it to return this "seal," as a token that he understands and agrees.

The room now fills with a bevy of young peasant maidens who have come to offer their homage and present bouquets to their gracious lady; among them are Barbarina and Cherubino, the latter dressed like the girls. They pipe an appropriately naïve little chorus, after which the action is carried on for a considerable time in recitative. The Countess has been particularly struck by the good looks and modest bearing of one of the girls—our friend Cherubino; and Barbarina explains that this is her little cousin, who had arrived last night to be present at the wedding. When the Countess accepts a bouquet from the "little cousin" the latter blushes painfully, and the Countess is struck by the resemblance of the child's features to those of the page. Susanna has only time for the ironical remark that this is quite natural when Antonio slips in, pulls off Cherubino's bonnet, and substitutes for it his regimental hat. The Countess is covered with confusion. The Count, who happens to be among those present, looks meaningly at both of them for an explanation. The Countess can do no more than stammer out a confession that it was precisely a little masquerade of this harmless sort that she and Susanna had been rehearsing when her husband had broken in on her that morning. Almaviva is sternly informing Cherubino that his disobedience shall be severely punished when the innocent Barbarina takes the wind out of his sails: "Oh, your Excellency always used to say, when you were kissing me, 'If you will only love me, Barbarina, I will grant you anything you may ask.' Now please let me marry Cherubino, and I will love you like my kitten." Well may poor Almaviva mutter to himself, "How is it that some one, some demon, some deity or other always steps in to frustrate me?"

23

A diversion is caused by Figaro, who enters protesting that if his lordship keeps all these maidens here much longer there will be no dancing. The Count, who of course knows something now which Figaro does not yet know he knows, has spirit enough left in him to wonder sardonically how the man can dream of dancing with a sprained ankle; but the valet explains that that is better now. How fortunate, the Count continues blandly, that the flower-pots he had landed among were clay; and the unsuspecting valet agrees that it was very fortunate. Antonio, who is not really such a half-wit as he looks, puts him further posers about the page having galloped to Seville and his commission being somehow in Figaro's pocket all the time; and the schemer is completely flabbergasted for a moment when the gardener tells him that the page—whom he now drags forward—has confessed that it was he who had jumped from the balcony. But soon Figaro is his foxy self again, as fertile in resource as ever. There is no law against jumping from balconies, he points out, and no particular difficulty about it; if he could do it, why not a page or anyone else? And he defies Antonio to produce any proof that it was not so in this instance.

A march is heard in the orchestra:

No. 27

the after-strain of which:

No. 28

has a faintly exotic tang that is very captivating. The Count and Countess having seated themselves the stage fills up with a joyous throng, among whom are the girls carrying bridal hats and veils for the two brides. Bartolo presents Susanna to the Count; she kneels before him, and he hands her the hat and veil; then the Countess performs the same office for Marcellina, who is presented by Figaro; and at the conclusion of the march the company sing a chorus of felicitation to the two happy couples, joined with praise of their noble master. This is succeeded by a fandango:

No. 29

While this is being danced, Susanna, on her knees before the Count, plucks him by the sleeve, surreptitiously draws his attention to the note, and keeps it in her hand while she adjusts her hair; pretending to put her veil straight he takes the note from her, conceals it, and then hands her over to Figaro; after which Marcellina is similarly given to Bartolo by the Countess. As the Count—still to the strains of the fandango—goes aside and furtively opens the note, he pricks his finger with the pin; this annoys him at first, but he philosophically reflects that it is the way of women to use a pin on all kinds of occasions: anyhow he understands the situation now and is greatly amused by it.

He has been observed by Figaro, who is also amused: some innamorata or other, he remarks to Susanna, has slipped his lordship a letter sealed with a pin; this has pricked his finger; he has let it fall, and he appears now to be searching for it. Well content with himself now, the Count dismisses the company until the evening, when they will all celebrate the dual nuptials in regal style, with music, feasting and dancing. They repeat their little chorus of homage, and the curtain falls.

24

Da Ponte makes a sorry mess of this episode. He follows Beaumarchais only as far as the moment when Figaro sees Almaviva reading the note and pricking his finger with the pin. Everything that ensues in the play immediately after that comes in perfect logical sequence. Beaumarchais's stage directions run: "The dance is resumed. The Count, after reading the billet, is folding it up again when he catches sight of the instruction on the reverse side to return the 'seal' to the writer by way of answer. [Obviously anything in the way of a reply either by letter or through an intermediary would be out of the question, the stage situation being what it is]. He looks round him on the ground, at last finds the pin, and fastens it to his sleeve." [Where it will be available for use as soon as circumstances permit]. This action of his also amuses Figaro: to the lover, he remarks indulgently to Marceline, the smallest object that once belonged to the loved one is dear.

A longish scene then follows in the play in which Basilio comes in and makes trouble over the marriage of Marceline, whom, as we have seen, he himself would like to marry. Still later, when Marceline and Figaro are left together on the stage, the former apologises to him for her earlier behaviour towards Susanna, to whom, she now admits, she had done wrong in believing that she was encouraging the advances of the Count. Figaro laughs to scorn the notion that he could ever entertain any suspicions of his wonderful Susanna. Just then little Fanchette (Barbarina) enters. She is looking for someone, she confides to them in her artless fashion—for her cousin Susanna, in fact, to whom she has been directed to return a pin. At once Figaro is on the alert. He leads Fanchette on by telling her he knows more about the matter than she imagines: it is the Count, is it not, who has sent her to Susanna with the pin that had fastened a little piece of paper he had had in his hand? Ah! the child counters, but there is something more that Figaro doesn't know—that the Count has given her a message for Susanna: "Deliver this pin to your lovely cousin, my little Fanchette," he had said, "and tell her that this is the seal of the big chestnut alley. Take care that no one sees you." (The chestnut alley had been named by Susanna as the place of the assignation: in the opera it becomes a pine-wood.)

Checking his rising rage, Figaro sends Fanchette on her way with the pin and the message; then he unburdens himself of his woes to Marceline, who, like a wise woman of the world, advises him not to jump to conclusions and condemn Susanna out of hand without a trial; after all, it may be the Count whom she is plotting to deceive. Figaro takes her advice; but he too, he says grimly, will be in the chestnut alley that night!

172

All this, in the play, occurs in its proper place, in logical connection, at the end of the third act, where it makes a first-rate curtain; and Da Ponte must have been fully aware of this. But the poor man was an opera librettist, not a dramatist, and so he had not a free hand. For one thing, convention suggested a choral ensemble, however short, as an "effective" ending for the act. For another, there are still four characters each of whom, by the rules of the game, is entitled to a solo piece of his or her own— Barbarina, Marcellina, Susanna and Basilio; and the only places Da Ponte can find for these solos are in the next act. So he most absurdly closes down, during the fandango, on Beaumarchais's well-constructed sequence of events before it has developed beyond its very first stage. We see only Figaro observing the Count reading the *billet-doux*, pricking his finger, dropping the pin and looking around for it. All that should follow straight upon this Da Ponte holds over to the next act; and when he does decide to use it there he makes a lamentable mess of it. And when he falls, as fall he does, he drags Mozart down with him—unless, as was by no means improbable, it was the composer who, for musical reasons of his own, insisted on the third act ending and the fourth opening in the way they do. Dictation or indolent acquiescence on the part of one or other or both of them? Who can say? But whether Mozart here acquiesced or dictated, he wrought his own undoing: from this point onwards the opera declines sadly for a time, not only in dramatic vigour but in musical interest. Nowhere else in the operatic output of his maturity has Mozart been so consistently mediocre for so long a stretch as in the first half of the fourth act of *The Marriage of Figaro*.

25

When the curtain rises for the final act we have passed on from late afternoon to night. The setting shows a garden, with a pavilion on the right and another on the left. It is as dark as is consistent with our just making out the characters and following the action: too dark, indeed, for the average spectator with no previous knowledge of the opera to grasp at a first seeing and hearing all the details of this final scene. Da Ponte begins where he had arbitrarily left off in the third act. Barbarina comes in, scrutinising the ground with a lantern for a pin she has lost, and, to a soft string accompaniment, sings an appropriately childish little cavatina as she does so: "Unhappy me! I have lost it! Where can it be? I can't find it. What will my cousin Susanna and his lordship say?" We are asked to believe, then, that all these hours, practically up to the very time of the assignation, the Count's message, *via* the "seal" of the note, has not yet reached Susanna!

Figaro enters with Marcellina, and the dialogue runs, in recitative, mainly on the lines of the corresponding situation in Beaumarchais's third act. Barbarina confides to Figaro that she is looking for a pin which the Count had ordered her to convey to Susanna, with the added injunction that no one else was to know anything about it. He palms off on her a pin he has taken from Marcellina's dress, and the child goes off on her errand to Susanna—and, what is more important to Barbarina, to her own secret assignation with Cherubino in one of the pavilions. When she has gone, Figaro breaks out in lamentations over Susanna's treachery. Marcellina, who, as we have seen, is now all pro-Susanna, advises her son not to condemn his bride too hastily; but he goes off fuming, swearing that now he knows where the assignation is—in the pine-wood —he will be there and will avenge himself and all other husbands. Marcellina, left alone, muses for a while on the situation: she will go and warn Susanna, whom she cannot bring herself to believe guilty; for fight as women may among themselves, when it is a question of dealing with the common enemy, peccant man, they fight as one. With this little soliloquy she goes off in the play; but Da Ponte makes it a "cue for song"—a long aria, with a liberal sprinkling of coloratura, on the universality of love in the innocent animal world and the reprehensible perfidy and cruelty of man towards woman. Unfortunately the aria is musically so banal that it is an act of piety towards the memory of Mozart to omit it from modern performances of the opera.

When Marcellina departs Barbarina makes another brief appearance, carrying a little basket containing some provisions she has managed to collect for Cherubino. As Figaro, Basilio and Bartolo enter she runs into the pavilion on the left, where she has arranged to meet the page. Figaro, now in savage mood, explains to the other two why he has summoned them here to meet him: on the very night of his wedding, he says, the Count and Susanna have come to an agreement behind his back, and he wants his friends' assistance in surprising them; [1] they are to wait until he whistles and then rush out on the criminals. With that he leaves them. The others discuss the eternal triangle problem for a moment, and Basilio seizes the opportunity to expound his own prudent philosophy in these matters in a long aria which we could quite well have dispensed with, for it is nothing more than a string of the musical commonplaces of the period. However, Bartolo had had *his* aria in the first act, and Basilio, with Da Ponte aiding and abetting him, feels that it is time to insist on his.

When at last he has made his exit Figaro comes into view again, and, with the end of all this fumbling in sight, the opera can begin to get into its musical stride again. Figaro, half-concealed in a long cloak and turned-down hat, indulges himself in an accompanied recitative and aria in which he rails against Susanna, himself, and the whole race of husbands, who, seemingly, will never learn what women really are. The aria is not Mozart at his very best, but at all events it is an improvement on what he has been ladling out to us recently:

No. 30

26

As Figaro almost disappears from our view Susanna and the Countess enter, each disguised in the other's clothes: with them is Marcellina, who is now wholly on their side in the intrigue; [2]

[1] In Beaumarchais he summons all and sundry, Antonio, valets, peasants, etc.

[2] It should be pointed out that Beaumarchais's Marceline is quite a different character from Da Ponte's: in the play, after the touch of comedy given her in the early wrangling-match with Susanna and later in the recognition scene, she is a very sensible wordly-wise woman, wholly pro-Susanna and giving excellent calm advice to Figaro, of whom she is very fond. Beaumarchais has put some lofty remarks into her mouth on the subject of the grievances of women. In the opera she becomes mostly a figure of the broadest fun. There is no need, however, for laying on the burlesque with the thick brush employed by the ordinary player of the part. Crude farce is always the last refuge of the actor or actress who cannot play comedy.

Figaro must be taught a lesson, and there could be no better preceptress than Susanna, who gleefully undertakes the rôle. To see and hear without being seen or heard Marcellina retires into the pavilion on the left into which Barbarina has gone. The Countess's nerve is inclined to fail her now that the hour of danger is approaching, and Susanna has to breathe something of her own courage into her. Knowing, through what Marcellina has said, that the lurking Figaro is listening to everything, Susanna asks her ladyship's permission to stroll off for a while into the wood to enjoy the fresh air. Having obtained it, she launches a lovely aria "Deh vieni, non tardar, o gioja bella":

No. 31

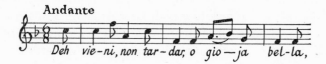

that shows Mozart in his best vein again; a tender romantic night-piece in which Susanna, serious for once, pours out all the love of her heart for some one unnamed.

We are to suppose that Figaro hears but does not see her very clearly, for of course she is dressed as the Countess: he accepts the amorous song as Susanna's, and is more perturbed and angry than ever at what he takes to be her perfidy. (Beaumarchais clarifies the situation for us by telling us, in a stage direction, that Susanna is now on one side of the stage, Figaro on the other.) While he is thus musing Cherubino appears. He is in high spirits, on his way to the pavilion where Barbarina and food are waiting him. But he catches sight of a woman, a spectacle always calculated to halt him dead in his tracks. It happens to be the Countess; but as she is in Susanna's clothes he takes her to be the maid, and at once proceeds to make love to her. A delightful duet follows: the ardent page cannot understand why the generally sprightly Susanna is so cold and coy, while the Countess is torn between fear of what will happen if the Count should arrive and annoyance at the boy's audacity.

Almaviva enters, very pleased with himself at having, as he thinks, found his Susanna at last; and everything is now set for the kind of ensemble in which Mozart revels. They are all in it, and all at cross-purposes. From opposite sides of the stage Figaro and Susanna comment on the present situation in their several ways. It is something the latter had not entirely foreseen. At last she recognises the page's voice, and feels that this unexpected turn of events has thrown a spanner into the works. Cherubino goes on with his eager wooing of the supposed Susanna, impudently reminding her that she need not put on virtuous airs with him, for was he not listening in the chair that morning when the Count had been making advances to her? The Countess tries in vain to get rid of him. Figaro and Almaviva are puzzled and enraged, in their individual ways, at the intrusion of this unknown person into the action. When at last Cherubino tries to kiss the supposed Susanna, the Count, unable to stand any more, steps between them and, to his vast annoyance, receives the kiss. The page, recognising him, runs off in terror. Figaro, who has come forward cautiously to see better what is happening, receives the cuff on the side of the head which his lordship had intended for the page, at which Susanna and the Countess break into laughter; everyone, in fact, is amused except Figaro, who, regretting his ill-timed curiosity, retires into the background again.

27

The imbroglio thickens. To a new strain in the orchestra:

No. 32

the Count begins his wooing of the fictitious Susanna; the Countess plays up to him admirably, while the amused real Susanna and the angered Figaro comment on the situation in their various ways from their several hiding-places. The Count gives the pseudo-Susanna a ring as a supplementary dowry, which makes Figaro boil over: "Everything's going marvellously," he mutters, "but the best is yet to come!" The Count directs his adored one's steps towards the pavilion on the right; and when she coyly comments on the darkness of it he assures her that it isn't to read that he has come there. As he himself is following her, Figaro confronts them: the Countess goes into the pavilion,

and the Count slips away and hides among the trees, promising
to see her again shortly. "Venus has taken cover," Figaro comments sardonically, "to meet her charming Mars; but I, the modern
Vulcan, will catch them in my net."

The pace and colour of the music change once more as Susanna,
in a feigned voice, calls on him to be silent. Taking her, of course,
for the Countess, he explains that his lordship has gone off with
Susanna, and now *he* is in command of the situation. She intends
to play up to him; but when she says "Speak more softly; I won't
stir from here, but trust me, I will be avenged," she forgets to
change her voice, which he recognises at once as Susanna's. Now,
he thinks, he sees his way clear before him: pretending to believe
still that this is the Countess dying to be revenged on her faithless
husband he will make love to her until the time for exposure shall
come: Susanna, for her part, sees through him and decides to
amuse herself with him for as long as may be necessary.

He stages a comic love scene, throwing himself at the pseudo-
Countess's feet and exhorting her to lose no time in co-operating
with him in giving Almaviva a dose of his own medicine. The
humorous point of this latest situation is that while Figaro knows
that she is Susanna, she does not know that he knows, and is
accordingly irritated at the passion he puts into the wooing of the
Countess. Her hand is itching to punish him: at last she can control herself no longer and boxes his ears heartily again and again,
resuming her proper voice and making it quite clear that she is
not the Countess but Susanna: this will teach him, she says, to
play the seducer. He is in the seventh heaven of delight at the
lesson; now he knows his Susanna's virtue is impregnable.

In a charming phrase:

No. 33

Andante

Pa-ce, pa-ce mio dol-ce te —so-ro! Io co-nob-bi la vo-ce che a-do-ro,

he asks her to make peace with him; he had known all along, he
tells her, by her adored voice, who she is, in spite of her costume.
Their voices blend in the happiest of duets.

Then the Count re-enters, calling "Eh, Susanna! Are you deaf?

Are you dumb?", and he goes into the pavilion where the Countess is. Susanna is relieved: she knows now that he had not recognised her ladyship in her disguise. She tells Figaro that it is time now to end the comedy, but they must first do something to "console" this "queer lover," with whom they have played long enough; this resolve they express to the heart-easing strain of No. 33. Delighted to co-operate with her, Figaro throws himself at the feet of the supposed Countess and makes love to her with exaggerated ardour: Susanna meets him halfway in this, and they go arm-in-arm in the direction of the pavilion on the left. But the Count has overheard them; he jumps to the conclusion that his wife is betraying him, and, seizing the presumptuous valet lover, shouts for his vassals, for he is unarmed. "My master!" ejaculates Figaro in mock terror as the Count seizes him, "I am lost!" Susanna slips into the pavilion. Basilio, Curzio, Antonio, Bartolo and a number of servants and peasants with lighted torches rush in. The Count tells them that the criminal he is holding has betrayed and dishonoured him: his depraved female accomplice they shall soon see for themselves. They register appropriate horror, while Figaro chuckles to himself. Retaining his grip on him, and telling him that resistance is in vain, Almaviva bids the supposed Countess come forth and meet the just punishment for her offence.

Receiving no reply he goes into the pavilion, and is very surprised by what he finds there. He hands out first Cherubino, who tries unavailingly to conceal his identity, then Barbarina, then Marcellina, and last of all the pseudo-Countess. The spectators are as astounded as he, as is evident from their turn-by-turn ejaculations:

The Count: "The Page!"
Antonio: "My daughter!"
Figaro: "My mother!"
Basilio, Antonio and Bartolo: "The Countess!"

The feigned Countess begs for mercy, which the infuriated Almaviva refuses, even when the others add their supplications to hers. The climax comes when the veritable Countess emerges from the other pavilion and remarks with gentle malice, "At least you won't refuse *me* when I ask you to pardon them."

The Count, recognising that this is really his wife disguised as the Susanna whom he has been trying to seduce, collapses like a deflated balloon. Humbly he implores pardon:

No. 34

She answers the poor repentant, outwitted sinner with magnanimous tenderness; and in a lively final ensemble the whole company express their delight at this happy ending to a "day of torments, caprices, follies":

No. 35

28

The equivalent in Beaumarchais of the aria (No. 30) in which Figaro laments his lot as a deceived husband is an eloquent three-pages-long soliloquy of the most serious and savage kind: it was this, more than anything else in the whole work, that gave the play its absorbing social interest for contemporary spectators. Apart from his railings against women, Figaro—here, more than anywhere else, speaking directly as Beaumarchais—poured out his gall upon the social structure of his period, in which mere birth counted for so much and ability for so little. In words that stab and sear he runs over his own chequered career, the straits to which he had been reduced time after time to keep his end up in such a world. He makes a vicious frontal attack on the French aristocracy, as symbolised by Almaviva, who enjoyed every advantage in life without ever having done anything to deserve one of them: "No, my lord the Count, you shall not have her [Susanna]; I say you shall not have her! Simply because you are a grand seigneur you flatter yourself that you are a great genius: nobility, fortune, rank, offices, these things make a man so proud! What have you done to deserve such a wealth of good things?

You have given yourself the trouble to be born, nothing more: for the rest, you are a very ordinary creature; while I, lost in the obscure crowd, have had to employ more knowledge and ingenuity merely to subsist than have gone to the governing of all the Spains in the last hundred years. And you dare to pit yourself against me!"

Two modern French authors, Jean Jacques Brousson and Raymond Escholier, have made this speech of Figaro's, that has more than a touch of prophecy in it, the starting-point for a play, *La Conversion de Figaro*, the setting of which is the Paris of a few years later than the *Marriage*. The Revolution has broken out: the Terror stalks through Paris. Figaro, in virtue of his brains, his courage, his gift for handling men, has become a person of some importance in the councils of the revolutionists, while Almaviva is now a mere cork on the swirling currents of events which he and his like cannot control and have barely managed to understand. The Count and Rosina are heading, as "aristos," straight for the guillotine, and it is Figaro who saves them from that fate, out of the affection and respect he has always had for Rosina, for the character and the intellect of the Count he still despises as of old. It has always seemed to me that *La Conversion de Figaro* might be made into a very effective opera by some librettist and composer of genius. There is no good reason why this amazingly vital character should remain for all time where Da Ponte and Mozart have left him.

Tosca

PUCCINI [1858–1924]

PRINCIPAL CHARACTERS

Floria Tosca	*Soprano*
Mario Cavaradossi	*Tenor*
Baron Scarpia	*Baritone*
Cesare Angelotti	*Bass*
The Sacristan	*Baritone*
Spoletta	*Tenor*

1

N order of composition *Tosca* follows the *La Bohème* of 1893–1896; but Puccini's attention seems to have been first drawn to the subject about 1889 (after the completion of his early opera *Edgar*), when he saw a performance of Sardou's play at the Teatro dei Filodrammatici in Milan. As he knew no more than a word or two of French he could have understood only vaguely what most of it was really "about"; but the main situations must have gripped him—especially the torture scene and the shooting of Cavaradossi—he could be in no doubt as to what Scarpia stood for, while the part of the impulsive, convulsive Tosca, played as Sarah Bernhardt played it, hardly needed words to explain it. Six years later, in a letter of the summer of 1895, we find Puccini telling his publisher Giulio Ricordi that he and his wife are "off to Florence, where they are giving [Sardou's] *Tosca* tonight." The next reference to the play in his published correspondence is on the 15th May 1898, when he writes to Ricordi from Paris, "I shall see Sardou in a few days and will settle definitely the question of that eternal Act I"; from which we gather that the opera was already on the stocks and that the first act, on the construction of which we shall have to turn a critical eye later, was even then a nut which neither he nor his librettists nor even the master-craftsman Sardou himself could crack.

In the years between *Edgar* (1889) and about 1897 a good deal happened. Verdi, whose sense of "theatre" was almost as lively as that of Sardou, had evidently had his eye on the French dramatist for many years; as far back as 1869, when rejecting a suggestion of his friend Camille Du Locle that he should write an opera based on Meilhac and Halévy's *Froufrou*, he had said that if he were going to write a work for Paris at all he would prefer something from Sardou with text by Du Locle. Some time in the mid-1890's the news reached Puccini's ears that another Italian composer, Alberto Franchetti, had had a *Tosca* libretto made for him by Luigi Illica, that this had been read to Sardou in Paris, and that Verdi, who was present, had bubbled over with enthusiasm for the subject, even, it was alleged, going so far as to say that if he were not too old for the task he would have written an opera on it himself. This was enough to convince Puccini that the subject must be his or no one's. Illica was his friend as well as Franchetti's; Ricordi was Franchetti's publisher as well as Puccini's— and Giulio saw more lire ahead of him with the composer of the successful *Manon Lescaut* and *La Bohème* than with the composer of *Asrael* and *Cristoforo Colombo*. So librettist and publisher got quietly to work on the innocent Franchetti, and by a piece of chicanery on which the moralist in us may frown but of which the opera-goer in us cordially approves, the good man was persuaded that Illica's book was a poor one and the theme quite unsuited to him—indeed, to the operatic stage. The day after the persuasion—some say the very same day—a contract for a *Tosca* was signed by Illica, Puccini, and the firm of Ricordi; and Giocosa was called in to collaborate in the making of the libretto.

2

Sardou seems to have played a considerable part in the enormously difficult business of boiling the play down for operatic purposes; otherwise, we may be sure, he would certainly not have said, as he is credibly alleged to have done, that the libretto was perhaps better than the original drama. Part of his enthusiasm, of course, may be accounted for by the fact that he had done so good a deal with Ricordi in the matter of royalties that he stood to profit handsomely by the success of Puccini's work. He certainly threw himself heart and soul into the first Paris production of the opera: and we are told that by that time the energetic old gentleman had almost managed to persuade himself that he had written the music also. But the final word all along in the many disputes with the librettists had rested with Puccini. Like Wagner and Richard Strauss, he would sometimes write the music for an episode before he had the text: we find him, for example, sending instructions to his librettists for a number of lines that *must* follow precisely the metrical scheme he indicates; even the alternations of Mario-Tosca must be observed. He always knew what he wanted, was determined to have it, and persisted till he got it. If he had set his heart on space for musical expansion at this point or that, space had somehow to be found; if he thought anything poor "theatre" it had to come out. The librettists had made Cavaradossi sing a sort of aria while he was being tortured; this may have been in the tradition of Italian opera, but Puccini would have none of it. In the original drama Tosca's death-leap from the parapet of the castle of Sant' Angelo had been simply "dans le vide." Sardou wanted the heroine of the opera to leap into the Tiber; and when Puccini pointed out to him that this meant a jump of some fifty feet horizontally on Tosca's part, seeing that the river does not flow, as the dramatist imagined, between St. Peter's and the Castello but on the other side, the great man, "calm as a fish," as Puccini said, merely remarked "Oh, that's nothing!"

Puccini had a keen sense of the difference in suggestiveness between two phrases that on the surface look practically alike. Thus for the "Tu mi odii?" ("You hate me?") which the librettists had put into the mouth of Scarpia in the scene with Tosca in the second act he insisted on substituting the cynically complacent "Come tu mi odii!" (How you hate me!"), which lends itself to a much more telling vocal inflection.

In Sardou's play the fourth act had ended thus after the stabbing of Scarpia: "She goes round the table to the glass," say the stage directions, "arranges her hair before it, then turns to the corpse of Scarpia. 'And it was before this that a whole town trembled!' A drum roll in the distance. Trumpets sound the morning call. She shudders: 'The call. Day has dawned!' She goes back to the space between the table and the dead man and blows out the lights on the table. 'And the safe-conduct? . . . What have I done with that?' " There follows the finding of the paper at last in the dead man's hand, the arranging of the lights on either side of the body, the laying of the crucifix on Scarpia's breast, and all the rest of the well-known effective "business" before her exit. Puccini was wiser. He saw, for one thing, that Tosca ought to say nothing at all after her remark about the one-time terror under which the city had groaned. Sardou's "And the safe-conduct? What have I done with that?" is something of an anti-climax; Puccini wisely left the feverish search for the document to be carried out in dumb show, knowing that with his orchestra he could convey a nervous tension far beyond the power of words. Moreover, it is to him that we owe the phrasing of Tosca's last words: "E avanti a lui tremava tutta Roma!" ("And before him trembled all Rome!"). The substitution of "all Rome" for "a whole town," with the cadential "Roma" as the final word, was a masterstroke on the composer's part. Incredible as it may appear, the librettists wanted to strike the line out, but Puccini insisted on its being restored; he knew better than they what would be the effect in the theatre of this line delivered in a low-pitched monotone that is virtually ordinary speech.

3

Over the big choral ensemble in the church at the end of the first act he took particular trouble. Apparently mistrusting his own knowledge of ecclesiastical usage he appealed to a friend of his, a Roman priest, Father Pietro Panichelli, to help him out. He outlined the scene for him—the abbot and the chapter emerging from the sacristy en route to the altar, the people watching the procession from either side of the stage, and the baritone "soliloquising independently, or nearly so," in the background. He wanted some prayers to be recited during the procession—whether by the chapter or the people did not matter much so long as the effect was obtained of a "murmuring of prayers in subdued and natural voices, without intoning, precisely as real prayers are said." The *Ecce sacerdos* he thought "too imposing to be murmured." He knew that it is not usual for anything to be said or sung before the Te Deum, which is given out when the high altar is reached; but whether it would be ecclesiastically right or wrong, he wanted something to be murmured during the passage from the sacristy to the altar, preferably by the people, because—a sound operatic reason, this!—"they are more numerous and therefore more effective musically." How his wishes were met will appear in our musical analysis of the scene. It may be added that for this church music Puccini drew to a small extent upon a Mass (still unpublished) written in 1880, in his twenty-second year.

The first performance of the opera was given in the Costanzi Theatre in Rome on the 14th January 1900, under Mugnone, with Ericlea Darclée as Tosca, Emilio De Marchi as Cavaradossi, Eugenio Giraldoni as Scarpia, Enrico Galli as Angelotti, and Ettore Borelli as the Sacristan. For one reason or another everyone's nerves were on edge, so that the performance as a whole was an indifferent one; but the work soon became a pronounced success, especially in London, where it was given in the summer season at Covent Garden in the same year, with Ternina as the first of a series of great Toscas and Scotti the first of several notable Scarpias.

4

The musical world pullulates with schools and instruction books for pianists, fiddlers, singers, conductors, composers and what not. It still lacks, however, a school for librettists. To recast a novel or a play as an opera text calls for a special technique; yet after three hundred years there is still nothing resembling a code for the guidance of a librettist in his fumbling hand-to-mouth practice. What generally happens is that the poet—to employ what in this connection is generally no more than a technical term—and the composer, after an infinity of discussion, correspondence, and from time to time heated recrimination, eventually settle down to a rough-and-ready compromise between the claims of the drama and those of music: despite the struggles of the poor librettist the composer always has the last word, and we know from history that it is not always the most rational word. So it pays us to compare now and then in some detail the text of an opera and that of the well-constructed novel or play from which it was derived, if only to get a rough idea of the difficulties attendant on this species of collaboration; and *Tosca* is about as instructive a subject for an enquiry of this sort as could be found.

Sardou's drama *La Tosca* had been produced in Paris on the 24th November 1887, with Sarah Bernhardt as the heroine. The play, with its five acts and twenty-three characters, had of course to be drastically condensed for the purposes of the opera, which is in three acts and has only nine characters in all, of whom four —Spoletta (the police agent), the gendarme Sciarrone, a gaoler and a shepherd—play only minor parts in the action. A fair amount of what happens in the play could be dispensed with in the opera without fatal dramatic loss; Sardou's effective second act, for instance, disappears *en bloc*. On the other hand, much of the Sardou drama that is vital to the spectator's understanding of the opera has been entirely eliminated or passed by with the most casual of hints.

Puccini had a consummate sense of "theatre," which, however, is not always quite the same thing as "drama." Moreover, his musical genius was on the whole a slow-moving one. His music seldom hurries; his strength lay to a great extent in unrelenting insistence on a motif once launched, the piling up of obsessional effect on effect in some episode or other that lent itself well to that kind of musical treatment. This psychological bias led him, now consciously, now unconsciously, to see a dramatic action as concentrated in a few peak-situations supercharged with musical emotion. If the dramatic layout as a whole lent itself to this sort of simplification, well and good. But if the action had been dependent, in the play or story on which Puccini founded his own work, on the dexterous piecing together of a number of small psychological motives or episodes, his own structure necessarily suffered to some extent by his sweeping all that aside in order to get more room for his music.[1]

[1] The general situation is summed up in a despairing passage in one of Giacosa's letters to Giulio Ricordi, written at the time when he was struggling with the far smaller difficulties of condensing the subject matter of *La Bohème:* "It is a terrible undertaking to reduce to the required proportions an act crammed full of events. I worked desperately hard, but on the one hand I have to make clearness my aim, and on the other I must not make the act longer than three hundred lines."

This is decidedly the case with the first act of *Tosca*: the critical spectator who sees it for the first time keeps wondering precisely who or what Cavaradossi, Tosca, Angelotti and "the Attavanti" are, how it comes about that Cavaradossi is painting in the church, why the Sacristan keeps mumbling serio-comic doubts about the artist's religion and morals, why Angelotti should be taking refuge in this particular church, why Cavaradossi should be so ready to assist him at the risk of his own liberty or even life, and so forth; and the full answers to these and many other questions are to be found only in Sardou's play, some knowledge of which should always be at the back of our minds when we are listening to the opera—as of course it was at the back of Puccini's mind when writing it.

5

The action of Puccini's first act is briefly as follows. Into the empty church of Sant' Andrea della Valle in Rome there steals, when the curtain rises, an agitated Angelotti; the stage directions tell us that he is "in prison garb," though how the spectator is to recognise the Italian prison garb of the year 1800 we do not know; all he sees is a panting man in rags. Angelotti proceeds to lock himself in one of the side chapels, the key of which he has found, after a little search, at the feet of a statue of the Madonna: for his sister, he obligingly informs the audience, has sent him—where? when? why? how? the spectator cannot help asking—a letter telling him that it is there he will find the key. The painter Mario Cavaradossi then enters, and, during and after a colloquy with the Sacristan, sets to work at a half-finished easel picture of a blonde and blue-eyed Magdalen. The garrulous old Sacristan recognises the face as that of an unknown lady he had seen in the church lately, praying to the Virgin; [1] and Cavaradossi informs him—though one fails to perceive why he should confide in him to this extent—that, fascinated by her features, he had begun

[1] That her identity should be a mystery to the Sacristan is incredible; the Marchesa Attavanti's face would be as well known in Rome as that of any other member of the local aristocracy. Moreover, no one can know better than the Sacristan that the chapel on the right of the stage is that of the lady's family: it is he, indeed, who points it out later in response to Scarpia's enquiry. This difficulty with regard to the recognition of the lady does not arise in Sardou.

188

painting her at her devotions without her having observed him; he has incorporated also in his picture something of the beauty of his mistress Floria Tosca, a miniature of whom he takes from his pocket and contemplates rapturously. Once more we are at a loss to understand why he should tell the Sacristan all this—and particularly that, unlike the original of the picture, his Tosca is a brunette and her eyes are black; the truth is, of course, that it is only in this way that the composer can convey the information to the audience. The Sacristan does a good deal of *sotto voce* grumbling about the artist's addiction to mundane things and his lack of pious interest in the saints, and mutters something about "these dogs of Voltaireans who are the enemies of the Holy Office"—a line to which the spectator cannot attach any meaning, and for the significance of which we have to go back to Sardou.

When the Sacristan leaves and all is quiet, Angelotti, believing the church to be empty now, turns from the inside the key of the chapel grille, apparently intending to make his escape. (Why he should have gone there in the first place, with the intention of leaving it so soon, has so far not been divulged to us.) Scared at the unexpected sight of a stranger, he is about to slip back into the chapel when, to his joy, he recognises in the painter an old friend of his, Mario Cavaradossi. At first the latter does not know him, for, as Angelotti explains, as much for our benefit as for Cavaradossi's, his imprisonment in the castle of Sant' Angelo has changed him greatly; but the painter eventually remembers him as "the Consul of the extinguished Roman republic"—a phrase incomprehensible to the audience—and hails him as such. Their very brief colloquy is interrupted by an off-stage call from Cavaradossi's mistress, Tosca: and giving the starving Angelotti his own basket of food and wine Mario hurries him back into the chapel and settles down to a long duet with Floria. Her suspicions have been aroused by his delay in unbolting the church door, and her jealousy by the picture, the original of which she recognises as a certain Marchesa Attavanti. However, Mario manages to placate her, and finally persuades her to depart and leave him to his work.

When she has gone Angelotti comes out of the chapel again, and Cavaradossi informs him that delightfully amorous as Tosca is she is very pious and given to telling her confessor everything;

for which reason he had had to be very guarded in his conversation with her. Angelotti now discloses his plan for flight. It appears that his sister the Marchesa had concealed a woman's clothes in the family chapel; he was to don these, slip out of the church at dusk, and so escape the clutches of the scoundrelly Chief of Police, Baron Scarpia. It is now arranged between the two men that Angelotti shall make his way over the fields to Cavaradossi's villa in the country, the key to which the painter gives him, promising to rejoin him there at night. There is no need to put on the female garments now, Cavaradossi explains; let him take them with him and make use of them later if need be. But just as Angelotti is going back to the chapel for the clothes the boom of a cannon is heard—the warning to the town that a prisoner has escaped. Cavaradossi and Angelotti leave the church hurriedly. The Sacristan and the populace come in, rejoicing over the news that has just reached Rome of the defeat of the French under Bonaparte. They are followed by Scarpia; and the remainder of the act follows on the purely operatic lines which will be familiar to the reader.

All this, however, leaves a great deal to be explained which it is necessary for us to know if we are to understand all that has happened before the rising of the curtain, and why Puccini had obviously earmarked the bulk of his space in the first act for two big musical show pieces—the duet between Cavaradossi and Tosca, and Scarpia's outburst of erotic frenzy, with the massive choral ensemble that accompanies this and brings the act to a sonorous close; he had consequently little space left for explanation of the core of the drama. For a fuller knowledge of the characters and the action we have to turn to Sardou.

6

The period of the spoken play is that of the invasion of Italy by the army of the French Republican Government. Puccini's score gives the date of the action as June 1800; Sardou, with his "17th June," is more explicit. His drama begins with a talk between the Sacristan (Eusèbe) and little Gennarino, Mario Cavaradossi's boy servant, who, when the curtain rises, is cleaning his master's brushes, preparing the palette, and so forth. It is the hour of the siesta, and Eusèbe is anxious to close the church and go home to his sleep; but he cannot do so until Cavaradossi arrives as usual, and the artist is late today. We gather from what the garrulous Eusèbe says that Cavaradossi has obtained permission from the authorities to work in the church at this hour each day, when he will be free from disturbance by worshippers, choir, organist and English tourists with their guides. Eusèbe, a pious plebeian of low intellectual development, has nothing against the artist personally, for he is liberal with his tips. But though the man comes of an old patrician family on his father's side, Mario's mother, Gennarino is informed, was French, which, for Eusèbe, accounts for everything that is morally wrong with the son. Cavaradossi, though he is decorating the church, never takes part in the services, never goes to confession; "a Jacobin, Gennarino, an out-and-out Jacobin." His father had lived a long time in Paris, where he associated with "the abominable Voltaire" and other reprobates of that kidney; and the son has imbibed the father's reprehensible opinions on religion and politics.

As for Eusèbe, he is looking forward gleefully to a festival at the Farnese Palace that evening in celebration of a great victory of the Austrian General Melas which has just been announced in the Roman news-sheets: Genoa has been captured, Masséna has barely escaped with a few thousand demoralised troops. And so her Neapolitan Majesty Queen Marie Caroline (daughter of the Empress Maria Theresa and sister of Queen Marie Antoinette of blessed memory), glorious and worthy spouse of his Majesty Ferdinand IV, being at the moment in Rome on her way to Vienna, has commanded a splendid concert and ball at the Palazzo Farnese and a public fête in the Piazza. Soon there will be an even greater victory to rejoice over. There is a lot of nonsensical street gossip about General Bonaparte being at Milan, but Eusèbe has it on the best authority that Bonaparte has died in Egypt, "drowned in the Red Sea like Pharaoh," and is now being impersonated by his imbecile brother Joseph, a farceur who is really trying to persuade people that he has crossed the Alps with all his cannon!

So we have gathered that this Mario Cavaradossi, while there is nothing definite against him on which the Church and the Government can fasten, is not in the best odour in Roman political and clerical circles. He enters the church now, dismisses

Eusèbe and Gennarino, and prepares to resume work at his easel. Absorbed in this he does not hear a key being turned from the inside in the grille of one of the chapels; but happening to turn round just then he sees a man making steathily for the door of the church, where he pauses and listens intently. (The reader will recall that in the opera Angelotti enters immediately on the rising of the curtain and slips into the chapel before anyone else arrives on the scene. In Sardou he has been there all the preceding night.) The stranger announces himself as a prisoner escaped from the castle of Sant' Angelo: he had been engaged, he says, in revolutionary activities in Naples, and on the failure of these he had fled to Rome, where once more his name—Cesare Angelotti—figures on the list of proscriptions. Having overheard Eusèbe's account of Cavaradossi and his "Jacobin" antecedents he is confident the painter will not betray him. Thus in Sardou Cavaradossi and Angelotti have no knowledge at all of each other before the action opens; the only link between them is that of a common detestation of tyranny and clericalism. This gives all the more point to Mario's resolve to save Angelotti even at the risk of his own life.

7

The painter assures Angelotti that they are secure from interruption for a good two hours; the church is closed, even the Sacristan being unable to enter except by a side door the bolt of which Cavaradossi has shot. How has Angelotti managed to escape from prison? he asks. Angelotti tells him in full detail. He has been helped by his devoted sister the Marquise Attavanti.[1] She had bribed one of his gaolers, a certain Trebelli, to unlock his fetters yesterday, and profiting by the confusion in the castle where they were busy repairing the damage done by the French during the occupation of it, he had made his escape in his prison clothes. But where was he to go first? From the evening to the morning Angelus the gates of the town would be closed as usual. He could not go to his sister's house, for her husband the Marquis is a fanatic for Church and throne and would assuredly deliver him up to the authorities. So his sister had concealed a woman's

---

[1] She herself does not appear either in the play or the opera, though her husband plays a part in the former.

costume, including a cloak, a veil and a fan—the purpose of this last, of course, being to hide his face if need be—together with scissors and a razor (Sardou thinks of everything!), in this family chapel, the key to which she had conveyed to him through Trebelli. The plan was that he should slip into the chapel before the church was closed, spend the night there, cut his hair and shave off his beard. In the morning Trebelli was to come for him at the hour of High Mass and accompany him—now made up as a woman—to a place where a carriage would be waiting for them; at Frascati, outside Roman territory, where he would be safe, his sister would join him. But this morning, Trebelli not having appeared, Angelotti had not known what to do, whether to wait or to make the dash for freedom alone; for it is possible that his escape from Sant' Angelo has been discovered by now, and Trebelli may have confessed everything under torture. The one encouraging feature of the situation is that so far the alarm cannon has not been fired from the castle.

Cavaradossi tries to reassure him; the delay in Trebelli's coming may be due to some trifling last-minute hitch that had not been foreseen. Angelotti had better wait until evening begins to fall before slipping out of the church disguised. If he does so now, as had obviously been his intention, he is certain to attract the notice of some of the women knitting at the doors, or of the children who are playing about; whereas after the church has reopened he can mingle with the crowd of comers and goers without fear of detection. He is anxious, however, he replies, about his devoted sister, with whom there is no way of communicating. Mario tells him that he understands now why the fair devotee whom he had surreptitiously painted had been so assiduous in her attendance at the church of late; and Angelotti tells him the full story of his sister and himself.

Some twenty years ago he had been living a life of pleasure in London. At Vauxhall one night he had made the acquaintance of one of the light-o'-loves who used to frequent the Gardens. The liaison had lasted only a week. Years passed, and on the death of his father he inherited considerable property in Naples. Dining one day at the house of Prince Pepoli he had been presented to the wife of Sir William Hamilton, the English ambassador in Naples; and to his stupefaction he realised that this famous Lady

Hamilton was none other than his casual Vauxhall pick-up of years ago, not yet the figure she became later by her association with Admiral Nelson, but already a power at the Neapolitan Court. Exasperated by the hostility she showed towards the revolutionists he had told the whole company what she had once been, and where and in what circumstances he had formerly met her. Two days later his house was searched and his papers seized. They contained nothing incriminating; but an agent provocateur had craftily slipped a copy of Voltaire among his books, and this was sufficient to send him to the galleys for three years.

After that, ruined, exiled, he had left Naples, to return only with Championnet. When the royal troops re-occupied the town he had fled to Rome, thus escaping the imprisonment and torture that were the fate of his fellow-libertarians. But when the French troops had to leave Rome he was arrested once more and thrown into Sant' Angelo, where he had spent a year. Thanks to his sister's social influence he had been shown a certain passive benevolence by the governor of the prison, who hoped that when a new Pope was elected Angelotti would receive an amnesty along with other prisoners. But the court of Naples had recently sent to Rome, as head of the police, a certain pitiless Baron Scarpia, whom Cavaradossi, who knows the man well, describes as a thorough-paced scoundrel who conceals his ambitions, his lechery and his lust for blood under a mask of religion and courtesy, "an artist in villainy, subtle in wickedness, delighting in cruelty, bloody even in his orgies, a foul unscrupulous satyr." Yes, says Angelotti, this scoundrel had pursued his sister the Marquise Attavanti, and having been repulsed, and sensing in advance a design on her part to rescue her brother, he had arranged for Angelotti to be sent three days hence to Naples, where Lady Hamilton would have the pleasure of hanging her one-time lover. In that, however, she will be disappointed, for in a ring given him by his sister he has poison enough to make an end of himself. At that moment there is a sound of battering at the church door. The two men's hearts go into their mouths; they listen in anxious silence for a while, but the noise proves to have been only that of the ball of some players in the street. This little episode is one of Sardou's most telling pieces of stage craftsmanship; the emotional tension gathers up into itself all that has so far happened, and

when the real coup de théâtre comes later—the thunder of the
Sant' Angelo cannon—it strikes us with double force.

8

The spasm of terror having spent itself, the two men resume
their conversation. Mario now tells Angelotti all about himself.
He is the son of a Roman gentleman who had spent the greater
part of his life in France, where he had been intimate with such
people as Voltaire and Diderot, and had married a great-niece of
Helvétius. Mario himself had been brought up in circles that
breathed revolt against the established political and clerical order.
Family affairs had made it necessary for him to return to Rome,
which he did at the very time when the French troops were leaving the city. Nothing kept him in the abhorred place now but his
passion for Floria Tosca, the great singer, the idol of musicians
and populace alike, who is at present performing at the Argentina
Theatre. He is madly in love with her: she has only two faults—a
tendency to crazy jealousy, and a religiosity which Cavaradossi
finds excessive. So he remains in Rome. He takes no part in
revolutionary activities; but his un-Roman way of behaviour and
his former Paris associations go against him with the authorities.
He would have come within reach of Scarpia's claws by now if it
had not been for his ingenuity in getting permission from the
chapter of Sant' Andrea to decorate gratuitously the walls of the
church. Soon Tosca will be leaving Rome to fulfil a season's engagement in Venice, and he intends to slip away quietly with
her. Till then, he believes, he is safe; anyhow he is prepared to
take the risk. He and Tosca meet freely, either at his villa in the
country or here in the church; she would have been here by now,
indeed, were it not that she is rehearsing for this evening's
concert.

Cavaradossi rejects the suggestion that he should let her into
the secret of Angelotti's identity. For one thing, he does not believe in bringing women into serious affairs of this sort; for another, he could not rely on a woman so subject to nervous crises
as Tosca is, and a fanatical royalist into the bargain. Moreover
she is very pious and hides nothing from her confessor. So, all in
all, the less she is told the better: "the only really discreet woman
is the one who knows nothing."

Just then a knock at the church door is heard, and Tosca's voice impatiently calling "Mario!" He hustles Angelotti into the chapel, saying he will cut Floria's visit as short as possible; then he opens the church door. At once she begins to vent her jealous suspicions. Why is the bolt shot today? With whom was he talking? Some old flame of his, no doubt? She piously protests against his kissing her hand until she has offered placatory flowers to the Madonna, which she does kneeling at the feet of the statue. This done, she becomes her normal amorous feline self again. They cannot meet tonight as usual, she complains, because she has to sing at a fête at the Farnese Palace. After that there is to be a ball, at which the Queen of Naples has reserved a special place for her; so it will be mid-day tomorrow before she can see her lover again. Her suspicious eye catches a look of relief which he has been unable to conceal. In a flash she becomes the jealous, suspicious Tosca once more.[1] Who is that woman he is painting? Why has he made her so beautiful? It must be some former mistress of his, through whom he is now recalling his memories and realising his secret desires. Why is her hair golden, Tosca's being black? Why are her eyes so blue? Then she recognises her —the Attavanti! He admits it, but patiently tries to explain that he has seen the original of the picture only here in the church, and that by hazard, she having come in to pray before the statue of the Madonna while he was at work: she had seemed so truly the ideal Magdalen that he had at once committed her features to his canvas, without her having been aware of it, without his having spoken a single word to her.

Floria traduces the character of her supposed rival: why does she not try to reform that villainous brother of hers, "an enemy of God, of the King and of the Pope, a demagogue, an atheist?" Mario tries to laugh all this off, but only succeeds in angering her more. He must himself be as bad as Angelotti, she rants, or he would not be so complacent about him. Now she thinks of it, does not Mario himself read Voltaire? Has he not given her to read—

[1] We see at every point that it was Sarah Bernhardt, with her capacity for rapid changes of expression, whom Sardou had in his mind's eye all along as his Tosca.

her, the pious Floria Tosca!—Rousseau's *La Nouvelle Héloïse*, a
book so infamous that her good confessor had given her the
choice of either burning it or herself burning in hell! though it
soon appears that her private feminine grievance against the
people in the book is that they are untrue to life—they talk too
much about love and practise it too little. Her confessor has
warned her against this artist lover of hers, denounced her passion
as abominable, and adjured her to convert him if she can. As a
preliminary sign of conversion, says the good priest, she ought
to persuade him to get rid of that moustache of his; it is a revolutionary symbol, and he flaunts it in the street with such assurance!
Then, with another of her kittenish quick changes, Tosca declares
that she will not obey the priest in this, for Mario's moustache
becomes him. Altogether she lives in a constant state of mortal
sin on his account, and dreads dying suddenly, in which case,
she feels, her chance of salvation would be small. Her only consolation is that she stands well with the Madonna, thanks to her
pious attentions to her. Mario listens to all this feather-headed
gabble calmly and indulgently. He knows his Floria too well to
take her tantrums very seriously; all the same, it is inconvenient
to have her carrying on so long in this style just now.

10

The problem of how to get rid of her is solved for him by her
servant, who enters with a letter for Tosca from the composer
Paisiello. This being read aloud, we learn—as does Angelotti
also, listening in the chapel—that the Queen has just heard from
General Melas that on the 14th he had completely routed the
French army under General Bonaparte at Marengo. Public prayers
and thanks are to be offered in all the churches. As for Paisiello,
in his loyal enthusiasm he has dashed off a cantata for the fête in
the Farnese Palace that evening, and he begs Tosca to come to a
quick rehearsal of it before the supper. The Queen's wishes, she
recognises, will have to be complied with; so she quite resigns
herself to seeing no more of her lover that day. For his part, he
promises her, he will work as long as the light allows, then sup
and sleep at his villa, and they will meet again at mid-day on
the morrow.

She goes away, leaving the two men in the depths of despair

over the bad news of the Austrian victory; Tosca's last words are a coquettish request to Mario to make the Magdalen's eyes not blue but black, like hers. Angelotti comes out of the chapel, and they hastily concoct a new plan. The church is now certain to be opened before the usual time for the prayers and thanksgiving that have been commanded: a great crowd will be there, and perhaps in the general excitement they will be able to get out of Rome before the gates are closed, without waiting for Trebelli. But at that moment the cannon of Sant' Angelo booms out: the escape has been discovered. Yet another plan is hastily improvised: Angelotti is to don his female disguise, slip out of the chapel by a grille on the other side, steal through the dimly-lit church, and join Cavaradossi at the great door. He goes back into the chapel just as Eusèbe enters,[1] followed by a number of women and children. Mario poses himself before the canvas, looking as unconcerned as he can. The Sacristan is in high glee; a notorious Jacobin, one Angelotti, he and Gennarino tell Cavaradossi, has escaped from Sant' Angelo with the connivance of his gaoler, who has confessed everything under torture. A price of a thousand piastres is set on Angelotti's head, and the hue-and-cry is on. While Eusèbe, with his back to the chapel, is gloating over the defeat of the farceur Bonaparte, Angelotti is vaguely perceived escaping by the other grille of which Cavaradossi had spoken and disappearing in the dim depths of the church. With a sigh of relief Cavaradossi makes his own exit, leaving Eusèbe still chattering. The church begins to fill, the choir is heard in the distance, and Scarpia, in pursuit of Angelotti, enters with his two henchmen, Spoletta and Schiarrone.

11

This detailed outline of Sardou's first act has been necessary to show what an ill-made piece of work, dramatically speaking, the first act of Puccini's opera is. The basis and essence of the original drama are political; it is the community of feeling between the

---

[1] He has come in by the main entrance to the church; the first thing he does is to draw the bolts of the side door from the inside. Sardou has not forgotten that Cavaradossi had assured Angelotti during the first few moments of their meeting that "the church is empty and completely closed. The sacristan himself cannot get in at that [side] door until I draw the bolts."

two men in that field that makes the painter ready to risk everything to save the life of a man whom he had never seen until that
day. In Sardou, not only has Eusèbe expressed to Gennarino his
disapproval of the moral character of this "Voltairean," this
"Jacobin," but Mario himself has told Angelotti at considerable
length the story of his early life and French associations and the
danger of his present position in Rome. In the opera all this
logical motivation disappears; the only attempt at a hint of it
(and it is so vague that the spectator who does not know Sardou's
play cannot possibly make anything of it) is in the Sacristan's
mumblings to himself about the painter being more taken up with
worldly than with religious things—a remark actually evoked by
the mere fact of Mario's rhapsody over the beauty of his mistress
Tosca.

The woman's-clothes motive, again, that is treated so plausibly
in Sardou, is clumsily handled in the opera, where the absence of
any mention of Trebelli results in a certain obscurity in the action
later. In Sardou, the moment we hear of the confession of the
gaoler we visualise everything that has happened at Sant' Angelo.
The full details of the plan to escape had been disclosed under
torture; that is why Scarpia has made straight for the church,
where he knows Angelotti had gone into hiding. His first words to
the Sacristan are "Listen to me. A criminal has escaped from Sant'
Angelo; he spent the night in this church; he may be here yet.
Where is the Angelotti chapel?" [1] Schiarrone is sent into the chapel

[1] In the opera this becomes the "Attavanti chapel." We may reasonably
wonder why the Marquise should be so imprudent as to deposit the female
disguise in the *Attavanti* chapel, which any member of that royalist family
might have visited! Sardou, who never leaves a loose thread of this kind
anywhere in a play, makes it quite clear from the outset, in the tale Angelotti
tells Cavaradossi, that no such danger could threaten the plan. "But where
was I to find shelter for the night? My sister had provided for that. The
Angelottis, whose ancestors had founded this church, have a chapel of their
own here to which they alone have the key: in this she placed the woman's
clothes. . . . She conveyed the key of it to me through Trebelli. I slipped in
before the church was closed. . . ."

In the play, almost Scarpia's first words to Eusèbe are "Where is the
Angelotti chapel?" A later remark of his, when the agent finds the fan, is
"This was part of the toilette." Obviously he has learned every detail of the
plot from Trebelli: that is why he has made at once for the church of Sant'

and returns with the news that there is no one there: all he has found that bears on his quest is "divers objets de toilette," a mirror, scissors, a razor, some hair on the ground—and a fan. Scarpia at once recognises the crest on the latter as that of the Attavanti family; Angelotti, he says, "must have forgotten it in his haste or decided he would have no use for it." This is consistent with what we have learned earlier in the play; the fan, Angelotti tells Cavaradossi, had been included by the Marquise in the bundle of woman's clothes in order that he might cover his face with it during his flight from the church. It is really upon the fan that the whole ingenious working-out of the action turns in Sardou; and it is a pity that operatic exigencies, particularly the need for compression in order to get plenty of space for the two big musical episodes of the first act, made Puccini and his librettists depart from Sardou's expert handling of the motive. On the general matter of music *versus* drama in the opera we shall have more to say later.

12

Let us now follow the dramatic and musical course of the first act of the opera in detail.

Three terrific chords, hurled at us by the orchestra without preamble:

No. 1

Andrea, and why he says to Schiarrone, "Nothing else? No woman's clothes? It is in that disguise, then, that he has fled."

Sardou makes it clear at the very opening of the play, in his stage directions, that the chapel was that of the Angelotti, not the Attavanti, family: ". . . the Angelotti chapel, with a grille . . . surmounted by the Angelotti arms." Puccini and his librettists missed or ignored the whole point—that the fugitive was safe for the night in that chapel because it was not accessible to anyone but a member of the Angelotti family. His sister was an Attavanti only by marriage.

first of all flash an image of the brutal, ruthless Scarpia upon our
inner eye. Then, the curtain having risen, we see a section of the
interior of the church of Sant' Andrea: on the right is the "Attavanti" chapel, as the stage directions describe it; on the left is
a low platform with an easel on it, and on the easel a large canvas
covered with a cloth; lying around are various implements of the
painter's craft and a basket containing food and wine. Towards
the centre of the stage is a statue of the Madonna, surmounting
a font of holy water. To a series of hurrying, stumbling, syncopated chords of this type:

No. 2

Angelotti staggers in by a side door—a broken, emaciated creature
in rags, out of breath, trembling with fear. After a rapid glance
round him he sees, to his relief, that he has taken the right direction; in his terror he had imagined that everyone in the streets
who had looked at him was a police agent. Another nervous
glance around confirms the fact that this is really the church of
Sant' Andrea; and he gives a sigh of relief as he sees at last what
have been staring him in the face all along—the statue and the
font. "At the feet of the Madonna, so my sister wrote to me . . .,"
he ejaculates for our information; and we hear in the orchestra a
motive obviously intended to be associated by us, in part, with
the sister who has been working for his life and liberty:

No. 3

He searches for a key that was to have been left at the foot of the
column supporting the statue, fails to discover it at first, and for

a moment gives way to despair. At last he finds it and runs with a cry of joy towards the chapel: "here is the key, and there is the chapel," he obligingly tells us. He looks round him, once more a prey to terror, then cautiously inserts the key in the lock of the grille, enters, and closes the gate carefully from the inside.

13

Hardly has he disappeared from our sight when the Sacristan enters from the back of the church with a bundle of paint-brushes in his hand. While he fusses about, seeing that everything is all right in the church, the orchestra gives out a couple of motives:

No. 4

and

No. 5

that suggest that he is the simplest of souls, easily pleased with his own little world and himself. To dispel any possible doubts we might have that he is intended to be a comic character Puccini tells us in his stage directions that he is afflicted with a nervous *tic,* a recurrent twitch of the neck and shoulders; and many a Sacristan with no voice to recommend him to us manages to get through the act quite successfully on the strength of that serio-comic twitch alone. The brushes are dirty, he tells us, dirtier, to use a professional simile that occurs to him, than a shabby priest's neckband. After a while it dawns on him, to his surprise, that the painter is not yet at his easel: "I could have sworn that the Cavaliere Cavaradossi would have been here by now." He peeps into the basket: the food and wine have not been touched. As the Angelus sounds he falls to his knees and mumbles a prayer: "Angelus Domini nuntiavit Mariae, et concepit de Spiritu Sancto. Ecce ancilla Domini; fiat mihi secundum verbum tuum. Et Verbum caro factum est et habitavit in nobis."

He rises to his feet as Cavaradossi comes in by the side door. The artist ascends the platform and removes the cloth from the picture; it is that of a Mary Magdalene with great blue eyes and a cascade of golden hair. He contemplates it for a while, the orchestra giving out a theme which we learn later to associate with the original of the picture, the Marchesa Attavanti: though some of Puccini's uses of it are rather puzzling:

No. 6

towards the end, following the bent of Mario's thoughts, it glides into one afterwards representative of Tosca and her lover. (See No. 12.) The Sacristan stares at the picture in amazement: he has recognised the subject of it as "the unknown lady who has been coming here lately to pray devoutly to the Madonna." [1] "Quite right," agrees Cavaradossi; "and she was so absorbed in her devotions that I painted her without her being aware of it." The Sacristan is scandalised; "Get thee behind me, Satan!" he cries. Mario sets to work, painting rapidly, and now and then stepping back to study the result, while the Sacristan potters about, washing the brushes in a bowl, etc.

Cavaradossi's mind is beset by thoughts of his Tosca:

No. 7

and, somewhat irrelevantly, he treats the Sacristan and us to a little professional discourse on the abstruse harmony that can exist between diverse kinds of beauty:

No. 8

Re—con—di—ta ar—mo—ni—a   di bel—læ-ze di— ver—se!

[1] As we have remarked already, it is incredible that the Sacristan should not have recognised the praying lady as the Marchesa Attavanti to whose family the "Attavanti" chapel belonged.

203

His ardent Tosca is dark and her eyes are black, while the unknown devotee he is painting is blonde, with eyes of the bluest
blue. "Yet Art, in its mysterious way," he muses to the accompaniment first of all of No. 7, "blends all kinds of beauty; while I am
painting this other it is still you, Tosca, who are the sole subject
of my thoughts." All through the soliloquy the shocked Sacristan
keeps mumbling *sotto voce* that "he amuses himself with puppets
and neglects the saints; these women of all sorts, rivals of the Madonna, emit a musty odour of hell. But with these dogs of Voltaireans, enemies of the Holy Office, it's best to have nothing to
do. All these fellows"—pointing to the artist though there is no
one to see or hear him but the audience—"are impenitents"; and
he makes the sign of the cross. This is the futile best that Puccini
and his librettists can do to cover the ground Sardou had been
over so fully in his account of Cavaradossi's antecedents and those
political and religious opinions of the painter that are so vital to
our understanding of his actions and motives in the Angelotti
drama.

14

It is time for the Sacristan, having played out most of his small
part in the construction of the drama, to leave us. But before he
does so there are one or two little bits of "business" he must go
through for our benefit. In the first place he has to make a final
assertion of himself as the comic relief of the piece; this he does
by hypocritical pretensions of regret, accompanied by some self-
satisfied hand-rubbing and snuff-taking, when Cavaradossi accounts for the fact that the basket of food is still untouched by
the further fact that he is not hungry. In the second place, the
Sacristan has to impress it on us that the basket is full when he
leaves the church, because, as we shall see later, this becomes, for
Scarpia, a link in the chain of evidence against Cavaradossi and
Angelotti; the whole episode, however, is managed more plausibly
in Sardou than in the opera.

With a final exhortation to Cavaradossi to close the church door
when he leaves, the Sacristan goes out, and the painter settles
down to work again, with his back, of course, turned towards the
chapel. "Angelotti," the stage directions inform us, "believing
the church to be empty now, appears behind the grille and inserts

the key, intending to open the gate." Why he should assume *both* speakers to have gone, seeing that he must have just heard the departing Sacristan tell the artist to make sure that he closes the church door when *he* goes, is an insoluble mystery to us. At a later stage of the same scene, after the colloquy between Cavaradossi and Tosca and the departure of the latter, Mario, according to the stage directions, runs at once to Angelotti, "who, of course, has heard the preceding conversation" of the lovers. If this overhearing occurs as a matter of course on that occasion, why should it not be just as much a matter of course in the earlier one? And, strange to say, when Angelotti now comes forward to open the gate his eyes serve him no better than his ears had done; he actually does not see Cavaradossi, who is right before his eyes only a few feet away. The truth is that for Puccini and his librettists the emergence of Angelotti from the chapel, and his recognition of Cavaradossi as an old friend, *had* to take place just at that point of the action and in just that way, whether plausible or not. Puccini, having in mind little beyond his lyrical expansions, troubles himself, for once, as little as need be with what he seems to have regarded as minor points of dramatic plausibility.

Cavaradossi, hearing the grating of the key in the lock, turns round with a startled cry of "Someone in there!" Angelotti, we are invited to believe, had inserted the key without seeing Cavaradossi painting within a few feet of him; it is only the noise made by Mario as he turns round on the platform that makes him aware that he is not alone in the church, as he had thought! The nervous No. 2 is now heard as he pauses in terror, and, for a moment, seems about to retreat into the recesses of the chapel. But "having raised his eyes," as the stage directions naïvely inform us, he "gives a cry of joy, which he immediately stifles in fear: he recognises the painter and stretches out his arms towards him, as if to an unexpected hope." "You, Cavaradossi!" he cries; "God has sent you!" It is a little while before Cavaradossi recognises his old friend, who has been greatly changed by his imprisonment. When he does so he ejaculates, "Angelotti! The Consul of the destroyed Roman Republic!" What meaning, if any, Puccini expected this to convey to the ordinary spectator we cannot imagine; but that he was anxious to force it on the attention of the audience is shown by his making the sentence stand out clearly without any accompaniment, and marking it "rapidly, declamatorily, loudly": manifestly he has an uneasy sense that somehow or other, somewhere or other, he must give at least a hint of that political background to the drama on which Sardou lays such stress.

15

But Angelotti has time to say no more than "I have just escaped from the Sant' Angelo castle," and Cavaradossi to reply "Count on me!", when the poor man has to make another hasty exit, for Tosca's voice is heard outside, impatiently crying "Mario!" The painter bids Angelotti get back into the chapel, telling him that the caller is "a jealous woman," and assuring him that he will get rid of her quickly. But Puccini's Angelotti is too well aware of the part the provisions basket is booked to play later in the opera to take cover there and then: instead, he staggers to the platform and says, "I am at the end of my strength; I can't hold out any longer"; whereupon Cavaradossi hands him the basket, telling him that it contains food and wine; and after a little interchange of "Hasten!" on the one side and "Thanks!" on the other, Angelotti re-enters the chapel, taking the basket with him, and Mario admits the fuming Tosca. Puccini has seen to it that that basket is forced on our attention.

Tosca, as soon as the bolt is drawn, sweeps in like the Italian prima donna she is, under full sail, with an armful of flowers:

No. 9

She is very angry at having been kept waiting, and Mario has difficulty in allaying her suspicion that he has been entertaining a rival. Puccini does his best to present her to us as the changeful, capricious creature of Sardou's play, by turns amorous and religious. Cavaradossi makes to embrace her, but she piously reproves him: "Oh! in front of the Madonna!" And so, to the accompaniment of the insinuating No. 9 and its no less insinuating ending:

No. 10

she arranges the flowers—"artistically," we are assured—at the feet of the statue, kneels, prays "with great devotion," crosses herself, and then turns to the painter, who artist-like, has been showing signs of wanting to get on with his work. She has come to tell him that she is singing that evening, but the opera is a short one; he is to wait for her at the stage door, and they will go straight to his villa in the country. A flash of the agitated No. 2 in the orchestra shows Mario wondering how all this is to be made to square with his plans for aiding Angelotti in his flight.[1] Whenever she speaks to him he answers her abstractedly. Abandoning herself to the luxury of her amorous imagination she paints for him the joys that await them in the villa, that hidden nest known only to them, full of mystery, warm with love:

No. 11

Non la so—spi—ri la nos-tra ca—set—ta che tut-ta a-
sco—sa nel ver—de ci a—spet-ta?

[1] Most conductors, being almost wholly intent on the music, to the neglect of the drama, dissipate much of the tension of this episode by failing to give its full value to one of Puccini's favourite devices for creating suspense—a sudden pause for both orchestra and voices. Puccini's handling of the present episode is admirably dramatic. After Tosca's "Wait for me after the performance and we will go off, just we two, to your villa," there is a quick reference to the Angelotti motive (No. 2) in the orchestra, and Cavaradossi interjects abstractedly "Tonight?!" The actor must convey to us this sudden sense on Mario's part of the difficulties that Tosca's plans bring into the arrangements made for Angelotti's flight. Tosca runs on thoughtlessly: "The moon will be full, the night scent of the flowers intoxicating." Then she senses a certain reserve on Mario's part. "Are you not pleased?" she asks him wonderingly, seating herself by him on the steps of the platform. It is at this point that the typical Puccinian pause occurs—a dead silence as Mario turns the situation over in his mind and then replies (according to the stage directions "absent-mindedly"), "Oh, of course!" That pause and its psychological implications cannot be too strongly impressed on the audience.

and we hear again the feline, caressing cadence that is so characteristic of her (No. 10).

Cavaradossi, while sharing her transports, cannot help adding, looking distractedly over her head, which is resting on his shoulder, towards the chapel, "And now leave me to my work!" She is hurt at being "dismissed," as it seems to her; and catching sight of the picture on the easel she asks who is this person with the blonde hair and blue eyes. "The Magdalen," he replies casually. After a closer scrutiny she recognises "the Attavanti," and by a misuse of the leitmotif principle—for there cannot be any possible association in Tosca's mind of the Marchesa with the prisoner who has escaped from Sant' Angelo—the orchestra gives out the Angelotti theme (No. 2). In many places in this first act Puccini uses motifs and fragments of motifs in a rather mechanical and meaningless way.

16

In vain Mario tries to calm her; now she is all jealousy. "It was she who was with you, the coquette!" she cries furiously. He patiently explains that it was by pure accident that he had lighted upon the unknown lady at her devotions. He assures her ardently that no eyes in the world can compare with Tosca's, and gradually gets her to see reason. Their voices unite in a passionate duet:

No. 12

that is the highest musical light of the opera so far, Mario calling Tosca affectionately "My jealous one!", and she repentantly accepting the description and accepting his pardon gratefully. Towards the end of the duet she becomes kittenish again, breaking from his embrace and reproving him for having ruffled her hair —in church! At last he manages to persuade her to leave him, after she has made him promise—a point that will become of importance later in the drama—that he will go on working till the evening, will not admit any other woman to say her prayers, and will change the eyes of the Magdalen from blue to black.

She leaves behind her a thoughtful and troubled Cavaradossi.

There comes another of those musical pauses that are so frequent and so significant in Puccini, or would be if conductors in general observed them as they should. Having assured himself that there are no signs of her returning, Mario brings Angelotti out into the open: "My Tosca," he explains, "is a good soul, but so pious that she tells everything to her confessor": that is why he had thought it safest not to confide in her. While the orchestra rings the changes on the motif shown in our No. 3 Angelotti, in response to Cavaradossi's enquiries, at last reveals his plan—either to get out of Roman territory or hide in the city, according to the immediate run of events. "My sister"—"the Attavanti!" Mario interjects for our benefit—"had concealed a woman's costume there under the altar, a dress, a veil, a fan"; at dusk he was to slip out of the church disguised. The orchestra perhaps justifies our identification of No. 6 with the Marchesa when it accompanies Cavaradossi's praise of her: now he understands her visits to the church, he says; at first he had suspected some amorous intrigue on the part of the unknown lady; but it was evidently just a sister's love.

She had indeed done everything she could, says Angelotti, to save him from the scoundrelly Scarpia. (No. 1 raises itself menacingly in the orchestra, then repeats itself in softer tones and more insidious colours, like something evil lurking in the shadows.) "Scarpia!" cries Cavaradossi passionately; "a bigot, a satyr, who conceals his lusts under a mask of piety, confessor and executioner in one! I will save you if it costs me my own life!" But for Angelotti to wait until night falls is dangerous. (No reasons are given, as they are in Sardou.) Better for him to go now. The chapel opens on to an enclosed kitchen garden, from which a cornfield leads to a villa of Cavaradossi's, to which he gives Angelotti the key, telling him to take the female outfit with him. He will rejoin him there at night, he says, No. 10 in the orchestra reminding him and us of his promise to Tosca to work until it grows dark.

17

Angelotti is making for the chapel to get the clothes, when Cavaradossi stops him: "If danger threatens you at the villa," he says, "run to the well in the garden: at the bottom of it is water, but half-way down is an opening leading to a large cave, inaccessible and safe." The words are hardly out of his mouth when the usual warning to the town of a prisoner's escape from the castle booms out. Cavaradossi now decides to accompany Angelotti, and the two men leave the church hastily.

Even while they have been talking we have heard in the orchestra the merry theme of the Sacristan (No. 4)—another instance of Puccini's haphazard use of leading motifs, for the Sacristan does not enter until the others have gone. He has returned, out of breath with excitement, to give the painter, to the accompaniment of Nos. 4 and 5, a piece of news that fills him with joy but is calculated to annoy the Voltairean Cavaliere. "Your Excellency! Not here? A pity! Whoever brings grief to an unbeliever gets an indulgence."

The orchestra becomes all jubilation as a crowd of clerics, choristers, small boys and others pours into the church, to whom the Sacristan gives the glad tidings of the annihilation of Bonaparte, who has gone where he belongs—to the Devil. To a gay new melody:

No. 13

everyone rejoices as the Sacristan tells them that in the evening there will be a grand torchlight procession, a fête at the Palazzo Farnese, a new cantata, expressly composed for the occasion and sung by Floria Tosca, and in the churches hymns to the Lord. There are loud cries of "Long live the King! Te Deum! Gloria!" But before they can complete the word "Vittoria!" they are hushed by the terrible No. 1 fortissimo in the orchestra and the appearance of the dreaded Chief of Police himself, followed by Spoletta and other minions of his. Scarpia upbraids the crowd for its scandalous uproar in the church. One by one they creep out silently. The terrified Sacristan would follow them, but Scarpia halts him. Sending the agents to search every nook and cranny of the church and chapel, he turns coldly on the Sacristan and bids him weigh his words carefully. A prisoner has escaped from Sant' Angelo and taken refuge here, he tells him, to the accompaniment of a sinister bass figure that runs through the whole of the ensuing dialogue:

No. 14

He may still be here. Which is the Attavanti chapel? "That is it!" replies the Sacristan. Going to the gate, he finds it, to his astonishment, open. "A good sign!" ejaculates Scarpia. He and the Sacristan go into the chapel; when they return, Scarpia is visibly annoyed at having found it practically empty except for a fan which he now dangles nervously.[1] There is a pause in the music prescribed at this point: it can hardly be too long for dramatic effect. Then Scarpia muses, "That cannon shot was a great blunder: the rascal has fled in haste. But he has left behind him a priceless clue—this fan! Who was his accomplice?" He stares long and thoughtfully at the fan: then his face brightens—"The Marchesa Attavanti's crest!" "Who painted that picture?" he suddenly asks. The trembling Sacristan replies "The Cavaliere Cavaradossi." (There is some irresponsibility, we cannot help thinking, in Puccini's use of leading motives during this episode.) "He?" says Scarpia, "Tosca's lover! A suspect! A Voltairean!"

[1] The librettists seem to have bungled here. In Sardou the female clothes are not in the chapel, because Angelotti has escaped in them. But in the opera they are, on the face of it, still there when Scarpia arrives. "Take the woman's clothing with you," Cavaradossi had told Angelotti (in the opera) when giving him his final instructions to make his way to the villa. Angelotti, according to the stage directions, "goes to get the clothes left by his sister." "Shall I put them on?" he asks. "No need at present," replies Mario, "for the road is deserted." As Angelotti is leaving the church Cavaradossi runs to him and tells him about the well in the garden. He has no sooner done this than the Sant' Angelo cannon booms out, and the startled pair make a hurried exit. Did the librettists intend to convey to us that Angelotti actually went into the chapel and returned with the bundle of clothes in his arms in the short space of time occupied by three bars of orchestral music, or are we to take it that his query to Mario," Ought I to don them?", and the latter's reply, "No need at present, for the road is deserted," imply that he had only *made towards* the chapel without actually going inside? It is all very unclear.

18

Meanwhile the Sacristan has been examining the basket which one of the agents has brought out of the chapel. "Empty!" he exclaims. Scarpia, who has overheard him, quickly drags the facts out of him. The basket belongs to the painter, he stammers; it contained his usual repast, and the Sacristan can vouch that it was full when he last saw it. Cavaradossi himself could not have taken it into the chapel, for he had no key to that; and besides, he had assured the Sacristan that he had no intention of eating, as he was not hungry.

All is now becoming clear to Scarpia. But just as the solution of his problem is dawning on him, Tosca, accompanied—for no good reason that we can see—by the Angelotti motive (No. 2), enters in nervous haste. At the sight of her Scarpia conceals himself, making an imperious sign to the Sacristan to remain where he is, by the easel. Not finding Mario where she had expected him to be, Tosca goes to look for him in the nave of the church. "She must not see me," Scarpia mutters; "to bring jealousy to the brink of frenzy Iago had a handkerchief: I have a fan!"

Tosca returns, calling impatiently "Mario! Mario!" and the Sacristan approaches her. "The painter Cavaradossi?" he says; "who knows what has become of him? Vanished: spirited away by witchcraft." With that he takes to his heels—which rather makes nonsense of his terrified obedience to Scarpia's imperious order to remain where he is. His going, however, accomplishes the composer's musical purpose, which is to clear the stage for the big scene between Tosca and Scarpia which he has long since been impatient to get down to. Thoroughly in his element now, Puccini launches the theme that is to dominate the episode, one of those typically Puccinian motives that lend themselves so well to his fondness and his genius for insistent repetition:

No. 15

(The church bells double the orchestral statement of the theme.) To this colourful accompaniment Scarpia comes forward, offers Tosca holy water, and, in his oiliest tones, tells her that while her art of itself is a stimulus to piety, not content with her triumphs on the stage she comes here to pray, very different in this respect from some shameless creatures—he points meaningly to the picture on the easel—who have the air and wear the robe of the Magdalen and play at love! Her suspicions now thoroughly aroused, Tosca demands proofs. Showing her the fan, he asks suavely if that is a painter's implement. He had found it on the platform, he tells her: someone must have entered and disturbed the lovers, and in her hurried flight the lady had dropped her fan. Tosca examines it and recognises the Attavanti crest: her forebodings have come true! To another of those repetitive phrases which Puccini always handles with such mastery she sobs, "And I who came here full of sorrow to tell him that in vain night would spread its dark mantle over the earth, for Tosca, the loving Tosca, is a prisoner of the royal jubilation"; i.e. she has been commanded to sing at the palace that night. (It may seem curious that she should confide all this, and in such flowery poetic terms, to the Chief of Police; but our surprise is diminished by the knowledge that only in this way can the librettists convey this vital information to us in the audience.) Her lament is punctuated by melodramatic asides from Scarpia.

Undeterred by his dread presence, and regardless of the fact that it is obviously intruding upon a private conversation, the public infiltrates into the church again, singly, in pairs, in groups, for of course it will be wanted very soon for the big choral ensemble that is to end the act in the best grand opera manner; but Tosca and Scarpia continue their colloquy as if they were still alone, with No. 15 pealing out again in the bells. Smoothly, insinuatingly, he regrets that cheeks so beautiful as hers should be bedewed with tears, and swears he would give his life to bring her consolation. She hardly listens to him: "and I," she moans, "consuming myself while he was laughing at my folly in the arms of another!" ("My poison works!" Scarpia interjects *sotto voce;* he has manifestly read *Othello.*) "If I could trap them!" she goes on. "For a double love, no doubt, the villa serves!

Traitor! Traitor! My lovely nest soiled with mud!" (Here the fate-laden No. 14 weaves its way through the depths of the orchestra, which is intelligible enough; what one fails to see is just why the Angelotti motif—No. 2—should also figure in the tissue as she cries, "I will surprise them there! You shall not have her tonight! I swear it!"). Scarpia piously reproves her for such a display of mundane passion in the church. She begs God's pardon, weeps, and goes towards the door, Scarpia accompanying her with feigned expressions of sympathy, while the orchestra depicts her meditating on her lost happiness (No. 12).

19

Tosca having departed, Scarpia summons Spoletta to him with a sign, the Angelotti motive (No. 2) showing us what is in his mind. He orders his lieutenant to follow Tosca in a carriage with three of his men and to meet him later at the Palazzo Farnese; and, melodramatic to the last, he apostrophises his victim ironically: "Go, Tosca! Scarpia has wormed himself into your heart!" From now onwards the psychological emphasis is on this satyr-like passion for the singer—a motive that does not appear in Sardou's handling of the action of this first act, and, indeed, in the play is subordinate throughout to Scarpia's desire to save his own head by the sacrifice of Angelotti's.

All this while the crowd has been growing in size. It is shepherded into two groups, one on each side of the stage, by the Swiss soldiers who have entered with the cortège of the Cardinal. The latter makes his way towards the high altar, blessing the people; Scarpia inclines himself in prayer as the prelate passes. To a broad theme that dominates the remainder of the act a service of thanksgiving to God is begun by choir and organ, the former murmuring their words, not singing them. The object of this procedure is obviously to give Scarpia freer play in his accompanying monologue; he is supposed to be communing with himself, regardless of his surroundings. He begins by explaining for our benefit ("ferociously," say the stage directions), that he has a double purpose in view—not merely to bring the escaped prisoner to the scaffold but to see love for himself flaming in Tosca's beautiful eyes as she satisfies his desire: (this "con passione erotica"), "the one" ("ferocemente") "to the halter, the other to my arms." It is in order that he may say all this as it were *sotto voce* and still be heard by us that Puccini, in addition to keeping down the organ and the orchestra, restricts the choral co-operation to a toneless murmur.

By now the scene is fully set for the final tableau, with all heads turned towards the high altar. Choir, orchestra, and organ launch a Te Deum, with bells and cannon joining in for greater effect. Scarpia alone stands aloof, staring into the void, as if lost in a dream. Suddenly rousing himself he exclaims "Tosca, you make me forget God!"; then ("con entusiasmo religioso") he thunders "Te aeternum Patrem omnis terra veneratur!" with the rest and the best of them; and after three fortissimo reiterations of No. 1 in the orchestra the curtain falls.

On the whole this first act, dramatically speaking, is a poor piece of work. Things happen in it not because they develop naturally out of what has gone before but simply because they have to be inserted at just that point and handled in just that way purely for the enlightenment of the audience. The episode of Tosca's return to the church is a case in point. That return may be vital in the opera—the reader will remember that it does not occur in the play—but while it is understandable that the sight of the fan shall kindle her jealousy it is imposing too great a strain on our credulity to ask us to believe that she *must* confide to the Chief of Police straight away that she had come back to tell her lover that she would be unable to meet him that night as they had arranged. And Scarpia, with his sudden transitions from the cruel to the erotic and then to the religious, his often ludicrous asides, and his sudden reminder to himself at the end that Tosca has "made him forget God"—a feeble attempt to show him as the bigot and satyr in one that Cavaradossi had described to Angelotti—is the merest villain of melodrama. It may be replied that Sardou's play is melodrama in every fibre of its being. That is true; but it happens to be such consummate melodrama, so thoroughly competent at playing the game according to the rules of the game, that while we are watching it we put our critical faculty in our pocket, having no use for it; as indeed we shall do later in the case of Puccini, whose second and third acts are melodrama of the most unblushing kind, but, in virtue of the musical expression, melodrama *in excelsis*.

Sardou's cunningly constructed second act was not drawn upon by the librettists until near the end of it. It shows us a Scarpia not in the smallest degree interested amorously in Tosca but himself in danger of his life, and only gradually seeing a way out of his difficulties. In the final scene of Sardou's first act Tosca had not been brought on the scene at all, as she is in the opera. Scarpia had learned from the terrified Eusèbe that the name of the painter who had been working in the church before the escape of Angelotti was Cavaradossi. "Ah!" he ejaculated, "we are getting warm! The Chevalier Cavaradossi! A Liberal, like his father." Next it appeared that the painter had often had a visitor—Tosca; and judging from the flowers by the figure of the Madonna, Eusèbe had said, she was here today while he was absent. Scarpia has no reason to associate her in any way with the Angelotti affair: "she is faithful to the Church and the King; all the same we will keep an eye on her," since her name has been mentioned. Nothing more can be done for the present, he tells his minion Colometti, the fugitive having escaped him by a few moments; so they will join in the general thanks to the God of Armies who has given them victory over the French, and pray to the Madonna "to bless our further efforts in our war on impiety." With that the first act closes abruptly. The spoken play, of course, could not give us, as the composer can, an elaborate thanksgiving service with music; moreover, mass effects of that kind had no part in Sardou's dramatic technique. All we hear at this point in the play, according to the stage directions, is a faint suggestion of prayers and chanting in the distance. There is no one at all by the Angelotti chapel in the final moments except Scarpia, his men, and Eusèbe. It is a pity, in some ways, that the musician in Puccini thought it necessary to end the first act of the opera as he did; one feels, indeed, that by a general curtailment of his lyrical expansions he could have indulged himself in the luxury of four acts instead of three and made a better drama of his opera.

Let us now see what happens in the second and third acts of Sardou's play.

The scene of the second is the great salon in the Farnese Palace, later in the same day. The room is filled with a great crowd of talkers and card players. Among them is the Marquis Attavanti, who is throughout a fatuous figure. Also present is one Trivulce, the sigisbeo of the Marquise—the male companion permitted by Italian custom to a married lady of quality, who might or might not be her lover in the ordinary sense of the term, the beau monde not troubling itself about a detail of that kind so long as a convention that suited all the parties to the triangle was discreetly observed.

The subjects of the conversation of a group in the foreground are the two great events of that afternoon, the reported defeat of the French and the escape of the republican Angelotti. The Marquise Attavanti, it appears, is not present at the fête, or even in Rome; she has gone to Frascati. Scarpia enters, preoccupied with his own grave problem, for as yet he has not succeeded in discovering Angelotti's latest hiding-place; Cavaradossi's town house has been surrounded and the servants questioned, but the painter has not put in an appearance there. The fox no doubt has several holes, Scarpia remarks to Schiarrone; what is certain is that Cavaradossi and Angelotti are together somewhere. Tosca, the police agents have discovered, went to her own house after taking part in the rehearsal for the concert, supped alone, and is now in the Farnese palace. Scarpia does not know what to make of it all. Is Tosca an accomplice? What if Cavaradossi has been astute enough to take into his confidence a woman whom everyone knows to be of the royalist and clerical party?

21

Tosca enters, and in a brief conversation with Scarpia shows the better side of her nature: her womanly sympathies are with this prisoner who, she has heard, has escaped a horrible death, and Scarpia cannot decide whether all this is the calculated bravado of an accomplice or real ignorance. The Queen of Naples enters, and goes straight to the point with the fretted Scarpia. "Be careful lest this affair should turn out fatally for you," she warns him. "You have many enemies; unpleasant rumours circulate with regard to you; people are pointing out that this Angelotti, after being in prison for a whole year, escapes a mere week after your arrival in Rome." The criminal's sister, the Queen insinuates, is rich and beautiful. "You had better find Angelotti, tonight if possible, for if not I shall have difficulty in curbing the King's ill humour." With that she leaves Scarpia to his gloomy reflections, which are not brightened by the cries of "Death to Angelotti! Death to Scarpia!" that float up from the excited crowd in the piazza. He turns the situation over in his worried mind. If Angelotti escapes, he himself is ruined; the person he fears most is not the Queen but Lady Hamilton,[1] who will not spare him if Angelotti is not recaptured and hanged. What is he to do? Arrest Cavaradossi when he turns up at his villa? But by that time Angelotti will be far away: Scarpia must somehow get hold of both men before the city gates close that night. Is the key to the affair, he wonders again, in the hands of this singer Floria Tosca? Does she really know nothing, or is she only pretending not to know? Against the other woman, the Attavanti, he certainly has a weapon of a sort—her fan. An idea strikes him: the Attavanti being out of his reach, why not use that weapon against Tosca? Here is a notoriously amorous, explosive, jealous woman upon whom, perhaps, he can work for his own ends; "a jealous woman is more useful than any police agent." Either she knows all and he will get it out of her, or she knows nothing, in which case she will want to find out for herself the truth about the fan—and so find out for him. Now at last, he thinks, he sees his way clear: "Iago achieved his ends by means of a handkerchief";[2] he will do likewise with a fan. That fan, it is becoming ever clearer, is the tiny point upon which the whole fateful action has been poised from the first.

He engages Tosca in further conversation and gradually entangles the unsuspecting woman in his coils. He begins by sounding her on the subject of Cavaradossi. Why did she take him for her lover, this man Roman by birth but French in his opinions, this Voltairean, this revolutionary? Her reasons, which she deems sufficient, are that she loves him and he is devoted to her. Is she sure of that? he asks, casually producing the fan which, he tells her, he had found in Sant' Andrea just after the Chevalier had

---

[1] The reader will remember that, as Angelotti had informed Cavaradossi in the first act, this Baron Scarpia had just been sent to Rome, as chief of the police, by the court of Naples.

[2] As we have seen, Puccini's librettists transferred this line to Scarpia's erotic monologue in the church.

left the church—about the hour of compline. This little sentence is the explosive spark. "He told me he would remain there until night!" she ejaculates.[1] Scarpia assures her (falsely, as we know) that he had found the fan on the painter's stool while examining the picture, and, innocently assuming it to be Tosca's, had brought it away to return it to her. She denies that it is hers, examines it, and, recognising the Attavanti crest, at once succumbs to the suspicious jealousy that constitutes one half of her weather-cock personality. Everything, she says, is crystal-clear now to her: the Marquise must have been concealed there when she arrived in the church, which explains why Cavaradossi had been so slow in opening the door to her and why he was so embarrassed and so anxious to get rid of her. She summons the Marquis Attavanti to identify the fan as that of his wife, which he, or rather the useful Trivulce, at once does. She becomes a raging fury, especially when she learns that the Marquise has gone to Frascati, where Cavaradossi has no doubt joined her by now. She swears she will go there and trap him, and crazily refuses to sing at the concert, Queen or no Queen, in spite of Scarpia's threat to arrest her if she disobeys the royal command. If she sings—a mere matter of a quarter of an hour, he reminds her—he promises he will assist her to find the guilty pair.

22

The Paisiello cantata is about to begin, Tosca raging madly all the time, and the company excusing her on the score of an attack of singer's nerves, when a courier enters and hands a message to the Queen from General Melas. Confident that it contains the news of another victory she reads it out to the company: but what Melas has to announce is the destruction of his army by Bonaparte at Marengo.[2] Tosca's only reaction is a glad cry that

[1] The reader will see at once how vastly superior Sardou's handling of this matter is to Puccini's. It is perfectly natural that in the spoken play Tosca should cry "He told me he would remain there until night" *after being told by Scarpia* that he had found the fan in the church after Cavaradossi had left; whereas it is mere theatrical mechanics for the opera Tosca to inform the Chief of Police that she had come back just to tell her lover that they could not meet that evening.

[2] The course of Sardou's action is quite in conformity with the historical facts and dates. Early on the morning of the 14th June the Austrians, under

now she need not sing in the victory cantata but can go straight
to her vengeance: she rushes out, followed by Scarpia and his
sleuths, Attavanti, much to his surprise, being ordered to go with
them. That is the end of the second act.

Sardou's third act takes place at Cavaradossi's villa in the
country, where Mario and Angelotti have at last arrived after a
perilous crossing of Rome. The house, built by one of his ancestors, had passed later into the possession of an Englishman,
from whom Mario now rents it, using it only for his secret meetings with Tosca. As no one in Rome has any reason to associate him
with the place the police are not likely to look for them there;
and when they further consider that no one has any cause to
link his name with that of the fugitive from Sant' Angelo it is
evident, he says, that they are perfectly safe. But if they should
after all be traced, he tells Angelotti, they still have a trump card
to play. The layout of the garden is as it had been when the
house was first erected on the site in the days of ancient Rome.
Someone, for safety's sake in the faraway days of barbarism, had
constructed a sort of well from the shaft of which, twenty feet
down, a small opening concealed by vegetation led to a chamber
of some size. This had served as a hiding place for a former
Cavaradossi who had got on the wrong side of the Medici
through a trifling matter of an assassination: Mario had stored
the chamber with all that would be required for his own retreat
in case he ever got into trouble with the Roman authorities, and
now it will serve to conceal Angelotti until it is safe for
him to leave Rome, not by the gates but by swimming the
adjacent Tiber. (We have learned already, by the way, from
the conversation between the two men in the first act, that

General Melas, had attacked the French at Marengo, and, by virtue of
superiority of artillery fire, had forced them to retire. Confident that his
victory was final, Melas went back to his headquarters at Alessandria, leaving
General Zach in command. The latter, instead of pursuing the French ener-
getically, as he had been ordered to do, paused to consolidate his forces.
Napoleon, who had arrived on the field just before a retreat became necessary, formed a new line of battle and advanced on and defeated the Austrians with heavy loss. The next morning Melas asked for an armistice. We
may therefore suppose his first false report of the annihilation of the French
to have reached Rome, as in Sardou, on the 16th or early 17th, and the
counter-news of Napoleon's victory on the evening of the latter date.

Angelotti is provided with poison if the worst should come to the worst.)

While they talk, someone is heard approaching; it can be no one but Tosca, for she alone, besides Cavaradossi, has a key to the garden. She enters, and there follows a long scene between her and Mario in which he eventually succeeds in ridding her of her suspicions with regard to the Marchesa Attavanti, clears up the mystery of the fan, and lets her into the secret of Angelotti's escape. With one of her quick changes of mood she admires him for the nobility of his conduct, humbly begs his forgiveness, and gives him the welcome news of Bonaparte's victory. She wishes to remain with him, but he persuades her to return to the city, where he will join her on the morrow, after Angelotti has made his escape. He is rather disquieted by the thought that Scarpia's men have in all probability followed her; but even if they come now, he says, they will not discover Angelotti's hide-out. He presumes she had returned to the church after he had left and thus found the fan; when he learns that it was not so, but that Scarpia had discovered it and given it to her, they both realise the danger he is in now; it was to trap Cavaradossi, and through him Angelotti, that Scarpia had played upon Tosca's jealousy.

Cavaradossi's old servant runs in with the news that police agents are at the garden gate, and Mario calls out to Angelotti that they have been tracked down. Angelotti, in his panic, is making for some ruins in the fields; but Cavaradossi tells him it is too late for that, and sends him to the well. Scarpia, Attavanti and the police agents enter. Cavaradossi calmly assures Scarpia that Tosca is there simply because she had come to satisfy her suspicions with regard to his fidelity; this is a purely domestic affair with which the State has nothing to do. Scarpia, however, informs him coldly that he is present in the exercise of his moral duty to the community as head of the police; the Marquis Attavanti would like to know how his wife comes to be in Cavaradossi's house at this hour. Mario denies that she is there, and Tosca corroborates him. Scarpia throws off the mask; he sends Attavanti back to his Rome house, where, he says, he will no doubt find his wife, she having been too prudent to accompany her criminal brother here; and he is to inform the King that it is only a matter of minutes now before Angelotti is caught.

Having made sure that the house is surrounded, Scarpia has Mario removed to another room, where he is put to the torture, with the agonised Tosca aware of every turn of the screw, as in the second act of the opera. Bit by bit Scarpia wears Tosca down emotionally until she admits that Angelotti was there when she arrived; and in the end, to save her lover from further suffering, and in spite of his exhortations to her to stand firm, she discloses that the fugitive is in the well in the garden—again as in the opera. The exhausted Mario is brought in: he faintly asks for an assurance from her that neither of them has said anything; all she can do is to sob out an evasive "No! No! You have said nothing! Nothing!" Just then one of the agents returns with the news that Angelotti has been found in the well—but dead by poison. Mario curses Tosca for having betrayed him, heedless of her cry that she had done so to save him. As the curtain falls, Scarpia orders Cavaradossi to be taken away—"for the gallows." "And the woman?" asks Schiarrone. "The woman too!" is the reply.

23

It would have been impossible, of course, for Puccini's librettists to reproduce all the detail of Sardou's second and third acts. Music has always to work on broader and simpler lines than spoken drama, condensing and simplifying an action in order to secure room for its own more elaborate emotional expression. The librettists, to do them justice, have done some ingenious things in the way of condensation, transposing a telling dramatic point from one scene to another, and so on; and as we know that Sardou himself collaborated with Illica and Giacosa we may assume that some at any rate of these ingenious transpositions originated in the agile brain of that master craftsman of the theatre. But when all is said we are still left with the feeling that a better job might have been made of the adaptation of the play to operatic ends. We may smile as patronisingly as we like at Sardou today, but the fact remains that what he did not know about dramatic construction is not worth knowing. He foresees and provides for everything and forgets nothing: there is a reason for everything; piece fits perfectly into piece, and every one of them is indispensable. Throw all or most of this cunning dovetailing of details to the winds for a purpose other than his, and what remains of the coherence of the play?

One's grievance against Puccini and his collaborators is that they have retained enough of the original to furnish forth a few particularly striking episodes, but not preserved enough to make these always plausible or endow them with the effect they have in the play. The fan motif has been bungled. In Sardou the significance of it only slowly dawns on Scarpia; at first, at the end of the first act, it means nothing more to him than that it tallies with Trebelli's story of the plan for escape in female attire. It is only in the second act that he manages slowly to piece the facts and the broad inferences from them together. The Attavanti's complicity in the affair is proved by her fan, but she is safe in Frascati; Cavaradossi's is suggested by his flight from the church at the same time as Angelotti's, and proved by the discovery of the empty basket of provisions. To find one of the men will be to find the other. But it will have to be done before the city gates open again, otherwise Angelotti will have slipped away—which means disgrace and ruin for Scarpia—and there will remain no valid evidence against Cavaradossi. Then comes the illuminating idea. He has only been a week in Rome, but he knows—it is the business of the Chief of Police in times like these to know everything!—that Mario Cavaradossi's antecedents and behaviour have made him politically suspect, and that his mistress Tosca is notoriously a woman given to hysterical accesses of jealousy. What if the key to unlock the mystery can be found in this jealousy of hers? By playing on that, perhaps he can send her away from the palace in furious search of the elusive Cavaradossi—and have her followed. And so the first wheel of the tragic dénouement begins slowly to revolve.

How is all this handled in the opera? Very lamely. The librettists' hands were to some extent tied: the second act would obviously have to be devoted mainly to the torture scene and the murder of Scarpia, and the third act to Cavaradossi's last moments, before which, he being an operatic hero, and a tenor at that, he would necessarily have a good deal of singing to do, including an affecting farewell to Tosca. So the only place in the opera for confronting Tosca with the fan was the end of the first act; and for this purpose the librettists had to resort to the lame device of Tosca returning to the church the moment after the fan had been discovered in the chapel. She had gone away to rehearse for the evening performance in the theatre; and the only reason given us for her return now is her odd description of herself—to Scarpia —as "the prisoner of the royal rejoicings." She stalks in, calling impatiently "Mario! Mario!" The Sacristan comes forward: "You mean the painter Cavaradossi?" he asks. "Who knows where he is? Vanished, spirited away by a magician"; whereupon the old man decamps and we see no more of him for a while. Tosca has time only to say "Deceived? No, no! he could not betray me!" before Scarpia, who has been hiding behind the Madonna column, comes forward and insinuates himself into her company. Was ever a vital moment in any realistic opera so badly, so unconvincingly handled?

Without the political background of the action, again, being made clearer than it is in the opera, much of what happens, and why, is unintelligible to the spectator. In the following analysis of the remainder of the work attention will be drawn to the rather helpless efforts of the librettists to remind themselves and the audience now and then that there *is* such a background. It is a fair assumption, indeed, that they were only too painfully conscious that something would have to be done in connection with the matter. For some time, we are authoritatively told, they clung to the idea of making Cavaradossi's farewell to the world "an excessively tedious and pedantic 'Latin Hymn,' embracing, amongst a number of other topics, the whole range of politics and the arts." Puccini was both musically and dramatically right in rejecting this ending: it would have had a chilling effect on the audience to have Mario spend his last few minutes in this world spouting the political theories of 1800 instead of bidding a poignant farewell to his Tosca. But the mere fact that Illica and Giacosa wanted to do this dreadful thing at just that point seems to be proof enough that it was a last desperate attempt on their part to do what they had striven in vain to do until then—to give the fundamentally political motivation of the drama a final glimmer of a chance to assert itself.

24

Puccini's second act is set in Scarpia's apartment on the first floor of the Palazzo Farnese. On the left a large window looks out on to the courtyard. It is now night.

When the curtain rises we see Scarpia seated at a table laid for supper near the window, brooding on his problems and feverishly awaiting the return of Spoletta with his report:

No. 16

Now and then he pauses in his eating and looks at his watch. Tosca is a good hawk, he muses: surely by this time his sleuths have the two men in their clutches? Tomorrow's dawn will see them both hanging from a halter; and at that comforting prospect the general quietude of the music is shattered for a moment by an upsurge of his motive (No. 1) in the orchestra.

Sciarrone (Spoletta's subordinate) enters with the news that Tosca has arrived at the palace. At a sign from Scarpia he throws the great window open, and from a room below, in which the Queen is giving a grand fête in honour of Melas, there float upwards the soft strains of a gracious gavotte:

No. 17

Evidently the diva is not in the salon yet, says Scarpia to himself, or the cantata would have begun: then, to Sciarrone, "Wait for Tosca's arrival there, and tell her I shall expect her here when the cantata is finished; or, better still," he adds, going to a writing-desk and scribbling a few lines, "give her this note."

He resumes his brooding: "she will come," he says to himself after Sciarrone has gone, "for love of her Mario—and will give

herself to my pleasure, for the deeper the love the greater the
misery"; and when once again No. 1 rears itself in the orchestra
it takes on a fresh psychological significance by appearing in new
colours, beginning *mf* and tapering off into a sinister *ppp*. Then,
to a broad melody, he surrenders himself in imagination to the
blend of ferocity and erõticism that is characteristic of him: "there
is more savour to a conquest by violence than to the most honeyed
consent." No insipid wooings by moonlight for him, no songs to
the guitar, no horoscope of flowers, no casting of sheep's eyes,
no turtle-dove cooings. He is all brutal desire: "God has created
every variety of beauty as of wine, and I would drain the divine
work to the last drop."

Spoletta comes in, and Scarpia seats himself at the table again
to interrogate him. The servile agent is trembling with fear: he
and his men had followed Tosca, he says, to a rural villa hidden
in a thicket. She had entered, but very soon came out again—
alone. Then he had scaled the garden wall and searched the house
from top to bottom—but found no Angelotti. Scarpia rises in a
fury, curses him, and threatens him with the gallows. The terrified
Spoletta stammers out the remainder of his story: he had come
upon Cavaradossi, whose ironical manner with him was proof
enough that he knew where the fugitive was hiding; so he arrested him, and now has him in the antechamber. "That's not
so bad!" says Scarpia, and the orchestra gives out a sombre theme
that will henceforth be associated with the sufferings of Mario
under torture:

No. 18

At that moment the choral cantata in honour of the Austrian
victory is heard through the open window, and Scarpia realises
that Tosca is there at last. The suave strains of the cantata:

No. 19

contrast dramatically throughout with the increasing tension and ever-darkening colour of the stage action that accompanies it, in which No. 18 plays a cumulative part.[1]

25

An idea strikes Scarpia. Seating himself at the supper table again he orders Spoletta to bring in Cavaradossi, Roberti ("the executor of justice"), the Judge of the Fisc, Sciarrone and a scribe. Mario faces him boldly, demanding to be told why he has been brought there. Scarpia replies with elaborate courtesy, begging him, to the accompaniment of the fateful No. 18, to be seated in a chair facing the table. Mario has hardly done so when Tosca's voice is heard soaring above the chorus: "Her voice!" he ejaculates with profound emotion. Scarpia begins his interrogation quietly, smoothly. The Cavaliere no doubt knows that a prisoner escaped today from Sant' Angelo. "I did not know that," says Cavaradossi. "Yet it is said that you met him in the church of Sant' Andrea, provided him with food and wine, and took him to your villa in the country." Cavaradossi denies all knowledge of the affair and demands proofs: "your police searched the place and found nobody." Scarpia continues with the utmost suavity of tone and manner. "That merely proves how well he was concealed." Mario, too sure of himself, only laughs at him.

Scarpia rises in anger. "This is a matter rather for tears!" he says: "have a care!" The cantata, which has been steadily increasing in volume as it rises to its climax, gets on his nerves, and he closes the great window violently. Turning to Cavaradossi he thunders, "Where is Angelotti? Do you deny that you gave him food, clothes, and shelter in your villa, and that he is hiding there now?" Then, changing his tone to one of paternal solicitude, he says, "Come, Cavaliere, reflect. Your obstinacy is unwise; a confession will save you much suffering"; and a dolorous phrase in the orchestra:

No. 20

---

[1] At one time Puccini thought of using some actual Paisiello music for the "cantata," but he wisely abandoned the idea.

gives a horrible emphasis to his warning. "For the last time, where is Angelotti?" Mario's replies to all his questions are simply "I deny," "I do not know."

Suddenly Tosca enters breathlessly, to a reminiscence of one of the fragments of melody associated with her; she has come, of course, in response to Scarpia's note. Surprised to find Cavaradossi there, she runs to him and embraces him. "Say nothing of what you saw at the villa, or you will be my death," he warns her *sotto voce*. She makes a sign of comprehension. To a thunderous enunciation of No. 18, which has been heard at intervals all through the scene, Scarpia warns Cavaradossi that the Judge is awaiting his confession, and Sciarrone, in response to a gesture from him, opens a door at the back that leads to the torture chamber. "Just the customary procedure at first," says Scarpia blandly to Roberti; "then as I shall direct." Roberti, the Judge and Sciarrone go into the inner room, taking Mario with them; Tosca remains behind, facing Scarpia, while Spoletta takes up a watchful position by the door.

26

Everything is now set for the tremendous scene in which Puccini rises to his greatest height as a master of the musical macabre. After some agonised phrases in the orchestra Scarpia addresses Tosca in the smoothest tones:

No. 21

Ed   or fra noi par-liam da buo-ni a—mi-ci

"And now let us have a little talk like good friends. Do not look so frightened. What about the fan?" he asks, leaning familiarly over the sofa on which Tosca is seated. "Mere foolish jealousy on my part," she replies with simulated indifference. "The Attavanti was not at the villa, then?" "No, he was there alone." "Alone? are you sure of that?" "Alone," she insists angrily. Scarpia turns towards the door and calls out to Sciarrone, "What does the Cavaliere say?" "He denies," says Sciarrone, appearing for a moment on the threshold. "Insist, then," says Scarpia; and Sciarrone goes back and closes the door. Tosca now tries irony: "Then to please you one must lie?" To a new theme:

No. 22

the effect of which Puccini intensifies as usual by repetition, Scarpia slowly, inexorably, breaks down her poor defences. No, he replies, but the truth might shorten a very painful hour; the law must be vindicated, justice must be done. He becomes all tigerish ferocity again as he tells her, to the accompaniment of No. 22, the sinister effect of which is now increased by the writhing turns, like a serpent's coils, given to the bass line:

No. 23

that her lover lies bound hand and foot, with an iron circlet pressing on his temples, from which blood gushes afresh at every denial on his part. Listening in nervous horror during a momentary silence in the room she hears a groan from the torture chamber. To her wild appeal for pity Scarpia replies that it rests with her to save her lover. Approaching the door he orders Sciarrone to unbind Cavaradossi. Tosca calls out Mario's name: he answers with a faint, dolorous "Tosca!": he assures her that the torture has ceased and bids her have courage and be silent.

The ever-resourceful Puccini finds music that surpasses in horror and frenzy all that has gone before as Scarpia approaches Tosca, and, disregarding her cries of "Monster! you are killing him!", first of all compliments her ironically on being more superbly tragic now than she ever has been on the stage, then suddenly reverts to the satyr and the beast of prey. He orders the door to be opened a little so that she may hear Cavaradossi's groans better as the torture is renewed. The climax comes with another reiteration of No. 23 as Scarpia asks her again and again, "Where is Angelotti? Speak! . . . Where is Angelotti?"

With the last refinement of cruelty he allows her a glance into the inner room. This comes near breaking down what remains of her power of resistance. "I can bear no more!" she moans, to a persistent sobbing figure in the orchestra:

No. 24

Bass: D

and she begs Mario's permission to disclose the truth. In a faint voice he forbids her to speak: "What can you say? What do you know?" This exasperates Scarpia, who calls out angrily "Silence him!" Tosca falls prostrate on the sofa: Spoletta, in an attitude of prayer, murmurs some lines from the *Dies irae*. Tosca appeals for the last time to Scarpia, who stands before her silent and impassive: "it is I whom you are torturing, my soul that you are torturing." He sees that she is weakening and that the decisive moment has come: without saying another word he goes to the door and gives a sign for the torture to be resumed. A deathly quasi-silence in the orchestra, followed by one of Puccini's usual significant pauses, is broken by a harsh reminder of No. 1, at the end of which Tosca murmurs brokenly, "In the well in the garden."

His end gained at last, Scarpia orders the torture to cease. "He has fainted," says Sciarrone, appearing in the doorway. "I must see him," Tosca insists, and at a word of command from Scarpia the victim is brought in, to dolorous accompanying figures in the orchestra. The fainting man is laid by the police agents on the sofa: Tosca runs to him, but recoils and covers her eyes with her hands as she sees the blood on his temples. Then, ashamed of her weakness, she covers his face with tears and kisses, while the orchestra gives out a poignant reminiscence of a phrase from their duet in the first act, to which Cavaradossi had then sung the words "What eyes in the world can compare with yours, eyes tender with love?"

The myrmidons of justice leave the stage, only Spoletta and the police agents remaining behind at a sign from Scarpia. Cavaradossi and Tosca murmur a few tender words to each other: then he asks her faintly, "Did I speak?" "No," she assures him. "Truly?" Once more she replies "No." But as No. 1 projects itself in the orchestra again Scarpia says loudly, "In the well in the garden. Away, Spoletta!" Hearing this, Mario turns on Tosca and curses her for having betrayed him.

Then for the first time in this act there comes a piece of poor dramatic construction.

28

We have seen that in Sardou the news of Bonaparte's victory at Marengo is brought to the company—which includes Tosca and Scarpia—assembled in the Palazzo Farnese to celebrate the supposed triumph of Melas. The incident serves there a double purpose, to bring the party and the act to a quick and telling dramatic close, and to make it unnecessary now for the impatient Tosca to remain in the palace to sing in the cantata; she is free to go away at once to surprise Mario, as she hopes, with the Marquise, and Scarpia can set Spoletta on her traces. In the opera the battle of Marengo has no bearing whatever on the dramatic action. Why then is it introduced into the opera at the point at which we have now arrived?

For no other *dramatic* reason—the musical reason will appear later—than that the librettists, uneasily aware of the importance of the political background of Sardou's play, but having had no opportunity as yet to make us acquainted with it, suddenly decided to create, by hook or by crook, an opportunity here. The composer had rightly rejected their desperate plan to make Cavaradossi spout political and other theories in the tense final scene of the last act. The opportunities in the first act for sketching in the background against which Angelotti and Cavaradossi play their parts had been sacrificed to Puccini's determination to devote the major part of his space in that act to the lyrical endearments of Tosca and Mario and the imposing grand opera finale. The close construction of his second act as a whole provided no moment for a political manifesto on Cavaradossi's part, so one had to be made; and in the nature of the case it could not possibly be made anywhere but here.

The episode that now follows, dramatically considered, will not bear critical examination. Not the slightest hint has been given us previously of any passionate interest taken by Cavaradossi in the Franco-Italian events of the day; nor, indeed, is any light thrown for us on the activities that had brought Angelotti to Sant' Angelo, apart from that meaningless recognition of him by Cavaradossi as "the Consul of the destroyed Roman Republic." The bringing of the news of Marengo, at the point in the opera which we have now reached, has not the smallest bearing on either the past, the present or the future of the action. And how is the news brought? Cavaradossi has just cursed Tosca, and the latter has replied with an appealing "Mario!", when Sciarrone runs in out of breath, stammering "Your Excellency, such news!" Scarpia is naturally surprised at the intrusion of his hireling. "A despatch announcing a defeat," says Sciarrone, "at Marengo. . . . Bonaparte is victor. . . . Melas is retreating." Can we imagine this cowed hound of a police agent, who, like Spoletta, is always in mortal fear of his Chief, presuming to break in in this fashion on a colloquy between Scarpia, Cavaradossi and Tosca?

As to the dramatic incongruity of the exhausted Mario suddenly finding strength to deliver a long tirade in praise of the French victory and liberty we need say little. After all, operatic tenors in general, and Italian opera tenors in particular, often manage to display a remarkable vigour of lung and larynx even when at the point of death; and we must bear in mind that this is the only opportunity the tenor of *Tosca* has had during the whole long second act to impress it on us that he *is* the tenor. So far he has had only an acting part, making an interjection here and there in merely conversational tones. The hero cannot be expected to leave the stage without giving us at least one taste of his vocal quality, to which end the composer now kindly gives him a liberal allowance of high A flats. So Puccini bows the knee to operatic convention; and after all we forgive him, if not dramatically at any rate musically, for Mario's outburst is of itself excellent, electrifying stuff.

29

"Cavaradossi," say the stage directions, "who has listened to Sciarrone with increasing eagerness, finds, in his enthusiasm, the strength to confront Scarpia threateningly," while the orchestra gives out—*ff, tutta forza*—our example No. 6. "Vittoria! Vittoria!" he cries, soaring at once to the high A flat: "The avenging dawn has come that will make the impious, the inhuman tremble":

No. 25

"Liberty raises its head once more; the tyrants go down in ruin! I rejoice in the martyrdom I have suffered; your heart quakes within you, Scarpia, hangman!" Tosca implores him distractedly to be silent. Scarpia merely laughs sarcastically; "Bluster, howl as you please," he says to Cavaradossi; "you are only showing me the depths of your criminal soul. Your last hour is nigh! The scaffold awaits you!"

Exasperated at last by Mario's outcry Scarpia orders the agents to remove him; they drag him off, in spite of Tosca's frenzied appeals. She would go with him, but Scarpia restrains her. He seats himself at the table again, composed and smiling, resumes his interrupted supper, and politely invites her to join him in a glass of Spanish wine, suggesting that perhaps between them they may after all find some means of saving Cavaradossi. Taking a seat at the table, leaning her elbows on it with her face cupped in her hands, looking at him with the profoundest disdain, she goes straight to the point. "How much?" she asks him: "your price?" He smiles imperturbably to the accompaniment of a suggestion of No. 6: "I know they call me venal," he remarks, "but I do not sell myself to beautiful women for money"; and he repeats the latter part of the sentence meaningly. He has long waited for this moment, he continues, has long been consumed by love for the great singer:

No. 26

but more than ever does he desire her now that he has seen her weep; her tears were lava to his passion, and the look of hatred she had darted on him had added an agreeable ferocity to his appetite. He rises and approaches her with outstretched arms. She flies from him, first taking refuge behind the sofa, then running to the window. The idea occurring to her to go to the Queen for protection she makes for the door. Divining her intention he stands aside, knowing that he still holds the trump card. "You are free to go if you wish," he remarks ironically, "but your hopes would end in nothing: the Queen's grace would be bestowed only on a corpse." She collapses on the sofa again, directing on him a look of supreme hatred and disgust. "How you hate me!" he remarks complacently. "This is how I would have you—convulsions of rage, convulsions of love."

30

The psychological argument is degenerating into a physical pursuit round the sofa, chairs and table when distant drum beats, coming ever nearer, are heard. Scarpia explains them to her; it is the escort of some condemned men who are going to their doom. Tosca recoils from the window in horror as he tells her that down there a scaffold is being erected: her Mario, thanks to her, has only one hour to live. The tattoo dies away again in the distance.

Tosca, exhausted with grief and terror, sinks on to the sofa; and while Scarpia, leaning against the table and pouring himself a glass of wine, keeps his cool cynical gaze fixed on her, she breaks out into a lament over her shattered life. For art and love she had lived, she says:

No. 27

$\textit{p}$ Vis-si d'ar-te, vis-si d'a-mo-re, non fe-ci mai ma-le ad a-ni-ma vi-va!

without doing harm to a single soul; the griefs of others she had assuaged. Always, she continues, to the accompaniment of the melody of No. 9, her prayers had ascended to the saints, always she had decked the altar with flowers. She has given her jewels for the mantle of the Madonna, her song had soared to Heaven. Why then does God desert her in her hour of misery?

Scarpia's only reply is a pitiless "Decide!" She falls on her knees before him, and to the accompaniment of a long orchestral lament humbly begs for pity. "You are too beautiful, Tosca," he tells her, with No. 6 making another appearance in the orchestra, "too loving. I yield"—that is to say, he will grant Cavaradossi his life: "a poor price for you to pay, but for me, a life." She repulses him with scorn. There is a knock at the door, and in response to Scarpia's cry of "Who is there?" Spoletta enters with the news that Angelotti had taken poison when they found him. "Ah well!" says Scarpia, "string him up on the gallows dead! [1] As for the other prisoner, wait a moment." He turns to Tosca with a laconic "Well?" There is another of those expressive Puccinian silences: then she moans "Yes!" and, bursting into tears, buries her head in the cushions of the sofa. "But I must have him set free this instant!" she interjects as Scarpia is about to give his instructions to Spoletta.

He explains to her, *sotto voce*, that dissimulation will be necessary: the pardon must be kept secret; it must be believed by everyone that Cavaradossi is dead. "This trusty man"—indicating Spoletta—"will see to it." To prove his good faith he will give the order in her presence. "Spoletta," he says, while the orchestra plays in sinister fashion on No. 1, "I have changed my mind: the prisoner is to be *shot*, like Palmieri: listen carefully—a fictitious execution, as in the case of Palmieri. You understand?" Spoletta has already conveyed by a glance that he has divined his Chief's sinister intention; now he gives his verbal assurance. Tosca's request that she shall be the one to tell Cavaradossi of the plan is granted. "At four in the morning," says Scarpia as he dismisses Spoletta, who goes out with a meaningful "Like Palmieri!"

[1] For the reason for this we have to go back to Sardou. The Queen, it will be recalled, had threatened Scarpia with the King's displeasure if he were cheated of the satisfaction of having Angelotti recaptured and hanged; the Roman mob too had been clamouring for the Chief of Police's head. So in Sardou's fourth act, Scarpia, for his reputation and his safety's sake, orders Spoletta to conceal the fact that Angelotti had tricked him by taking poison, and to hang the dead man on the scaffold: "leave the body there, in the view of all, until the hour of High Mass."

Scarpia now turns, full of passion, to Tosca: "I have kept my promise," he tells her. "Not yet," she replies; "I want a safe-conduct out of the Roman States for myself and him." The dramatic atmosphere now darkens, in a way that is possible only to music among the arts, by the whispering in the orchestra of a new motive that warns us to look beyond Scarpia's smooth perfidy to the tragic end of the drama:

No. 28

The poignant sequel to this:

No. 29

becomes of particular importance later. It is to repetitions of this motif that Scarpia seats himself at the desk and writes out a safe-conduct—"*via* Civita Vecchia,"[1] as she insists. While he is thus engaged she goes to the supper table and with a trembling hand takes up a glass of wine. But as she does so her glance happens to fall on a sharp-pointed knife; and a sudden startling surge in the orchestra suggests that a plan has occurred to her. Carefully concealing the knife behind her as she leans against the table, she waits until Scarpia, having signed and sealed the safe-conduct, brings it to her with arms outstretched to embrace her. He has barely time to ejaculate "Tosca, mine at last!" before she strikes the knife into his heart: "This is Tosca's kiss," she tells him. Writhing in agony he calls raucously, incoherently, for help. (The orchestral turmoil here is curiously suggestive of the furious outburst that follows the slow movement of the Ninth Symphony.) She gloats over his death agonies: "Your blood chokes you? You

[1] Where the Roman writ does not run.

have tortured me enough: now you die, killed by a woman! Die damned! Die! Die! Die!"

The sombre No. 28 coils and uncoils itself still in the orchestra as she washes her right hand in water from a carafe, adjusts her hair before a mirror on the wall, runs to the desk and searches feverishly for the safe-conduct, only to discover in the end that it is still in Scarpia's hand. She nerves herself to loosen the grip of the dead fingers on it, and as she gazes down on the body she ejaculates, on a note in the lowest part of her voice, "And this was the man before whom trembled all Rome!"; then she takes two candles from a bracket, lights them from the candelabra on the supper table, and extinguishes the latter. While the Scarpia motive (No. 1) repeats itself three times in ghostly orchestral tones that harmonise with the darkened atmosphere of the room she lays a candle on either side of the head of the corpse: then, catching sight of a crucifix hanging on the wall, she takes it down, kneels by the dead man, and slowly drops it on his breast—a last supremely ironic tribute to the loathsome piety of the satyr: then she stealthily steals out, closing the door noiselessly behind her. So ends the most macabre, and the most impressively macabre, scene in all opera.

32

Between the terrific tension of the second act and the even greater tension of the final stage of the drama the spectator's nerves would obviously need a little rest; and this Puccini supplied in full measure in the opening scene of the third act. Before the curtain rises, however, there is a short orchestral introduction —sixteen bars only—the tragic significance of which will not be manifest until later: the horn quartet gives out fortissimo, in unison, a melody which Cavaradossi and Tosca will sing later in the last few delusive moments of their life together on earth.

The curtain opens on a parapet in the castle of Sant' Angelo. On the left of the stage is a casemate, and in front of it a table (with writing materials, a large register, and a lantern) and a chair; in the background is a bench. On one of the walls of the casemate is a crucifix, with a hanging lamp in front of it. On the right we see the top of a small staircase that communicates with the courtyard below. In the far background the Vatican and St.

Peter's are visible. The air is clear, the night sky studded with stars: it is the early morning after the murder of Scarpia.

A series of descending thirds and fifths in the orchestra:

No. 30

conveys a curious sense of morning freshness and serenity: towards the end of the prelude, however, there are sinister suggestions of No. 1. In the distance, growing fainter and fainter, we hear a tinkling of cow-bells; and to the accompaniment of the tranquil pastoral No. 30 a shepherd boy, far away, sings a simple little song in the vernacular. The first grey of dawn appears, and a distant sound of morning bells at different pitches trembles for a while on the quiet air, over a subdued, slow-moving strain in the orchestra, one phrase of which:

No. 31

is particularly insistent.

An immense early morning peace is still brooding over the scene as a gaoler comes up the staircase with a lantern from which he lights first the lamp at the foot of the crucifix, then the one on the table; then he goes to the end of the parapet and looks into the courtyard below for the military picket he is expecting, bringing with it Cavaradossi. He exchanges silent greetings with a sentry on patrol, then seats himself outside the casemate and falls into a doze. All this time the strain of which No. 30 is part persists in the orchestra, with a faint reference at one point to the theme of the duet between Cavaradossi and Tosca in the first act (No. 12).

While the bells sound nearer and nearer, the picket, accompanied by a sergeant, appears on the parapet, bringing Cavaradossi with it, and the orchestra gives out the main phrases of the aria he will shortly sing:

No. 32

No. 33

No. 34

At the sight of the sergeant the gaoler rises and salutes; the former gives him a paper which he reads; then he opens the register and enters the interrogatories and the replies: "Mario Cavaradossi? You have an hour to live. A priest is at your service if you desire one." The sergeant, having signed the register, goes out with the picket by way of the stairs.

33

Cavaradossi rejects the offer of the consolations of religion, but begs, to the accompaniment of No. 12 in the most poignant tones of the violoncellos, the granting of a last request. He is leaving a dearly loved one behind him: will the gaoler deliver a last message to her? He offers the man his sole possession, a ring; the gaoler, after a moment's hesitation, gives a sign of assent, takes the ring, and retires to the bench in the background. Cavaradossi seats himself at the table and begins to write, the violoncellos once more singing the tender No. 12.

He begins his famous aria, "E lucevan le stelle," at first reciting the substance of it as he writes, then abandoning the pen as memories of Tosca overwhelm him: the orchestral tissue is built up out of the examples shown above as Nos. 32, 33, 34. He recalls his ecstatic hours in the villa with Floria: No. 34, to which he sings of her kisses and caresses, is of particular importance; it becomes the expression of his passionate grief at the shattering of all his hopes of happiness, and will be chosen later for the final summing-up of the tragedy. No. 33 is more especially associated with his cry of "I die despairing."

No. 12 is heard again in soft tones in the orchestra as Spoletta enters by way of the staircase, bringing with him the sergeant (carrying a lantern) and Tosca: with a silent gesture to the latter, indicating where she will find Cavaradossi, he goes out again, taking the sergeant and the gaoler with him, leaving the sentry, however, and bidding him keep an eye on the prisoner. There is a passionate outburst in the orchestra as Tosca runs to the weeping Mario, and, unable to speak for joy, raises his bowed head and shows him the safe-conduct. He takes it from her and they read it together: "Permission for Floria Tosca and the Cavaliere accompanying her. . . ." The signature awakes a slight suspicion in him. "This is Scarpia's first act of grace," he says. "And his last," adds Tosca grimly, for with the help of the Madonna and the saints she had killed him after procuring the safe-conduct, in the very moment of what he thought was his triumph over her; and we hear again in the orchestra the sinister strains of No. 28.

In an access of gratitude and admiration Mario takes her hands in his—the white hands that had been dipped in blood for his sake: "dear hands, so gentle, so pure, made for caressing children, for culling roses, for raising in prayer":

No. 35

At the words "You dealt him death, victorious hands," we hear another brief reminiscence of No. 28 in the orchestra.

She tells him of the arrangements she has made for their flight —a carriage, money, jewels—and of the plan agreed upon with Scarpia for a sham execution. The guns will not be loaded; as they fire, he is to fall and simulate death; the soldiers will go away, and they two will make straight for Civita Vecchia, where a vessel will carry them across the sea to safety. They revel for a while in imagination in the joys of freedom and a new life together; then, recalling themselves to reality, she gives him his instructions once more: he must act the death fall realistically, but without injuring himself, just as she herself, with her experience of the stage, would do!

34

As the firing squad under the command of an officer emerges from the stairway the lovers indulge in a final ecstasy of love and hope—a repetition of the unison melody for the horns with which the act had begun; there it had had a certain sombre impressiveness; here, sung by soprano and tenor alone, without any supporting harmonies in the orchestra, it reveals itself as one of Puccini's least distinguished inventions. While the officer is marshalling his men in the background the sergeant, the gaoler and Spoletta appear, and the police agent gives the myrmidons of the law their instructions. A lugubrious prison bell tolls the hour of four; whereupon the gaoler removes his cap, and, going up to Cavaradossi, points to the officer and then descends the stairs, taking the register of condemnations and executions with him. Laughing quietly to herself Tosca reminds Mario once more to be sure to fall flat the moment the volley is fired, and, himself smiling, he promises to do so "like Tosca on the stage"; then they remind each other of the necessity for a façade of seriousness.

At that moment the orchestra strikes in softly with the most tragic theme in the work, the motive of the *real* execution—"as in the case of Palmieri":

No. 36

Cavaradossi, having bidden Tosca a last farewell, follows the officer and the sergeant to the spot by the wall pointed out to him. Tosca places herself opposite, by the casemate, the better to observe him. The sergeant would bind his eyes, but Mario motions him away with a smile. It is now almost day. Tosca becomes impatient at the tedious slowness of it all; "Why this delay?" she asks them; "I know it is all a comedy, but you make this suffering seem endless. Come, present arms!"; and No. 36, which has been repeating itself incessantly, maddeningly, in the true Puccini manner, modulates and rises to a climax of anguish [1]:

No. 37

Bass: F♮ B♭ Eb Ab D♮ G

35

The officers and the sergeant arrange the procedure of the execution, giving each man his separate instructions. As the officer is about to give the order to fire by lowering his sword, Tosca puts her hands over her ears, impulsively murmuring, however, "How splendid my Mario is!" and as the volley rings out she cannot help adding "See, now he is dying! What an artist!" And she sends him a kiss with her hand.[2] The sergeant inspects the

[1] There can hardly be the least doubt that when Puccini wrote the music for this episode he was subconsciously recalling the Transformation Music in *Parsifal*: apart from the basic resemblances of manner between the two—certain similarities of melodic and harmonic procedure, the cumulative effect of persistent repetition, etc.—we have only to compare our No. 37 with this passage from the climax of the Transformation Music:

Bass: A D——E———————A——D———— G——B♭——C——

Puccini's admiration for Wagner knew no bounds. A friend who called on him in his last years found him hypnotically absorbed in the score of *Tristan*: he put it aside with the resigned comment, "After this, what are we all but a lot of mandoline strummers and dilettanti? . . . This terrific music reduces us to nothingness. . . ." His greatest admiration was for *Parsifal*; we are told that he would play the Prelude, the Transformation Music and the Good Friday Music without the score for hours on end. The amazing thing is that in spite of this powerful German influence his genius went its own appointed way in perfect self-assurance from first to last, always Italian and never anything but Puccini.

[2] In no other opera of Puccini, with the exception of *Madam Butterfly*, are the stage directions so numerous and so detailed as in *Tosca*. Many of them

body carefully and is about to give the *coup de grâce* when Spoletta restrains him.[1]

All this while the orchestra has been thundering out Nos. 36 and 37. The officer, the soldiers, the sergeant, the sentry and Spoletta having all left the stage by the stairway, Tosca rushes to Mario's body and bends over it: her consuming fear is that he may be imprudent enough to move too soon. She looks cautiously over the parapet, then returns to him, with a warning "Not yet! Do not move!" At last, her fears allayed, she tells him to rise: "Mario! Up! Quick!" Touching him, she realises the horrible truth and throws herself in desperation on his body, sobbing "Mario! Your poor Floria!" From below there now come the muffled exclamations of Spoletta, Sciarrone and the soldiers: "It is true . . . Stabbed! . . . Tosca!"; for the murder of Scarpia has been discovered. "She must not escape! Watch the stairs!"

The sobbing Tosca has the prostrate body in her arms when they pour upon the scene from below. Spoletta, shouting "You shall pay dearly for his life!", tries to seize her, but she pushes him away violently towards the staircase. "With my own life!" she cries: "Oh Scarpia, before God!" She hurls herself over the parapet, leaving Spoletta and the others gazing after her in blank incredulity; and half-a-dozen bars devoted to a fortissimo enunciation of No. 34 in the orchestra bring the blood-curdling scene to a close.

There cannot be many operas in which the mortality rate is so high as in *Tosca*; not one of the principal characters is left alive at the finish. Sardou's appetite for slaughter seems to have grown with what it fed on. "He wants that poor woman dead at all

---

are taken directly from Sardou, who, like the first-rate craftsman he was, always gave his actors every possible assistance in this line. In the play, however, Tosca leaves the stage at the moment of firing, her feelings being too much for her; she returns, when all is over, to find Spoletta bending over the body. We shall probably not be far wrong in assuming that the copious stage directions for the scene in its changed operatic form were Sardou's work. They are from first to last in his vein.

[1] This little stroke of stagecraft, which is not in the play, is surely Sardou's; he had not forgotten that in the opera Tosca is still on the stage, and that the comedy of the mock execution has to be played out to the end with this last cruel refinement of suspense.

costs," Puccini wrote humorously to Giulio Ricordi in January 1899. "Now that Deibler's [1] sun has set, the Magician insists on being his successor. . . . On Tuesday morning I must go to see Sardou again. . . . Perhaps he will insist on killing Spoletta too. We shall see." However, Spoletta was allowed to survive.

[1] The famous Paris executioner of the period.

Fidelio

BEETHOVEN [1770–1827]

PRINCIPAL CHARACTERS

LEONORA (FIDELIO)	*Soprano*
FLORESTAN	*Tenor*
MARZELLINE	*Soprano*
JACQUINO	*Tenor*
ROCCO	*Bass*
PIZARRO	*Bass*
FERNANDO	*Bass*

1

HE COMPOSITION of Beethoven's only opera *Fidelio* in its first form belongs to the fertile period of about 1803–1806, which saw the inception or completion of such works as the Waldstein and Appassionata piano sonatas, that in F major, op. 54, the triple concerto for piano, violin and violoncello, the Eroica symphony, the G major piano concerto and the fourth and fifth symphonies.

At the outset of an enquiry into the origins of the opera we come upon one of the many ticklish problems connected with it. In the Leipzig *Allgemeine Musikalische Zeitung* for the 30th March 1803 the Vienna correspondent of that journal announced that "Beethoven and the Abbé Vogler are each writing an opera for the Theater an der Wien." The *Zeitung für die elegante Welt* of the 2nd August contained a similar communication from Vienna: "Why is it that we Germans have so few good opera texts and always have to make do with translations, or else composers have to set mediocre libretti? Thus the Abbé Vogler is now writing an opera to a text by H.,[1] and Beethoven one to a text by Schikaneder." Three months later, on the 2nd November, we find Beethoven writing to the painter Alexander Macco, declining, for the present, the offer of a libretto by a certain A. G. Meissner, on the grounds that he is "just beginning his opera," the composition and then the production of which will keep him occupied until the following Easter. The Beethoven biographers have never quite known what to make of all this; but they have agreed that it can have no reference to *Fidelio*. What then was the opera on which Beethoven professed to be, and was believed to be, engaged at that time?

In 1872 Nottebohm, who was the first to undertake a systematic study of Beethoven's Sketch Books, published in his *Beethoveniana* a hitherto unknown "piece from an uncompleted opera": it is contained in an autograph manuscript in the archives of the Vienna Society of Friends of Music, and it had figured in the posthumous catalogue of the composer's manuscripts as "No. 67, a vocal piece with orchestra, complete, but not fully orchestrated." Some eight years later, in 1880, in his famous work *Ein Skizzenbuch von Beethoven aus dem Jahre 1803* ("A Beethoven Sketch Book of 1803"), which set forth in great detail the composer's preliminary work at the Eroica, Nottebohm dealt also with some fragments (from the same Book), which he described as "sketches for two pieces from the Schikaneder opera which Beethoven, before embarking upon his *Leonora*, intended to compose for the Theater an der Wien." Of these two pieces the one that concerns us here is a scene for four voices and orchestra the whole text of which—running to 75 lines—Nottebohm prints, together with the music (a trio) to lines 68–71. The characters are Porus (bass), Volivia (his daughter, soprano), Sartagones (Volivia's lover, tenor), and a second tenor, the rival of Sartagones, who is not named; he takes no part in the trio, in which, after the usual misunderstandings, a happy ending to the drama is evidently reached:

Volivia and Sartagones: Never was I so glad as today: never have I known such joy.

---

[1] The opera in question was presumably Vogler's *Samori*, the libretto of which was by Franz Xaver Huber.

Porus: Look down, benevolent gods, and bless their pure affection.
May their love be true to the grave,

The concluding four lines of the text, the music to which Nottebohm does not print, are a repetition of these sentiments by the
two lovers. The chief interest of the trio for us today resides in
the fact that Beethoven drew upon the theme of the words "Nie
war ich so froh wie heute" ("Never was I so glad as today"):

Nie war ich so froh wie heu-te

for the duet "O namenlose Freude" ("O joy beyond expression")
in the penultimate scene of *Fidelio*, in which Leonora and Florestan pour out their rapture at being restored to each other again.[1]

2

Notwithstanding Nottebohm's and Thayer's confident attribution of the text to Schikaneder, it has to be pointed out that there
is no evidence to connect him with it. How then does he come
into the story?

In April 1800, having received notice from Prince Starhemberg
to quit the theatre on the latter's Freihaus property—on the
grounds of the risk of fire—Schikaneder obtained a "privilegium"
from the Emperor to build a new theatre.[2] He had had in tow for
some time a rich Viennese merchant of the name of Bartholomäus
Zitterbarth, whose ambition it was to cut a figure in the theatrical
world. Schikaneder persuaded him to buy the house No. 26 an
der Wien and put up on the site a fine theatre, exceptionally well-
equipped mechanically, and boasting the largest stage in Vienna.
It opened on the 13th June 1801, much to the annoyance of Count
von Braun, the director of the Court Theatre, to which the new
establishment became a troublesome rival. In May 1802 Schikaneder sold his interest to Zitterbarth, being kept on, however, as
"poet and actor." In the following year Zitterbarth's ignorance
of the practical side of theatre management compelled him to

[1] See Musical Example No. 36 in the following analysis.
[2] For the previous career of Schikaneder see the chapter on *The Magic
Flute.*

re-engage Schikaneder as director; but by that time the poor patron was virtually ruined and soon had to sell out to Count von Braun. Then the comedy began afresh: Braun in his turn got rid of Schikaneder, but before long had to bring him back as director (in September 1804).

Schikaneder is alleged to have asked Beethoven more than once to write an opera for him, but apart from the reports of the musical journalists quoted above we have nothing that can be regarded as evidence to that effect. The question arises whether the contemporary journalists had any first-hand knowledge of the matter, or whether they were merely reporting Viennese gossip. If Beethoven was really engaged on an opera to a text by Schikaneder why has nothing survived of this but the setting of the seventy-five lines quoted by Nottebohm? This scene is manifestly the final one of the work in question. We know that when writing *Fidelio* Beethoven composed the music number by number in the order in which they appeared in the libretto. Is it likely that in the case of the alleged Schikaneder opera he began at the end? Again, the subject of the work is obviously connected in some way or other with the legends that had clustered, in the operatic world, round the Indian campaign of Alexander the Great.[1] Now in 1801 there had been produced at the Theater an der Wien an *Alexander* of which the text was by Schikaneder and the music by one Tayber, in which the former had indulged to the full his mania for smashing stage effects—in the final scene, we are told, Alexander and the Indian Queen appeared in a golden triumphal chariot drawn by four horses and escorted by forty mounted guards. Is it probable that Schikaneder would have written *another* Alexander opera for Beethoven so soon after that of 1801? Evidently the problem of the alleged Schikaneder-Beethoven connection is insoluble. Can the suggestion be ruled out that in the (anonymous) piece printed by Nottebohm Beethoven was trying his prentice hand at opera composition without any more definite object in view than that, and beginning at the end of some text or other because that was the situation in it that appealed to him most strongly?

But this is not the only mystery surrounding *Fidelio*. As the reader will already know, there were ultimately three versions

[1] Metastasio had written an *Allessandro nelle Indie* in 1729.

248

of the work, for which Beethoven wrote in all four overtures; [1] and there are baffling problems connected with all these.

Apparently Beethoven had received, at some time or other, a commission to write an opera for the Theater an der Wien. This contract automatically came to an end when the theatre was transferred to Braun; but at some date which cannot accurately be determined now, though it was presumably early in 1804, Braun entered into a new agreement with Beethoven. It is probable that the latter had actually begun work on the opera before receiving the formal commission for it—as early, indeed, as the end of 1803. [2]

3

The theme of *Fidelio* was one very much "in the air" just then. The troublous times that immediately succeeded the Revolution of 1789 and the ensuing Terror had brought into being a number of French dramas and operas dealing with the perils, the sufferings and the heroisms of that feverish epoch. One of the most popular works of this type was the *Léonore, ou l'amour conjugal* of J. N. Bouilly and Pierre Gaveaux, which was produced in the Feydeau Theatre, Paris, on the 19th February 1798: [3] according to Bouilly, his libretto was based on an incident that had actually happened during the Terror, at a time when he himself held an official appointment in Tours, though for his own safety and that of his family, he tells us, he had transferred the scene of the drama to Spain. The vogue of his opera in France led to the subject being taken up in Italy. A libretto that departed considerably from the original was made in 1804 for Ferdinand Paër, a composer of great repute in his own day, and his opera *Eleonora, ossia l'amore conjugale* was produced on the 3rd October 1804 in Dres-

[1] There are indications that he planned a fifth.

[2] His copious sketches for it are contained in what are known today as the Sketch Books of 1803 and 1804. The reader will find detailed discussions of them in Nottebohm's *Ein Skizzenbuch von Beethoven aus dem Jahre 1803*, pp. 66–69, in his *Zweite Beethoveniana*, pp. 409–549, and in the second volume of the German Edition of Thayer's *Life of Beethoven* (edited by Hugo Riemann) chapter 13.

[3] The only French opera of this genre that has survived to our day is Cherubini's *Les deux journées* (Englished as *The Water Carrier*), which was produced in Paris in 1804.

den, where Paër was at the time Kapellmeister at the Italian Opera. In the following spring another opera on the same theme, *L'Amor conjugale*, by Simon Mayr (1763–1845), was given in Padua; this time the librettist, Gaetano Rossi, thought it advisable to transfer the action to Poland and to give the characters such names as Zeliska, Moroski and Floresca; and by dint of a good deal of curtailment and the elimination of the character Jacquino, Rossi managed to compress the action into one act. In the Bouilly-Gaveaux opera the villain Pizarro is Florestan's enemy on political grounds; in Mayr's, the trouble has arisen from Moroski (Pizarro) having been in love with Zeliska (Leonora), the young wife of Amorveno (Florestan).[1]

The making of the libretto for Beethoven's opera was entrusted to Joseph von Sonnleithner, the secretary of the imperial theatres, who did wisely in modelling his action on that of Bouilly, but unwisely in spinning out the two acts of the original into three.[2] Beethoven finished his opera in the summer of 1805, and it was produced in the Theater an der Wien on the 20th November of that year, before an audience consisting, it is said, mostly of French soldiers, for Napoleon had occupied the town a week earlier, and most of the Viennese who had not fled from the city thought it prudent to remain in their homes. The reception was so discouraging that after two more performances, on the 21st and 22nd, Beethoven withdrew his score. The opera seems to have been inadequately rehearsed, and the singers, for the most part, were unequal to their tasks: the Leonora, Anna Milder, who later had a distinguished career under her married name of Milder-

[1] The reader who may wish to follow this matter up will find an analysis of Mayr's *L'Amor conjugale* in Vol. II, pp. 41–50, of Ludwig Schiedermair's *Beiträge zur Geschichte der Oper um die Wende des 18. und 19. Jahrh. Simon Mayr* (1907–1910).

[2] Sonnleithner turned out another opera text at the same time—*Faniska*, which was produced in Vienna in February 1806. Beethoven decided on *Fidelio*. Adolph Bernhard Marx has reasonably suggested that Beethoven must have received the commission for *Fidelio* before it became generally known that Paër was engaged on his *Eleanora*—which was produced, as we have just seen, in Dresden in 1804; otherwise Braun would hardly have allowed Beethoven, whose capacity as an opera composer was as yet unproved, to embark on a competition with a man of Paër's great reputation in Vienna.

Hauptmann, was at that time an inexperienced girl of twenty, while the Florestan, Demmer, was a tenor of limited vocal and intellectual capacity. It has been suggested, too, that one reason for the failure of the work was not the absence of the Viennese from the theatre but the presence there of an anti-Beethoven cabal. The overture played at the production of this First Version of the opera was that now known as the Leonora No. 2.

According to J. A. Röckel, a young tenor who had recently joined the an der Wien company,[1] a meeting of some of Beethoven's sincerest well-wishers was held in Prince Lichnowsky's house in December to consider ways and means of setting *Fidelio* on its feet again; and after a stormy session lasting from seven in the evening until one the next morning Beethoven was persuaded to perform a drastic surgical operation on his work, three numbers being cut out entirely and the action reduced from three acts to two. (The re-arrangement of the libretto was the work not of Sonnleithner but of Stephan von Breuning). The new *Fidelio* was put upon the stage on the 29th March 1806, with Röckel as Florestan in place of Demmer: the overture played on this occasion was that known today as the Leonora No. 3. A second performance followed on April 10th. There were signs that in this second version the work was well set for popularity when Beethoven quarrelled with Count Braun and withdrew his score. That was the last that was heard of *Fidelio* for several years.

4

In 1814 three members of the Court Theatre company, Saal, Vogel and Weinmüller, who were entitled to a benefit performance, decided, in view of Beethoven's great popularity in Vienna just then, that the best box-office card to play would be *Fidelio.*[2] They approached the composer, who agreed to let them have his work on the dual condition that it should now be given in yet another revised form and that the recasting of the text and the action should be entrusted to Georg Friedrich Treitschke, the official poet and stage manager at the Kärnthnerthor Theatre.

[1] He became later the father of the August Röckel who figures so largely in the Wagner biographies in connection with the Dresden rising of 1849.
[2] In this revival Saal was the Don Fernando, Vogel the Pizarro, and Weinmüller the Rocco.

Treitschke's stage experience suggested many dramatic changes both in the older wording of the libretto and the musical-dramatic design, all of which met with Beethoven's approval. Typical of them is the handling of the opening scene of the second act, in which, on the rising of the curtain, Florestan is discovered in his dark dungeon. "The second act," Treitschke tells us, "confronted us at the outset with a great difficulty. Beethoven wanted poor Florestan to have an aria in which he could distinguish himself; but I pointed out to him that a man at the point of death by starvation could not possibly sing bravura. We tried this and that idea, till finally I was convinced I had hit the nail on the head—I wrote some lines that depicted a last blazing up of life within the man before its extinguishment." The lines Treitschke proceeds to quote are those of the closing section of Florestan's aria in its present form: the weary prisoner sees in imagination an angel of consolation standing by his pallet—his Leonora, who leads him out of his dungeon to freedom and heaven. This ecstatic vision makes the exhausted man's sudden access of vitality plausible.

To the Treitschke revision we also owe the change to bright daylight for the closing scene of the opera; the fact that in the earlier *Fidelio* the whole of the concluding action took place in the gloomy dungeon must certainly have gone against the work. Beethoven, whose heart had always been with this dearest child of his sorrow, as he (or was it Schindler?) called it, and who must have heaved many a sigh over it during the eight years or so in which it had disappeared from public view, was delighted with Treitschke's emendations: "they determine me," he wrote to him in March 1814, "to rebuild the desolate ruins of an old castle." But the re-writing, for one reason and another, proceeded slowly.[1] "The first act will be finished in a few days," we find him telling Treitschke in the spring of 1814, "but there is still much to be done in the second, as well as a fresh overture to be written—which, however, will be the easiest part of all, because I can make it entirely new." By the time of the first performance of the new *Fidelio*, however—in the Kärnthnerthor Theatre on the 23rd May—the overture still not being ready, the performance had to begin—or so the biographers have assured us—with that to *The*

---

[1] Changes, small or large, were made in the music of every part of the original version except the March.

Ruins of Athens. The new overture—the one in E major, now known as the *Fidelio*—was heard, however, at the second performance, on the 25th. In its third and final form the opera soon became popular both in Austria and in Germany.

5

Beethoven's autographs of the full scores of the First and Second Versions of the work are lost or dispersed, though the manuscript of the Leonora Overture No. 2 and some fragments of the opera itself have survived. Of the Second Version Breitkopf and Härtel published in 1807 three numbers only—(1) a trio in E flat major, "Ein Mann ist bald genommen," (2) the "canon" quartet in G major, "Mir ist so wunderbar," (3) a trio in C major, "Um in der Ehe froh zu leben." Of these only the second was incorporated in the final version of the opera. In 1810 the same publishers brought out a piano score of the Second Version which lacked, however, the finales and the overture (i.e. the Leonora No. 3): they followed this up later in the same year by an issue of *the orchestral parts only* of the latter, which was described as "Ouverture de *Leonore* à grand orchestre." In August 1814 and October 1815 appeared reprints, edited by Moscheles and Czerny respectively, of the portions of the Second Version that had seen the light (in a pianoforte arrangement) in 1807, together with the overture Leonora No. 3 (also in piano score). None of the three overtures was published in full score in Beethoven's lifetime. The Leonora No. 3 appeared in 1828, the Leonora No. 2, in a curtailed form, in 1843; this, says Josef Braunstein, "was actually the first portion of the First Version of the opera to be published." (About the Leonora No. 1 we shall have something to say later.) In the early 1850's Breitkopf and Härtel brought out a piano score of the Second Version (1806) of the opera that was the result of many years' skilled labour by Otto Jahn, who set forth in a preface the details in which this Second Version had differed from that of 1805. He followed this up with an issue of the Leonora No. 2 overture in its complete form, in orchestral score. More than half a century after that—in 1905—Erich Prieger embodied the results of twenty-five years of laborious research work in an edition of the full score of the First Version.

6

There remains to be considered the overture known today as the Leonora No. 1. This has had a curious history, of which only the barest outline can be given here. The Viennese publisher Tobias Haslinger (afterwards owner of the Steiner business) professed in 1828 to have bought, at the sale of the dead Beethoven's effects, "a packet of dances, marches, etc." which he found also to contain "the full score and the orchestral parts of an entirely unknown grand characteristic overture, which the Master, as Schuppanzigh [1] recalls, had rehearsed some years ago, as is shown by the corrections made by him in red crayon." (The manuscript was not an autograph but a copy, Beethoven's holograph of the overture being lost.) This story of Haslinger's is not accepted quite at its face value today; the probability is that the manuscript was one of several that he had bought from the composer many years earlier but, for shrewd business reasons, had not found it convenient to publish at the time. The overture was first performed in Vienna in February 1828 (some eleven months after Beethoven's death), and published by Haslinger in 1832 as op. 138.

In that year Seyfried's book containing Beethoven's youthful studies in counterpoint, thoroughbass and composition was published.[2] Seyfried contributed some personal recollections of the composer, and said, à propos of *Fidelio*, that "for the Prague theatre Beethoven wrote a new and less difficult overture, which Haslinger bought at the auction of effects and will probably publish soon"—i.e. the opus 138. In the *Journal des Luxus* of January 1808 a correspondent had stated that "Beethoven's opera *Fidelio*, which, despite all contrary reports, has extraordinary beauties, is to be performed in Prague in the near future with a new overture." This performance, however, did not take place.

Nottebohm found some sketches for this overture and drew from them the conclusion—in an article *Die Ouverture op. 138*, in his *Beethoveniana* (1872)—that it was written in 1807. As this seemed to confirm the story about a Prague production set going

[1] A Viennese violinist, leader of the Schuppanzigh string quartet.
[2] Seyfried had been Kapellmeister at the Theater an der Wien until 1828. The Beethoven studies also had been bought by Haslinger.

by Seyfried and the *Journal des Luxus* the chain of evidence seemed to be nicely complete; and as Nottebohm was at the time regarded as an infallible authority on the Beethoven Sketches it soon became an article of faith that the true order of the composition of the Leonora overtures was not No. 1 (i.e. op. 138), No. 2, No. 3, but No. 2, No. 3, No. 1. Confident statements to this effect began to appear in the musical dictionaries—in the earliest *Grove*, for instance—and these have been submissively copied since then in encyclopedia after encyclopedia, edition after edition of the same encyclopedia, biography after biography, programme note after programme note. Almost from the beginning, it is true, several scholars questioned the validity of Nottebohm's arguments and conclusions, but as their articles appeared in this or that German periodical they were not generally accessible and soon disappeared from public view.

7

Criticism of the Nottebohm legend never quite ceased, however, and in 1927 Josef Braunstein dealt it its death-blow in his book *Beethovens Leonore-Ouverturen, eine historisch-stilkritische Untersuchung*. Nottebohm's methods of dealing with the Beethoven sketches are not accepted today as ideally scientific, and many of his conclusions are open to question: the mere fact that a given sketch is found in a certain place in a certain Sketch Book is not now regarded as proof of the date when it was committed to paper; and it is not disrespectful to the great researcher to surmise today that in the matter of the opus 138 he merely believed what he was predisposed to believe. He accepted the story of the overture opus 138 being written for a projected Prague performance of 1808 as confirming his attribution of the sketches in question to 1807, and then regarded the supposed proof of 1807 as the date of the sketches as confirming the story put in circulation by Seyfried. The trouble is that as neither leg of his thesis, when critically examined, can stand by itself, their "confirmation" of each other is illusory. It is anything but certain that the sketches found by Nottebohm belong to 1807, and there is nothing in the report of the *Journal des Luxus* of January 1808—which Seyfried was obviously repeating twenty years later—to justify our believing that the "new" overture which, according to current

255

report, was to be used for the Prague performance, was "new" in the sense of "newly-composed for the occasion."

What the scribe of 1808 had said was merely that "*Fidelio* is to be performed in Prague in the near future with a new overture." [1] That rumor no doubt came from within the Beethoven circle, and its ultimate origin may have been the composer himself. But "new" could easily have meant, for Beethoven, not "newly-composed" but "new to the public." This was not the only occasion on which he had employed the term in this latter sense. When the Third Version of *Fidelio* was being given for his benefit in July 1814 it was announced, as a special attraction, that two new arias would be included. One of these was Rocco's now well-known aria in praise of money—"Hat man nicht auch Gold beineben." But this aria, as we know, was in the First Version of 1805, though it had been deleted from the Second Version of 1806. As it had not been heard for nine years, and then only in two performances of the opera which, as we have seen, had been attended by merely a few Viennese, Beethoven would feel himself justified in describing the aria as "new" to his audiences of 1814, though not new in the sense of "recently composed." Again, in the announcement of a concert he was giving on the 27th February 1814 he spoke of "a quite new not yet performed trio." The trio in question was the "Tremate, empi, tremate" of 1801. Evidently, then, for Beethoven, "new" could signify merely "new to the public"; and there seems every justification for believing that it was in this sense that he used the word in connection with the overture to be performed at the projected Prague production of

[1] No correspondence relating to any such projected performance exists; and *Fidelio* was given for the first time in Prague in November 1814, with Weber as conductor. Braunstein suggests that what had happened in 1808 was simply that Beethoven, having so many members of the Bohemian aristocracy among his patrons, had conceived the idea of the possibility of a revival of his opera in Prague.

It has been conjectured that the author of the *Journal des Luxus* paragraph was none other than Seyfried himself, who is known to have done a good deal of journalism. As conductor at the Theater an der Wien he had had to do with the *Fidelio* rehearsals and performances of both 1805 and 1806. He was in close personal contact with Beethoven at that time and later, and it may well have been that the composer had told him of his hopes for a performance of *Fidelio* in Prague and said something about a "new" overture for the occasion.

1808. We know that for the original production of the opera in Vienna in 1805 he had written an overture which was actually rehearsed privately but discarded as too "light" for the drama, whereupon he wrote the Leonora No. 2; and the evidence as a whole suggests that this discarded overture was the one he had intended for the Prague production, as perhaps being more within the capacity of the local orchestra than either the No. 2 or the No. 3, and that the true chronological order of composition of the Leonora overtures is No. 1, No. 2, No. 3.[1]

8

One other little error remains to be corrected before we proceed to an analysis of the opera. The legend still endures in some quarters that in 1805 and 1806 the work was produced as *Leonora*, Beethoven's desire to have it called *Fidelio* being overruled on each occasion by the theatre management. This story—the precise reverse of the truth—had its origin in a letter from Stephen von Breuning of the 2nd June 1806 to his sister. Beethoven had been annoyed, he said, because he had not been able to have the opera billed as *Fidelio*, "as it is called in the French original." Strange as it may seem, the words "Leonora" and "Fidelio" were some-how transposed either in Breuning's actual letter or in the copy

[1] I have, of course, been able to give only the barest outline of the evidence as a whole. For the marshalling of it I must refer the reader to Josef Braun-stein's book.

On pp. 252–3 it has been hinted that the generally accepted story of the first performance of *Fidelio* in 1814 with the *Ruins of Athens* overture may be open to question. Treitschke, in his reminiscences, said the overture then played was that to the ballet *Prometheus*. The biographers rule this out, but accept Seyfried's statement that the work performed was the overture to *The Ruins of Athens*; a contemporary notice of the production in the maga-zine *Der Sammler* also says that the overture given in 1814 "was originally written for the opening of the theatre in Pesth"—i.e. *The Ruins of Athens* (1812). As the score of this was not published until 1823, it is possible that Seyfried and the *Sammler* correspondent may have been mistaken. Schindler said that the overture played at the first night in 1814 was "an overture to *Leonore*" (i.e. the first *Fidelio*). Hugo Riemann remarks that "it is very difficult to believe that Beethoven would consent to his opera being prefaced by either of these overtures [the *Prometheus* or *The Ruins of Athens*]. Could the one performed have been the first of the *Leonora* overtures (op. 138)? In that case Schindler would be right."

of it that found its way later into print. In the "French original," as everyone knows, the title was not *Fidelio* but *Léonore*. The theatre posters of 1805 and 1806 place it beyond question that on both occasions the opera was billed as *Fidelio*. The printed text-book of 1805 gives the title as *Fidelio*; and the opera is referred to as *Fidelio* in the contemporary press notices. It was Beethoven who from first to last desired his work to be known as *Leonore*, but the theatre authorities insisted on *Fidelio*. The new *text-book* prepared for the Second Version (1806) did indeed bear the title of *Leonore, oder der Triumph der ehelichen Liebe,* as did the imprint in 1810 of the (incomplete) piano score of the opera and the orchestral parts of the overture Leonora No. 3. (See above, p. 253.) But these were matters in which the theatre management had no power to restrain Beethoven from doing as he wished. They no doubt overruled him in the theatre out of regard for Paër, whose *Eleanora* had been given in Dresden in 1804. For the revival of his work in 1814 Beethoven again desired the title *Leonore*, and the text book used for these performances actually bears that name: in the copy preserved in the archives of the Vienna Opera, however, "Leonore" has been struck out and *Fidelio* substituted for it in red crayon; once more Beethoven had been unable to assert himself publicly against the theatre management. The work was given once more as *Fidelio*, and it was under that title that Beethoven himself, giving up the struggle, published the piano score.

9

Fidelio is technically a singspiel, that is to say, an opera in which the action is carried on and the situations explained largely by means of spoken dialogue.

Two years before the action opens, a certain Florestan, an official in the service of Don Fernando, a high-minded, humanistic Spanish Minister of State, had mysteriously disappeared from human ken. By his probity and the liberalism of his political opinions he had incurred the enmity of a typical member of the reactionary party, one Pizarro, who had secretly consigned him to a prison of which he was the governor. For the world of men Florestan is dead; only his devoted wife, Leonora, has not accepted the current story, and she has made it the mission of her life to find him if he is still alive. At the period when the opera opens she suspects that he may be languishing in Pizarro's prison; and in order to carry out her search for him without raising suspicion she has entered, disguised as a man, the service of Rocco, the jailer, who holds this "Fidelio," as he calls himself, in high esteem for his zeal and efficiency. In an exhaustive article *Zur Dramaturgie des 'Fidelio,'* in the *Neues Beethoven-Jahrbuch* for 1924, Hermann von Waltershausen demonstrates that we are to think of Florestan as a man of about forty and Leonora a young Spanish woman of about twenty-five, of a build that makes it easy for her to wear a man's clothes without arousing any doubts as to her sex. Unfortunately, however, she has to be also a dramatic soprano with a high and powerful voice, which makes it only too likely, the world of opera being what it is, that on the stage we shall be confronted with a woman of fairly ripe age and matronly build, calling for a good deal of polite credulity on our part.[1] The first great Fidelio, Wilhelmine Schröder-Devrient, whom Wagner saw in his young days and who remained to the end of his life the ideal player of the part, was only eighteen when, in 1822, she amazed the German world by her combination of fine singing and fine acting as Leonora and did much to extend the vogue of the opera; but Schröder-Devrient was unique.

Unless the player of the part can wring from us an admission that she could credibly pass herself off as a man in the daily round of the jailer's household the opening scenes of the opera are bound to be a slight strain on the gravity of the ribald spectator; for not only does no one there entertain the least suspicion that this Fidelio is not a man, but the jailer's daughter Marzelline is actually head over ears in love with him, to the annoyance and anguish of the young porter of the prison, Jacquino, who, until Fidelio's appearance on the scene, had been paying his addresses to the maiden with good hope of success.

When the curtain rises we find Marzelline and Jacquino engaged in what is evidently only the latest of many tiffs over the present state of affairs in the kitchen. For a long time in the nineteenth century there was much head-shaking over this first scene,

---

[1] Romain Rolland shuddered at what he described as "the visceral amplitude" of some of the high-powered dramatic sopranos of yesterday and to-day.

the bourgeois domesticity of which, it was argued, would have been more in place in a drama less tense and lofty than that of *Fidelio* is soon to become. We generally end, however, by not being hypercritical about the matter. Here, as in the case of many another opera, a great deal of subtle argument can be spared us if we take a simple commonsense view of the case. To do that, all that is necessary is to see the situation as it must have presented itself in terms of actual stage practice to the librettist and the composer. If the opera was to occupy a whole evening there would have to be a second soprano and a second tenor, and something would have to be found for them to do. In the main tragic action there would of course be little room for them. By tradition they would have to be subsidiary characters, of a lower social standing than the principal ones. No prominent place could be found for them except at the very beginning, for as soon as the real action of the drama began they would virtually have to fade out as quietly as possible. The only practical thing to do was to make the second soprano the daughter of the jailer, and the second tenor her lover or wooer. This of itself constituted a stage pattern familiar and acceptable to the audiences of that day and put no great strain on the invention of either librettist or composer. The general pattern would determine the particular procedure: there would have to be somewhere a duet for the characters, and a solo for at any rate the soprano. The only alternative to this layout would have been to concentrate the drama into a single supremely tense act, which would have been technically difficult for both dramatist and composer and would have confronted the management with the awkward problem of how to fill up the rest of the evening.

Marzelline and Jacquino, therefore, came into being simply because the operatic apparatus of the epoch was what it was. It is superfluous for us today to psychologise very seriously about the two characters; all we have to do is to accept them and the situation and make the best of both. We are perfectly well aware from the start that the opening scenes are only a sort of "fill-up" until the real action begins; and as Beethoven has written some charming music for these domestic episodes we are quite willing to enjoy this for its own sake and then forget all about the matter until the next time we hear the opera.

10

The curtain rises on the courtyard of the prison, the main entrance to which is at the back, where there are also a postern gate in the wall and a porter's lodge. The cells are on the left, behind heavily barred and bolted iron doors and windows; nearer the foreground on this side is the jailer Rocco's house. On the right are the trees of the castle garden and a gate opening on to this. Outside Rocco's house is a table at which Marzelline is busy ironing. By the little lodge stands his assistant Jacquino, who opens the postern gate every now and then to admit people carrying parcels. His main occupation, however, is pleading his cause with Marzelline. "At last we are alone, dearest," he begins, "now we can have a confidential talk":

No. 1

Why cannot they go back to the old footing, when they were as good as engaged, and fix the day for their wedding? But she fends him off with a mixture of coquettish indifference and mild affection of a sort; and she is relieved when a knock at the door:

No. 2

calls him away for a moment. She is sorry for Jacquino, she soliloquises, but since this Fidelio came among them she has no room in her heart for anyone else. A tender little phrase in the oboe and bassoon:

No. 3

accompanies her breathing of the beloved name. Jacquino has to leave her to answer the door, and when he returns again she begins to be cross with him. Why keep on plaguing her, she asks him, since she has no intention of ever changing her mind? His reply is that he still hasn't given up hope.

The musically pleasant little duet having run its leisurely course, the characters drop into ordinary speech. For the third time Jacquino, to his annoyance, has to break off the dialogue to attend to people at the gate; and then, just as he is settling down to another appeal to Marzelline's better nature, he hears Rocco calling peremptorily for him. Reluctantly he goes off, telling Marzelline that he will be back again in a couple of minutes and that she is to stay there until he returns. This leaves the stage free for her to indulge in a little aria, in which she confesses her love for Fidelio. Nothing is wanting to her happiness now, she says, but a little reciprocity on the young man's part and the consent of her father: "Oh, if I were but united to him! But alas, a maiden is not allowed to reveal more than half of what is in her heart":

No. 4

Andante con moto

O wär ich schon mit dir ver-eint, und dürf-te Mann dich nen-nen!

Still, she will go on hoping for the happy day when she will be his, sharing his burdens, rejoicing in his love. Beethoven surrounds the simple aria with a wealth of expressive decoration in the orchestra.[1]

At the conclusion of it Rocco enters with Jacquino. Has Fidelio not returned yet? he asks his daughter; he should have been back by now with the despatches which the jailer will have to take to the Governor. "Perhaps he has been detained at the blacksmith's," Marzelline suggests. But almost before the words are out of her

[1] In the First Version of the opera the order of opening was the reverse of that of the present *Fidelio*: Marzelline's aria (our example No. 4) came first and the duet with Jacquino (our No. 1) second. There followed (before the canon quartet) a trio for Marzelline, Jacquino and Rocco in which the jailer expounded his philosophy of matrimony: "A man soon finds a woman, a woman a man; but it isn't long before regrets come on both sides." This trio does not appear in the final *Fidelio*.

mouth there is a renewed knocking at the door: Jacquino opens it and Leonora enters. The librettist describes her costume in detail—"a dark red doublet, a red vest, dark pantaloons, high boots and a broad black leather belt with a copper buckle." From the blacksmith's she has come laden with purchases appropriate to the prison, the weight of which is manifestly almost too much for her woman's strength. Rocco naïvely attributes the young man's admirable zeal in the performance of his duties to a desire to look well in Marzelline's eyes; but a broad hint to that effect is passed over by Leonora, and without more ado the characters settle down to a quartet (with orchestral accompaniment) that is one of the wonders of the work. The strings preludise with a brief but profoundly moving strain:

No. 5

Then Marzelline leads off with a vocal phrase—"How marvellous it is! My heart will burst! He loves me, that is clear; my happiness is certain":

No. 6

The quartet is framed on canon lines, each voice when it enters striking into the existing texture with a restatement of the original melody (No. 6). Each actor speaks, so far as the words are concerned, in character. Marzelline, as we have just seen, indulges herself in dreams of happy union with Fidelio. Leonora, who follows her, scents danger to her plans in this infatuation that is no stranger to her: "Great is the peril! How weak is the semblance of hope! She loves me, that is clear; oh unutterable, unutterable torment!" Rocco, who comes into the texture third, expresses himself thus: "She loves him, that is clear. Yes, maiden, he will be thine. A worthy young pair; they will be happy"; while Jacquino, who enters last, takes an entirely different view of the situation: "I am horrified. Her father gives his consent. Marvellous it seems to me; there is nothing I can do."

11

Now any other dramatic composer would presumably make it his first care in an ensemble of this kind—as Verdi, for instance, did in the great quartet in *Rigoletto*—to differentiate the characters musically so far as that was possible. Why does Beethoven, having on his hand four characters reacting psychologically in four different ways to the one situation, choose as his medium the canon form, in which, by the very nature of the technical procedure, all are irrevocably committed to saying precisely the same musical thing? [1] How, we ask, can one and the same melody express, for example, the joy of Marzelline at the happy turn of events as she sees them and the anxious foreboding of Leonora? Why, again, should Beethoven decide to treat with such tremendous gravity a situation which we in the audience have so far been able to see only as slightly comic, a mere light filling-in before the real business of the drama gets going? For the orchestral preamble itself, with its great ground-swell of emotion and the solemn throb of the basses, is of a gravity and an intensity for a parallel to which we have to wait for the slow movements of Beethoven's last piano sonatas and quartets. The answer seems to be that the moment Leonora has stepped on the stage his whole great heart has gone out to her. He sees the others and their minor interests only through her eyes heavy with suffering, her concentration on the noble purpose to which she has dedicated her young life. That entry of hers on the scene with a physical burden almost beyond her strength is, whether the librettist intended it to be so or not, symbolic; it was thus that Beethoven no doubt saw it and it was this that suddenly moved him to his depths. Although her voice is only one of four, and she is held fast musically in the technical armature of the canon, it is she whose sublime spirit dominates it all; and the last thing that remains in our ears is her

---

[1] "Rossini," says Berlioz in his article on *Fidelio* in À *travers chants*, "has written a number of delightful things in this form—the canon 'Mi manca la voce,' for example, in his *Moses in Egypt*." True, but there all the characters are expressing the same sentiment, whereas in the *Fidelio* canon each is supposed to be moved in a different way from the others.

repetitive "Oh unspeakable, oh unspeakable, unspeakable, unspeakable pain!" [1]

The quartet having come to an end, the characters drop for a little while into spoken dialogue. Rocco declares, to the joy of Marzelline and the embarrassment of Leonora, that Fidelio shall become his son-in-law the day after the Governor has gone to Seville. Then—for even the second bass in the opera must have his little aria—he warns the young pair that love is not enough to ensure happiness in marriage. Money also is necessary, for, as he puts it, what are two loves in themselves but a mere nothing plus nothing with precious little as the answer to the sum? This philosophy he expounds in the famous "Gold" aria:

No. 7

Allegro moderato

Hat man nicht auch Gold bei-ne-ben, Kann man nicht ganz glück-lich sein!

which had been omitted from the Second Version of the opera but was restored in the Third at the seventh performance. [2]

12

After this the drama is carried on for a time in speech. Leonora makes by a roundabout route for the plan of action she has already decided upon—somehow to get admission to the dungeons and so find out if Florestan is among the prisoners. She values Rocco's confidence in her, she tells him, but at the same time is concerned about the toll his work is taking of his health, for he is

[1] The quartet cost Beethoven a great deal of trouble: the Sketch Book of 1803 contains at least a dozen attempts, all of them ultimately discarded, to find the right melody for the opening words. It is clear, however, as Nottebohm says, that his intention from the beginning was to cast the number in canon form.

[2] This seventh performance, on July 18th, was for Beethoven's benefit. Treitschke had made some changes in the text of the aria. The number is sometimes omitted today. There is no justification for this.

Berlioz was of the opinion that Gaveaux's "Gold" aria was the one number in his score that suffered least by comparison with Beethoven: if the latter's setting has the virtue of vigorous vitality, he says, Gaveaux's commends itself to us by its melodic ease, its excellent handling of the words, and its piquant orchestration.

no longer young.[1] Marzelline, taking her father's hand affectionately, agrees with Fidelio; and Rocco admits that one of these
days he will have to ask the Governor's permission to depute some
of his work to his assistant. There is one cell in the secret dungeons, however, into which no one but himself is allowed to enter.
The occupant of this, opines Marzelline, must be the prisoner of
whom her father has sometimes spoken; and Leonora grasps the
opportunity to ask how long the man has been there. "Just over
two years," is the reply. "Two years!" Leonora repeats feverishly;
then, mastering her emotion, she remarks, "He must be a great
criminal!" "Either that or he has powerful enemies, which comes
to much the same thing," replies Rocco, who evidently knows
the political world. But he knows, too, the value of prudence for
a mere underling like himself: he cannot tell them the name of
the prisoner or whence he came, for Rocco has always closed his
ears when the man has shown an inclination to talk about himself.
"The fewer secrets the likes of us know the better for us," he
says; "and anyhow the man will not be troubling me much
longer." "Oh God!" ejaculates Leonora under her breath.

When Marzelline affectionately begs her father not to subject
the sensitive Fidelio to such an ordeal as the sight of this unfortunate man, Leonora asks the jailer eagerly, "Why not? Do you
doubt my courage and strength?" "Well spoken, my son," replies
Rocco, and a trio is launched in which Leonora's resolution is
made manifest at the outset in a recurrent figure in the orchestra:

No. 8

She will brave any horrors that may confront her in the execution
of her duties, she declares. Marzelline exhorts her Fidelio to think
only of love and marriage; while Rocco assures them that this
very day he will ask the Governor's permission to share his work

[1] As Hermann von Waltershausen has pointed out, "Rocco does not mean
it literally when he describes himself as having one foot in the grave," and
consequently it is mistaken zeal on a producer's part to show us an old
fellow "always weak on his pins and looking like a greybeard who has escaped from the poor-house."

in the cells with his assistant, for he feels that his own health will not last out much longer. Towards the end of the long trio Beethoven depicts admirably the contest between the happiness of the unsophisticated little Marzelline and the grief of Leonora by the simplest device imaginable—the flattening of a single note and the consequent darkening of the mood when the latter replies to Marzelline's innocent cry of "Oh sweetest tears!":

No. 9

with an anguished "Oh bitter tears!": [1]

No. 10

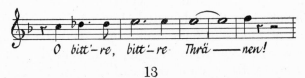

13

Seeing Pizarro approaching, Rocco takes the despatch box from Fidelio and hands it to the Governor Pizarro on his entrance. Marzelline and Fidelio go off. Officers and soldiers come upon the scene, and, to the accompaniment of a short march, "newly composed" for the revival of the opera:

No. 11

with its after-theme of true military character: [2]

No. 12

[1] The point is apt to be obscured in translations of the opera intended for singing. It is essential, though not always practicable, that Marzelline's "sweet" and Leonora's "bitter" shall be sung to D natural and D flat respectively.

[2] In the First Version the second act had begun here.

they mount guard under Pizarro's curt directions; "Three sentries on the wall! Six men day and night on the drawbridge, and another six in the garden! Anyone who approaches the moat is to be brought before me at once!" As he takes the despatches out of the box his eye is caught by a letter the handwriting of which seems familiar to him, and he hurriedly reads it aloud. It runs: "For your information. It has come to the ears of the Minister that in the State prisons over which you preside there are several victims of arbitrary power. He is setting out tomorrow [that is to say, the today of the opera] to pay you a surprise visit of inspection. Be on your guard." For a moment Pizarro is dismayed: "What if he should discover," he ejaculates, "that here I have in fetters the Florestan whom he has so long believed to be dead?" Then, recovering his self-command, he cries, "There is one way out for me. One bold deed can make an end of all my fears!"; and he breaks into the celebrated "Revenge" aria, in which all his hatred of Florestan finds expression: "Ha! the moment has come! Now will I wreak revenge on you! Your doom is sealed! Oh, what joy to strike you to the heart!":

No. 13

"Once I lay almost in the dust, a mock to all men; but now it is my turn the slayer himself to slay":

No. 14

The aria, on which the soldiers comment from time to time in low, fear-stricken tones, is a tempestuous expression of blood-lust: this Pizarro is evidently a man crazed by imaginary wrongs and beyond the pale of ordinary human feelings. As he plunges the dagger into his victim's heart he will cry "Triumph! Victory is mine!" The orchestral accompaniment is a swirl of passion culminating in leaping syncopated figures of this kind:

No. 15

His furious outburst over, the action reverts to speech again. Pizarro's first care is to accomplish his deed of vengeance before the Minister arrives. Summoning the Captain of the guard he orders him in low tones to mount the watch-tower, taking a trumpeter with him: he is to keep his eyes on the Seville road, and as soon as he sees a carriage with outriders approaching he must tell the trumpeter to give a signal; "You understand? on the instant! or your head will answer for it!" Having posted the guards, he calls Rocco to him: Fidelio, unobserved, listens to their conversation. "I must win this man over," says Pizarro to himself; "without his help I can do nothing." Then, raising his voice, he tells the jailer, to an agitated orchestral accompaniment, that he has the opportunity now to become rich. "You are a man of cold blood, of intrepid spirit, hardened by long years in your profession." "What would you have me do?" asks Rocco. "Murder!" is the reply:

No. 16

The jailer quails at this, but Pizarro presses him hard: "You tremble. Are you a man? We have no time to lose, for in the interests of the State a quick end must be made of an evil creature." While Rocco stammers out his horror at the proposition made to him, Pizarro communes feverishly with himself: "He must die or I am ruined; when he is dead I shall be safe." To Rocco's protest that murder is no part of his duties Pizarro replies, "If your courage fails you, I will see to that. As for you, merely go down to the cell of that man below—you know the one I mean." "The one who is already nigh to death?" asks Rocco, "hardly more than a tottering shadow?" "The same," replies Pizarro. The jailer is to descend and dig a grave in an old well in the dungeon; Pizarro himself will wait in the background, and, when the grave is ready, steal in with his face concealed and end the matter with a single blow:

No. 17

Even then the end will be too quick to sate his hatred. Rocco, for his part, though he is horrified at the idea of murder, reflects that after all that the poor prisoner has suffered, death will be a merciful release.

14

As Rocco and Pizarro leave the stage Leonora comes forward. Now she begins to see her way clear before her: she has realised that a murder is to be committed in the dungeons, though as yet she does not know for certain who the victim is to be. And now she reveals herself, for the first time in the opera, in her full stature as Beethoven saw her, the incarnation of love and of the strength that love can give.[1] In an agitated recitative, "Abscheu-

---

[1] Incredible as it may seem, in the First Version of the opera there came between the departure of Pizarro and Rocco and the launching of the great aria a duet between Marzelline and Fidelio, in which, greatly to the latter's embarrassment, the maiden gave naïve expression to her views on marriage and motherhood. Evidently Sonnleithner, having the rather impossible Marzelline on his hands from the beginning, felt that he had to insert her here and there in the later action, but was at his wits' end to know just where and how; Beethoven weakly followed him. Treitschke's elimination of this episode was one of his greatest services to the composer and to us.

licher! Wo eilst du hin? Was hast du vor?" ("Fiend incarnate! Where are you going? What is your foul purpose?"), she pours out her horror and loathing of Pizarro. He reminds her of a tossing sea of malice, over which, however, she sees a rainbow rising that awakes old memories in her and kindles new hopes. A short adagio orchestral introduction, in which the horns play a prominent melodic part:

No. 18

serves to launch the great aria, "Come, Hope, let not the last star of the weary one fade in the sky: light up for me my goal, for however far off it may be, Love will reach it":

No. 19

A change of tempo and of mood comes in the latter half of the aria, where she affirms her resolution to allow nothing to turn her from her resolve to find and rescue the beloved man for whom she has suffered so much:

No. 20

As may be gathered from the foregoing quotations, the aria makes great demands on the singer, who has to be a dramatic and a coloratura soprano in one. In the First Version of the opera the coloratura of the aria was much more luxuriant than it is in the present *Fidelio*. The first Leonora, the young Anna Milder, jibbed at it, and it is doubtful whether many dramatic sopranos of today would attempt it more than once. Beethoven did wisely in using the pruning hook vigorously on the aria in 1814.

After Leonora's exit we lapse again into spoken dialogue, in a rather superfluous scene in which Jacquino once more gets at cross purposes with Marzelline with regard to this intrusive young Fidelio. The cue for something more apposite to the real drama is given by Leonora, who, having returned with Rocco, asks him whether this is not a good opportunity to keep his promise to her to admit the poor prisoners into the fortress garden: he has more than once promised her this, but always put it off. "Today it is so fine," she pleads, "and the Governor never comes here at this hour." As Rocco still hesitates to give the prisoners even the briefest liberty without Pizarro's express permission, Leonora artfully suggests, "Perhaps there is some service he wants you to do him that will make him less rigorous?" Rocco seizes on this; the service he is about to render the Governor will certainly give him, he feels, a momentary claim on him. He gives Jacquino and Fidelio permission to open up some of the cells; meanwhile he himself will go to Pizarro, he says, and keep him engaged in conversation—this with a meaning glance at his daughter. Greatly pleased, she kisses his hand. He goes out: the gates are unlocked, and Fidelio, Marzelline and Jacquino retire into the background as the prisoners slowly emerge from their cells, Fidelio, however, anxiously scrutinising the face of each of them in turn.

They enter slowly and hesitantly, with subdued expressions of their joy at seeing the light and breathing the air of day once more, the orchestra surrounding their halting words with tender phrases of this type:

No. 21

"The prison is a tomb!" they mutter from time to time:

No. 22

One of them ventures to breathe a hope that by God's help they will one day be free; but another softly warns him to speak low, for everywhere around them are hostile eyes and ears:

No. 23

and they resume their pathetic cries of delight at the small mercy that has been vouchsafed to them.

As they drag their feeble bodies towards the garden Rocco re-enters, bringing Fidelio the news that Pizarro not only sanctions the marriage with Marzelline but consents to Fidelio being allowed to descend into the dungeon with the jailer that very day. She gives a great cry of "To-day! Today!" "Yes," replies Rocco; "in a few moments we two will go down to the man who for weeks now has been given less and less to eat"—for he is now to be "set free" in the most sinister sense of the words: within an hour his grave is to be dug. "Is he dead, then?" asks Leonora. "Not yet, not yet," is the reply. "Are you going to kill him, then?" she asks with a shudder. The jailer reassures her as to this. He himself will commit no murder; "the Governor himself will enter and strike the fatal blow; my duty and yours is simply to prepare the grave." "Perhaps my husband's grave!" Leonora mutters, aghast.

15

Then, at a stroke, mainly by means of a complete change of harmonic colour, Beethoven plunges us by anticipation into the atmosphere of the prison cell itself. A new phrase:

No. 24

is passed through one sombre metamorphosis after another as Rocco describes how Fidelio is to help him in his distasteful work—the digging of a grave in a ruined well—a task, he fears, for which the youth's tender constitution unfits him. The lad is almost weeping, he observes, and he offers to spare him the ordeal and carry out Pizarro's orders without his help; while Leonora, for her part, tries to make light of the emotion that is racking her, protesting that she will go through with her task whatever may befall her.

Marzelline and Jacquino break in upon their colloquy with the news that Pizarro, having learned from the officer of Rocco's indulgence to the prisoners, is breathing fire and vengeance. He storms in, cursing the jailer for his presumption, and is only calmed down a little when Rocco craftily reminds him that this is the name-day of the King, when a little indulgence may surely be permitted: let the Governor be content with the extinction of the prisoner he hates most, and spare the others. Thereupon Pizarro orders him to go below at once and dig the grave; meanwhile the prisoners are to return to their cells, and Rocco is not to permit himself such disobedience again.

So, with the whole company now on the boards, we glide into

the big ensemble that ends the act in the approved manner; the prisoners lament the briefness of their taste of light and air:

No. 25

Pizarro repeats his frenzied commands to Rocco, the jailer deplores the task laid upon him but which he dares not refuse, Leonora asks herself distractedly if justice has vanished from the earth and evil-doers reign supreme, Marzelline expresses her sympathy with the abject creatures as they slink back, cowed, to their cells, and Jacquino almost manages to forget their misery, so full is he of his own trouble, his blind jealousy of Fidelio. The drama has worked up to its highest point of tension so far, and everyone has his part to play in the ensemble; but as it is difficult for us to understand what each of them is saying, for all are saying different things at the same time, it is the total musical effect alone that counts in the theatre. The act ends with a few quiet chords in the orchestra that attune us to the mood of what is to follow.

16

The second act takes us into the dark dungeon in which Florestan is immured. At the back a wall and a flight of steps are dimly visible; there is a low entrance on one side; on the other everything seems to be in ruins. Florestan, fastened by a long chain to the wall, is seated on a stone.

The act opens with a sombre, slow-moving orchestral introduction in which there figures largely an anguished chromatic phrase:

No. 26

that anticipates the idiom of Tannhäuser's story of his pilgrimage to Rome. Tremolandos in the strings over throbbing figures in the kettledrums add to the gloom and horror of the scene. Florestan breaks the sinister silence with a cry of "Oh God! what darkness here!" ("Oh silence full of horror and solitude!"), No. 26 in the orchestra adding a poignant commentary on his words.[1] His trial is hard, but he will not murmur at his fate, for God's will is just, the recitative continues: and after a short orchestral preamble he breaks into the main melody of the first part of his aria—"Happiness has deserted me in the springtime of my youth; I dared to speak the truth, and these chains are my reward; now my days are ending in shame, my sole consolation being the thought that I did my duty":

No. 27

Then, as the tempo quickens and lighter colours spread through the orchestra, he sings ecstatically, but calmly, of the softer and sweeter air that seems to fill his cell; on the threshold of the grave a light strikes on him, and in it he sees an angel having the semblance of his Leonora and conducting him to freedom in another and better world:

No. 28

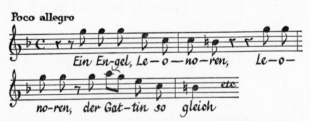

[1] The humorists have not failed to observe that although Florestan has been in the dungeon a good two years it is only now, apparently, that he has really noticed how dark and quiet it is in this living tomb of his. The laws of verisimilitude in real life do not always apply, however, to opera.

The final section of the aria is liberally besprinkled, as befits a tenor solo, with high A's and B flats. The orchestra continues in the same excited way for a few bars after the voice has ceased, then subsides into a series of ejaculations that shade off by a slow diminuendo into three bars of pianissimo chords.

This was the aria which, as we have seen, Beethoven had to recast in 1814 to meet the demands of the tenor for a show piece in which he could "distinguish himself" and earn his round of applause.[1] Röckel, in his reminiscences, said that "in order to satisfy in some measure the new Florestan, the Italian Radichi, who wanted applause after his aria—which, after the pianissimo ending (with the violins muted), and having regard to the situation, was neither possible, proper nor desirable, except by writing a new aria—Beethoven cut the adagio [of the older version] in two and concluded with an allegro in the singer's high register: but as the din of applause would not have been of any help to Rocco and Fidelio—who enter there and then with the intention of digging the grave of the probably dead prisoner, Beethoven decided to end the bustling allegro with a short new pianissimo coda, by which means the stillness necessary for the succeeding scene would be re-established." This is not ideally lucid.[2] If the audience were to break in, as audiences are inclined to do, immediately the singer had ended on his top notes, Beethoven's pianissimo orchestral coda might just as well not have been written, for it would be quite inaudible; while if they waited until the coda had run its course and *then* applauded the singer, the original difficulty would still remain—Rocco and Fidelio would have to enter after a din quite out of keeping with the solemnity

---

[1] We can only regret that Beethoven did not leave Florestan's aria in its 1805 form, which is superior to the later one not only musically but in psychological appropriateness.

[2] The Thayer-Krehbiel English *Life of Beethoven* makes matters worse by a woeful mistranslation at one point: "da aber das Geräusch des Applauses Rocco und Fidelio . . . nicht bestärkt haben würde" ("but as the din of applause would not have been any help to Rocco and Fidelio") is nonsensically rendered "but as the noise of applause would not have been *increased by* Rocco and Fidelio, who enter at this moment," etc. What Röckel meant is that the situation, so far as Fidelio and the jailer were concerned, would be ruined by the two gravediggers entering while the audience was applauding the singer.

of the scene. It looks as though Beethoven's idea was that the orchestra should cease playing after the cadence in F major at the end of the aria and let the audience have its minute or so of enthusiasm and the tenor his minute or so of triumph—not as Florestan but as "the Italian Radichi,"—and then resume with the quiet coda which leads without a break into the music that accompanies the entry of Fidelio and Rocco. Quotation of the sixteen bars that follow the F major of the orchestra (shading off in a sempre diminuendo to a double pianissimo) may help the reader to see the situation more clearly:

No. 29

Of course if the audience is intelligent enough to wait until the orchestra has finished before applauding the tenor the difficulty foreseen by Beethoven will not arise.

17

The final F major of our last quotation joins up with the basic F of what follows. This episode is what was known in those days as a melodrama, i.e. an action carried on in speech with the orchestra joining in descriptively here and there. Rocco and Leonora are now in the vault, which, as it lies deep underground, strikes cold into the latter's young blood. Rocco points out to her the almost invisible form of Florestan, who, during the orchestral coda shown in No. 29, has sunk down exhausted. She fears that the man is dead, but the jailer assures her that he is only sleeping. Leonora tries in vain to distinguish his features: "God help me if it is he!" she ejaculates under her breath. To reminders of No. 24 in the orchestra Rocco gropes about until he finds the opening of the old well; then he begins digging, watched by the trembling Fidelio. The muted strings keep up a persistent dull throbbing under which we hear from time to time a sinister figure in the double bassoon:

No. 30

Leonora helps him as well as she can, assuring him in moving phrases that her zeal will not falter:

No. 31

and all the while trying to make out the prisoner's features. To the best of her strength she helps Rocco to dislodge a heavy stone.[1] Still to the same fateful orchestral accompaniment as is shown in No. 30 the grisly work goes on, with Rocco urging his assistant to greater efforts, for Pizarro will soon be there, and Leonora, still anxiously scanning the face of the sleeping man, vowing to herself that whoever he may be she will somehow loosen his chains and set him free. So runs its slow course one of the most moving episodes in the whole range of opera.

At last Rocco pauses in his work for a drink of wine, and Leonora observes that the prisoner is awake. "Awake?" repeats Rocco; "then he is sure to ask me a thousand questions as usual, so I must speak with him alone." He clambers out of the grave, bidding Fidelio take his place there and make the clearance necessary for opening up the old well. He goes over to Florestan

[1] In his Sketch Book Beethoven has twice written at this point "They take breath," accompanied by a sketch for appropriate descriptive music. This realistic touch, however, does not appear in the score.

and asks him if he has had a little rest. "Rest?" is the weary reply; "where could I ever find rest?" Faint as his voice is, Leonora thinks she recognizes it: "If only I could see his face for a moment!" Suddenly, while the prisoner is reproaching his jailer for his harshness to him he turns his face in the direction of Leonora: recognising him now, she falls senseless on the edge of the grave.

"What would you have of me?" Rocco asks the prisoner gruffly; "I merely obey my orders." "Surely," says Florestan, "you can tell me now, at last, who is the Governor of this prison?" "Don Pizarro," is the reply. "Send someone as quickly as you can to Seville," the prisoner implores him, "to find Leonora, wife of Florestan, and tell her that I lie here in chains, in the power of the cruel Pizarro." ["Oh God!" murmurs Leonora; "if he knew that I am here, digging his grave!"] "If I am doomed to end my days here, make my time of suffering short: give me, for pity's sake, just a drop of water." All that Rocco can offer him is what is left of the wine in his bottle, which he tells Fidelio to bring to him.

She hastens with it to Florestan's side, with a cry of "Here it is!" At the sound of her voice a faint memory of the past stirs in him. "Who is that?" he asks. "My turnkey," Rocco replies, "and in a few days my son-in-law." While Florestan is drinking what remains of the wine Rocco notices how strangely moved Fidelio is, and asks the reason. Perturbed and embarrassed, she can only reply, "But you too, sir, are moved." "True," says the jailer; "there is something in his voice . . ." "Yes," Fidelio continues significantly, "something that goes to the very depths of one's heart!"

Florestan's thanks—"You will have your reward in a better land, for it is heaven that has sent you to me":

No. 32

are the beginning of a trio in which Rocco too expresses his pity for the human wreck before him, whose last hour it appears to be. Leonora's soul is divided between sorrow and hope; for Florestan and herself it is now either death or rescue. Florestan cannot comprehend why not only the boy but the jailer himself is suddenly so moved. In a brief episode that tears at one's heartstrings Leonora begs to be allowed to give the prisoner a piece of bread she has brought with her, which request Rocco, with some misgivings on the score of duty, finally grants. She gives it to Florestan—"Oh take this morsel of bread, poor wretched man!":

No. 33

He stammers his thanks, and the trio continues with a repetition of No. 32: hope is beginning to dawn in Leonora's heart, Florestan promises her a reward in heaven for her kindness, and Rocco too is filled with pity for the prisoner's long sufferings, the end of which is apparently near.

18

There is a moment's silence after the trio: then the action is carried on for a little while in speech again. Rocco feels that it is time he gave his master the signal that all is ready, and going to the back of the stage he opens the door and blows a whistle. "Is that my death-knell?" asks Florestan, and to himself he murmurs, "Oh, my Leonora! shall I ever see thee again?" Mastering her own emotions she exhorts him to be calm: "Be calm, I tell you. Remember, whatever you may see and hear, that there is a Providence over all." She goes back to the well as Pizarro enters, closely muffled in his cloak. In a feigned voice he asks if everything is ready. "Yes," replies Rocco, "it remains now only to open the well." At Pizarro's bidding he orders Fidelio to leave them, whereupon she retires to the background, while Pizarro mutters that to secure his own safety afterwards he must make an end not only of his prisoner but of the jailer.

Rocco is about to remove Florestan's chains when Pizarro stops him, draws his dagger, and breaks out into another ferocious denunciation of his victim; "He shall die! But first of all he shall know who it is that finds vengeance in his death!"; and throwing

back his cloak he reveals himself as the Pizarro whom Florestan
had once opposed: now *his* day has come, the day of revenge, he
repeats frenziedly. This outburst launches a great quartet. Calmly
and scornfully Florestan stigmatises him as a common murderer.
Pizarro, blind with fury, attempts to stab him; but Leonora rushes
forward, covers Florestan with her body, and defies the murderer
to do his worst: it is he, not his prisoner, who shall die. Pizarro
hurls her away; the astonished Rocco also urges Fidelio to stand
back out of harm's way. But she is now in almost complete control
of the situation. She sobers them all with a great climactic cry of
"Kill first his wife! (Turning to Florestan) I am Leonora! (Addressing Pizarro) Yes, I am his wife; I have sworn consolation to
him and perdition to you!" "You both shall die," Pizarro cries, and
he presses forward to the pair. Leonora halts him by drawing
a pistol and presenting it at him; [1] and as the excitement of the
quartet rises to its climax there comes from without a trumpet
call: [2]

No. 34

—the warning from the tower that the Minister's cortège has been
sighted on the Seville road. This is the trumpet fanfare that makes
so profound an effect in the Leonora No. 3 overture—now the
most frequently performed of the three—in the concert room,
and here, as there, it is followed by a sweeping phrase in the
orchestra that seems to spread great consoling wings over the
scene:

[1] Schröder-Devrient shook Berlioz to the depths of his being when he
saw *Fidelio* in Paris: in this episode he describes the womanly "trembling of
the hand" that held the pistol at Pizarro's head and the "convulsive laugh"
that accompanied the action.
[2] Beethoven is thought to have derived the idea of using the trumpet signal
in the Leonora overtures No. 2 and No. 3 from the overture to Méhul's *Helena*
(1803).

No. 35

Through the quiet texture of it we hear Florestan and Leonora,
locked in each other's arms, pouring out their gratitude to heaven,
and the ejaculations of the stunned Pizarro and Rocco at this
unexpected turn of events. Then the trumpet signal rings out
again, this time nearer. Jacquino appears at the top of the staircase, accompanied by two officers and soldiers carrying torches,
and tells Rocco that the Minister and his entourage are already
at the gates. The jailer, whose heart has never really been in his
horrid work, is rejoiced at the news. "God be praised!" he ejaculates under his breath. "We will come at once," he says to
Jacquino; "let those men with torches come down here and light
the way up for my lord the Governor." The soldiers descend,
their torches now lighting up the stage: and Jacquino and the
officers go out by the way they came.

There follows a vigorous quartet, in which Leonora and Florestan give wild expression to their joy in the triumph of love over
hatred and revenge, Pizarro calls down curses on those who have
frustrated him and made him an object of scorn, and Rocco is
torn between fears for his own future and relief at having no
longer to serve as the reluctant instrument of Pizarro's cruel will.

The torch-bearers escort Pizarro out by way of the stairs, Rocco
following them. With cries of "Leonora!", "Florestan!", husband
and wife fall into each other's arms, and, in an ecstatic duet—
"Oh joy beyond expressing!":

No. 36

pour out their gratitude to heaven for the grace that has been
vouchsafed them.[1]

[1] This was one of several places in which Treitschke's tightening up of
the action was not quite successful. In the present *Fidelio* this duet seems

The scene changes to an open space outside the prison. An exuberant orchestral introduction in C major leads into a chorus in which the people and the liberated prisoners praise the new day that has dawned for all now that justice and pity have so suddenly and unexpectedly joined hands. As the chorus rises to its climax the benevolent Minister of State Fernando enters, together with Pizarro, who is escorted by a guard. In a majestic recitative the Minister expounds the laudable sentiments that were very much in the air in the post-Revolution days and especially dear to Beethoven: "The best of kings has sent me hither to dispel the dark clouds of evil under which you have so long cowered. No longer bend the knee in slavish fear: no cruel tyrant shall ye find in me: let brother seek out brother, helping where he can"; sentiments which the people greet with enthusiasm.

Rocco forces his way through the guards, accompanied by Leonora and Florestan, whom he commends to the Minister as objects specially worthy of his pity and protection. Fernando is astonished to recognise in the broken creature standing in fetters before him the friend of other days who had fought so nobly for humanity and whom he had long thought dead, and still more astonished at the sight of Leonora in such a place. The voluble Rocco explains that she had come to him in male disguise in pursuit of her great purpose, served as his assistant, and been so scrupulous in the performance of his duties that he had accepted him as his future son-in-law. The disclosure of Fidelio's sex naturally fills poor Marzelline with confusion. "This inhuman monster," continues the jailer, pointing to Pizarro, "was on the point of murdering Florestan." "With his assistance," interposes Pizarro, not without some show of reason; "only the arrival of your Excellency frustrated the design." The people demand the punishment of Pizarro, who, at a sign from Fernando, is taken away by the soldiers.

The Minister takes a lenient view of Rocco's share in the matter: "You dug his grave," he tells him; "now be it your deed to strike off his fetters. But stop! yours, noble lady, be that task!" To a solemn strain in the orchestra Leonora gratefully does so. Flores-

suddenly to drop in from nowhere in particular: in the First Version it was led up to by an expressive recitative.

tan voices his own happiness, Fernando praises the justice of
heaven, Marzelline and Rocco echo him, and soloists and chorus
join in a great ensemble of thanks to God. This first section of the
finale ends with Leonora soaring to the high B flat.[1] The second
section is a hymn of praise to womanhood and its incarnation in
Leonora—"Let all who have won for themselves a gracious wife
join in our jubilant song":

No. 37

(The two lines are taken, with a small verbal alteration, from
Schiller's Ode to Joy: they recur in the finale of the Ninth Symphony.) The strain is launched by the chorus, with Florestan,
Leonora and the others, including Marzelline and Jacquino, joining in one by one; and the opera ends in universal rejoicing.

20

It has been suggested in some quarters that in the final scene
Leonora should not appear as Fidelio but in clothes appropriate
to her sex, thus giving more point to the universal laudation of
womanhood in the last chorus. Several minutes have elapsed before Florestan and Leonora appear after the change of scene
from the dungeon to the open air, and so, the argument runs,
there would be ample time for Leonora to drape herself in some
sort of mantle supplied by one of the women in the crowd that
has assembled to greet the Minister, and to let down her hair;
while for Marzelline's dismayed ejaculation "Woe's me! What do
I hear?"—after Rocco has disclosed that his assistant Fidelio is
not a man but a woman—it is proposed to substitute, "What do
I see? What do I hear?" All in all, however, it is perhaps best to
leave the matter where Beethoven and his librettists did.

On the 20th November 1905, the hundredth anniversary of the
first performance of the first *Fidelio*, the work in its original form,

---

[1] No doubt the singer (Anna Milder) had asked for something of this
kind, for among the sketches of 1814 for the opera is a memorandum by
Beethoven, "high B flat for Milder."

as reconstructed by Erich Prieger from a number of sources, was given in Berlin. The fact that it had only a few performances was due, in part, to the soprano's fear that some of the more exacting passages would do her voice permanent harm, especially the coloratura in the big aria to which reference has been made above, and the high notes in the duet "Oh joy beyond expression" (No. 36), which, in the First Version:

No. 38

O na—men, na—men—lo—se Freude,

ran virtually on the lines shewn in the quotation on page 247. Naturally, after that, no other singer was keen to take on the part, which here and there demands a vocal agility which no present-day dramatic soprano can reasonably be expected to have. It is hard, however, to reconcile ourselves to the complete loss of the First Version, which, though generally inferior to the final one in dramatic concision, is musically superior to it in some places. Hence the suggestion made in 1925 by Hans Joachim Moser that a "Fourth Version" of the opera might well be attempted now, that would incorporate all that is best in the first and the third. This would mean rather a longer *Fidelio* than the present one, but, as Moser pointed out, the opera is actually one of the shortest in the repertory, and a good deal of time could be saved by omitting the unnecessary Leonora No. 3 overture. Everyone who knows the original version will agree with Moser that "we would be essentially richer for the restoration of all that is best in the *Leonora* score [i.e. that of 1805], which deserves a better fate than a second century of sleep in the libraries."

21

There remain to be considered the four overtures to the opera.

In the theatre the Leonora No. 1, No. 2 and No. 3 are equally impossible, the first because it cannot hold its ground in our minds against the mighty No. 2 and No. 3, while each of these too completely summarises the dramatic action and lives at too

high a tension for us to be able to adapt ourselves after them to
the domestic scene played out before our eyes when the curtain
rises: as Romain Rolland put it, "how can we descend from these
epics to the babblings of the jailer's family?" It became the practice in the nineteenth century to play the No. 3 during the course
of the opera, generally between the prison scene and the finale.
But while we are all willing to listen to the overture purely for
its own great self at any time, the inclusion of it in the opera at
this point is dramatically an error, if only because its tumultuous
final section sums up and rounds off the inner meaning of the
drama with such overwhelming emotional power that we feel it as
a drop to earth again when the curtain rises on the scene in which
the Minister comes in as the *deus ex machina.* The proper place
of the No. 2 and the No. 3 today is in the concert room.

The fourth overture—the *Fidelio*—is the right one with which
to begin the opera, for it dispenses with the vast symphonic structure and the highly dramatic narrative of the Leonora No. 2 and
No. 3 and enables us to tune in without difficulty to the domestic
atmosphere of the first scene. It begins with four bars expressive
of joyous resolution:

No. 39

succeeded by a soft adagio phrase derived perhaps from the
orchestral postlude to Florestan's aria:

No. 40

After a repetition of No. 39 and No. 40 the strings begin, pianissimo, a gentle undulation that rises gradually to a fortissimo:
then, after another quiet reference to No. 40, the main allegro of

287

the overture begins. This is based on a simple development and contrast of two subjects, both expressive of joy:

No. 41

No. 42

Towards the end, exploiting a device often used by him, Beethoven reverts once more for a few bars to the quiet No. 40, then takes up in a mad presto the joyous figure shown in the first bar of No. 39 and No. 41. His concern throughout has been not to traverse afresh the course of the drama, as in the two mighty Leonora overtures—for apart from No. 40 there is no reference to the music of the opera itself—but to suggest the happy ending of it all.

Don Giovanni

MOZART [1756–1791]

CHARACTERS

DON GIOVANNI, "an extremely licentious young nobleman"	*Baritone*
DONNA ANNA	*Soprano*
DONNA ELVIRA	*Soprano*
ZERLINA	*Soprano*
DON OTTAVIO	*Tenor*
LEPORELLO	*Bass*
THE COMMANDER	*Bass*
MASETTO	*Bass*

1

THE PROBABLE sources of the Don Juan saga have been investigated with great thoroughness by many scholars. Though the elements of the story are found in the folk lore of more than one country, including Iceland, there may have been an ancient tradition in Seville of a young rapscallion of noble birth whose career of crime came somehow to a violent end in a church; while folk stories are fairly abundant of a grisly supping of living people with the dead. It is possible that in the Spain of the sixteenth or seventeenth century these two cardinal dramatic factors had begun to coalesce in the imagination of either the people or the playwrights. With matters so purely antiquarian as these we need not trouble ourselves here; our concern is simply with the first literary results of that coalescence, the forms the story took in the hands of later dramatists, and the bearing of it all on the Mozart-Da Ponte opera *Don Giovanni*.

The original shaper of the complete tale as we now have it

seems to have been a Spanish monk named Gabriel Tellez (1571–1648), who wrote under the name of Tirso de Molina. Later reports as to his scandalous way of living seem to have no foundation in fact; he ended his days as Prior at Soria, "renowned as a preacher of most tranquil, virtuous life." The legend of his immorality no doubt sprang from the intimate acquaintance his plays show him to have had with the seamier and more adventurous side of human nature; but "it appears to be forgotten," as a historian of Spanish literature remarks, "that Tirso spent years in the confessional—no bad position for the study of frailty." [1]

The first part of his "theatre" was published in 1634, the fifth in 1637. His *El Burlador de Sevilla* appeared in Barcelona in 1630 as the seventh of *Twelve New Plays by Lope de Vega Carpio and Other Authors,* where it is described as a "famous comedy" by "the Maestro Tirso de Molina." The "famous" suggests that by 1630 the play had already been before the public for some time. Its popularity is shown by the number of editions it went through in the seventeenth and eighteenth centuries. Tirso's authorship has been questioned in some quarters, but it is now generally accepted. In 1878 a copy was discovered of a drama, dating from the first half of the seventeenth century, entitled *Tan largo me lo fiáis,* and stated on the title page to be the work of "Don Pedro Calderón." [2] No doubt the vogue of the subject led to more than one contemporary imitation of Tirso; and today his right to be regarded as the true creator of the long-lived saga is generally admitted. But even this might have gone the way of the rest of his large output, surviving to be read now only by specialists in Spanish literature, had it not been for one remarkable feature of *El Burlador de Sevilla, y Convidado de Piedra* [3]—the terrifying and edifying part played in the punishment of the hero-villain by the statue of a murdered man. It was this that quickly captured

[1] James Fitzmaurice-Kelly, *A History of Spanish Literature*, p. 308.

[2] This is now accessible to students in the complete annotated edition of Tirso's plays by Emilio Lotarelo (two vols., Madrid 1906–7). "Tan largo me lo fiáis" is an expression frequently in the mouth of Tirso's Don Juan; it seems to have been a catch-phrase of the period.

[3] "Burlador" means "scoffer," "jester," "mocker," "trickster," and other things of that sort. Perhaps the best colloquial rendering of it in the Don Juan connection today would be "playboy." "Convidado de piedra" means "the stone guest" (at a meal).

the interest of the Spanish, French and Italian world. Without some knowledge of Tirso's play it is impossible to understand how Da Ponte's libretto came to have not only the virtues but the faults we are now conscious of in it. It will be as well, therefore, to tell the story of the Spanish drama in some detail.

2

It opens not in Seville but in Naples. The scene is the interior of the royal palace; the time, night. A door opens, and we see Don Juan, his face carefully concealed in his cloak, being ushered out stealthily by one of the great ladies of the court, the Duchess Isabela. "Come this way, Duke Octavio," she whispers; "it will be safer." She would like an assurance that the favours she has just bestowed on him will find their legitimation in marriage. This the cloaked man promises fervently, but when she talks of bringing a light to facilitate his exit he protests vehemently that if she does so he will extinguish it. Her suspicions are now aroused; and discovering that he is not, as she had thought, her fiancé the Duke Octavio, she cries out for help. The clamour brings on the scene the King of Naples—with a lighted candle— the royal guard, and Don Pedro Tenorio, the Spanish Ambassador to the Neapolitan court. In the obscurity of the room the King cannot recognise either the man or the woman, for Isabela, like Don Juan, prudently keeps her face covered; but he orders the guards to arrest both culprits, consigns them to the custody of Don Pedro, and departs. Having sent Isabela away with the guard, Don Pedro turns for an explanation to the audacious young cavalier, who has sworn he would kill anyone who dared lay a hand on him. He claims, in a manner of speaking, diplomatic immunity; he is a gentleman, he says, attached to the Spanish embassy. To Don Pedro, however, when they two are left alone, he discloses his identity—he is Don Juan, Don Pedro's nephew. Asked by his startled uncle what he has to say in excuse for his conduct he brazenly declares that his youth and his ardours justify him in everything he does, including his recent triumph, disguised as the Duke Octavio, over the virtue of the highly respected Duchess Isabela. His uncle upbraids him for his crimes and his impious pride in them, but for family reasons feels bound to save him from punishment and disgrace; so he lets him escape *via* the

291

balcony, bidding him fly to Milan or Sicily and there go into hiding.

When the King returns, Don Pedro tells him that his intrepid prisoner has managed to escape; though badly injured, he says, the man had fought off the soldiers who would have arrested him and had leaped from the balcony. Don Pedro gives the astonished King the further information that the lady in the case is the Duchess Isabela, and that her ravisher, according to her own story, was the Duke Octavio. The King orders her to be brought before him; she is either too confused or too crafty to disclose the whole simple truth of the affair, so the King orders her to be imprisoned; Duke Octavio also is to be arrested, brought before him, and made to put things right by marrying Isabela, who now consoles herself with the sage feminine reflection that, after all, if the Duke marries her not much harm will have been done.

The scene changes to a room in Octavio's house in Naples, where we find him rhapsodising to his servant Ripio over the charms and virtues of his adored Isabela. He is interrupted by the entry of Don Pedro, who tells him he has been sent by the King to arrest him. A seducer, it appears, had been found that night in the chamber of the Duchess Isabela. The libertine had escaped, but the lady herself had assured the King that he was none other than her betrothed, Duke Octavio. The Duke's grieved and angry protestations at the lady's perfidy are of no avail. Don Pedro kindly offers to connive at his escape; so the Duke goes off to Spain, there to rail at fate and the inconstancy and unveracity of woman.

3

The next scene is the beach at Tarragona, where the beautiful and chaste Tisbea, who lives in a nearby cottage, is congratulating herself at great length on her freedom from the ordinary weaknesses of her sex; her love is sought by all, but to their sighs and pleas she is indifferent. Just then two men are cast up on the beach by a storm that has wrecked their boat: they are Don Juan and his servant Catalinón. It all ends, of course, with the accomplished seducer triumphing over the virtue of the proud country maiden under the customary promise of marriage, and the soon-forsaken one registering the furies and despairs traditionally regarded by the poets as appropriate to such occasions. When the valet remonstrates with his master, as he often does, for living so evilly, and warns him that he will pay for his crimes after his death, Juan replies with a jaunty phrase that he employs throughout the play on such occasions, like a kind of leitmotif, and which we may render colloquially, for our purposes, as "Time enough for that." Before the climax of the Tisbea affair is reached, however, we have been taken to the Alcazar at Seville, where King Alonzo of Castille is congratulating a worthy gentleman, Don Gonzalo de Ulloa, on his recent loyal services as ambassador at the Lisbon court. Anxious to reward him for these, the King, having learned that he has a beautiful daughter, Doña Ana, declares that he will bestow her in marriage on a certain gentleman of his court, one Don Juan Tenorio.

In a later scene in the Alcazar we find the King receiving Don Diego Tenorio, the father of our hero, who gives him the latest news he has received from his brother Don Pedro, the Spanish ambassador in Naples—that the young Juan had been found at night in the apartment of one of the beauties of the court, the Duchess Isabela. The seducer and his valet, it appears, are now in Seville. The King is shocked, but out of regard for Don Diego consents to pardon Don Juan if he marries Isabela; meanwhile the young man must leave at once for Lebrija. As for the unfortunate Duke Octavio, he shall be properly indemnified for his prematrimonial misfortune. Then the King remembers that he has already promised Don Gonzalo that Juan shall marry Doña Ana. The situation looks like becoming a trifle awkward, but the keen royal intellect perceives a way out: the King will compensate Don Gonzalo by making him Grand Majordomo.

Just then a servant announces the arrival of Don Octavio. The alarmed Diego implores the King to forbid the duel that must inevitably follow a meeting between Octavio and his dear son Juan, whose peccadilloes, he pleads, are merely the product of his youth and high spirits. Octavio having entered and begged the King's support in his quest for vengeance on the author of his wrongs, Alonzo assures him that while he fully sympathises with him he has made a false step in leaving Naples. However, he will urge the King of Naples to restore him to his former condition, while he, Alonzo, will marry him to a lady far superior in beauty to Isabela, none other than the pearl of Castille, the virtuous Doña Ana, daughter of Don Gonzalo de Ulloa, Commander of Cala-trava. Octavio leaves the royal presence overwhelmed with joy. In the street he runs into Don Juan and Catalinón. (He does not know, of course, that it is to his friend Don Juan that he owes all his troubles in Naples.) Each of them courteously assures the other that he is wholly at his service on all occasions; and the dupe and the rogue part on the best of terms.

Octavio and his man Ripio having left the scene, a new charac-ter is introduced—Don Juan's boon companion in Seville debauch-ery, the Marquis de la Mota. We are concerned with him here only in so far as he contributes unconsciously to the downfall of Juan. Accident places in the latter's hands a letter from Doña Ana to her lover the Marquis: "My faithless father has secretly disposed of my hand without giving me any choice. . . . If you value my love and my volition as they deserve, and if your love for me is sincere, now is the time to prove it. Tonight at eleven my door will be left open for you. Come to me; your hopes shall be fulfilled and your love receive its recompense. To ensure that my duennas will let you pass, wear a coloured cape. . . .[1] Adieu, my unfortu-nate lover!" Thereupon Juan, perfidious as usual even towards his closest friends, goes to the Marquis, tells him that he has been entrusted with a message for him, and gives him the purport of the letter, making the hour of assignation, however, not eleven but midnight.

4

There follows another scene between Don Diego and Don Juan, in which the distressed father tells his son that all Seville knows now of his evil behaviour in Naples, and warns him that God will one day exact an account from him. The young man's reply is his usual one: "Time enough for that! Life is long!" Don Diego gives him the King's message—he is to go at once to Lerija and remain there until Octavio has received due satisfaction and the scandal has died down. Juan merely laughs at the distressed old man. Soon we find him encountering the Marquis again

[1] "In former times," we are told, "the cape was a military distinction worn by noblemen." Thus clothed, Mota's rank would be manifest, and the servants of the household presumably would not dare to bar his way.

(whom he recognizes in the darkness by his cape). Mota is waiting for midnight outside Don Gonzalo's house with a body of musicians for the serenading of Doña Ana. To help Juan in an alleged amorous adventure of his own, Mota lends him his cape; thus all the winning cards come, as usual, into Juan's hands. He steals into Don Gonzalo's house, whence there soon come frenzied cries from Ana: "Traitor, you are not the Marquis! I have been duped!" The venerable Gonzalo, coming to the rescue of his daughter, is killed by Juan. There follows a brief colloquy with the still unsuspecting Mota, after which Don Juan, having returned the cape, and told him of the fatal end to the adventure of which he had spoken, seeks safety in flight with Catalinón.

Lights and cries from the direction of the Alcazar attract Mota's attention. He is taken for the murderer of Gonzalo and arrested by Don Diego: then the King arrives, who promises him execution on the morrow. "As for the Commander," says the King, "bury him with royal splendour and solemnity; make a tomb for him of bronze and stone, surmounted by his statue, and engrave on it the story of his murder and the chastisement of the crime. Obsequies, statue, tomb," his Majesty adds grandly, "all at my expense." Doña Ana, it appears, has placed herself under the protection of the Queen.

5

The scene changes to Dos-Hermanas, where the still unrepentant Juan has the good luck to stumble on the wedding feast of a simple country couple named Aminta and Batricio, and in due course, under the usual promise of marriage, he seduces the bride. Then, highly pleased with himself and in defiance of danger, he makes his way back with Catalinón to Seville.

Next we meet with Isabela and Fabio (her servant) at Tarragona, on their way to Seville. Isabela, while regretting the Naples incident, is on the whole not displeased with the turn in her fortunes—to be the wife of "the noble Don Juan," whom the King has made a Count—but anxious that her "honour" shall be in no way publicly compromised. She falls in with a young woman bewailing her fate in flowery seventeenth century style. It is Tisbea once more, who tells the great lady of her deception and ruin by a villain who had been cast up on the shore by a tempest—a certain Don Juan Tenorio. It ends with the horrified Isabela taking Tisbea with her to Seville, in the hope that justice may be done to both of them.

Meanwhile Don Juan and Catalinón are back in Seville again. They find themselves in a church, in the chapel of which is a tomb surmounted by a statue. The valet warns his master, as he had often done before, of the perils in which he has managed to involve himself: Octavio, it appears, has at last learned the truth about the Naples affair and is hot upon the traitor's track; Mota has discovered the ruse of the letter and the cape; Isabela has arrived for her wedding to Juan; and so on. Juan cuts him short with threats and blows; what harm can come to one so bold and resourceful as he, especially here, on the sacred ground of the church? While he is chuckling over his exploit at Dos-Hermanas a curtain glides aside, revealing the tomb of Don Gonzalo. Juan gaily compliments the defunct gentleman on the magnificence of his present habitation, and reads the epitaph placed on it by order of the King: "Here, awaiting the vengeance of heaven on a traitor, lies the most loyal of gentlemen." This excites Don Juan's hilarity: "how can you," he gaily asks the statue, "an old man with a beard of stone, avenge yourself?"; and he lays an irreverent hand on the beard. Pursuing his jest, he addresses the statue: "this evening I will await you at dinner in my house; then, if it is vengeance you want, you can defy me. But what sort of a fight could you put up with your stone sword? If you are to have your revenge, curtail your sleep, for if you wait till I too am dead you may say goodbye to hope. You will have to nurse your anger a long while! Time enough yet for all that!"

Catalinón hurries him away, and the scene changes to a room in which servants are laying the table for Don Juan's supper. He forces Catalinón to sit down with him. Suddenly knocking is heard without. The trembling valet opines that it is the ministers of the law; but Don Juan angrily bids him go to the door and see who or what is there. Catalinón does so and staggers back in terror; what he has seen he cannot bring himself to say, for he dares not believe his eyes: "I saw him, I swear it!" he stammers, "He spoke to me. I answered him. I saw him . . . " But who it was he had seen he cannot or will not say. Don Juan, in a rage, himself takes a candle and goes to the door. It flies open, and he sees Don Gonzalo in the shape he had borne in the chapel. Juan mechanically draws his sword, but recoils. The statue advances slowly towards him, and, forcing him back to the middle of the stage, announces that he has come in response to his invitation. With much bravado on Juan's part and craven buffoonery on Catalinón's, and to the accompaniment of music from behind the scenes, the grisly meal goes on, till at last Juan orders Catalinón and the servants to leave him alone with his guest. "Now then," he says: "the door is closed and I await your will. Shade, vision or phantom, what do you desire of me? If your soul is in torment and demands satisfaction of me, speak, for I give you my word to do whatever you wish." The statue, "slowly, in a voice that seems to come from another world," bids him give him his hand as pledge of the word of a gentleman. Defiantly Don Juan does so: "you should have my hand if you came from hell itself!" Grasping the hand, the statue makes him swear to be his guest at ten the next evening in the church: "and see you keep your word as I have kept mine."

6

It goes out slowly, leaving·Juan, for the first time in his life, troubled and a little afraid, for strangely enough the stone hand had seemed to burn his flesh. Then, with a great effort, he masters himself: "Bah! all this is pure imagination. Fear of the dead is the worst, the most craven of all fears. Tomorrow I will go to supper in the church, for all Seville admires and marvels at my courage."

There follows a short scene in the palace, where the King and Juan's father, Don Diego, are awaiting Isabela. Diego has heard that she has arrived in Seville in an ill humour: the King, still ignorant of the real character of Don Juan, commands him to be sent for; if he shows any signs of a good disposition he will make him a Count and endow him with a fief. Isabela, says the King, should be satisfied with the way things have turned out: true, she has lost a Duke, but she has won a Count. This day Doña Ana too shall be married, though not to Octavio: that would perhaps be asking too much of that honourable gentleman. Ana has begged the Queen to obtain a pardon for the Marquis de la Mota, whom she wishes to marry. This pardon the King now grants. Everything seems, especially to Don Diego, for the best in the best of all possible worlds, when Octavio enters and demands the royal permission to execute personal vengeance on Don Juan. There is a brief quarrel and a threat of a duel between Diego and Octavio, but the King intervenes: after he is married, he tells the Duke, he will be able to talk at greater length. "As for Don Juan, he is a gentleman of my household, my liegeman, and the son of Don Diego here: respect him!" And so Octavio resigns himself to having a bride provided for him by the King on the morrow.

The King having left, the forsaken Aminta and her father Gaseno enter and innocently ask Don Octavio, who is evidently a gentleman of the court, where they can find a certain Don Juan Tenorio, of whom they are in search, for the young cavalier is Aminta's husband. They have come to Seville to complain to the King if justice is not done her. The light dawns on Octavio at last; now, he is convinced, he holds Juan in the hollow of his hand and can have his revenge on him; and he takes Gaseno and Aminta with him to see the King.

7

But vengeance from quite another quarter overtakes Juan. The scene changes to a street outside the church in which Don Gonzalo is buried. Juan and Catalinón enter. The former tells the valet with glee how excellently his recent audience with the King has gone off: he is in full favour, and that very evening he is to be married to Isabela. But first of all he has another engagement to fulfil—his promised supper with the statue. Catalinón tries to dissuade him, but Juan insists: has he not pledged the word of a gentleman? They go into the dark church, where they are greeted by Gonzalo (in statue form). He rouses Juan's ire by taunting him with cowardice in having run away the night he had murdered him. "I fled," Juan replies, "only for fear of being recognised. Now I face you here. Tell me what you would have of me." "I would have you sup with me," says Gonzalo. The intrepid Juan raises the cover of the tomb, and a black table set for a feast is disclosed. Two black-robed figures draw up chairs for the statue's guests, and the meats and wines are served—scorpions and vipers, vinegar and gall. Juan, for all his bravado, is secretly ill at ease. The meal over, the statue says to him, "Have no fear: give me your hand." Scorning the suggestion that anything can

298

make him afraid, Juan does so. Once more, at the touch of that hand, he feels he is being consumed by fire—a faint foretaste, the statue tells him, of what is in store for him. "Such is the divine law; what a man sows, that he reaps." Juan cries out in impotent and incoherent rage: "I am burning! Do not stifle me! I will drive my dagger through you! My blows pierce only the air! I did not outrage your daughter: she saw at once through my guile." "That avails you nothing," is the reply: "you made the attempt." Then Juan's spirit breaks. He calls wildly for a confessor to absolve him of his sins. But it is too late: still crying out that he is on fire, he falls dead. The tomb sinks into the earth, taking with it Juan and the Commander: there is a noise like thunder, and the terrified Catalinón crawls out, calling incoherently on God and all the saints to save him: "I will take the news to his father! St. George! St. Agnus Dei! See me to the street!"

There follows a scene in the palace in which Batricio, Gaseno, Tisbea and Isabela tell the story of Don Juan's perfidies and demand reparation; then the Marquis de la Mota denounces Juan as the real murderer of Don Gonzalo, and even Don Diego turns against his criminal son. The horrified King orders Juan's arrest. But just then Catalinón rushes in with a strange story of how his master had impiously plucked the beard of the statue and otherwise insulted the murdered Gonzalo, invited the statue to supper, confessed that he had failed in his attempt on Ana, and been duly punished by heaven for all his crimes. Octavio, who is one of the company, now demands the hand of his injured Isabela, Mota claims that of Ana, Batricio that of Aminta; and the King orders the sepulchre of Don Gonzalo to be moved to Madrid and given a place of honour in the church of St. Francisco.[1]

[1] There is a modern French version of Tirso's *El Burlador de Sevilla* by Jean Cassou and Jean Camp that is reasonably representative, for the most part, of the original, though occasionally a speech is allotted to a wrong character, which is a trifle confusing. The translation ends, however, with the flight of the terrified Catalinón from the church. There is no justification for this. Tirso's final scene in the palace is a dramatic necessity, for naturally we want to know how matters are finally arranged between the various lovers, while it is equally necessary for all the characters to learn how the vengeance of heaven had overtaken the libertine at last.

8

As the reader will see, here are all the basic constituents of the Don Juan story as it was to be reproduced in many forms in European literature before it came into the hands of Da Ponte and Mozart—a reckless, impious adventurer among women, a half-assenting, half-protesting valet who is a mixture of servility and impudence, the seduction of two great ladies under the cover of darkness, the murder of the father of one of them when he comes to her rescue, comic relief of a sort in the adventure of the hero among maidens and their lovers of a lower degree than his own, the vengeful pursuit of him by the gentleman whom he has most wronged, the insult to a statue, the acceptance of an invitation to supper, and the final judgment of heaven on the villain. Reshape the characters and select and rearrange the episodes as future dramatists might according to their fancy, the essential pattern remained the same: Tirso de Molina had created a genuine saga, a story that could take on as many forms as future dramatists might choose, and into which each epoch, each culture, could read itself afresh over a period of some three hundred years. Molière, in his *Don Juan, ou Le Festin de Pierre* (1665), gave a turn and a complexion of his own to the saga. Shadwell, in his play *The Libertine* (1676), endowed Don Juan liberally with new and worse debaucheries and impieties. Goldoni, in his *Don Giovanni Tenorio, o sia Il Dissoluto*, upon which Da Ponte drew to some extent, as he did upon everyone and everything that could be useful to him, aimed at ridding the story of some of the buffooneries that had become part and parcel of its very being by this time, and to that end dispensed with the character of the valet. Two French seventeenth century plays on the subject, each entitled *Le Festin de Pierre, ou le Fils Criminel*, by Dorimon (1659) and de Villiers (1660) respectively, have been made accessible to modern students in a reprint by Gendarme de Bévotte.[1]

[1] G. Gendarme de Bévotte, *Le Festin de Pierre avant Molière . . . textes publiés avec introduction, lexique et notes*. Paris, 1907. He reprinted also the Italian text of Cicognini's seventeenth century play *Il Convitato di Pietra*.

9

During the seventeenth and eighteenth centuries the story of the "Dissoluto punito" was highly popular also not only with the actors of the Italian impromptu comedy—the commedia dell' arte—but the German puppet booths, where, as might have been expected, it suffered a progressive degradation. For the gaping mob everywhere the two great things in the story came to be the farcical antics of the valet and the vengeance of the statue on the young criminal. We are fortunate in the possession of a document that gives as a close-up view of what the part of the valet had already become as early as the middle of the seventeenth century. In 1658 an Italian company of commedia dell'arte players drew all Paris with a version of their own of *Le Festin de Pierre*; it was this production, indeed, that moved de Villiers to write his five-act play.[1] The part of the valet (Trivelin) seems to have been played in Paris originally by the manager of the troupe, Locatelli, but he was replaced in 1662 by a certain Biancolelli, who wrote out with great complacency a full account of his buffooneries in the part. (The original Italian manuscript has been lost, but there survives a French translation of it made in the eighteenth century, by one Thomas Gueullette, that is now in the Paris Bibliothèque Nationale.)[2] From this we get an excellent idea of the devices to which the valet had recourse to extort the tribute of a guffaw from the groundlings; and evidently some of the buffooneries of the part had become traditional by Mozart's time. Goldoni protested against this and other degradations of the subject: he tells us in his memoirs that audiences were accustomed, in the scene of the shipwreck of Don Juan and his valet, to see the latter save his life by floating ashore on a couple of bladders, while the aristocratic hero somehow made his way through the sea without so much as his coiffure being disarranged or his fine clothes getting wet.

By Mozart's time the saga had crystallised into an excellent working formula for opera purposes—the hero-villain and his

[1] In the commedia dell' arte the actors improvised their dialogue and their miming within the framework of a dramatic action the main lines of which were already agreed upon.
[2] It is printed in the book of Gendarme de Bévotte already mentioned.

rascally buffoon of a servant; a dignified victim of Don Juan's sensuality; her aristocratic lover; a lady of somewhat lower social rank who had previously been seduced and deserted by Juan and who follows him about with her heart equally divided between love for him and the desire to be revenged on him; a group of peasants, with a bride and bridegroom at their head, to provide a lighter *décor* for Juan's amorous exploits; and, of course, a murdered father who reappears, as the avenging instrument of heaven, in the form of a statue in the closing scenes. So conceived, an opera would have everything that an audience of all degrees of taste and intelligence could require for its delectation—gaiety, gravity, tragedy, psychological variety, action, humour, farce, religion. Tirso de Molina had builded more wisely than he knew. And, on the whole, he had builded better than many of those who succeeded him. "Of these later artists," says Fitzmaurice-Kelly, "not one has succeeded in matching the patrician dignity, the infernal, iniquitous valour of the original. To have created a universal type, to have imposed a character on the world, to have outlived all rivalry, to have achieved in words what Mozart alone has expressed in music, is to rank among the great creators of all time."

10

Parallel to some extent with the story of Don Juan Tenorio, though apparently later in origin, there ran a Spanish story of a Don Juan de Marana, at the end of which the hero found not hell fire but heavenly grace. This other legend seems to have travelled to France early in the nineteenth century. It was the theme of an excellent short story—*Les Âmes du Purgatoire*—by Prosper Mérimée (1834), and it was turned by the elder Dumas into a drama, little known today, that is one of the curiosities of the French romantic stage—*Don Juan de Marana, or the Fall of an Angel, a Mystery in five acts, in nine tableaux*, produced at the Porte-Saint-Martin Theatre, Paris, on the 30th April 1836. The lively action takes too long to be set forth in detail here; it can only be said that it concerns the struggle, with God's permission, between a Good and a Bad Angel for control of the soul of the depraved young Don Juan de Marana. "One of my ancestors, if not one of my race," the hero boasts, "descended alive into hell, where he supped with a Commander whom he had killed after dishonouring his daughter. I have always been jealous of this man's reputation; and I want to surpass him, so that the Devil himself will not know which of the two to prefer, Don Juan de Tenorio or Don Juan de Marana." In a fit of terrified repentance he becomes a Trappist for a while: then, having killed his brother José, he muses, "upon my word, it looks as if the Devil doesn't want me to become a hermit"; and he takes to debauchery and crime again.

In the ruins of an old castle the phantoms of his victims appear to him and dance a ballet "in the style of the nuns in *Robert the Devil*." The finale of the drama is one of Dumas' most magnificent flights into the very stratosphere of the prodigious. To his rival Sandoval, whom he has wronged, Don Juan says, "Listen! God has given me one hour in which to repent: I give Him a quarter of an hour in which to strike me with His thunderbolt!" There follows a duel with Sandoval, whose sword, as it crosses that of Juan, darts flame. Juan is dismayed. A shade rises out of the ground: it is Juan's former love Caroline; she is followed by a Vittoria, a Teresina and an Ines. At the back of the stage is a great fiery clock, with flames for hours and minute fingers; the pendulum swings slowly between two points, one of which is marked "Never!" the other "For ever!" The time is five minutes before midnight: our nerves are now on edge. Caroline ascends the steps leading to the clock, and, to Juan's horror, advances the minute hand one degree. Then come Vittoria, Teresina and Ines, each of whom inexorably registers another minute on the clock. Juan, terrified at last, falls on one knee. But now comes a certain Martha, with angel's wings and a star on her forehead, and accompanied by angels; she had loved the wicked Juan, she says, when she was alive, and still loves him now she is dead; and in the name of that love she exhorts him three times, with increasing urgency, to repent. He cries out despairingly, "It is too late! Midnight is about to strike!" But Martha arrests the hand of the clock and once more cries "Repent!" This gives Juan a second's grace. With a last great effort he raises himself and then falls at her feet. "O Lord, thou has heard him!" she ejaculates. A song of angels is heard: the background opens, showing heaven in all its splendour. Juan is convinced that he is dying, but Martha assures him that this is a delusion on his part, and that his eyes will reopen to eternal life.

Thus did Don Juan de Marana, according to Dumas, by a grand last-second spurt win the Eternity Stakes by the shortest of short heads. He probably developed into heaven's champion bore, telling the story again and again to each new arrival and to as many of the older club members as he could buttonhole, no doubt finishing in the style of the Duke of Wellington's classical description of the battle of Waterloo to Mr. Creevey—"It was a damned near thing, sir, the nearest thing you ever saw in your life!"

Out of this Dumasian farrago, however, Arnold Bennett, by concentrating on the saner elements of the play, succeeded in constructing the libretto for Eugene Goossens' opera *Don Juan de Mañara*, which was given at Covent Garden in 1935.[1]

11

The Don Juan saga as established by Tirso has been a favourite subject with the poets, dramatists and novelists in many countries for something like three centuries.[2] Christian Dietrich Grabbe (1804–1836) made a characteristically German attempt, in his tragedy *Don Juan und Faust* (1824), to run the two sagas in harness; but the venture was more praiseworthy than successful. In our own day Edmond Rostand has treated the theme in quite a new way in his play *La dernière Nuit de Don Juan*, which might be turned into an excellent opera by a librettist and a composer of genius; and Suzanne Lilar, in her drama *Le Burlador*,[3] has shown once more how adaptable the great drama is to all the psychological changes that humanity undergoes in the course of the centuries. Mme Lilar's original and searching reading of the soul of Juan is perhaps one that only a woman could have accomplished. One thing is very significant in the modern literary his-

[1] The libretto was adapted by Bennett from a play of his own on the subject written in 1913, but never performed. It was published in a limited private edition in 1923. He had followed Dumas in his spelling of "Marana": in the opera the more correct "Mañara" is restored.

[2] The most comprehensive survey of the various treatments of the theme is Gendarme de Bévotte's *La Légende de Don Juan, son évolution dans la littérature des origines au romantisme* (1906).

[3] Produced in Paris in December 1946; published in Brussels in 1947.

tory of the saga—the gradual disappearance from it, as it were by tacit consent, of the two features that accounted for most of its popularity in the beginning and as late as the eighteenth century—the comic character of the valet and the moral ending in hell fire. With these primitive elements the story can now quite well dispense; it is the psychology of Don Juan and of some of the women into whose orbit the Fates throw him that is now the really important thing, and the possibilities in this field seem infinite.[1]

12

The stupendous popularity of *The Marriage of Figaro* in Prague in 1786 had made the impresario of the local theatre, Bondini, eager to have another opera from Mozart's pen; and naturally the composer turned for his text to the collaborator who had served him so well already. The Prague commission was particularly acceptable to Mozart just then, for his operatic stock did not stand very high in Vienna at that time, both the Court and the public preferring the simpler art of the Spaniard Martin y Solar's *Una cosa rara* and Dittersdorf's *Doktor und Apotheker* to what were regarded as the complexities of *The Seraglio*. Da Ponte, for his part, was eager to add to his growing reputation in Vienna as a writer for the theatre. He has left us his account of how he set to work on receiving the new commission in the early part of 1787. So great was his vogue just then that three text-books were commissioned from him at the same time. For Mozart, he says, he chose the subject of Don Giovanni, and for Martin y Solar that of *L'Arbore di Diana*; while for Salieri he had only to make an Italian adaptation of the *Tarare* that had already proved a success in Paris. (It was based on Beaumarchais's play of the same name.) The total task was certainly a formidable one, having regard to the short time at his disposal and the very different natures of the three subjects; but Da Ponte managed to pull through, he tells us, with the assistance of some bottles of excellent Tokay, a good

---

[1] I need hardly remind the reader of Shaw's brilliant *Man and Superman*, nor, in the operatic sphere, of the Pushkin-Dargomizhsky *Stone Guest*. The *Don Giovanni* of Bertati and Gazzaniga, which alone bears directly on our present study of Da Ponte and Mozart, will come up frequently for discussion later.

supply of Seville snuff, and the company of a charming young girl of sixteen, living in the same house, who brought him, whenever he rang for her, a cup of coffee, a biscuit, or a loving disposition, according to his requirements at the moment. To the Emperor he said, according to his own story written many years later, "I shall write for Mozart at night, regarding it as reading Dante's *Inferno*; in the mornings for Martin, which will be like reading Petrarch; and in the evenings for Salieri, which will be my Tasso."

If we are to take his word for it, his first night's labour produced the first two scenes of *Don Giovanni*, two scenes of *L'Arbore di Diana*, and more than half of the first act of *Tarare*, the title of which he changed to *Assur*. "The next morning I took these three texts to the respective composers, who could hardly believe their eyes; and in sixty-three days I had finished the Mozart and Martin texts and nearly two-thirds of *Assur*." But even a genius of the first order, as Da Ponte frankly admitted himself to be, could hardly have turned out three masterpieces in two months; and the libretto of *Don Giovanni* in particular is far from perfect.

As was his custom, he paid various predecessors in the same field the compliment of borrowing from them whatever he found useful to him in his work. He evidently knew the *Don Juan* of Molière. But the work he principally laid under contribution was one by Bertati,[1] with music by Gazzaniga, that had been given in Venice in 1787 and had had a great success there and elsewhere.[2] This was constructed on a formula much in vogue in those days—in the first part the manager of a travelling opera company discusses with his personnel the necessity of finding something new to attract the public, while the second part consists of a performance of the work finally decided upon, in this case a version of the Don Juan story in one act (twenty-five short "scenes").

The Bertati opera opens, as that of Mozart does, with the valet (Pasquariello) awaiting the return of his master from the nocturnal adventure with Donna Anna and the duel in which the

[1] Who later wrote the text of *Il Matrimonio Segreto* for Cimarosa (1792).
[2] It seems to have been originally produced in 1782, and to have undergone various modifications in various revivals between then and 1787, and again later.

Commander has been killed. There follows the regulation episode of the seduction of a country maiden (Maturina, whose betrothed is Biagio), while Bertati adds a second lady of higher degree, Ximena, to the traditional Elvira. As far as its limited time-scale allows the opera follows for a while the familiar course, till in the nineteenth scene we find Anna's lover, Ottavio, of whom we have seen and heard nothing since the opening episode, giving a stonecutter instructions as to the carving of an inscription on the base of the equestrian statue of Anna's father. After he has left the stage the drama runs its expected course—Don Giovanni's encounter with the statue, the fateful supper, and the descent of Giovanni into hell—after which Ottavio, Lanterna (another of Giovanni's servants), Maturina, Elvira, Ximena and Pasquariello (but not Anna) pour into the room to take part in a buffo ensemble.

13

Even where he stole from Bertati, Da Ponte often improved on him. He wisely dispensed with Donna Ximena, and fused Pasquariello and Lanterna into one. But in one instance he blundered badly. That his and Mozart's Ottavio is a woeful "stick," dramatically considered, few would question today. Even when he is convinced that Giovanni was Anna's assailant he does nothing about it. It is true that here and there a critic has racked his brains to discover some profound psychoanalytical reason for this irresolution and inactivity; some of them have even managed to persuade themselves that poor colourless spineless Ottavio is another Hamlet. Others have surmised that, like the good law-abiding citizen he is, he feels that it is not *his* task to execute vengeance on the reprobate, whose punishment should be left to the officers of the law. But it is always a waste of time and intellectual energy to go about beating the bush for a subtle explanation of a simple fact when an equally simple commonsense explanation of it stares us in the face. Obviously the reason why Da Ponte can never bring matters to a head as between Giovanni and Ottavio is that if a duel were to take place between them either Ottavio would be killed—in which case the opera would from that point onward be without a tenor and the drama without its virtuous counterpart to the wicked baritone, all which is operatically unthinkable—or Don Giovanni would be killed—in which case the performance would come to a summary end, and the audience would be cheated of its prescriptive right to the dreadful ethical joy of witnessing the Statue's vengeance on the murderer of Anna's father.

All the dramatists had been aware of this dilemma, and consequently had seen to it that the two male protagonists did not arrive at the decisive moment of meeting too soon. In Molière, for example, Don Alonso, a brother of Elvira, tracks Juan down in the third act and is about to take vengeance on him there and then. He is restrained, however, by his brother Don Carlos, whom, as it happens, Juan has just saved from being robbed and murdered by some brigands. (Carlos has never seen Juan before, but Alonso has.) As Carlos' Spanish sense of honour will not permit him to consent to Alonso's slaying his benefactor out of hand, he persuades his brother to postpone vengeance for one day. Before the trio can meet again, however, Juan has his first encounter with the Statue (in the mausoleum), invites it to supper, and so starts the train of events that leads swiftly to his end. Carlos comes upon him in the cemetery and insists on his marrying Elvira. Juan refuses, hypocritically pretending that he cannot do so as he has seen the error of his ways and is resolved to adopt the religious life, and therefore cannot fight a duel. The furious Carlos swears he will have vengeance, but recognises that to kill his man on consecrated ground would be sacrilegious. Juan leads him to believe that he will soon be passing through a small street leading to a convent, where they can settle their differences. Carlos departs, but before the two can meet again the Statue has avenged him on the betrayer of his sister. It is only Da Ponte who has been maladroit enough to give Ottavio too soon not only the justification but the opportunity for vengeance on Don Juan, so making it dramatically impossible for him to act decisively—to do anything, in fact, but be the mellifluous tenor of the production.

Da Ponte was partly forced into this awkward situation by the necessity imposed on him of finishing the libretto in the shortest possible time. In his initial hurry he took over Bertati's first four scenes very much as they stood—Leporello waiting for his master, the emergence of Giovanni and Anna from the house, the latter's frenzied expostulations, the arrival of her father, the duel, the opportune entry of Ottavio, Anna's grief for her father's fate, Ottavio's affectionate attempts to console her, and his vow that he will discover and punish the criminal. Had Bertati's opera been a longer one he too would at some point or other have been confronted with the difficulty that ultimately floored Da Ponte—that of keeping Ottavio inactive and yet interesting after Anna had revealed the name of her assailant. But Bertati was saved from this by the fact that his opera—mainly a buffa one at that—was in one act only. By the time he had regaled the audience with the conventional humorous scenes between Don Giovanni on the one hand and Elvira, Ximena, Maturina and Biagio on the other it was necessary for him to go without more ado to the hungrily expected closing scenes—Giovanni's parley with the Statue, the supper, and heaven's punishment of the young rake. As we have seen, Ottavio does not appear anywhere in Bertati's text between that introductory scene between himself and Anna and the near-final scene in which he is found telling the stonecutter what to carve on the Commander's tomb. Donna Anna too disappears completely from the action after that early scene: she would go into a retreat, she had told Ottavio, until the villain had been tracked down and punished; and so stoutly does she adhere to this resolution that Bertati does not even bring her on with the others, as Da Ponte does, for the buffo ensemble that ends the opera.

14

Mozart must already have been as well acquainted as Da Ponte was with the popular Don Juan story and Bertati's handling of it, and possibly he knew something also of Gluck's *Don Juan* ballet, which had been produced in Vienna in 1761. If we are to take literally Da Ponte's chronology (of a much later date), Mozart must have been engaged from about the middle of May to the end of August (1787) on the composition of *Don Giovanni*. In the early days of September he went to Prague to study the local conditions on the spot, as was generally necessary in the operatic world of that day, when the extent of the resources of a company and the capacities or limitations of individual singers had always to be taken into consideration. Da Ponte followed him shortly afterwards, but had to return to Vienna before the first performance. Mozart, who was an excellent producer of his own works, must have done a good deal of coaching of the Bondini troupe in collaboration with the gifted regisseur of the Prague theatre, Guardasoni. Apparently the only sections of the score remaining to be composed in Prague were the overture, Masetto's aria "Ho capito, Signor, sì!", an expansion of the recitative that had originally opened the second act into the present duet ("Eh via buffone") between Giovanni and Leporello, and the closing ensemble of the opera. Many minor details in the action would of course be modified in rehearsal.

It had been Bondini's intention to produce the new opera on the occasion of the visit to Prague, on the 14th October 1787, of the newly married couple the Archduchess Maria Theresa and Prince Anton of Saxony; but that plan fell through owing to the slow progress made with the rehearsals for one reason or another. Possibly, for one thing, the work confronted the singers with difficulties of a kind rather new to them; for another, Bondini's company seems to have been so small that he had to work on a narrow margin of safety.[1] On the 21st October Mozart wrote thus to his Vienna friend Gottfried von Jacquin: "Yet another delay has been caused by the indisposition of one of the female singers. As the company is a small one the impresario is in a constant state of worry; he has to take the greatest care of his people for fear of some sudden ailment or other that may mean no performance at all! Consequently everything here moves by slow stages, since the actors, out of sheer laziness, won't do any work on days when there is a performance at night, and the impresario is too scared to put any pressure on them." It was not until the 29th that the opera could be produced, with the following cast: Don Giovanni, Luigi Bassi;[2] Anna, Teresa Saporiti;[3]

[1] The Masetto had to double the part of the Commander.
[2] He had just turned twenty-one. He had joined the Bondini company in 1784. A legend has sprung up that he was not very intelligent and gave Mozart some trouble, causing him in particular to rewrite the duet with Zerlina—"Là ci darem la mano"—no less than five times. Proof is lacking for all this: Mozart's manuscript shows the duet to have had its present form before he left Vienna. In 1816 Bassi became regisseur of the Dresden Opera. Eight years later we find Beethoven speaking of him as a "fiery Italian." He died in 1825.
[3] Apparently she survived her trying experiences as Donna Anna rather

Ottavio, Antonio Baglioni; Elvira, Catarina Micelli; [1] Zerlina, Catarina Bondini (the impresario's wife); the Commander and Masetto, Giuseppe Lolli; Leporello, Felice Ponziani. Mozart conducted. The opera was an instantaneous success: "Evviva Da Ponte! Evviva Mozart!" Guardasoni wrote exultantly to the librettist in Vienna; "every impresario, every artist must extol you to the skies, for as long as we have such men among us there will be no more talk about the theatre being in a bad way!" Mozart, in the seventh heaven of happiness among his good friends and admirers in Prague, delayed for some weeks his return to Vienna.

A new crop of difficulties sprang up for him in connection with a production in the capital. The new singers made fresh demands on him, which Mozart had to meet; the result being a series of changes that have meant a headache for producers and audiences ever since. The new Ottavio, Francesco Morella, felt himself unequal to the exacting "Il mio tesoro," so Mozart wrote a new aria, the less difficult "Dalla sua pace," in substitution for it; and as both are included in modern productions the right places for their insertion are to some extent a matter for conjecture and caprice. The Elvira (Catarina Cavalieri) demanded an extra show piece, and was gratified with the great recitative and aria "Mi tradì quell'alma ingrata," which is today placed either near the beginning of the opera—after Leporello's Catalogue aria—or near the end—just before the churchyard scene. In the place of "Il mio tesoro" there was inserted a grossly farcical scene between Zerlina and Leporello ending with a duet, "Per queste tue manine"; all this is omitted in present-day performances, out of respect for Mozart's reputation and for the intelligence of the audience. One result of these changes being to prolong the opera unduly, the final sextet was omitted. The opera was given in its new form on the 7th May 1788. It was too much in advance of Viennese taste to have much success; and after fifteen performances it disappeared from the repertory for the remainder of Mozart's lifetime. [2]

more than eighty-one years, dying in March 1869 at the age of a hundred and six—nine days before Berlioz!

[1] The contemporary view of her voice seems to have been that it was "flexible but not agreeable": she appears to have been best in soubrette rôles.

[2] Owing to the haste in which the libretto was put together, and the vague-

15

Little importance attaches to the fact that the overture was not written until the night before the final rehearsal of the opera; for Mozart must have had it completely worked out in his mind long before then, and putting it on paper would be a mere act of penmanship.

The orchestra seems, by modern standards, a small one for the tremendous dramatic effect obtained at the very commencement— strings, two flutes, two oboes, two clarinets, two bassoons, two horns, two trumpets and kettledrums. The overture, which is in the so-called "French" form—a slow movement followed by a fast one—begins with an andante introduction the thematic material of which is drawn from the final supper scene. The full orchestra first of all gives out a suggestion of the impressive chords (see No. 44) that seem to strike the startled Giovanni full in the face when he flings open the door and sees confronting him the statue he has rashly bidden to supper:

No. 1

It is rather curious that Mozart's marking for the chords in the overture is simply forte, whereas in the opera fortissimo is prescribed; strange, too, that when he came to enter the motifs in the "Catalogue of my Works" in which it was his habit to record the completion of a work and quote the opening bars of it, he should

ness of some of the scenic indications, the staging of the work bristles with problems for the modern producer. Already there is quite a literature dealing with this subject. It would carry us too far afield to attempt to deal with all the ramifications of it: we must content ourselves with an analysis of the opera as it stands in the score. Nor need we waste any time debating whether *Don Giovanni* is an "opera buffa" or not. We can afford to take the simple common sense view that for comic purposes Mozart wrote comic music, and for serious purposes serious music, and leave it at that.

have failed to remember that in the score the bass D in the second bar and the C sharp in the fourth, in the bassoons, violas, 'cellos and double basses, being of minim length, continue to sound after the crotchets of the upper chords have ceased to be heard. (We meet with the same procedure in the opera itself.) Quoting the passage in his "Catalogue" on the 28th October 1787 he cuts the bass D and C sharp down to crotchets.[1]

There follows, in quieter tones, a six-bars repetition of the impressive rhythmic figure:

No. 2

to the accompaniment of which the Statue declaims the words, "Don Giovanni! You have invited me to sup with you. I have come!"

There has been much futile debate as to whether the overture to the opera is "programmatic" or not. What is certain is that the andante introduction follows so closely the pattern of the corresponding scene in the drama that we are compelled to read into it the various significances the music has there. A vacillating syncopated figure in the first violins:

No. 3

that follows immediately upon our No. 2, depicts unmistakably the agitation and self-doubt into which Giovanni is thrown by the appearance of the supernatural guest. For a moment he loses

[1] A facsimile of the precious little *Verzeichnis aller meiner Werke* was published in a limited edition a few years ago.

his normal arrogant self-poise. "Never would I have believed it!" he stammers; "but I will do what I can. Leporello, have another table laid at once!"

Next come, in the overture as in the opera, a few bars connected with the half-serious, half-farcical tremors of the valet, and the rejection by the Statue of the idea of serving earthly food to beings who have passed beyond all that. "I come here on a graver matter," it says; and a grisly gliding figure in flutes and violins in octaves, with alternating crescendi and diminuendi:

No. 4

surrounds the words with a sinister meaning.

But now Mozart departs from the procedure of the opera and enters upon a feverish symphonic development (molto allegro) of new motifs, beginning with one in sixths in the violins:

No. 5

which is capped by a fanfare in the whole orchestra except the strings:

No. 6

Though there is no longer any following of a dramatic "programme," the general psychological implications of the themes that follow are obvious—Don Giovanni is posed before us in all his youthful levity and audacity. In the following example we seem to see him answering a threat with his usual gay mockery:

No. 7

Mozart dwells with particular insistence on this antithesis, and, towards the end of the overture especially, on the "threat" portion of it:

No. 8

Our quotation, taken from almost the closing bars of the overture, shows him settling down into the key of F major; there is no "recapitulatory" return, such as we would have expected him to make if he had been writing an overture for its own formal sake, to the prime key of the allegro, D Major.

16

The modulation to F major was foreordained by the fact that he had already begun the stage action with Leporello's monologue in that key (see musical example No. 9). Evidently, then, he wanted the action to follow the overture without a break; and that being so, it behoves the conductors to make the transition from the one to the other as natural as the composer intended it to be. But few of them do this. They mostly fall into two errors. In the first place they try to impose a more or less self-existent formal structure on the overture by introducing a rallentando in the last half-dozen bars or so, oblivious of the fact that, as will be seen from our example No. 8, Mozart has already achieved all the rallentando *he* desired by the simple process of changing his time-values from crotchets to minims: an additional slowing down on the part of the conductor is not only superfluous but harmful, suggesting, as it does, a sort of concert close to the overture never intended by the composer. In the second place the conductors and singers, with rare exceptions, take Leporello's opening solo too slowly. Mozart, who knew perfectly well what he was about, had marked that molto allegro—the same tempo as he prescribes for the allegro of the overture.[1] The over-slow tempo mostly adopted for the solo today is due to the irresistible inclination of a long line of basses to angle for the public guffaw.[2] In that process something of the real character of Mozart's Leporello is lost. Only a rapid tempo can bring out the impatience and bad temper of this ill-conditioned underling whom, when the curtain rises, we dimly see keeping watch by night in the garden of the Commander's house; his only objection to his master's villainies is that the gentleman regales himself with all the fruits of debauchery while the valet does no more than keep an eye on the tree. "Wearing myself out night and day, in wind and rain," he grumbles:

No. 9

[1] The marking for the *Nozze di Figaro* overture in the score is presto; but when Mozart entered it in the thematic Catalogue of his works on the eve of the first performance he marked it allegro assai. The latter is the marking for the *Don Giovanni* overture in the Catalogue, while in the score it is molto allegro. So again with the overture to *Der Schauspieldirektor*: in the score presto, in the Catalogue allegro assai. It is evident that for Mozart the terms allegro assai, allegro molto and presto meant the same thing, a point which conductors and singers of his operas would do well constantly to bear in mind. If they did, we might be spared some of the nonsensical tempi under which we suffer during performances of *Don Giovanni* in particular.
[2] It is perhaps a small point, but one worth taking into consideration that when Beethoven uses the Leporello theme (our No. 9) as the basis of the 22nd of his Diabelli Variations he not only marks it "Alla 'Notte e giorno faticar' di Mozart" but reproduces the "molto allegro" direction of the score. That variation is always, and rightly, taken at a great pace by pianists, not at the leisurely tempo adopted by our present-day Leporellos for their solo, which is untrue both to the *molto allegro* marking and to the psychological atmosphere of the episode in the opera.

"eating badly and sleeping badly, and for what? I too would like to play the gentleman, not the lackey. A nice gentleman indeed! he inside there with the lovely lady, while I just act the watch-dog"—"the watch-dog!" he repeats three times with surly sarcasm.[1]

But soon he hears confused sounds proceeding from the house, and at once he smothers his envy and resentment and becomes the craven lackey anxious before all else for his own safety. As he hides himself Donna Anna rushes from the house, holding Don Giovanni firmly by the arm; he is concealing his face in his cloak. In an agitated trio, for which a pelting molto allegro is a *sine qua non*, Anna swears she will discover who her assailant has been, even if it costs her her life:

No. 10

Non spe-rar, se non m'uc-ci-di, ch'io ti la—sci fug-gir mai!

Giovanni swears that she shall not; and from his hiding place Leporello comments, "What a tumult! My master in another scrape!" As the distracted and furious Anna becomes more troublesome Giovanni becomes angrier and more threatening: he bids her be silent or take the consequences. (This episode again is taken from Bertati, but Da Ponte has given both greater dramatic energy to the action and more point to the words. In Bertati, Don Giovanni tries to score a debating point by saying, "If it had been the Duke Ottavio you would not have had a word to say"; [2] to which Anna replies, "Never has the Duke done anything base." This little verbal interchange has been omitted by Da Ponte— on the whole, we feel, wisely. He has been dramatically right, again, in expanding the scared comments of Leporello, whose sole fear is that this latest escapade of the libertine master whom he serves so unwillingly may get *him* into trouble.)

[1] Da Ponte took the general idea of the monologue from Bertati; but there is a more malicious bite in his own lines, and Mozart's skilful phrases give them an extra curl of the lip. Note particularly the fermata over the first syllable of the final repetition of "sentinella"; Leporello seems to dwell on it to get the last drop of acid comment out of it.

[2] Here we get a distant echo of Tirso's play, in which the woman who figures in the opening scene is not Ana but Isabela.

17

At last Anna's father, the Commander, enters, bidding the unknown interloper draw his sword and give him satisfaction. Giovanni, about whom there is always a certain aura of cavalier *grandezza*, will not deign to fight a man so much older than himself. It is only when the Commander taunts him with cowardice that he loses his self-control and says gravely, *mezza voce*, "Wretched man! So be it, if you are bent on dying!"

A few orchestral bars suggest the crossing of the swords, the thrust and parry. As the Commander falls, mortally wounded, Mozart for the first time changes the tempo. In a short andante trio in F minor, of the most impressive quality, the old man gasps out his farewell to the world; Giovanni, still with a certain nobility about him, laments the tragic turn events have taken; and even Leporello is moved to a seriousness not hitherto observable in him. Was it by chance or by design, by the way, that Mozart used the phrase to which, in her furious dialogue with Giovanni, Anna had sung "I will pursue you like a desperate fury":

No. 11

for the *sotto voce* comment of Don Giovanni with which the tragic trio opens, now, of course, in the minor—"Ah! unhappy man! Already his agonising soul is leaving his miserable body"?

No. 12

As the Commander breathes his last a wailing chromatic descending phrase in the orchestra sings his elegy: [1]

[1] Most conductors, desirous of an easy "effect," turn these few orchestral bars into a languishing adagio. This is quite wrong: the tempo of the trio should be andante from beginning to end, as Mozart has marked it; and "andante" in that epoch had its literal meaning of "walking"—"going" at an easy, natural pace, as Leopold Mozart puts it in his *Violinschule*.

No. 13

Giovanni and Leporello are now alone, for Anna had fled into the house on her father's entry. The two take their new bearings in a brief recitative. "Bravo!" says the valet ironically; "two pretty deeds accomplished—a girl ravished and a father killed!" "He willed it so," replies Giovanni sombrely; "his the blame." "And Donna Anna?" asks Leporello slyly; "did she will it too?" But Giovanni quickly checks his insolence, for which he is in no mood just now: "Keep your mouth shut and come with me, unless you want something to happen to you as well"; and the valet, cowed as usual when his imperious master asserts himself, follows him off the stage, muttering "I want nothing, Sir; I will not say another word."

As they disappear in the darkness Anna enters with Ottavio. Her object in running into the house had evidently been to find him, though how and why he happened to be there at that time of night is something Da Ponte does not pause to explain. Anna, not having seen the duel, believes her father merely to be in some peril. Ottavio, of course, assures her that he will shed the last drop of his blood to help the old man. "But where is the villain?" he asks her. "I left him just here," she replies; and then, to her horror, she sees the body on the ground.

Once more the tempo whips up—or should do—to allegro assai as Mozart plunges into one of the finest scenes of the opera. Stabbing phrases in the orchestra accompany Anna as she laments her loss, followed by wailing figures as she points to the old man's wounds. It is in this episode that the conductors are generally seen at their worst. They slow down the time to adagio at this point and that, making Anna dwell pathetically on her loss, whereas she should be in a frenzy of despair that allows her no time, just then, for indulgence in the luxury of self-pity. Such slowing down as is required is once more amply provided for by Mozart by a change from crotchet to minim time-units.

Some servants with torches have come in, and these Ottavio, always fertile in good advice, sends back into the house for smelling-salts and cordials to revive the fainting Anna, over whose drooping body he bends with gestures of tender compassion. He bids the servants carry the body away, and exhorts her to take heart again. She abandons herself (*allegro*) to a passion of grief: "Leave me!" she cries; "let me die!":

No. 14

Ottavio and the orchestra vie with each other in tendernesses and solicitudes; "put away these sad memories," he exhorts her; "in me you have father and spouse in one":

No. 15

but she is inconsolable. The tempo slows down as she solemnly exacts from him an oath to avenge her father's murder: this he swears by her dear eyes and by their love. With a return to the previous rapid tempo they reaffirm, in duet, their oath, and go into the house.

18

This scene had run differently in Bertati. After the exit of Giovanni and his valet, Ottavio, Anna and some servants come upon the stage. In a few short lines the body of the Commander is discovered and taken away, and then Bertati feels that some explanations are due for the benefit of the audience. "Duke," says Anna, "my father is dead, and I do not know who the dastard was who has slain him." Naturally Ottavio asks, "But how did the villain get into your apartments?" She reminds him that, in virtue of their being betrothed lovers, she had given Ottavio an assignation in her room.[1] Her waiting-woman having left her, a

---

[1] Bertati is at pains to make it clear to his audience that the assignation was quite open and innocent:
"A voi, Duca, stringendomi
La promessa di sposa, io me ne stava

man enveloped in a cloak had entered, whom she had taken to be the Duke. Without saying a word he had embraced her passionately. Covered with confusion she had shaken him off and said, "How dare you, Duke? What are you doing?" But the man had only renewed his assault, calling her his dear one and protesting his love. This naturally induced something like paralysis in her; and taking advantage of her weakness the vile intruder had resumed the assault. She defended herself as best she could and called out to her maid; whereupon the villain had turned to flee. She tried to unmask him, at any rate, and called for her father, immediately on whose appearance she had fled from the dreadful scene; and then the assassin had run the old man through.

Her story told, Ottavio (in Bertati) protests that he is absolutely on fire with rage: it will not be long, he assures her, before the miscreant is discovered, and then his punishment will fit the crime. However, he goes on to say, Anna can surely console herself with the reflection that if she has lost her father she still has her lover and the sure prospect of a happy union. She tells him, however, that for the present there can be no more talk of marriage: until the murderer of her father is found and punished she means to go into a retreat. With that she leaves him and disappears from the opera—for good. Ottavio, left alone, bewails, tenor-like, his hard lot in an aria, hopes for the dawn of a better day, and disappears, in his turn, until the cemetery scene.

One of Da Ponte's most effective strokes was to substitute a construction of his own for this of Bertati's. He saw that what was required at the moment was not cold explanation but passionate emotion; so—perhaps at the urging of Mozart, whose imagination the scene had evidently captured—he allowed Anna full scope for the expression of her grief. Her explanation to Ottavio he brought in in a later scene, with excellent dramatic effect.[1] But he

---

Ad aspettarvi nel mio appartamento
Pe' l nostro concertato abboccamento":
(in virtue of their being betrothed, she had arranged with Ottavio for a "colloquy" with him in her room). Here the distant affiliation with the opening scene of Tirso is obvious; but Tirso's Isabela and the Anna of the opera are quite different characters.

[1] And of course, with three-fourths of the first act and a long second act before him, Da Ponte could not make *his* Anna go into a retreat there and then!

overlooked one point when laying out that scene. Bertati does at least give us, for what it is worth, some sort of explanation why, in the first place, Anna was not surprised at the appearance of a man in her room at that hour of the night, and, in the second place, why Ottavio should so conveniently be on the premises just then. Anna had actually given her lover an assignation in her room, regarding his promise of marriage as justification for doing so. But in the later scene in Da Ponte in which she tells Ottavio what had happened that night, her story is that when sitting alone in her room she saw a man enter, wrapped in a cloak, whom at first she took to be the Duke. But just *why* the mild Ottavio, whose morals are beyond reproach and whose behaviour is always scrupulously correct, should have been calling on a virtuous Donna Anna at that hour of the night, unknown to her father, is something that remains quite unexplained. Da Ponte seems to have no better reason for making him be on the spot than the fact that he is necessary for Anna's great scene after the discovery of the body of her father.

19

The setting now changes to "a street": the time is "early morning"—possibly the morning of the following day, for Leporello speaks at one point of it "now being full dawn"; and already, at the first change of scene, we find Da Ponte burdening himself and us with some awkward problems of time and place. According to dramatic tradition the valet takes it on himself on one occasion and another to reprove his master for living so dissolute a life; and Da Ponte chooses this point at which to introduce the theme. From their colloquy (carried on in recitative) we learn that, far from repenting and reforming, Giovanni has a new adventure in prospect. He has captivated, and been captivated by, a young beauty who has promised to come to his country house— or so it seems—that night. He breaks off abruptly as his trained senses detect what he calls an "odour of femininity" in the air. Just then a woman enters, and Giovanni, taking Leporello with him, retires into the background the better to spy out the land.

The newcomer is Donna Elvira, who has just arrived in the neighbourhood, hot on the traces of the deceiver who has triumphed over her in Burgos under the usual assurance of marriage

322

and then basely abandoned her. She gives vent to her outraged feelings in a passionate aria, the substance of which is that if she can only come upon the scoundrel again she will be satisfied with nothing less than cutting out his heart. It is a distinguishing feature of the score of *Don Giovanni* that often the main burden of psychological expression is borne not by the voice but by the orchestral texture, in which Mozart revels in felicity after felicity of characterisation.[1] Elvira's present aria ("Ah! chi mi dice mai quel barbaro dov' è"), for example, derives its driving and cutting power less from the vocal line than from pelting and stabbing orchestral figures such as this:

No. 16

and this:

No. 17

Giovanni and Leporello eavesdrop on her for some time before they recognise her, and, in a trio that is one of Mozart's little masterpieces in the way of fusing the serious with the humorous, they comment on the lady's tantrums with mock pity. "Poor little thing!" says Giovanni; "we must try to console her"—"As you have 'consoled' some eighteen hundred already," Leporello comments sardonically. Giovanni approaches the angry lady ingratiatingly, and the swift disconcerting recognition is mutual. The malicious valet is amused and delighted by this unexpected turn of events. Giovanni, soon recovering something of his normal aplomb, addresses Elvira with elaborate courtesy. She interrupts him with a lengthy and furious recital of the wrongs she has suffered at his hands: "she reels it off like a printed book!" interjects Leporello

[1] During the period of gestation of *Don Giovanni* his instrumental genius was functioning with rare ease and power, as witness in particular the great string quintet in G minor and the *Kleine Nachtmusik*.

admiringly, borrowing a phrase from Molière. Giovanni turns the awkward business of explanation over to his servant, disappears, and leaves the ground clear for Leporello and his Catalogue aria.

20

We may enlarge our view of this episode a little by going back to Bertati. He describes the scene as "in the country, with rustic dwellings and a fine country house, outside the walls of Villena" [1] (the general scene of the action in Bertati). From the dialogue between Giovanni and Pasquariello we learn that the former's new conquest—the "pretty lady" of Da Ponte—is a certain Donna Ximena, who had arrived "yesterday" at her country house— evidently the one shown on the stage—for the purpose of having secret meetings with Don Giovanni. While master and man are talking Elvira enters. She is a lady of quality attended by two servants, who has just arrived from Burgos in a splendid carriage: she decides to put up for the present at an inn in "this village" rather than in the town, the better to keep an eye on the comings and goings of the man who had deceived and abandoned her after a mere three days of sham wedlock. When, after their short colloquy, Giovanni, with apologies for having to leave her "on pressing business," deputes his valet to explain his past behaviour to her, he "goes into the casino" (the country house), manifestly to keep his assignation with Ximena. At the conclusion of the Catalogue aria Elvira simply "exits," presumably to make her way to the inn.

Bertati had all along a clear and consistent idea of the setting and the action: his next scene (following on the "Catalogue" episode between Pasquariello and Elvira), shows us Giovanni and Ximena in amorous communion inside the house, she trying to pin him down to a promise of wedlock, the consummate confidence trickster taking evasive action as usual. But Da Ponte was in too much of a hurry to think very hard about it all. He sensibly abolished Ximena, whom he could hardly have made use of now without having her on his hands for the rest of the evening. It was precisely Ximena, however, who, in Bertati, had accounted for the "casino," for Don Giovanni being stationed outside it, and for his running away so unceremoniously from Elvira. Bertati

[1] In Aragon.

makes it perfectly clear that Giovanni and Pasquariello are so
early out of their beds—or not yet in them—because the assignation with Ximena in her country house is for that very hour.
What Giovanni says to Leporello in Da Ponte, however, is this:
"Know that I am in love with a beautiful lady who loves me; I
have seen her, I have spoken to her, and she will come with me
to the casino [whose? presumably his] *tonight.*" The "tonight"
makes sheer nonsense of it all. Truly Da Ponte could be the most
slovenly of craftsmen at times: the best he can do now in the way
of getting his hero off the stage is the direction "Don Giovanni
escapes"!

21

Let us take up the dropped thread of the Da Ponte opera.
Giovanni having been got out of the way by hook or by crook
the stage is now set for one of the most famous show pieces of the
work—the Catalogue aria, the subject of which has a place of its
own in the history of the Don Juan drama.

There is nothing resembling it in Tirso's *El Burlador*: Tirso was
too good a dramatist, and wrote for too cultivated an audience,
to bring the minor character of the lackey too much to the forefront. But it was inevitable that in proportion as the Don Juan
story descended to the smaller European theatres and the puppet
shows and the chawbacon public it should drift more and more
into common clowning in the places where the comic character
could assert his traditional rights.[1] This process of degradation
set in first in Italy, where the commedia dell' arte specialised in
characters whose prime concern it was to lay the fun on with a
trowel. It was in Italy, apparently, that the Catalogue of the
Spanish hero's conquests first came into being. The motif appears
to have made its first, or at all events an early, appearance in
Cicognini's *Il Convitato di Pietra, opera esemplare in prosa*, produced shortly before 1650. (The first Venice imprint bears no
date; but it is generally agreed that the author died about 1651.)
This Cicognini was a prolific and highly popular writer for the
Italian theatre in the first half of the seventeenth century. He
obviously played to the gallery: a later historian of Italian litera-

[1] Think of the often dreadful buffoonery, for the delectation of the groundlings, in some of Shakespeare's and Marlowe's finest tragedies!

ture, Crescimbeni, regarded him as on the whole a degrading influence.

Cicognini's *Il Convitato di Pietra* is accessible to students today in the reprint of Gendarme de Bévotte. It is a very free handling of Tirso's story, often coarsened by the influence of the commedia dell' arte. In the eleventh scene of the first act Don Giovanni and his servant Passarino, having escaped from the wrecked ship, make the acquaintance of the fishermaiden Rosalba (Tirso's Tisbea at a considerable remove). As soon as he has recovered from the effects of his immersion Giovanni observes that Rosalba is uncommonly pretty. "Vedi che buon bocconcino" ("A nice little mouthful, this"), he remarks *sotto voce* to Passarino, who comments, "Another one for the list!" That is all, for the time being, in Cicognini; but in the thirteenth scene, when Giovanni is about to leave Rosalba and she is reminding him of his vows, Passarino remarks that if his master had kept all the promises of marriage he had made he would now find himself with four thousand wives. (We are already very far from Tirso, it will be seen, well on the way towards the broad farce of later days.) As Giovanni leaves Rosalba, the valet, according to the stage directions, throws the list *at the audience*, bidding them see for themselves how many hundreds of names there are in it; and with that he leaves Rosalba to bewail her lot alone. As yet, then, there is no actual reading from the list; the mere mention and exhibition of one was presumably enough to set the audience in a roar.

22

The treatment of the motif remains much the same in the Biancolelli scenario (1622) of which mention has already been made.[1] When, in this Italian production in Paris, Don Juan abandons the fishermaiden after having betrayed her under a promise of marriage, Arlequin (the valet) tells her, by way of consolation, that she is only one of more than a hundred damsels who have been similarly honoured. "I say to her," so Biancolelli's scenario runs, " 'Look, here's the list of all the others in the same case as yourself; I'll add your name.' Then I throw the scroll into the pit, keeping hold of one end of it, and I say, 'Gentlemen, just see if the name of one or other of your own female relatives isn't down

[1] See p. 301.

here.'" The theme, it will be seen, was capable of all sorts of comic variations.

Dorimon and de Villiers make the valet reel off to the forsaken maidens the names of some others of the hero's victims, and show them the scroll. In Molière, where the valet is not the ordinary Italian buffoon but a shrewd, brainy fellow, coolly critical of his master and rather contemptuous of him, there is neither production nor mention of a "list." The play opens with a scene between the valet (Sganarelle) and Gusman (the majordomo of the abandoned Elvire), who has been commissioned to find out why Juan has behaved so callously to his mistress. Sganarelle assures Gusman that his master, about whom he has no illusions, simply does not know the meaning of the word honour. "It costs him nothing to contract a marriage; that's his usual trap for women. He marries right and left—high-born lady, young girl, bourgeoise, peasant, none is too warm or too cold for him. If I were to tell you the names of all the women he has married here, there and everywhere, it would keep me going till nightfall. You look surprised at this: you change colour; but it is a mere sketch of the man, and to complete the portrait would mean many more brush-strokes. Suffice it to say that one of these days the wrath of heaven will overtake him. I would rather belong to the Devil than to him. . . ."

But Molière was writing for a Paris audience with some claims to intelligence and taste. The Italian small town public was satisfied with lower standards: there a clowning servant was a well-established figure of fun, and it was in the Italian tradition that Bertati and Da Ponte were content to work.[1]

---

[1] The register of a lady-killer's operations was no doubt something of a stock comic apparatus even before the Don Juan saga acquired its vogue. In John Fletcher's play *The Wild-Goose Chase* (probably about 1621) the hero Mirabell (the "Wild-Goose") is described in the list of dramatis personae as "a Travell'd Monsieur, and great defyer of all Ladies in the way of Marriage, otherwise their much loose servant, at the last caught by the despis'd Oriana." He is, in truth, merely a harmless young poseur whom no one, and least of all the women, take very seriously; but he keeps a register of his alleged conquests and shows it confidentially to his friend De-Garde— "this book, this inventory," as De-Garde describes it, "the debt-book of your mistresses."

We have left Elvira alone with Leporello, who has been commissioned by his master, before he "escapes," to tell the lady just why she has been treated so scurvily. He takes this as his cue to reel off the expected Catalogue; Elvira is to console herself with the knowledge that she has had many forerunners, in proof of which Leporello holds out to her the "little book" of names and places, inviting her to read it with him—in Italy six hundred and forty, in Germany two hundred and thirty-one, a hundred in France, ninety-one in Turkey (it will be seen that Don Juan has travelled a good deal since Tirso's days), and here in Spain no fewer than a thousand and three, making a grand total of two thousand and sixty-five.[1] His master's tastes, Leporello assures Elvira, are catholic—from the princess and the marquise, the baroness and the countess to the lady's maid and the bourgeoise, blonde or brunette, old or young, the plump being more fancied in the winter, the slim in the summer; in fact, virtually anything in petticoats, but in general novices preferred. Da Ponte as a verbal artist has improved here on Bertati, and for every one of the many piquancies of the text Mozart finds the perfect musical characterisation, the ribald chuckle of the orchestra, for example, as Leporello reads out the score in Italy, Germany and elsewhere:

No. 18

[1] Giovanni's record does not surpass that of Alphonse Daudet's Brichanteau, who confessed to having in some forty-five years seduced six hundred young girls, saved seven or eight hundred persecuted female orphans, married thousands of *jeunes premières*, and even violated ladies of quality. These exploits, however, were performed by him merely in his capacity as an actor, "between the footlights and the back curtain," as he explains. But even a stage character of this vital sort takes some sort of living up to. Has any of us ever seen a Don Giovanni who suggests the veracity of Leporello's laudatory account of him? Many of them put us in mind only of a good-looking barber's apprentice with a respectable score at purely local targets. A few are so frankly undemonic as to be incredible; they put us in mind of that Don Giovanni whom Berlioz saw in Paris, who ought to have been

The aria, thanks to Mozart, practically sings itself, so that most of the farcical by-play that the average bass over-zealously insists on in the delivery of it is superfluous.

Having finished his "consolation" Leporello goes off. It is almost incredible that Da Ponte keeps Elvira on the stage all through this long ordeal, enduring the lackey's suggestive insolences without saying a word; but that was what the librettist was reduced to through having departed from Bertati without taking due thought of all the consequences. In Bertati the Catalogue is shorter and less farcical in its exaggerations: Elvira cuts the rascal short, refusing to listen any more; she orders him away, and when she is alone she voices in a few lines of recitative her determination to find out if she has a rival, and, if so, to deal appropriately with her. In Da Ponte the equivalent recitative put into her mouth seems so feeble after the lengthy Catalogue aria that some producers dispense with it, sending her off the stage along with Leporello. Others feel that she ought to be allowed to make her exit with more dignity than this, so they tack on to her words the recitative ("In quali eccessi, O Numi") and aria ("Mi tradì quell' alma ingrata") which Mozart added to the score for the Vienna production of the opera. But there the recitative and aria had been rightly placed near the end of the work: they are the last expression of Elvira's feelings, fluctuating between anger with Giovanni and pity for the doom she is now sure will overtake him, after the further proofs she had experienced of his perfidy and levity since the opera opened. To remove this aria from its proper place to the few minutes following on the Catalogue aria is to drift into sheer nonsense. For the difficult situation now created, however, only Da Ponte can be held responsible.

24

Towards the end of the present scene, when he is promising to marry Zerlina, Giovanni says to her, "This casinetto is mine. There we will be alone, and there, my jewel, we will be made one"; and again, at the commencement of the duet "Là ci darem la mano," "See, it is quite near: let us go there." Now in an earlier scene, as the reader will remember, Giovanni had spoken of the

given, he said, the *prix Montyon* (a prize awarded to the most outstandingly virtuous Paris schoolboy of the academic year).

country house in which his unnamed latest conquest had arranged
to meet him that night. All this had made better sense in Bertati,
where there really is a new conquest—Donna Ximena—and it is in
her house, shown on the stage, that the meeting is to take place.
But in *Don Giovanni* we hear no more of that assignation, for
Da Ponte dispenses entirely with Donna Ximena. Having taken
over from his predecessor the notion of a "casino," yet having
failed to make use of it in circumstances that would have been
appropriate to it, he now decides to work it into the Zerlina episode. In this there was certainly a touch of ingenuity. But Bertati
had throughout a better construction in mind. He makes the entry
of Giovanni and Ximena into the latter's house, and their exit
from it a little later, not only dramatically credible but sugges-
tively operative as regards time. All this goes for nothing in Da
Ponte: he makes Giovanni "escape" at a critical moment, but where
he escapes to we do not discover. Leporello "goes off" after reel-
ing off the list to Elvira; but again we are not told, nor can we
discover, where. In Bertati it had all been quite simple and logical,
as well as scenically economical. Da Ponte requires two settings
—first the "street" in which Giovanni and Elvira accidentally meet
in the early morning, followed by the Catalogue aria and so on,
and afterwards the "open country" near Giovanni's house, where
the peasants are merry-making. In Bertati *one* scene suffices—"the
open country, with rustic dwellings and a handsome villa, outside
the walls of Villena." Giovanni is hanging about the house—
Ximena's—because that lady had arrived there yesterday and
would receive him today. There follow, in logical sequence, the
chance meeting and mutual recognition of Giovanni and Elvira,
the slipping of the former "into the villa," as we are expressly told,
Leporello's detention of Elvira by means of the Catalogue aria,[1]
the later emergence of Ximena and Giovanni from the house, and
their brief dialogue. With the exit of Ximena, Bertati at once
brings the peasants on the stage. There is no need, as in Da Ponte,
for any change of scene. This is all provided for in the one setting:
to celebrate with song and dance the nuptials of Maturina (Zerlina) and Biagio (Masetto) all that the villagers have to do is to

[1] What was meanwhile happening in the villa we can infer from Giovanni's
closing remark, *sotto voce,* as he leaves Ximena: "I must be off and enter her
in the list."

come out of their cottages into the "open country" near the patrician house. When Giovanni succeeds in wearing down Maturina's resistance the pair leave the others and, according to the stage directions, "go into Maturina's house"—obviously one of those "rustic dwellings" described by Bertati as forming part of the stage setting.

Moreover, Bertati's transition from the previous scene to the present one is much more logically and naturally managed than Da Ponte's, where we see Giovanni "escaping" from Elvira—whither and why? Next Leporello escapes from Elvira—where? Master and man reappear together after the opening ensemble of villagers, and from Giovanni's first words, "Good riddance! But see, what a number of pretty girls . . .", we gather that the pair have met again just after the exit of Elvira. Bertati has a better sense of timing. After the Catalogue aria Pasquariello obviously strolls around on his own account, waiting for the return of his master from Operation Ximena in the villa; and when Giovanni and Ximena leave the stage the former as obviously goes off trusting to come upon his valet sooner or later. Da Ponte makes the mistake, in terms of stage time, of bringing master and man on together in the villagers' scene. Bertati is defter: he brings Pasquariello in again almost as soon as Maturina and the peasants have burst upon the scene and begun their little song and dance; clearly he has not been far away since he turned his back on Elvira. At first he listens and watches in concealment; then, unable to repress the amorous ardours he shares with his master, he runs into their midst, takes Maturina by the hand, and makes her dance with him, until the hackles of the jealous Biagio rise and he packs the other villagers off and turns roughly on Pasquariello, who, attempting an imitation of his master's technique, tries to pass himself off as a gentleman of the name of Don Giovannino. It is while the two are quarrelling that Giovanni enters, contemptuously puts the lackey in his place, and then turns his attentions to Maturina. Bertati's Giovanni, then, we can assume to have been wandering about for a little while in search of Pasquariello after his exit from Ximena's house. Da Ponte's construction, in which master and man—the former ejaculating "That's a good riddance!"—meaning Elvira—enter together without any credible time-interval, is a lamentably feeble piece of work in comparison. Further, Bertati's more extended treatment of the scene, with the consequently more gradual breach of Maturina's defences, is dramatically superior to Da Ponte's, which hardly gives Zerlina any time to do more than say first "I want to and yet I don't" and then "Yes," before she goes off towards the house with Giovanni.

25

Let us return to the point in Mozart's opera in which Giovanni and Leporello find themselves in the midst of a number of villagers who are celebrating the espousals of two of their number, Zerlina and Masetto.

Giovanni, who knows every move in the game he has played so successfully for so long, soon insinuates himself into the favour of the pretty bride, whom he promises to take under his gentlemanly protection; while a little commotion among the other girls is explained by Leporello having suggested taking one or two of them under *his* protection. Poor Masetto tries to assert his rights, but the peasant is soon cowed by the veiled threats of the nobleman. He vents his rage in an aria (allegro di molto) that is one-third craven cringing, one-third rough irony and one-third surly threat: "Yes, I understand, Signor. A cavalier like you can wish a man like me nothing but well. But as for you, you slut [turning to Zerlina] my calamity, my ruin! . . . [Then to Leporello, who is shooing him out] Yes, yes, I'm going! [To Zerlina again, sarcastically] The fine gentleman here will make a fine lady of you, I'm sure!"

As soon as Masetto has been hustled off the stage Giovanni turns on little Zerlina the blend of charm and flattery that has always worked with her sex. She is too pretty, he assures her, to be the wife of a country bumpkin like Masetto: he, Don Giovanni, will make a lady of her forthwith: "so let us slip into my villa here, where we will be made one":

No. 19

P Là ci da-rem la ma-no, là mi di-rai di sì.

She takes very little persuading; her defences are soon down, and she becomes as ardent for the adventure as Giovanni himself.

As they are leaving for the villa, arm in arm, they are confronted by Elvira, who has overheard their colloquy and now intervenes to save "this poor innocent girl" from the cavalier's "cruel claws." At this Zerlina naturally hesitates, and for a moment or two Giovanni's craftsmanship is put to a severe test. To Elvira, whom he addresses cajolingly as "my idol," he explains in a rapid aside that he is merely amusing himself with a country maiden, which draws from her the acid comment that *she* knows only too well what "amusing himself" means. In another aside he tells the puzzled Zerlina that this poor excited lady is crazily enamoured of him, and to keep her quiet he has to pretend, out of the sheer kindness of his heart, to be in love with her.

But Elvira is not so easily fooled. In a vigorous aria, "Ah, fuggi il traditor":

No. 20

she warns Zerlina that the plausible gallant is a rogue and a liar, and ends by hustling her away. Giovanni takes his frustration philosophically. "Everything seems to be going wrong with me today," he soliloquises; "the Devil seems to be amusing himself at my expense, opposing all my pleasant little plans." "But this is the last straw!", he ejaculates disgustedly as Ottavio and Donna Anna enter. Ottavio, as usual, is more heart than head; and as he comes into view we hear him bidding Anna not to give way to vain tears but to think about vengeance for her father. Before he can get even as far as talking about this, however, he and Anna catch sight of Giovanni. He is well known to both of them, it appears. Anna's opening words to him are, "My friend, we meet you in the nick of time. Have you courage, a noble soul?" ("Now I wonder," he mutters under his breath, "if the Devil has been

putting ideas into her head!") He courteously places himself at
her disposal, however, and, with a sigh of relief, discovers from
her next words that he is in no danger of recognition. "Fair Donna
Anna, why are you weeping?" he asks; "has any villain dared to
grieve you?" He is hers to command, he protests; his relations,
his friends, his possessions, his good right arm, his sword, all are
at her service if she has been wronged.

26

But before she can satisfy his generous curiosity on this point
Elvira breaks in upon them with the remark "Ah! do I find you
again, perfidious monster?"—which, considering she had left him
in that very place only a minute before, can hardly be regarded
as a masterpiece of dramatic construction on Da Ponte's part.
There seems to be no valid reason why she should return at this
point except the fact that a quartet has now been called for by
the composer. She begins by taking Anna under her protection
as she had done Zerlina: "Wretched one, put not your trust in
this ribald rogue: he has already betrayed me, and now he would
betray you":

No. 21

Anna and Ottavio are impressed by the nobility of her bearing
and the signs of suffering in her face.

Giovanni resorts to a technique that has served him well before;
the poor creature, he informs the others confidentially, is mentally
deranged; if they will leave him alone with her he will see if he
can calm her down. For a while Ottavio and Anna do not know
which of the two to believe; but gradually Elvira's passionate
reiterations of Giovanni's perfidy have their effect on them, and
the masterly quartet, in which each personage is aptly character-
ised by Mozart, ends as it were on a note of interrogation. Don
Giovanni has not lost his case; nor, on the other hand, has Elvira
entirely won hers.

Da Ponte now wants to have the stage clear for the decisive

"explanation" scene between Ottavio and Anna, which opens with
an agitated orchestral figure:

No. 22

suggestive of Anna's horror at the realisation that the murderer
of her father was Don Giovanni. He cannot be altogether congratulated as a dramatist, however, on the way he brings this
about. He can think of nothing better than to make Elvira leave
the stage—just at the point when the dramatic tension has reached
its climax!—and send Giovanni hot-foot after her, with a lame explanation to Ottavio and Anna that he must see that the poor
deluded creature does not do herself some injury. With polite
apologies and a renewed assurance that if he can be of any service
to Anna and Ottavio they will find him in his villa, Giovanni bids
them goodbye and hastens after Elvira.

Da Ponte's handling of Elvira so far, and for some time later,
is the great blot on the libretto; what should be the most *positive*
female character in the work—for Anna is throughout more
negative than positive—is apt to become in performance a mere
figure of fun, popping in and out of the action like a jack-in-the-
box as she does; in particular her sudden appearance in the present scene within a minute or so after she has bundled Zerlina off
to safety has an effect of sheer farce that the most seriously disposed audience cannot resist. For this unfortunate result Da
Ponte's reliance on Bertati in general outline and his departure
from him in matters of detail are about equally responsible. Bertati, with only a few minutes now to fill in before coming to the
decisive mausoleum scene for which his audience has been eagerly
waiting, decides to pile on the fun thick and fast. After the exit of
Giovanni and Maturina into the latter's cottage he has a comic
scene in which Giovanni, on his reappearance, plays off Elvira
and Ximena against each other, whispering to each of them in
turn that the other is mentally deranged. Ximena having left the

stage, he repeats the process with Elvira and Maturina. Then he goes off, leaving these two to indulge in a lively duet in which each of the supposed "wives" slangs the other in true Italian buffo style, and the great lady Elvira is brought down to the peasant girl's level. They go off, still exchanging insults, and the scene changes to the mausoleum and the episode with the Statue, for which, by this time, the audience can be presumed to be getting impatient.

Henceforth Da Ponte is left to his own resources: his opera being in two acts, he still has a large canvas to fill in before he can arrive at the climactic Statue scene. He will do so with some difficulty, as we shall see: meanwhile it is important to take note of the awkwardnesses in which he has already landed himself by playing the in-and-out game he has done with Bertati's construction, and especially by his having dispensed with the character of Ximena.

27

It does not seem to have been observed by the writers on the *Don Giovanni* subject that of all the Don Juans of literature and the drama that of Da Ponte is professionally the most futile. (We are not talking now of the Don Giovanni of Mozart.) He is the last poor ineffectual scion of an illustrious race of conquerors. Tirso's Don Juan would have refused to sit at the same table with anyone so inefficient; Shadwell's Libertine would have scorned to be seen raiding the same nunnery in his company. For when it comes to action Da Ponte's Giovanni accomplishes simply nothing to justify his reputation. Bertati's hero, in his short innings before he is given "Out!" by the Great Umpire, at least manages to run up almost before our eyes the respectable score of three. It is clear that he had been successful with Donna Anna: "Bravo!" says Pasquariello to him after the death of the Commander; "Two heroic deeds—Donna Anna violated and her father run through the body!", and the hero, be it noted, does not deny either impeachment; witness also his cynical remark to Anna when he was trying to escape from her—"If it had been Duke Ottavio you wouldn't have had anything to say about it." Later he retires into the villa of the enamoured Ximena, and does not reappear until after an interval long enough to allow the audience to draw its own conclusions as to how he had occupied his time

336

there. So again when he goes off with the equally amorous Maturina into the latter's cottage, with a scene's convenient time-interval between that disappearance from our view and his next appearance on the stage.

But in Da Ponte his record is one of continuous frustration and failure. In the critical case of Anna he confronts us with two alternatives—either we are to come to the conclusion that her story to Ottavio of the merciful frustration of Giovanni's attempt is deliberately false, in which case what becomes of our conception of "the noble Donna Anna"?—or we must accept her story as unquestioningly as Ottavio does, with a similar sigh of relief, in which case Giovanni's first adventure in the opera must rank as his misadventure number one. It is true that there is some confusion, even among Mozart students, with regard to this. Alfred Einstein, for instance, confidently lays it down that "what is true is that she is one of the hero's victims, that Don Giovanni in the dark of the night, disguised as Don Ottavio, has reached the summit of his desires, and that the curtain rises at the moment when Donna Anna has come to the realisation of the terrible truth of her betrayal. In the eighteenth century no one misunderstood this." For all these *ex cathedra* assertions Einstein offers no evidence at all. There is nothing whatever *in the text* to lead us to believe that Anna is "one of the hero's victims." The "eighteenth century"—whatever, if anything, that may mean in this connection—would be aware that in Bertati it had been made tolerably clear that Anna had been outraged. But why should it collectively assume that in Da Ponte also she had been, when neither in the text of the opening scene of the opera nor in that of the "explanation" scene with Ottavio is there a single line to warrant that assumption? [1] To invoke the whole "eighteenth century" in this

[1] To this it may be objected that in the short dialogue in recitative that follows the murder of the Commander, Leporello says "Bravo! two pretty affairs; the daughter outraged, the father killed." To this Giovanni makes, in effect, the sombre reply, "What he got he asked for." Then, when the lackey asks insinuatingly, "And Donna Anna, did *she* ask for it?", his master checks his impertinent familiarity with a curt "Silence: do not annoy me: come away with me [drawing his sword] unless you want something to happen to *you*." All this is consistent with the view that Giovanni had *not* succeeded with Anna, but was for the moment sobered by the thought of the consequences of the killing of her father. The parallel dialogue in Bertati suggests

high-priori manner in support of a theory that is nothing but guesswork on Einstein's part is going a trifle too far.

Einstein seems to have worked on the vague notion that Da Ponte's Anna is the equivalent of Tirso's Isabela. But though Isabela confessedly succumbed to the seducer at the beginning of the drama, the daughter of the Commander whom *his* Don Juan slew was Doña Ana, with whom, as he himself admitted, he had failed. The fact that neither Da Ponte nor Bertati took the trouble to make a self-consistent unity out of the two women of the original saga is regrettable but beside the present point: what we are finally left with is the *Don Giovanni* libretto of Da Ponte, and this contains no warrant for Einstein's obiter dictum that Anna is lying to Ottavio when she gives him her account of what had happened in her chamber. "It goes without saying," he writes, "that in the famous recitativo accompagnato in which she designates Don Giovanni to her betrothed as the murderer of her father she cannot tell Don Ottavio the whole truth; and his 'Respiro' [his sigh of relief when he hears her story] has always had a tragi-comic flavour for every understanding listener." Einstein, in his confident invocation for his own purposes of "the eighteenth century" and "every understanding listener," and his question-begging "it goes without saying," is throughout merely taking for granted the very thing he has to prove. And the final result of his disquisition is not only to make Anna out to be a slut and a liar but to make the simple Ottavio look a positive fool in the eyes of the audience, in which "every understanding listener" can see at a glance what is hidden from him!

It cannot be emphasised too strongly that the Anna of the opening scene of Da Ponte's *Don Giovanni* is *not* the Isabela of Tirso's first scene, and that all the usual misunderstanding—Einstein's for example—of the character of the Anna of the opera is due to the librettist's clumsy attempt to fuse Tirso's Isabela and his Ana into one. In *El Burlador* Isabela is obviously no better than she should be: she is a woman of the world who has no

---

no such psychological dilemma: when Leporello says "Bravo! two heroic deeds, Donna Anna violated and her father stabbed," Giovanni merely rejoins "I have told you before now that I don't want any criticisms of my conduct ["rimostranze"—"remonstrances"] from you. Follow me, and keep your mouth shut."

objection to being "seduced" so long as the "seducer" is her lover Ottavio. In the later stages of Tirso's play Isabela is a coolly calculating creature for whom our sympathies are never sought. Tirso's Doña Ana, the daughter of the Commander, is another character altogether, and Giovanni, as we have seen, admits that he had failed with her. The confusion between the two on Da Ponte's part landed him in another difficulty—one not of psychology but of dramatic structure. To open his opera with a Donna Anna who was originally a Doña Isabela, then to make *her* the daughter of the Commander, was to make the murder of the latter the *first* and worst of Giovanni's crimes (in the opera), whereas, as Tirso's surer dramatic instinct had told him, it should be the last and worst, after which the laws of God and man closed in inevitably and inexorably on the Burlador. And from this cardinal blunder, as has been pointed out already, arose the failure to make Ottavio anything more than the tenor windbag of the opera.

Later we find Giovanni boasting to Leporello of an assignation with some enamoured lady (unnamed) who is accompanying him to the villa "tonight." Of this adventure, which appears, so far as the opera is concerned, to exist only in the hero's imagination, we hear no more. Later still all seems to be going well with him in the Zerlina affair, till at the last moment the girl is snatched from his clutches by Elvira. Much later, his attempt on Zerlina in an inner room of his villa is frustrated by her shrieks for help. Later still, it is true, he tells Leporello gleefully of a successful adventure he has had on his way by night to their last rendezvous —with a young woman (seemingly Leporello's wife) who at first took him for the valet and discovered her mistake too late. But for this, let us remember, we have only his word; and the braggart's reputation for veracity has been proved to be none of the best.

All in all then, what conclusion can the realistic spectator in a modern opera house come to but that, judged by purely professional standards of achievement, Da Ponte's Don Giovanni is the merest impostor? He owes his reputation with our trustful modern audiences entirely to the questionable book-keeping of Leporello. Pasquariello, in Bertati, while anxious to glorify his master and annoy Elvira, had not let his imagination run away with him in the Leporello fashion. He had contented himself with assuring Elvira that the list ran to a hundred or so in Italy and Germany, plus he did not know how many in France and Spain. Perhaps Da Ponte's Leporello believed, like Hitler, that if you are going to tell a lie at all you may as well make it a whopping one. Or perhaps, on the other hand, he was simply a bad secretary and his list merely the irresponsible arithmetic of an amateur in accountancy. Anyhow, having regard to all the known facts of the case, we are surely entitled now to ask for an independent audit.

28

As we have remarked, Da Ponte, after the "explanation" scene between Anna and Ottavio, has still a long sail before him, unpiloted now by Bertati or anyone else, before he can reach the sure harbour of the Statue scene. Great as his ingenuity is, the voyage will task it to the utmost. Obviously tragedy, or even, on the whole, a high degree of seriousness, is ruled out for the next stage hour or so, for the spectator's stronger emotions must not be allowed to suffer any preliminary dissipation on smaller matters before the falling of the terrific blow of the final scene. So from now onwards, until shortly before the end of the work, the prevailing element in the libretto is bound to be the buffo one, or something near that. With this the genius of Mozart was exceptionally competent to deal musically, with ample left over for the interweaving of a serious thread in the humorous texture when an opportunity for that should present itself.

By the laws of the operatic game Da Ponte's immediate object must now be to manœuvre his characters in such a way that all of them who matter will be in the same place at the same time for the big finale to the first of the two acts; and he has decided that the place of the assembly shall be in Don Giovanni's house. He could easily have arranged for this to happen fairly quickly after the recognition by Anna and Ottavio of Giovanni as the murderer of the Commander; but he has rather more time on his hands than he quite knows what to do with, so he falls back on safe operatic routine. Anna, after her story to Ottavio, is given an aria in which she tells her lover that now he knows who her assailant was she looks to him to avenge her on the dastard: "Remember the wound in my poor father's breast and the blood that drenched the ground around him," she says, and let this lover of hers now nerve himself to avenge her wrongs. After saying this at considerable length and with much repetition she leaves him, whereupon, as usual, Ottavio becomes the man of sentiment rather than the man of action. "Is it believable," he asks the universe distractedly, "that a cavalier like Don Giovanni could be guilty of so black a crime?" He must take all steps, leave no stone unturned, explore every avenue, he continues, to bring the truth to light. Two voices are speaking to him, one of them that of the lover, the other that of the friend; his duty is clear before his eyes—he must either undeceive Donna Anna as to the identity of her assailant or avenge her father's murder on this monster of a Giovanni.

His first practical step towards one or other of these ends is to sing an aria, "Dalla sua pace," in which he sets out to explain (either to himself or to the audience, for he has no other listeners) that upon Anna's peace of mind depends his own—whatever pleases her gives him life, whatever grieves her means death for him; when she sighs or weeps so does he; in a word—though, owing to the exigencies of an eighteenth century opera aria, it is rather a long word—he knows peace of mind only when she does. This is the aria spatchcocked into the score for the Vienna performances as a sort of consolation prize to the local tenor who was unequal to the bravura of the great tenor show piece of the Prague production, "Il mio tesoro"; and a lovely piece of music it is—in the concert room. In the opera house it serves only to slow down the action and to confirm us in the suspicion that has been slowly stealing over us from the commencement that whatever else Ottavio may turn out to be it will not be one of history's leading men of action.

Ottavio having left the stage Leporello returns. He begins, in recitative, a new variation on his favourite theme—he will remain no longer in the service of this crazy master of his; but before he has got very far with it he is interrupted by Don Giovanni, who seems to the lackey to be even more debonair than usual, carrying himself as if he had nothing on his conscience and not a care in the world. Leporello reports progress—as his master had commanded, he had taken the villagers off to the house, where he had entertained them with small talk, cajoleries and lies *à la* Don

Giovanni; he had calmed the jealous Masetto down; and all of them, men and women, had been drinking themselves tipsy, some of them singing, others larking, when who should walk in but Donna Elvira and Zerlina, discussing Don Giovanni and finding nothing good to say about him. With much address Leporello had enticed the great lady into and then out of the kitchen garden, and locked the gate on her. His master commends his ingenuity; with the troublesome interfering Elvira out of the way he can now settle down to serious work among the country maidens; and he launches his great aria—the only one he has in the whole opera:

No. 23

Fin ch'han dal vi—no cal-da la tes—ta, u—na gran fe-sta
va pre-pa—rar.

a feverish, explosive canticle (presto), the burden of which is that all his guests are to drink, dance and make merry while he adds, before morning, another half-score or so names to his already bulging list.

29

Master and man go out, and the scene changes to the garden of Giovanni's house, where a number of country folk are enjoying themselves, while Zerlina is trying to get a very sulky and cantankerous Masetto to see reason. What does she mean, he growls, by abandoning him for another man on the very day of their wedding? His fears are groundless, she blandly assures him; the fine gentleman had not so much as touched her with the tips of his fingers. To soothe and soften her angry spouse she sings him an enchanting aria, "Batti, batti, o bel Masetto," in which she assures him that he may beat his poor little Zerlina as he pleases, tear out her hair, pluck out her eyes, and she will kiss the hand that maltreats her if only he will believe her innocent: why should they not make peace and live in happiness together day and night for ever and ever?

The little witch, as he calls her, succeeds in calming if not quite convincing him. There is sound stuff in this Masetto, country bumpkin though he be; he will keep his suspicious peasant's eyes open, we learn. His meditations are interrupted by the voices of Giovanni and Leporello without. Zerlina turns pale: if there were only some hole, she stammers, into which Masetto could creep! This confirms his suspicions: now he understands and will investigate. He sees a recess in which he can conceal himself yet see and hear all that goes on between Zerlina and the cavalier. There is an agitated duet (allegro assai) between him and his bride, in which she vainly tries to dissuade him from his plan; and as he slips into the recess Giovanni enters with a number of his servants, who, at his command, conduct the country folk into the house, where they are given every opportunity to enjoy themselves.

Giovanni and Zerlina are left alone on the stage, with Masetto in hiding; and Mozart proceeds to turn his full genius upon a situation in itself of the most ordinary kind. Wagner used to maintain that the art of composition is the art of transition—leading the listener on imperceptibly step by step, from one musical mood, one dramatic situation, to another. The ten pages or so that now follow in the score show us Mozart at the height of his musical-dramatic power; they are as remarkable in their quiet way as the terrific Statue scene is in another. The music keeps changing perpetually; yet we feel all the time that one great line encloses it all, psychologically as well as musically.

As the crowd had left the stage the trembling Zerlina had tried to take cover behind some trees, but Giovanni, who has never lost sight of his prey, now begins to weave his spells about her. A gracious, insinuating figure in the violins:

No. 24

gives us a hint of the courtly charm he can exercise when he feels that to be the right technique for the occasion. Conscious of her danger, and mindful of the watching Masetto, Zerlina implores the cavalier, for pity's sake, to let her go to the others; but in soft cajoling terms he urges her towards an alcove where, he assures her, her good fortune shall be crowned. The alcove happens, however, to be the one in which Masetto is concealed; and at the unexpected appearance of the surly peasant the seducer, thrown off his guard, stands for a moment as if petrified. Here is the situation as Mozart has depicted it musically, with Giovanni's startled ejaculation "Masetto?" and the peasant's grim reply "Yes, Masetto!":

No. 25

It will be observed that Mozart still keeps going in the orchestra the curious quiet tread of the quavers shown in the opening bar of our quotation No. 24; but what a different suggestion they carry now, especially with their changed harmonic basis! The tread is now as menacing as it had formerly been ingratiating: here, emphatically, is the unity in variety and the variety in unity which the aestheticians laud as the acme of art.

Giovanni, as usual, soon regains his poise. In the smoothest of tones, but with mocking laughter playing about them in the orchestra, he assures Masetto that his lovely Zerlina has been feeling quite lost without him. Masetto is not fooled: "I understand, Sir, I understand," he growls. But Giovanni cuts him short. Music is heard from inside the house: the musicians are tuning up, he says; should they not join the rest of the merry throng? Zerlina eagerly agrees, and Masetto also succumbs to the seductive lure—or appears to do so.

As they leave the stage Donna Anna, Elvira and Ottavio enter, all masked. They are nerving themselves and each other to expose Giovanni and deal sternly with him. The most resolute of the three is Elvira, who, true to her character from the beginning of the opera, cannot forget her own wrongs at his hands: Ottavio is trying to keep up the courage of Anna, who is apprehensive of what may befall her lover. Notable in the orchestral accompaniment are hurrying ascending figures in sixths:

No. 26

Progressions of this kind seem to have had for the eighteenth century certain connotations which they have now lost: they have been a telling feature of the theme (No. 7) in which Giovanni is first introduced to us.

From within the house come the strains of a minuet:

No. 27

and the sensitive listener will feel, in the rhythmic structure of this, the same pulse as in our Nos. 24 and 25. This minuet will dominate a great deal of the later texture of the scene; and we cannot sufficiently admire the art that with such simple technical means can give such psychological unity to the changeful action.

Leporello, opening a window from within, draws his master's attention to the maskers—evidently people of quality. Giovanni orders him to invite them in; and in his smooth, courteous tones the pursuers find fresh confirmation of their suspicions. Still to the dignified strains of the minuet Leporello invites the maskers to enter. They accept, and when Leporello has closed the window, thereby shutting out the music from within the house, the whole character of the music changes as Anna, Elvira and Ottavio unite in a grave trio in which they once more exhort each other to have courage and pray for the protection of heaven. The decisive moment of the action has arrived, we feel; the die is cast.

30

The scene changes to a brilliant ballroom, where a dance has evidently just been concluded. To the gayest of strains in the orchestra:

No. 28

Giovanni is politely urging the women to rest for a moment, while Leporello is busy persuading the men to take some refreshment before beginning the revels again. Zerlina's simple mind is delighted by it all. Masetto thinks it well to warn her to be on her guard, but she only laughs at him, much to his annoyance. Both Giovanni and Leporello see that it will be necessary in the interests of the Catalogue to get the jealous peasant out of the way somehow or other; but while they are discussing this the three masks enter. They are greeted politely first by Leporello, then by Giovanni, who, on an occasion of this kind, he assures them, keeps open house. The general tempo of the music has now changed to maestoso. The maskers thank Giovanni gravely for his courtesy, and then join him in a paean to liberty.

He invites the company to another dance, and the minuet is resumed, Giovanni selecting Zerlina as his partner, while Ottavio dances with Anna. It is with dismay that she and Elvira have observed that Zerlina is among the company. Giovanni, seeing that Masetto is showing fresh signs of restiveness, orders Leporello to "take care" of him. Here a second stage orchestra begins a country dance, and a little later a third orchestra strikes in with a waltz. There is thus something in the way of music and dancing for all tastes, the formal courtly minuet for the gentry, more popular fare for the rustics; and Mozart weaves all three strains into a contrapuntal whole, though it is rightly the minuet that mainly engages our attention, for it is between Giovanni and the maskers that the dominant dramatic issue now lies.

Giovanni manages to edge Zerlina into an adjoining room against her will, and soon the storm breaks. Even Leporello, who, under Giovanni's instructions, has been forcing Masetto to dance with him, cannot help ejaculating "Now there's going to be a crash!" Anna, Elvira and Ottavio realise that the decisive moment has come; "Now the criminal has put the noose round his own neck!" they say. Suddenly the minuet ceases, there is a drastic change of key, and over a pounding figure in the orchestra (allegro assai) we hear from the inner room a frenzied cry from Zerlina: "Help, good people! Villain!" The musicians hurriedly leave the scene, the company breaks up in confusion, and the three maskers, headed by Masetto, declare, in true operatic fashion, that they must rush to the maiden's assistance, remaining, however, rooted to the spot the while. The tempo has been whipped up to the highest pitch of excitement; but it slows down again to an andante maestoso as the ever-resourceful Giovanni comes out of the inner room holding Leporello by the ear, stigmatising him as the ruffian who had assailed Zerlina, and vowing that he himself will be the first to punish him. The lackey plays his part well in the momentary tragi-comedy, whining for mercy as his master pretends to set about killing him.

But the game, it would appear, is now up, the fox cornered. Anna, Elvira and Ottavio unmask and deride Giovanni's clumsy attempt to impose on them: Ottavio even goes so far as to produce a pistol—an act no less impressive in its own way than Mr. Snodgrass's removal of his coat and his announcement to the company that he is about to go into action. But this is opera, and before the characters take whatever steps may be regarded as appropriate to the occasion they have to join in a big end-of-the-act ensemble; besides, it is foreordained that Giovanni shall get out of the net, tightly as it appears to be closing about him, or what will become of the second act? So Ottavio does nothing with his pistol but flourish it. In a massive finale Masetto, Anna, Elvira, Ottavio and Zerlina warn the villain that vengeance is now about to overtake him, while Giovanni—a trifle perturbed for a moment—and Leporello bow for a while before the storm. It is not long, however, before Giovanni regains full possession of himself, and, with the orchestra hammering away repeatedly at a figure of this type:

No. 29

he and Leporello are heard through the turmoil declaring that they fear nothing, even though the heavens fall. Giovanni draws his sword and makes his escape with his lackey as the curtain descends.

31

Da Ponte has still another long act to fill up, and for some time after the rising of the curtain for the next scene his invention is not at its best, only the genius of Mozart keeping him afloat. The none too bright idea has occurred to the librettist of endowing Elvira with a serving-maid, and showing Giovanni in pursuit of her. (She plays no part in the action; we have only Da Ponte's word for her existence.) The setting shows a street, on one side of which stands Elvira's dwelling, which has a balcony. It is now night, and we find Giovanni and Leporello in conversation. The valet is once more swearing that he will stay no longer in the service of a master who gets the pair of them into such terrible scrapes; and Giovanni, in the gayest spirits, is telling him not to be a fool but to take all that has recently happened as just good clean fun. The recurrent theme of the lackey's revolt has begun to be a trifle tiresome by now—or would be, had not Mozart made it the subject of a racy colloquy in the purest buffo style. Leporello turns to go: Giovanni, taking out his purse, persuades him to reconsider his decision; and the remainder of the episode is played out in recitative. The valet hopes that his master's thoughts are not still running on women; but Giovanni assures him that he will not be satisfied until he has subdued the whole brood of them; they are more vital to him, he says, than the food he eats, the air he breathes.

Leporello, as usual, gives in, and Giovanni discloses to him the plan of a new adventure that has taken his fancy. He has discovered that Donna Elvira has a charming serving-maid; she has kindled his acquisitive appetite, and his scheme now is to woo her under the guise of Leporello—for, as he explains to the staggered lackey, young women of that class are rather apt to be on their guard when a well-dressed gentleman begins to tell them the old, old story. Leporello is still reluctant, and only a burst of anger on his master's part makes him consent to an exchange of cloaks and hats.

No sooner has this been effected than Elvira appears on the balcony, to breathe out the affliction of her soul over this deceiver of a gallant whom she hates for his perfidy but for whom she still cannot help feeling a certain tenderness and pity. As usual with him when there is something in an ostensibly humorous situation that is also capable of a serious interpretation, Mozart puts into Elvira's mouth music of the most heartfelt kind:

No. 30

Even when Leporello and Giovanni, from their hiding-place, begin to comment *sotto voce* upon the unforeseen turn of events—"Softly!" whispers Leporello, "it's Donna Elvira; I recognise her voice":

No. 31

—we are conscious of something in the music that goes rather deeper than the words and the buffo situation: Mozart, we feel, has too much interest in and compassion for his Elvira to involve her any more than he can help in the buffoonery of the lackey and his master.

Giovanni resolves to exploit the comic possibilities of the situation. Standing behind Leporello, who makes the gestures appropriate to a serenading lover, he sings of his love to Elvira, in phrases that are an echo of hers (No. 30); but it is upon No. 31 that Mozart draws to blend, in the way of which he has the secret, the serious with the humorous aspects of the scene. There is no need whatever for it to be so grossly clowned as it generally is on the stage by actors who know no mean between humour and thick-thumbed farce; the comedy is inherent in the situation, but curiously interfused with pathos, and to reduce it all to mere buffoonery is to pay a poor compliment to Mozart's consummate art of blending humour and seriousness so subtly that we cannot say where one ends and the other begins.

When Giovanni launches into a snatch of song that sounds— whether by accident or design it is impossible to say—rather like an anticipation of the serenade he will shortly sing (No. 32) to the invisible serving-maid, and Elvira replies that she can no longer believe him and Giovanni protests that he will kill himself if she does not, and Leporello, in low tones, swears that if the fun goes on much longer he must either laugh or burst, the comedy element in the scene necessarily comes more to the forefront, but even now it should not degenerate into yokel clowning. When at last the voices unite in a short trio, in which Giovanni chuckles over the success of his little stratagem and Leporello mockingly invokes the protection of heaven for this latest victim of his master's wiles, it is Elvira who commands almost the whole of our attention with lovely music, of the type of No. 30, that is wholly serious and heartfelt: the composer's sympathies are evidently with her, though he never loses sight of the comedy of the imbroglio.

Overcome, in spite of herself, by Giovanni's pleading, Elvira leaves the balcony to join him. There follows a brief recitative in which Giovanni gives Leporello his final instructions; when Elvira descends he is to overwhelm her (as the supposed Giovanni, of course) with caresses and cajoleries, mimicking his master's voice as best he can, and then lead her off somewhere so as to leave the course clear for his master. When she reappears, Giovanni recedes into the background to watch the fun. Elvira tells the supposed Giovanni that she now believes in the sincerity of the return of his heart to her, and forgives him for all the tears he has made her shed. The comedy thickens: the more pressing Elvira becomes for the renewal of her happiness the more Leporello, to Giovanni's quiet amusement, actually becomes interested in the part he is playing. But once more let it be said that the fun should not be laid on with the broad and rather soiled trowel that is the only comic tool of which the average Leporello has any command; anything of the nature of crude farce is always quite alien to Mozart, the subtle master of fine shades and border-line states of mind, always himself, even when the less delicate sensibility of his librettist is edging him towards the domain of the chawbacon grin and the loud guffaw. It occasionally happens with Mozart that, if not openly at variance with a librettist, he does not walk exactly in step with him.

32

The situation is broken up by Giovanni, who descends on them in the manner of a footpad; as they run away a light appears in the supposed maid's window, and Giovanni sings, to a mandoline accompaniment, the enchanting canzonetta, "Deh, vieni alla finestra, o mio tesoro" ("Come to the window, my treasure, come and take pity on my woe, or you will see me die before your eyes, o maiden with mouth sweeter than honey, with sugar at the centre of your heart"):

No. 32

and once more we see Mozart declining to go as far as his librettist in the way of facile exaggeration. The canzonetta is purely appropriate to the occasion, to the situation and to the mentality of the supposed serving-maid, and to nothing and no one else in the whole opera—for Mozart's dramatic instinct even in little things of this sort is well-nigh infallible: but for all that the song breathes the purest Mozartian atmosphere.

In what follows we get further and further away from the central current of the opera, and have little more to do than to accompany Da Ponte in his rather desperate efforts to fill up the space that still intervenes between where he is now and the climactic point that, foreordained for him as it is, still lies uncomfortably far ahead of him. It has apparently occurred to Masetto that whatever the others may think of doing next it is his business, and at last within his capacity, to bring the dissolute cavalier to book. He enters now, carrying a musket and a pistol and accompanied by some villagers, also armed after their fashion. They are searching for Don Giovanni. He and Masetto catch sight of each other in the dim light simultaneously. In a longish recitative Giovanni pretends that he is Leporello, tired beyond further endurance of his criminal master, and willing to co-operate with Masetto in his desire to track the miscreant down and murder him. In a long aria Giovanni-Leporello expounds to the others his plan of campaign: they are to hunt about until they come upon a man and a young woman in the piazza, or perhaps making love under a window. The man will be wearing a hat with white plumes, a great cloak over his shoulders, and a sword at his side. This is the villain they are in search of. The villagers are to disperse, some going in this direction, others in that; Masetto is to accompany the pseudo-Leporello, "and you will soon see what happens," the latter assures him with sinister humour. The aria is unduly spun out by repetition, but both Da Ponte and Mozart obviously have more stage time on their hands just now than they quite know what to do with.

The villagers having all departed, and Masetto having assured the pseudo-Leporello that nothing short of wallowing in the miscreant cavalier's blood will content him, Giovanni gets the musket and the pistol from him on the pretext of examining them, then turns on the poor fellow and beats him savagely before leaving him. Zerlina, who has heard his howls, enters with a lantern. In another long recitative Masetto tells her how he has been maltreated: she cannot resist the temptation to tell him that he has brought all this on himself by his jealousy, but having done that she invites him into the house, where, she says, if he will promise to reform she will apply a remedy that will make him forget his bruises; whereupon she sings her aria "Vedrai, carino, se sei buonino, che bel remedio ti voglio dar." Her words, water them down as the translators may, leave us in no doubt as to what her "remedy" is, and are intended to leave no doubt in Masetto's; it is "natural," "not to be obtained at the apothecary's," "far from unpleasant," "a sure balsam," his for the asking. "Would you know where I keep it? Place your hand on my heart and feel its beating." She has no difficulty in persuading him to try her sure specific; and as he limps off with her the orchestral accompaniment to the cajoling melody, which has been wonderfully soft and insinuating so far, develops into a sort of ironic paean with laughing trills rippling along the surface of it. Masetto has put up a good fight so far in the opera, but this is decidedly the artful Zerlina's round.

33

Da Ponte now feels it is time to return to Leporello and Elvira. We come upon them again in what the libretto informs us is "a dark courtyard before the house of Donna Anna." The lackey's one thought now is how to get away from this nuisance of a love-struck lady; and while Elvira, maintaining her own characteristic idiom, tries to tell the supposed Giovanni of her love and fears he keeps feeling along the wall for a door through which to slip. But before he can succeed in this they are joined in the darkness by Anna and Ottavio, both in mourning, and preceded by servants bearing torches. They bring, of course, a psychological atmosphere of their own with them, which Mozart suggests by the simplest of means—three bars of bold modulation in the orchestra from the key of B flat to that of D major:

No. 33

and a dignified rhythm appropriate to the two patrician lovers.

As usual, Ottavio is heard exhorting Anna to dry her tears and have courage; her constant weeping, he says, can only bring more sorrow to the shade of her beloved father. (Throughout the opera it is obviously the murder of her father, rather than the assault on herself, that is Anna's grievance against Giovanni.) When she begs to be allowed at least the consolation of grief it is to a melody that carries on, in the minor, the strain launched by Ottavio; and in every bar of the brief duet Mozart plays "symphonically" and expressively upon orchestral mutations of this short figure:

No. 34

which leads, by the most natural of transitions, into a descending chromatic figure of lament:

353

No. 35

Bass C ——————— B♮ —————— C —————— F♯ —————— G

as Elvira (who is of course invisible to Anna and Ottavio in the darkness) bewails having lost sight of her supposed lover, and Leporello, his nerves now on edge, catches sight of a door in the wall through which he thinks he can escape. But before he can do so Zerlina and Masetto rush in on him. At the same time Anna and Ottavio perceive him, and of course assume from his costume that he is Giovanni. The phrase shown in our No. 35 comes into its full expressive rights as they all comment on the new situation, Elvira pleading with Masetto and Zerlina to spare her "husband," and all of them being as astonished as Anna and Ottavio are to find Elvira in their midst.

On one thing, however, all except Elvira are resolved, that the cornered criminal shall die. Sinking down upon his knees, Leporello, to descending orchestral phrases derived from No. 35, begs them to have mercy on him; and once more we light upon a distinguishing feature of Mozart's genius, his capacity for describing a scene in musical terms that are at the same time comic in relation to the episode and serious in themselves.

The discovery that the supposed Giovanni is really Leporello throws the minds of all of them for a moment into confusion, which they express in their various ways, while Leporello is full of self-pity in the tight fix in which he finds himself. With masterly hand Mozart weaves all the moods in a single whole, in a sextet that is one of the high-lights of the score.

Anna having gone away with her servants the others turn upon Leporello. Elvira is furious with him for having passed himself off as his master, Zerlina and Masetto for having, as they think, maltreated the latter, Ottavio for no stated reason: the one thing they are agreed upon is that the valet shall be punished. In a lively aria Leporello protests to each of them in turn his innocence, laying the blame for all that has happened on his tyrannic and unscrupulous master. At last he finds a door and runs out. The others would pursue him, but Ottavio stops them, for he has an important announcement from the chair to make to the shareholders' meeting: "My friends, after these unspeakable iniquities we can no longer have any doubt that the impious murderer of Donna Anna's father was Don Giovanni.[1] Remain you in the house for a few hours; I will have recourse to the proper authorities, and I can promise you that before very long you shall be avenged. . . ." That is in recitative; the aria that follows—the long and technically difficult "Il mio tesoro intanto"—is in the same vein: "Meanwhile go you and console my dear one and help her to dry her eyes. Tell her that I have gone to avenge her wrongs, and that I will return only as the messenger of death." With these brave words the heroic Ottavio goes out on his grim errand, taking Masetto and Zerlina with him.

34

Elvira remains behind, for she, able at last to shake herself free of the buffoonery that has surrounded her for so long, also has an aria to sing.[2] The recitative, in the grand eighteenth century manner, is held together by an arresting figure entrusted to the orchestra:

No. 36

She is appalled at the further evidences Giovanni has given of his wickedness; for these, surely, retribution must fall on him, and

---

[1] Here Da Ponte becomes unintentionally but irresistibly funny: it apparently takes such "unspeakable iniquities" as the crude befooling of Elvira and the lambasting of Masetto to convince Ottavio finally that Giovanni was the murderer of his beloved's father! Ottavio seems to have anticipated De Quincey in his fine perception of the insensibly merging degrees of criminality. "For," says the author of *Murder as a fine Art*, "if once a man indulges himself in murder, very soon he comes to think little of robbing; and from robbing he comes to drinking and Sabbath-breaking, and from that to incivility and procrastination. Once begin upon this downward path and you never know where you are to stop. Many a man has dated his ruin from some murder or other that perhaps he thought little of at the time."

[2] Between Ottavio's aria and that of Elvira there comes, in the scores, a scene between Leporello and Zerlina that is always omitted in performance. On this matter see *infra*, pp. 367 ff.

already in imagination she sees the destroying thunderbolt from heaven and the abyss opening to receive him. But there is room in her tender breast for other sentiments than personal vengeance, as is shown by the expressive orchestral figures that accompany the final part of her recitative:

No. 37

(It is the bad practice of many conductors to drag these passages out to an adagio. There is no warrant for this in the score: Mozart's general marking of allegro assai still holds good, and presumably he knew better what he wanted than any conductor can do.) The aria that follows—"Mi tradì quell' alma ingrata"— is on the same grand scale as that in which Mozart has indulged himself in Ottavio's aria and will shortly indulge himself again in one allotted to Donna Anna. The burden of the present aria is that in spite of all the wrongs done her by this one-time lover of hers Elvira feels for him, if no longer love, at least a great pity. True, when she remembers the pain he has inflicted on her something within her cries out for vengeance; but when she thinks of the dangers that now environ him her heart trembles. Yes, from now until the closing scene the dominant emotion in Elvira's breast is pity for her betrayer.

With her exit Da Ponte and Mozart have at last shaken themselves free of the low-comedy padding they had had to fall back on to fill out the big time-scale of their opera, and can set their course for the tragic dénouement. The next scene shows us a churchyard in which stands a Statue of the Commander. Giovanni, in excellent spirits, leaps over the wall; in this churchyard, he is sure, he will be safe from any pursuit by a woman (unnamed) whose problematic identity will be revealed to us later. It is a lovely moonlit night, as bright as day, an ideal night for the amorous hunt; and it is still only two o'clock. He would dearly love to know how Leporello had managed with Elvira and if he had been adroit enough to get out of the scrape. Just then Leporello himself appears on the wall, still sore in body and spirit from his recent experiences. His master makes light of his complaints and tells him that if he will join him in the cemetery he shall hear something that will interest him. Leporello jumps from the wall, and after the pair have exchanged cloaks and hats Giovanni tells him of one adventure that night that had particularly delighted him—the conquest of a very young and pretty girl he had encountered, who, mistaking him for her "caro Leporello," had loaded him with caresses. He had taken appropriate advantage of this mistaken identity, and then, somehow, the girl had discovered the facts of the case and screamed; so Giovanni, hearing footsteps, had given her the slip and jumped the cemetery wall. "And you tell me all this quite calmly?" protests the lackey. "What if it were my wife?" at which Giovanni laughs uproariously.

35

This ribald laugh of his, in such a place, at such an hour, sets the avalanche moving that will before long engulf him. A deep voice is heard addressing him in slow, solemn tones: "You will have finished with laughter before the dawn!" [1] "Who spoke there?" Giovanni asks sharply. "Some spirit from the other world," Leporello suggests ironically, "who knows you inside out." Giovanni silences him and again asks "Who spoke there?", this time slashing angrily with his sword at some of the tombs and monuments. The voice of the Commander sternly bids him respect the dead. Thereupon Giovanni orders Leporello to read the inscription on a certain tomb. The valet, who is beginning to be scared, protests that his education never got as far as reading by moonlight; but as his master insists he at last reads out the inscription: "Here I await vengeance on the impious one who dealt me death." Giovanni laughs at the "old prince of jokers," as he calls him, and at his command the trembling Leporello invites the Statue to supper with his master. The episode is one of Mozart's masterpieces of characterisation, the terrified stammerings of Leporello, the impressiveness of the Statue's curt "Yes!", and the comments, half genuine courage, half bravado, of Giovanni all being woven into a consummate musical whole.

[1] Here, for the first time, the trombones make their appearance in the score, with awe-inspiring effect.

It ends with Giovanni hurrying off to give orders for the festive meal, Leporello being only too glad to accompany him.

To fill up the necessary interval between this scene and that of the supper Da Ponte draws once more upon Anna and Ottavio. The new setting is a room in the house of the former. Ottavio enters to assure her once again that justice will soon be dealt out to the author of all her woes; meanwhile he suggests a marriage on the morrow as an aid to forgetfulness. To his astonishment she rejects the affectionate proposal, not because her heart is not his, but from the rather curious consideration of what the world will say: let him not doubt, however, her constancy. Into her recitative there has stolen a moving fragment of melody in the orchestra:

No. 38

which, transposed into the key of F major, becomes the generator of her exquisite aria "Non mi dir" ("Say not, beloved, that I am cruel: you know how truly I love you; but no longer grieve unless you would have me too die of grief"). These last words are accompanied in the orchestra by one of the most searching expressions of tenderness that ever came from Mozart's pen:

No. 39

to which conductors and orchestras rarely do anything like justice. But it is not long before Mozart realises that he has on his hands a coloratura soprano whose appetite for applause he must satisfy; so with a change of tempo to allegretto moderato he launches a bravura second section that has always been a source of pain to most of his admirers, who find it difficult to understand why the singer should suddenly cease to be the sympathetic and noble Donna Anna and become transformed into a mere Madame This or Madame That, angling for applause.

Berlioz, in his *Mémoires*, bewails this lapse into bad taste on his adored Mozart's part. The first section of the aria, he said, is "a song of profound sadness, in which all the poetry of love pours itself out in sorrow and tears"; but the roulades that follow are "of such shocking impropriety that one wonders how a composer like Mozart could have been guilty of them . . . Anna seems suddenly to have dried her eyes and broken out into indecent buffoonery. The words of this passage are 'Forse un giorno il cielo ancora sentirà-à-à-à'—here comes an incredible roulade in the worst style imaginable—'pietà di me.' Surely this is a strange way for the ill-used noble lady to express the hope that 'some day heaven will have pity on her'! I found it difficult [in his young days] to pardon Mozart for such an enormity. Today I feel that I would shed my blood to erase these shameful pages and certain others of the same kind found in his works." To this, in later years, Berlioz added a footnote: "Even the epithet 'shameful' seems to me hardly strong enough to blast this passage. Mozart has committed one of the most odious and senseless crimes in the whole history of art against passion, feeling, good taste and good sense." [1]

Having finished imploring heaven to take pity on her, in a concluding flourish on high A's and B flats, Anna departs, leaving Ottavio, before he too quits the stage, to assure us, in three lines

[1] The justice of the indictment cannot be gainsaid; one listens to this second section of the aria with a wry face. And no one seems to be aware that Mozart himself, were we able to tackle him now on the subject, would probably agree with Berlioz and the rest of us. In 1849 one Joseph Cornet, the director of the Hamburg theatre—who comes into Wagnerian biography by reason of his production of *Rienzi* in Hamburg in 1844,—published a book entitled *Die Oper in Deutschland und das Theater der Neuzeit* (*Opera in Germany and the Stage of the Present Day*), in which he comments severely on the vogue of senseless coloratura in the first half of the nineteenth century and the bad effects it had on the genuine expression of feeling in opera; it was the singers who insisted on it, because it won them the applause of the unintelligent mob. Cornet had known Mozart's widow, and he assures us that she had told him more than once that the composer, while bowing to the spirit of his time in this connection, did so with his tongue in his cheek, so to speak, "and always had it in mind to alter these numbers later." We shall meet with Cornet again in our discussion of *The Magic Flute*.

of recitative, that it will be his privilege to ease her burden by
taking some of it on himself.

36

The scene now changes to a room in Don Giovanni's house,
where a table is laid for supper; there is also a small band of
musicians, for Giovanni, being a man of quality, likes music with
his meals. After a few bars of lively orchestral introduction he
enters with Leporello: some producers show him accompanied
also by a bevy of gay ladies, but there is no warrant in the text
for this. The music is throughout spirited and joyous; Mozart,
the lover of fun and movement, the inveterate dancer, is always
in his element in such situations as this. The tide of life is rising
high in Giovanni's veins; while there is breath in his body he will
drain the cup of pleasure to the dregs. He bids the musicians
strike up, seats himself at the table, and is served by Leporello.
The first tune he recognises, with delight, as one from Martini's
opera *Una Cosa Rara*, which had been produced with great success in Vienna a couple of years earlier. The second part of the
melody:

No. 40

is particularly captivating; Mozart evidently knew a good thing
when he heard it, by whatever rival of the moment it may have
been written. He falls to with renewed appetite, and is equally
gratified by the next tune the musicians give him, one from Sarti's
opera *I due litiganti*:

No. 41

which goes well with the excellent marzimino wine and the
pheasant that Leporello has just served. The third tune the lackey

knows, he says, only too well: it is the "Non più andrai" from *Figaro*, which all Prague had been singing, humming, and whistling for the last eighteen months or so. This section of the supper scene is primarily Leporello's; by long custom it was here that the lackey, gormandising and guzzling surreptitiously on his own account, had full licence to indulge in all the robust humours of the commedia dell' arte and the buffo operatic stage.

37

The gay music, so full of the carefree joy of life, comes to a sudden end as Elvira runs in distractedly. There is a change of tempo to a feverish allegro assai as she tells Giovanni that she has come to give him the last proof of her love: she has forgiven him all the wrongs he has done her, and her one desire now is to save him from justice. This episode derives ultimately from the impressive one in Molière's *Don Juan*—by way, of course, in Da Ponte's case, of Bertati. In the latter's libretto Elvira begins by announcing that she is "another Elvira" than the one we have seen hitherto. Her former passion for Giovanni has now turned to a protective pity: all his intrigues have been unmasked, she tells him, everyone knows him to be the slayer of the Commander, and outraged justice is about to exact the penalty from him; but before that can happen she implores him to save himself by true repentance and a reformation of his ways: as for herself, she intends to go into a retreat for the remainder of her life. Giovanni's mocking reply to this appeal is an invitation to her to put up for the night in his house.[1] She tells him with dignity that her carriage is waiting outside for her, and goes out with a final passionate exhortation to him to think not of her but of himself—pausing only long enough to deliver herself of an aria that begins with a renewed assurance of her love if he will reform, and ends, after further ribald caricature of her on the libertine's part, with an exasperated revulsion of feeling: "Ah, miserable man, you still laugh at me! I see now that you are a tiger at heart! [2] But perhaps the thunderbolt is not far away."

[1] In Da Ponte she receives a similar impertinent invitation.
[2] In the original, "Di tigre le viscere già che avete." In Molière it is the valet Sganarelle who comments ironically that Giovanni must have a "cœur de tigre." No doubt all expressions of this kind derive ultimately from

In Da Ponte the episode, though similar in sentiment and lay-out, is more condensed; his sense of the theatre told him that the action should now hasten on to its catastrophe without unneces-sary delay; and Mozart seconds him nobly, weaving all the con-tending elements, the anxiety of Elvira, the reckless mockery of Giovanni and of his sycophantic echo Leporello, into one in-comparable whole. There are two other strokes of genius on the part of the collaborators: first the entire hedonistic being of Don Giovanni is summed up in an immortal phrase (repeated several times), in praise of women as "the sustenance and glory of hu-manity":

No. 42

So-ste-gno e glo-ri-a d'u-ma-ni-tà,   so-ste-gno e glo-ri-a d'u-ma-ni-tà.

and second, Elvira does not walk off, prima donna fashion, at the conclusion of her aria as she does in Bertati, but receives full in the face the first impact of the coming tragedy. As she turns from Giovanni with a final cry of "Remain, then, monster of iniquity!" and Leporello comments with indecent irony, "If all this grief of hers doesn't move him he must have a heart of stone!", the or-chestra whips up the excitement with mounting phrases of this sort:

No. 43

Allegro assai

which culminate; as Elvira reaches the door by which she has entered, in a stabbing chord of the diminished seventh that seems

---

the "Hyrcanian tigresses" of the abandoned Dido's passionate reproach of Aeneas:

> Nec tibi diva parens generis nec Dardanus auctor,
> Perfide, sed duris genuit te cautibus horrens
> Caucasus Hyrcanaeque admorunt ubera tigres,

which had become a classical tag for situations of this sort.

to halt her in her tracks. She recoils with a wild cry and rushes out by a door on the opposite side. "Why does she scream like that?" asks the exasperated Giovanni; and he sends Leporello off to investigate.[1] Repetitions of the feverish No. 43 accompany the lackey on his way, with another culmination in a diminished seventh chord as he gives a wild cry from the other side of the door.

He returns in abject terror, closing the door behind him, with only enough breath left in him to stammer out that the "white man of stone" is outside; and he describes as best he can the pounding "ta! ta! ta!" of the Statue's footsteps. There is a heavy knocking at the door. No threat of the angry Giovanni can induce Leporello to go near it; instead he crawls under the table. So Giovanni, taking a light with him, flings open the door himself.

38

Then Mozart strikes like a thunderbolt. The whole orchestra, including the trombones, seems to blare out our example No. 1 in Giovanni's face as the Statue strides in with the words, "Don Giovanni! You invited me to sup with you. I have come!"

No. 44

Andante

[1] Here Da Ponte's superior sense of the stage asserts itself. In Bertati, as we have seen, Elvira had flounced out prima donna fashion after her vain appeal, and there had followed a long buffo scene in which Giovanni and Leporello resume the banquet; the latter indulges in more and more of the buffooneries traditional at this point, and the gaiety of the pair culminates in a toast to Venice as *the* city of pleasure and to the Venetian ladies as the finest flower of womankind. (This would be appropriate enough in the Venice production of the Bertati-Gazzaniga opera.) Then comes a repeated knocking at the door, and, at long last, the entry of the Statue. Da Ponte and Mozart did wisely in cutting all this out and going straight from the failure of Elvira's exhortation to the dénouement.

Giovanni tries to brazen it out: "I would never have believed it," he says, "but I will do what I can"; his words are accompanied in the orchestra by the unsteady No. 2, the purport of which in the overture now becomes manifest. He bids Leporello have another cover laid for the guest, but the lackey is too terrified to move. The Statue bids master and man not to trouble about earthly food for one who has passed beyond the needs of the mortal body. It has come with a graver purpose, the solemn voice goes on, accompanied by the sequences, ascending and descending, alternately forte and piano, shown in our No. 4. The Statue's summons becomes more and more emphatic: "You invited me: I have come; now will *you* come and sup with *me*? Answer me! Decide! You will come?" Leporello manages to get in a word or two in character: he must be excused; he has no time: "tell him no, Sir." Giovanni's courage still holds: he accepts the grisly invitation. The Statue demands his hand in pledge; an icy cold creeps through Giovanni's veins at the touch, but his hand he cannot release, struggle as he will. "Your last moment is near: come: repent!" the voice thunders on, the ever-useful chord of the diminished seventh supplying the necessary touches of horror in the orchestra. "Never!" replies Giovanni, "never, old fool that you are!" They bandy their "Yes!" and "No!" for a while, till the Statue, as a solemn hush comes upon the orchestra, abandons the unrepentant sinner to his fate: "Your time has come!" it says, and disappears.

The tempo now whips up; flames shoot out in all directions, and the earth trembles. From below comes a chorus of invisible spirits, bidding Giovanni join them, and warning him in hollow tones of the eternal punishment awaiting him for his crimes. Now at last he breaks down, while Leporello comments gibberingly on his dismay. There is a final "Come!" from the spirits, followed by a tortured "Ah!" from Giovanni as he disappears in the depths.

This is the end preordained for him by the saga; but it is not the end of the opera. For the grand finale we are spirited off into the buffo, though a buffo with some serious moments. Anna, Ottavio, Elvira, Zerlina and Masetto enter, crying in unison, "Where is the villain? Vengeance on him!", Anna adding ferociously on her own account that only the sight of him in chains will compensate her for all she has suffered through him. Leporello advises them to give up hope of laying hands on him, for he has gone far away. Bit by bit, and rather disconnectedly, he tells them what had happened—the stone man had come and handed his master over to the Devil, who had dragged him below. The others can hardly believe it, though they realise now that this must have been the apparition seen by Elvira when she opened the door—a thought on which they dwell for some time. Then the tempo slows down to a larghetto, and one by one they speak of their future plans. Ottavio begins with an appeal to Anna: now that heaven has avenged them all, he pleads, surely she will not keep him waiting long for his happiness. Gravely she asks for a year in which to forget her grief for her father, and the pair renew at some length their assurances of mutual devotion. Elvira, for her part, vows that she will enter a convent and there end her days. The more materially minded Zerlina and Masetto decide to make for home and dine in style; while Leporello will go off to the inn and try to find another and better master. The three subsidiary characters indulge in a brief trio in which, displaying more classical learning than we would have expected of them, they consign the villain of the piece to Proserpine and Pluto, and exhort the others to join them—which Anna and Ottavio do—in repeating the joyous ancient song, "See now the end of all bad people, whose death befits their life":

No. 45

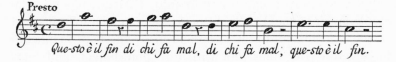

Que-sto è il fin di chi fa mal, di chi fa mal; que-sto è il fin.

It was the fashion for a long time to omit this final scene in performance, and modern British producers glow with pride when they restore it. But more than a century ago Thomas Love Peacock was protesting against the barbarous excision in the name not only of Mozart but of good taste. The original ending to the opera, he wrote, is "one of the finest things in dramatic music, and the most appropriate possible termination of the subject; and yet is this most noble composition, this most fitting and genuine conclusion, sacrificed [in London] to a dance of devils flashing torches of rosin, for no earthly reason but that so ended the Drury Lane pantomime."

Two points in connection with the opera remain to be considered that could not have been dealt with in the text without interrupting the narrative unduly.

1. The first relates to what occurs in the second act between the escape of Leporello from his tormentors [1] and Elvira's recitative ("In quali eccessi, o Numi") and aria ("Mi tradì quell' alma ingrata"). In his score the reader will find the following sequence: (A) In a short aria after the sextet Leporello begs for mercy from the people who have cornered him (Elvira, Ottavio, Zerlina and Masetto; Anna has by now left the stage), protesting that he has been, as usual, the innocent victim of the wiles of his unscrupulous master. At the end of all this he finds a door and escapes. (B) A short comment of the others in recitative:

> *Elvira:* Stop, wretch, stop!
> *Masetto:* The rascal's feet have wings!
> *Zerlina:* How artfully he has got away!
> *Ottavio:* After misdeeds so enormous who can doubt, my friends, that the impious murderer of Donna Anna's father was Don Giovanni? Go now into this house for a while. I myself will go to the authorities concerned, and I promise you that you shall be avenged, as is demanded alike by duty, compassion and love.

(C) Ottavio's aria "Il mio tesoro intanto" ("Meanwhile go ye and console my dear one"). (D) A comic scene in which Zerlina, with a razor in her hand, drags Leporello in by the hair, manhandles him severely, threatens him with dire punishment, and finally, with the help of a peasant, ties his hands. (E) An excessively long duet, "Per queste tue manine," in which he begs her to have pity on him, which she refuses: he and his wicked master, she says, should both receive the punishment they deserve. At last she goes out, leaving him tied to a chair, and the chair to a window-frame.[2]

---

[1] See p. 354.

[2] Manifestly, then, episode (D) takes place inside a room; yet the setting of the scene so far had been "a dark courtyard, with three doors, before Donna Anna's house"! No doubt when (D) was spatchcocked into the opera in the Vienna production (1788) a change of scene was made here, regardless of the pre- and post-context. Nobody seems to have reflected then on the absurdity of the peasant girl's making free of the great lady Donna Anna's

Leporello appeals to the peasant for a glass of water—apparently hoping by this ruse to get his knots untied; but the man goes away without saying a word. Thereupon Leporello, by means of a great tug at the chair, manages to wrench out the window-frame to which it is fastened, and so makes his escape, dragging the chair and frame behind him. (F) Zerlina returns, bringing with her Elvira, and the following brief dialogue ensues:

> *Zerlina:* Come, my lady, and you shall see how I have fixed the rascal.
> *Elvira:* Ah, I will vent my rage on him.
> *Zerlina:* Heavens! How has the scoundrel managed to escape?
> *Elvira:* His wicked master must have got him away.
> *Zerlina:* He it was, without a doubt. We must inform Don Ottavio, and trust him to avenge us all.

(G) Zerlina having left the stage, Elvira sings her recitative and aria—"In quali eccessi, o Numi" and "Mi tradì quell' alma ingrata" ("In what excesses of crime the wretched man has involved himself . . . This ungrateful creature betrayed me . . ."). At the end of her aria she leaves the stage, and the scene changes to the churchyard, where Leporello and Giovanni find each other again.

The reader will already be aware that Ottavio's aria "Dalla sua pace" and the duet—"Per queste tue manine"—were additions to the score made by Mozart for the Vienna production of 1788. Surely nothing but dire theatrical necessity could have induced him to consent to Leporello being brought back after his escape, tied up by Zerlina and the peasant, and then made to escape for the second time. By common consent this miserable piece of clowning is omitted from modern performances. Dramatically the action goes to pieces at this point if we accept the present scores at their face value. After Leporello's first escape—which really coheres with the drama—the other characters comment briefly on the matter, as in our (B), and then dismiss it from their minds. Their thoughts are now concentrated on the punishment of Don Giovanni: Ottavio sings his "Il mio tesoro," and all leave the

---

house in this fashion. The great thing for the groundlings would be Leporello's comic exit with the chair and the window-frame trailing behind him; and for these stage properties a room was of course necessary.

stage, upon which, as we have seen (D), Zerlina drags Leporello in for the farcical scene of the razor, the tying up and the second escape.

There follow next our (F) and (G), and we naturally ask ourselves why Zerlina's discovery that the Leporello she had tied up is no longer there should lead to such grave ethical reflections on Elvira's part on the tragical iniquity of Don Giovanni; Elvira feels now that he is doomed irrevocably by his crimes and his constitution, yet her heart is filled with compassion and affection for him.

40

The mystery was solved for us in 1938 by a fine piece of research work on the part of Alfred Einstein. Various people had had their doubts for a long time as to the authenticity of the recitative in which Leporello asks the peasant to get him a drink of water: "for pity's sake, friend," he says, "a drop of fresh water or I shall die. Just see how tightly that murderess [Zerlina] has tied me up. . . ." ("Guarda un po' come stretto mi legò l'assassina"). In the recitative as we have always known it in the scores the word "legò" is accented musically on the first syllable instead of on the second, a blunder of which Mozart would have been incapable; the inference seems to be that the recitative is someone else's work, someone with no more than a passing acquaintance with Italian verb-tenses.

Einstein was able to prove that the recitative as it appears in our scores is not by Mozart at all; it was evidently a substitution for the original, inserted in some Prague performances of the opera after 1787. A manuscript of *Don Giovanni* discovered by Einstein in Florence is plainly a copy of Mozart's autograph score for the Vienna production of 1788; and there the recitative in question is given in an entirely different form—Mozart's own form—which Einstein printed in full for the first time in an article in *Music and Letters* for October 1938.

But that is not all. In the Vienna libretto of 1788 there occurs a little episode which is not to be found in our scores, but which is absolutely vital to our understanding of the situation. In the scores all we have is our (F), after which Elvira plunges without any apparent rhyme or reason into her intensely serious recitative and aria (G). But in the score as it left Mozart's hands there was more than this. After Zerlina's ejaculation "Heavens! how has the scoundrel managed to escape?", Masetto enters accompanied by two peasants. Zerlina impatiently asks him where he has been all this time, and Masetto's explanation supplies what has hitherto been lacking—the reason for the great emotional disturbance set up in Elvira's soul, and consequently the justification of the horror and pity expressed in her recitative and aria. The authentic Mozartian text runs thus:

Masetto, entering after Zerlina's "How has the scoundrel managed to escape?": Never has there been a soul so vile!
Zerlina: Ah Masetto, Masetto! Where have you been all this while?
Masetto: It was heaven's will that I should save an unfortunate young woman. Hardly had I left you when I heard cries from the opposite path. I ran there with the others, and found a woman weeping and a man in flight. I tried to overtake him, but he disappeared from my view. From what the girl said to me, however, from the behaviour of the man, from his appearance and his bearing, I concluded it was that rascal of a cavalier.
Zerlina: It was he without a doubt. This, too, let us report to Don Ottavio: to him we look to act for us all and exact vengeance.

What the author of the Prague forgery has done is to retain these last sentences of Zerlina—see our (F)—but to make them apply to Don Giovanni's conjectural participation in Leporello's (second) escape, whereas, as we have just seen, they refer, in the original, to the horror created by Masetto's story of yet another crime on Giovanni's part.[1] As Einstein rightly remarks, the episode with the Masetto narrative supplies what otherwise has been lacking to us—the reason for the serious sentiments expressed in Elvira's aria. The recitatives which appear in our present scores were forgeries made in Prague for some performance or other there and innocently included in the first edition of the full score (1801) in the belief on the publisher's part that they were Mozart's own.

It is fairly easy to see what must have happened in Vienna in 1788. Somebody or other steeped in the Italian buffo tradition must have decided that a bit of farcical relief was called for between Ottavio's aria and Elvira's, so Mozart, no doubt for peace' sake, consented to the addition of the episode of Zerlina dragging

[1] Mozart's musical setting of the scene in recitative is quoted in full in Einstein's *Music and Letters* article.

Leporello in by the hair of his head, the duet ("Per queste tue manine") in which he pleads for mercy, the tying of him up with the aid of a conveniently handy peasant, and his ultimate escape, dragging behind him the chair and the window-frame—which could be counted on to bring the house down. Mozart has noted in his "Catalogue of my Works" the exact dates of composition of "Per queste tue manine" and "Mi tradì quest' alma ingrata"—the 28th and 30th April 1788 respectively. (The first Vienna performance took place on the 7th May.) The Masetto recitative discovered by Einstein was obviously intended to supply the necessary motivation for the new "Mi tradì" aria which had been demanded of the composer by the player of the part of Elvira. The dramatic intention is better than the realisation of it: it strikes us as rather odd that in the moment or two beween Masetto's rushing to the aid of the girl and the escape of her assailant he should have been able to divine from the latter's appearance and bearing that he was Don Giovanni—for it will be remembered that the episode takes place in semi-darkness; besides, if the criminal were really Giovanni he would be in Leporello's clothing, which makes it all the more difficult for us to understand how Masetto could deduce from the man's appearance and his bearing that it was not a valet but a cavalier that was fleeing from him!

It will be remembered that in the scene that follows Elvira's aria, where Giovanni and Leporello meet again in the churchyard and each changes back into his own cloak and hat, Giovanni tells the valet of an adventure he claims to have just had with a young woman whom the startled Leporello surmises may have been his own wife. It would be interesting to know whether the Masetto recitative was designed to fulfil a double purpose—not only to afford Elvira a "cue" for her aria, but also to add a touch of verisimilitude to Giovanni's story of his alleged recent conquest.

41

2. The second point concerns a supposed participation of Casanova in the text of the Da Ponte-Mozart opera.

In 1784 the famous amorist had settled down, at the age of sixty-three, in the castle of Dux, in Bohemia, as librarian to Count Waldstein. He became friendly with the Prague impresario,

Bondini, and with various local notabilities in the circle that formed round Mozart during his stay in the town in 1787. A contemporary letter from a man in Brünn to one in Tschaslau, dated the 4th November, indicates that Casanova was in Prague at the time of the production of *Don Giovanni*: "Casanova is in Prague; his letter to me is dated the 25th October." He had gone there to arrange for the publication of a novel of his, *Icosameron*. In the list of subscribers to the book appears the name of Franz Duschek, the husband of the singer Josepha Duschek whose hospitality Mozart enjoyed during his stay in the town; and as the first performance of the new opera took place on the 29th October it is a fair presumption that Casanova attended it.

In 1937 Paul Nettl announced in the Alt-Prager Almanach the discovery at Schloss Hirschberg, in Bohemia, of a document undoubtedly in Casanova's writing, with a number of emendations in the same hand, that is obviously a sketch for what follows in the score of *Don Giovanni* immediately after the sextet in the second act. The few lines from the document printed by Herr Nettl on that occasion were sufficient to show that they formed part of an alternative version of the aria—"Ah, pietà, signori miei"— in which Leporello pleads with his captors for mercy, obviously playing for time until he can find a door through which to escape, as eventually he does.

The fragments quoted by Herr Nettl gave rise at the time to the conjecture that Casanova was helping Da Ponte and Mozart out of a little difficulty. Da Ponte, it will be remembered, being pressed for time, had had to return to Vienna some days before the first performance of *Don Giovanni*. The conjecture was that Mozart had come to the conclusion in Prague that some alteration in the libretto was necessary at this point, and, Da Ponte not being available and time being short, he had called Casanova in to supply the necessary words, the latter's contribution consisting of (*a*) the brief recitative that follows the sextet, (*b*) Leporello's aria "Ah pietà," (*c*) the recitative of the other characters that comes after his escape and before Ottavio begins his "Il mio tesoro."

Against this theory it has to be pointed out, in the first place, that the Leporello aria was composed before Mozart left Vienna for Prague; [1] and in the second place that any collaboration of Da Ponte with Casanova is extremely improbable. We know comparatively little of the relations of the two adventurers, but we have evidence that Casanova's failure to rate Da Ponte's poetical efforts as highly as that gentleman did himself was always a sore point with the latter. Casanova, one imagines, would be the last person in Europe whose intervention in the matter of the *Don Giovanni* libretto would have been agreeable to the vain and touchy librettist; and in the absence of even the smallest direct evidence as to Casanova's "collaboration" we shall perhaps do wisely to rule it out.

42

In 1938 Herr Nettl printed the Casanova document in full, with a facsimile of the manuscript, in his book *Mozart in Böhmen*. It consists of a single sheet of paper, divided vertically into two halves by either a line drawn down the middle of it or by it having been folded from top to bottom. At the end of each half is the word "Fugge," i.e. [Leporello] "Flees." This had given rise to the conjecture in 1937 that the paper—of which, it will be remembered, Herr Nettl had at that time quoted only a few lines—contained two alternative sketches for the episode. Now that we have the complete text it is more probable that there is only one sketch; for Herr Nettl, I venture to suggest, may have transcribed them in the wrong order in his book. He begins with the text on the right-hand side of the paper and then continues without a break with the text on the left-hand side; but if we reverse that order the sketch, I think, makes something like complete dramatic sense. The left-hand side obviously begins where we should expect the episode to do after the completion of the sextet and the departure of Donna Anna. Leporello confesses that he is cornered and confused and has no defence. He begs for pardon, which Elvira, Ottavio, Zerlina and Masetto refuse. He makes another appeal, which is also rejected, his captors telling him that they would like to tear his insides out, or, as an alternative, see him dangling from a gibbet. For a third time he appeals abjectly to them, only to be

---

[1] The numbers of the opera composed in Prague are written on a different-sized paper, with a different ruling, from those Mozart brought with him from Vienna.

greeted with the same contumely and threats; and for the third time he repeats his refrain, "My fate is in your hands alone: my beating heart asks for your clemency." That brings us to the foot of the left-hand page, and the terminal word "Fugge."

The right-hand half seems to follow naturally on this. It is allotted wholly to Leporello. He explains how he comes to be in the position he now occupies. His tyrannical master, he says, had forced him to exchange clothes with him, and is the *fons et origo* of the whole imbroglio. The basic trouble is Giovanni's passion for the female sex, that traditional root of all evil. Leporello addresses an *argumentum ad hominem* to each of them in turn—as he does in the opera—explaining, for instance, that it was his master, not he, who had thrashed Masetto and dictated the burlesque wooing of Elvira. "What I am telling you is the truth," he concludes. "It is with Don Giovanni alone that you should be furious. Let me go free." By this time, apparently—again as in the opera—he has managed to find the door he has been searching for, and he escapes, as is indicated by the final stage direction "Fugge." If the two halves of the sheet are taken in the order I have suggested, which happens also to be the order shown in the facsimile, it all constitutes a dramatic unity. Taken in the reverse order the two halves necessarily look like two alternative treatments of the episode. The *double* "Fugge," however, must be admitted to be inexplicable; only the second, agreeing as it does with the course of events in the opera, makes stage sense.

We may dismiss, I think, the theory that Da Ponte and Mozart were concerned in any way in the matter. We have evidence, as Herr Nettl shows, that in Prague it was the custom to insert broadly farcical improvised passages in buffo scenes for the amusement of the groundlings; and the discovery of Einstein to which reference has been made above is proof enough that after Mozart's death the local hacks took liberties of one kind and another with *Don Giovanni*. We shall perhaps be correct in assigning the Casanova document to that period. Casanova, by the way, died at Dux in 1803, at the age of seventy-eight.

The Tales of Hoffmann

JACQUES OFFENBACH [1819–1880]

PRINCIPAL CHARACTERS

HOFFMANN	*Tenor*
OLYMPIA	*Soprano*
GIULIETTA	*Soprano*
ANTONIA	*Soprano*
NICKLAUSSE	*Mezzo-soprano*
LINDORF	*Baritone*
COPPELIUS	*Baritone*
SPALANZANI	*Bass*
DAPPERTUTTO	*Baritone*
COCHENILLE	*Tenor*
PITICHINACCIO	*Tenor*
SCHLEMIL	*Baritone*
CRESPEL	*Bass*
DR. MIRACLE	*Baritone*
FRANZ	*Tenor*

1

HE REAL name of the composer who achieved fame as Jacques Offenbach was Jakob Eberst. His grandfather, Juda Eberst, was a poor music teacher who lived in Offenbach-on-Main, not far from Frankfurt. This man's son, Isaac Juda, inheriting his father's love for music, made a living of sorts partly as an itinerant fiddler, partly as a cantor in any synagogue to which his wanderings might lead him. The future composer of *The Tales of Hoffmann*, born on the 20th June 1819, was the second son and seventh child of this

Isaac Juda. Some musical encyclopaedias still repeat the legend that in Paris he adopted the name of Offenbach because he had been born in Offenbach-on-Main. The truth is, however, that he first saw the light in Cologne,[1] in and near which town his father mostly sought his livelihood, now as musician, now as bookbinder, from about 1802. Because he had come from Offenbach he was colloquially referred to in the Cologne neighbourhood as "the Offenbacher," and he appears to have accepted the name of Offenbach as a matter of course.

The young Jakob seems to have received little in the way of formal musical education, and probably heard little music of the higher kind during his boyhood. As he showed talent first as a violinist, then as a 'cellist, it became his task at a very early age to help his father to support his large family. In November 1833, with a view to making a 'cello virtuoso of him, his father took him to Paris, where, after a few weeks, he left him to fend for himself. The boy worked at his chosen instrument at the Conservatoire for a year, then decided that he was learning too little there to make it worth his while to stay in the institution any longer. He managed to eke out a meagre living by playing the 'cello in the orchestra of the Opéra-Comique, where he remained three years. He could not have learned much about music in the larger sense of the word in those years, but he did pick up much that was of use to him in his later career. He attended performances at the Opéra whenever he could, where he assimilated a good deal, especially from Meyerbeer; and all the time he was busy composing in a light theatrical vein and trying to make connections that would be useful to him. From 1850 to 1855 he held the post of conductor at the Théâtre Français, where his job was mainly to provide music during the intervals and compose a song or a piece of incidental music whenever a dramatic situation called for one. For a production of Alfred de Musset's *Le Chandelier* he wrote a love song for the character Fortunio that was to maintain its popularity for many years after the event;[2] and when, in 1861—

[1] One of Offenbach's little jokes was to describe himself as "O. de Cologne."
[2] The actor Delaunay, who played the part of Fortunio in the Musset comedy in 1850, had so mellifluous a speaking voice that Offenbach took it for granted that he would be a tenor; so it was for a tenor that he wrote the song. But as Delaunay's singing voice turned out to be a bass, the song had to be shelved.

by which time his reputation was established in Paris—he wrote a one-act operetta entitled *La Chanson de Fortunio,* the song played a leading part in it.

As he grew more and more aware of his talent for broadly comedic music the desire sprang up in him for a theatre of his own. In 1855 he leased the tiny Bouffes Parisiens, exchanging this later for another bandbox, the Théâtre des Jeunes Élèves. In both places he was for a time subject by law to some curious restrictions; in the former he was not allowed to produce pieces with more than three characters, and in the latter with more than four—difficulties out of which he wriggled now and then by having characters who neither sang nor spoke, but displayed their words to the audience on placards. But in these places he was at any rate free to try out new notions of his own for opera bouffe and experiment technically to his heart's content; and all the while he was developing his sense of "theatre" and his own peculiar musical capacity. It was not long before he became the purveyor most in fashion of the particular operatic goods in which the Parisian world of the period most delighted.

2

He first made his real mark with *Orphée aux Enfers* (1858, revised in 1874); this was followed by a long succession of works which sooner or later became the rage of the town—*Geneviève de Brabant* (1859), *La Belle Hélène* (1864), *Barbe-bleu* (1866), *Les Deux Aveugles* (1866), *La Vie Parisienne* (1866), *La Grande Duchesse de Gérolstein* (1867), *La Fille du Tambour-Major* (1879)—and several others that are of less repute today. But all the time he seems to have cherished a conviction that he was capable of something more distinguished than opera bouffe, and he was quietly feeling his way towards first operetta, then comic opera. After the war of 1870–1871 he was quick to sense a change in the mentality of the Paris public. He had achieved his enormous popularity by supplying that public for many years with the fare most after its own heart. Few Frenchmen of any intelligence in the 1860's believed that the Second Empire, for all its pomp and glitter and apparent prosperity, had a very long life before it. People had a suspicion that they were living on a volcano that might erupt any day; and as they could do nothing about it they wisely decided to dance and drink and sing on their narrow foot-hold on the edge of the crater while the dancing and drinking and singing were still good. Open criticism of the régime being dangerous, the public turned with delight to stage works into whose ostensible fantasies and innocencies they could read satiric comment on highly-placed personages and the political events of the day. Offenbach's touch was unique; his work had a peculiar quality—a sort of ingratiating impudence and irreverence—that was as delightful as it was indefinable. He and his librettists made people laugh at things the world had been taught never to approach except with raised hat and bended knee—the gods and heroes of old Greece, for example: who could forbear to laugh when, for instance, he saw Orpheus, the legendary master musician whose song could move rocks and trees and tame savage beasts and win back his dead Eurydice from Hades, re-incarnated as the incompetent director of the Thebes Conservatoire of Music, a professional fiddler who so bores his wife Eurydice with his violin concerto in E major that she flings herself into an affair with Pluto, while in the underworld Jupiter dances a minuet that develops into a cancan of the gods?

3

The *Tales of Hoffmann* was not Offenbach's first excursion into opera proper. Towards the end of 1864 he wrote for Vienna a romantic opera entitled *Die Rheinnixen*; it ran to only eight performances, but one number in it, a "Goblin's Song," was destined to win world-wide popularity later as the Barcarolle in *The Tales of Hoffmann*. Offenbach wisely reverted to the genre in which he had made his reputation. It was after the war, in 1873, that he began to feel his way again towards opera, in the larger sense of the term, with *La Jolie Parfumeuse*. By this time he was doing some serious thinking about himself and his art. In the changed postwar world the public appetite for the kind of opera bouffe in which he had specialised seemed to be diminishing, and Offenbach was shrewd enough to sense the change; declining health, too, and some financial reverses played their part in giving his mind a more serious tinge. Apparently it was about 1876, after his tour in the United States, that the Hoffmann idea took possession of him. He had of course long been familiar with the works of the

German romantic writer (1776–1822) whose vogue was at its highest about the middle of the nineteenth century not only in his own country but in France. In 1851 a play entitled *Les Contes Fantastiques d'Hoffmann*, by two expert theatrical craftsmen of the period, Jules Barbier and Michel Carré, had been produced at the Odéon Theatre in Paris; Offenbach appears to have been struck at the time by the operatic possibilities of this, but for many years yet had his hands too full with his comic operettas to devote much attention to it. The subject, however, was no doubt subconsciously active in him in all the years between 1851 and 1876. When, in the latter year, he decided to set it to music he found that Hector Salomon, the chorus-master at the Opéra, had almost completed a setting of his own of a Hoffmann libretto by Barbier. Salomon having generously abandoned his plan as soon as he heard that Offenbach's heart was set on the subject, the latter could now devote the last and best of his energies to the work that mostly keeps his name alive in the opera house today; the ageing and ailing man who had survived into a world very different from the one in which his career had begun no doubt seemed to himself to be some such fantastic figure as the original E.T.A. Hoffmann might have created.

On the 18th May 1879 he had some of the finished sections of the opera performed in his house before a small audience of friends and theatre directors, as a result of which the work was claimed for the Opéra-Comique by Carvalho, at that time director of the institution. The prospect of entry at last upon that august scene must have done much to hearten Offenbach, as did the great success of *La Fille du Tambour-Major* at the Folies Dramatiques in December of the same year, and the commission from the Théâtre de la Renaissance for a new operetta, *La Belle Lurette*.

The first performance of *The Tales of Hoffmann* had been arranged for the winter of 1880. Offenbach, now a desperately sick man, worked with feverish haste at his opera, a piano score of which was finished by September. On the 5th October death claimed him. Ernest Guiraud put aside a work of his own to revise and complete the scoring of the dead master. Offenbach's sketches and alternative readings, however, proved to be so many and so various that the construction of a more or less definitive score for publication was a matter of considerable difficulty. The first performance, on the 10th February 1881, was hardly representative of the work as the composer had conceived it. The Giulietta act—which, by the way, was originally intended to be the third, as it was in the play of 1851—was taken out, as it was feared that the opera would prove too long for the Paris public; but as no one could find it in his heart to sacrifice the charming Barcarolle it was inserted in the Antonia act, the scene of this now being laid not in Munich but in Venice. The work, for all that, was a great success. In December of the same year it was given in the Ringtheater in Vienna; but the disastrous fire that broke out there on the night of what would have been the second performance not only ended its career in Austria but made other theatres superstitiously fight shy of it. Then, as the comic works of the composer gradually lost their vogue, *The Tales of Hoffmann* passed more or less out of sight and sound with them. One of the first to revive it was Sir Thomas Beecham, who gave it at His Majesty's Theatre, London, in 1910.

4

Offenbach's collaborator, Jules Barbier, performed very well the difficult task of making an organic whole out of the immense body of unconnected material afforded him by the stories of the German romancer and credibly placing the man himself at the psychological centre of it all. Not only must he have had an intimate acquaintance with all Hoffmann's work, but out of the scanty biographical material available in the mid-nineteenth century he managed to achieve a plausible reconstruction of the man himself. Barbier divined that many of the characters and incidents in the stories were fictional disguises of the complex Hoffmann himself and his amatory experiences; he realised, for instance, the great part played in the novelist's emotional life by the sixteen-years-old Julia Mark with whom he had fallen in love at one time, and who probably appears in several guises in his stories.

The central subtlety of Barbier's work is apt to go unnoticed by the casual listener to the opera—the presentation of the incidents of each of the three acts as a phantasmagoria in the brain of Hoffmann, and the enclosing of the actual formal opera in the armature of a realistic prologue and an epilogue in which we see the phantast first of all entering the kingdom of macabre dream and then returning from it to the world of common day. This essential point is completely lost when, as has sometimes happened, Offenbach's work is given simply as a three-act opera, the prologue and epilogue being omitted. Barbier may not have achieved all he aimed at in the way of symbolisation—had he done so with complete success in the medium he chose there would be no need today to instruct audiences and producers in these matters. But unless we bear his purpose in mind we are not seeing and hearing *The Tales of Hoffmann* as Barbier and Offenbach intended us to see and hear it. The work is an eerie psychological drama played out in and around the soul of Hoffmann, the three female characters—Olympia, Giulietta and Antonia—being diverse dream-projections of the same romantic illusion, and Hoffmann's enemies and frustrators—now Coppelius, now Dappertutto, now Dr. Miracle—simply one fantastic reincarnation after another of the Lindorf who, in the prologue, is Hoffmann's rival for the love of the flesh-and-blood Stella. In the ideal cast for the work not only would these four male characters be played by the same baritone but the three female parts would be represented by the same soprano. The latter plan has been carried out in some performances, but it is obviously not easy to find a singer whose voice is equally capable of the coloratura of the mechanical doll Olympia, the voluptuous timbre of the mature and experienced Giulietta, and the febrile ring of the consumptive young Antonia.

5

Barbier had to throw his net wide to draw from the vast Hoffmannesque sea just the kind and the quantity of fish he required for his and the composer's dramatic purposes. The prologue and epilogue were his own idea. For the first of the three "Tales" of the opera he drew upon a story of the actual Hoffmann entitled *Der Sandmann* (No. 1 of the *Night Pieces*)—a story of a young student (Nathanael) bedevilled in the first instance by a sinister dabbler in black magic of the name of Coppelius, who, after some experiments that had cost Nathanael's credulous father his life, disappears from the German scene for a while and then returns in the guise of an Italian, Giuseppe Coppola, a maker of barometers and optical instruments of all kinds, specialising in necromantic eyes. He allies himself with the professor of physics

(Spalanzani) [1] at the local university, and between them they construct a life-like automaton who passes in the town for the professor's daughter Olympia. She is very beautiful, sings and dances nicely, and is greatly admired at local tea parties, where not the least of her attractions is that she never utters more than a syllable or two. Nathanael, seeing her through bewitched glasses made for him by Coppelius, falls crazily in love with her, to the total neglect of his own betrothed Clara; he even reads his poems to Olympia, and takes her upturned eyes and occasional solitary ejaculation of "Ah!" to betoken an understanding of and an admiration for them too profound for words. His illusion is shattered when one day, having called on her as usual, he hears a terrific shindy going on inside the house, and finds Coppelius and Spalanzani fighting for possession of Olympia and tearing her to pieces in the process; the two rogues have in fact quarrelled over their respective shares in the construction of the automaton and in the possible advantages to be derived from their creation. The scales, of course, fall at once from Nathanael's eyes. His sanity returns to him, but only for a time; imprudently using one day one of Coppelius's sinister spy-glasses while out with Clara he goes mad again and tries to throw her from the top of a tower; only the opportune arrival of her brother Lothar saves the poor girl from a horrible death. Catching sight of the evil Coppelius among the crowd that has assembled something snaps in Nathanael's brain and he throws himself from the tower. That is the end of him; Clara, we are glad to learn, marries a young man as free from optical and other illusions as herself and lives happily ever after in his company and that of their two children.

6

Barbier's second act was derived, with sundry modifications, principally from the *New Year's Eve Adventures* that constitute the second part of Hoffmann's *Fantastic Pieces in Callot's Manner*; Pitichinaccio, however, is imported from another story, that of *Signor Formica* in *The Serapion Brethren*.

From another story in this latter collection, that of *Councillor*

---

[1] In the excellent English version of the text of the opera Spalanzani is described as "a doctor." This is a mistranslation of the French "physicien"— a physicist, a natural philosopher.

Krespel, Barbier got the material for his third act; and as the underlying dramatic motives of this act are not always apparent to the ordinary listener it may assist him to be given a summary of the story as the original Hoffmann tells it.

Krespel is a worthy and capable City Councillor whose eccentricities are the talk of the provincial town in which he lives. But, as Hoffmann explains in one of those psychological divagations of his in which he anticipates the science of a later day than his own, the man is not "mad," as most of his fellow-townsmen think: his is merely one of those curious cases "in which Nature, or some mysterious fatality or other, has deprived a man of the outer envelope underneath which we other beings carry on our crazy activities unseen. He resembles one of those insects with an integument so thin that their busy muscular movements, plainly visible to us, appear to be all confusion, though everything soon falls into a regular routine. What in other people remains just thought, in Krespel finds expression in action. The bitter scorn which the ordinary soul often feels, encased as it is in earthly impulses and actions, in Krespel is externalised in frantic gesticulations and adroit hare's-leaps. But these are just his lightning conductors; what comes to him out of the earth he returns to earth again, but the heavenly he retains, so that all is lucid in his inner consciousness despite the seeming craziness of his behaviour."

Bit by bit the supposed teller of the tale had managed to fit together the pieces of the psychological puzzle that was Krespel as his friends saw him. In his youth he had been passionately devoted to the study of the great old Italian violins, the secret of whose construction he tore out of them by the simple but destructive process of taking one after another of them to pieces. Always eccentric in manner and speech, he becomes more mysterious than ever to his fellow-townsmen when one day they discover that he has in the house with him a young girl, Antonia, who had been heard singing divinely: he would not allow her to sing for other people, however, and became satanic in his fury when anyone at this party or that was indiscreet enough to press her to do so. It was not until some time later that the mystery was solved. In his youth, it appeared, he had lived for a while in Venice, where he had fallen in love with a brilliant prima donna named Angela. They had married in secret, Angela refusing either to give up her

operatic career or to be known to her public by the barbarous
German name of Krespel. With the usual caprice of her tempera-
mental species she had made his life a misery to him, till one day,
after she had smashed a favourite violin of his in a fit of temper,
he threw her out of a window—not a high one—and went back
to Germany.

They continued to correspond, however, on friendly terms,
and after the birth of a daughter (Antonia) she became quite a
pleasant human being. The child gave promise of becoming an
even more gifted singer than her mother. A young composer
named Theodore fell in love with her,[1] but Angela having died
the day before the wedding Krespel brought his daughter to live
with him in Germany. Every day her singing became more and
more divine; but Krespel soon discovered that when she put her
whole soul into it, for it was her very life, two dark red spots appeared on her cheeks, and he learned that she was consumptive.
The medical verdict was that she must either give up singing and
live long and happily, or sing and resign herself to dying young.
Father and daughter thereupon agreed that she should sing no
more; the young composer also appeared to accept the mournful
situation, though Krespel doubted his ability to endure it for
long. Antonia begged to be allowed to see her lover once more,
and then die. Krespel unwillingly granted her request. The composer came, and Antonia sang to his accompaniment on the piano,
Krespel joining in on his favourite violin. Suddenly the dark red
spots appeared on her cheeks, and she fell into a swoon. The
furious father thereupon turned the young man out of the house,
threatening to murder him if he ever returned.

After this, the now repentant Antonia showered more affection
than ever on her father. She refused to sing for anyone. When
Krespel acquired one day a new violin of the most exquisite tone
she begged him to spare this one the fate of its predecessors: so
instead of dismembering it he used to play his best on it, and she
would hear her own tones in it and declare that it was not the
violin but her own soul and body that sang. All went well until
one night Krespel, unable to sleep, heard a preludising on the
piano in the next room, and recognised at once the touch and
style of the young composer. Then Antonia's voice soared in

[1] Hoffmann's second name, be it noted, was Theodore.

383

ecstasy in a beautiful aria that her lover had once written for her; and the distracted father had a vision of the pair locked in a passionate embrace. But a paralysis of all his limbs seemed to hold him fast to his bed, and after a while he lapsed into a profound coma. When he came to himself again he hurried to Antonia's room: he found her lying dead on the couch, a beatific smile on her face. A visitor to the house after the funeral found all the violins draped in crape—with the exception of the master instrument, in whose accustomed place on the wall there hung only a wreath of cypress: when Antonia died the sound-post had shivered to pieces with a rending noise. Krespel buried the violin in her grave, and never made or played on another.

7

The librettist and the composer must have realised from the beginning that the original story was unsuitable for their particular purpose. For one thing, it was too psychological in essence; for another, its centre of interest was Krespel, and they could not possibly allow the final act of their opera to deal mainly with a character who had no *raison d'être* in the dramatic scheme as a whole. At the same time the story played, in some respects, straight into their hands. Antonia does not sing merely because as an operatic personage she is committed to doing so but because singing is the character's natural mode of self-expression. The young composer who is in love with her could rationally be linked up with the Hoffmann of the first two acts. Krespel could still figure as the unhinged father, and his frenzied violin playing be quite plausibly introduced—in another connection—into the climactic episode in which the mad desire to sing would take fatal possession of Antonia. But some other agency than the father had obviously to be invented to account for Antonia's unconquerable desire to sing despite Krespel's efforts to restrain her, despite the warnings she herself had had of the consequences of doing so. Barbier's solution of the problem was a twofold one: in the opera she should be encouraged in her dangerous passion for singing by a crazy physician, Dr. Miracle—who is fanatically convinced that by his magnetism and his potions he can control fate—and by her hearing the voice of her prima donna mother. For the rest, an occasional passing touch of comedy could be achieved by the introduction of a servant of Krespel's who, being deaf, misunderstands everything that is said to him. The essential point was that the demoniac element of the original story, which had there been incarnated in Krespel, could now be given full opportunity to express itself musically in the evil genius of the Antonia drama, the crazy Dr. Miracle.

Each act of the opera is fundamentally tragic in spite of its bizarrerie. In the first act it is a mentally deranged Hoffmann who falls absurdly in love with a mechanical doll. In the second act we are taken into a crazy world in which the young idealist's soul is entrapped by means of a reflection in a mirror. Over the whole of the last act hovers the shadow of death; when that closes in on Hoffmann the young idealist's dreams of love are over, and his only refuge in his disillusionment is the tavern in which we had first found him.

8

The prologue is set in the moonlit wine cellar of Luther's tavern in Nuremberg, which happens to be located in the same building as the opera house, where *Don Giovanni* is being performed, with the famous Stella, a prima donna from Milan, singing the part of Donna Anna. The interval has just been reached. Offenbach sensibly contents himself with nine bars for the orchestra in lieu of the customary overture; anything of that formal nature was hardly possible, in view of the diversity of characters and interests in the opera. From the wings we hear a short chorus of Spirits of Wine and Spirits of Beer, singing the praises of the beverages respectively associated with them as dispellers of the melancholy of man.

Lindorf, a bourgeois Councillor of the town, enters to a pompous motif:

No. 1

which we shall meet with again more than once in the course of the opera; for, as has been pointed out already, it is this Lindorf

of the real world who is supposed to project himself, in one transformation after another, into the dream world of Hoffmann's love
life. He brings with him Andreas, the servant of the enchanting
Stella, who has a letter in his hand. By dint of a threat and a bribe
Lindorf manages to get possession of this: as he had imagined, it
is from Stella to Hoffmann. Women are queer fish, Lindorf muses
bitterly; how can a Stella—to whose charms he himself has succumbed—take for lover a poet and a drunkard of the Hoffmann
sort? He breaks open the letter: it is a confession of love on Stella's
part, and enclosed in it is the key to her room. Lindorf breaks
into an appropriately gauche aria, the burden of which is that
though he is too old and of the wrong temperament to play the
languishing lover he still feels himself to be the very devil of a
fellow where women are concerned, emitting a sort of satanic
electricity that makes him irresistible; and he intends to make good
use of the key that has now fallen into his hands. He has two
hours before him (i.e. before the opera ends): meanwhile he will
keep an observant eye on his rival Hoffmann, who, he knows, is
in the habit of coming to this tavern to drink and talk with other
young fellows as wild as himself.

Luther enters, accompanied by a number of waiters who, at his
bidding, prepare the tables for the irruption of the young enthusiasts who will fête the enchantress from Milan. Soon a crowd
of students, prominent among whom are Nathaniel, Hermann
and Wilhelm, surge gaily upon the scene, demanding a supply
of Luther's best, and declaring, in a four-part chorus, their intention of drinking till the morrow:

No. 2

to the lovely Stella, who, Nathaniel swears, is the pearl of nature
and the triumph of art, Mozart's Donna Anna incarnate. But
where is Hoffmann? they ask; why is he not here to join them in
the toast? ("To the devil with this Hoffmann!" Lindorf mutters
under his breath).

Hoffmann enters to the cue, accompanied by young Nicklausse, his satellite, his constant friend, and always his cool, ironic critic and counsellor, the sympathetic spectator of his romantic illusions but never himself the victim of them. It is Nicklausse who introduces the distrait Hoffmann to the company now with a sly bantering quotation of Leporello's opening words and music in *Don Giovanni*—"Never resting, day or night!" But Hoffmann, who is evidently in an ill humour, cuts him short, sits down at one of the tables, and buries his head in his hands. His friends comment that he has changed beyond recognition of late. He confesses that his present view of life is a gloomy one, for which the only remedy seems to be drinking. Tonight he is even more melancholy than usual, for in the theatre he had thought he had caught a vision again—"but why reopen an old wound?" he breaks off; better drink and laugh and sing the clouds away.

In response to a demand for a song from him he sings the bizarre story of Kleinzach—the protagonist of one of the original Hoffmann's fantastic stories, *Klein Zaches genannt Zinnober*, the other students joining in from time to time. This Kleinzach was a misshapen little creature at the court of Eisenach:

No. 3

On his head he used to wear a *colbac* (a military bearskin cap), and when he walked his legs went click-clack. He was everything in the French language that rhymes with zach and Eisenach and clac; his feet sprawled as if they were in a *sac*; his nose was stained with *tabac*; his head always went *cric-crac*. The cadence of the song sums him up—"Clic-clac! that was Kleinzach":

No. 4

As Hoffmann is about to launch into a second stanza continuing the description of Kleinzach's odd appearance a veil seems to descend over his mind. The others stare at him in astonishment as, sunk in a dream, he muses in feverish tones on the features not of Kleinzach but of a lovely creature whom he had encountered one day and with whom, forgetting house and home, he had wandered through the woods and valleys, intoxicated by her hair, her eyes, and above all her wonderful voice, singing to the listening stars in heaven:

No. 5

Molto animato

Ses che—veux, ses che—veux en tor—sa—des som — bres,

As the song ends and the last echo of No. 5 dies away in the orchestra, and his puzzled listeners ask him of whom he is speaking, the mists of his dream float away; he returns to reality and takes up the story of Kleinzach where he had left it off. Kleinzach, he tells them, ugly and grotesque as he is, is worth more than the other apparition; and he launches into another round of jocular rhymes, the students joining in with him as before. Having come thoroughly down to earth again he curses the beer and calls for punch: they put the candles out, Luther lights the punch that has been carried in, and the students sing a chorus in mock laudation of the tavern keeper.

9

Nathaniel opines that Hoffmann is in love. He rejects the impeachment with scorn, whereupon Lindorf breaks into boorish laughter. Led by Nicklausse, the others ironically beg indulgence for all married men, including this poor Lindorf. Hoffmann and Lindorf bandy polite insults for a little while, finally coming almost to blows as the former raises his glass in an ironic toast to Madame Lindorf which infuriates the Councillor beyond endurance. The cool-headed Nicklausse steps between them; but Hoffmann, pointing to Lindorf, surmises that some evil is about to overtake him (Hoffmann), for whenever he comes across this philistine fellow everything is sure to go wrong with him—if he is gaming, he loses; if he is drinking, the stuff goes down the wrong way; if he loves . . . whereupon Lindorf interjects with a sneer, "Oh, so our gentleman does fall in love sometimes, then!"

Nathaniel, rather under the influence of the punch, protests sentimentally that there is nothing to blush for in being in love—"Our friend Wilhelm here is all afire for Leonora, whom he thinks divine; Hermann is in love with Gretchen; and I am ruining myself for Fausta." This provokes a torrent of contemptuous invective from Hoffmann—Leonora, a mere virtuosa, Gretchen, a doll with a heart of ice, Fausta, the courtesan with a front of brass! The mistress of his own heart, Stella, is three women incarnate in one, three souls in a single soul, artist, young maiden and courtesan. "My mistress? No! Say rather three mistresses, three enchantresses who have enslaved me in turns. Would you like to hear the story of these three mad loves of mine? I can promise you that before it is time for me to relight my pipe you will have come to understand me."

Luther warns them that the curtain will soon go up on the second act of *Don Giovanni*. But all the students are now for listening to Hoffmann rather than to Mozart, while Lindorf tells himself, in an aside, that he too will have time to hear this tale of Hoffmann's before the opera finishes—when, of course, he intends to make use of the key that has fallen into his hands. So all settle down to drink and smoke again and listen to Hoffmann's recital of his three loves that were really one love. He will begin, he says, with the first of them, Olympia; and with that the curtain falls on the now static figures of the prologue, very much as—apart, of course, from the punch and the tobacco—Dido and her Carthaginians composed themselves to listen to Aeneas' long account of the disaster that befell Troy:

> *Conticuere omnes intentique ora tenebant*
> *Inde toro pater Aeneas sic orsus ab alto.*

The reader will not fail to have observed that Hoffmann, in his description of the three women embodied in one, three souls fused into one, had named the trio in this order—the artist (the singing doll, Olympia), the young maiden (Antonia), and the courtesan (Giulietta). We can perhaps detect in this an original intention of Barbier and Offenbach to make the Venice episode the final one of the opera, as it had been in the Barbier-Carré play of 1851.[1]

[1] See *supra*, p. 379.

10

So far Offenbach's music has been mainly in an unassuming opera bouffe style; now it takes on the more ambitious manners of comic opera.

The first act opens with a short orchestral intermezzo in minuet rhythm:

No. 6

The curtain having risen we see a room in the physicist professor Spalanzani's house; curtains are drawn over the rear and side doors, thus hiding from our view, for the time being, a gallery at the back of the scene. Spalanzani enters. He raises a curtain on the right and rubs his hands with satisfaction as he peeps into an inner room and sees that his masterpiece, the mechanical puppet Olympia, is sleeping tranquilly, looking not only beautiful but modest and wise. From his brief soliloquy we learn that he hopes by means of this triumph of mechanical ingenuity to recoup himself for the five hundred ducats he has recently lost through the insolvency of a Jewish banker of the name of Elias. It is true, he adds, that his accomplice Coppelius may give him some trouble by claiming a share of the profits he hopes to make out of his waxwork figure; and a reminiscence in the orchestra of the latter part of our musical example No. 1 advises us at the outset of the opera that in this Coppelius we are to imagine another incarnation of the crafty, unscrupulous Lindorf. Spalanzani, however, is confident that if it should become necessary he will be able to outwit his fellow rogue.

His musings are broken in upon by the entry of one of his students—Hoffmann—who modestly hopes he has not called at an inconveniently early hour. Not at all, Spalanzani assures him. He has great hopes of this Hoffmann; if he will only cease to bother about such things as poetry and music and stick to the physical sciences Spalanzani will undertake to make a professor of him some day. He promises also to introduce him to his daughter Olympia, whose smile is ravishing. The young man cannot quite see what connection this damsel can have with physics, but he keeps his thoughts to himself.

Calling for his servant Cochenille, Spalanzani bids him light up everywhere and bring up the champagne. The pair go off to make the necessary preparations for a coming party; and Hoffmann, left alone, vows that he will work hard and become a veritable fountain of learning. His romantic mind, however, is really running all the time on the fair Olympia, whom he surmises to be in the adjoining room. Cautiously raising the curtain he gets a glimpse of the lovely creature, evidently sleeping; and he sings of his hopes of lifelong union with this ineffable being in an ardent little romance that takes us back in spirit to Hoffmann's invocation of his ideal love in the prologue. He is interrupted by the entry of Nicklausse, who, coolly detached and ironic as usual, advises his moonstruck friend to wait until he knows this Olympia rather better before he makes any plans with regard to her, for as yet Hoffmann has set eyes on her only once, from the window of his own dwelling, which overlooks that of the professor. She is not aware of his existence; for he has never dared to speak to her, dared even to write to her. Nicklausse suggests singing to her, but Hoffmann points out that Professor Spalanzani is prejudiced against music. Nicklausse, who seems to know, or at any rate to suspect, a good deal more about the true state of affairs than his friend does, sings a little ditty, obviously intended to carry a double meaning, about a doll who used to flirt with a little copper cockerel that stood by her, the pair dancing and singing and prattling with each other so naturally that anyone would have sworn they were alive, the doll making eyes at the cockerel and sighing "I love you!"

11

Coppelius, heralded by No. 1 in the orchestra, enters furtively carrying a sack; he has evidently come to spy out the land, and is not at all pleased to find a couple of strangers present. Going up to the curtain and looking over the self-absorbed Hoffmann's shoulder, he realises that the young man is lost in contemplation of what Coppelius calls "Our Olympia," a description which Nicklausse repeats in a mock aside. Having at last succeeded in attracting Hoffmann's attention by tapping him on the shoulder he introduces himself. His name is Coppelius, he says, a friend of Monsieur Spalanzani. As for his profession, this will be evident from the stock-in-trade he produces from the sack—barometers, hygrometers, thermometers, all going cheap for cash. There are also spectacles and opera glasses that make everything look as black as jet, others as white as ermine. Coppelius can even fit you up with new eyes, he continues in a song the melody of which is manifestly a variant of No. 1:

No. 7

eyes that will enable you to see right through a human body to the innermost soul, or even, in exceptional cases, to see life where there is no life, or to detect whether the heart of a woman is pure or vile, or to persuade yourself that it is the former when in fact it is the latter.

The eager Hoffmann takes a pair of the glasses that Coppelius is forcing on him and looks through them into the inner room, where he sees an Olympia of dazzling grace and beauty. The price is only three ducats, which Nicklausse obligingly hands over to the charlatan. Just then Spalanzani returns, rubbing his hands. He is a little abashed for a moment by the unexpected sight of Coppelius. The two rogues spar warily with each other for a while, to the accompaniment of ironic figures of this type in the orchestra:

No. 8

It now appears that Spalanzani, having at last put the finishing touches on his automaton, had thought to rake in the whole profit on it for himself. He reminds Coppelius that there had been a sort of gentlemen's agreement between them, to which the other replies that there was nothing in writing, and since there is money in prospect for this marvellous doll he intends to have his share. "Am I not Olympia's father?" asks Spalanzani loftily; to which Coppelius replies, "Pardon me, her eyes are mine." Begging him to speak more softly, lest they should be overheard, Spalanzani pretends to see the force of his confederate's reasoning and offers him an extra five hundred ducats for all rights in Olympia, including her eyes. Coppelius having agreed, Spalanzani hands him a draft for that amount on the Jew Elias, who, he assures him, is solvency itself. Coppelius gives him in exchange a memorandum acknowledging the professor's rights, and the happy pair embrace each other effusively to the accompaniment of the humorous No. 8. Before he hurries off to cash the draft Coppelius has a bright idea which he propounds to Spalanzani—why not marry Olympia to that young simpleton over there, who is evidently in love with her? The precious pair shake hands once more; then Coppelius rushes out with his cheque, chuckling, to the accompaniment of the latter part of our No. 1, at his own cleverness and wit. Spalanzani, not to be outdone in humour, turns with a professorial air to this romantic young fool of a Hoffmann, gravely exhorting him to devote himself wholeheartedly to the study of the physical sciences.

12

Heralded by Cochenille, the guests invited by Spalanzani to Olympia's coming-out party now pour upon the scene, singing the praises of their generous host to the minuet outlined in our musical example No. 6. All are agog to meet this daughter of his; "At last," Nicklausse remarks ironically to the bemused Hoffmann, "we are to see this unparalleled marvel at close quarters!" Spalanzani enters, escorting Olympia, on whose grace and beauty the guests comment in excited chatter. His gifted daughter, the professor announces, will sing an aria for them, to the accompaniment of anything they like, piano, guitar or harp: he himself decides in favour of the harp, which Cochenille runs off to fetch. Seating himself by it the fond father exhorts his daughter not to be nervous, and at a touch of his finger on her shoulder she pipes out a staccato "Yes! Yes!" After a little harp prelude by Spalanzani she begins her naïve aria, which is all about the spring, the birds, the stars and her own innocent heart:

No. 9

Les oi-seaux dans la char-mil———————————— le

the guests joining in from time to time. As the aria proceeds it blossoms into more and more exuberant coloratura, in which, with great art, Offenbach gives a satiric touch of the mechanical to the runs and turns and trills that are the stock-in-trade of the coloratura soprano:

No. 10

Voi-là la chan-son gen-til ———————————— le

When it is all over Cochenille takes the harp away, and Olympia acknowledges the applause first with one hand, then with the other.

The company now clamours for supper as a preliminary to dancing. The infatuated Hoffmann approaches Olympia and begs the honour of the first dance, and Spalanzani having stepped between them adroitly and pressed the spring in her shoulder, she manages once more to emit her mechanical "Yes! Yes!" She is a little tired after her singing, Spalanzani explains, so perhaps Hoffmann will not mind waiting a bit; meanwhile no doubt he will stay and keep her company while the other guests go in to supper, which they do to the tune of No. 6. Spalanzani is enjoying the fraudulent farce immensely and looking forward to seeing the student make a still bigger fool of himself. Going behind the wax figure he gives the mechanism a turn or two: Nicklausse hears the creaking spring and asks sharply what it is. "Nothing, my dear sir," replies Spalanzani airily; "Physics, just physics"; and carefully seating Olympia in a chair he goes out with his guests into a room at the back.

13

Hoffmann pours out his amorous soul to Olympia in passionate strains, and happening to emphasise his remarks by touching her shoulder she of course ejaculates the inevitable "Yes!" At the end of his ardent declaration of love he takes her hand and presses it fervently: this sets another bit of mechanism going within her —she rises from the chair, gyrates aimlessly about the stage, and finally disappears through one of the doors, negotiating the curtain without laying a hand on it. Hoffmann, fearing he has offended her maidenly modesty, makes to follow her, but is intercepted by Nicklausse, who asks his friend cynically if he knows what the talk is in the other room about Olympia—that she is dead, or rather, that she has never been alive. But Hoffmann is in no mood for listening to reason; he is as sure, after what she has said to him, that Olympia loves him as he is that he loves her; and he rushes out after her.

The stage is no sooner empty than Coppelius enters by a door on the left. He is in a furious temper: Spalanzani's cheque on Elias has turned out to be a dud; the Jew is bankrupt; Coppelius has been fooled and robbed, and he means to have revenge, even if it means murder. As the curtains at the back open he slips into Olympia's room.

To a charming waltz the whole company flocks back for the grand finale. At another touch of the spring by Spalanzani the automaton gives its arm to Hoffmann. While the chorus sings the waltz theme the pair dance themselves off the stage into the gallery and then back again, the pace, set by the now thoroughly wound-up Olympia, becoming faster and faster. Nicklausse tries to stop them, but is brushed aside and falls into a chair. Spalanzani presses the spring in Olympia's shoulder; she stops suddenly, and the released Hoffmann drops half-dead upon a couch. The professor tries to control his daughter, but a touch on another spring sets her careering off again to the right, gratifying the company with a final brilliant exhibition of coloratura as she at last floats out,[1] followed by Cochenille. Nicklausse turns anxiously to the exhausted Hoffmann, fearing that he is dead; but Spalanzani, after examining him closely, declares that the worst that has happened to him is that his eyeglass is broken, and that he will soon come round again.

While the company is condoling with the "poor young man"

---

[1] As all she can say, apart from an occasional "Yes!", is "Ah!", she has the vocable most suited to a display of coloratura technique.

the orchestra strikes in with a rending dissonance, and Cochenille cries out from the wings, "The spectacles man is here!" A
noise of disintegrating machinery is heard off stage. Spalanzani
cries out in terror and anger, "Olympia! Smashed!" The dazed
Hoffmann repeats his words and rushes out to find his beloved,
just as Coppelius enters shouting with glee at his triumph over
the crooked Spalanzani. The pair of rogues vituperate and manhandle each other. Hoffmann returns, pale and distracted: "It was
only an automaton!" he cries despairingly, and falls into a chair,
where Nicklausse does his best to comfort him. In a final ensemble
the company laughs at the farce that has been played at the young
romantic's expense; the broken-hearted Spalanzani and the exultant Coppelius exchange insults and blows; and so ends the tragi-
comic story of the first of Hoffmann's loves.

14

Over the externally voluptuous second act there broods the
spirit of tragedy. The setting is the terrace of the sumptuous
palace, overlooking the Grand Canal, of the Venetian courtesan,
Giulietta. When the curtain rises she is entertaining a numerous
company, among whom are Hoffmann, Nicklausse and one of the
minor aspirants to her favours, Pitichinaccio. The general atmosphere of sybaritic languor is first of all suggested in a brief
orchestral introduction that outlines the melody of the famous
Barcarolle. This is taken up by Nicklausse:

No. 11

and then by Giulietta; their theme is the beauty of the present
night and the rapture of abandonment to love—mortal love, that
is unfortunately only too fleeting. It is a beguiling melody that
loses none of its nostalgic charm by any amount of repetition. As
the last strains of it die away Giulietta and Nicklausse, who have
been duetting from the gallery at the back, come upon the stage.
Hoffmann dissipates the pensive atmosphere evoked by the
Barcarolle in a song in praise of livelier love and laughter, with

Bacchus called in to reinforce or supplant the fascinations of Venus: "to the devil with him who is foolish enough to weep for two beautiful eyes; for us the diviner intoxication of song in a single hour of bliss." The company agrees with these sentiments in a chorus.

Giulietta's accredited lover of the moment, Schlemil—the shadowless man of Chamisso's famous story *Peter Schlemihl* (1814) —now comes forward, accompanied by his hanger-on Pitichin-accio. Giulietta introduces to Schlemil the young poet, Hoffmann, who has lately joined her circle: the two men greet each other in none too friendly fashion. Giulietta, rising, invites the company to card play in an adjoining room: Hoffmann offers her his arm, but Schlemil forestalls him. Hoffmann and Nicklausse are left alone on the stage. True to his constant rôle in the opera, the latter gives his friend, whose capacity for illusion he knows, a word of warning; he keeps two horses always saddled, and at the first sign of any infatuation on Hoffmann's part he will whisk him away. The poet laughs to scorn the notion of his falling in love with a courtesan, and cares nothing for the enmity of either Schle-mil or that Mephistopheles incarnate, Dappertutto. The latter, ostensibly a captain, appears while they are talking; he is a som-bre, sinister figure, clad in black; and his filiation with the Lindorf of the prologue is made clear to us by the appearance of No. 1 in the orchestra.

The two friends having left the stage, Dappertutto soliloquises: he is bent on possessing himself of the soul of this Hoffmann as he has already secured that of Schlemil, and he will use Giulietta as his instrument, winning her over by the gift of a great diamond that sparkles on his finger. This is the kind of bait no woman can resist, he says in an aria:

No. 12

With it he will not only entrap the courtesan but obtain for himself the soul of the poet.

15

Giulietta returns, and at once succumbs to the fascination of the diamond that Dappertutto places on her finger; she is willing to do anything her master may command her. She has already entrapped Schlemil, he tells her; and now he wants her to get for him Hoffmann's reflection; this will be an easy matter for her, for the young poet is given to romantic dreaming; and the conquest of him ought to be particularly agreeable to her, for has he not just been audacious enough to flout the charm of all that she and her like stand for? He shall become her plaything, she promises Dappertutto. As Hoffmann enters, Dappertutto kisses Giulietta's hand and takes his leave. Hoffmann, having left all his money at the card table, is in melancholy mood. Feigning regret at the thought of his leaving her she bursts into tears, whereupon he confesses that he loves her. Craftily she advises him to flee, for her love may prove fatal to him; Schlemil will kill him if he finds him that night in her arms. This draws from him a passionate declaration of love:

No. 13

O Dieu, de quelle i-vresse— em-bra-ses-tu mon â-me,

that is the emotional high light of the opera thus far; from this point onwards the dark clouds of the present act thicken.

If he must go, she replies, let him at least leave something of him with her that will be a consolation to her—his reflection in the mirror she now shows him, which she will transfer from the glass to her heart. He is fascinated by the idea, yet appalled by it, for he knows that the captured reflection means the loss of his soul. They debate the matter in a long and agitated duet. Heralded by our example No. 1 Schlemil enters,[1] followed by Dappertutto, Nicklausse, Pitichinaccio and others. We realise from the recurrence of the motif that the satanic Dappertutto's poison has already begun to work. Schlemil is in a surly humour—Giulietta,

[1] The motif applies equally well to Schlemil as to Dappertutto, for the former is merely the fated instrument of the latter.

he tells the company, is about to abandon them all for this Hoffmann! The young man begins to feel vaguely that a net is closing round him, but Giulietta quiets him in an aside: "Be silent!" she says, adding meaningly, "He has my key!" [1]—which takes us back in imagination to the episode of Stella's purloined key in the prologue. "Shall we kill him?" Pitichinaccio asks Schlemil, who merely replies "Patience!" "You look pale," Dappertutto remarks sardonically to Hoffmann, handing him a mirror that he may see for himself. To his horror Hoffmann can see no reflection of himself in it, nor in any of the large mirrors that adorn the room; and he gives a wild cry of "I have lost my reflection!" "For Madame," interjects Nicklausse, with an ironical glance at Giulietta. Nicklausse urges him to flee before he loses his soul also; but Hoffmann is already as good as lost. In an agitated aria he curses the passion that now consumes him: he loves Giulietta and at the same time hates her:

No. 14

The others take up the strain one by one and build it up into a septet of the principal characters with a four-part accompaniment by the rest of the company. Dappertutto ironically compassionates Hoffmann on his betrayal by a kiss; Giulietta professes still to love him, but pleads that, she being a woman, the bribe of the diamond was more than she could resist; the despairing Hoffmann is torn between love and hate for her; Nicklausse comments pityingly, as usual, on his friend's abnormal capacity for romantic illusion.

16

There comes a short pause after the massive ensemble: then the orchestra gives out some quiet suggestions of the Barcarolle.

[1] The point of this remark is apt to be missed by the casual spectator. With these four words Giulietta signs Schlemil's death warrant: to get the key to her room that night Hoffmann will kill his rival. Dappertutto is thus everywhere triumphant; through Giulietta and the diamond he puts an end to his victim Schlemil's days and possesses himself of Hoffmann's reflection.

Pitichinaccio once more suggests killing Hoffmann there and then, and once more Schlemil bids him wait. The remainder of the act is dominated by the Barcarolle, which sings out in full in the orchestra while the drama works itself out to its destined close. "Here are the gondolas," says Giulietta, singing on a monotone; "it is the hour of barcarolles, the hour also of adieux." What follows in the next couple of minutes is extraordinarily dramatic by reason of the actors speaking, not singing, through the luscious tissue woven by the Barcarolle in the orchestra. The conversation runs thus:

> *Nicklausse* (to Hoffmann): Are you coming?
> *Hoffmann:* Not yet.
> *Nicklausse:* Very well; but I shall stay with you and watch over you.
> *Schlemil:* What are you waiting for?
> *Hoffmann:* Until you give me a certain key I have sworn to have.
> *Schlemil:* With it will go my life.
> *Hoffmann:* I will take both, then.
> *Schlemil:* We shall see. Come on!
> *Dappertutto* (to Hoffmann): You have no sword: take mine.

Hoffmann takes the sword offered to him by the evil genius of the piece, and in the duel that follows Schlemil is killed. From the dead man's neck Hoffmann takes a key, with which he rushes into Giulietta's room. Pitichinaccio looks cynically down at Schlemil's body, making sure he is dead. All this while the Barcarolle has been singing out in the orchestra: it is now taken up by the chorus in the wings, to the words that accompanied it at the beginning of the act. As the distracted Hoffmann returns from his fruitless quest of the faithless Giulietta we catch sight of her in a gondola, laughing at her poor dupe. "I give him to you," she says cynically to Dappertutto. Pitichinaccio enters the gondola, where Giulietta takes him in her arms. Hoffmann gives a cry of rage and despair as Nicklausse, warning him that the watch is coming, drags him away from the scene of the wreck of another of his illusive loves.

17

The tragic ending of the third act having been foreshadowed in a few sombre bars of orchestral introduction, the curtain rises on a room in Dr. Crespel's house in Munich. Its appearance is

suggestive of its monomaniac owner as we already know him
from the German Hoffmann's story—a strange room, with a
harpsichord on the right, the walls hung with violins, and at the
back, between two doors, a portrait of Crespel's dead wife, the
one-time prima donna. At the harpischord the frail Antonia is
seated, singing a simple sad little song to a lover from whom she
has been parted:

No. 15

the musician Hoffmann, whom she has met on her travels with
her father, but whom the fretted old man, obsessed as he is with
the fear of his consumptive daughter's early death if she is allowed
to excite herself too much with music, is anxious that she shall
not meet again. She has been forced by her destiny to flee from
this love of hers: will she ever meet him again? she asks in pathetic tones.

As she sinks wearily into a chair her father enters. When he
reproaches her for having broken her promise to him never to
sing again she pleads that the spirit of her dead mother had been
too strong within her; and we hear in the orchestra a motif that
will afterwards be specifically associated with the mother whose
whole being had expressed itself in song:

No. 16

Repentant now, Antonia vows that she will not distress her father
again by breaking her promise; and she goes out slowly to a
regretful echo of No. 15 in the orchestra. But Crespel is ill at ease.
He has seen once more the tell-tale spots on his daughter's cheeks,
and has fears for her life. It is that Hoffmann, he says angrily,

who has filled her veins with something that can find expression only in song—Hoffmann, to escape from whom he has fled to Munich with Antonia. He orders his servant Franz, who has come into the room while he has been soliloquising, not to admit anyone into the house; then he goes out, leaving the stage to Franz. This is the one broadly comic person in the whole opera: he is very deaf but hardly realises it, always misunderstanding what is said to him and making irrelevant replies.[1] Perhaps Barbier and Offenbach felt that a little farcical relief was needed somewhere in the opera, and that this was the only place at which it could be worked in; or it may have been that a certain space had to be filled before Antonia could credibly return and go through her duet with Hoffmann, and they could think of no better way of filling it than by an aria in the opera bouffe style. This Franz now sings. He is better at dancing than at singing, he informs us, the great thing in both arts being not technical accomplishment but "method"; his own method in dancing, however, does not save him from a stumble and a collapse from exhaustion in a chair.

He is roused by Hoffmann, who, accompanied by Nicklausse, has obviously managed to get access to the house through Franz being more intent on his dancing and singing than on attending to his duties at the front door. After the usual series of little misunderstandings due to the old servitor's deafness Hoffmann manages to get rid of him, and, seating himself at the harpsichord, reads the piece of music he sees open on it—"a song of love," he comments quietly, "sad or mad, that comes and then flies away:

No. 17

Antonia having entered, Nicklausse recognises that he is now *de trop* and makes a quick exit.

[1] In the first act Offenbach had rung the comic changes on another infirmity: Spalanzani's servant Cochenille has a stammer.

18

The lovers fall into each other's arms. They have found each other again, says Hoffmann, and now the future is theirs; tomorrow she will become his wife, a prospect that fills her with joy. Their first transports over, Hoffmann reveals what is at the back of his mind: he is jealous only of music, which, he fears, Antonia loves more than him. She tries to smile his fears away: it is Hoffmann that she loves in music, she assures him, and music that she loves in Hoffmann. Surely when they are married he will not forbid her to sing, as her father has done? The young man has a vague disturbing sense of something febrile in her eyes and in the trembling of her hand; but for all that he joins her in the song of love they used to sing together (No. 17, which we now hear in a more extended form). But the effort is too much for Antonia, who, at the conclusion of the duet, clutches at her heart and seems to be about to faint.

At that moment Crespel is heard returning. Antonia, greatly perturbed, goes out. Hoffmann is about to follow her, but changes his mind: he will stay and try to find the explanation of the mystery that he feels is in the air around him. To that end he conceals himself in a window recess just as Crespel enters. The old man curses Hoffmann, whom he surmises to have been with Antonia. To add to his trouble, Franz comes in with the news that Dr. Miracle has arrived. Frenziedly Crespel orders him to deny the charlatan admittance—this no-doctor, as he calls him, this assassin, this gravedigger, who had killed Crespel's wife and would now kill his daughter with his quackeries! But he is too late; the clinking of his phials that will characterise Miracle throughout is heard, and the malign figure appears in the doorway, laughing demoniacally. Franz runs away.

Miracle is overjoyed at meeting again this dear old friend of his by whose side he deems it his duty always to be. "How is our Antonia?" he asks; "does the dear creature still suffer from the malady she has inherited from her mother? But we will cure her"; and he demands that he shall be taken to her. As the furious Crespel refuses, threatening to throw the intruder out of the window, Miracle draws up a couple of armchairs, in one of which he seats himself with a professional air; the other he feigns to be

403

occupied by Antonia, whom he will examine and prescribe for at a distance. Hoffmann, who has seen and heard everything, trembles with terror: Crespel too is so shaken that he can make only a few feeble protests as the charlatan goes through his sinister routine. Miracle makes some magic passes in the air; the door to Antonia's room opens, and though she does not appear, he indicates by his gestures that he is taking her by the hand, leading her to the chair, and motioning to her to sit down there. "How old are you?" he asks. "Only twenty? The springtime of life! Give me your hand." To a throbbing rhythm in the orchestra he goes through the mummery of feeling her pulse. "Ah!" he says, "rapid and unsteady; that's a bad sign! Now sing!" Crespel makes an impotent gesture of protest, but suddenly the voice of the still invisible Antonia is heard in a loud trill and a long chromatic cadential descent from the D *in alt* to the D two octaves lower. "See," says the doctor, "her face lights up, her eyes are aflame; she lays her hand on her pounding heart. It would be a pity," he concludes, rising from his chair, "to let death claim so beautiful a prey!"

19

Crespel roughly pushes back the other chair, bidding him be silent. But there is no stopping the crazy Miracle, who, to a bass rhythm and a melodic figure:

No. 18

that between them will dominate much of the music that follows, and with much maddening jingling of his flasks, begs the father to let him try his skill once more, promising him a happy outcome. With Crespel protesting wildly in the foreground and the horrified Hoffmann joining in from his place of concealment a macabre trio is built up, to which extra point is given by stabbing figures in the orchestra:

No. 19

Still prescribing volubly, Miracle is at last turned out of the room by Crespel: but no sooner has the door been closed on him than he reappears through the wall, and the feverish trio is resumed until the quack is once more expelled, making his exit backwards with much rattling of his phials. The angry Crespel follows him.

Hoffmann emerges from his hiding place: how, he asks despairingly, can Antonia be induced to make so great a sacrifice as giving up her art? Just then she herself enters and asks him what her father has said. He will not tell her now, he replies, but later she shall know everything. A new pathway through life is opening out before them, but she must give up her dreams of public glory and be content with his devoted love. After a moment's significant silence she consents, to his great joy; and the orchestra sings softly the melody (No. 17) already associated with the happy days of their first love.

20

Hoffmann having left her, Antonia muses sadly on his capitulation, as it seems to her, to the wishes of her father. Still, she has given her word: she will sing no more; and she sinks into an armchair. But at once we hear again the motif (No. 1) that throughout the prelude and the opera has symbolised the malign fate that dogs Hoffmann's footsteps at every turn, with its sardonic sneer in the final trill; and Miracle appears once more. Again he begins to weave his spell around Antonia, whispering in her ear that it was foolish of her to have given father and lover the pledge she has; so huge a sacrifice is not to be expected of one with her talent, her beauty, her charm; what can domestic felicity, even with a hearthful of brats thrown in, weigh in the scales against the applause of the adoring multitude?

Antonia does not turn round, but she asks herself, with a shudder, whether this voice that is whispering in her ear comes from heaven or from hell. She decides to choose love; but at once the tempter sets to work on her again. Hoffmann, he says, loves her only for her present beauty; when that fades he will desert her for another and younger woman. With that he leaves her. In her despair she casts about her for help; who will save her from this demon, from herself? Her mother, perhaps; and her eyes turn to the picture on the wall. Suddenly Miracle reappears; "Your mother?" he says; "how can you call on her; is it not she, ungrateful girl, who is speaking to you through me? Think of the splendour of her fame, which you would cast aside." The portrait comes to life with a cry of "Antonia!"; and the spirit of her mother sings to her, imploring her to listen to her loving counsel before it is too late:

No. 20

(See also No. 16).

With the voice of the tempter also sounding in her ears, telling her that the spirit of her beloved mother will live again if only she consents to sing, Antonia's resolution begins to waver. A trio follows, then a duet in which Miracle's solicitations become still more urgent, then another trio on the theme of No. 20. When at last Miracle plays madly on a violin Antonia breaks down; she asks heaven feverishly for just one moment of life before her soul ascends to the skies; then she falls dying on a couch, the animated picture on the wall reverts to its old still form, and Miracle, his end achieved, vanishes in the earth with a burst of mocking laughter. Crespel rushes in, crying "Where is my daughter, my Antonia?" With her last breath she tells him, to a soft enunciation of No. 16 in the orchestra, that the spirit of her mother has called her; then her thoughts go back to the song of her and Hoffmann's love (No. 17). As Crespel, wild with grief, bends over her dead body Hoffmann and Nicklausse enter. Crespel curses the lover as the murderer of his daughter, and calls frenziedly for his blood to reanimate the cheeks of his child. Hoffmann sends Nicklausse in search of a doctor. There is an instant tragic-ironic reply to his message—Miracle, to the accompaniment of his macabre No. 18, suddenly materialises, bends over Antonia, takes her hand, and as it drops helplessly, ejaculates "Dead!" Franz enters and falls on his knees by the body. Crespel breaks out into a wild lament. Hoffmann gives a despairing cry of "Antonia," and the curtain falls.

21

A little time must necessarily elapse before the stage can be set for the epilogue; and Offenbach's way of filling it is to set the orchestra playing the Barcarolle again. There is no dramatic justification for this: he probably said to himself that as it was likely to prove the most popular number in the work, the public could hardly hear it too often. After the Barcarolle there comes an orchestral entr'acte of twenty-eight bars; then the curtain rises once more on Luther's cellar, with Hoffmann telling the company that they have now heard the story of his three loves, the memory of which will never leave him. From off stage come enthusiastic cries of "Stella!" from the theatre audience. "No longer any need to fear him!" says Lindorf in an aside; "the diva is mine!" Hoffmann, rather to the puzzlement of Nathanael, also cries out "Stella!", and it falls to Nicklausse to explain that the Olympia, Giulietta and Antonia of whom the young poet has been telling them were actually not three women but separate incarnations of the same woman—none other than this living Stella.

The company is for drinking the health of the lady, but Hoffmann, rising in a fury, swears that if he hears another word from them he will annihilate them as he has just smashed the glass he has hurled to the ground. A reproach from the faithful Nicklausse, who feels himself to be included in the objurgation, brings about a revulsion of feeling in Hoffmann. "I am mad," he cries; "let us fly to the intoxication of the spirits of wine and beer, forgetting everything in our folly." Punch is brought in, and the company sings the joyous chorus shown in our No. 2, to the same words as formerly in the prologue. "Well, Hoffmann?" says Nicklausse; but the poet, deep in thought, makes no reply. "He is quite drunk," comments Wilhelm as he follows the rest of the company from the stage, taking Nicklausse with him. But the exhausted Hoffmann's drunkenness is of the poetic spirit, not of the flesh. The huge cask at the back of the tavern lights up, revealing what the librettist calls the Muse. "I am your faithful friend," she says to him, "whose hand shall wipe the tears from your eyes, through whom the sorrow of your soul shall drift away to the skies in dreams, and your passions find rest. The man is no more: let him be born again as poet, Hoffmann; become wholly mine"— all this to a reminiscence in the orchestra of No. 13. Hoffmann takes up the impassioned strain in ecstasy: the gentle eyes of the Muse have filled his heart with a fire at once searing and sweet: "Beloved Muse, I am yours!" he cries. He sinks down completely intoxicated—whether with poetry or wine or both we are not informed. The door opens, and Stella enters and goes slowly towards him, "He is asleep," she says. "No, Madame— dead drunk," remarks Nicklausse, who has now returned with a few of the roystering crew, who burst into No. 2 for the last time. Among them is Lindorf, to whom Nicklausse tries to draw Hoffmann's attention. Lindorf clasps Stella to him, but her eyes remain fixed on Hoffmann, who, under the protection of the Muse, is still oblivious to everything around him. And on that German-romantic tableau the final curtain falls. The symbolism of the epilogue is hard to realise convincingly on the stage, and producers in general prefer to handle the epilogue in diverse ways of their own. With these, however, we have happily no concern.

Carmen

BIZET [1838–1875]

PRINCIPAL CHARACTERS

CARMEN	*Soprano or Mezzo-soprano*
DON JOSÉ	*Tenor*
ESCAMILLO	*Baritone*
MICAËLA	*Soprano*
FRASQUITA	*Soprano*
MERCÉDÈS	*Soprano*
ZUNIGA	*Bass*
MORALÈS	*Baritone*
LE DANCAÏRE	*Buffo Tenor*
LE REMENDADO	*Buffo Bass*

1

ARMEN was produced at the Opéra-Comique, Paris, on the 3rd March 1875, and its composer died three months later, in the night of the 2nd–3rd June. Sentimental legends die hard, and that of Bizet's untimely death having been brought about by the "failure" of his opera still survives in some quarters. Whether *Carmen* was a "failure" or not depends on the meaning we attach to that term. It received thirty-five performances during the three months that remained of the 1875 season; that it lay under a cloud in Paris for some time after that can be accounted for by a variety of circumstances not at all uncommon in opera houses, with their changing managements and shifting fortunes. Despite the abuse the work had received from some of the critics the public remained interested in it. When, under a new management, it was revived at the Opéra-Comique under a new director, Carvalho, on the 21st April 1883, there was a general outburst of anger in the

Press and among the public, not because a "failure" had been revived, but because Paris had been so long deprived of what had by this time been accepted elsewhere as a masterpiece. The day before the composer died he had signed an agreement with the Vienna Opera for a production there; and the hard-boiled directors of opera houses do not usually approach a composer for rights in a new work that has obviously proved a "failure."

The first Vienna performance took place on the 23rd October of the same year. Brussels took the opera up in February 1876, St. Petersburg, New York, London, and other towns followed suit during the next couple of years. By the end of 1883 it had attained its hundredth performance at the Opéra-Comique alone, and by 1904 its thousandth there: in the meantime it had consolidated its position all the world over as one of the three or four most popular operas of all time.[1] Camille Du Locle, the director of the Opéra-Comique when *Carmen* was commissioned, jibbed, as many other people did at first, at some of the startling new features of the libretto; but had he regarded the work as a "failure" he would hardly have suggested, as he did almost immediately after the first performance, a new opera by the same composer and the same librettists. Finally, ill as Bizet was in March, we find him working at the plan for an oratorio on the subject of St. Geneviève of Paris; which of itself suggests that the legend of his being crushed by the "failure" of *Carmen* is as much indebted to the sentimental imagination of the authors of it as to the simple facts.

That he was greatly depressed at times after the first performance of the work is undeniable—and quite understandable. He had always overworked a constitution none too strong, teaching and doing hackwork for publishers as well as composing; and the mere proof-reading and rehearsing of *Carmen*, with all the maddening stage and back-stage annoyances inseparable from the production of any new opera, must have been a grievous physical and mental strain on him. The stupidity of many of the critics must also have struck him to the heart. But hundreds of other composers have undergone these vexing experiences without any noticeable effect on the mortality statistics; so we must look else-

[1] By 1951 it had been given some 2,700 times at the Paris Opéra-Comique alone.

where for a reasonable explanation of the depression in which his friends found Bizet from time to time. He was already a very tired and sick man; and a long-standing malady of the throat—perhaps also of the heart—saw the opportunity it had been waiting for and struck.[1] He would in all probability have died when he did had the Press notices of *Carmen* been as sensible and kind in general as, in point of fact, they were imbecile and cruel.

Nor had Bizet's short life been a disheartening struggle for recognition. Both in the concert room and in the opera house he had had more opportunities than came to the lot of most young composers in a not very musical capital in which the competition was fierce. He was only twenty-eight when the *Pearl-Fishers* was produced at the Théâtre-Lyrique; it had eighteen performances. The *Fair Maid of Perth* followed at the same theatre four years later, with a total of twenty-one performances. The one-act *Djamileh*, in 1872, had only a short run, but he himself hardly questioned the justice of the popular verdict: "the poem," he wrote to his friend and pupil Edmond Galabert, "is really anti-theatrical, and my soprano surpassed even my worst fears. For all that, I am very satisfied with the results obtained." The Press, though critical, had taken the work with gratifying seriousness; "never before has an opera in one act been so earnestly, I would say passionately, discussed." The significant fact is that he had had the work performed; and he was still only thirty-four.

2

As a composer he had been in search of himself for many years. There were times when he was tempted to believe that his vocation lay in the field of instrumental music; his symphony in C major, written at the age of seventeen, a work of great charm, dashed off in about a month in 1855, must have done something

---

[1] There were other complications. A few weeks before his death he had brought on severe rheumatism and partial paralysis by bathing in cold river-waters. On the 31st May he told his friend Guiraud that he had gone deaf in his left ear. His widow thought the immediate cause of death was a tumour in the ear on which the surgeons were afraid to operate. His librettist Ludovic Halévy surmised, in his contemporary diary, that Bizet's rheumatism had suddenly gone to the heart. Paris, of course, was full of rumours: some people spoke of suicide, others of marital and extra-marital complications, and so *ad infinitum*.

to confirm him in this belief.[1] An inner voice, however, kept urging him more and more insistently towards the stage. There it was some time before he really found himself—it was not until *Carmen*, indeed, that he fully succeeded in doing so. He had much to acquire by practice and reflection, much dead wood to cut out of himself; and probably no one was more conscious of all this than he was. His published correspondence with Galabert (*Lettres à un Ami*), which extends from 1865 to 1872, throws a good deal of light on his struggle towards self-realisation. Galabert was engaged on an opera the completed sections of which he would send to Bizet for criticism, and we find the latter turning an extraordinarily penetrating eye on his pupil's occasional failures to conceive his dramatic action and his music as an organic whole—and this at a time when Bizet's own operatic practice left a good deal to be desired. As an artist he never had much bent towards the purely speculative—he would never have tried to formulate, for instance, an aesthetic of opera and drama, as Wagner and others have done. He was always the practician, the craftsman concentrating on a particular problem of expression or procedure that confronted him at a given moment. When he made "concessions," as he called them, to the poor taste of his Parisian audience, he did so in perfectly cold blood, and afterwards had no hesitation in pleading guilty to the charge he himself had been the first to bring against himself.

The first impression the casual listener gets from a hearing of *The Pearl-Fishers, The Fair Maid of Perth* and *Djamileh* is that of a musician somewhat regardless of the special problems of the musical stage, yielding too readily to the temptation to write delightful music—of which there is an abundance in these three works—for its own delightful sake. That first impression, however, corrects itself to some extent as one comes to know these early operas better; again and again we light upon some touch or other in them that only a musician with the *dramatic* root of the

---

[1] It was neither published nor performed during his lifetime. The manuscript was one of several of early Bizetiana presented to the Paris Conservatoire by Reynaldo Hahn. In 1933 Mr. D. C. Parker, the author of the first English biography of Bizet (1926, second edition 1951), drew Weingartner's attention to it, and the German conductor performed it for the first time at Basel on the 26th February 1935.

matter in him could have achieved. Still, we are a long way as yet from the Bizet of *Carmen*, the musician always drawing with his eye on the object, and in doing so accomplishing a unique fusion of the lyrical and the dramatic. The change from the musician often using a dramatic situation only as a pretext for lovely music to an artist in whom fine music and dramatic characterisation or dramatic movement are simply different aspects of the same thing, was a curious phenomenon to which we cannot persuade ourselves that we have the key. We can say, if we like, that the final Bizet is a quite natural evolution from the first; but this, true as it is in broad outline, does not answer all the questions we find ourselves asking. There is no unbroken line of evolution observable, nor can we find anything in his letters to suggest that the remarkable change in him of which *Carmen* is the evidence was the product of any willed or desired new orientation on his part, or indeed that he was aware of any fundamental change in himself.

3

Certainly he had always had spells of critical self-examination. A sort of minor crisis seems to have come in the summer and autumn of 1868. In July of that year we find him writing to Galabert, "Nothing new to report. My spirits are low; all black, black, black." The root cause of it may have been physical: he has been very ill, he says—"a very complicated quinsy." But the bodily depression and the following convalescence evidently led, as so often happens with artists, to some soul-searching on his part. "There is an extraordinary change going on in me," he writes later. "I am changing my skin, both as man and artist; I am purifying myself; I am becoming better; I feel it! Come, I shall find something in myself if I search hard enough." In August he develops the theme: "There is going on within me so radical a change, from the musical point of view, that I can't venture on my new manner without some months of preparation. I shall test myself in September and October." For all that, the statement in the text above remains broadly true: there is no conscious, undeviating line of evolution traceable in him even in the field of music drama: three years after the letter just quoted we find him contentedly accepting the libretto of the essentially undramatic *Djamileh.*

After *Djamileh*, on the 17th June 1872, he writes to Galabert, "What gives me more satisfaction than the opinion of all these gentlemen [the critics] is the absolute certainty of having found my path [meaning, one surmises, that he now recognised opera as his true vocation]. I know what I am doing. A three-act work has just been commissioned from me by the Opéra-Comique. Meilhac and Halévy will do the libretto. It will be *gay*, but with a gaiety that permits style." In the same breath, however, he confesses to having "some symphonic projects," a theme that recurs in a letter to another correspondent in which he speaks of the probability of his being asked to write something for the Opéra. The Opéra-Comique commission was to be realised ultimately in *Carmen*, though that subject may not have yet been decided upon. Yet something of the vacillation, the self-doubt, that was characteristic of him all his life at intervals is evident even now. After having got his hand thoroughly in with *Carmen*, early in 1873, he put that work aside in order to write, in the summer and autumn of the same year, a five-act opera on the subject of the Cid.[1] Then, when *Carmen* was probably under way again, he lost interest in it, vowed that he had finished with the stage, and asked the librettist Louis Gallet to provide him with a text for an oratorio on the St. Geneviève subject. And still the indecision persists: he tells his fellow-composer Guiraud that he has lost faith in his capacity to fill an Opéra bill, but believes he can make his mark at the Opéra-Comique, where he hopes to "expand and transform the genre." A man of genius more divided against himself, so little the servant at that time of a daemon driving him inexorably in the direction the Fates had decided upon for him, it would be difficult to find in the whole history of music.

Yet some compulsion there must have been, though he himself was only dimly conscious of it, and that intermittently. It has sometimes been asked, with all respect towards him, whether *Carmen* may not have been just a lucky accident, something the like of which he would perhaps never have accomplished again. The question evades answer, but it persists in obtruding itself. The mere fact that even while under the spell of *Carmen* he could

---

[1] Seemingly, though completed in his head, not much of this *Don Rodrigue* was actually worked out on paper. The death-blow to the scheme was given by the burning down of the Opéra in October 1872.

seriously think of plunging into oratorio, a genre for which he had never shown the suggestion of any aptitude or any sympathy is of itself calculated to set us wondering whether he was even yet fully aware of what is now so obvious to the rest of the world —that he had a genius of the first order for musical drama, and that he ought now to devote himself heart and soul to developing his capacities in that field.

4

Manifestly a great subconscious change had somehow taken place in him, a remarkable growth both in extent and depth. But what was the meaning of that change? What was the origin of it? Was he himself aware of it, or was it just that he set to work at his latest subject believing himself to be still the same Bizet fundamentally who had written the earlier operas—though of course with more stage experience now—and then found that by the operation of some mysterious psychical chemistry in him he had become something quite different, the talent having somehow developed into a genius? It is generally as the result of a slow change of tissue and temperature within, not through some sudden violent impact from without, that certain highly-strung men have become radically different from what they were: much more must have gone to the transformation of a Saul into a Paul, for example, than hearing a voice and seeing a light one day on the road to Damascus. Various attempts have been made to account for the transformation in Bizet. Outside influences can probably be ruled out. Sentimental musical biography has always been inclined to overrate these in the psychology of a composer—the influence of Schumann's marriage on some of his songs, for instance, or the attribution of the general sunniness of the *Meistersinger* to the change wrought in Wagner's material circumstances by the patronage of King Ludwig. The truth is that in the mysterious complex of forces that we call the artistic consciousness doors open more often by slow silent pressure from within than by sudden assault from without; the poet or the composer simply becomes a different being by an internal metamorphosis of which he himself is unaware at the time.

In the case of Bizet the supreme achievement of *Carmen* seems to have been partly due to the immense good fortune of his coming upon the right subject at the right time. He had always been attracted by the exotic in general and the gipsy in particular; and in the *Carmen* subject he found ready made for him, in Mérimée's great story, a gipsy the windings of whose being he had only to follow in his music curve by curve. But, once again, we feel that Carmen herself might have come to not much more fullness of stage life than his Mab in *The Fair Maid of Perth* had done had there not been an internal change of substance in him by then. Something within him seems to have been impelling him for a long time towards the probing of certain of the darker depths of human nature. There is a hint of a Carmen-José complex *avant la lettre* in his conception of the Myrrha of *La Coupe du Roi de Thule*, who throws an evil spell over the fisherman Yorick. In a letter of December 1868 Bizet is shrewdly critical of Galabert's mishandling of the scene of the entry of Myrrha: "Had you been describing her in words," he remarks, "you would have done just the opposite of what you have done in the music you send me. This Myrrha is a courtesan of the antique mould, sensual as Sappho, ambitious as Aspasia. She is beautiful, intelligent, and full of charm, the proof of which is the extraordinary fascination she exercises on Yorick. In her eyes there must be that palegreenish look that is the unmistakeable sign of sensuality and egoism pushed to the length of cruelty." The colloquy between the pair should be supported by an instrumental passage suggesting her fascination for Yorick, commencing at the words "Je tremble au seul bruit de ses pas." "The serpent has come, and the bird is half paralysed. . . . This is how I see the situation. Left to himself Yorick is free: he gives passionate, delirious expression to his love, addressing the clouds, the stars. In the presence of Myrrha he is extinguished." Bizet shows how the most can be made of this entry of the enchantress: "she is leaning on the arm of Angus; she comes in slowly, absent-mindedly, as if lost in a dream; her eyes take in all around her, and then settle almost disdainfully on Yorick." We shall find this psychological situation reproduced, in broad essentials, in the first act of *Carmen*.

Perhaps something that had been set going in the depths of him by his brooding upon the problem of Myrrha had been slowly maturing in him in the years between *La Coupe du Roi de Thule* and *Carmen*.[1] On the 1st October 1872 Alphonse Daudet's play *L'Arlésienne* (*The Woman of Arles*) had been produced at the Paris Vaudeville Theatre, with incidental music by Bizet. In this remarkable score we see him at last coming into his own; already he is a master. The dramatic and psychological substance of the play is akin to that of *Carmen* in some respects—Frédéri is fascinated by the Arlésienne (who does not appear in person in the play but is sensed as an ever-present destructive, irresistible force in the background), very much as Yorick had been by Myrrha and Don José will be by Carmen. Moreover, in both *L'Arlésienne* and *Carmen* there is a contrasted purer element, in the former the humble unreciprocated love of Vivette for Frédéri, in the latter the Micaëla who strives, but in vain, to rescue Don José from the clutches of the gipsy siren. Frédéri, unable to square his account between the irreconcilable worlds of pure love and blind fascination, commits suicide by throwing himself from a window of the farm: José kills Carmen and then goes with sombre resignation to meet his own fate.

When Bizet received the commission to write a new work for the Opéra-Comique the Carmen subject appears to have been his own choice. He must have been well acquainted with Mérimée's story long before then; but evidently it was only after his experiences with *L'Arlésienne*—or contemporaneously with them—that it took complete possession of his imagination. Only then was he dramatically and musically ripe for it. Out of this combination of outward circumstances and a new complex of inner forces came the masterpiece that is *Carmen*. It is the most Mozartian opera since Mozart, the one in which enchanting musical invention goes hand in hand, almost without a break, with dramatic veracity and psychological characterisation. The Bizet of the earlier works has here developed a new weight and strength with-

[1] After putting Galabert to work at *La Coupe du Roi de Thule* he decided to set the text himself. His score was never completed and little of it has been published; the prelude was performed at a Colonne concert in Paris on the 12th December 1880 under the title of *Marche funèbre*. What remains of the manuscript is in the Paris Conservatoire. For further information regarding the opera the reader must be referred to Mr. Winton Dean's admirable book on Bizet (1948)—indispensable to every student of the composer—and his article in the October 1947 number of *Music and Letters*.

out losing any of his old litheness. This is indeed music muscled in the Mozartian way, the fascinating way of the cat-tribe, the maximum of power being combined with the maximum of speed and grace and the minimum of visible effort. The Bizet of the earlier works had been marvellously gifted by the gods with beauty of melody, expressiveness of harmony, and an exquisite sense of colour-values in orchestration. All this endowment was now concentrated, in a heightened form, on a single work.

5

The first performance of *Carmen* took place at the Opéra-Comique on the 3rd March 1875, with spoken dialogue, as was *de rigueur* in the genre to which it belonged. After Bizet's death his friend Guiraud rewrote much of the dialogue as musical recitative, some of which was used in the Vienna production of October 1875, in which several extraneous elements suited to the local taste were introduced. It became a sort of opera-ballet, the procession of toreros and picadors (the latter on horseback) in the fourth act being made a pretext for a dazzling stage picture. It was not until 1900 that Mahler succeeded in ridding *Carmen* of these excrescences in the Austrian capital. In 1901 the work was given in the Nîmes arena with the added attraction, for southern eyes, of a real bull-fight, the singing Escamillo being replaced for the time being by an actual torero.

At the first performance of the opera in Paris the Carmen was Célestine Galli-Marié, the first of a long line of famous gipsy heroines.[1] The tenor, Lhérie, seems to have been no more than ordinarily competent, either vocally or histrionically. The Escamillo (Jacques Bouhy) and the Micaëla (Mlle Chapuy) were on the whole better. That the opera should have got off to a rather bad start was in the nature of things. The Opéra-Comique was the favourite haunt of the sentimental bourgeois, who were shocked by the drastic realism of the action and the deplorably low social standing and defective moral sense of some of the characters,

---

[1] She seems to have been an intelligent woman, who went direct to Mérimée's story for her conception of the part. Oddly enough, in 1864 Victor Massé, the composer of *Les Noces de Jeannette,* had contemplated writing a *Carmen* in conjunction with Sardou; and as his Carmen he had in view Galli-Marié.

particularly the gipsies, and jibbed especially at the uncompromis-ingly tragic finish, which was out of keeping with the happy-ending tradition of the house. Furthermore, the average patron of the Opéra-Comique was unused to a harmonic idiom so ad-vanced as Bizet's, and puzzled by the seeming "formlessness" of much of the music. He liked to know where he was, with solos, duets and so on of which he could see clearly the beginning and the end: it is significant that the three numbers which drew the most response from the audience were "set" pieces conforming more or less to the accepted patterns—the duet of Don José and Micaëla in the first act, the Toreador's song in the second, and Micaëla's aria in the third. Ludovic Halévy, whose testimony can be relied upon, for it appears in his diary under the date 16th March 1875, tells us that the trouble as regards the general musi-cal idiom and especially the harmony of the work was simply that it took everyone a little time to get inside them. The company had at first found them strange, but in the course of the three or four months during which the rehearsals had lasted had become not only reconciled to them but enthusiastic about them. As Halévy says, the misfortune was that the first-night public had not gone through a similar education.

6

Bizet had as his librettists two seasoned craftsmen of the theatre, Henry Meilhac and Ludovic Halévy: the latter was Bizet's wife's cousin, son of Leon Halévy, the brother of Fromental Halévy, the composer of *La Juive*, who had been Bizet's teacher. Their task was not an easy one, and it is rather surprising that they should have performed it, on the whole, so well. There is nothing dramatic or theatrical about Mérimée's immortal story, which had appeared in 1845. There the story is told in the first person: Mérimée, touring Spain for archaeological and historical purposes, one day falls in with a sinister-looking character who turns out to be a notorious brigand, a certain José, the terror of the country-side. The story-teller does the hunted man one or two little kind-nesses and wins his confidence. The brigand, on whose head there is a price, goes off into the mountains, and Mérimée to Cordova, where he falls in with La Carmencita, a gipsy "of a wild and strange beauty," as he describes her; "her eyes in particular had an expression at once voluptuous and fierce that I have never met since in any human glance." Mérimée studies her as a curious case, for gipsies have always interested him. He goes to her home, where she begins to tell his fortune. A man in a bad humour breaks in on them; it is José, who remonstrates angrily with her for a way of life to which he has had reason to object many times before. From her excited gestures Mérimée surmises that she is urging the brigand to cut the stranger's throat; but José ushers him out. When Mérimée returns to his inn he finds that his watch has been stolen by Carmen.

He bothers no further about it but goes off again on his scientific quest. After some months' wandering he finds himself once more in Cordova, where a Dominican Father of his acquaintance, relieved to find that he has not been assassinated, as he had feared, tells him that not only has his watch been recovered but the ruffian connected with the matter, a brigand and murderer known as José Navarro (though actually he is a Basque with an outlandish name which no one can pronounce), is now in jail. Next day Mérimée is allowed access to the prisoner, who is to be garrotted shortly; and now the brigand tells him the story of his life. He was Don José Lizzarrabengoa of Elizondo, a Basque of the old Christian faith: he had been intended for the church, but a quarrel during a game of paume (hand tennis) had led to a fight with lethal weapons, and he had had to flee the country. He enlisted in the Spanish dragoons, soon rose to be a corporal, and was well on the way to becoming a quartermaster when one day he was placed on guard at the tobacco factory in Seville, where some hundreds of girls worked. He was not interested in them, his mind being always on the girls of his own country, with their blue skirts and braided hair.

The story proceeds for a while along the lines of the first act of the opera. José had been punished and degraded for allowing Carmen to escape while ostensibly conducting her to prison. He happens to fall in with her again, when she is the mistress of the colonel at whose door José is doing sentry duty. She upbraids him for so cravenly submitting to his punishment; never could she love anyone of so poor a spirit. Her fascination for him increases, and his mood becomes one of deepening and darkening exasperation. One day he finds her in the company of a young lieutenant of his regiment who roughly and contemptuously orders the common soldier away. A fight ensues, in which the lieutenant is killed. José is taken away into safety by Carmen, and soon he finds himself compelled, if he does not want to lose her, to join a band of smugglers of which she is an active member, the head of it being one Dancaïre. Time goes on, José becoming more and more exasperated by the refusal of Carmen to confine her affections to him. One day he learns that she is actually the wife now of the ugliest of the smugglers, a repulsive ruffian known as Garcia the One-Eyed: this adds fuel to his jealousy. The smugglers are caught in an ambush; most of them take to their heels, only Carmen, José, Garcia, Dancaïre and a fine young fellow named Remendado being left. In their headlong flight through the mountains, under the fire of the soldiers, Remendado is wounded; and Garcia callously disposes of him by shooting him through the head.

7

So it goes on for a long time, the net of jealousy and enforced crime closing ever more closely round José. At last a grand smuggling *coup* is in train, in which it is the business of Carmen to draw an English officer whom she has befooled in Gibraltar into a trap in the hills. A quarrel over cards leads to José killing Garcia: Dancaïre's cynical comment on it all is "To the devil with love affairs! If you had asked him for Carmen he would have sold her to you for a few piastres." So now only Dancaïre, Carmen, José and two or three more of the band are left. Dancaïre is killed in a surprise attack by the soldiers, and José himself is wounded and has to hide in a wood. Carmen nurses him back to health and then takes him with her to Granada. He implores her to make an end of this life of outlawry and crime and go with him to the New World; but, as usual, she pours scorn on the idea. Another grand smuggling scheme is on foot; she means to see it through, and José must work with her or lose her. He discovers that in Granada she has made the acquaintance of a noted picador named Lucas, of whom she characteristically proposes to make use for her own unscrupulous ends. He is a man, she tells José, whom it will be easy for her to handle; he has earned a good deal of money in the bull-ring, and one of two things must happen—either they will

421

get possession of this money, or she will inveigle him into joining their band.

The picador leaves for Malaga, and José continues his work as smuggler. (It was at this late point in his career, we now learn, that he and the teller of the story had first met.) One day Carmen goes off to Cordova. All José's jealousy boils up in him again when he discovers that there is to be a bull-fight there. He follows her and finds her on a bench in the arena. It falls to Lucas to play the first bull; it charges him, unhorses and crushes him. José takes Carmen away and once more implores her to go to America with him and there lead a decent life. He is very weary of killing her lovers, he tells her; it is she whom he will kill next. But now she is in a fatalistic mood; she had long foreseen the end, she says—"me first, then you." He goes to mass. On his return he finds Carmen gazing into a bowl full of water with melted lead in it, absorbed in one of her gipsy incantations. He takes her away on his horse and makes a last appeal to her: her reply is "Yes, I loved Lucas for a while, but perhaps less than I did you. Now I love nothing, and hate myself for having loved you. . . . I will follow you to death; but I will never live with you again." They are now in a solitary gorge. He pulls up his horse, and Carmen jumps to the ground. "Is it here?" she asks. "You wish to kill me, I can see. It is decreed; but you will not make me yield." He pleads with her abjectly, but she is immovable. She will fence with him no longer, she says, tell him no more lies: as her *rom* he has the right to kill her; but free she was born, and free she will die. He draws his knife, hoping at least that he can make her afraid. "But that woman was a demon," he tells his listener; her only reply was to take from her finger a ring he had given her and throw it into the bushes. Then he loses control of himself and stabs her twice with the knife that had killed Garcia: she falls without a cry. He remembers that she had told him once that she would like to be buried in a wood. He dug a grave for her with his knife and laid her in it, placing beside her the ring and a small cross: then he galloped straight to Cordova and gave himself up at the first guard-house he came to.

8

As will be seen from this swift summary, Mérimée's story covers a much larger extent of space and time than the opera. This was the first of the difficulties the librettists had to face. In the nature of the case, most of what gives the story its unique impressiveness—the atmosphere of unrelieved gloom, the slow inexorable transformation of a decent young Basque boy into the bandit and murderer of the after years—has had to be sacrificed. It is true that José is a different being in each act of the opera; the librettists have managed this very well, and Bizet's genius has heightened their every stroke. But music is always a voracious devourer of stage time; and it was inevitable that a great deal that goes to the mental and moral make-up of the Don José of Mérimée should have to be sacrificed to the peculiar exigencies of opera.

Then there was the difficulty that always attends the transfer of an action from the book page to the theatre, where everything that happens has to do so before our eyes in the person of someone or other. In Mérimée there are really only two characters—Carmen and José—; Lucas, Dancaïre and Remendado each receive only a few lines of mention. But a full-scale four-act opera with only two characters is unthinkable; and so not only had the more or less negative Lucas to be enlarged into the very positive Escamillo, and even Dancaïre and Remendado made to play their musical part in the whole, but an entirely new character had to be invented in the person of Micaëla. In the story we are conscious of the purer, happier, more innocent Basque background of José's youth only by way of hint and inference, as we are, in another way, of the sinister Arlésienne.[1] It is dimly conceivable that the authors of an ordinary play on the *Carmen* subject might have managed to present in symbolical form the antithesis between the

[1] At the beginning of José's story of his life he says, "I am a Basque and of the old Christian faith. I was intended for the Church and forced to study for it; but it profited me nothing. I was too fond of paume, and that was my undoing. When we Navarros play at paume we forget everything else. . . ." Meilhac and Halévy manifestly thought it of importance that the audience should know all this, for in the spoken dialogue between José and the lieutenant in the first act they reproduce Mérimée's text almost verbatim. But the dialogue does not appear in the vocal scores now current.

world of trickery and crime in which the later José finds himself trapped and his nostalgia for the Basque environment of his youth; certainly this could have been done in a spoken drama with incidental music on the *L'Arlésienne* pattern. Even in opera—though hardly in that of Bizet's day apart from Wagner—a musical-dramatic tissue might somehow have been woven in which all that Micaëla stands for could have been suggested without bringing her on the stage in the flesh. But in the French opera of the eighteen-seventies this was an impossibility. For purely technical and practical reasons alone there had to be a female voice contrasting with Carmen's; and so the creation of a Micaëla was a sheer necessity. "Contrast" of more than one kind has indeed been thus effected; over against the dark gipsy, for instance, as the incarnation of hard unscrupulous reality, there was now posed a regulation stage blond ingénue symbolising virtue. The librettists and the composer could not have done otherwise than they did: but while admitting that what they did achieved every possible effect of theatrical "contrast"—like the two constrasting subjects of a symphonic movement—we cannot help feeling that the Micaëla of the opera remains something of a lay figure, a *dea ex machina* to be pushed forward when required and afterwards withdrawn without any further or deeper concern with her on the librettists' part or ours. It is only the music that Bizet has given her that keeps us interested in her while she is on the stage; when she is not, we are inclined to forget about her.

Escamillo, as we have seen, is entirely the librettists' creation, and a legitimate one, a development of the merest hint given them in Mérimée's Lucas, the picador Carmen's interest in whom takes her to the bull-fight and so brings about the final tragedy.

9

The overture to the opera is of the simplest and, at first sight, the most innocent kind. Bizet had no thought of making it in any way a symphonic epitome of the characters and the dramatic action: there is no hint in it, for instance, of either José or Micaëla. It is with the animated theme of the music associated with the entry of the bull-fighters in the last scene of the work that he chooses to begin. (See our example No. 32.) On to this he tacks, in an abrupt modulation from the key of A major to that of F

424

major, the refrain of the Toreador's song in the second act; it is played the first time piano, the second time fortissimo. (See musical example No. 17.) Another nonchalant key-leap brings him back into A major and a repetition of the arena music with which he had begun. Then, in the final twenty-seven bars of the short prelude, he introduces his Carmen, whom he impresses on our imagination once for all in a theme, in which the interval of the augmented second is prominent, that stands out commandingly in the 'cellos, a clarinet, a bassoon and a cornet [1] against an ominous string tremolando:

No. 1

Whether we are to regard this theme as representing Carmen the actual woman, or, as some contend, the Fate of which she is the instrument, is an interesting subject for debate but finally immaterial to the dramatic issue. As the motif develops, the augmented second characteristic of it defines itself more and more clearly as part of the chord of the diminished seventh, that has always proved itself so useful in suggesting the sinister; and it is on a double-fortissimo chord of the diminished seventh that the overture ends—or rather remains suspended, arrestingly, questioningly, in the upper air.[2]

The curtain rises on a square in Seville. On the right is the great tobacco factory, employing some hundreds of women, of which Mérimée has given us so interesting an account. On the left is a military guard-room, in front of which is a small covered gallery elevated slightly above the ground by two or three steps.

[1] Not a trumpet, as in the modern miniature orchestral score. Bizet wrote for cornets, not trumpets, throughout *Carmen*.

[2] As Henry Malherbe has pointed out, the *Carmen* prelude follows the same plan as that of *L'Arlésienne*, (a) the theme of the bullfighters paralleling that of the "Marche de Turenne," (b) the Escamillo motif that of the Innocent, (c) the *Carmen* motif that of the Arlésienne.

Near the guard-room we see a rack holding the dragoons' lances, adorned with red and yellow banderoles. Along the back of the stage stretches a bridge. Grouped about the guard-room are a dozen or so dragoons of the Almanza regiment; some are sitting and smoking, the others leaning on the balustrade of the gallery; among them is the brigadier Moralès. Citizens are strolling about, each intent on his own affairs. Moralès and the others join in a charming chorus the burden of which is the pleasant spectacle afforded the idle observer by this endless ebb and flow of Seville humanity: note the piquant accentuation of the chorus and the orchestral bass ascending step by step—this latter a favourite procedure of Bizet's:

No. 2

To the accompaniment of a tripping little melody in the violins Moralès draws the attention of the others to a new arrival. It is Carmen's antithesis Micaëla, complete with Basque blue skirt and hair in braids; and she is evidently a stranger in the place, for she comes in hesitantly and, sighting the soldiers, a trifle apprehensively. They gallantly place themselves at her disposal. She is in quest of a brigadier, she explains, a certain Don José; and the orchestra limns her sufficiently for the time being in a modest little motif:

No. 3

They know him, they tell her, but he does not happen to belong to their company, though he will be putting in an appearance shortly, at the changing of the guard. The hand of the matured

426

Bizet is already apparent in this short episode; as in Mozart, the music is all ease and charm yet everywhere germane to the characters, the words and the situation. Micaëla politely declines their pressing invitation to wait for the brigadier in the guard-room, despite their assurance that due respect will be paid to her there. She will return later, she says—"when the guard coming on duty has relieved the guard going off," she adds, singing the words, with a delightful touch of quiet irony, to the tune to which they themselves had formerly sung the words. Moralès and the soldiers take their rebuff philosophically, and, to the strain of our No. 2, they resume their former occupation of watching the crowd with amused eyes.

At the end of the page of the opera we have now reached the reader will find, in the French scores in current use, the instruction to "join up to No. 2." If he takes any notice of this—in all probability he does not see it, but turns over as a matter of course to the next page—he will be puzzled to discover that this is headed not "No. 2" as he expects, but "No. 3." If he retraces his steps he will find that "No. 1" is the overture, while the scene we have just been describing is marked "No. 2," at the end of which he is now rather surprisingly invited to "join up to No. 2." The explanation of the mystery is that in the original lay-out of the opera there came, between the scene we have just been analysing and the next one—the chorus of street urchins—an extended episode in which, to the great amusement of Moralès and the soldiers, a young wife, promenading on the arm of her elderly husband, is pursued through the crowd by a young lover, who finally manages to slip a letter into her hand. All this was omitted when Carvalho re-staged *Carmen* in 1883, and taken out of the published score; the primary object of the librettists seems to have been twofold—in the first place to give the player of the part of Moralès an opportunity to exhibit his vocal powers in three stanzas of song, in the second place to help fill up the necessary stage time between the exit of Micaëla and the arrival of José. The complete text of the episode, together with the directions as to the miming of it, is easily accessible today in the imprint of the *Carmen* libretto in the collected works of Meilhac and Halévy.

10

We are a fairly long way as yet from even an adumbration of the Carmen-José tragedy hinted at in the closing bars of the overture. The makers of the work have decided, not without reason, that there ought to be a slow approach to this by way of light relief and local colour; and both are liberally supplied in the episode that now follows. In the distance is heard a military cornet fanfare: the new guard is on its way. The retiring guard take up their lances and line up before an officer; and soon the relieving company comes into view, to the strains of a march in the high-piping tones of the piccolos:

No. 4

The incoming guard is followed by a number of small boys—Meilhac and Halévy's instructions to the producer are that they shall be "as tiny as possible"; later come José, the lieutenant Zuniga, and the dragoons with their lances. While the new and the old guard line up smartly in front of each other, the urchins, marching with exaggerated military discipline, sing their own praises in a delightful chorus to the melody of No. 4; and at the end of the usual ritual of the changing of the guard, the saluting, and all the rest of it, they strut out with the departing troop with the same air of self-importance with which they had entered. Meanwhile Moralès, before leaving the scene, has had time to get in a word with José. He tells him that a young girl in a blue skirt and with her hair in plaits has been enquiring for him. "It must be Micaëla!" exclaims José, after the violins have repeated softly the tiny motif (No. 3) that had accompanied her entry. (We should probably regard José's remarks as a private expression of surprise rather than a piece of information for Moralès' benefit; otherwise it is difficult for us to understand why the news of Micaëla's unexpected presence in Seville should be taken so nonchalantly by José. We shall see in a moment that it was necessary for the librettists' purposes that Moralès should give José this information before he leaves and that he should be overheard by the lieutenant of the incoming guard, a pretext thus being provided for the later talk between José and the lieutenant in which the former manages to give the audience a sketch of his early life.)

The real significance of Moralès announcement and José's curt comment on it comes out in the scene that follows next in the opera, but not so clearly there as in the original libretto. In the former all we get is this brief conversation in recitative between José and the lieutenant of the new guard, Zuniga:

Zuniga: Is not that big building opposite where the girls who make cigars work?
José: It is, sir; and assuredly a flightier lot are not to be found anywhere.
Zuniga: They are pretty, I suppose?
José: I know nothing about that; I don't concern myself with gallantries of that sort.
Zuniga: I know well what occupies *you*, my friend . . . ! [here the orchestra gives out a reminder of No. 3] . . . a charming young girl of the name of Micaëla, in a blue skirt and with her hair in plaits. What do you say to that!
José: I say it is true, that I love her. As for the work-girls here and their beauty, judge for yourself; here they come.

Whereupon there begins the "chorus of the cigar-makers," in which the townspeople take part, for these damsels, as Mérimée explains in considerable detail, are one of the sensations of Seville.

11

But in the original libretto the spoken dialogue between José and the lieutenant had run to much greater but by no means unnecessary length. The former favours Zuniga with much more information about the girls: it appears that there are some four or five hundred of them, and as they discard most of their garments when at work—the younger among them in particular—men are not allowed to enter the factory without permission. To the lieutenant's question "Are they pretty?" José replies with a careless laugh, "I suppose so; but to tell you the truth I am not quite sure, for although I have mounted guard here several times I have never looked very closely at them. As a matter of fact these Andalusian women rather frighten me. I don't quite understand them—always joking, never saying a sensible word." Zuniga remarks quizzingly that perhaps José prefers blue skirts and plaits down to the shoulders—from which it becomes clear that he has overheard Moralès' parting words. José admits the soft impeachment; blue skirts and plaits, he explains, are the marks of the girls of Navarre, and mention of them reminds him of his native land. He regales the lieutenant with a short chapter of autobiography, in very much the words that Mérimée puts into his mouth in the prison. He is Don José Lizzarrabengua, he says, a Navarro of the old Christian faith, and there follows the account of his training for the Church and of the game of paume with its unfortunate sequel. He had been forced to flee the country and enlist as a soldier in Spain. His father was already dead; so his mother had followed her son and settled a few miles from Seville with little Micaëla [1]—an orphan whom his mother had adopted and who is inseparable from the old lady. (This Micaëla is only seventeen years old, a detail which producers and singers should do their best to live up to.) José's story having ended, the lieutenant remarks drily that he understands now why the young man does not know whether the cigar-girls are beautiful or ugly. Just then the factory bell tolls. "In a moment," José tells the lieutenant, "you will be able to judge for yourself. As for me, I am going to make a chain to hang my *épinglette* [priming-iron] on."

It will already be suspected that Guiraud did Bizet no great service in general in substituting recitative for much of the spoken dialogue of the original text, and more particularly in cutting down this conversation between Zuniga and José (which occupies two-and-a-half pages of the Meilhac-Halévy text) to the few lines of dialogue in recitative given on page 429. The longish conversation between the pair is really necessary in order to acquaint the audience with the pre-history of the Basque José, to explain how

[1] There is nothing of this, of course, in Mérimée: it was an invention practically forced on the librettists once they had decided to create Micaëla. It serves to account for the Navarre girl now being within such easy distance of Seville, and provides an explanation for her being at present in the town, as the bearer of a message from José's mother. Her convenient residence in the neighbourhood further explains her being able to penetrate to the smugglers' haunt in act three in order to sing an aria that is no more than the soprano's due—for this is opera.

he comes to be in Seville, and to emphasise the native simplicity
of the young soldier who is soon to be entangled in the web
woven for him by the Fates with Carmen as their instrument.[1]

The lunch-bell has brought the usual crowd of idlers into the
square to see the girls erupt from the factory. Even the soldiers
come out of the guard-room: of them all, only José remains indifferent, concentrating placidly on his chain. A number of infatuated young men go through what is evidently the established
ritual of laying their hearts at the girls' feet, in a charming little
chorus of tenors in unison, the harmonies and modulations of
which are just pleasantly piquant to the ears of today but no
doubt were a bit of a problem to the typical Opéra-Comique
audience of 1875: we see Bizet at work here with one of his usual
devices—switching the harmony into a seemingly remote key,
poising for a moment on an alien chord, then serenely and surely
making his way back to the main key of the piece.

As the cigar-girls saunter across the stage nonchalantly smoking
their cigarettes—somewhat unfeminine behaviour, one imagines,
in respectable Paris circles in the 1870's—the basses among their
young admirers [2] comment on their saucy self-assurance in a little
unison chorus; then the girls break into a song in praise of the
cigarette; in the lazy curl and glide and swaying syncopations of
the music we seem to get the aural equivalent of the floating
patterns of the smoke:

No. 5

<hr/>

[1] At the top of the page (of the present score) on which the chorus of the
cigar-girls begins there still remains the direction, "Cue [i.e. for the resump-
tion of the music after the spell of conversation]: 'Quant à moi, je vais faire
une chaîne pour attacher mon *épinglette*.'" These are the final words of José
to the lieutenant in the Meilhac-Halévy text; they do not of themselves make
sense in the score, where the brief conversation in recitative ends with José's
"There goes the bell, and now you will be able to judge for yourself," and
the direction is given to "run on to No. 4 (the chorus)." In the Italian-
German score the "cue" is omitted.

[2] In the original text it is the soldiers.

Bizet develops the vocal and orchestral ensemble with the finest art. The scoring of the episode is a miracle of delicate suggestion —muted strings, sustained harp chords, wood-wind, and muted first violins and violas playing softly with the lulling syncopations of our No. 5 etc.

The young men have no sooner commented on the regretted non-appearance of la Carmencita when she enters, with a bouquet of cassia in her corsage and a flower of the same species in the corner of her mouth: she is accompanied in the violins by a new version—expressive now not of Fate but of Carmen herself—of the motif given out at the end of the overture (No. 1):

No. 6

It is punctuated now by full-volumed staccato chords in wood-wind and brass. The motif is repeated frequently during what immediately follows—an appeal from the young men (tenors) to be informed when she will begin to love them. Her opening words—"I do not know: perhaps never, perhaps tomorrow"— are a magical musical stroke on Bizet's part, the key-shift in the second half of the phrase and the sudden drop from forte to piano being curiously impressive:

No. 7

In the score she is instructed to address these words to the men "after a rapid glance at Don José." But this is surely a plain mis-direction: she has not been on the stage a minute, and so far has been besieged by her eager young adorers. It is difficult to suppose that she has no sooner burst out of the factory than she fastens her eyes on the brigadier sitting apart from the others on the left of the stage, whom she has never seen before, and vows by implication to love *him*, if ever, perhaps tomorrow. Meilhac and Halévy's directions were quite different: "Enter Carmen . . . accompanied by three or four young men; they follow her about, surround her, speak to her; she coquets with them. José raises his head; he glances at Carmen, then sets to work tranquilly again at his chain."

12

"But not today, that is certain," are her final words before she expounds her happy-go-lucky philosophy of love to her adorers in the famous habanera, the thesis of which is that love is a rebellious bird that comes when it wills, not when it is summoned.[1] Threats and prayers are alike in vain: love is gipsy by nature, recognising no law; and she, Carmen, is a true gipsy whose philosophy is "I will love you whether you love me or not; and if I love you, beware!"

The words of the habanera are almost entirely by Bizet himself. He is said to have composed the piece only because he was importuned to do so, and to have rewritten it a dozen times to suit the caprice of Galli-Marié, who wanted an effective show piece immediately after her first entry. The habanera, by the way, is one of the few numbers in *Carmen* that have a Spanish, or at any rate Spanish-American, origin: the tune was the work of one Sebastian Yradier (1809–1865). Bizet, who had been familiar with it for some years, appears to have taken it for granted that it was a folk-song. He has improved considerably on the original. A good deal of ink has been wasted on the question of whether Bizet ought not to have given a more authentically "Spanish" cast as a whole to his "Spanish" opera; the point having been overlooked that *Carmen* is a French opera set in Spain. We might as well censure Mozart for not having given a more specifically Neapolitan tinge to his *Così fan Tutte* by bestrewing it with specimens of the folk-music of the locality, or disapprove of Strauss's *Elektra* because its music is not in the least ancient Greek but wholly modern German.

[1] The librettists no doubt took their cue from José's remark to Mérimée in the prison, to the effect that women and cats are alike in this respect, they "come not when they are called but when they are not."

The habanera, which is interspersed with ejaculations from the chorus, begins each stanza in the minor but terminates in a refrain in the major:

No. 8

p L'a-mour est en-fant de Bo-hême, il n'a ja-mais, ja-mais con-nu de loi.

that is of more direct dramatic significance, embodying as it does Carmen's persistent warning, "If you love me not, I will love you; and if I love you, then beware!"

13

At the end of the song the young men begin again to flock round Carmen and make their appeal to her, but by this time she has lost interest in them. The allegro tempo changes to andante moderato as the Carmen-Fate motif (No. 1) asserts itself in the clarinets, violas and 'cellos, gradually fading out in an interval of a diminished seventh that is like a question mark. Evidently a crucial point in the drama has been reached. The stage directions in the score read thus: "Carmen looks at the young men who surround her, then turns her eyes on Don José. She hesitates, takes a few steps towards the factory, then returns and goes straight to José, who is still engaged on his chain. She takes a cassia flower from her corsage and throws it at him." According to the libretto there comes "a moment of silence" *before* this piece of dumb-show. But obviously the silence should come *after* her approach to José. No specific provision is made for it in the score, but the place for it is clearly after the interval of the diminished seventh in the 'cellos referred to above. This is followed by a silent fermata in the orchestra which the conductor should force upon our attention: it is during this moment or two of complete silence in the orchestra and on the stage that Carmen's fateful resolution is taken; and the precise moment of its taking is when the cornets and trombones strike in with a single brusque staccato dissonant chord.

Then comes the brief dialogue that does not appear in the current scores, and for which we have to turn to the libretto:

Carmen: What are you doing there, my friend?
José: I am making a wire chain to hang my *épinglette* on.
Carmen (with a laugh): Your *épinglette!* Upon my soul! Your *épinglette*, pin-maker (*épinglier* [1]) of my heart!

It is then that she throws the cassia flower at him. It strikes him between the eyes; he rises angrily, and it falls at his feet. The factory bell rings for the second time—the summons to return— and the stage empties, Carmen and the other girls going into the building, Zuniga and the soldiers into the guard-room, to a derisive repetition by the sopranos of the habanera refrain, "L'amour est enfant de Bohème" (No. 8), while the orchestra accompanies the general exit with a sweeping melody and mocking reiterations of No. 1:

No. 9

The gipsy poison has begun to work.

Guiraud now steps in with a short scene in recitative (numbered No. 6 *bis*) in which José muses upon the audacity of Carmen and the pungency of the scent of the flower she has hurled at him; then Micaëla appears. In the original the spoken text is rather longer, though to the same general effect; it is only during this soliloquy that José picks up the flower, not, as in the ordinary French vocal score, during the short orchestral postlude that accompanies the emptying of the stage. He repeats Mérimée's tag about the similarity between women and cats, and smiles at Carmen's effrontery. It is only when he smells the flower that we detect the beginning of a subtle change in him: "assuredly if there are sorceresses," he remarks, "that woman is one of them."

For the time being, however, she is swept out of his mind by Micaëla, who returns to tell him that she has come with a letter and a message and a small gift of money from his mother. There

[1] The play on words—*épingle,* pin, *épinglier,* pin-maker, *épinglette* (priming-pin for a gun), is necessarily unproduceable in translation. In Mérimée there is an added touch of insult: "Ah!" says Carmen, "the gentleman makes lace, since he has need of *épingles*"; and the onlookers laugh at the mortified soldier, whose blood rushes to his face, but who can think of no retort.

follows a tender duet, the most significant section of which, for the analyst, is that in which she delivers the mother's message to her son:

No. 10

Allegro moderato ♩=88

Et — tu lui di-ras que sa mè-re Son-ge nuit et jour— à l'ab-sent,

whom she has pardoned, for whom she prays day and night, and whom she hopes to have restored to her soon. Micaëla has been further commissioned to convey a kiss from mother to son. José's heart is flooded with tender memories of his village home and native land. A shadow darkens the picture for a moment as he thinks of "the demon whose prey I had nearly become," and Micaëla asks anxiously what is the meaning of his words. But he brushes the question aside and the tender duet is resumed. Micaëla is leaving Seville that evening and will be with his mother on the morrow; she is to assure her that her son will always be worthy of her; and José sends a return kiss by way of a pledge.

14

The scene that follows the departure of Micaëla is a condensation of the original text; José reads his mother's letter—to an expressive quiet breathing of No. 10 in the strings—promises to obey her exhortations, and vows he will marry Micaëla; and he dismisses "the witch and her flower" with a shrug of the shoulders. But just as he is about to remove the flower from his tunic there comes a hullabaloo from inside the factory, from which the girls soon pour out in great excitement; "it was la Carmencita!" some of them are crying. The noise brings the lieutenant and some soldiers out of the guard-house. There ensues a masterly musical ensemble, in which every feature of the animated episode is dexterously hit off—the ceaseless cackle of the women and the vain attempts of Zuniga to make himself heard. As to what had happened to cause all this uproar it appears that there are two schools of thought among the women, some siding with Carmen, others with her antagonist Manuelita; there had been an interchange of contumelious repartee between these two ornaments of the factory, ending in a reciprocal pulling of hair.

When at last the lieutenant can make himself heard he sends José into the factory with a couple of soldiers to find out what it is all about. They return with Carmen, the orchestra accompanying her entry with the broad melody that had formerly accompanied her exit. The cackling mob of women having been shooed to the back of the stage by the guard, José reports that the matter is rather more serious than had been thought at first. Among some three hundred excited women in the factory he had found one screaming blue murder and asking for a confessor; a cross had been scored on her cheek with two knife-cuts; standing opposite her was la Carmencita, who "said not a word, but ground her teeth and rolled her eyes like a chameleon." He had accordingly "asked mademoiselle to follow him." For a moment it had looked as if she wanted to resist; "then she became resigned, and followed me as meekly as a sheep." This is the whole truth, on the word of a Navarrais, he concludes. At the word "Navarrais" Carmen turns round quickly and fixes her gaze on José: evidently a line of action has suggested itself to her—she will work on the young man's sympathies by pretending that she is a compatriot of his. This little point cannot be too clearly brought out in the stage action; but it is completely frustrated by the omission of the lengthy spoken dialogue and the substitution for it of a few bars of recitative, after which Carmen begins a nonchalant "Tra la la la," followed by the words, "You can cut me, you can burn me, but not a word will you get out of me. I defy everything, fire, steel, and heaven itself. My secret is mine, and I will keep it well; I love another, and will avow it with my dying breath":

No. 11

The melody to which these words are sung was taken by Bizet from one current in Spain, to which Sarasate (who had been a fellow-student of his at the Paris Conservatoire) may possibly

437

have introduced him: Bizet, however, has decidedly improved on the original.

The words themselves have a rather curious prehistory. They were taken by the librettists almost verbatim from *Les Bohémiens,* a prose translation by Mérimée of a poem (*The Gipsies*) by Pushkin which tells of an alien youth, Aleko, who elects to live among the gipsies, with one of whom, Zemfira, he falls deeply in love. One day he is perturbed to hear her singing, half to herself, a wild song of her tribe in which a wife addresses her husband in this wise: "Cut me in pieces, if you will, burn me; I fear neither knife nor fire. I hate and despise you; I love another, and will die loving him. . . ." Like Carmen she prizes liberty before all else, and soon the inevitable catastrophe comes—she ceases to love Aleko and gives herself to another lover. Aleko surprises them and kills them both, the gipsy girl, like Carmen, defying her jealous murderer to the end—"I fear you not; I scorn your threats! Assassin, I curse you! I love another, and loving him I die." [1]

15

Carmen, still to the strain of No. 11, treats with brazen effrontery the attempts of Zuniga to make her behave herself, even going so far as to threaten another of the women with bodily assault. The soldiers finally drive the excited crowd off the stage, and Zuniga calls for a rope to bind the dangerous Carmen's arms. Quite politely he sends her off to prison, where the jailers, he says, will be able to form their own opinion of the quality of her gipsy songs. He consigns her to the custody of José. Left alone with him she switches off her impertinence and becomes as mild as milk. She persuades him to loosen the rope, which is hurting her hands; he does so, but his manner remains professionally aloof. Once more we have to pass the recitative by and resort to the original text to understand fully what happens next. As in Mérimée, Carmen begins with an unblushing attempt at bribery; she offers to give José a piece of the *bar lachi,* a magic stone one fragment of which will make all women fall in love with him. Finding that this does not work she tries another line. She has gathered that he is a Navarrais; she now asserts herself to be a

[1] Pushkin's poem was drawn upon by Rachmaninov for his early one-act opera *Aleko.*

438

native of Etchalar, which is only a few miles from José's birthplace, Elizondo. According to her story, in which of course there is not a word of truth, she had been abducted by gipsies and taken to Seville, where she has been working in the factory with the object of saving enough money to take her back to her poor mother, of whom she is the only support; the Spanish women hate her because she is a Navarraise and proud of it.

José tells her bluntly that he does not believe her story, that everything about her, her mouth, her eyes, her complexion, testifies that she is a gipsy. Thereupon she frankly confesses that she had been lying, and changes her strategy once more. Yes, she is a gipsy, she admits; but all the same the soldier will do whatever she asks, because he loves her, one proof of which is that he has kept the flower she had thrown at him: it is useless to throw it away now, she continues as he makes an angry gesture, for the charm has already worked. He forbids her to say any more. Very well, she replies; but if she is not allowed to speak she can at least be permitted to sing. There follows a tiny musical episode that has been the subject of some comment, the meaning of which, however, is perfectly clear if we follow the guidance of the librettists' text. José's angry ejaculation, "Do you hear me? Speak no more! I forbid you to speak!" is clinched by a furious gesture in the orchestra, terminating in a single peremptory fortissimo F minor chord. But instantaneously the mood of the music changes, the explanation of this being afforded by the stage direction in the original text after Carmen's "You forbid me to speak? Very well, I will speak no more"—"She fixes her gaze on José, who recoils." It is obviously to this psychological turn in the action that the short orchestral passage that follows the F minor chord relates: a quiet, insinuating melody first in the violas, then in the violins, supported by an occasional pizzicato string chord:¹ Carmen's glance and José's recoil mark the first under-

---

¹ It is often said that Bizet knew nothing of Wagner's music later than *Lohengrin*. This is hardly credible. In 1871, in a letter to his mother-in-law, he had praised Wagner's music to the skies. By the mid-eighteen-seventies the scores of *Tristan*, the *Meistersinger* and much of the *Ring* had been published; and we ask ourselves whether it is at all likely that so passionate an admirer of the German composer as Bizet was would have been content to let his acquaintance with him terminate with *Lohengrin*. In the case of our

No. 12

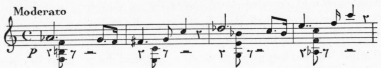

mining of his defences. As Bizet himself had said to Galabert à *propos* of Myrrha and Yorick, "the serpent has come, and the bird is half paralysed."

With an enharmonic change, the A flat of the last bar of our No. 12 now being treated as G sharp, the music makes towards the new key of F sharp. Three bars suffice for this harmonic shift; then, over the characteristic seguidilla rhythm:

No. 13

Carmen sings the captivating seguidilla, with its piquant fluctuations between major and minor:

No. 14

At Lillas Pastia's tavern near the gates of Seville, she sings, she will dance the seguidilla and drink manzanilla, but not alone. Her new lover will accompany her there; lovers she already has in plenty, but now she is José's and José hers. Distractedly he bids her be silent, but she protests that she is singing only to herself, thinking only of a certain officer, not a captain, not even a lieu-

---

example No. 12 the later-Wagnerian filiation is surely obvious. Nor is it the only instance of the kind in the *Carmen* score.

tenant, merely a brigadier, whom she is capable of loving to her heart's full content. In vain the bird struggles in the net; when José stammers his protests it is to the intoxicating rhythm of her song that he does so; he sees things now only through Carmen's eyes, his blood beats now only to her pulse. Finally his defences collapse: "I am like a drunken man," he cries; "if I give myself up to you will you keep your promise, Carmen? You will return my love?", and he unfastens the rope that binds her hands. Her reply is a reiteration of the seguidilla, ending in an exultant "Tra la la la."

The atmosphere changes, and we have the feeling of coming down to realistic earth again, as Zuniga comes out of the guard-room with the order for Carmen's committal to prison; he is entirely the soldier, concerned with nothing but the unpleasant but necessary practical business in hand:

No. 15

Carmen sits down demurely, her hands, now quite free, behind her back. To José she says *sotto voce*, "On the bridge I will push you as hard as I can. Fall down; the rest leave to me." Nonchalantly humming the refrain of her habanera, "L'Amour est enfant de Bohème" (No. 8), she places herself between the two men. By now the crowd has come upon the stage again, though the soldiers keep it at a distance from the protagonists. When Carmen and her escort reach the bridge her habanera suddenly merges into a derisive reiteration of No. 15 in the orchestra as, to the amusement of the crowd, she gives José a push and runs. He pretends to fall. Carmen throws the rope over the parapet of the bridge in triumph and disappears, while as the curtain falls the factory girls surround Zuniga and burst into peals of mocking laughter.

16

In the second act we see Bizet really getting into his stride as a musical dramatist; for every smallest turn in the action, serious or humorous, he will now find the right music.

Before the rise of the curtain there comes a short orchestral entr'acte in which he makes use of the theme of the unaccompanied ditty that José will sing later (see No. 20) on his way to the tavern of Lillas Pastia, after spending a month in prison for his connivance at Carmen's escape. There seems at first sight no very logical dramatic reason why the song should put in an appearance now; but, as Henry Malherbe has pointed out, it is subtly apposite to the occasion. Its scoring has throughout a burlesque tinge, with its predominance of clarinet and bassoon colours, its trills, and its drum-taps marking the rhythm: and the general dynamic effect, with its gradual decline to a quadruple pianissimo at the finish, is that of a march-past. Bizet is artfully preparing us for a second act in which the military will play a considerable part, and that not a very dignified one. It is in a sense light relief, but light relief of a curiously appropriate kind.

José's assignation with Carmen in the first act had been at Lillas Pastia's tavern that stands near the city gate: it is a regular meeting-place of the band of smugglers of which Carmen is now one of the leading lights. It is also the resort of some of the army officers, who obviously come there, as on the present occasion, to enjoy the company of the gipsy girls, a couple of whom we see dancing as the curtain rises, while the others are smoking cigarettes with the officers, for dinner has just ended. The music of the dance is a lively affair, with the melody mostly given out at first by the flutes in thirds over a pizzicato accompaniment in violas and 'cellos, many piquant key-shifts, and an orchestral texture in which cymbals, triangle and tambourine play an occasional part:

No. 16

Carmen, sitting apart from the others, has for companion the lieutenant, Zuniga, to whom, however, she seems to be paying little attention. Suddenly she rises and breaks into a *chanson bohème*. This song of hers, descriptive of the intoxication of gipsy song and revel, sets the dancers in swift motion again, while in her cadences Carmen is joined by two of her companions, Frasquita and Mercédès. After the final mad dance Carmen sinks panting on to a bench. Then, in the original text, the others fall into a discussion, in ordinary speech, of the situation of the moment. Lillas Pastia is anxious to close for the night, for the magistrate, it appears, is none too favourably disposed towards him, though he professes not to know why. Zuniga tells him pleasantly why; it is because his tavern is known to be the resort of all the smugglers of the neighbourhood; and he hazards the guess that the real reason why Lillas Pastia wants to put up the shutters now is that he and his contraband friends have some business to discuss. However, as he has no desire to get the tavern keeper into trouble with the authorities, he suggests to the girls that they shall go off to the theatre for an hour or so with him and his companions. At a surreptitious sign from Pastia they politely decline, Frasquita and Mercédès acting as their spokeswomen. Zuniga then appeals to Carmen, but her refusal is uncompromisingly blunt.

He thinks he can account for her manifest animus against him, and in doing so he makes the audience acquainted, as it has a right to be, with what has happened since the curtain had fallen on the first act. The authorities had sent to prison for a month, as in duty bound, the soldier who had obviously assisted Carmen to escape, and who had been suitably degraded. This seems to be news to Carmen, who repeats after him in serious tones, "Degraded and imprisoned?" She is rejoiced to learn, however, that the peccant soldier had been released the day before. "If he is free," she cries, "all is well"; and with a flourish of her castanets she advises Zuniga and his friends to make themselves scarce as soon as possible. They resign themselves to their brusque dismissal; but before they can depart there comes from off-stage a joyous chorus of welcome to the most skilful and intrepid of toreros, one Escamillo, who is on his way to the tavern accompanied by a torchlight procession of his admirers. The situation being explained to the soldiers, Zuniga and Moralès, blandly ignoring the local licensing regulations, gallantly declare that they will stay where they are and drink a toast in the torero's honour; and the lieutenant, going to the window, invites Escamillo, in spite of Lillas Pastia's protests, to join them within. All this is very

443

skimpily treated in the recitative that Guiraud has substituted for the spoken text.

17

Zuniga having greeted the new-comer courteously on behalf of them all and proposed the toast of "the great art of tauro-machy," Escamillo thanks him in half-a-dozen words, and then, without more ado, plunges into the famous "Toreador's Song"— a splendid piece of swagger against which the voices and the eyebrows of purists have long been raised in vain.[1] He gives us a colourful description of the thrills and dangers of the bull-ring, including the occasional overthrow of a picador, the scattering of the banderilleros, the panic of the spectators, and even a real-istic and most effective imitation of the roar of the maddened bull—or such, at any rate, it appears to be—in a low G flat in the trombone and double basses. Yet even in these perilous circum-stances, it appears, the torero should remember that a pair of dark eyes are fixed on him all the time, and that the loving owner of them is waiting for him. This constitutes the theme of the refrain of his song: [2]

No. 17

It is taken up vigorously by the whole company after each verse. At the conclusion of the song the enthusiasts crowd round the hero, shaking his hand and drinking his health. Shortly before

[1] Bizet is alleged to have thought so little of the Toreador's song that he remarked to the conductor, "Well, they want muck; here it is!" If he really thought it "muck," why did he afterwards give it so prominent a place in the prelude to the opera? The truth underlying the traditional story appears to be that Halévy wanted an "aria" at this point and sent his proposed verses to Bizet, who, after jibbing for a while, at last set the lines to music and handed the whole thing over to Halévy with the ironic remark, "Voici ta saleté!" In any case, no one with any sense of humour and any knowledge of the artistic temperament takes rough-and-ready remarks of this sort seri-ously: they are spoken with a smile, and should be taken with one.

[2] Bizet's marking for the refrain—"Toréador, en garde"—in both verses is "avec fatuité." He also directs it to be sung quietly, not bellowed at us, as is the way with baritones.

444

the exuberant end of the ensemble there comes an extraordinarily impressive series of cadences by Frasquita, Mercédès, Carmen and Escamillo on the words "L'Amour":

No. 18

during the last two of which, according to the stage directions, Carmen looks intently at Escamillo and Escamillo at Carmen; the latter's low D flat has a curious clinching quality.[1]

The spoken version of what immediately follows is more il-luminative than Guiraud's condensation of it in recitative. In response to a renewed appeal from the worried Pastia the com-pany begins to break up; and as it thins out, Escamillo finds him-self close to Carmen, who has apparently captivated him at first sight. The remainder of the scene is carried on in spoken dialogue. Escamillo asks her name, and learns that it is Carmen or la Carmencita, whichever he prefers. Gallantly he declares that it is her name he will speak, according to torero custom, when he kills his next bull. And what if he should say he is in love with her? he asks. She replies that she has no objection to this, but that he can dismiss the notion that she will love him in return. In that case, he says, he will wait in hope: her careless reply is that there is no law against waiting, and to hope is always pleasant.

Moralès and Zuniga now try once more to persuade Frasquita and Mercédès to depart with them, but at another sign from the tavern-keeper they decline. The two officers take their second rebuff in good part, but Zuniga tells Carmen *sotto voce* that he will return in an hour, after the roll-call. She advises him pointedly not to, but he only reiterates his promise; then, accompanied by Moralès and the others, he joins the cortège that is to escort Escamillo home, and, to a repetition in the orchestra of the refrain of the Toreador's song (No. 17), the stage gradually becomes

[1] For some unimaginable reason or other these magical bars are sometimes omitted in performance. I have been told of one conductor who did not even know they were in the score, and had to have them pointed out to him. Perhaps they were crossed out in the theatre score he was using.

empty of all except Pastia, Carmen, Frasquita and Mercédès. "Why were you so anxious to get rid of them?" Frasquita asks Pastia, "and why did you motion to us not to go away?" He explains that he is expecting Dancaïre (the leader of the smugglers' band) and Remendado, to discuss with them "affaires d'Égypte," which is the smugglers' euphemism for their contraband activities. The two worthies in question have been waiting outside for the departure of the crowd. Pastia now opens a door and signs to them to come in; and when they have done so he closes the doors and the window-shutters, and they all settle down to business. Remendado has a strain of irresponsible humour in him which Dancaïre has to check from time to time; the librettists no doubt felt that the habitués of the Opéra-Comique were entitled occasionally to a little comic relief. Dancaïre's news is that they have just come from Gibraltar, where a ship has unloaded some English goods which it is the intention of the band to intercept somewhere in the mountains. To this end they need the assistance of the three girls, not, as Carmen laughingly suggests, to carry bales, but because this is one of the situations in which the natural talent of the female of the species for lying and bamboozling will be of inestimable value. The discussion is carried on in a quintet (Frasquita, Mercédès, Carmen, Remendado, Dancaïre) of incomparable verve and musical wit.

18

At the end of it Frasquita and Mercédès say they are willing to set out with the smugglers at once, but Carmen demurs. While the orchestra carries on with the basic melody of the quintet she explains, to the general horror, that *she* cannot accompany them because she is in love. Remendado and Dancaïre remark ironically:

No. 19

p La cho-se, cer-tes, nous é -tonne, Mais ce n'est pas le prem-ier jour.

that this is no new experience for her; all the same, where business is concerned love must take second place. All through this scene it is clear from the words and the music that these are comic opera smugglers, not taking themselves or their profession too seriously; and we feel that José could afford to throw in his lot with them without undergoing anything of the slow moral degeneration of the José of Mérimée's sombre tale. But in the main we can regard the second act up to now as a sort of dramatic scherzo, designed for the light relief of the audience. Matters, so far as the smugglers are concerned, will take on a more serious tinge in the third act.

Carmen, to the strain of No. 18, replies in the same vein of polite irony; thanks to the genius of Bizet, these smugglers and gitanas, for all their bad upbringing, have perfect manners. In the present instance, she assures them, business will have to come a bad second to love. The others, in another light-footed ensemble, appeal almost plaintively to her better nature; but she is immovable. For the full understanding of what immediately follows we have to by-pass Guiraud and the current score and glance at the original spoken text. Dancaïre makes the mistake of throwing his weight about as leader of the band, entitled to obedience: this of course calls out all that is most rebellious in Carmen's nature, while Dancaïre aims a kick at Remendado, who has mistakenly tried to be facetious once more. To the general dismay Carmen declares that she cannot join them until tomorrow; for tonight she is expecting a man she loves—the poor devil of a soldier who had been put in prison for doing her a service, and whom, a fortnight ago, as Frasquita now discloses, Carmen had tried to liberate by sending him a loaf of bread in which was concealed a gold piece and a file, of neither of which, however, had he availed himself.[1] "You see," says Dancaïre scornfully, "your soldier was afraid of further punishment: tonight too he will be afraid. It's no use your opening the shutters to see if he is coming; I wager that he won't." "You will lose your wager," Carmen retorts; and at that moment José's voice is heard in the distance, singing (unaccompanied) a buoyant little canzonetta in dialogue form:

[1] All this is as in Mérimée. It is important for the light it throws on José's psychology at that stage: he knows that the file will set him free in a few hours, and divines that it has come from Carmen; but he declines to use it because his honour as a soldier forbids; "desertion seemed to me a great crime," he tells his interlocutor in his last hours.

"Halt! Who goes there? . . . A dragoon from Alcalà. . . . Where are you going, dragoon from Alcalà? . . . True and faithful I come where my loved one calls me! . . . Pass then, my friend! . . . Affairs of honour, affairs of love, these mean everything to dragoons from Alcalà!":

No. 20

In the Meilhac-Halévy text it is "Almanza"; but that means nothing so far as the drama is concerned, while "Alcalà" means a great deal. In Mérimée's story the loaf containing a file which was brought to José in prison is described as "un pain d'Alcalà"; and in a footnote Mérimée explains that "Alcalà de los Panaderos" (Alcalà of the Bakers) is a small town not far from Seville famous for the delicious quality of its rolls. For us who know our Mérimée, therefore, the reference to Alcalà in José's song on his way to the tavern has a certain dramatic meaning: Carmen, and she alone, knows at once that it is José who is approaching. The unfortunate thing is that there is nothing in the text to make this clear to the audience—which, no doubt, is why in the Meilhac-Halévy imprint of the text Josè is made to come from Almanza.

During the first verse of the song Dancaïre, Remendado, Carmen, Frasquita and Mercédès have thrown open the shutters to observe the singer. The smugglers like the appearance of this new admirer of Carmen's and opine that he would make a valuable recruit for their band. She half agrees with them, but for the moment can think only of her love for him,[1] so she answers evasively. Obviously the time is approaching when she and José must be left alone on the stage for their big scene; the librettists' way of effecting this is to make Dancaïre chase Remendado out for a remark unusually fatuous even for him, and for Frasquita and Mercédès to follow the pair to make peace between them.

[1] This is made clear enough in the spoken dialogue, but not in the score. Gipsy honour demands that a debt shall be repaid.

All this while José has been drawing nearer and nearer, and his timing is excellent; he manages to make a most effective tenor entry on the last note of his song, a prolonged high G.

19

The dialogue that follows the meeting of the pair is compressed by Guiraud into a few bars of recitative, after which Carmen dances a gipsy *romalis* for José. In the lengthy spoken dialogue, however, a good deal is said that it is necessary for us in the audience to know. José, we learn, has only just been released from prison. Carmen asks him why he had not made use of the file to escape: he replies in the words of Mérimée, that his honour as a soldier forbade him to desert, while the gold piece he now returns to her with a noble gesture. With this unexpected wealth in her possession she summons Pastia and bids him prepare a feast—a detailed later episode in Mérimée being thus condensed and brought within the orbit of the second act of the opera. José tells her of his degradation in rank, which, with all the rest of his punishment, he bears gladly for her sake. She becomes for a minute or two quite kindly and likeable, paying off her debt, as she says the gipsies always do, by pressing on José the oranges and bonbons that Pastia has brought; she herself gormandises like a happy child. She tells him that his lieutenant and other officers had been there a little while before, that she had danced a *romalis* for them, and that the lieutenant had vowed that he adored her. As José shows signs of jealousy on hearing this she promises to dance for him also. In a somewhat similar scene on another occasion in Mérimée, as no castanets are available she breaks a plate and makes do with the two pieces of china. But this, of course, would not do in opera; so the librettists, after first of all making her, quite unnecessarily as it turns out, lose her castanets and then break a plate, find the operatically indispensable castanets for her—they have been on the table all the time!

José having seated himself where she has indicated she performs a dance for his sole benefit, humming a constant "La la la" and marking the rhythm with her castanets. But soon there are heard, from a distance, the cornets sounding the retreat; and Bizet combines the military call with the melody of Carmen, in this fashion:

No. 21

The sound has been too faint as yet to attract the notice of Carmen, but the soldier in José is sensitively aware of it. When he
draws her attention to it—for now it has come nearer—she is at
first merely amused and resumes her dance. But when she realises
—the retreat sounding more and more insistently—that José is
bent on obeying the summons of duty her fury knows no bounds.
In a magnificent piece of musical rhetoric she vents her rage and
scorn on him: she has been dancing for him, and now he would
leave her at the call of "duty"—for by now he has taken up his
cartouche-box and put on his sword-belt. Blind with rage she at
last throws his shako at him and bids him begone. His mournful
humble protestations of his consuming love for her and Carmen's
torrent of abuse are admirably differentiated by Bizet without the
smallest loss of unity of musical tissue. At last, as proof of his
love, José takes from his tunic the flower she had thrown at him
in the first act and shows it to her: he has kept it on him all
through his imprisonment, where it has been his one consolation
for all he has suffered. A very different José now from the one who
had sung of his boyish love for little Micaëla—for the character
of the man is now developing subtly in the imagination of Bizet,—
he tells her, in the Flower Song, how he had kept this cassia flower
in his prison, breathing in its perfume night and day, for it brought
Carmen close to him. At times he had cursed the fate that had
brought her into his life; yet for all that his one desire had been
to see her again.

The Flower Song is unusual in its structure; it flows on, page
by page, with hardly a repeat of phrase, weaving an unbroken
musical web. It has practically nothing of the symmetries of
pattern of the conventional opera aria. In this respect it has a few
notable older and newer confrères: the *Marseillaise* is another of
these continuous melodies, while songs like Strauss's *Seitdem dein*

Aug' and Wolf's *An die Geliebte* belong to the same non-repetitive
or hardly repetitive type. The ending of the Song is a sore trial
to any tenor. First of all there comes, to the words "Et j'étais une
chose à toi," a slow ascending scale that culminates in a long-held
high B flat; and the marking for both voice and orchestra is
pianissimo! The passage, while psychologically veracious, is undoubtedly a technical blunder on Bizet's part, for it leaves the
ordinary tenor confronted with only two alternatives, each of
which is fatal to the intention of the phrase—he must either sing
it fortissimo, or, if his artistic conscience will not permit him anything but a pianissimo, resort to an anaemic falsetto. Now in 1869
Bizet had censured Galabert for having written a phrase for the
Claribel of *La Coupe du roi de Thule* expressive enough in itself
but inconveniently high in the vocal register; "How can you expect anyone," he had asked his pupil, "to enunciate distinctly at
this exceptional pitch and at the same time produce a smooth,
sweet, unforced tone?" Yet in 1875 we find the admirable theo-
retician flying in the face of his own sound precepts!

Nor is he entirely happy in the phrase that follows—the final
cadence of the Song:

No. 22

where the curious brief evasion by the orchestra (the high wood-
wind) of the key of D flat not only makes any departure from
the pitch on the tenor's part all too evident, but even today has
an air of calculated oddity. To the ears of the Opéra-Comique
audience of 1875 it must have been a puzzle and a trial.

20

Carmen is sobered by José's confession óf devotion. When the
brief orchestral postlude to the Song has come to a quiet and

expressive end she mutters on a low D flat—a most effective touch, this—"No, you do not love me!", and then launches one of the most curiously enigmatic passages in the whole work, in which the six-eight rhythm seems at variance with, and yet is subtly inwrought with, the melancholy of the words. The gipsy is overcome by nostalgia for the mountains, whither, she says, Josè must follow her—to the mountains, where both will be free of the pressure of other lives on theirs, where José will carry her on his saddle with no officer to give him orders, no retreat to obey, where they can breathe the divine air of liberty. José is drawn into the stream of her song and her thought. For a while he is on the point of succumbing; then the soldier in him asserts himself once more, and he begs her despairingly, in a splendid phrase in which passion and despair contend for the mastery, to have pity on him, for follow her he cannot:

No. 23

Hé-las! hé-las! pi-tié Car—men,—pi-tié! O mon Dieu! hé—las!

(This moving cry appears to be one of Bizet's own touches; the words do not appear in the Meilhac-Halévy text.)

At last he manages to shake off the fascination; recalling his honour as a soldier he tears himself from Carmen's arms. Thereupon her mood changes: she tells him she hates him, and furiously orders him out. He bids her a sad farewell for ever; but just as he reaches the door a knock is heard. "Keep silent!" Carmen whispers to José. The door opens, and with a confident cry of "Holà! Carmen! Holà!" Zuniga enters. Catching sight of José he addresses an ironical reproach to Carmen—"A misalliance! Taking up with a common soldier when you might have had an officer!" Roughly he orders José to make himself scarce, and when he twice refuses the lieutenant strikes him. Swords are drawn and bloodshed seems imminent; but at a wild cry from Carmen the smugglers and gipsies pour in, and the great finale begins.

At a gesture from Carmen, the lieutenant is seized by Dancaïre and Remendado and disarmed. A masterpiece of musical irony follows; Carmen politely condoles with Zuniga for having had the bad luck to arrive at an inopportune moment, and Dancaïre and Remendado, with their pistols pointed at his head, take up the polished argument; they are all under the necessity of leaving the tavern at once, and the lieutenant will be good enough to accompany them—"just a promenade," Carmen tells him. Zuniga, not to be outdone in politeness, assures them that no one on earth could resist such potent arguments as theirs, but, still apparently in the best of humours, he advises them to have a care later. The menace beneath his polished phrase is admirably hit off by Bizet in three bars of trills in the strings—even the double basses joining in—that are like the hissing of a pit of serpents, but serpents with Chesterfieldian manners:

No. 24

"War is war," replies Dancaïre philosophically, "and now have the goodness to come along with us quietly." The lieutenant is conducted out by four of the gipsies, each presenting a persuasive pistol at his head. Then, as the company takes up joyously the strain of Carmen's paean to liberty, she herself has a quiet word with José. "You will be one of us henceforth?" she asks. With a sigh he answers, "I have no choice!" She comments drily that though the reply might have been given with a better grace, it will do; and the whole company, turning to José, assure him, still to the strain of Carmen's previous appeal to him, that no life is finer than theirs—an open sky, a wandering life, and above all the intoxication of liberty.

José is now fairly in the net: henceforth he will be, as regards his outer life, a smuggler, an outlaw, and as regards his inner life the slave of Carmen's whims and passions. Necessarily the opera cannot depict for us in such grim detail as Mérimée could permit himself the slow disintegration of the man's soul, his inevitable drift from crime to crime, the mad jealousy aroused by Carmen's amorous caprices: but for all that the librettists, with Bizet's help, have done very well. It is really José, not Carmen, who is the psychological centre of the drama, just as in Prévost's story it is Des Grieux, not Manon Lescaut, who should claim our main attention and sympathy; for it is the men who go through one psychological transformation after another, whereas the two women are basically the same from first to last. Carmen is the same Carmen in each act of the opera, while, thanks almost entirely to Bizet, José is a different being each time we meet him. So pronounced is the difference between the José of the first act and the José of the last that even vocally they seem to call for different types of voice and style—an agreeable lyric tenor for the first act, a powerful dramatic tenor for the fourth.

21

As is his way, Bizet places an orchestral entr'acte between his second and third acts. This is an exquisite miniature, with much melodic dialoguing and interwining between the wood-wind instruments. It was originally intended for the *L'Arlésienne* score, where its pastoral quality would have been quite in place. There has been much discussion as to its appropriateness here in the opera: some critics have censured it as having no justification at all on dramatic grounds; others have welcomed it as bringing with it a momentary contrast to, and relief from, the gradually darkening atmosphere of the tragedy. Both are right in their way; neither can be confuted because there is no common ground for argument between them. The only sensible thing to do seems to be to accept the entr'acte for the lovely delicate thing it is and not enquire too closely into its dramatic relevance.

The concluding E flat major chord of the entr'acte is continued for a couple of bars in the orchestra after the curtain rises. The scene is "a wild and picturesque rocky place in the mountains: the solitude and the darkness are complete." A few smugglers are seen here and there lying on the ground, wrapped in their cloaks; gradually others become visible, carrying bales of merchandise. In the orchestra we seem to see and hear their cautious, laboured movements, to sense an air of secrecy and danger in all they do:

454

No. 25

Note the steady step-by-step tread of the bass (in this case violas and 'cellos) so characteristic of Bizet. This sense of slow wary movement as the smugglers exhort each other to be on the alert becomes intensified in the pianissimo orchestral accompaniment to their chorus:

No. 26

and reaches its climax in a series of descending chromatics in which they sing "Take care not to make one false step":

No. 27

The atmosphere lightens for a moment as the three women, with Dancaïre, Remendado and José—for he is irrevocably one of the smugglers now—unite in a sextet; then the sombre No. 26, No. 27 and No. 25 are resumed. The ensemble ends with a general cry of "Take care! Take care!" that tapers off into a meaningful pianissimo.

In the text proper there follow now some pages of spoken dialogue. Dancaïre addresses the band; anyone who wishes to sleep can do so; he himself, taking Remendado with him, will

455

reconnoitre their chances of getting the goods into the town. There is a breach in the wall at one point at which an official will be keeping guard: Lillas Pastia has assured him that the man will be in their pay, but they must not be too confident. Meanwhile some of the gipsies have lit a fire at which Frasquita and Mercédès seat themselves while the men wrap themselves up in their cloaks to sleep. José seizes the occasion to have a few words of explanation with Carmen. They have evidently quarrelled recently, and he is anxious to make peace. She is unfriendly and hard: she loves him less than she had done, she says, and if he continues to pester her it will end in her not loving him at all, for her liberty means more to her than the love of any man. He speaks sadly of a village only a few miles away in which is an old woman—his mother—who still believes that her son is an honest man. Carmen scornfully advises him to go back to this mother of his, for the smuggler's life plainly is not one for such as he. When he threatens her she replies, "Perhaps you will kill me? Very well! I have often read it in the cards that you and I will die together." With a clack of her castanets she turns her back on him and seats herself near Frasquita and Mercédès, where she watches in silence their consultation of the cards. José, after a moment's hesitation, walks away and stretches himself on a rock.

All this is replaced in the score by a few pages of recitative, into which, at the mention of José's mother, there is introduced a reminiscence in the orchestra of our No. 10 from the first act, and, when Carmen hints that José should leave the band, another of our No. 1; and after she has suggested that some day he may kill her, with the added reflection that after all Fate is master, she makes her way to the card players.

22

The scene of the cards is an enchanting musical vignette, giving not only our ears but our spirits a grateful relief until Carmen shall step into the forefront of the action again and spread a sinister cloud over it. Her two companions are reading their fortunes in the cards. Frasquita sees a romantic young lover who carries her off on his horse into the mountains, where he becomes a famous chief with a hundred men in his service: Mercédès is wooed by an elderly lover who marries her, loads her with gold and jewels, and then, most considerately, dies, leaving her his sole legatee. Twice the prattle of the girls is rounded off by a charming duet:

No. 28

in which they exhort the cards to tell them truly who will love and who will deceive them.

The duet dies away in an orchestral postlude based on the final bar of our last musical example; and this, by a stroke of genius, Bizet instantaneously metamorphoses into the typical Carmen motif (No. 6):

No. 29

For Carmen, who so far has been watching the two girls, has now begun to turn the cards herself. "Diamonds! Spades! Death!" she mutters; "I first, then he. Death for both of us!"; and she points to the sleeping José. Still throwing the cards she muses sombrely, over a throbbing orchestral accompaniment, on the infallibility of this mode of divination—if your fate is settled you may cut the cards hopefully twenty times, but the pitiless answer will be always the same—death! So nothing matters; she will be fearless to the end. Her gloomy monologue terminates in a cadence of extraordinarily tragic power; but the words are hardly out of her mouth before Frasquita and Mercédès, wholly absorbed in their own game, break in with their light-hearted No. 28; and this time Carmen weaves through the bright texture her own dark thread of foreboding.

By now Dancaïre and Remendado have returned with the news that the breach in the town wall is guarded not by one official but by three. The women cheerfully profess themselves capable of dealing with these in their own way, whereupon José turns furiously upon Carmen. Dancaïre roughly orders him to put his jealousy in his pocket, for this is neither the time nor the place for it; daylight is almost on them, and they must act. José is left behind, posted on a rock from which he will have a good view of the country all around; his task is to guard such of the bales of merchandise as the smugglers are leaving behind them for the present. This bit of spoken dialogue—not provided for in the recitative in the score—is essential to the spectator's understanding of what happens a little later; for Dancaïre's final words to José are, "You will be able to see if we are followed: if you should sight anyone, you have my permission to deal with him in the appropriate way."

All except José now make their exit in the best of spirits, singing gaily, in a rousing ensemble, of their confidence in their ability to handle the douaniers if occasion should arise: the orchestra continues the vigorous strain for a little while after their departure. As the stage will be wanted in a minute or two by Micaëla for her aria it is now necessary for the librettists to get José off the stage as plausibly as they can. So they make him follow the smugglers out, examining as he does so the priming of his carbine, presumably to make sure that if a minion of the law should appear he will be able to deal with him according to Dancaïre's instructions. The next thing we see and hear in the score is Micaëla, after a brief orchestral prelude and a recitative, breaking into her aria. How has the simple girl managed, the spectator asks himself, to find her way in the dark with such certainty to this wild place? The opening words of her recitative are hardly sufficient explanation: "This is the usual resort of the smugglers. Here I will find him, and discharge without a tremor the duty laid on me by his mother." But in the text proper she appears dialoguing with a guide, who, in reply to her expression of surprise that there are no smugglers there, explains that they have just left, but will return soon for the remainder of their goods. Micaëla, he says, is to keep her eyes open, for it is the custom of these gentry to leave a sentinel somewhere, and if he sees her the consequences to her may be awkward. He congratulates her on the courage she has so far shown, even when they had found themselves in the middle of a herd of savage bulls in the charge of "the celebrated Escamillo." (This is the librettists' rather innocent way of preparing us for the bull-fighter's popping up a few minutes later.) Since Micaëla is bent on staying where she is the guide takes leave of her; he has accompanied her thus far, he says, only because she has paid him well, and if she should need him again she will find him where she had hired him, in the inn at the foot of the mountain. And so, invoking all the saints of paradise to protect her, he leaves Micaëla to her fate and her aria, the first section of the latter being devoted to assuring herself that her courage will not fail her, the second to a resolve to confront the evil woman who has caught her José in her toils and rescue him if she can, and the third to a *da capo* repeat of the first section, with a final prayer to heaven for its protection.

She drops into plain prose as she catches sight of José on a rock not a hundred feet from her; she calls to him, but apparently he has not seen her and does not hear her. He is looking at someone in the opposite direction, at whom he fires; whereupon Micaëla, declaring that she has "presumed too much on her courage," flies in terror, and we see no more of her for some time.

23

What we do see now is Escamillo, studying his hat, which has a bullet hole in it: "an inch or two lower," he nonchalantly informs us, "and it would not be I who would be fighting the bulls I am taking to the Seville arena!" José comes into view with a drawn knife, and Escamillo introduces himself—a toreador from Granada. José has heard of him, and gives him a friendly hint that it might have been better for him to have stayed in Granada. Escamillo agrees in principle, bulls, seemingly, being less dangerous than smugglers bearded in their lair, but points out that he is obeying the call of love. The woman he adores is a gipsy, a member of the smugglers' band, a certain Carmen, who at one time had been in love with a soldier whom she had befriended; Carmen's liking for him, however, had not lasted six months. All this—and the discovery on Escamillo's part that the "soldier" was the smuggler now standing before him—leads of course to a quarrel, during which, while José loses command of himself, Escamillo remains invincibly polite and ironic. As regards the fight with knives that follows, the score and the Meilhac-Halévy text take different lines. In the former the end comes quickly:

Escamillo's knife breaks, and José is about to finish him off when Carmen and the others enter. In the latter there are two stages to the combat. First of all José is at the mercy of Escamillo, who magnanimously grants him his life. As he remains defiant the fight is resumed: this time Escamillo slips and falls, and Carmen arrives just in time to save him. There is no good reason operatically for all this: one round of the fight, we feel, is enough, more especially as Bizet is in the main not at the height of his form in this episode. He finds himself again, however, in the grave phrase in which Escamillo thanks Carmen for having saved his life. Politely, as usual, he promises José to resume their combat at the first convenient moment.

At this point Dancaïre intervenes: there is no time for any more of this bickering just now, he says, for business calls them. He bids adieu to Escamillo, who courteously invites them all to the bull-fight at Seville, where he will do his best to earn their approval; "anyone who loves me will be there," he adds with a glance at Carmen. The smouldering José makes a furious gesture and is about to attack Escamillo again; but the toreador waves him aside, in a telling passage in which the calmness of his words and manner contrasts with the veiled menace of the orchestra:

No. 30

Bizet's handling of this episode has been throughout a remarkable fusion of the dramatic and the musical.

Escamillo departs with great dignity to an expressive slow reminiscence in the orchestra of the refrain of his song in the second act (No. 17), this time in the lower key of D flat major and with richer harmonies.[1] José, menacingly, but with outward self-restraint, warns Carmen that he has reached the limit of the

[1] Once more we may be permitted to wonder why, if Bizet regarded the Toreador's Song as "muck," he should put it here to such gravely expressive use.

suffering he can bear on her account; but she merely shrugs her shoulders and walks away. The others are preparing to depart when Remendado catches sight of an interloper. He drags forth Micaëla, at the sight of whom Carmen not unnaturally ejaculates, "A woman!" Equally natural, in the circumstances, is José's enquiry, "Micaëla, what are you doing here?" Gravely, once more to the melody to which, in the first act, she had delivered his mother's message to him (No. 10), she implores him, in his mother's name, to return with her. Carmen harshly advises José to obey the summons, for at heart, she says, he is not one of them. "So that you may be free to join your latest lover!" he retorts; "no, I will stay, even though it costs me my life":

No. 31

$\quad$ *Dût-il m'en coû-ter la vi-e, Non, Car-men, je ne par-ti-rai pas!*

This is one of the finest psychological strokes of the whole score; in this single cry of his we already have the José of the last act, the man goaded beyond endurance, capable now of anything. "The chain that binds us," he continues, "will endure until death. You do not love me? What matters that, since I love you, and I am strong enough to rule you? I hold you in my hand, accursed woman, and I will force you to submit to the destiny that links your life with mine." His frenzy rises; we hear No. 31 again, this time more urgently, in a higher key. There is a general cry of horror; in an agitated ensemble the others, Micaëla among them, exhort José to save his life by flight. His spirit breaks only when Micaëla, to an expressive change in the texture and the colour of the music, tells him quietly that his mother is dying, and with her last breath wishes to pardon him. "Let us go," he cries wildly to Micaëla; and then, turning to Carmen, "You have your way. I go —but soon we too will meet again." The sinister Fate theme (No. 1) is heard for a moment in the wood-wind, then dies away into silence, and in the distance is heard the voice of Escamillo singing once more the refrain of his Song in the second act (No. 17)—"On your guard, toreador! and in combat remember that two dark eyes are fixed on you, and that love awaits you." Carmen impulsively makes as if to follow the call, but José menacingly bars her path. The smugglers set out on their journey to the accompaniment in the orchestra of the march-like motif to which they had come on the scene at the beginning of the act (partly shown in our example No. 26), and the curtain falls.

24

An animated orchestral entr'acte in Spanish-Flamenco style, abounding in piquancies of melody and rhythm and in those swift transitions from major to minor in which Bizet delighted, prepares us for the ebullient gaiety that is to characterise most of the fourth act: [1] evidently all Seville is thinking of the coming

---

[1] In 1920 a Spanish musicologist, Rafaël Mitjana, in his history of Spanish music in the *Encyclopédie de la Musique et Dictionnaire du Conservatoire*, alleged that this prelude to the fourth act was derived from a polo (a variety of Spanish song and dance) in a comic operetta of 1804 by Manuel Garcia, *El Criado Fingido (The Feigned Servant)*. (Garcia himself used to sing the tenor parts in his own works). This particular polo, said Mitjana, became so universally known in Spain that it was ultimately regarded as a folk-song; and Bizet, believing it to be such, "made use of it for the famous prelude to the fourth act of *Carmen*. I have never seen any mention of this curious analogy, which, however, as regards the opening phrases and even the contour of the preliminary bars [in the orchestra], leaps to the eye, and proves how well the brilliant young composer had 'documented' himself before writing his immortal masterpiece."

Far from the "analogy" between the two pieces "leaping to the eye" it is barely apparent to anyone but Mitjana. For one thing, Bizet's prelude is all movement and fire (it is marked allegro vivo), while Garcia's polo is an andante serenade of the feigned servant to his inamorata. The melodic line of the prelude resembles that of the polo at scarcely any point. There is indeed a slight similarity between the third and fourth bars of the short orchestral prelude to the polo and the long rippling figures that Bizet inserts every now and then between the limbs of his melody; but little Spanish clichés of this sort he could easily have picked up anywhere in the course of his investigations into Spanish music. He must often have discussed that subject with his friend the great singer Pauline Viardot, who was Manuel Garcia's daughter. Furthermore, during the war of 1870/1 he spent some time in Bordeaux, where he is known to have taken an interest in Spanish music and story.

Henry Malherbe has justly argued that if Bizet had knowingly made use of a Garcia original for his prelude he would have said so in a footnote at the relevant place in his score, as he did in the case of the Yradier habanera.

bull-fights. When the curtain rises we see, according to the stage directions, "an open place in Seville, with the walls of an ancient bull-ring in the background; the entry to this is covered by a long curtain." [1] Edgar Istel has pointed out how easy it is for stage designers and producers to misunderstand this; it is difficult to imagine the murder of Carmen taking place in a public square. In Spain they know better; in a Madrid production, says Istel, the setting showed "a small narrow space between the horse-stables and the bull-ring, through which the *Cuadrilla* (the company of fighters) proceeds to the ring. . . . When it has disappeared the space is closed off laterally by a heavy cross-beam so that it now forms a sort of pen, from which there is no escape for Carmen—a kind of symbol of destiny inescapable."

An animated orchestral prelude and a following chorus show the populace eagerly awaiting the opening of the courses, with fan-sellers, orange-sellers, programme-sellers, water-sellers, ciga-rette-sellers and so on pressing their wares on the crowd. Among the latter are Zuniga and two other officers, one with Frasquita, the other Mercédès on his arm. Zuniga, in a brief interlude of spoken dialogue, asks the girls where Carmen is. She will be here soon, Frasquita replies, for Escamillo is performing today, and where he is, Carmen will never be far away. She is more infatuated with him than ever, it appears; as for José, he had been seen in the village where his mother lived; an order for his arrest [as a deserter], had been issued, but when the soldiers arrived he was no longer there. "If I were Carmen," Frasquita comments, "I would not feel very comfortable about it all."

The short colloquy is broken in upon by joyous cries from the crowd as the Cuadrilla makes its appearance, with lances flashing in the sunlight and sombreros held high in the air. After the toreros come the alguazils (the constabulary), and later the banderilleros and the picadors—all to the gay tune with which the overture to the opera had begun:

[1] It may just be mentioned here that after Bizet's death some theatres, following in the footsteps of the Vienna production, began the fourth act with a ballet, drawing upon *The Fair Maid of Perth* and *L'Arlésienne* for their musical material. This is an intolerable insult to Bizet's dramatic sense: there is no place in the tragedy for the irrelevant antics of ballerinas.

No. 32

(Note once again, in bar 5 of this quotation, the sudden key-shift that always gives such vigour and elasticity to Bizet's style.)

A group of children pipe a satirical greeting to "the alguazil with the ugly face," and the men join in with them with a cheery cry of "Down with the alguazil!" Similar greetings fall in turn to the lot of the chulos, the banderilleros and the picadors; till at last the star of the occasion, Escamillo, enters, accompanied by Carmen, gorgeously arrayed; for Escamillo the uproarious welcome takes the form of a choral delivery of No. 17.

Suddenly the mood changes as Escamillo addresses Carmen quietly but passionately: "If you love me, Carmen, soon you shall be proud of me." To the same warm melodic strain she replies, "Yes, I love you, Escamillo, and may I die if I ever love anyone but you."

25

Escamillo disappears from our view, acclaimed enthusiastically by the crowd, which pays its respects also to the alcalde (mayor), who makes his majestic entry into the arena accompanied by alguazils and followed by the Cuadrilla. But the "march," as the text styles it, that accompanies their exit is not imposing, as we might have expected, but curiously, deceptively quiet, for now Frasquita and Mercédès seize the opportunity to approach Carmen and warn her to be on her guard, for José is there, lurking among the crowd. She replies calmly that she has no fear of him; she will remain and face him.

To another brief outburst of the rousing No. 32 the crowd pours into the arena, Frasquita and Mercédès following it. José, whom the thinning-out of the crowd has made visible, and Carmen, whose motif (No. 9) is heard for a moment or two in the violins, then in the violas, are now alone. They begin their last colloquy in sombre tones, Carmen telling him that she had been warned that he was near and that her life was in danger, but she had scorned to fly. In humble, appealing tones:

No. 33

he implores her to forget, as he is willing to do, all that is past and begin a new life with him elsewhere. He is asking the impossible, she replies; Carmen has never lied, and between José and her all is ended. The temperature of the music rises as José, in one of the most poignant expressions in all opera of blended love and grief, implores her to let him save the woman he adores. But she is inflexible: in low, level tones she tells him that she knows that he will kill her, and then, in a sudden access of passion, declares that whether she lives or dies she will never yield.

"There is yet time," he repeats; but in vain. "Then you no longer love me?" Her answer is a tranquil "No"; nothing, indeed, in this remarkable scene is more admirable than Bizet's avoidance of the temptation to let Carmen step out of her present character; she never meets storm with storm, but is always stoically resigned. As he repeats still more passionately his distracted appeal to her, her refusals become more sombrely fatalistic. He promises now to remain a bandit for her sake, to do anything she asks of him, if only she will not leave him: but her unvarying reply is, "It is useless. Carmen will never yield. Free she was born and free she will die!" At this point the crowd in the arena, to the accompaniment of No. 32, hails the approaching triumph of Escamillo. Carmen makes a joyous gesture and moves towards the entrance, but José intercepts her. The contest between them is resumed, this time with more desperation on both sides, José maddened by the thought that it is Escamillo who is the rival for whom she is abandoning him, Carmen reiterating that even in the face of death she will cry to the world that she loves the toreador.

There comes another exultant cry from within the arena, and the emotional tension reaches its highest point in a series of thunderous statements in the orchestra of the Fate theme (No. 1). José's reason snaps: for the last time he asks Carmen if she will follow him, and for the last time she refuses; herself now a raging fury, she tears from her finger a ring he had once given her and throws it away. This is the last straw; with a cry of "Accursed woman!" he strides towards her just as fanfares and voices are heard from inside the arena acclaiming Escamillo's triumph and the crowd begins to make its way out. It is at the entrance to the bull-ring that José catches the fleeing Carmen and stabs her. By now the crowd has debouched upon the stage, and as No. 1 thunders out again for the last time in almost the full orchestra José throws himself upon Carmen's body with a great cry of "It was I who killed her! O my Carmen, my adored Carmen!" And that is all: letting the tragedy speak for itself, without any further comment of voices or orchestra, Bizet and his librettists wisely bring the curtain down at once.

Madam Butterfly

PUCCINI [1858–1924]

PRINCIPAL CHARACTERS

CHO-CHO-SAN (MADAM BUTTERFLY)	*Soprano*
SUZUKI	*Mezzo-soprano*
KATE PINKERTON	*Soprano*
LIEUTENANT B. F. PINKERTON	*Tenor*
SHARPLESS	*Baritone*
GORO	*Tenor*
PRINCE YAMADORI	*Baritone*
THE BONZE	*Bass*
YAKUSIDE	*Baritone*
THE IMPERIAL COMMISSIONER	*Bass*

1

UCCINI'S Muse was a lady with a passion for travelling. She took him first of all, in *Le Villi*, to the German Black Forest, and abandoned him at the last, in *Turandot*, in China, having meanwhile whisked him through Paris, Florence, Rome, the Wild West of America and Japan; and it was only by resolute evasive action on his part that he prevented her from carrying him off to India (in quest of the Buddha) and various other places—for no composer has ever considered and rejected a greater multiplicity of opera schemes than he. In 1900 it became the turn of Japan. In the early summer of that year he happened to be in London, helping Covent Garden to produce *Tosca*, and friends took him to the Duke of York's Theatre, where he saw the American David Belasco's *Madam Butterfly*, which had been based, with many alterations, on a story by another American, John Luther Long. He was unable to understand a word of the text;

467

but the story and the effective theatrical handling of it struck deeply into his artistic subconsciousness. For one thing, here was yet another incarnation of the type that always fascinated him, the woman who suffers cruelly through love. For another, the drama gave him a change of milieu that was a life-long necessity to him if his creative imagination was to be continually refertilised. Finally, there was much in the play which he must have instinctively felt called out for musical treatment, especially the moving episode of Butterfly's lonely vigil between the first and second scenes of the one-act American drama, fourteen minutes of miming and clever scenic effects without a word being spoken. Puccini no doubt felt that with his music he could make that interlude even more emotionally telling than Belasco had done, master of "theatre" as he was.

There followed, in course of time, the usual struggles with his librettists—in this case Illica and Giacosa—and with his own self-doubts and technical difficulties. One of these latter, which beat him for a long time, was the length of the second (the final) act of the opera, which, as it turned out, went against the work at its first performance. It was not until near the end of 1903 that he finished his score, and the opera was given for the first time, with Rosina Storchio, a fine singer and actress, as Butterfly, at the Scala, Milan, on the 17th February 1904. (Giuseppe de Luca was the Sharpless: the conductor was the experienced Cleofante Campanini.) It was a complete fiasco; never before or since, in all probability, has an audience, even an Italian operatic audience, treated the world to such an exhibition of bestial malignity towards a composer; the only valid explanation of it all is that the opposition was organised by some of Puccini's rivals and personal enemies.[1] The composer and his publishers withdrew the work next day. Puccini proceeded to make sundry alterations to it, the most drastic of which was to divide into two acts the overlong second, which originally ran to something like an hour and a half. In its revised form the work was given at Brescia on the 28th

[1] It is sometimes urged that it was the length of the second act that exhausted and exasperated the audience; but it is clear from contemporary accounts that the hostility of a large section of it had been evident from the beginning of the performance.

May 1904, with Salomea Krucenisca as Butterfly, Storchio not being in Italy at that time. It was now a resounding success, and quickly became popular in one country after another.

The minor changes in the score consisted for the most part in the excision of a number of details insignificant in themselves but theatrically harmful, slowing down the main action as they sometimes did. They had crept into the original score because of Puccini's over-anxiety to impress the Japanese milieu of the work on the audience. As he was to do years later in the case of *Turandot*, he had laboured conscientiously during the gestation of *Madam Butterfly* at getting the exotic milieu of the work thoroughly into his blood and bones, reading a good deal about Japan and Japanese customs, getting hold—with the assistance of the wife of the Japanese Ambassador to Italy—of such fragments of Japanese music as he could, and so on; and the knowledge he himself had found necessary he thought equally necessary to the audience.[1] We must disabuse ourselves, however, of the notion that he was trying to be authentically "Japanese" in his opera, any more than in *Turandot* he tried to be specifically "Chinese"; it was simply the Italian composer Puccini expressing himself within a framework of Japanese characters and Japanese surroundings.[2] When, at a later date, he was producing *The Girl of the Golden West* in New York, he said, somewhat naïvely but quite sincerely, that he believed the work to be really American. After assuring an interviewer that "the music cannot really be called American, for music has no nationality," he went on to say, "For this drama I have composed music that, I feel sure, reflects the spirit of the American public, and particularly the strong, vigorous nature of the West. I have never been West, but I have read so much about it that I know it thoroughly." So it had been with the "Japan" of *Madam Butterfly*, and so it was to be again with the

[1] Mme Ohyama, the Ambassador's wife, criticised adversely some of the Japanese names in the libretto. "Yamadori," for instance, she declared to be "feminine."

[2] Or rather pseudo-Japanese. The general European view of the Japanese in general and Japanese women in particular at that time was largely derived from Japanese prints and Pierre Loti's *Madame Chrysanthème*. "Japanese" musical comedy had come into fashion in the London theatre in the late nineties; *The Geisha* dates from 1896, *San Toy* from 1899.

"China" of *Turandot*. He would have agreed, had the point ever been put squarely to him, that what he "knew thoroughly" was not the actual Japan or the actual China, but the Japan or China of his own imagination. He was perfectly within his rights as an artist in giving his music here and there—by means of unusual scales, unconventional harmonies, quaintly-turned melodies, orchestral colouring, piquant effects and so on that would have been out of place in an opera less exotic—a shape and a tinge appropriate to the "Japanese" milieu as he imagined it. All we in our turn are asked to do is to play the musical game on his terms, as we play it on Verdi's terms in the "Egyptian" *Aïda*.

2

The opera has no formal overture: it begins with a quasi-fugal elaboration of an animated theme first heard in the violins:

No. 1

which, with a later pendant:

No. 2

defines for us at once the main outlines and the dimensions of the world in which the drama is going to be played, a small and, in the amused eyes of a young American naval officer, a quaint world, in which small quaint people are fussily occupied with small quaint things.[1] When the curtain rises we see a Japanese house with its little terrace and garden on a hill overlooking Nagasaki, the town itself and the harbour being visible below in the background. From the house emerges the marriage broker Goro, bowing and scraping obsequiously as he points out the vir-

[1] It becomes evident from some of his later uses of our No. 2 that Puccini wishes us to associate it more or less specifically with Nagasaki.

tues of the house to the new lessee, Lieutenant B. F. Pinkerton [1] of the United States Navy. Goro shows how a sliding partition can transform the aspect and the utility of the place, how the rooms can become whatever the occupant may desire at any given moment: here is the nuptial chamber, there the hall, though everything can be changed at will, the inside becoming the outside and vice versa, the view from the terrace being open or closed by a mere touch of the finger on a partition. All this explanation goes on to the incessant chattering of No. 1 and No. 2 in the orchestra, and with many bows and genuflections, graphically represented in the music, on the part of the deferential Goro. Pinkerton is enchanted with the novelty and the convenience of everything.

There is a change in the music as the broker reveals other amenities of this desirable suburban residence. He claps his hands three times and a woman and two men enter and make deep obeisances to the Lieutenant: they are (1) the devoted maid (Suzuki) of the new mistress of the house, (2) the cook, (3) the man-of-all-work, and bear respectively the poetic names of Miss Gentle Cloud of Morning, Ray of the Rising Sun, and—even the respectful Goro permits himself a discreet smile at this—Aromatic Odours. [2] Pinkerton decides that it will be simpler for him to call them "Mug One," "Mug Two," and "Mug Three." Suzuki politely ventures to remind him of the value of a smile in all human relations; but as Pinkerton looks bored with her flowery language Goro claps his hands thrice and the servitors all run off into the house.

Goro now prepares Pinkerton for a number of expected visitors—the bride, her relations, the Official Registrar and the American Consul; the bride's relations will include her mother, her grandmother, cousins male and female, about a couple of dozen other collateral branches, and an uncle, the Bonze (Priest), who, however, is hardly likely to grace the proceedings with his august

---

[1] In performances in English he becomes F. B. Pinkerton. This inversion of the initials is quite inexplicable; what *could* B. F. be taken to stand for but "Benjamin Franklin"?

[2] There was once a Japanese heavyweight boxing champion with a knockout punch on whom his countrymen bestowed the poetic name of Plum-Blossom Fist.

presence. So much for the ascendants; as for the descendants, Goro, with a smirk, leaves all that to the Lieutenant. Running through all this colloquy is a dainty theme:

No. 3

to which Puccini gives a quiet little touch of the exotic by the simple insertion at one point of a B flat into a melody that is otherwise C major pure and simple.

A voice is heard at a little distance; it is that of the American Consul, Sharpless, who enters to the accompaniment of two new conjunct themes, each on the miniature scale of all that has gone before:

No. 4

The Consul, rather out of breath after his climb, looks out admiringly at the town and the harbour and the sea below. While Goro and a couple of servants are setting out two wicker lounge chairs, two glasses, and the materials for whisky and soda, Pinkerton, very pleased with himself, tells Sharpless how he has acquired this fantastic little dream-place on a nine hundred and ninety-nine years' lease with the option of terminating the agreement any time at a month's notice, legal contracts in Japan, he says, being apparently as elastic as the houses.

3

So far the music has all been on an appropriately miniature scale, a number of tiny motifs being woven skilfully into a continuous texture. (This would be a virtue in the score which a first-night audience would hardly be likely to appreciate.) But with the passage of the action into what may be called the American zone a change comes over the musical idiom; the melodies are now more sweeping, the harmonies less exotic, the whole texture more solid. Pinkerton expounds for the Consul's benefit his own hedonist philosophy of life. The Yankee, he says, wanders over the earth:

No. 5

Do-vun- que al mon-do   lo Yan-kee va-ga-bon-do

intent on business or pleasure, casting anchor where and when it suits him, until he runs into a squall, and then—as is apparently the case with him just now—life isn't worth living unless he can solace himself with the best of the pleasures and the loves of the country in which he happens to find himself; this he now means to do, marrying "in Japanese fashion" for nine hundred and ninety-nine years (with a monthly escape clause). From time to time the Consul, an older man, breaks in with a word of friendly criticism of "this easy-going gospel," to a phrase that impresses itself on our memory:

No. 6

The Lieutenant, however, brushes aside the counsels of prudence with a toast of "America for ever!", in which Sharpless joins him as in duty bound.

The music reverts imperceptibly to the dainty "Japanese" manner, with a repetition of the tiny motifs shown in our No. 4, as Pinkerton enlarges poetically on the beauty and charm of his bride—"and all for a bagatelle," Goro interjects, "a matter of a mere hundred yen." He offers his professional services as marriage broker to the Consul, who laughingly declines them.

At a peremptory order from the impatient Lieutenant, Goro goes down the hill to usher in the bridal company, and Pinkerton seizes the opportunity to rhapsodise once more about the fragile beauty, the butterfly lightness and simple charm of his bride,

Puccini, with consummate art, striking a middle course in his music between the everyday reality of the American human element and the exotic pseudo-Japanese. The former predominates as Sharpless tells how Butterfly had called at the Consulate a few days ago; though he had not seen her, he had been struck by a mysterious something in her voice that seemed to breathe sincerity of affection; it would be a pity, he says, to break those delicate wings, and with them a trusting heart. The irresponsible young Lieutenant brushes the well-meant counsel of the older man aside; he does not propose to break those wings but to launch them on a flight of new love; so there is nothing for Sharpless to do but to toast bride and bridegroom and wedding in another whisky and soda.

We revert to the more exotic idiom again:

No. 7

as Goro returns with the news that the bridal cortège is in sight. Before we see Butterfly we hear her voice in the near distance soaring above the chorus of the accompanying women, and, in the orchestra, the soft tones of a motif that will henceforth be characteristic of her:

No. 8

a melodic and harmonic germ that is rich in possibilities of modulation and sequential treatment. "One more step to climb," she sings; "over earth and sea a vernal breeze is blowing, and I am the happiest girl in Japan, nay, in the world, for I have obeyed the call of love." Her song, which rests upon a soft choral accompaniment, reaches its height of ecstasy in a great cry of "at the call of my heart I stand now upon the threshold of the house where all blessings, be they of life or death, await me":

No. 9

It is manifest at once that she is of a different, a superior substance not only to Goro and the rest of her compatriots, but to the thoughtless, devil-may-care young American who has acquired her. Cunningly interwoven with her ardent solo are the congratulations of her female friends; but this choral accompaniment has to be taken in by the ear alone, as part of the total musical fabric, for little of what they are saying is intelligible on its own account.

4

At last the little company debouches on the stage, all carrying open sunshades of gay colours. At a word of command from Butterfly they close their parasols and go down on their knees to Pinkerton; and for a moment we revert to the "Japanese" idiom in a motif that will become of importance later:

No. 10

Butterfly pays her new lord and master some pretty compliments, and gravely assures him, to the strain of No. 10, that she has many more at her command if he cares to hear them. In reply to Sharpless she says she is from Nagasaki (here No. 2 comes out quietly in the orchestra), but as her family, at one time rich, had met with misfortune she had had to go as a geisha to earn her living. Her mother, she says, is very poor. To a question from Sharpless as to her father she replies curtly "Dead!", and her friends fan themselves furiously to hide their embarrassment. There is a moment of painful silence; then Butterfly goes on to say proudly, to the melody of No. 10, that she has another relation, an uncle who is a Bonze, whom her friends eagerly declare to be a veritable fountain of wisdom. There is yet another uncle, it appears; about him, however, the less said the better, she hints, for he is of rather weak intellect and a frequenter of pot-houses. All this Pinkerton laughs off as delightfully quaint.

While he is talking to her Goro is busy introducing some of her friends to the Consul. He turns after a while to Butterfly and asks her age, and with an archly apologetic air she admits she is rather old—no less than exactly fifteen: at this he is rather horrified, while Pinkerton, who never strikes us as abundantly blessed with either brains or tact, treats it as quite a charming joke. At his order, Goro in his turn bids the three house servants hand round sweetmeats and wines of the comical sort that presumably appeals to the quaint Japanese taste in such things. While this is being done a reminder of No. 2 in the orchestra is presumably intended to direct our attention once more to Nagasaki, from which fresh arrivals are now beginning to appear; among them are the Imperial Commissioner and the Official Registrar. Pinkerton takes Sharpless aside and laughingly draws his attention to the comical crowd of Butterfly's relations, who, for their part, for all their kowtowings, regard the two Americans somewhat suspiciously. To Pinkerton it is all a huge joke—Japanese relations acquired, like his house and his bride, on monthly terms; he is pretty sure he has a mother-in-law somewhere among those present. The women comment rather unfavourably on Pinkerton's appearance and general eligibility, one of them going so far as to swear that Goro had offered him to her before planting him on Butterfly. All this and other chatter takes place mostly to the accompaniment of the tripping No. 3; it is clear that some of Butterfly's companions are very jealous of her and hope the marriage will not last long. Her mother, on the other hand, who does her best for a while to keep out of sight, quite approves of Pinkerton's looks, while Uncle Yakuside, the family disgrace, the nitwit and toper, is already on the trail of something alcoholic. Mainly on the foundation of No. 3 an animated ensemble is built up, in which Pinkerton and Sharpless join, each according to character, the former fatuously certain that he is in for the best of luck with this charming bride of his, the latter warning him of possible trouble, for Butterfly is obviously in love and takes the union with the utmost seriousness.

5

The relations, including the mother, are duly presented to the condescending Pinkerton, who is particularly amused at the tipsy Uncle Yakuside. Like the experienced craftsman he was, Puccini weaves all his threads together with a masterly hand, and we who now know the opera well can see how all this detail fits neatly into the general plan. But there was much more of it in the first version, Puccini being over-anxious to make the exotic milieu convincing; and the first-night audience may be excused for wondering now and then when the real drama of Pinkerton and Madam Butterfly, with the expected tally of big emotional moments and vocal high lights, would get going. And Puccini has some way to travel yet before this can happen.

First of all the Consul, the Commissioner and the Registrar go with writing materials to a table and draw up the formal marriage contract. Heralded by the typical Butterfly motif (No. 8) there now follows a colloquy between Butterfly and Pinkerton in which the former is the principal source of interest; she is to be allowed to exhibit for a while the more kittenish side of her character—for she is only fifteen. Childlike she brings forth from her ample sleeves a number of the little objects she treasures most. She is a little afraid of offending him by all this, and Pinkerton, in a brief moment of comprehension of her, asks "But why, my lovely Butterfly?", to a tiny phrase in the orchestra that shows him to be sincerely touched by her affectionate simplicity and innocence:

No. 11

Her few possessions consist of some handkerchiefs, a pipe, a girdle, a small silver clasp, a mirror, a fan and a little jar of carmine: this last she throws away because Pinkerton appears to disapprove of it. Finally she produces first of all something which she gravely declares she holds sacred—a knife sheath; and it falls

to Goro to explain that the weapon was sent to her father by the
Mikado with an invitation, which he had dutifully obeyed, to
suicide. The sinister significance of the story is emphasised by a
harsh figure in the orchestra:

No. 12

Next come out of her sleeve the Ottoké, small figures representing
the souls of her ancestors. Humouring her in this quaint fancy,
Pinkerton pays the Ottoké his respects; but she goes on to explain
that, unknown to her friends and relations, she had gone yesterday to the Mission, abjured her own religion, and adopted that of
her lover, who has generously paid no less than a hundred yen
for her. This confession becomes important in the action a little
later.

Silence having been imposed on the crowd the Commissioner
reads out the contract of marriage between Lieutenant Pinkerton,
of the American gunboat *Abraham Lincoln*, and the spinster
Butterfly, of the Omara quarter of Nagasaki. Bridegroom, bride
and relatives all sign; and after the usual congratulations the
Consul, the Commissioner and the Registrar depart.

The matter of Butterfly's abjuration of her own faith had
obviously been introduced to prepare the way for a dramatic later
episode in which her uncle the Bonze was to call down the wrath
of his gods on her for her apostasy—the basic reason of it all being
to emphasise the completeness of Butterfly's abandonment to her
love for Pinkerton. But this further episode could not well be
inserted immediately; so Puccini fills in the necessary brief interval
with a scene which from the dramatic point of view could well
have been dispensed with, in which, urged on by the Lieutenant,
the toper Uncle Yakuside shows what he can do in the way of
potations. Then the atmosphere is rent by a raucous cry of
"Cho-Cho-San!" from the path that leads to the hill. At the sound
of the dreaded Bonze's voice the friends and relations huddle

together terror-stricken; Goro alone has courage enough to ask petulantly why this spoil-feast could not have spared them his presence, but even he thinks it prudent to make himself scarce. Soon the strange figure of the fanatical Bonze appears, holding out his hands threateningly towards Butterfly and breathing fire and slaughter. The sinister motif of the Curse:

No. 13

dominates most of what follows. The Bonze had learned that Butterfly had renounced the religion of her fathers, and now he calls down on her the maledictions of the gods of Japan. The angry Pinkerton quells him with a single curt sentence and he deems it wise to retire, taking with him the relations and friends, all shouting "We renounce you!" at the dazed Butterfly, who all this while has stood apart, immobile and silent. The lovers are now alone and everything is set for the great closing rhapsody of the long act. Evening steals over the scene. Pinkerton takes the fainting and weeping Butterfly in his arms and whispers tender consolations, while in the background Suzuki is heard murmuring in her own tongue her evening prayers.

6

Drawing Butterfly towards the house Pinkerton begins the final duet with a deeply-felt melody:

No. 14

to which Butterfly sings of her happiness in spite of her renunciation by her kindred. Suzuki and some servants enter for a moment and silently slide some of the partitions of the house, giving point to Butterfly's murmured words, "Yes, now we are alone, the world shut out!" Suzuki puts Butterfly's night robe on her, and at a sign from Pinkerton she and the others retire. The unvarying theme of Butterfly is her profound happiness in becoming Pinkerton's wife, in spite of everything, even the angry curses of the Bonze, whose motif (No. 13) cuts menacingly at one point across her ecstatic song. She tells of her reluctance to listen to Goro when first he had come to her with an offer of marriage from a barbarian—she hastily apologises for the thoughtless word—a man from America; but she had liked him from the first moment, and now he is all the world to her, for he is so tall, so strong, his laugh so frank. "Love me a little," she begs him, "just a little, as you would a baby, for I come of a people accustomed to and grateful for little."

When he calls her "Butterfly" it reminds her of something she has heard—that in his country when a man captures a butterfly he runs a pin through it and fastens it to a board; and the menacing Curse motif (No. 13) thunders out again in the orchestra. Pinkerton tells her soothingly that it is only that the man wants to make sure of possessing the lovely thing forever, as he will her. The passion of the music grows steadily, one ardent theme following straight on the heels of another. Finally Butterfly, to the accompaniment of No. 8, sings rapturously of the beauty of the starlit night, and the climax comes with an ecstatic elaboration, in unison, of No. 9, the melody with which she had made her appearance on the scene a little while before. The song ends, the pair go slowly from the garden into the house, and the last word is left to the orchestra, which dies down from a fortissimo to a pianissimo as the curtain falls on a chord that seems less a conclusion than a question to which the answer must be sought in the future.

7

The second act of *Madam Butterfly* is a masterpiece of invention, style and craftsmanship, working hand in hand. Puccini never surpassed it as a musical-dramatic unity; it is a mosaic of a hundred small pieces, but greater as a whole than in any of its parts. Most masterly of all is the art with which he passes by the most natural transitions from the music of the "quaint" pseudo-Japanese milieu to that of the larger operatic utterance; we are

480

always conscious of the psychological difference between the two, but never of any break in the consistency of the musical style as a whole.

Three years have elapsed since the close of the first act: Pinkerton has long ago sailed away, leaving with Butterfly the child of the marriage and never communicating with her; yet her love for him is as ardent, her faith in him as profound as ever. The second act—as it is still called in the score—is played within the little house on the hill. When the curtain rises after a short orchestral introduction we see the room in semi-darkness, with Butterfly standing motionless by a screen, and the faithful Suzuki, before an image of the Buddha, murmuring a prayer in her own language and from time to time ringing a ritual bell: "Grant that Butterfly may weep no more," she prays. In the orchestra we hear again and again, in the following enlarged form:

No. 15

the tragic motif (No. 12) associated with the suicide of her father, as Butterfly reproaches the gods of Japan for their indifference to her; surely the American God should be more accessible to those who call upon Him as she does, but alas, He seems not to be aware of her. Motif after motif is woven smoothly into the texture as she asks Suzuki how much money now stands between them and starvation, and learns that only a few small coins remain. Yet her belief that Pinkerton will return is unshakable; had he not intended to do so would he have fitted the house with locks as he had done, to keep out her pests of relations and to provide protection for his wife (No. 8), his little Butterfly? When the devoted but more worldly-wise Suzuki remarks that she has never yet heard of a foreign husband returning to his Japanese nest Butterfly turns upon her angrily, and in a tender melody in which she tries to imitate Pinkerton's loving accents:

No. 16

tells how, when he left her, he had promised to return when the roses bloomed again and the robin redbreasts—whose twittering is charmingly suggested in the orchestra—were building their nests once more. She brushes Suzuki's scepticism aside; one of these days, she insists in her well-known aria, limning the whole scene with her gestures, they will see a thread of smoke on the far horizon, and a white ship making for the harbour, and she, Butterfly, will stand on the brow of the hill, waiting unweariedly for the return of the man she loves. Soon a speck will appear in the distance, coming from the town. It will be he; and when he reaches the top of the hill he will call out "Butterfly!", and she will not answer at once, half in play, half so that she shall not die of happiness:

No. 17

and he, a little troubled at heart by her silence, will cry out to her as he used to do, "Dear little wife of mine, my little verbena blossom!" And so let Suzuki banish her fears, for he will come, of that she is sure; and No. 17 rings out passionately in the full orchestra, only to fade away in a pianissimo almost immediately. She sends Suzuki away, looking after her sadly.

8

The substance and the colour of the music change in a moment, reverting temporarily to the idiom of the childlike Butterfly of former days, as Goro and Sharpless enter from the garden, accompanied by the "Nagasaki" motif (No. 2) which we have learned to associate also with the Consul. Butterfly greets him joyously, and Suzuki returns to arrange a stool and cushions and set out a table with smoking materials. In the long scene of varied musical expression that follows, the embarrassed Sharpless tries to communicate the contents of a letter he has received from Pinkerton. But in her joy at hearing the beloved name she interrupts him time after time, so that his story never gets fully told, or even fairly begun. She asks when the robins nest in America, for it was then that Pinkerton had promised her he would return; here in Japan they have nested three times since he left, but perhaps they do so more rarely in America? She tells how, as soon as the Lieutenant had gone away, Goro had begun to pester her with other offers of marriage; and latterly he has been trying to tempt her to wed a rich simpleton, for her relations have all cast her off and she is in the depths of poverty. This latest suitor, Goro explains to Sharpless, is one Yamadori, who now enters in pomp, attended by servants bearing gifts of flowers. Goro and Suzuki greet him obsequiously, and the latter places a stool for him between the already seated Butterfly and the Consul. Butterfly twits Yamadori unmercifully on his hopeless passion for her in spite of the many wives he has had already and divorced. Goro is out of patience with her for refusing so rich a suitor, and yet more for deluding herself that she is still married to Pinkerton. She replies that it is true that in Japan a marriage can be ended by the husband opening the door and turning his wife out; but in America that cannot be done, and she is an American now.

While Butterfly goes aside with Suzuki for a moment Goro manages to whisper to Sharpless and Yamadori that Pinkerton's ship has already been sighted. Yamadori remarks distractedly "And when she sees him again . . ."; but the Consul tells them that the Lieutenant does not want to meet Butterfly; indeed, it was to break this news and that of Pinkerton's American marriage to her as gently as possible that he has come to the house. Sadly Yamadori turns to depart, Butterfly laughing unkindly at the piteous figure he cuts. One does not quite know what Puccini's intentions were with regard to Yamadori: his stage directions make it clear that he wants him to appear almost as ridiculous in our eyes as he does in Butterfly's, yet he characterises him musically throughout the scene in a motif of deep feeling, which rings out passionately in the orchestra as he and his servants finally leave the stage, followed by Goro.

483

9

Now that Sharpless is alone with Butterfly he tries once more, with deepening gravity, to tell her the contents of Pinkerton's letter, which she eagerly takes from him and kisses before he can begin to read it. Having regained possession of it he begins to read it to her, but only broken phrase by phrase because of her constant ecstatic interjections. The reading is accompanied by a persistent motif in the orchestra to which it is difficult to attach any precise label, though frequent use is made of it in the present scene and later: perhaps it was connected in Puccini's mind in some way with the simplicity of Butterfly's soul, and her pathetic obsession with the idea of Pinkerton's return:

No. 18

In its later stages it appears topped by a broad melody in octaves:

No. 19

The letter, the reading of which Sharpless is never allowed to finish, begins thus: "Dear Friend, please seek out that lovely flower. Three years have gone by since she and I were happy together, and perhaps Butterfly remembers me no more. If she still cares for me and expects me, I rely on you to prepare her discreetly for the blow. . . ." As she evidently senses nothing sinister behind these last words he resignedly puts the letter away again and tries another line of approach. What would she do, he asks her gravely, if Pinkerton were never to return to her? Sobered at the very suggestion of that calamity, she bows her head like a child submissive under punishment, and stammers, "Two things I might do—go back to where I came from and entertain people

with my singing, or else—and better—to die!" As the Consul
holds up his hands in sheer helplessness Butterfly summons Suzuki
and bids her show him out, then repents of her harshness and
draws him back and begs him to forget what she had said under
the first shock of the wound he had dealt her. All through this
episode there runs an orchestral figure, insistently repeated, of
the kind which Puccini so often relied upon to create a cumulative effect of mental suffering.

Butterfly repudiates the idea that Pinkerton can have forgotten
her, and to a rapturous outburst in the orchestra runs into the
inner room, returning with her baby on her shoulder. She shows
Sharpless the child, asking him if ever a Japanese baby was born
with such blue eyes and golden curls. Sharpless admits the resemblance to Pinkerton, and asks if the Lieutenant had ever
been told of the coming of the child. No, Butterfly replies, but
surely when he knows he will hasten back to Japan; and in a great
lyrical outpouring she asks the baby if he understands what the
Consul has had the hardness of heart to suggest—that she should
take her little one in her arms and go through the city in rain and
tempest, trying to earn her keep and his by singing and playing
and dancing. Her excited imagination running away with her, she
sees the crowd open and the Emperor appear at the head of his
warriors, and she will say to him, "Great Ruler, tarry a moment
and deign to look at these blue eyes, blue as the heaven from
which the Emperor himself has come." The vision is accompanied
in the orchestra by a strongly accented motif:

No. 20

Andante mosso ♩ = 112

of which Puccini will make powerful dramatic use at the end of
the opera.

"And the good Emperor will stop," she continues, addressing
the child in a strain at once tender and exalted, "and graciously
create you the greatest prince of his kingdom," and she presses
him passionately to her heart. Sharpless is on the verge of tears.

Feeling that it is hopeless to try any longer to pierce through Butterfly's mystical exaltation with anything in the nature of sober fact he takes his leave, she asking him to convey a message to Pinkerton from the child, whose name now, she tells him, is Grief, which on the day of his father's return shall be changed to Joy—this to a reminiscence of the rapturous No. 17 in the orchestra.

10

When Sharpless has gone Suzuki returns, dragging in the terrified Goro, whom she is threatening to murder; she has caught him, it seems, at his usual game of spreading the tale in the town that no one knows who is the father of Butterfly's baby. The marriage broker tries to explain that all he meant was that in America a child born under such conditions lives under a curse, rejected and scorned by all from birth to death. Blind with fury Butterfly takes down the paternal dagger that is hanging up by a shrine and rushes at Goro, who howls with fright. Suzuki carries the child to an inner room; and Butterfly, quickly repenting of having allowed herself to be betrayed into taking part in such a degrading scene, allows the howling Goro to escape. Putting away the dagger again she turns once more in thought to the child, pouring out her heart to it in a flood of tenderness: soon, she says, his father will come and take them both away with him to his own country.

Suzuki runs in excitedly as the distant boom of the harbour gun is heard. In soft strains the orchestra takes us back to the music of Butterfly's rapturous account of how some day Pinkerton will return. Trembling with excitement she takes a telescope from the table and runs out on to the terrace; and the reminiscent music soars to a great climax as she reads the name of the ship— the *Abraham Lincoln*. Triumphantly she turns to Suzuki; now, she says, the maid will see the folly of doubting; just when everyone was counselling her to weep and despair, love and faith had triumphed; "he has returned, and he loves me!" Now begins the charming episode in which the two women prepare the house for the home-coming of the beloved: "Shake the cherry-tree," Butterfly bids Suzuki:

No. 21

pdolce Scuo-ti qud-la fron-da di ci—lie-gio e m'in-non-da di fior—

"till it drowns me with its blossom and drenches me with its perfume." Will he be here in an hour? Two hours? The house is to be gay with flowers to greet him, peach-blossoms, violets, jessamine and whatever else they can find; though this may strip the garden bare as in winter, within the house it shall be spring. Excitedly they strew flowers everywhere, to one happy little melody after another, the climax coming with:

No. 22

as the two women sing, "Let us scatter in handfuls violets and tuberoses and verbena, petals of every flower."

Butterfly, looking sadly at her worn face in a mirror, bids the tenderly caressing Suzuki make her beautiful for the home-coming of her lord; the baby's cheeks too are to have a touch of carmine, lest the vigil before them make him even paler than he is now. A suggestion of the Curse motif (No. 13) is heard in the orchestra as Butterfly angrily recalls the Bonze and his prophecies of evil, giving way to the Yamadori music as her mood lightens and she remembers half-humorously the piteous pleadings of that rejected suitor; soon will come her triumph over them all. The music of the love duet in the first act (No. 14) steals in for a moment as she dons her wedding garment and puts a scarlet poppy in her hair, while Suzuki wraps the baby up in light loose fabrics.

Suzuki closes the shosi (the sliding shutters) at the back of the room, and Butterfly punches three small holes in them, the highest one for herself to see through standing up, a lower one for the crouching Suzuki, and the lowest one of all for the baby, seated on a cushion. So the three look out into the deepening darkness, through which the moon is now beginning to steal, and wait for the dawn and the coming of Pinkerton; the orchestra, however, envelops the rigid silent figures in a phrase expressive of grief and ending with a muttered hint of the Curse (No. 13), thus playing something of the part of a Greek chorus: it knows what Butterfly as yet does not, knows how her hopes of happiness will all end, and it communicates its sad prescience to us who are listening and watching. This First Part of the act is played out to complete silence on the stage, the orchestra alone continuing with the strains of No. 18 and its companion No. 19. The baby is the first to fall asleep and drop down on his cushion as the vigil goes on; then Suzuki succumbs to fatigue and she too sleeps; Butterfly alone remains as motionless as a statue, staring out into the night as the curtain slowly falls.

11

Before the Second Part opens on the stage there comes in the score an orchestral interlude in which Puccini plays in masterly fashion on motives old and new, the impression we get being one of ecstatic reminiscence shot with foreboding. At this point a little explanation is perhaps due to the reader who is accustomed to seeing *Madam Butterfly* played in *three* acts. The original plan of the librettists had been for an opera in the customary three acts; and included in the scheme was a scene in which Butterfly, calling at the Consulate, encountered the American Mrs. Pinkerton there, whereas in the present version the whole action, after the first act, takes place in Butterfly's house. Towards the end of 1902 Puccini became convinced that the opera ought to be in two acts only. "The Consulate," he wrote to his publisher Ricordi on the 16th November, "was a great mistake. The action must move forward to the close without interruption, rapid, effective, terrible! In arranging the opera in three acts I was making for certain disaster. You will see that I am right." Three days later, evidently in reply to some objections on Ricordi's part, he writes "Have no fear; I am sure of my ground . . . that the opera, with the division which I have adopted [i.e. the orchestral interlude] will be very effective indeed. The dilution of the work with the Consulate act is a mistake. This [opera] is a little drama which, once begun, must proceed without interruption to the end. . . . Illica agrees with me, and makes the same suggestion of cutting out the Consulate act; only he would like to keep the three acts—but to drop the curtain and raise it again on the same scene does not seem to me desirable." When the score was completed except for the orchestration Puccini felt that "it has turned out splendidly, the action moving forward straight and logically in the most satisfying way. Ah, that act at the Consulate was ruining everything!"

It was thus that the long second act came to assume its present form in the score—two parts linked by an orchestral interlude. In most performances, however, the interlude does not link the two parts but separates them: the curtain comes down on the First Part at the point where Butterfly, Suzuki and the baby have begun to look through the holes in the shosi; then, after an interval, the audience returns for the "third act," to which the interlude forms a prelude. All this is purely and simply a concession to the poverty of human endurance in the average audience—or supposed poverty, for today people manage quite well to keep their unbroken attention on such long one-act works as the *Rhinegold*, *Salome* and *Elektra*. From the artistic and the dramatic standpoint Puccini was right; we should remain in our seats while darkness gradually descends upon the room, and, under the guidance of the interlude, live imaginatively with Butterfly through those night hours of weary waiting.[1]

12

We have arrived, then, at the point where, after the orchestral interlude, Butterfly's long vigil is nearing its end. From far away

[1] The constant references to "three acts" in any study of *Madam Butterfly* is apt to confuse the reader. He should remember that when Puccini himself speaks of "three acts" in his correspondence he is referring to the *original form of the libretto*, of which the "Consulate act" formed an integral part; by insisting on this being cut out he reduced the opera to the two-act form on which his heart was set. The present three-act lay-out did not come into being until the Brescia revival, and it amounted to no more than a simple division, for theatrical convenience, of the long second act into a second and a third. It is therefore rather misleading to speak, as some analysts have done, of Puccini having "gone back to the original plan of three acts." There was no "going back to the original plan," which had included the "Consulate act." All that happened at Brescia (and afterwards) was that at the point where the orchestral interlude occurs an interval was made in order that the audience might relax for a while. The published score of 1906 was not "in three acts" but in (1) act one, (2) act two, first part and second part.

in the bay come inarticulate human calls and murmurs, accompanied by the clanging of ships' chains and anchors from the harbour; and when at last the curtain rises again we see the first rays of dawn stealing into the room, with Suzuki and the baby asleep by the shosi, and Butterfly still like a figure carved out of stone. The orchestra swells to a blaze of light and colour as the sunshine gradually floods the room. Butterfly is the first to move; she wakens Suzuki with a touch on the shoulder and then takes the baby tenderly in her arms. The recurrence of a motif that had been heard previously at the point where she had held the child up for the Consul's admiration tells us that it is the little one that is in the forefront of her mind as she now confidently assures herself that soon Pinkerton will come:

No. 23

"Sleep, my love," she croons to it as she carries it off to a room above; "you are with God and I with my sorrow," to which Suzuki adds a reflective "Poor Butterfly!"

A grave motif to be later associated with the thoughtful, good-hearted Sharpless (see No. 24) is dwelt on for a little time by the orchestra as we enter upon the next vital stage of the action. Suzuki, opening the door to the Consul in response to some knocking, is staggered to see that he is accompanied by Pinkerton; the pair enter with an air of stealthy secrecy. Suzuki informs the Lieutenant that not merely has her mistress been waiting and watching the whole night for him but not a ship has entered the harbour during the last three years without her anxiously scanning its flag and colours; while last night, in the sure expectation of his coming, she had insisted on having the room strewn with flowers. Suddenly Suzuki catches sight of a foreign lady in the garden, and she asks the men anxiously who this may be. Pinkerton, who never cuts an impressive figure in the drama, dares not tell her: all he can bring himself to say is "She has come with me." It is left to Sharpless to tell her, quietly but resolutely, that this is Pinkerton's wife, whereupon Suzuki breaks into a wild cry of despair—"Souls of my ancestors, for my little one the light of the sun has gone out!", and she sinks on her knees with her arms raised to heaven and her face turned to the ground.

In vain the Consul tries to comfort her; they had come so early in the morning, he tells her, in the hope of finding her alone and being able to count on her guidance and support. In grave, sympathetic tones:

No. 24

he breaks it to the dazed and anguished Suzuki that while they all know how Butterfly must suffer they feel that their first care must be for the child.[1] The voices unite for a moment in a trio in which Pinkerton muses sadly on the unchanged appearance of the room in which he and Cho-Cho-San first plighted their love, and Suzuki, the one who feels most deeply for Butterfly, bemoans the new turn of events: "Souls of my forefathers," she wails, "this is the end of all for my poor little one!"

13

Pinkerton sends her out into the garden to join Kate. The Lieutenant, unable to bear up under this load of misfortune for them all, decides to follow Suzuki: Sharpless, reverting for a moment to the music of his fatherly talk with him in the first act, reminds him of his disregarded warning on that occasion. Pinkerton abjectly admits his own recklessness and heartlessness, but can get no further in the way of redemptive action than to give Sharpless some money for the support of Butterfly. Taking up the strain of No. 24 he bids a mournful farewell to what had once been the scene of his love:

[1] As the reader will remember, Butterfly had told Sharpless that she had never sent Pinkerton news of the birth of a child. We must therefore presume that the Consul had given the Lieutenant this news after his return from his interview with Butterfly; in which case Mrs. Pinkerton's resolution to adopt the child must have been rather sudden.

No. 25

Ad—di—o fio—ri—to a—su di le—ti—zia e d'a—mor,

Then he goes out with bowed head, leaving to Sharpless the task of disclosing the whole dreadful truth to Butterfly. He is decidedly not a "sympathetic" figure anywhere in the opera, and least of all here; but it is difficult to see in what other guise the librettists could have presented him to us, the original drama being what it was.

The Lieutenant having left, Suzuki and Kate Pinkerton enter from the garden, a conversation there having evidently been just concluded. "You will tell her, then," says the latter, "and advise her to trust me, for I will tend him as a son of my own"; to which Suzuki mournfully assents, stipulating, however, that she shall be alone with Butterfly when the blow falls on her, for her heart will be broken. Just then Butterfly is heard calling from a room above, and presently we see her at the head of the staircase and beginning to descend. In vain the maidservant tries to hold her back. She has come in the confident expectation of finding Pinkerton there, but seeing only Sharpless and Kate she begins to be alarmed. "Who are you?" she asks the American woman. No one dares to answer her, but the orchestra fills the stage silence ominously, some descending phrases in the whole-tone scale being particularly expressive. At last Kate Pinkerton ventures to speak to the dazed Butterfly; "I am the innocent cause of all your woe. Forgive me." "How long is it since he married you?" asks Butterfly. "A year," is the reply, "and will you not let me do something for the child? I will give him the most loving care." Motif eloquently succeeds motif in the orchestra (No. 23, No. 6, No. 15, No. 13), to which is entrusted all the delineation of what is going on in the stunned soul of poor Butterfly. Sadly she felicitates Kate on her marriage to Pinkerton; "Under the great vault of heaven there is no woman happier than you. May you always remain so. Feel no sadness for me; but do this for me—tell him I shall find peace"; and she declines, though not unkindly, the friendly hand the other woman proffers her. She has always been pathetic; now we see her in process of becoming inwardly great.

Overhearing an enquiry addressed to Sharpless, Butterfly tells Kate that Pinkerton shall have his son if he will come for him—in half an hour from now, she adds meaningly: her great resolution has been already formed. Suzuki having shown Kate and the Consul out, Butterfly, mastering herself with a great effort, bids her shut out the sunlight that is now flooding the room: spring has died within her, and she wishes to forget its presence in the world. Suzuki closes the curtains and doors until the room is in almost total darkness, the orchestra meanwhile enveloping the scene in an ominous twilight of its own. When Suzuki proposes to bring the child to Butterfly she tells her to go and join him in his play; but the weeping maid cannot bring herself to obey. There comes one of those long Puccinian silences to which the conductor should give the utmost possible value; then Butterfly murmurs the words of a sad mysterious old song: "He came through the closed gates; then he went away, and left us with nothing, nothing—but death!"

Imperiously she bids the sobbing Suzuki leave her. Then she lights the lamp in front of the large image of Buddha, before which she bows her head for a few moments. She shudders convulsively as she recalls the Bonze's prophecies of woe (No. 13 in the orchestra), then goes to the shrine, draws the white veil from it and throws it over the screen, takes the dagger out of its sheath on the wall near the Buddha, holds the haft in her two hands, kisses the blade, and reads out softly the words engraved on it—"Better to die with honour than to cling to life in dishonour." The tempo and colour of the orchestral music change for a brief spell as the door on the left opens and Suzuki appears with the child, who, at her urging, runs towards his mother. In a convulsion of tenderness and grief Butterfly kisses him and holds him to her breast: "You must never know," she cries, "that it was for you, for your dear innocent eyes, that Butterfly died, so that you may go away beyond the sea and not recall with regret the mother who abandoned you." She sings a last passionate invocation to him, this angel who had come to her from Paradise, to look well at his mother's face for remembrance in days to come:

493

No. 26

O a me, sce—so dal tro-no del -l'al-to Pa-ra—di-so,

"Farewell, my love, my little love," she ends her cry, "and now go and play."

She seats the child on a stool, gives him the American flag and a doll to play with, and tenderly bandages his eyes; then with her own eyes fixed on him she goes behind the screen. The dagger is heard falling to the ground, and the white veil that was on the screen is snatched away. Butterfly comes tottering from behind the screen, the veil wound round her throat. She gropes her way to the child, gestures to him with her hand, gives him a last embrace, and falls beside him. The voice of Pinkerton is heard off-stage, calling "Butterfly!", and the orchestra crashes in with a phrase of climactic poignancy:

No. 27

The door is flung open; Pinkerton and Sharpless enter and run to Butterfly, who points feebly to the child as she dies. Pinkerton falls on his knees, while the sobbing Consul picks up the child and kisses him. Then Puccini's genius finds the right musical ending to the drama; the orchestra thunders out the motif (No. 20) that had accompanied Butterfly's ecstatic vision of the Emperor some day catching sight of the child, and, moved by his beauty, making him the foremost of the princes of his empire. It is a masterstroke of tragic irony, of a type of which music alone among the arts has the secret; but it is in the nature of the case one of which a first-night audience could not be expected to be conscious. It is only after long acquaintance with *Madam Butterfly*, indeed, that we become fully aware of the many subtleties that have gone to the making of it.

Der Freischütz[1]

CARL MARIA VON WEBER [1786–1826]

PRINCIPAL CHARACTERS

Cuno, Head Ranger	Bass
Max, a Young Forester	Tenor
Caspar, a Young Forester	Bass
Kilian, a Peasant	Bass
Prince Ottokar	Baritone
A Hermit	Bass
Agathe, Cuno's Daughter	Soprano
Ännchen, her cousin	Soprano

1

MAX MARIA VON WEBER, in the second volume of his Life of his father, has told us how, on the first appearance of the *Gespensterbuch* [2] of August Apel and Friedrich Laun in Leipzig in 1810, the composer and the librettist-to-be of *Der Freischütz* (Friedrich Kind) felt at once that heaven had placed within their hands the ideal stuff for a "romantic" opera. The *Gespensterbuch* was a collection of poems, folk-tales, original stories and what not, the first tale being a long one by Apel entitled *Der Freischütz, a Folk-Saga*. Weber and Kind, however—so Max Weber informs us—were for a time not easy in their minds about two things: would it be prudent to put a hermit and Satan on the operatic stage, and would the German censorship approve of a story so rank with popular

[1] Literally "The Freeshooter," a marksman who obtains an advantage over his rivals by means of "free" bullets of special efficacy, because they have been made in collusion with the devil.

[2] *Gespenst* (plural *Gespenster*) means spirit, ghost, apparition, spectre, etc.

superstition as this? But as it happens there is no hermit in Apel's story and no character of the name or nature of Satan—for the sinister Samiel advances no claim to that brevet rank. From all this we infer that Max Maria von Weber had never seen the *Gespensterbuch*, which would already have become a volume of great rarity even by the 1860's.

These trifling errors of his were in due course corrected by German scholars who had access to the old book, but it was not until 1872 that one Meynert lighted upon the actual source of Apel's story. The latter, in swift outline, runs thus.

One Wilhelm, a clerk in a small town adjoining a forest, is in love with Käthchen, the daughter of a forest ranger named Bertram, who, to his constant regret, is the last male of his line. It appears that in the distant past the hereditary rangership had been bestowed by the local prince on an ancestor of Bertram's, a certain Kuno, by way of reward for a deed of exceptional skill and daring. The huntsmen had one day seen a stag racing along with a man tied to its back. The clement prince was revolted by the explanation of the matter given him by his suite—that this was the local hunters' drastic way of dealing with captured poachers, the delinquent being strapped to a stag and left to die an agonising death by violence or slow starvation. The prince would put an end to this cruelty. He promised a handsome reward to whichever of the huntsmen could kill the flying stag without harming the man, with the proviso, however, that he would receive dire punishment if the latter were injured. All shrank from the test except the young Kuno, who, commending his bullet to heaven, accomplished the deed to perfection. As his reward the prince made the rangership hereditary in his family. But malicious tongues were soon heard whispering that the incredible feat had been performed by the aid of diabolic arts—by means of a "free shot" (*Freischuss*) which would bring down anything that ran or flew, for the devil had had a hand in the casting of the ball. So the prince decreed that each successive holder of the office must first prove his skill by a "trial shot," the target being the ring in the beak of a wooden bird perched on a pole.

Käthchen is very sad when she hears this ancient domestic story one day from the lips of old Bertram, who has no objection to Wilhelm *per se* but can accept as a son-in-law only a youth who can qualify for the rangership succession by acquitting himself with glory in the trial shot. Wilhelm, however, mere quill-driver though he be, is not dismayed, as he does not lack experience as a marksman. Still, the danger of his failing in the trial is real. Rejoicing at the discovery that the young man has some skill in shooting, Bertram provisionally sanctions his bethrothal to Käthchen, though it is to be kept a secret until the day of the trial, which is to take place during the visit to the neighbourhood of the prince's grand master of the chase.

But now things begin to go wrong with Wilhelm. His shots either miss altogether or land on something he has not aimed at, such as a tree trunk. Sometimes his game bag for the day consists not of partridges but of ignoble jackdaws and crows; on one occasion, aiming at a hare, he had brought down a cat. The good old ranger has to speak very severely to him about it: either he must improve on these performances or he can say goodbye to his hopes of ever marrying Käthchen.

Wilhelm now loses his nerve and goes from bad to worse. The game seem positively to saunter round him in derision. Three times he fires at a roebuck at ten paces; twice the gun does not go off, the third time the bullet lands indeed on the buck, which, however, trots off into the bushes unharmed. As Wilhelm flings himself on the ground in deep dejection he is accosted by an old soldier with a wooden leg, to whom he tells his sad story. The soldier, having examined the young man's gun, assures him that it is bewitched. But there are such things, he says, as magic bullets, and giving the young man one of his own he points to a far-away speck in the sky and bids him fire. The incredulous Wilhelm does so, and brings down the biggest vulture ever seen in those parts. The making of magic bullets, the soldier assures him, is an art that can be learned. He will give Wilhelm a lesson some time, but now he must leave him, as the village clock has just struck seven. (We shall meet with this "seven o'clock" motif in the opera.) Before going away he gives the young man a handful of his own bullets. Wilhelm tests one of these against one of his own: the latter fails miserably, as before; with the former he has incredible luck.

2

This, of course, is the beginning of the end for poor fated Wilhelm. Back in the ranger's house, where all rejoice over his bag for the day, he learns that there has been a little accident during his absence; a rusty nail on which the portrait of the original Kuno was hung had given way at exactly seven that morning, and the picture had crashed to the ground. Wilhelm remembers uneasily that it was precisely at that hour that the uncanny old soldier had told him he must leave him. He intends to keep the charmed bullets for the trial, but is compelled to use some of them on his hunting expeditions with the ranger. At last he is down to two—and the visit of the grand master of the chase is announced for the morrow! Wilhelm thinks he is safe now; but a messenger arrives with the news that the visit is put off for a week, and meanwhile a plentiful supply of game is to be collected for the notables' consumption. Wilhelm has to sacrifice one of his remaining trusty bullets, but determines to keep the other for the trial. But Bertram reproaches him for once more returning with a poor bag; and so in the end the last bullet has to go. From a conversation between the ranger and one of the huntsmen (Rudolf), Wilhelm learns that once upon a time there was a certain Georg Schmid, a promising young marksman of rather wild disposition, who had boasted that soon he would be the best shot of the neighbourhood. One day his body was found fearfully mangled; he was taken to Prague, and before he died he confessed that with the assistance of an old hunter in the mountains he had made magic bullets warranted to bring down anything they were aimed at, but that owing to some oversight or other on his part the devil had made him pay for his acquisitions with his life. He described in detail the dreadful nocturnal rites he had observed with the huntsman towards midnight at the cross roads; we shall meet with these at first hand when we come to our analysis of the opera. In an access of terror he had leaped out of the charmed circle, whereupon the devil had fallen on him with tooth and claw.

3

After a night of torturing dreams Wilhelm goes again into the forest in search of the old soldier. Not being able to find him either that day or the next, he resolves to put into practice by himself all he had learned from the story of Georg Schmid. On the night before the day of the trial—which he hopes will be the day also of his wedding to Käthchen—he goes to the cross roads in the forest, more than ever ill at ease, for the portrait of grandfather Kuno has not only broken loose once more from its nail but wounded Käthchen on the forehead in its fall. In the depths of the forest, by the ghastly light of the moon, with owls and bats and birds of prey hovering over him and croaking horribly round the skulls and bones with which the place is strewn, he sets to work. A shadowy figure stretches out its hand towards him in despairing supplication: an owl's wings fan the dying coals into life for a moment, and in the sinister light Wilhelm recognises the figure as that of his dead mother. It disappears, and once more, with horror piling on horror all round him, he addresses himself to his work. As he is nearing the end of it—sixty of the regulation sixty-three bullets having been cast—he hears a voice frenziedly calling his name, and he sees his Käthchen trying to escape from a maniacal old woman, and the one-legged soldier barring her way. At the end of his strength, Wilhelm ceases his work and is about to leap out of the infernal circle when the clock strikes midnight, the vision disappears, the owls take flight, the coals die out, and Wilhelm sinks to the ground exhausted. A rider on a black horse approaches slowly and claims *his* share in the night's work—sixty bullets for Wilhelm, three for him—the sixty will hit any mark, the three will befool him. ("Jene treffen, diese äffen.") The young man refusing to deal with him, the Black Rider leaves him with a threat of punishment for his insolence.

Käthchen and her parents are horrified by Wilhelm's ghastly aspect when he returns to the house after midnight, but he explains it as the effect of the night air: then he admits that something portentous has happened to him, but begs that it may remain a secret for another nine days. He retires to his own room, and, torn between his conscience, his hopes and his fears, swears he will renounce all the magic bullets but one—and surely heaven will condone that one, for his object is simply to win Käthchen with it.

4

In due course the huntmaster arrives, and, on the grounds that the real test of a marksman is in the chase, insists on Wilhelm accompanying him into the forest for a day's shooting before the regulation trial. The young man has no choice, though he knows it means the expenditure of the last bullet on which he can rely. Meanwhile preparations for the wedding are going on. The priest arrives. Old Anne, Käthchen's mother, cannot produce the bridal wreath, owing to the jamming of the lock of the drawer in which she had placed it; so a child is sent off in hot haste to a florist's, with instructions to bring back the most beautiful chaplet in the shop. He returns with a funeral wreath that has taken his innocent fancy. For a moment Käthchen and Anne stand aghast at the omen; but by good fortune the lock is now made to work and the true bridal wreath is taken out and placed on Käthchen's head.

When the hunters return, the hunt-master is loud in his praises of Wilhelm's prowess; it seems ridiculous, he says, to subject so superlative a marksman to the formality of a trial shot. Still, the traditional routine must be followed, for appearance's sake; so he orders Wilhelm to fire at a white dove that has perched on a pillar. Käthchen cries out in protest; she had dreamed the night before, she tells them, that she was a white dove. Her mother had fastened a ring round her neck; then Wilhelm had fired at it, and her mother had fallen bathed in blood. Wilhelm lowers the gun he had raised to his shoulder, but the hunt-master twits Käthchen on her lack of nerve and orders the young man to fire. He does so, and Käthchen falls to the ground with a death-cry—her forehead has been shattered, and the bullet is still in the wound. By the side of his dead bride Wilhelm sees the one-legged old soldier laughing eerily at him, and hears him say "Sechzig treffen, drei äffen." The young man draws his hunting-knife and rushes at him, but his strength fails him and he sinks down by the corpse of his bride. "The master of the hunt and the priest," the story as told by Apel concludes, "tried in vain to console the old couple who had lost their child. Hardly had the mother laid the too prophetic funeral wreath on the dead Käthchen's breast when her own life ebbed away with her tears. The father followed her to the tomb before long. Wilhelm ended his days in a madhouse."

5

Apel had described his story as a "folk-saga," and as such it was regarded all through the first half-century of the opera's existence: the original playbill describes it as "an opera in three acts, founded in part on the folk-tale of the free-shot." Kind himself, in the first edition of his libretto, said that "the subject, as is well known, is derived from an old Bohemian folk-saga." It was reserved for Meynert, in 1872, to track this legend of an "old Bohemian folk-saga" to its source. He had come upon a curious collection of "Discussions from the Spirit-World" that had appeared in Leipzig in 1729 and the following years. The two interlocutors, Andrenio and Pneumatophilo, discuss, as the preamble to their fifth conversation puts it with Teutonic concision, "the nature of spirits, their fall, their characteristics before and after their fall, whether and how it is possible for them to take bodily form, to what extent God in His holy ordinance has permitted them to control the earthly elements, what can be done in the way of magic, pacts with spirits, the finding and keeping of hidden treasures, the state of those possessed by spirits, together with the various opinions held as to the souls of the dead, their apparitions, how much truth there is in the many stories about spirits: the whole examined in the light of Holy Scripture, the ancient Church Fathers, the best philosophers and other famous men, and placed at the service of the learned world and other lovers of such marvels by Andrenio and Pneumatophilo."

It is in their fifth conversation, as has just been said, that these two learned men take up the question whether or not the archfiend sometimes enters into pacts with human beings for their destruction. Pneumatophilo has no doubts about it; and to prove his case he tells in full the story of Georg Schmid, a young Bohemian of no more than eighteen years, a clerk by profession. The misadventure befell him in the year 1710. He had quite a reputation as a target shot, but his ambition rose higher than that; in particular he wished to put his skill to good financial use. So he sought out a huntsman in the mountains who had the reputation of being well up in magic arts. On the night of the 30th July the pair went to the cross roads and there began the manufacture of sixty-three magic bullets, to the accompaniment of all the hair-raising horrors described in Apel's story and later exploited by the librettist and the composer of *Der Freischütz.* When their work was completed a Black Rider approached and claimed all the bullets as rightly his. When the hunter refused to give up more than the regulation three, the horseman took himself off in so terrible a rage that the pair fell half-dead to the ground. There they remained until the dawn, when the hunter managed to pull himself together sufficiently to pick up the bullets, return to the village, and tell the villagers that a poor sick man was lying at the cross roads. Georg Schmid, brought before both a civil and an ecclesiastical court, confessed his crime and was sentenced to be beheaded and his body burnt.

6

The story of Georg Schmid was not really a "folk-saga," as Apel styled it, but the official record of a criminal process in some small Bohemian town or other, probably Taus, in the year 1710. That Apel was acquainted with the *Unterredungen von dem Reiche der Geister* of 1730 is beyond question: his copy is still in possession of the Apel family, and there can be no doubt that the story of Georg Schmid as told by Pneumatophilo is the *fons et origo* of Weber's opera. It forms the core of Apel's novel: to what extent the general setting of it there is purely Apel's own work, or whether he was indebted for some of his details to yet other legends, we do not know.

Max Maria von Weber tells us that his father and a certain Alexander von Dusch made the acquaintance of Apel's *Gespenst-erbuch* on its publication in 1810 and at once saw the possibilities of an opera in it. Dusch went so far as to draft a scenario and elaborate some of the episodes; but as his occupation as a lawyer left him with no time to complete the text, Weber threw himself into the composition of his *Abu Hassan,* which was produced at Munich in June 1811. Towards the end of 1816 he was placed by the King of Saxony in charge of the German Opera in Dresden. There he renewed a recent acquaintance with one Friedrich Kind,

⌐tired lawyer ⟍ ⊃ fancied himself greatly as a man of letters, and discussed wi. him the question of an opera text. Their choice fell on Apel's ⌐ory of *Der Freischütz*, and the libretto was completed in a few ⌐eks' time. The problem of whether the censorship would aut. ⌐ise the stage representation of such a story of gross popular superstition was solved by Kind's transference of the action to the period following the Thirty Years' War. A happy ending was substituted for Apel's sombre dénouement, and innocence was shown prevailing over evil.

To bring this about a pious hermit had to be invented, who was to engineer the happy ending in a way which will appear later, in our analysis of the opera. For an explanation of the appearance of the hermit in the final scene of the opera we have to go to the opening scenes of Kind's original libretto. There the action began in a woodland, complete with hermit's hut, a cross covered with white roses, and an altar of turf before which the holy man is kneeling in prayer when the curtain rises. Suddenly he looks round him in horror, for he has seen a dreadful vision—the foul fiend lurking in the shadows, and stretching out his great hand towards an innocent lamb—none other than the heroine of the piece, Agathe—and her bridegroom, towards whom his intentions are obviously of the evillest. The hermit rises to his feet, not quite certain whether old age is not playing sorry pranks with his poor mind. "Cold flows the blood in the veins of age! And then come visions from God! For three days I have not seen Agathe, and already evening is about to fall. But over there, if my eyes do not deceive me . . . Yes! It is she!" Agathe and her companion Ännchen enter, the former carrying a pitcher of milk, the latter a basket containing bread and fruit for the holy man. Agathe tells him how much she loves him, apologises for not having called on him earlier, and confides in him that the Max to whom she is betrothed has fallen into a melancholy mood; he is worrying about the trial shot on which so much will depend on the morrow. The hermit tells her that he too is ill at ease, for a vision he has just seen forebodes some evil or other, he knows not what. He will pray for them both, he says; and as further protection he gives her some of the white roses growing on his bush, which had been brought from Palestine by a pilgrim to his predecessor in the hermitship; the roses, when pressed, have a reputation in the neighbourhood as a guard against sickness and misfortune. The hermit and Agathe blend their voices in a duet rich in pious sentiments, and the curtain falls.

Kind's text, which bore in the first instance the title of *The Trial Shot*, and later *The Hunter's Bride*, was submitted to the judgment of Weber's fiancée, the singer Caroline Brandt, who advised the excision of these preliminary scenes and a plunge straight into the third scene, that of a popular merry-making in front of the village inn. Weber agreed with her, and Kind fell in unwillingly with their wishes, though out of pride of authorship he included the two discarded scenes in his own imprint of the text. In his later years (he died in 1843) he denied that he was specifically indebted to Apel for his story. In the early 1780's they had been fellow-students at the St. Thomas School in Leipzig, the Conrector of which allowed them to help him in his work in the Town Library, of which he was superintendent. According to Kind's story he had himself found there an old volume which, by his description of it, might or might not have been the *Unterredungen* of about 1730; but as later librarians have all denied that such a book had ever been in the Leipzig library, Kind's account of the matter has not been accepted by scholars. The probability is that his knowledge of the legend had no other source than Apel's *Gespensterbuch* of 1810.

7

The composition of *Der Freischütz* occupied Weber, off and on, from July 1817 to May 1820. The work was produced on the 18th June 1821, not in Dresden, however, where Weber was still Kapellmeister, but in Berlin on the opening night of the newly built Court Theatre. It was an immediate and immense success: both the subject and the musical treatment of it appealed to all that was most romantically German in the German romantic consciousness of the day. In form it is a singspiel, i.e. a stage action carried on in large part by means of speech, with music striking in every now and then to raise the lyrical or dramatic expression to a higher emotional plane.

The overture—still one of the most popular things of its kind—should be listened to even in the concert room with a full knowledge of the dramatic significance of each theme and each sector of it: analysis of it had therefore better be deferred until we have made our acquaintance with the opera itself.

The curtain rises on an open space before a tavern on the edge of a forest. The local rustics have been engaged in a shooting contest, and at the moment when the action opens the winning shot is being fired by the peasant Kilian; it shatters the last remaining star on a wooden target in the background. The feat is greeted by the spectators with cries of "Victoria! Victoria!": even the young huntsman Max, who is sitting moodily aside from the others, with his mug of beer in front of him, rouses himself sufficiently from his dejection to congratulate his successful rival. Then, bringing the butt end of his rifle down violently on the ground, he asks himself, half in anger, half in despair, what has gone wrong with him: "have the sinews of this hand lost their strength? Have I gone blind?"

The peasants sing the praises of the victor in a rousing chorus, accompanied by exuberant rushes in the strings. Then the elated Kilian calls for some "Bohemian mountain music," which Weber supplies in full measure in the form of a march in the popular vein, to the tune of which the peasants parade in procession, some carrying what is left of the target and the pewter prizes they have won, and all of them lauding Kilian as the prince of marksmen. As the procession passes Max they greet him with ironic acclamations. Finally Kilian plants himself arrogantly in front of him and bursts into a rough song in praise of himself and mockery of his humiliated rival, commanding them all, Max included, to doff their hats to him:

No. 1

Schau der Herr mich an als Kö-nig, dünkt ihm mei-ne Macht zu we-nig?

until Max, unable to endure their derision any longer after the third stanza, draws his hunting knife and seizes Kilian by the throat, crying "Leave me in peace, or—!" Weber gives an extra loutish touch to the song by doubling the voice part in the bassoons, while the flute and violoncellos finish off their phrases with a guffaw:

No. 2

As the others seize and manhandle Max, the head ranger, Cuno, enters with Caspar and other foresters, and demands to be told why so many of them are attacking one, and that one a lad in his employ. Kilian, sobered and scared, explains whiningly that it has all been in the way of kindness: it is the harmless fashion of the little shooting community to have a good laugh at the expense of the loser, especially when, as in the present instance, the common farm hand has beaten the professional hunter. In reply to a horrified query by Cuno, Max has to admit that he has failed lamentably; and another young forester, Caspar, ejaculates aside, "Thanks, Samiel!" (We shall discover presently that Caspar has already placed himself in the power of the sinister Samiel, the Black Hunter, by accepting his aid in the making of some magic bullets: his period of grace having almost expired, he must either pay the regulation penalty for his impious rashness or find a fresh victim to take his place. He now sees his chance to use Max's misfortunes to save his own skin.)

Max has been bewitched, Caspar tells him, and he will never shoot well again until he has broken the spell. He should go next Friday to the cross roads, draw a circle round him with his rifle or a bloody sword, and call three times on the Great Hunter. Cuno, cutting him short, reproves Caspar for his impiety: he has always been known, he says, as an idler, a gormandiser, a cheat at dice; let him take care that he doesn't get the reputation of being something even worse. Then Cuno admonishes Max: fond as he is of him, if the young man fails in the contest tomorrow he will not only lose his bride but will have to leave the ranger's service. (At this point of the libretto, as published by Kind, Cuno, at the request of Kilian and the others, tells them at full length the story of the institution of the hereditary rangership in his distant ancestor's time, the malicious whisperings there had been then about a "free bullet," and the injunction that henceforth each new aspirant to the post must "prove himself" with a trial shot on his wedding day.) Kilian tells the others that he has heard from his grandfather about these magic bullets, of which six are guaranteed to hit the mark while the seventh goes where the foul fiend wills.[1] Caspar swears it is all nonsense, but does not forget to mutter his saving catchword, "Help, Samiel!" This spoken episode can safely be omitted from modern versions of the opera, it being taken for granted that the listener knows all about it by this time. The explanation, however, must have been as vital to the audiences of 1821 as that of Gurnemanz to the squires in the first act of *Parsifal* still is to us. But Gurnemanz's explanation of what had happened before the commencement of the opera, with its constant interplay of leading motives, has an organic musical interest; whereas Cuno's is in the bald prose of everyday.

There follows a short trio, in which Max bemoans his ill luck and looks forward sadly to the morrow:

No. 3

and Caspar, to a strain of the type of Kilian's song (No. 1), with the bassoons once more supplying the appropriate rustic colouring, exhorts him to pluck up courage. The chorus also advises him, to a melody in the true German folk vein, not to lose heart:

No. 4

Cuno orders the huntsmen to prepare for the next day's chase, and they and the peasants break out into a joyous chorus:

[1] Kind and Weber found it necessary, for obvious reasons of stage time, to cut down the number of bullets cast at the cross roads from sixty-three to seven.

No. 5

Allegro moderato

Wir las — sen die Hör-ner er-schal-len,wir las —sen die

through which the horns blow lustily in four parts.

8

The gay company of hunters goes off, Kilian and the villagers remaining behind. Kilian now approaches the more than ever dejected Max, wishes him good luck at the trial, invites him to drink in the tavern with him, and suggests his joining the others afterwards in a dance. Max, however, feels no more like the one than the other; so Kilian leaves him to his gloomy brooding. Kilian and the peasants indulge in a "Bohemian waltz" of the simplest kind:

No. 6

Couple by couple they all drift into the tavern, leaving Max alone on the now darkening stage. He can bear the burden of fate no longer, he cries. For what sin is he being made to pay this dreadful penalty? He recalls his happiness in the past, when he roamed the forest:

No. 7

Moderato

Durch die Wäl-der, durch die Au-en zog ich leich-ten Sinns da —hin!

revelling in his skill as a marksman, and his joy when, at nightfall, he would return to his loving Agathe. Suddenly the atmosphere of the scene changes: as he cries "Has heaven, then, forsaken me?" there is a tremolando in the violas (reinforced by sinister low notes in the clarinets) that gradually extends to the higher strings and is punctuated by throbbing octaves deep down in the kettledrums and basses; it is the distinguishing tab of Samiel throughout the opera:

No. 8

The chord of the diminished seventh, destined to play so large a part in the romantic apparatus for the musical expression of horror, has now established itself firmly in the score. The evil Samiel is dimly seen, a more than life-size figure, standing motionless among the bushes in the background; he is dressed in dark green shot with flame-colour and gold. He disappears as Max asks the universe what his fate is now to be—is he doomed to ruin? Will blind chance decide his fate?

The mood and the texture of the music change again as Max thinks of his Agathe sitting at her open window, straining her ears for the sound of his returning footsteps. But the idyllic atmosphere of this section of his monologue is suddenly rent by a harsh chord in the clarinets, bassoons and violas, which leads into the next main section. Doubt and despair once more take possession of him: "the powers of darkness spin their web about me; I am a failure and a scorn"; and Samiel (invisible, of course, to Max) traverses the back of the stage with giant strides. Max's agitation is expressed in a series of stumbling syncopations in the orchestra:

No. 9

"Will no ray of light pierce the darkness that surrounds me?" he cries, to the accompaniment of agitated tremolandos in the strings:

No. 10

"Does blind fate govern all things? Is there no God?" At the mention of the deity Samiel shudders convulsively and disappears, leaving Max to continue his harangue in ever-increasing despair.

For a while the music is replaced by dialogue. Caspar enters stealthily and accosts Max; he has come, he says, to put into operation for his friend's benefit an idea that has just struck him. Let him not take too much to heart the crude derision of the peasants. Caspar calls to the tavern for wine to replace Max's beer, for in beer, he says, there is no inspiration for him or any other man. Max is reluctant to drink, for his head is confused enough already. (Samiel appears for a moment in the background.) Caspar craftily proposes three toasts, not one of which, he knows, can Max refuse to honour—first of all the head ranger Cuno, then Agathe, and finally the prince. Between the drinking of the toasts Caspar breaks out into a crude song in praise of the consolatory properties of wine:

No. 11

each stanza of which ends with shrill demoniac laughter in the piccolos:

No. 12

(The piccolos sound an octave higher than written.) The realistic effect—a novel one in the orchestral writing of that day—is still found worthy of quotation in our manuals of orchestration.

There follows another long spell of dialogue. Drop by drop Caspar pours his poison into Max's reluctant ear. There are certain secret powers of nature, it appears, certain innocent hunter's arts, that can be pressed into the young man's service if he goes the right way about it. (At the mention of these Samiel comes into sight once more, listening in silence.) Caspar can help Max to get a bullet that will ensure his winning Agathe on the morrow. Forcing his own rifle into the young man's hands he bids him fire at a speck in the sky: Max does so, and brings down a huge golden eagle. This will stagger the peasants, Caspar assures him; this will rejoice Agathe's heart; and to the latter end he plucks out some of the eagle's feathers and fastens them in Max's hat.

In spite of the horror all this inspires in him Max becomes more and more impressed. "What kind of a bullet was that?" he asks. Has he never heard of a "free shot"? Caspar replies. Old soldiers know all about these things: it is with the aid of bullets of this sort that the sharpshooters bring down their man through all the powder-clouds of battle; it was such a ball that slew the King of Sweden at Lützen, notwithstanding his leather jerkin. But to make these bullets a special art is required. Unfortunately the ball he had given Max was the last of his own store. But more can be made this very night, when there will be a total eclipse of the moon. It is the chance of a lifetime for Max—the rangership and Agathe both won with one shot!

Max gradually succumbs as Caspar craftily plays on his hopes and fears. He promises to meet his tempter in the awe-inspiring Wolf's Glen at midnight, uncanny as the hour and the locality are, and there learn the art of casting "free" bullets. At the moment of his complete surrender Samiel appears and gives his minion Caspar an approving nod. Max goes away, promising again, for Agathe's sake and his own, to keep the midnight rendezvous. After his departure Caspar breaks into a song of mocking triumph: "Hell's net is closing round you: nothing can save you now. Gather round him, ye powers of darkness: already he is in your toils! Triumph! Revenge is mine": [1]

---

[1] This melody well illustrates a characteristic of Weber's style—his inclination towards a type of phrase that swings, as it were, up and down on a pivotal note; in the present example, short as it is, we see the swing taking place twice. This Weberian "fingerprint" reveals itself hundreds of times in

No. 13

ff Der Höl-le Netz hat dich um-garnt, der Höl-le Netz hat dich um-garnt!

9

The second act presents us first of all with a domestic scene of the old German type. When the curtain rises we see an antechamber in Cuno's house. Evidently in days gone by this has been the hunting lodge of some prince or other, for the walls are decorated with weapons and trophies of the chase. On one side of the stage is Ännchen's spinning wheel; on the other a table with a lighted lamp, and Agathe's white wedding gown trimmed with green ribbon. In the background is a balcony, the curtains in front of which are at present closed. On a ladder stands Ännchen, giving the final hammer blows to the nail from which the time-honoured portrait of the original Cuno had broken loose, injuring Agathe in its fall: when the action begins we see her removing a bandage from her forehead. Her costume suggests that she is about to retire for the night.

Ännchen, whose frivolous spirits are intended as a foil to the more serious Agathe, playfully apostrophises the nail: the rogue, as she calls him, has had his bit of fun at their expense, but the thrashing she has just given him will keep him in his place for another hundred years. She rallies her cousin on her woebegone look; she herself is all for dancing and laughter, while Agathe is silent and thoughtful even on her wedding eve. Agathe confesses that she is worried about her Max: "How lonely and quiet it is here without him!" she sighs. Ännchen agrees that there must be pleasanter places for a young woman to spend the night before her wedding in than this eerie old place, especially when ancient dodderers about whom no one cares a farthing take it into their heads to crash down on her. For her part, she sings in a sprightly little arietta—for of course the second lady of an opera is as much entitled to her show piece as the first:

his works; it is seen, for instance, in our *Freischütz* analysis, in Nos. 4, 6, 15, 17, 18, 28, 29. In his dramatic music it sometimes has the disadvantage of giving much the same physiognomy to quite different characters in different psychological circumstances.

No. 14

Kommt ein schlan-ker Bursch ge-gan-gen, blond von Lo-cken o-der braun,

if a good-looking young fellow should come her way, be he fair or be he dark, though she would cast down her eyes in maiden modesty, she would lose no time in bringing him to the point. The arietta is decorated with many innocently roguish little touches in the orchestra.

Agathe admits that she is not as free from care as she ought to be; particularly since she returned from a visit she had paid the hermit that afternoon a load has seemed to lie on her heart. At her cousin's request she tells her the story of the hermit's vision, his warning of danger threatening her, and his gift of the consecrated roses. She is willing now to believe that the "danger" he had foreseen was from the picture, which might have killed her in its fall. The roses the holy man had given her are doubly dear to her now, and she agrees with Ännchen's suggestion that they shall be placed outside the window in the cool night air. But in answer to her cousin's advice that she shall now go to bed she cries, "No, not until Max is here!" Thereupon Ännchen, with a shrug of the shoulders at the foolish fancies of people in love, leaves her to her own devices.

10

Agathe now has the field to herself for her great scena. How tranquil was her sleep, she muses in a short recitative, before she gave her heart to Max; but love and grief always go hand in hand. She draws the background curtains, and we see a landscape stretching out under a sky studded with stars. She steps out on to the balcony, raises her hands in prayer, and to a gently swaying accompaniment of muted strings and violas begins her famous aria, "Softly, softly, my song, ascend to the starry heavens, bearing with you my prayers":

No. 15

pp Lei-se, lei-se from-me Wei-se, schwing' dich auf zum Ster-nen-krei—se!

513

But over the far-off mountains a storm seems to be gathering, she continues in another short recitative, and sinister clouds are already lowering over the nearby wood. She resumes, to the strain of No. 15, her prayer for the protection of heaven. Where is her beloved now? she asks to a new melody:

No. 16

She can hear only the gentle rustling of the trees—an effect suggested in the orchestra—and the crickets and the nightingale rejoicing in the silence of the night. She believes she hears her lover's footsteps at last, and waves a greeting to him with her handkerchief. Unless the moonlight deceives her there is a nosegay in his hat, betokening his victory in the contest. This is a good omen for the morrow, and the final stage of the aria begins with an expression of hope and gladness:

No. 17

The climax comes with a great cry of gratitude to heaven:

No. 18

after which the exuberant No. 17 is taken up again.

Max enters, followed shortly afterwards by Ännchen, and for a while the music is replaced by spoken dialogue. Max is obviously in a state of great agitation; and Agathe's heart sinks as she perceives that his hat is adorned not with the expected trophy but with an eagle's feather. He tells her, to her astonishment and dismay, that he must leave her again immediately, notwithstanding the gathering storm. He throws his hat on the table, thus extinguishing the lamp and leaving the room in darkness except for the faint light from the night sky. But Ännchen, sagely remarking that if it were not for the moon the place would be in darkness, immediately relights the lamp; and we are left wondering why the episode was introduced at all.

To the girls' eager enquiries as to what he had won at the shooting contest Max replies, in obvious embarrassment, that he had not taken part in it, but that he had been fortunate enough to bring down a huge eagle. Then he notices the wound in Agathe's forehead. She and Ännchen explain that it came about through the picture of old Cuno breaking loose from its nail just as the village clock was striking seven. Max remembers with a shudder that it was at the stroke of seven that Caspar had begun to spread his evil toils round him. To cover his confusion he tells the anxious Agathe that he has had another big stroke of luck besides the eagle: he had shot down a great stag, which he must bring in at once before the peasants find it and rob him of it. It lies, he says, in the depths of the forest—not far from the Wolf's Glen.

At this point the music begins again. The girls recoil in horror at the mention of that sinister place, with its associations with the Wild Huntsman, and a trio follows in which they try to dissuade Max from his purpose, which he justifies as best he can, though he is obviously ill at ease. A little figure that begins in the violoncellos and weaves its way in and out of much of the texture of the trio:

No. 19

well conveys the agitation that possesses them all.

In the doorway Max pauses to pour out his love for Agathe in a sad little melody in Weber's tenderest vein:

No. 20

Doch hast du auch ver—ge——ben den Vor-wurf, den Ver-dacht?

in which he asks her forgiveness for having hurt her. She herself takes up the phrase and the trio is resumed; Max protesting that his destiny calls him away before the moon shall have quite disappeared, Agathe assuring him of her love but warning him of the risks he is running, and Ännchen commenting on it all in her usual irresponsible fashion. At last Max rushes out with a final cry of "My fate tears me away!"

11

The scene changes to the Wolf's Glen—a fearsome ravine surrounded by high mountains, down the side of one of which a waterfall pours. The moon is full and pallid, and two storms from opposite directions seem to be contending for possession of the place. Near the foreground is a blasted tree, so rotten internally that it emits a ghastly putrescent glow. On one side of the stage a great owl is perched on the gnarled branch of a tree; on other trees are ravens and other forest birds. All the best accredited stage "properties" of the romantic horror of the early nineteenth century are now assembled, and no musician in Europe in that epoch was better qualified to put them to effective use than Weber.

Blood-curdling mutterings in the violins and violas over long-held chords in the clarinets and a descending line in the violoncellos and basses, punctuated now and then by threatening growls in the trombones, bring it home to us that we are in the Wolf's Glen at midnight as forcibly as any stage setting can do. In the dim light we catch sight of Caspar, hatless and in his shirt-sleeves, but otherwise complete with hunting-bag and knife, making a circle of black stones with a skull as its centrepiece; a few feet away lie an eagle's wing, a casting-ladle and a bullet-mould. From all sides come the voices of invisible spirits intoning a spell: "Uhui! Uhui! Moon's milk on the leaves, spiders' webs bedewed with blood! Uhui! Ere the dawn the tender bride will lie dead! Ere the night has run its course shall the sacrifice be offered!

Uhui!" At each "Uhui!" there is an uncanny owlish outburst of diminished sevenths in the orchestra:

No. 21

As a distant clock strikes twelve Caspar completes the circle of stones, draws his hunting-knife, plunges it into the skull, raises the ghastly symbol aloft, and calls on Samiel to appear.

A rock is rent in twain and Samiel appears, to the accompaniment, as usual, of No. 8. "Who calls me?" he asks. Caspar prostrates himself before his master. Accompanied by an agitated figure:

No. 22

that persistently winds its way in and out in the orchestra, the pair go over the terms of their compact of old. Caspar's time expires the next day, and Samiel categorically refuses him an extension. Thereupon Caspar proposes to provide a substitute, a young associate of his who wants some magic bullets: "Sechse treffen, sieben äffen" ("Six hit the mark, seven befool"), says Samiel grimly. The seventh, Caspar suggests, shall be directed by Samiel against the young man's bride; this will reduce both him and the girl's father to despair. "Over her as yet I have no power," Samiel complains. "Will the young man suffice, then?" Caspar asks eagerly. "That remains to be seen," is the reply; meanwhile Caspar is provisionally given another three years' grace, at the end of which time he must provide the Black Hunter with yet another victim. "By the gates of Hell, then—tomorrow either he or thou!" Samiel vanishes to the accompaniment of a thunder-crash in the orchestra.

A new syncopated figure:

No. 23

which, as will be seen, terminates in the crazy laugh of No. 12 in the wood wind, depicts Caspar as he slowly pulls himself together after the departure of Samiel. The knife and the skull disappear, their place being taken by a small hearth with glowing coals and some faggots. He wipes the sweat from his brow, takes a swig at his flask to steady his nerves, and blesses the name of Samiel. His only anxiety now is as to whether Max will keep the tryst. The glow of the coals begins to fade; he bends down and puts on some faggots, and owls and other birds obligingly fan the embers with their wings.

12

Caspar's fears are set at rest when Max appears on the top of the rock opposite the waterfall. He is appalled by the horrors of the hour and the scene—the dark abyss at his feet, the reek of hell in the atmosphere, the distant thunder, the fading of the moon, the ghostly forms flitting about in the darkness, the blasted tree that seems to stretch out rapacious fingers towards him, and the beating of eerie wings in the bushes; all these grisly effects being pictorially suggested in the orchestra. At last, to Caspar's great relief, he summons up courage enough to descend a few steps with the desperate intention of braving his fate. But on the opposite rock he sees in the faint moonlight the spirit of his dead mother, urging him with a gesture to retrace his steps. Caspar calls on Samiel, who at once substitutes for the apparition the figure of Agathe with all the attributes of stage madness, including straw in her loosened hair; she seems to be on the point of throwing herself into the waterfall. This decides Max: as the apparition disappears he descends with a wild cry into the hollow.

Feverishly he asks Caspar what he has to do now. He refuses to undertake the casting himself; that is contrary, he says, to their agreement. So Caspar takes charge of the ceremony. He bids Max enter the charmed circle, which is a protection against all powers between heaven and hell; and whatever he may see or hear he is not to be dismayed, even, he adds with a malicious laugh, if it were a Black Rider on a black horse breathing fire: "but when you see *me* tremble, come to my aid and repeat what I shall say. If you don't, we are lost."

By this time the moon has almost totally disappeared. Caspar initiates the shuddering Max into the magic art, the ingredients for which he takes out of his game-bag and throws one by one into the crucible. "First the lead; then a bit of glass from a broken church window; a morsel of quicksilver; three bullets that have already hit their mark; the right eye of a hoopoe and the left eye of a lynx. *Probatum est!* And now for the blessing of the bullets!" Three times he prostrates himself, to ominous quasi-silences in the orchestra; then, as No. 8 pulsates in the strings and kettle-drum, once more he invokes his master: "Thou who watchest in the darkness, Samiel, Samiel, be near me this night till the magic rites be finished. Anoint for me the herb and the lead, blessings give them seven, nine and three, and give them magic power! Samiel, Samiel, hither to me!"

13

The contents of the crucible begin to effervesce and hiss and emit a greenish-white light. A cloud creeps over what is left of the moon, so that now the scene is lit only by the glow from the hearth, the great owl's eyes, and the putrescent gleam of the rotten wood of the tree. Caspar casts a bullet, drops it out of the mould, and calls out "One!":

No. 24

As echo repeats the word nightbirds descend and surround the circle, hopping about and flapping their wings:

No. 25

After "Two!" and its echo a sinister figure in bassoons and double basses worms its way time after time through shuddering chords in the strings:

No. 26

while a black boar crashes out of the bushes and runs wildly across the stage. Even Caspar is startled, but he manages to call out "Three!", and as the echo repeats the word a hurricane arises that rocks and rends the trees and sends sparks shooting up from the fire, with the characteristic figure of No. 26 now swirling madly in the heights and depths of the orchestra. So it goes on through "Four!", "Five!" and "Six!" The air is filled with the din of clattering wheels, cracking whips and galloping horses. Four wheels dart fire and flame as they career across the stage, though their speed makes it impossible to distinguish the outlines of the vehicle they carry. Next there comes a baying of hounds and a neighing of horses in the air, a mellay of hunters mounted and on foot, flying stags and pursuing hounds on the heights. The Wild Hunt is on:

No. 27

Invisible tenors and basses intone on a reiterated A flat (apart from a single excursion to a G) what Kind describes as a "fearful song": "Over hill and dale, through gorge and cavern, through dew and cloud, storm and night, through hollows, marshes, chasms, through fire, earth, air, land and sea! Jaho! Jaho! Wau! Wau!" Pitch darkness descends upon the scene: the various hurricanes collide to the accompaniment of peals of thunder and flashes of lightning, torrents of rain, eruptions of flame from the ground, will-of-the-wisps on the mountains. Trees are torn up by the roots; the waterfall goes plumb crazy; rocks come crashing down; the earth itself seems to totter blindly. Two frenzied motifs that will play their part in the overture:

No. 28

No. 29

take possession of the orchestra as Caspar, now writhing in convulsions, manages to scream "Six!" and then "Seven! Help, Samiel!" He and Max are caught up by the hurricane and tossed hither and thither: the former at last falls to the ground in the last stages of terror; Max manages to leap out of the circle, seize one of the branches of the blasted tree, and shriek, in his turn, "Samiel!" At that instant the storm begins to abate its fury: the tree disappears, and in its place Samiel is seen, reaching out for the young man's hand. "Here am I" he cries. Max, after making the sign of the cross, falls senseless to the ground, the violins depicting the last catches of his breath:

No. 30

521

As the clock strikes one, silence descends on the scene. Samiel has disappeared. Caspar is still lying with his face to the ground. With a last convulsive effort Max manages to rise to his feet, and the curtain falls.

14

In the ordinary vocal score of the opera the third act opens with a short orchestral introduction descriptive of a hunter's merrymaking, the main substance of it being a joyous melody in the brass:

No. 31

which Weber has marked "scherzando": then the curtain rises, disclosing Agathe in her chamber. For an explanation of the orchestral entr'acte, the relevance of which to Agathe is anything but apparent, we have to go to the orchestral score or to Kind's text. Actually there comes a whole scene before we are introduced to Agathe again. It is set in an open space in the woodland, with the joyous music of the hunters sounding off-stage; the time is the morning after the second act. Two of the prince's huntsmen are congratulating themselves on the change from last night's storm; apparently the devil had been let loose in the Wolf's Glen, for in the forest several great trees lie uprooted. But today, they say, they have ideal hunting weather. Caspar and Max enter, the latter flushed and agitated. The two huntsmen discuss in an undertone the astonishing skill as a marksman he has displayed that morning, and the certainty of his finding favour in the prince's eyes: then they depart.

Max feverishly asks Caspar for some of his magic bullets. "Three for me, four for you," Caspar reminds him sardonically; "could any share-out have been more brotherly?". "But I have only one left," Max protests; "the other three have just gone on those lucky shots that so astonished the prince. What have you done with yours?" Caspar takes a couple of magpies out of his game-bag: these, he explains, account for two of his bullets, leaving him, like Max, with only one; and anyhow, what concern of his are the prince and the rest of them? Max frenziedly demands the third bullet, but Caspar will not give it to him; surely the one Max has in his pouch will be all that is necessary to ensure his success in the trial? At this point a hunter enters with the news that the prince desires to see Max at once, to settle a dispute that has arisen among them as to the range of the young man's gun. Max again pleads for the gift of Caspar's last bullet, and is again roughly repulsed. He curses his false friend and leaves him. Caspar, left alone, plays his trump card; loading his gun he fires at a passing fox. That makes in all six used bullets; the fatal seventh, the devil's own, is the one left in Max's pouch; and with that, Caspar gloats, the young man will lose his bride, his ranger-ship, and everything else.

This first scene of the third act in its original form is in spoken dialogue throughout. It is vital to our understanding of the later course of the drama, for it explains why Max is left at the time of the trial shot with only one of his four bullets, the disastrous seventh.

<h2 style="text-align:center">15</h2>

After the departure of Caspar the scene changes, and music enters into its own once more. We see Agathe in an old-fashioned room of the house, at one side of which stands a prie-dieu on which is a vase containing a bouquet of white roses. She is in a bridal costume of white trimmed with green, and is kneeling at the prie-dieu. Her cavatina is introduced by an expressive violon-cello solo that plays a prominent part in all that follows:

No. 32

To this heartfelt strain she begins her song, which expresses her simple faith in sunshine after cloud and storm and in the protec-tion of heaven, for the world, surely, is not governed by blind chance. This is the most deeply-felt piece of music in the whole opera.

Ännchen enters—also in bridal finery—and asks why her cousin has been crying. Agathe explains that she has been racked with anxiety for Max all through the terrifying storm of last night. In a dream she had seen herself transformed into a white dove, at which her lover had fired; she had fallen, whereupon the dove vanished and she was once more Agathe, with a great bird of prey lying bleeding at her feet. Ännchen essays a naïve optimistic interpretation of the dream which fails to convince her cousin; so by way of reviving the latter's spirits she launches into a long—an over-long—mock-horrific aria which tells, to the accompaniment of shudders in the violins and violas, how an aunt of hers had dreamed one night that she was confronted in her bed by a fearsome monster with fiery eyes, which, however, turned out to be only the old house-dog, Nero. But all Ännchen's laborious efforts to dispel Agathe's despondency are in vain, though they take up an unconscionable amount of our time.

Their colloquy is interrupted by the entry of the bridesmaids, come to place the regulation bridal wreath on Agathe's head: they sing a simple little melody that instantaneously became a German national possession:

No. 33

(In 1821 the eight-years-old Richard Wagner played this "Jung-fernkranz" melody on the piano to his parents the night before Geyer's death. "Has he perhaps a talent for music?" the dying man asked the mother.) The naïve ditty runs on for four stanzas, each with the same refrain—"Schöner, grüner Jungfernkranz! Veilchenblaue Seide!"

At the entrance of the bridesmaids Ännchen had slipped out to get the bridal wreath that had been ordered from the neighbouring town. She returns with bad news: during the night the troublesome Cuno had once more broken from his nail and this time brought much of the plaster of the wall away with him. But this is not the worst. When Agathe opens the bandbox it is found to contain a silver funeral wreath, owing to a mistake on the part either of the florist or of the half-blind old maidservant who had been entrusted with the commission. All are duly horrified by this latest contretemps, though Agathe resignedly regards it as an admonition from heaven; when giving her the white roses the hermit had advised her to make her bridal wreath of these. She now orders this to be done; as she philosophically remarks, white flowers accompany a maiden to both the altar and the tomb. Ännchen twines the roses in her cousin's hair, the bridesmaids sing the "Jungfernkranz" chorus once more, and the curtain falls.

16

The next scene shows us a great gathering in the open country, strewn with the tents of the prince and his guests, most of whom are banqueting at tables on the sward. Scattered about are dead boars, stags and other game. Prince Ottokar is dining in his own tent: Cuno is seated at the end of the princely table, and Max stands by him, leaning on his gun, sunk in thought. On the other side of the stage Caspar is spying and eavesdropping behind a tree.

The huntsmen are doing just what is to be expected of them in an opera—singing in a lusty chorus the praises of the chase, to a tune:

No. 34

which counterpoints with No. 31 in the orchestra: at the finish they roar applause and clink glasses. The prince then recalls the company to the business of the day. He congratulates Cuno on his choice of a son-in-law whose only fault seems to be an excess of youthful impetuosity. "Where's the girl?" Caspar mutters uneasily; "help, Samiel!", and he climbs up into a tree to get a better view of things. Max takes a bullet out of his pouch, looks at it gloomily, and murmurs, "I've kept you till the last. Magic ball! Infallible! But you weigh a hundredweight in my hand!"

The prince expresses a desire to see the bride, of whom he has heard so much that is good. Cuno tells him that she is on her way, but begs that the trial may take place before her arrival, for the bridegroom has had a great deal of trouble lately, and the presence of the bride may fluster him. The prince smiles indulgently; this young forester is certainly a trifle peculiar, he says, though he had fired three excellent shots that morning; and he asks Cuno slyly whether perchance he has an older assistant whose years entitle him to priority of consideration. This causes Cuno much perturbation; but the prince cuts short his stammerings, explains that he merely feels that he must follow the traditional procedure, and orders Max to get ready: "one more shot like your first three today and you are safe!" At the veiled reference to a rival Max had shuddered: "Caspar no doubt still has the last of his magic bullets," he mutters: "he might—!" Then, hastily loading his gun, he ejaculates, "This once, but never again!"

Pointing to a white dove perched on a bough the prince gives him the order to fire. As Max brings the gun to his shoulder Agathe and her companions arrive at the tree on which the bird is standing. "Don't fire!" she cries; "I am the white dove." The bird flutters towards Caspar's tree, from which the villain descends hurriedly. Max aims at the dove and misses; but both Agathe and Caspar fall to the ground, shrieking. The hermit suddenly appears, raises Agathe, and then disappears among the crowd.

17

There is a general cry of horror—a massive chorus round which the orchestra plays feverishly; then a great cry of relief goes up as Agathe, evidently unhurt but naturally suffering from emotional strain, is led to a small mound, where the distracted and penitent Max falls on his knees before her. Ännchen, the bridesmaids, the prince and most of the huntsmen gather round her; others rush towards Caspar. There is a chorus of thanksgiving for Agathe's escape, interrupted for a moment by a cry from Caspar—who is writhing in convulsions on the ground, bathed in his own blood—and by a brief duet between Agathe and Max.

Caspar has no doubt now about his own fate: he had seen the hermit standing by Agathe when Max fired, and it was his own heart that the fatal bullet had reached. Behind him, though invisible to all the others, Samiel rises, accompanied by the sinister, shuddering No. 8. "You, Samiel?" Caspar groans; "here already? Is this how you keep your promise to me? Take then your prey; I hurl defiance at death and damnation and curse heaven and you!" He raises his clenched fist in a final defiant gesture, then collapses in a death agony. Cuno and the others comment in awe-struck tones on his evil life and horrible end.

At an order from the prince some of the hunters take away the miscreant's body to throw it into the Wolf's Glen. Then Ottokar turns to Max and sternly demands an explanation of it all. The young man's confession is prefaced, and later accompanied, by a mournful figure in the bassoon:

No. 35

that has quite a Wagnerian air. He admits that in a moment of grief and despair he had strayed from virtue's path and had re-course to magic arts: the last four bullets the prince had seen him fire were all "free" ones. In an access of anger Ottokar pro-nounces a sentence of banishment on him, coupled with the loss of Agathe's hand. Cuno, Agathe, Ännchen and the huntsmen plead for him, but the prince is inflexible: it must be either exile or imprisonment. The situation is saved by the venerable hermit, who now enters to solemn harmonies in horns and bassoons. They all listen with respectful attention—even the prince removing his hat—as he preaches a little sermon on the obligation of charity in our judgment of our fellow-mortals, for which of us, if he searches his own heart, is in a position to throw stones at others? He sug-gests that an end shall be made of this ceremony of the trial shot, and, to the accompaniment of a tender little melody in the flute, begs that Max, in virtue of his previous good behaviour, shall be put on probation for a year; at the end of that time, if his conduct has been satisfactory, he is to have his Agathe.[1] To this the prince

[1] Wagner used to tell the story of how, in his youth, an opera company that toured the smaller German towns found itself in the last act minus the player of the hermit's rôle. The problem of how to carry on without him was brilliantly solved. At the moment when he should have appeared to clear matters up a messenger came in with a missive for the prince—actually

agrees, the bystanders lauding his wisdom and clemency. Max breaks out into a song of gratitude that derives from the flute phrase that had accompanied the hermit's appeal for mercy:

No. 36

Die Zu — kunft soll —— mein Herz — be—wäh-ren

The four principals and many of the bystanders take up the strain; all fall upon their knees to receive the hermit's blessing, the orchestra gives out the melody (No. 17) to which, in the second act, Agathe had poured out her love for Max and her faith in a happy ending to their love; and upon this, together with the exuberant cry that had prefaced No. 17 in the original aria, the opera is brought to a jubilant C major close.

18

We are now in a position to follow the programmatic course of the overture.

It begins with one of those evocations of the spirit of field and forest so dear to the German musical heart—an introductory phrase in strings and wood wind:

No. 37

followed by a melody of quiet beauty in the horns:

No. 38

the music of the hermit's solo. "Ah," said Ottokar, "a message from my good old friend the hermit; let us see what the holy man has to say": and opening the roll he himself sang the hermit's part.

But over the idyllic peace of the forest a shadow creeps; shuddering strings and the throb of double basses and kettledrum (No. 8)
hint at the lurking Samiel, while sobbing phrases in the violoncellos suggest the lamentations of the victims he has caught in
his toils. Then comes a molto vivace section based on the latter
part of Max's aria in the first act, in which, with Samiel hovering in
the background, he had poured out his confession of despair and
doubt (No. 9 and No. 10); the latter is given out by a solo clarinet
over a fortissimo tremolando in the strings, and Weber has marked
the passage "con molta passione." The theme of Agathe's love
and hope (No. 17) inserts itself into this agitated tissue, and for
a while we see Max's soul as the battleground of the forces of
good and evil, the climax coming with a wild outburst of the
frenzied music of the Black Hunt at the end of the scene in the
Wolf's Glen (Nos. 28 and 29). The latter receives an extended
development, and the fight between the two principles is long and
fierce; it is noticeable that when, in the course of it, Agathe's
No. 17 reappears timidly three times in the oboe it is answered by
threatening growls from the trombones:

No. 39

No. 9 comes upon the scene again and the combat is renewed
with the same fury as before, until a gentle melody in violins and
bassoon:

No. 40

gradually gains the mastery over the demoniac No. 8, Samiel
disappears from the scene, and after a pianissimo followed by a
prolonged silence the good principle ꞌat last gets the upper hand,
with Agathe's No. 17 triumphant in the full orchestra.

La Traviata

VERDI [1813–1901]

PRINCIPAL CHARACTERS

Violetta Valery ("La Traviata")[1]	*Soprano*
Flora Bervoix	*Soprano*
Annina	*Soprano*
Giorgio Germont	*Baritone*
Alfredo Germont	*Tenor*
Gastone, Viscount de Letorières	*Tenor*
Baron Douphol	*Baritone*
Marquis d'Obigny	*Bass*
Dr. Grenvil	*Bass*

1

ARIE Duplessis, the heroine of Dumas *fils' La Dame aux Camélias*[2] and of Verdi's *La Traviata*, is one of the few people who have achieved such immortality as art can bestow on anyone within a few years of their death. As the reader will be aware, she was the most famous Parisian courtesan of an epoch that was peculiarly rich in that fauna. But to see her merely as that is to underrate her. She is psychologically the most intriguing and the most baffling crea-

---

[1] "Traviata" is the past participle feminine of the verb "traviare," meaning "to go astray."

[2] Dumas persisted in spelling the word thus until the end of his days. When it was pointed out to him that there should be two l's he replied gaily that George Sand before him had spelt it with one, and he would rather write incorrectly with Mme Sand than correctly with other people.

ture of her type that the modern world has known—"one of the mysteries of our epoch," as she was described by Jules Janin, who knew her well. Abundant testimony as to her strange beauty and her unanalysable charm is to be found in the writings of those of her contemporaries who have left us their reminiscences of her; and no doubt others, such as Liszt, who refrained from doing so—in public—would have grown equally lyrical over her had they written about her.

Jules Janin has recorded the impression she made on him on that day in 1845 when he and Liszt encountered her in the foyer of one of the minor Paris boulevard theatres. Her appearance was so charming, he says, her look so innocent, her manner so natural, "at once bold and becoming," that she gave one the impression of belonging to the highest society. "Her face was serious, her smile imposing; and merely from her carriage one would have deduced that she was, as Elleviou said of a certain court lady, either a demi-mondaine or a duchess." She could be in no company, private or public, bourgeois or aristocratic, without all eyes being drawn to her. Liszt, we are told, after a few minutes' conversation with her sang her praises to Janin with the discriminating enthusiasm of one who was a connoisseur where the other sex was concerned. The young woman—she would be about twenty-one at that time—seems to have been equally impressed by the great pianist, for to Janin she had hardly a word to say. Shortly afterwards Liszt became a visitor at her house.

A critical scrutiny of the Liszt-Duplessis affair in its entirety reveals several errors of time and fact in Janin's famous preface to *La Dame aux Camélias*. With all this, however, we cannot concern ourselves here; it belongs more properly to Liszt biography, which now calls for re-writing at many points. Whatever blunders —or perhaps intentional manipulations or concealments?—there may be on Janin's part does not affect his account of the impression Marie Duplessis made on him at his first meeting with her and later. Liszt was undoubtedly one of her lovers, though his biographers seem to have been unaware of it.

2

Marie was "tall," we are told by Dumas *fils*, who came into her orbit about 1844, and "very slender, with black hair and a pink and white complexion.[1] Her head was small, her eyes long and lacquer-like, resembling those of a Japanese, but delicate and animated; her lips were cherry-red, and she had the loveliest teeth in the world; she put you in mind of a Dresden figurine. . . . She was one of the last and the few courtesans with a heart: that, no doubt, was why she died young. She lacked neither intelligence nor disinterestedness. She died poor [2] in a sumptuous apartment that had been distrained on by her creditors. She had an inborn distinction, dressed with taste, and carried herself gracefully, almost nobly. Sometimes she was taken for a lady of high society: mistakes of that kind are made every day now." Théophile Gautier describes her as "a young woman of exquisite distinction, a pure and delicate type of beauty."

3

She is popularly supposed to have been unable to endure the scent of any flowers but camellias, and Dumas, in his novel of 1848, says that no one ever saw her with any other flower—that at the florist's shop kept by Mme Barjon she was known as "la dame aux camélias," a nickname that has stuck to her. In a preface of 1867, however, to a new edition of his play—which was later than the novel—he said categorically that she was never known, during her lifetime, as "la dame aux camélias": he appears to imply that this characterisation of her was as much his own invention as the name he bestowed on her, Marguerite Gautier. The truth seems to be that she decorated her apartment lavishly

[1] On two of her passports, issued at different periods, her height is given as 1 metre 65 and 1 metre 67, that is to say, about five feet four inches. One official described her eyes as black, the other brown. A captious critic here and there wrote her down as thin for her height; "no sculptor," said one of them, "would have chosen her as a model." The disturbing beauty of her face no one ever questioned. There exists a painting of her which confirms the judgment of her biographer Johannès Gros that her face and form were the purest expression of the "keepsake" type of female beauty in vogue in the early nineteenth century, fragile, virginal, spiritual, vaporous, expressive of melancholy and tender aspiration. In order to come as near as possible to the sylph ideal the fashionable woman of that epoch, so the Comtesse Dash assures us, ate as little as possible: this practice, combined with late nights and perpetual excitement, no doubt increased Marie Duplessis' tendency to consumption, even if it did not originate it.

[2] This is not true, as we shall see later.

with flowers according to the season, but disliked the proximity of strong-scented ones, such as roses, which made her feel faint. A camellia she could wear in her corsage without discomfort. Moreover, camellias were the "correct thing" in fashionable Paris circles at the time when Dumas was dramatising her. "La dame aux camélias" was probably just a novelist's licence on his part, on which he sometimes let his fancy play irresponsibly. "During twenty-five days of each month," he says slyly in the novel of 1848, "the camellias were white, but during the other five red: one never understood the reason for this variation of the colours, which I record without being able to account for it." He brings in this change-of-colour motif, as we may call it, at a decisive point in his novel.

The matter is complicated somewhat by his saying that on her monument in the Montmartre cemetery her name—her true name, Alphonsine Plessis—was surmounted by "a crown of artificial camellias affixed to the marble in a glass casket." The solution of this little mystery seems to be that this ornament was placed on Alphonsine's grave some time after her death, when Dumas' drama, which had stirred the sensibilities of all Paris, especially the women, had fixed indelibly in the public mind the poetic image of her as the lady of the camellias. The play was written in 1849, soon after the novel, but not produced, owing to difficulties with the censor, until 1852. Dumas's illuminating preface to it was written in 1867, for a definitive edition of his *Théâtre complet.*

4

To the making of this exquisite flower of a Marie Duplessis there had gone a considerable quantity of mud. We know much more about her now than her contemporaries did; thanks to the reminiscences of many of those who had known her, and to much patient French research among the official archives of the region in which she was born, we are able to reconstruct her short life with considerable accuracy. She was the daughter of one Marin Plessis, a mercer in a small way of business in Nonant, in the department of the Orne, a man of bad character and vicious heredity. His wife, Marie Louise Michelle Deshayes, whom he married in 1821, came from a family of better standing than his. There were two children of the marriage; the second, Rose

Alphonsine—the future "dame aux camélias"—was born on the 15th January 1824. At some date which we cannot fix precisely Marie Louise Plessis had to be saved from the brutalities of her husband by a relative on her mother's side, who obtained for her a post as housekeeper to a certain "Lady Anderson Yarborough," who lived now in Paris, now in Geneva. Apparently the mother never saw Alphonsine again.

The child was put by her father to work on a farm, where, as might have been expected, her singular beauty soon attracted the notice of the youth of the countryside. Finding her no doubt something of a problem her father took, or sent, her to Paris at about the age of fifteen, and left her more or less to her own resources. She appears to have worked for a while in various shops, but soon found a more agreeable scope for her natural talents among the students and small shopkeepers of the quarter. Paris was dance-mad at that time, and Alphonsine was an assiduous frequenter of the dance-halls. An excursion one day to Saint-Cloud with a small tradesman no longer in his first youth ended in her being installed in an apartment in the rue de l'Arcade as his mistress. It was not long before she was filched from him by a young man of birth, wealth and fashion who has been identified as Agénor, Comte and later Duc de Guiche, and later still Duc de Gramont and Prince de Bidache, Napoleon III's Minister of Foreign Affairs. The grisette was now fairly launched in the fashionable world.

She must have been a strange blend of voluptuousness, love of luxury, simplicity and disinterestedness. When the young Dumas first met her she was little more than twenty, and one could see, as he puts it, that she was still "à la virginité du vice." Part of her inexplicable charm lay in what would have been called, in a woman of rank, her high breeding. "She had an inborn tact, an instinctive elegance," said one who knew her well. We have abundant testimony that in the most riotous company she was generally quiet, discreet in her gaiety, speaking little, laughing rarely, with a shade of sadness in her smile, as though in the depths of her being she had a premonition of an early and tragic end. When she chose to talk, we are assured, her conversation could interest the most sober and sensible of men. The catalogue of the sale of her effects after her death listed books by Byron, Marivaux, Chateaubriand, the elder Dumas, Goethe (*Werther*), Molière, La Fontaine, Rousseau (*La Nouvelle Héloïse*), Lamartine, Victor Hugo, Walter Scott, Thiers (eleven vols.), and Rabelais. The few letters of hers that we possess are quiet in tone and sensible in substance. She was no vulgar, flashy gold-digger, and, contrary to popular belief, she "ruined" none of her rich lovers; she merely accepted the luxury in which they voluntarily and gladly indulged her. They were men of the highest Parisian society, on whom crudity of speech or vulgarity of manner would have grated. In her train she had poets, artists, and men of letters; and not one of that critical entourage has a word to say against her on any score. A greater feminine mystery the world has perhaps never known.

One of the legends connected with her is that while she was taking the waters at Bagnères, whither she had gone to escape for a while from the exhausting whirl of her life in Paris, hints of consumption having already forced themselves on her, she met with an old duke who had recently lost, through tuberculosis, a daughter of the same age as hers and resembling her physically; it ended in his taking her under his protection as a second daughter when she returned to Paris. The one element of truth in all this is that there was such a person, and Marie became his mistress in 1844. He was the Comte de Stackelberg, an elderly diplomat—he was approaching his eightieth year—living with his wife at No. 7 of the rue de la Chaussée d'Antin; a generation earlier he had functioned at the Congress of Vienna as Russian ambassador to Austria. He figures in Dumas' work as the Duc de Mauriac. "The legend," Dumas assures us, "of the consumptive daughter whose traits the duke found again in Marie Duplessis is pure invention. The Count, notwithstanding his great age, sought in her not, like Oedipus, an Antigone, but, like David, a Bathsheba." He installed her in a sumptuous apartment at No. 11 of the Boulevard de la Madeleine, with a carriage, jewels, furs and everything else that her luxury-loving heart could desire.

It was while she was living under the protection of this elderly nobleman that the acquaintance with Dumas *fils* began. That story, however, had better be told later, in closer connection with the play and the opera. Of the last two years of Marie's short life there is otherwise not much to tell.

5

At the end of 1845, after her rupture with Dumas, her accredited lover was a certain young Édouard, Vicomte de Perrégaux, who corresponds vaguely to the Comte de N . . . of the novel and the Comte de Varville of the play.[1] On the 25th January 1846 Marie obtained in Paris a passport—in her actual name of Alphonsine Plessis—and early in February she and Perrégaux set out for London, where they lodged at 37 Brompton Row, Kensington. On the 21st they were married at the Kensington Registry Office; on the certificate the bride's age was correctly given as twenty-two, while Perrégaux knocked some sixteen months off his, giving it as twenty-nine. Presumably it was for family reasons that he chose to have his marriage with the *dame aux camélias* celebrated in London rather than in Paris; but why it took place at all is a mystery still unsolved. Nor can we understand why, a little later, in a calm and friendly letter, the original of which has survived, Marie—signing herself "Marie Duplessis"—wrote to him thus: "My Dear Édouard, Of the many things touched upon in your letter there is only one to which you appear to wish me to reply: you desire me to say in writing that you are free to do whatever seems to you good. I told you this by word of mouth the day before yesterday: I now repeat it and sign myself, Marie Duplessis." No doubt there were family reasons at the back of all these moves; but that the marriage was legally valid, and that Perrégaux acknowledged it after her death, is proved by the fact that it was he who obtained permission from the authorities to have her body exhumed and re-interred.

Her vitality and her fortunes began to decline markedly in the spring of 1846. The summer of that year she spent in a feverish search for health and distraction at Spa, Wiesbaden, Ems and

---

[1] His grandfather was a celebrated financier whom the first Napoleon had raised to the Senate and made first Governor of the Bank of France; on his mother's side he was related to the Duc de Tarente. Édouard's father had been created a count by Napoleon. Édouard's elder brother, who came into the title in 1842, entered the French embassy service. Édouard chose the army, without showing any great zeal to carve out a military career for himself. He seems to have been of an amiable disposition, with an inclination to romantic melancholy. Eight short letters to him from Marie have survived and have been published.

other resorts. She could no longer doubt that she was consumptive and that the end could not be far off; and we may reasonably suppose that it was fear of the dread malady that accounted for the general neglect of her by her friends during the last few weeks of her life. When Dumas, in his preface of 1867 to a new edition of his play, described her as dying "poor, in a sumptuous establishment that had been seized by her creditors," he was speaking in relative terms. In the play and the opera she does indeed die in poverty, having come to the end of the sale of all her possessions, with only her maid and a certain Gaston remaining devoted to her to the end. The facts are, however, that although some of her creditors, obviously sensing that her star was setting, were pressing her for payment, and she was realising her possessions to satisfy them, she was far from anything resembling poverty. Her debts at the time of her death amounted to no more than about 20,000 francs; the four days' sale of her effects, which included jewellery, a considerable quantity of clothes, much table silver and porcelain, various objects of art, some elegant furniture, a fine horse, a carriage and a pony, realised more than 89,000 francs. The beneficiary of the estate seems to have been her sister Delphine, who had married one Constant Paquet.

Marie died on the 3rd February 1847, shortly after completing her twenty-third year, and was buried on the 5th.

In the final scene of the play and of the opera, which had to be made as romantically harrowing as possible, the only friend who remains faithful to Marie during her last weeks of agony is the impecunious young "Gaston" who had first introduced Armand to her. There is little reason to doubt, however, that Perrégaux visited her, and certainly he and the old Comte de Stackelberg accompanied her body to its temporary grave in the Montmartre cemetery. It remained there only a few days. On the 12th February Perrégaux bought for 526 francs a "concession" in the new quarter of the cemetery "for the sole and perpetual burial place of Mademoiselle Alphonsine Plessis." Four days later her remains were exhumed and re-buried: her final resting-place bore the simple inscription "Here reposes Alphonsine Plessis, born the 15th January 1824, died the 3rd February 1847. De Profundis."

6

Thanks mainly to Dumas' various prefaces and some scattered references of his in later life to the affair, we know now accurately enough how much in the novel and the play is fiction and how much fact. The reader will remember that the opera, which follows in the main the structural lines of the play, opens with a gay party in Marguerite Gautier's [1] house at which she meets Armand Duval [2] for the first time. In essentials this scene is drawn from life. After a chance meeting at one of the Paris theatres the young Dumas seems to have been taken to the house of Marie Duplessis by a friend who figures in all three versions as "Gaston"; the intermediary was a certain "Prudence Duvernoy" (in the opera "Flora Bervoix"), a former demi-mondaine one of whose windows almost touched one of Marie's; ostensibly in business now as a milliner, she made herself useful as Marie's confidante and woman of affairs, and borrowed money from her which she never had any intention of repaying. The large supper party of the opera owes its existence solely to the usual necessity for big vocal ensembles: at the actual supper the only people present were Marie, Prudence Duvernoy, "Gaston" and Dumas. The future novelist and dramatist was then a boy of twenty-one—the junior of Marie by some six months. An unhappy childhood had woven a thread of romantic melancholy into the texture of an ardent temperament; and there was in him already a good deal of the social moralist—especially where women and the preservation of French family life were concerned—with whom his books have made us familiar. On that fateful evening Marie's interest in him had been stimulated by the revelation that the boy had long worshipped her from afar, and that during her recent severe illness he had several times enquired at the house about her without leaving his name.

We have his assurance in later years that the account of what happened at the supper is not fiction but fact. Marie, suddenly seized with a fit of consumptive coughing, had to leave the table.

---

[1] This is her name in the novel and the drama. In the opera she becomes Violetta Valery.

[2] It will be observed that Dumas' hero has the same initials as Dumas himself.

She was followed anxiously to her room by Dumas: [1] the others were more or less indifferent, having been the witnesses of several previous attacks of this kind. Marie was touched by the young man's solicitude and his love, in which she saw interwoven a troubled pity for her manner of life that betokened a profound understanding of her. For the first time in her febrile career she realised that she was loved for her own sake; and though she neither desired nor conceived it possible to be "rescued" in the sense that he and the world of their epoch attached to that word, she was profoundly moved by and grateful for the delicacy of feeling he showed. Their talk ended in her accepting him as her lover; and Dumas has vouched for the literal truth of the episode in the novel in which, as a symbolic sealing of their compact, she plucked a red camellia from a bouquet of those flowers and placed it in his buttonhole. To his enquiry when he could see her again she replied with a smile "Later; it isn't always possible to carry out the terms of a treaty the day it is signed." "When, then, may I see you again?" Armand asked. "When the camellia has changed colour," was the reply. "And when will that be?" "Tomorrow, between eleven and midnight."

Apparently their rapturous idyll lasted only a few weeks; then the inevitable complications began. Loving and being loved disinterestedly for the first time, Marie dreamed of a *solitude à deux* for a while that summer in the country near Paris, the world forgetting, by the world forgot. As the young Dumas' modest income would be quite insufficient for that purpose, she expected him to leave the financial side of the matter to her. Against this both the lover and the chevalier in him rose in protest. Both Marie and Prudence had tried to make it clear to him that the idyll of young romantic love in temporary seclusion from the world could be only a chord of delicious harmony in the feverish dissonance of Marie's life. That life, she gave him clearly to understand, she could not change; she needed luxury on her present scale, with which Dumas would be quite unable to provide her even in their country retirement, and the whirl of excitement to which she had been accustomed was a physical and moral necessity

[1] In the play and the opera, of course, it is the guests who retire, the vital scene between Marie and Armand having to be played out in view of the audience.

for her if she were to live at all. She told him that as she knew she had not long to live she must live faster than other people. He, for his part, was too young and too poetic, too self-consciously literary, to be able to see the matter with her curious mixture of disinterested idealism and practical realism. He had read *Manon Lescaut*, and Marie's refusal to cut loose the economic tie that bound her to the generous old "Duke"—the Comte de Stackelberg—on whom her very existence depended, and her proposal that Dumas should not concern himself at all with the expenses of their temporary flight into the country, seemed to him a suggestion that he should be another Des Grieux living on another Manon supported by the purse of another M. de B. . . . The young man's jealousy also played its part in the tragic dénouement. Marie made no secret of the fact that she had other and richer lovers whose purses were at her disposal, for the scale of her expenditure went beyond even the liberal allowance of the venerable Comte. It all ended with a frenzied outburst on his part—half common jealousy and wounded amour-propre, half honourable revolt—during which he wrote her a letter that ended their association, though not the pathetic love of each of them for the other.

7

What purports to be this letter is given us, in slightly differing forms, on page 149 of the novel and in Act II of the play: the latter, being the shorter of the two, can be quoted here:

"It does not suit me to play a ridiculous part, even in connection with the woman I love. The moment I left you, the Comte de Giray entered your house. I am not as old as Saint-Gaudens,[1] nor am I of the same disposition. Pardon my only fault, that of not being a millionaire, and let us both forget that we have known each other, and, for a moment, believed that we loved each other. When you receive this letter I shall already have left Paris. Armand." In the novel, the lovers are soon reconciled, thanks to Marie's quiet good sense; she returns the letter to Armand and he destroys it. The course of events in real life was very different.

By a curious freak of fate the actual letter of the real "Armand"

---

[1] A ridiculous elderly character in the play who is led by the nose by the cocotte with whom he is in love.

has survived. It no doubt went to Marie's sister after her death, along with her other possessions, and in due course found its way first of all, apparently, to a collector of autographs, then into the auction room or the catalogue of some dealer in merchandise of this sort. Dumas bought it. In the early 1880's Sarah Bernhardt took up the part of Marguerite Gautier in a revival of *La Dame aux Camélias*; and Dumas was so moved by the memories she brought to life within him at a performance at the Théâtre de la Porte Saint-Martin in January 1884 that he presented her with the letter, enclosing it in a copy of an edition of the novel which by then had become a rarity. The letter, he assured her, "was written by the actual Armand Duval some forty years ago."

It is dated "Midnight, 30 August"; the year, according to M. Gros, can only be 1845, as in August of the following year Dumas was apparently not in France. It runs thus:

"My dear Marie,

I am not rich enough to love you as I would wish, and not poor enough to be loved as you would desire. So let both of us forget— you a name which should be almost indifferent to you, I a happiness that has become impossible for me. There is no need for me to tell you that I am sad, since you know already how much I love you. Adieu, then. You have too much heart not to understand why I write this letter, and too much intelligence not to be able to pardon me for it.

A thousand souvenirs,
A.D."

Whether she replied to this letter we do not know, or even whether she ever saw Dumas again. Be that as it may, the arguments he puts into Marguerite's mouth at her meeting (after the letter) with Armand Duval in the second act of the play are probably the very ones Marie employed to bring Dumas to reason all through the pitiful period of their association: he had enough of the objectivity of the dramatist in him to depict her as his superior in logic, knowledge of the world, good sense and good feeling.[1] As to whether the tragic dénouement came about through

---

[1] This is the finest section of the play, and perhaps the most important chapter (No. 15) of the novel. It is a pity that not the smallest use was

anything even remotely resembling the action of the play at this point—Marie's silent self-sacrifice to save the "honour" of a respectable family—we need have no hesitation in writing that down as an invention of the dramatist. It is even doubtful whether the rupture was brought about by any lavish expenditure on Marie's part for Dumas's benefit. In the preface of December 1867 to the new edition of the play he says expressly that "Marie Duplessis did not have all the pathetic experiences I have given to Marguerite Gautier, though she would not have shrunk from them. If she sacrificed nothing to Armand, that was because Armand did not wish her to do so; to her great regret, she was called upon to play only the first and second acts of the drama." The whole trouble, culminating in the rupture, seems to have come from the young man's resentment at Marie having other lovers, coupled with the bitter knowledge that he was not rich enough to ensure himself the sole possession of her by supplying her with the means to live to the full the kind of life that had become second nature to her. Of the sincerity of their love for each other, and of his later remorse for his behaviour towards her, there can be no question. We have a precious record of both his love and his remorse in a number of poems, inscribed to "M.D.," that form part of a very rare little volume—*Péchés de Jeunesse*—which he brought out in 1847, not long after her death. Only a hundred copies were printed, and only fourteen of these were sold.

8

It was no doubt to try to forget his sorrows that in the autumn of 1846 he went with his father and some friends on a trip to Spain and North Africa, where he found temporary consolation, as indeed he frequently did in later years, in some lighter loves. It was apparently in Algiers that he heard that Marie was gravely ill; and according to the *Péchés de Jeunesse* he wrote to her that he would return to ask her forgiveness:

> *Je vous avais écrit que je viendrais, Madame,*
> *Pour chercher mon pardon, vous voir à mon retour.*

made of this material by Verdi's librettist, for it constitutes the psychological core of the tragedy.

But apparently there was no reply from Marie, who was no doubt by that time too weak and too broken to write; so Dumas continued with the itinerary of the party. On the 4th January 1847 they arrived at Toulon. The father hurried back to Paris to attend to his dramatic affairs; the son stayed on at Marseilles until the 10th February. He was preparing to return to Paris when the news reached him of Marie's death a week earlier. When, a few days later, he arrived in Paris, it was too late either to attend her funeral or to be present at the sale of her effects.

The poignancy of his grief was enhanced by a chance return in the first days of June to the countryside in which he and Marie had spent so many happy hours. He sought relief from his anguish in the writing of his novel, which took him, he tells us, no more than three weeks. The play was written in 1849, but, as we have seen, trouble with the censorship delayed the stage production of it until the 2nd February 1852—five years, all but a day, after Marie's death.

As Verdi was living in or near Paris about the time when Dumas' novel was published we may be fairly certain that he made the acquaintance of the Lady of the Camellias then, and that he felt at once that this was the kind of subject—simple, moving, passionate but not "stagey" as he once put it—for which something within him kept crying out as a relief from the gloom of *Rigoletto* and *Il Trovatore*. When later he saw the play at its first appearance in the Paris Vaudeville Theatre in February 1852 he could no longer doubt that he had found what he wanted; and as soon as the play was published he sent it to his friend Piave to be turned into a libretto for him. Verdi's sketches for *La Traviata* have survived. They show with what ardour he worked at the congenial theme, laying out first of all, as was his general practice, the broad dramatic lines of the opera and then concentrating on the more emotional "numbers." What is musically the finest section of the whole work—the orchestral prelude to the third act—was evidently realised, just as it now stands, in a single hour or two of inspiration.

The new work was intended for the Fenice Theatre, Venice. From the beginning Verdi had difficulties with the casting of the rôles. He could never visualise the plump Signora Salvini-Donatelli as his Violetta, and would apparently have preferred almost any other capable soprano for the part: [1] he even received an anonymous letter warning him of "a stupendous fiasco" if he did not get another soprano and another bass. When he arrived in Venice in February 1853 to take charge of the rehearsals he found a Violetta quite as disillusioning to the eye as he and others had feared, and, in addition, a tenor (Graziani) who had lost his voice, and a baritone (Varesi) who obviously could not work up any interest in his rôle of the elder Germont.

The first performance took place on the 6th March 1853. The audience was favourably disposed towards the work until the middle of the second act, when Varesi sang "Di Provenza il mar" so badly as to set the house against him. With the third act came out-and-out disaster, the spectators, with the expansive figure of Salvini-Donatelli before their eyes, being quite unable to take seriously the doctor's diagnosis that the consumptive Violetta had no more than a few hours to live. "Sorry to have to bring you bad news," Verdi wrote with his customary curt stoical frankness to his publisher Ricordi the next morning, "but I can't hide the truth from you. *La Traviata* was a fiasco. Let us not waste time asking why. It just was." His message of the same day to his friend Emanuele Muzio was even more laconic: "*La Traviata* a fiasco last night. My fault or the singers'? Time will show." And two days later he wrote in the same resigned vein to Luccardi after the second performance: "Fiasco! out-and-out fiasco! I don't know who is to blame, and the less said the better. I'm off tomorrow to Busseto."

9

The legend still survives that the audiences of the 1850's in general jibbed at the novelty of operatic characters appearing in contemporary costumes; but the fact is that in the second production [2] the action had been put back a century and a half, and the costumes were those of the reign of Louis XIII. [3] Nor is there any more truth in the second legend sometimes associated with the fiasco—that the moral susceptibilities of some members of

[1] She was the second wife of the great Italian actor Tommaso Salvini.
[2] See p. 545.
[3] In present-day productions the setting of the opera is rightly that of the play—the Paris of the 1840's.

the audience were outraged by the subject of the work. That had undoubtedly been the case in Paris, where Dumas' play was stigmatised in some not normally prudish quarters as "an encouragement to immorality." To see how the sterner moralists of the period regarded Dumas' *La Dame aux Camélias* we have only to turn to Comte Horace de Viel Castel, who devoted a couple of corrosive pages in his diary to the play after seeing it on the 10th February 1852. The purpose of the censorship, he said, had been precisely to protect public morals against such outrages on them as this: "the play is a disgrace to the epoch that patronises it, to the government that tolerates it, and to the public that applauds it." Viel Castel, who knew Dumas *père* and Dumas *fils* well, detested them both. "Alex. Dumas *fils*," he continued, "is a young good-for-nothing to whom, I must say in justice to him, everything has been lacking—domestic education, moral instruction, decency of environment. The only company he has ever seen in his father's house is that of loose women. His father and he have often had the same mistresses and wallowed in the same orgies"; and he records a cynical dialogue between the father and the son that cannot be reproduced in English.

As for the opera, it is evident from the enthusiasm with which it was greeted at its second production that the Italian audience found nothing in the subject calculated to damage anyone's morals. This second production came about through one Antonio Gallo, the proprietor of a music business in Venice, and a great believer not only in Verdi but in the artistic value of *La Traviata*. He took the slighted work in hand, engaged a different company for it, and produced it in his own theatre at San Benedetto (Venice) on the 6th May 1854. It was an instantaneous success, and was quickly taken up by other theatres in Italy and abroad. For the new production Verdi made some changes in the score, mostly in the second act.

It is no disparagement of his work—a remarkable one for its epoch, and still very much alive—to say that the time is ripe for a new operatic treatment of the subject by some dramatist and musician of genius. The old conventional apparatus of the play and of the opera should be scrapped, and the theme treated on fresh lines, as a psychological study not of the fictitious Marguerite Gautier and Armand Duval but of the actual Marie Duplessis and Alexandre Dumas *fils*. Neither the imagination of the mid-nineteenth century nor the musical idiom and technical apparatus of the Italian opera of the period was equal to the task of limning so complex a character as Marie Duplessis in music. One sees her today as a psychological problem of profound interest, an unstable compound of the sensual and the spiritual, complicated, as cases of that kind so often are, by an hereditary tendency to tuberculosis. The borderline between the two temperaments is frequently a very uncertain one, and the merest chance may decide in a particular case on which side of that line the subject's life will be lived. It is impossible to read the effusions of the female saints, with the frequent tinge of the sensuous in their imagery, without feeling that by a single slight turn of the wheel of fate, a single small change in the chemistry of some gland or other, a single abnormality in this cerebral centre or that, the great saint might easily have become a *grande amoureuse*. Conversely, there are psychological grounds for believing that by the merest difference in the blending of the constituents of a Marie Duplessis, and in the epoch and the milieu of the blending, she might have become not a courtesan but a mystic, the knowledge that she was doomed to an early death filling her with a desire not to live more feverishly in this world but to aspire towards spiritual love.[1] Awakened sexually at a very early age and thrown into an environment that accelerated her development primarily along the lines of sex, she was predestined to be what she became. Modern music, with the instruments for psychological probing forged for it by Strauss in his Salome, his Elektra and his Don Quixote, would be much better equipped for the realisation of a character so complex as that of Marie Duplessis than the Italian music of Verdi's days was; it could show the subtle interworkings of the sensual and the spiritual in such a woman in a way that even poetry might find it hard to achieve. Piave and Verdi, even if they had been conscious that an interesting pathological problem existed, had not at their disposal the technical means for stating it. The Verdi of the 1850's could think of no better way of characterising the more frivolous side of Marie's nature than by giving

---

[1] Dumas himself described her as "a virgin of whom a nothing had made a courtesan, a courtesan of whom a nothing could have made the purest virgin."

her a passion for coloratura. No doubt his experiences of the prima donna of the period had made him suspect that facility in coloratura and mental negligibility were interchangeable terms; but that naïve way of dealing with the Traviata will hardly do today. The whole subject should be taken up and thought out afresh by some composer of the present day—if he can find the right librettist.

10

Piave's libretto, dramatically considered, is a mediocre piece of work, though it is difficult to see how he could have made a much better job of it, the operatic conventions of the period being what they were. For us today the most vital part of Dumas' play is the second act, in which Marguerite quietly lays all her cards on the table in her argument with Armand as to ways and means, and we realise how inevitably the conflict between her mentality and the scruples and jealousy of her lover must end in catastrophe. This part of Dumas' second act is completely ignored by Piave and Verdi. For the rest, while the general structure of the play is followed in the libretto, it is psychologically trivialised in the opera at many points simply in order to make it "opera." There are indications that Verdi himself, in later years, did not regard the part of Violetta as putting much strain on the intellectual powers of a prima donna. In 1886 the young Gemma Bellincioni was suggested to him as a possibility for his Desdemona, seemingly on the strength of the success she had had as Violetta. Before coming to a decision, Verdi wrote to Ricordi, he would like to see her in some other opera: "one could not judge her by *Traviata*; even a mediocrity could shine in that work and be very bad in every other."

The brief prelude to the opera is based on two themes, each of which delineates Violetta. The first:

No. 1

is an expressive melody which we shall not hear again until the third act, when it will be put to the finest uses: its appealing plaintiveness and its tenuous texture characterise the heroine in her last hours of suffering and resignation. The second theme:

No. 2

also depicts Violetta, this time as *amoureuse*; we hear it for the first time in the opera itself in the second act, at the point when, after the crucial scene with Germont *père*, she bids Alfredo a passionate farewell. (See Ex. No. 21.) In the prelude the orchestra sings the melody twice, the second time with a decorative counterpoint of smaller notes intended to suggest simultaneously the more frivolous side of her character. The composer's intentions are rational enough, but the realisation of them is not always beyond reproach. Here and there the ornamentation is musically rather naïve, suggesting an "air with variations" of a technically very rudimentary order; but in the end Verdi's sincerity silences any criticism we might feel impelled to make on that score.

The curtain rises on the drawing-room in Violetta's house. In the background there is a door leading to another room; there are also two lateral doors. On the left is a fireplace surmounted by a mirror; while in the centre of the room stands a richly laid out supper table. We find ourselves in a scene of revelry of the established operatic kind. Violetta, sitting on a sofa, is chatting with some of her friends, among whom is Doctor Grenvil, while others are hastening to greet some new arrivals, who include the Baron Douphol and the Marquis d'Obigny, the latter with Flora Bervoix (Violetta's confidante) on his arm. Violetta rises and goes to greet the newcomers, promising them and herself an evening of pleasure. The general atmosphere of careless gaiety is suggested at once by a sparkling melody in the orchestra:

No. 3

Pleasure, Violetta explains to her friends, is the drug that reconciles her to living.

A new and soberer theme breaks in suddenly on the lively No. 3:

No. 4

as the Vicomte Gastone enters, bringing with him a young man whom he introduces to Violetta as his friend Alfredo Germont—another of her many admirers, he assures her. Alfredo kisses her hand, and greets the Marquis, whom he already knows.

11

By this time the servants have completed the laying of the table, and Violetta, to the effervescent strains once more of No. 3, invites her guests to be seated. They arrange themselves so that Violetta is between Alfredo and Gastone, with Flora opposite her between the Marquis and the Baron; the others sit where they like. The orchestral texture of the scene is always admirably homogeneous, the transitions from No. 3—which depicts the company as a whole—to No. 4—which relates more specifically to Alfredo—and back again being managed without any break of continuity. It is No. 4 that comes into the foreground as Gastone tells Violetta that she is never out of Alfredo's thoughts; during her recent illness the young man had called at the house every day to enquire after her—"which is more than you did," she remarks maliciously to the Baron, who at once takes a dislike to this young newcomer who is obviously finding favour already in Violetta's eyes. The gay No. 3 ripples out again as she fills the cup of the shy and mostly silent Alfredo. The company clamours for a toast; and the Baron (the company's butt as well as Violetta's) feeling no inspiration, Alfredo is prevailed upon to try his powers.

The orchestra breaks into a lively melody in three-eight time, to which Alfredo launches a toast:

No. 5

They are to drink to youth and beauty and love, and especially to the bright eyes of Violetta. The company echo his sentiments enthusiastically, and Violetta tells them how happy she is among them, exhorting them to live like her, for pleasure is fleeting and youth soon over. After this, Cupid gets to work quickly, as he always does in the fantastic kingdom of opera. The Alfredo who had been too shy even to leave his name when he called daily to ask after Violetta in her illness is now bold enough to talk to the dashing courtesan about love. For the moment they get no further, for after another bacchanalian chorus to the strain of No. 5 a sparkling waltz is heard behind the scenes:

No. 6

and Violetta, regardless of the fact that the supper has only just begun, invites her guests to join her in a dance in the next room. They accept with alacrity, and are all moving off when Violetta suddenly turns pale—we are not told how this physiological transformation is to be conveyed to the audience—totters a step or two, and is obliged to sit down again. It is just an attack of faintness, she assures them, and bids the others go into the adjoining room, where she will join them shortly. All but Alfredo obey her, the dance music continuing in the orchestra without a break.

Going to the mirror to look at herself she perceives that Alfredo is still with her; and with a change in the waltz strain:

No. 7

the action takes a new turn. He exhorts her earnestly to give up this feverish life, which will surely kill her. How is it possible for her? she asks him sadly. If she were his, he tells her, he would watch over her and tend her. She cannot believe her ears; is it possible that anyone should feel like that towards *her*? With the lively No. 7 still coming from the adjacent room Alfredo assures her that until now no one has really loved her. She laughs neurotically at the idea that anyone should love a woman like her disinterestedly, and is still incredulous when he tells her that he has done so for a whole year:

No. 8

since the day, indeed, when he first saw her. This is true love, he assures her passionately, to a melody that will frequently appear like a leitmotif later:

No. 9

love that is the heart-beat of the universe, mysterious, noble, at once a torment and an ecstasy:

No. 10

Mi-ste-ri-o ——so, mi-ste-ri-o-so,al-te ——ro, cro-œ, cro-œ e de-li-ʒia,

She answers him in accordance with her character as seen by Verdi, that is to say, she tells him, soaring into coloratura, to fly from her:

No. 11

Ah_se ciò è ver, fug—gi—te—mi, so-lo a-mi-sta—de io v'of-fro; a-

mar——non so, nè sof————fro un co—sì e-roi-co a-mò——re.

for she herself cannot love, nor can she expect from him a devotion so heroic. She will be frank with him; let him seek another love and forget her. He replies with No. 10, to which, by way of emphasising her incorrigible flightiness, she contributes more irresponsible coloratura.

The waltz music is resumed, and Gastone appears for a moment in the doorway to ask, in his usual carefree way, what the devil she is doing. Just indulging in nonsense, she assures him, and he discreetly retires. Turning to Alfredo once more, she advises him not to speak to her again of love; but as he is on the point of leaving her she halts him, takes a flower from her corsage, and tells him to preserve it . . . and bring it back to her when it has faded. That must mean tomorrow, he opines; and she coquettishly agrees. Still to the accompaniment of the waltz music he swears once more that he loves her, kisses her hand, and bids her, for the present, farewell.

12

The dancers, to the melody of No. 3, return and break into a chorus in which the guests assure Violetta and each other that as day is dawning it is time for them to leave and replenish their capacity for pleasure by a little sleep. After a great many resolutions and reciprocal assurances to this effect, as was the way in Italian opera finales of that period, they take themselves off, leaving Violetta with the stage to herself for the great scena that is to close the act. It is strange, she muses in a preliminary recitative, how deeply Alfredo's obviously sincere words have engraved themselves on her heart. Would a serious love bring her disaster? She will leave the answer to her throbbing heart, which no man has yet warmed into real life. She has never known the joy of loving and being loved; and shall she turn away from it in disdain now, to continue her present feverish life? Then she launches her famous aria, "Ah, fors' è lui che l'anima, solinga ne' tumulti, godea sovente pingere?" ("Ah, was it he, perchance, whom, lonely in all my dissipations, I so often saw in imagination?"):

No. 12

She recalls the words and music (Nos. 9 and 10) of Alfredo's little song in praise of love. She repeats the whole of this first section of the aria to other words, her mind going back to the dreams she had had of such a lover in her childhood.

For a moment or two she remains silent, lost in thought; then she recalls herself to reality with a cry of "But this is folly, delirium! In the crowded desert that is Paris what can a poor lonely woman hope for? What can she do but seek distraction in the giddy whirl of pleasure?" A coloratura flourish points her final words, and prepares us for the next phase of the aria.

In an allegro brillante:

No. 13

she declares that she will think of nothing but novelty after novelty in the way of folly, confirming her resolve with a flight into coloratura that takes her up to the high D flat. But now there comes a true operatic touch—the voice of Alfredo is heard from beneath the balcony, singing his No. 9 once more, with its No. 10 sequel. The only effect it has on Violetta is to send her off into a repetition of the feverish No. 13; and while Alfredo continues with his canticle to love she surrounds his melody with coloratura more and more brilliant; and the curtain falls with a final assurance on her part that henceforth pleasure shall be the lodestar of her life. Granted that in the operatic world of the 1850's it was in some such form as this that feminine frailty and frivolity had to find expression, the thing could not be better done: a century of familiarity with the aria has not robbed it of the smallest particle of life.

13

But after all this we must confess to a slight feeling of surprise when at our next meeting with Violetta we find that she has done everything which she had vowed so copiously she would never do, even for the affectionate and ardent Alfredo. In Dumas' play the psychological change in her and in the drama comes about quite naturally. At the end of the first act there is no grand scene for the heroine alone: Armand, having received a pledge of love in the form of the flower, says goodbye to Marguerite, who rejoins her guests and encourages them to dance: it is perfectly evident that she is already in love. At the commencement of Dumas' second act we find her broaching to Armand a "combination" that has occurred to her: in a fortnight she will have realised her plan to be free to spend the summer with him in the country near Paris. Armand does not take kindly to the scheme, for the reason that, as he puts it, he cannot reconcile himself to playing the part of a Des Grieux, living with his Manon at the expense of a rich M. de B. . . . Marguerite fences dialectically with the jealous young Armand, and it is arranged that he shall call on her again on the morrow. Left alone, she indulges in a little soliloquy: "Who could have told me, a week ago, that this man, whose existence I did not even suspect, would come to occupy as he does, and so quickly, my heart and my thoughts? Besides, does he really love me? Do I even know that I love him, I who have never been in love? But why deny oneself a pleasure? Why not follow the caprices of one's heart? What am I? A creature of chance; then let chance do with me what it will. What does it matter? It seems to me that I am happier than I have ever been. Perhaps that is a bad omen. We women always foresee that we will be loved, but never that we ourselves will love, and that so profoundly that at the first assault of this unforeseen trouble we lose our bearings."

In the play, then, only a few days have elapsed between the first act and the second. In the opera the first act takes place in August, the second in January of the following year; yet not a word is vouchsafed us in explanation of the change in Violetta's feelings towards Alfredo and towards life in general during those five months. In the second act we are suddenly confronted with a new Violetta, all tenderness and goodness and self-sacrifice, without so much as a coloratura trill or roulade left in her. The stickler for dramatic logic may jib at all this, but Verdi gives us ample musical compensation. This second act of his reveals to us a new Verdi, a fine-fingered musical psychologist.

14

In the second act of the opera, then, Violetta and Alfredo have long been lost in the felicity of their seclusion in the country. When the curtain rises we see a room on the ground floor of their villa near Paris. On the background wall, facing the spectator, is a mantelpiece with a mirror and a clock, and on each side of it a glass door opening on the garden. In the foreground are two other doors facing each other. The room is furnished with chairs, tables, books—and writing materials, the dramatic necessity for which we shall discover later.

After a quiet orchestral introduction Alfredo enters in hunting costume. Putting down his gun, he declares, in an expressive quasi-recitative, that when Violetta is away life has no joy for him. Three months, he muses aloud for the benefit of the audience, have gone by since Violetta turned her back, for his sake, on all her former pleasures and associates, and still she scorns them all; he too is a new man, vivified and purified by her love. In a following aria:

No. 14

De' miei bol-len-ti spi-ri-ti   il gio-va-ni-le ar-do—re

he describes how by her love and her always gentle smile she has calmed and strengthened him; their retreat in the country has become a paradise to him.

Annina, Violetta's maid, enters hurriedly, out of breath. Alfredo's questions elicit the information, bit by bit, that she has been to Paris, commissioned by her mistress to sell her horses, her carriages, and what other possessions she can dispose of quickly, for this quiet life in the country has proved very expensive to her. Learning that the amount now required is a thousand louis, Alfredo declares that he himself will go forthwith to Paris and raise that sum; meanwhile Annina must not breathe a word of his intention to Violetta. Pausing only long enough to deliver himself of an aria:

No. 15

Oh, mio ri-mor-so! ohin-fa-mia! io—— vis-si in ta-le er—ro—re!

in which he reproaches himself passionately for his blindness all this time—Violetta has been his silent protectress against the hard realities of life, and he must wash himself clear of that shame—he rushes out.

Violetta now appears and learns from Annina, to her great surprise, that Alfredo has left hurriedly for Paris but will return before night. Her manservant Giuseppe brings her a letter, which she surmises to be from a business man whom she is expecting, and who was to have been shown in as soon as he arrived. Annina and Giuseppe having left her she opens the letter, which turns out to be from Flora, who, it appears, has discovered the secret of her retreat and now invites her to a dance at her apartment in Paris that evening. They will expect her in vain, says Violetta quietly. Just then Giuseppe returns with the news that a gentleman has called to see her. Assuming him to be the man of affairs whom she was expecting she orders him to be shown in. The visitor, however, proves to be an elderly stranger, who, after making sure that he is addressing Mademoiselle Violetta Valery, announces himself as Alfredo's father. He at once reproaches her roughly for having brought his poor boy to the brink of ruin. Quietly correcting his lapse from good manners in his way of speaking to a lady in her own house, she assures him that he is mistaken in his facts. "He is about to make over his property to you," the father insists.[1] Violetta denies it; Alfredo would never have dared to suggest that, nor would she have accepted anything from him. By way of enlightening him as to the true state of affairs she shows him a paper which proves that it is she who is selling her possessions. Perhaps it is her past that is accusing her? he suggests. The past no longer exists, she assures him; she loves Alfredo, and God has allowed her to cancel out her past by repentance. (Evidently the part she is to play henceforth in the opera is that of the penitent magdalen—always an interesting character in the nineteenth century novel and drama.) Germont, struck by a nobility of soul in her which he had not expected, is now emboldened to ask a sacrifice of her. The happiness of both his children, he says, lies in her hands, for besides his son he has a daughter, pure as an angel:

No. 16

Allegro moderato ♩=84

dolcissimo Pu—ra sic-come un an—ge-'lo se Al-fre-do ne-ga rie-de-re in
Id-dio mi diè una fi——glia;

se—no alla fa—mi—glia;

whose marriage to a certain worthy young man can never take place unless the stain inflicted on the family honour by Alfredo's association with the courtesan is removed. (Germont is the operatic "heavy father," another type very much in favour in drama

[1] The course of events is made clearer in Dumas: Germont has heard from his Paris lawyer that his son is proposing to make over to Violetta the inheritance he had received from his mother.

and fiction a hundred years ago, the inflexible guardian of family morals. In Dumas he is a highly respectable provincial receiver-general, whose wife had died some three years before the action of the play begins.)

15

Violetta opines that Germont merely wishes her to separate from Alfredo until the daughter is married: that sacrifice would be grievous for her, she assures him, but she is willing to make it. But when she learns that he expects the renunciation to be permanent she is horrified: Germont does not realise, she protests in agitated accents, how deeply she loves his son:

No. 17

P Non sa—pe—te quale af—fet—to   vi-vo, im-men-so- m'arda in pet-to?

Since she has known him, all the rest of the world has ceased to exist for her. And is Germont not aware that she is the prey of a dread malady the inevitable end of which she knows to be not far off? Separation from Alfredo would mean, for her, suffering so great that she would prefer her life to end at once.

The father is full of sympathy for her now, and by way of consoling her he points out that his son is very young, the heart of man is liable to change with the years, and the day will come when he will weary of her—for unions such as theirs have not received the blessing of heaven. His aria:

No. 18

Un di, quan-do le   ve—ne—ri il tem-po a-vrà fu-

ga——te, fia pre-stoil te-dio a sor-ge-re: Che sa-rà al-lor?

is another illustration of that peculiarity of Verdi's early style to which attention is drawn in our analysis of *Il Trovatore*—a tendency to reiterate the same figure (here seen in bars 2, 4, and 6 of our quotation) till it comes to have an unintentionally comic effect.

Violetta sorrowfully admits the unblessedness of her union with Alfredo, and, seeing that she is weakening, the father presses his advantage home, exhorting her to make an end of this mad dream of hers and save the honour and happiness of his children by listening to what he assures her is the voice of heaven itself. There is a sudden dramatic change from the major key to the minor as Violetta breaks into a wild lament over the lot of women like her, on whom the doors of hope are closed and barred; for even if God forgives them, man has no mercy on them. With tears in her voice she sings a song of resignation that is one of the most moving passages in the work:

No. 19

"Go tell your daughter that she shall have a victim whose one comfort in her misery will be that she has sacrificed herself and is ready to die." Equally moving is Germont's reply: "Weep, weep, unhappy one: I know well how great is the sacrifice I am asking of you: have courage, and your noble heart will win its victory":

No. 20

She accompanies his efforts at comfort with another mournful reiteration of her willingness to make the sacrifice demanded of her. This whole episode is musically the most moving one of the whole act; we can see that Verdi himself has been profoundly moved, and has drawn upon all that was most finely spun in his own nature to deal with the situation. We feel for Violetta as for a hurt, uncomprehending child: Verdi will never again achieve anything quite like this until the death scene of his Desdemona.

Violetta humbly awaits Germont's commands. "Tell him you do not love him," he advises. "He will not believe me," she replies. "Then leave him." "He will follow me." She asks him to embrace her as a daughter, and as he does so she comes to her great decision. Alfredo will soon be back: let his father be here to console him in his affliction. Telling Germont to go into the garden to await the return of his son, Violetta sits down at her writing-table. She will not tell Germont what her plan is; she will die, and if some day Alfredo learns the truth, let him not curse her memory. The father tries to console her with the prospect of life and happiness, but she reiterates her acceptance of death: she desires only that Alfredo shall know some day that her self-sacrifice was born of her love for him, and that she was his until the end.

16

With another embrace they part, Germont going out by the garden door, and Violetta, with a prayer for strength, sitting down again to write a letter the address of which surprises Annina when she gives it to her with instructions to deliver it herself. Then, to a wailing figure in the orchestra, she writes and seals another letter, which she conceals in confusion when Alfredo enters hurriedly. He sees, however, that she has been writing, and asks to whom. "To you," she replies; but she refuses to give him the letter just then. Alfredo tells her that he is uneasy in his mind because he has had word that his father has come to Paris. He has not seen him, but has had an angry letter from him: still, when his father sees Violetta he is bound to love her. Keeping back her tears with difficulty she begs that she shall not be present when the son and father meet; Alfredo will take her to his father later, when he has explained everything and calmed him, and then she will fall at Germont's feet and all will be well. Meanwhile she begs Alfredo passionately to give her his assurance that he loves her; she ends with the great cry (No. 2) which has already figured in the prelude, but is here heard in the opera itself for the first

time: "Love me; Alfredo! Love me as much as I love you!
Farewell!": [1]

No. 21

She runs into the garden. The uncomprehending Alfredo sits
down, opens a book, and is wondering whether his father will
come now, for it is late in the day, when the excited Giuseppe
rushes in with the news that his mistress has gone off in a coach
to Paris, and that Annina too has disappeared. Alfredo is not perturbed by this; he assumes that Violetta has gone to Paris to speed
up the sale of her property, but believes that Annina will check her.
(The reader will remember that he had told Annina that he himself would raise the 1,000 louis Violetta needs.) He catches sight
of someone in the garden, and is about to go out to see who it is
when he is stopped by a commissionaire, who hands him a letter
for a "Monsieur Germont" that had been given him by a lady
not far away from the house. Alfredo opens it, reads no further
than the opening words—"Alfredo, when this comes into your
hands . . ."—, assumes that he has been betrayed, turns round
with a wild cry, and finds himself in the arms of his father, who

[1] The resemblance has often been pointed out between this melody and the
one sung by Lida in Verdi's *La Battaglia di Legnano*:

Many similar "echoes" can be found in his operas; it was not that he was
"repeating himself," but simply that he unconsciously employed very much
the same basic formula whenever he fell into the same mood. "Fingerprints"
of this kind—inveterate *tics* of characterisation—can be found in abundance
in all composers.

has entered from the garden. Germont exhorts his son to return and be once more the pride and glory of his home: then, while the despairing Alfredo remains seated with his head in his hands, the father sings the famous appeal to him that cannot quite escape the charge of sentimentality but is still very effective in its proper setting. What has blotted out from Alfredo's mind, he asks, the memory of the soil and the waters of the beautiful Provence that gave him birth:

No. 22

where he had been so surrounded by love, and where kind hearts are now aching for his return? [1]

The furious Alfredo is not to be reasoned with: he has surmised, not knowing the full truth, that Violetta has wearied of him and the country and has gone back to Baron Douphol (the Varville of the play), and he can think of nothing now but vengeance. In vain does his father, in another aria in which a little figure resembling that of bar 2 of our example No. 18 is regrettably insistent, exhort him to return to the family that has been mourning his absence, where love and forgiveness await him:

[1] In Dumas' drama, where the whole course of events is more natural than in *La Traviata*, there is no scene between father and son corresponding at all to that in the opera, which was probably inserted only in order that the baritone might be indulged in the luxury of another aria. In the play, Duval *père* has entered from the garden unobserved while the commissionaire was handing Violetta's letter to Armand. The latter reads the first few words of this, gives a cry of rage, and, turning round, sees his father: he throws himself sobbing into the latter's arms, and the curtain falls there and then.

The destination and the contents of the two letters written by Violetta may not be clear to the casual spectator of the opera. In the play everything is clear: Prudence Duvernoy (the Flora of the opera) enters and is given the first letter, to take to Paris. She is astonished when she reads the address— evidently that of one of Marguerite's lovers, Arthur de Varville: she realises that Marguerite is forsaking Armand and returning to her old life.

No. 23

Assai moderato
♩ = 96

pp No, non u-drai rim—pro—ve—ri; co-priam d'oblio il pas-

sa-to — l'a-mor che m'ha gui-da— to sa tut-to per- do —nar.

(There is too much repetition here—more than the general quality of the music given to Germont *père* can comfortably carry.) The appeal evidently has no effect on Alfredo, who, after his father's final harangue, tears himself away, catches sight of Violetta's letter on the writing-table, opens and reads it, and rushes out with an angry cry of "She has gone to the party! I will have vengeance for this betrayal!"

17

The next scene takes us back into "opera" again. The actual drama will be resumed—indeed, worked up to its climax—later in this act; but the librettist and the composer have to fill in a certain time-space before that can happen. When the curtain rises once more we see a richly furnished and illuminated gallery in Flora's Paris mansion; for Verdi's Flora is not a mere sponging, cadging confidante-of-all-work, like the Prudence Duvernoy of Dumas' play, but a demi-mondaine in a large way of business on her own account. There is a door in the background, and another on each side of the gallery. On the right stands a gaming-table, on the left a table with flowers and refreshments, and elsewhere chairs and a sofa. According to the score, the second act of the opera takes place in January, the third in February. Dumas' chronology is more in accordance both with the historical facts and with credibility: the first half of the second act shows us Armand and Marguerite still happy in their summer retreat in the country, while the second part relates to a month or so after Marguerite's flight, and the exact time of the third act is the following New Year's day.

Verdi paints in the liveliest colours the revels in Flora's house, where, as the curtain rises, we see Flora herself, the Marquis d'Obigny, Doctor Grenvil,[1] and a few early arrivals engaged in conversation, from which we learn that both Violetta and Alfredo have been invited to the party. If the former comes it will presumably be with the Baron Douphol, in whose company she had been seen by one of the guests the day before. The conversation is interrupted by the entry of a number of lady guests disguised as gipsies, prepared to tell anyone's fortune; after them comes another crowd (among them Gastone) masked as Spanish matadors and picadors. For all this gay, irresponsible bustle, as well as for a little tiff—soon smoothed out—between Flora and the Marquis, Verdi finds appropriate music, if not music of the highest order.

As the men unmask and stroll about or seat themselves at the gaming-table the moody Alfredo enters. He curtly denies any knowledge of Violetta, and sits down to play. Soon Violetta enters, on the Baron's arm. He informs her in a whisper that Alfredo is there, and grimly warns her not to address a single word to him. She gives a cry of distress that, coming where it does and being what it is—the first expression of deep feeling in this scene—is one of Verdi's most telling dramatic effects:

No. 24

Allegro agitato

Ah, per— chè—— ven-ni in-cau-tal pie-tà, gran Dio, pie-tà, gran Dio, di me!

("Oh why was I so rash as to come here? Have pity on me, O God, have pity.") Twice in the later course of the scene the same phrase will strike in, with the same electrifying effect.

Some of the guests seat themselves at the gaming-table, others stroll about. An insulting remark by Alfredo about Violetta's treachery towards him nettles the Baron, who suggests that he and Alfredo shall pit themselves against each other at play; Alfredo's extraordinary luck so far, he says ironically, suggests that

[1] Why the Doctor, who has really no part to play in the opera until the death scene in the third act, should appear both in the first and the second, each time in surroundings hardly of a strictly professional kind, is a mystery. Perhaps Piave and Verdi felt that as they had to have a bass of some capacity for the final scene he might as well be made to earn his fee by putting in a bit of work in the earlier scenes, in each of which, however, except for a sentence or two, he merely adds his voice to the concerted pieces.

it is the traditional compensation for being unlucky in love. The game begins, the other guests, including Violetta, gradually leaving the room, only Alfredo and the Baron remaining behind. Not for long, however; Alfredo's luck still holding, the Baron proposes to postpone his revenge to another occasion. They go off to rejoin the others. The orchestra dies down slowly into an ominous silence, then lashes itself into life again as Violetta returns, agitated, breathless. She has sent word to Alfredo to join her, and she is certain he will come, she says, for his hatred of her will have more weight with him than her appeal. When he appears, she beseeches him to leave the house at once, for she dreads a quarrel between him and the Baron. Alfredo refuses to quit the field: if he kills the Baron, he tells her, he will have the satisfaction of having deprived her of her lover and her protector with one stroke. To Violetta's anguished cry that it is *he* for whom she fears, he replies that he will go on one condition—that she will accompany him. This, she says, is impossible; let him leave her and forget her, for she has promised another, on oath, that she will blot Alfredo out of her life. He asks if this other is Douphol; "Yes," she replies, and adds, summoning up all the strength that remains to her, "I love him."

Insane with fury, Alfredo opens the door and calls to the company to return. When they have done so he points to Violetta, who is leaning exhausted against the table, and brutally denounces her: "This woman, for love of me, squandered her money on me, and in my blindness I accepted the sacrifice. But now the time has come to cleanse myself of this stain. I call you all to witness that thus I discharge my debt"—and he flings a purse contemptuously at Violetta's feet. She faints in Flora's arms and the guests turn on him in anger. Meanwhile Germont *père* has entered unobserved.[1] He now comes forward, and, in the noblest heavy-father style, renounces this son of his as unworthy of him. Alfredo's rage has by now spent itself, and he is contrite and broken. A big ensemble is built up, which is hushed for a moment as Violetta, in a feeble voice, reproaches Alfredo for his unkindness, which he would have spared her had he known that what she had done to him she did to prove her love. Time will enlighten him, she

---

[1] That Germont should put in an appearance at the demi-mondaine's house is incredible.

goes on as the ensemble is resumed; and when that day comes may God lighten his burden of remorse! Finally Germont *père* drags the distracted Alfredo away, the Baron following them. Flora and the Doctor take Violetta into the adjoining room, the guests disappear, and the curtain falls.

18

The third act opens with a prelude for the strings that is the finest piece of purely instrumental music ever written by Verdi— a miniature symphonic poem, flawless in every imaginative and technical respect, with each idea growing so naturally, inevitably out of its predecessor that the whole seems to be contained in one great line. It is the sick Violetta that he shows us here, Violetta nearing her end, a pathetic figure. The prelude is based on two themes; the first, breathing the purest spirit of emancipation from this painful world, is that with which the opera had opened (No. 1). In the second:

No. 25

we have the veritable accent of passion, but now passion purified: it seems to soar into the skies, then descends in a series of broken sobs:

No. 26

and at last dies away into tremulous silence.

The curtain rises on Violetta's bedroom, with the bed at the back, the curtains half-drawn, and near it a stool with a bottle of water, a glass and various medicines. In the centre of the stage stands a dressing-table and a sofa, and a little way off a piece of furniture on which a night-light flickers. In the grate a fire is burning. Violetta is asleep on the bed; her maid Annina, worn out with watching, dozes by the chimney. The time is seven o'clock in the morning.

Violetta awakens and asks in a faint voice for a glass of water, which Annina gives her. At her bidding the maid opens the shutters, looks into the street, and announces the coming of Doctor Grenvil, who arrives in time to assist Violetta to rise from the bed and stumble towards the sofa. All this while the orchestra has been musing softly upon No. 1; and as the Doctor is feeling her pulse and Violetta tells him that though her body suffers her soul is tranquil, for last evening a priest had brought her the comfort of religion, we hear, for the only time in the act, a brief pallid reminiscence of No. 25. Grenvil assures her that she will soon be convalescent, but with a sad smile she dismisses the assurance as merely the sort of kindly untruth with which doctors try to hearten the sick. As he is leaving, Annina has a few subdued words with him and learns that her mistress has only a few hours to live.

Annina returns to Violetta and exhorts her to take heart, for all Paris is on holiday, gaily celebrating the carnival; "but God alone," Violetta interjects, "knows how many unhappy souls there are in the town today." How much money is there in the drawer? she asks. "Twenty louis," Annina replies. Violetta bids her take them and give them to some poor souls, and in response to Annina's protests that this will leave little for herself she assures her that however little it is it will be enough. Annina having left her, Violetta takes a letter from her bosom and reads it aloud in the quietest of tones. It is from the elder Germont: "You kept your promise. . . . The duel took place. . . . The Baron was wounded, but is recovering. Alfredo has gone abroad. I myself told him of your sacrifice; he will return to you to ask forgiveness. . . . Take care of your health. . . . You deserve a better future. . . . Giorgio Germont." The orchestra accompanies the reading with a barely audible enunciation of Alfredo's song in praise of love in the first act (No. 9 and No. 10).

19

She rises, looks at herself in the mirror, and murmurs sadly, "I wait for him, I wait, but still he does not come! How greatly

I have changed—yet the Doctor bids me hope, while I know I am doomed!" She sings a pathetic little song of farewell to all the lovely dreams of the past:

No. 27

Her end is nigh, and though no one will weep over her grave and bedeck it with flowers, God will have mercy and forgive her.

Suddenly the air is rent by a bacchanalian chorus from the street in praise of the Fatted Ox of the Paris Carnival. Why did Verdi see fit to introduce this unnecessarily jarring note? Presumably only for purposes of "theatre": he may have been afraid that the audience would find a whole act devoted to a death scene somewhat monotonous, and have felt that in any case Alfredo's entry, which was due shortly, would be more effective set against this noisy background than against the quieter one of Violetta's lament. We must respectfully disagree with him on both counts.[1] When the shouts of revellers have died away Annina returns hurriedly, to prepare Violetta, to the accompaniment of an agitated figure in the orchestra, for the great news she is bringing—the return of Alfredo. The latter follows close on her heels. The lovers embrace passionately: Alfredo implores Violetta's forgiveness, while now she half-believes that death will after all stay his hand. Gently he exhorts her:

No. 28

[1] It was no doubt in order to get this rather crude contrast of the atmosphere of the death chamber with the noisy, thoughtless world without that he placed his third act during the carnival, instead of on New Year's Day as in Dumas.

to turn her back with him on Paris for ever and seek new health in a happier clime—the thought of which gives poor Violetta strength enough to indulge herself for a while in a certain amount of fioritura. But the emotional shock of her lover's return has been too much for her. She sinks exhausted in a chair, forcing a sad smile and explaining to the terrified Alfredo that it is just a passing weakness and that she is better already.

She calls to Annina to help her to dress. But her strength fails her: she throws the garment down with a gesture of defeat, and gives a despairing cry of "Oh God! I cannot!" Annina is sent off to summon the Doctor again: "tell him that Alfredo has returned and that now I want to live." Then, turning to Alfredo, she tells him that if his coming cannot work the miracle of restoration nothing can save her. Summoning up her last reserves of strength she sings a wild protest against the cruelty of death for one so young as she:

No. 29

Alfredo, mingling his tears with hers, takes up the passionate, despairing strain, and their voices blend in a duet.

As Violetta falls exhausted on the sofa Germont *père* enters—somewhat superfluously, we cannot help thinking, though Verdi manages to invest the scene that follows with a good deal of pathos. Germont has kept his promise, he tells Violetta; he has come to take her to his heart as his daughter. But she has no illusions left now, she assures the Doctor, who by this time is also of the company; her one consolation is that she will die in the arms of those who love her. At the mention of death Germont becomes wildly remorseful: "I have been a foolish old man! Now, too late, I see the evil I have wrought!" Violetta summons Alfredo to her side, and while the orchestra reiterates one of those figures of volleying chords:

No. 30

Andante sostenuto ♩=56

ppp

which Verdi so often employed as a symbol of impending doom,[1] she takes a miniature of herself from a casket and gives it to Alfredo; it will remind him, she says, of their days of happiness together, and if one day he should meet some pure and tender girl and make her his wife, he can give her this and tell her that it is the portrait of one who is praying in heaven for her and for him. Verdi builds up an impressive quintet, with Germont pouring out his regrets, Alfredo imploring Violetta not to leave him, and she reiterating her pious charge to him in the matter of the miniature.

As her physical forces ebb she becomes spiritually transfigured. While the orchestra breathes the softest of reminiscences of Alfredo's love song (No. 9) she has a momentary illusion that life is returning to her; but at last she falls back once more on the sofa. The Doctor, feeling her pulse, tells the others that the end has come, and a few hammered octaves in the orchestra bring the opera to a close. We cannot help feeling that Verdi could have devised a rather more moving ending than just these blunt octaves: a German composer would no doubt have played for a while in the orchestra on the exquisite No. 1 and No. 25.

[1] See the *Trovatore* analysis, pp. 607–8.

Rigoletto

VERDI [1813–1901]

PRINCIPAL CHARACTERS

RIGOLETTO	*Baritone*
DUKE OF MANTUA	*Tenor*
GILDA	*Soprano*
MADDALENA	*Contralto*
SPARAFUCILE	*Bass*
MONTERONE	*Baritone*
MARULLO	*Baritone*
BORSA	*Tenor*
COUNT CEPRANO	*Bass*
COUNTESS CEPRANO	*Mezzo-soprano*

1

ERDI's "middle period" may be said to have extended from the *Luisa Miller* of 1849 to the *Don Carlos* of 1867. The latter part of this long period comprises the *Simon Boccanegra* of 1857 (afterwards revised), *Un Ballo in Maschera* (1859) and *La Forza del Destino* (1862), all of which still keep their place in the repertory. The early part of the period saw the creation of three works in which Verdi can be said to have first truly found himself—*Rigoletto* (1851), *Il Trovatore* (1853) and *La Traviata* (also 1853). The popularity of these three works has been uninterrupted from their day to ours.

In March 1850 the Fenice Theatre, Venice, commissioned an opera from Verdi for production during Lent of the following year. The composer's mind was about that time full of plans and ideas of all sorts, among them a *King Lear*, a *Hamlet*, and the

Spanish drama that ultimately became *Il Trovatore*; but in the end he decided on Victor Hugo's play *Le Roi s'amuse*, which had been produced in Paris some seventeen years earlier without establishing itself, the public finding it hard to follow the poet in his bold contention that drama, and indeed art in general, was as capable of dealing with the "ugly" as with the "beautiful," with thoroughly repulsive characters as with attractive or borderline ones. Hugo had indeed set himself a formidable task—to win his audience's sympathies for a leading character not only physically but mentally and morally deformed, having only one redeeming trait, his love for his daughter. (Other considerations, such as the cynical immorality of the King in the case, were subordinate to this.)

When he published his play Hugo prefaced it with a *pièce justificative* that revealed what had been at the back of his mind when he created the character of his Triboulet. He had imagined, he said, a man labouring under a triple disadvantage—he was physically deformed, he was unhealthy, and fate had allotted him the rôle of a buffoon at a corrupt court. Under these stresses his nature had gone to pieces. He had become hate incarnate, hating the King because he was the King, the noble courtiers because they were courtiers, "and men in general because they do not have a hump on their backs." His dominant passion is to bring them all down to ruin by playing them off against each other: the King he encourages in his vices, off the courtiers he scores by making even them the victims of his master's villainies, incessantly pointing out to him "some wife to seduce, some sister to abduct, some daughter to dishonour." All are puppets in his hands; the viler he makes them the more voluptuous is his sense of triumph over them; till the day comes when, as he imagines, the arch-criminal of them all, the self-indulgent, unscrupulous King himself, having committed his worst crime—the seduction of the buffoon's daughter—unconsciously delivers himself into his hands for vengeance.

2

The conception is admirable, and the threads of the action are cunningly interwoven; but the stage realisation is not altogether successful. What might have become drama of a very fine kind tends to become in Hugo's hands merely melodrama. Later generations, unable to take the violences of the French romantics as seriously as they did, are inclined to see the personages as puppets rather than flesh-and-blood characters: the late nineteenth century view of the play in general seems to have been voiced by the dramatic critic William Archer, who described it as "a nightmare of a play, in which changes are rung upon cynicism, lust and cruelty until exhausted nature cries 'Hold! too much!'. In Triboulet [the Rigoletto of the opera] we have an instance of that 'system of predetermined paradox' (to use Mr. Myers's phrase) which has vitiated so much of Victor Hugo's work. He has told us how he determined to take the vilest of beings, a physical monstrosity placed in the most despicable of situations, and then to give him a soul, and place in that soul 'the purest sentiment known to man, the paternal sentiment' . . . This sublime sentiment . . . will transform before our eyes this degraded creature; the small will become great, the deformed will become beautiful."

Turning later to Hugo's actual handling of his characters and his theme, Archer remarked that "Melodrama [in which category he places *Le Roi s'amuse*] is illogical and sometimes irrational tragedy. It subordinates character to situation, consistency to impressiveness. It aims at startling, not at convincing, and is little concerned with causes so long as it attains effects. Developments of character are beyond its province, its personages being all ready-made, and subject at most to revolutions of feeling. Necessity and law it replaces by coincidence and fatality, exactitude by exaggeration, subtlety by emphasis."

What is true of Hugo's drama is equally true of the opera libretto; one finds it hard to sympathise entirely with the misshapen thing of evil that is the Rigoletto of the opening of the work, even when his love for his daughter is thrown into the scales in his favour. Under the seductive influence of music, however, we are more charitably inclined towards him than we can be towards the Triboulet of Hugo; and anyhow opera audiences have never been as exacting psychologists as the students of dramatic literature are. Verdi himself was over head and ears in love with his subject. It was a drama, he wrote to one friend and another, with some terrific situations, full of vitality, variety and pathos. He rather loved violence in a story, for he aimed, he said, before everything at "passion." He did not mind very much whether people found his music "beautiful" or "ugly" so long as he felt it to be true to the character and the situation of the moment; why then should he shrink from trying to make "a repulsive and ridiculous hunchback" *sing* melodiously with the best of them? He was convinced that the Rigoletto subject was the best he had so far come upon in his search for an opera libretto.

3

After the unfriendly reception *Le Roi s'amuse* had had in France, Verdi and his librettist Francesco Piave expected a certain amount of trouble with the censorship and perhaps with the Italian public, but they were hardly prepared for all the difficulties that sprang up in their path. The Austrian censor jibbed, as high circles in Paris had done years before, at the stage presentation of no less a personage than a king as an out-and-out immoralist. Verdi offered to make simply a prince of him, but in the end had to reduce him to the rank of a mere sixteenth-century Italian duke. The very title of the opera stuck in the censor's maw. Verdi had wanted to entitle it *La Maledizione*, for was not the curse laid on the brutal, cynical jester by the wronged Monterone the very core of the tragedy? [1] They took curses very seriously in those days, and the censor feared that religious susceptibilities might be deeply wounded by seeing one of them in actual operation on the stage. Finally the opera was named after the hunchback himself, at first *Triboletto* (an Italianisation of Triboulet) then *Rigoletto*. The music was written in quite a short time, and the opera produced at the Fenice on the 11th January 1851 with enormous success.

Verdi has his gloomy drama well in hand from the beginning. The orchestra opens with the vital motif of the Curse in the solemn tones of the brass:

---

[1] As Hugo himself said in his polemic against his critics, "The real subject of the drama is *The Malediction of M. de Saint-Vallier*."

No. 1

It swells for a moment to fury, then subsides into a descending wailing figure of a type frequently employed by Verdi to express anguish, becomes its ominous self again for a few bars, and finally leaves us with an imposing gesture; thirty-five bars of slow music have sufficed to place us at the core of the tragedy.

The pace changes to allegro con brio as the curtain rises, showing the foremost of a series of splendid apartments in the palace of the young Duke of Mantua, with cavaliers and ladies passing to and fro, some talking, others dancing. A succession of lively tunes in the orchestra, which are repeated again and again, depicts the carefree gaiety of the company. Against this gay background the Duke enters from an inner room with Borsa, one of the gentlemen of his court, telling him complacently that soon he hopes to bring to a happy ending one of the latest of his amorous adventures—the pursuit of a maiden, as yet unknown to him, whom he has seen at her devotions in the church each day for the last three months, though his pursuit of her has so far brought him no further than the discovery that she lives in a remote quarter of the town, in a humble house that is visited every night by a man about whom the Duke has been able to learn nothing.

These two, we surmise already, are the court buffoon Rigoletto and his daughter Gilda. We hear, however, no more of them for some time, for the Duke has several other amorous affairs on his hands. In the well-known ballata "Questa o quella":

No. 2

he sings to Borsa of the delights of promiscuity in affairs of gallantry; to him, as to Don Giovanni, all women are attractive, and to pursue and take them is a law of his nature. At the court he is mainly interested at the moment in the Countess Ceprano, the wife of one of his courtiers; with her he now has a brief surreptitious colloquy, during which the lady's husband watches him suspiciously, while some of the other guests comment amusedly on the familiar situation. The brief furtive episode ends with the Duke taking the Countess out on his arm, while Rigoletto insults Ceprano with a word or two of mock sympathy. Then he turns to the courtiers with a cynical shrug of the shoulders: it is always thus with the Duke, he says, who spends his time between gaming, drinking and lovemaking—in this latest instance with Count Ceprano's wife—while the rest of them enjoy the fun. Some of the company dance a perigodino (a piquant dance in 6/8 time), and when this is over another courtier, Marullo, enters with a piece of news which the others swallow eagerly, the orchestra playing round the conversation with the lively tunes with which the opera had opened. The news is certainly startling: Marullo believes he has discovered that the ugly, deformed, misanthropic court buffoon secretly plays the gallant like the rest of them. The courtiers are highly diverted by this metamorphosis, as they express it, of the hunchback into a Cupid. But for the moment this new dramatic motif recedes into the background as the Duke re-enters with Rigoletto, whom he is consulting as to the best way of getting rid of the inconvenient Count Ceprano. The buffoon reveals his evil nature in almost the first words he utters: he advises the Duke to put Ceprano in prison, or, failing that, to exile him, or, if that is impracticable, to settle the matter once and for all by having him beheaded. The cynical advice is overheard by Ceprano and some of the other courtiers, who turn angrily on Rigoletto. The latter is complacently sure of his master's protection in whatever rascality he may devise for him, but the Duke, who evidently despises his servile minion as heartily as the others do, bids him not to be too sure of that. The long-smouldering hatred of the courtiers for the evil-natured buffoon finds spirited expression in a big ensemble in which they call for vengeance on him. The light-hearted Duke, however, who takes nothing seriously but his own pursuit of pleasure, manages in time to make them all forget their grievance against the jester.

The atmosphere of gaiety that has enveloped the drama until now is suddenly dissipated by the entry of an elderly nobleman, Count Monterone, who forces his way into the company in spite of the efforts of the servants to restrain him. With his entry we find ourselves at once under the shadow of the Curse (No. 1). The old man has come to vent a personal grievance: the Duke has abducted and outraged his daughter. Before the Duke can say a word, Rigoletto takes it on himself to impersonate him. To the accompaniment of various orchestral figures that are meant to suggest the tortuosities of his own evil soul, such as:

No. 3

and

No. 4

he insults the old man, who, turning from him contemptuously, warns the Duke that even if he sends him to the scaffold his curse will pursue him to the grave and beyond it. And in that curse he includes Rigoletto: "it was not well done, Duke," he declares, "to set your hound upon the dying lion; and as for you"—turning to Rigoletto—"viper that could mock the sorrow of an old man, my malediction be on you!" The buffoon recoils in horror; and in an agitated ensemble the Duke and the courtiers, half in fear, half in anger, warn Monterone of the consequences of his audacity. At a sign from the Duke the old Count is led out between two halberdiers, and the remainder of the company follow them.

4

The scene now changes to a deserted alley in which stands the humble home of Rigoletto, the retreat in which he tries to conceal the one being he loves, his daughter Gilda, from the world he despises and hates so bitterly. A wall runs round a small court-yard, to which a door in the wall gives access, while above it some arches support a verandah, which can be approached from a door on the first floor of the house. On the other side of the street is a high wall, over which we have a view of an angle of the Ceprano palace. It is now night.

Rigoletto comes in slowly, closely wrapped in a great cloak. A sombre bit of tone-painting in clarinet, bassoon and lower strings:

No. 5

shows him stealthily and thoughtfully making his way through the darkness to his home. From his opening words it is evident that he is still brooding superstitiously over the recent events in the ducal palace: "that old man laid a curse on me!", he mutters:

No. 6

(The operatic world of the first half of the nineteenth century attached great importance to curses, and, for some reason or other, particularly to those of a father. The curse of a mother, a sister, a brother, a son, a daughter or even an aunt never attained the same high level of dramatic potency; it was from a father's curse alone that the best horrific results could be obtained.)

Rigoletto has been followed at a little distance by someone who now draws level with him and accosts him—a sinister figure also wrapped in a cloak, from beneath which a long sword pro-jects. It is Sparafucile, by profession an assassin, and by operatic convention a cavernous bass. Verdi limns him for us convincingly in a sinister theme that winds its way slowly through the orchestra as if, like Sparafucile himself, it was cautiously feeling its way in the uncanny dark:

No. 7

To the accompaniment of this theme the pair dialogue for a moment. The bravo—his name, he tells Rigoletto, is Sparafucile—places his professional services at the disposal of this stranger should he ever require them. Everyone, he suggests, has some rival or other whom he would gladly see removed from his path. "How much would you charge for a nobleman?" Rigoletto asks tentatively. "More, of course, than for a common man," is Sparafucile's reply. His terms, he says, are reasonable—half down before the murder, the balance after it. His methods are as safe as they are simple: either he disposes of his victims quickly in the town, or his lovely sister lures them to their conveniently secluded house, where his good sword—which he draws for his interlocutor's inspection—does the deed smoothly in no time. But to his regret Rigoletto declines his services for the present. Sparafucile informs him that he is to be found in this neighbourhood every night should his new friend have need of him; and the pair part company.

5

Left alone, the buffoon, considerably chastened by his recent encounter with Monterone, makes, in a long recitativo accompagnato, a bitter comparison of himself with the assassin who has just left him: "I murder with my tongue and my laughter, he with his sword!" Suddenly he recalls the Curse (No. 6), and he breaks into a passionate lament over his unhappy lot in life. Nature and men have between them made him base and vile, deformed in soul as in body. Each day his young, handsome, tyrannic master demands a new amusement from his buffoon, and he is compelled to obey. How he despises and hates humanity in general and these courtiers in particular! "Come what may, I must laugh: the tears that are the solace of other men are denied me. If I am vile, it is you who have made me so." (For the first time in the opera he becomes sympathetic to us.) But here in his humble home, he continues while a gentle figure steals out timidly in the flute, he can generally be another man; tonight, however, he cannot rid his tortured mind of the curse that the old man had laid on him. "Is it an augury of woe?" he asks.

As he goes into the courtyard his daughter—who must be assumed by the spectator to be much younger and more prepossessing than the average prima donna player of the part—runs to meet him, and the whole character of the music changes: it is now all childlike joy:

No. 8

as Gilda throws herself into the arms of this mysterious father whose name, even, she does not know; her mother she has never known. In mournful tones he tells her of that good woman who, deformed and poor though he was, had loved him and thrown in her lot with his; too soon death had taken her from him, leaving him only this dear child to console him in his loneliness. Gilda pours out her love for him in rather florid phrases:

No. 9

for she is a coloratura soprano as well as an affectionate daughter. Once more he refuses to tell her who and what he is, but warns her that he has many enemies, some of whom fear him, while others curse him.

It is three months since they came to this house, Gilda reminds him, and all that time he has kept her in strict seclusion, for his constant fear is that some man or other, perhaps one of those whom he has derided and injured, will rob him of her. She assures him that she never goes into the town in his absence. Rigoletto calls out his servant, Giovanna, and passionately demands assurance from her that no one has ever observed him entering the house and that the door is always kept locked; and he begs her piteously to watch unceasingly over his child.

At the conclusion of this perhaps over-long scene Rigoletto opens the courtyard door and goes into the street for a last look round. As he does so the Duke slips into the courtyard, throws a purse to Giovanna with a gesture that commands silence, and conceals himself behind a high tree. Returning after this rather naïve piece of byplay Rigoletto asks the servant if anyone has ever followed his daughter on her way to and from the church, and is falsely assured that no one has. He bids Giovanna see that the door is opened to no one in his absence. "Not even to the Duke?", she asks. "To him least of all" is the reply. Meanwhile the Duke, from his place of concealment, has recognised Rigoletto, and from the buffoon's parting words to Gilda—"Good night, my child"—he makes the surprising discovery that she is his hireling's daughter. Gilda and Rigoletto wish each other a fond good night, she all affection, he in accents in which tenderness is shot with anxiety.

6

When he has left the scene Gilda reproaches Giovanna and herself for having concealed from her father that a young man has been in the habit of following her from church—a young man whom she confesses that she already almost loves. The worldly-minded servant points out that one so generous with his money as this stranger is perhaps of noble birth; but Gilda, in simple words and music that contrast markedly with her former coloratura, vows that she would prefer a lover who is as poor as herself. On this cue the Duke, having dismissed Giovanna with a gesture, comes forward, throws himself at Gilda's feet, and declares his love; and she recognises him as the man she had first seen in the church. He bears down her maidenly resistance in a passionate aria:

No. 10

PP E il sol dell' a-ni-ma, la vi-ta è a-mo—re

to the later strains of which she contributes a florid counterpoint. (Gilda is not consistently drawn throughout; Verdi's music for her alternates between childlike simplicity and showy coloratura, seldom achieving an organic unity of the two).

She longs to know his name, she tells him; and just as he is informing her that he is Gualtier Maldé, and only a poor student, Giovanna enters in great agitation, for she has heard footsteps without. (They are those of Borsa and Ceprano.) Gilda fears that her father has returned, and the Duke is hastily ushered out *via* the house, his voice and that of Gilda joining in a final feverish duet. Left alone, Gilda muses fondly upon the supposed name of her lover, that is now so dear to her—"Dear name that first awakened my heart to love": this is the famous "Caro nome" aria, a remarkable combination of psychological expression and vocal exhibitionism.

As she slowly makes her way from the verandah into the house to a final rapturous sighing of her lover's name the prowling courtiers enter stealthily, to phrases that unintentionally acquire a somewhat comic air by their regular alternations of forte and pianissimo:

No. 11

Rigoletto, still brooding on the Curse (No. 6), runs into them in the dark, and they at once recognise him. The abduction scene that follows was evidently taken by Verdi with the utmost seriousness, but it is often undesignedly comic in its effect on the spectator. Revealing themselves, in reply to Rigoletto's enquiries—for he has not been able to identify them in the dark—as Marullo and his court associates, they carry out their heartless jest at the expense of the detested buffoon. Their design, they say, is to carry off Ceprano's wife, a project that at once appeals to the evil element in Rigoletto's nature. The problem will be, he says, to get admission to the Count's house, which stands on the other side of the road. Ceprano, whom the jester has not recognised, hands over his key, the crest on which Rigoletto manages to decipher with his fingers. He consents to being masked, like them, and without his knowing it he is blindfolded in addition; then he is allotted the task of holding the ladder while the conspirators climb the wall not into Ceprano's house, as he imagines, but into his own. (They, of course, are still under the impression that the girl in the jester's house is his inamorata.) We dimly see them entering the house, the chorus to which they accomplish their purpose once more bringing a disturbing note of the comic into the scene. Next we vaguely see them emerging from the house carrying a protesting Gilda calling distractedly on her father. Rigoletto apparently does not hear her, and this jest in the dark now begins to pall on him. Realising that he is blindfolded as well as masked he tears off the bandage, picks up a lantern which one of the conspirators has left behind him, and by its light recognises on the ground a scarf that had become detached from Gilda in her struggle with her captors. He runs wildly into the house, and comes out again dragging with him a bewildered Giovanna. At last the truth dawns on him. "The Curse! the Curse!" he cries despairingly, and falls down in a faint.

7

At the beginning of the second act, which is staged in an antechamber in the palace, we find the Duke, in great agitation of soul, lamenting the misfortune that had befallen him the night before—the loss of the girl who for the moment had become the guiding star of his life. Who were the abductors? Where had they taken her? They shall suffer for it when he discovers them! He has hardly concluded an invocation—one that sits none too convincingly on his lips—to this lost angel of purity when the courtiers, headed by Borsa, Marullo and Ceprano, break in upon him, bursting with the news that they had taken possession of the buffoon's lady-love. Mightily pleased with themselves, they tell the diverting story of the abduction in an ensemble that is of a type rather too frequent in the Verdi of the second period: the intention is half-serious, half-humorous, but the realisation somewhat ludicrous; one sees the circling handle of the barrel-organ rather too plainly:

No. 12

The Duke, remembering Rigoletto's "Good night, my child!" of the night before, realises that his new love is not the mistress but the daughter of his jester; and when he learns that the girl is now actually in the palace he expresses his joy, and avers his willingness to give up his kingdom for her, in some lyrical strains that do not ring quite convincingly; while the courtiers, to music equally lacking in distinction, comment surprisedly, as well they might, that they have never seen their ruler in such a state as this before. Rigoletto enters, vainly endeavoring to conceal his anxiety under a façade of indifference:

No. 13

His eyes wander about the room, probing for a clue to what has happened since the abduction of the night before. The courtiers play heartlessly with him. He lights upon a handkerchief at the back of the salon, but soon satisfies himself that it is not Gilda's. A page appears with a message that the Duchess would like to speak with her husband; and from the evasive replies of the courtiers Rigoletto gathers that his master, ostensibly out hunting, is in the palace but does not wish to be disturbed. The buffoon senses now that Gilda is somewhere in the palace, and throwing off the mask, he tells the courtiers that the girl they had carried off is his daughter, and passionately demands their help in finding her. They bar his exit from the room, and he breaks out into a savage denunciation of them and all they stand for: then his tone changes to one of heartfelt love for his child.

Before the others can say anything in reply Gilda bursts into the room in a state of wild agitation, throws herself despairingly into the arms of her father, and tells him that the Duke has dishonoured her. Rigoletto impetuously orders the courtiers out, declaring that even if his master himself should come now he would bar his entry. His fury cows them and they depart, muttering among themselves, leaving the stage free for a long duet in which Gilda tells her father of her first encounter with a stranger youth in the church:

No. 14

of his intrusion upon her last night, proclaiming himself to be a poor student who loved her ardently, and of her abduction. In spite of the coloratura into which she cannot help breaking towards the end, her music is sincere and moving. Rigoletto becomes once more wholly sympathetic to us as he speaks of the pains he has been at to preserve her from the world's harm, but Gilda's tearful praise of his love is too liberally festooned with coloratura to impress the modern opera-goer as much as it was meant to do. "Thus," laments Rigoletto, "has the world about me changed in a single day!" He and she will leave this dreadful place at once, he assures her.

Just then Monterone passes across the stage, being conducted to prison by some halberdiers; he is accompanied in the orchestra by one of those volleying rhythmic figures, rising from pianissimo to a mighty fortissimo, which Verdi knew so well how to handle. A portrait of the Duke on the wall catches the old man's eye: he pauses before it and ejaculates, "So my curse was laid on you in vain! No thunderbolt has struck you down! You will live on, happy as before!" As the halberdiers take him out, Rigoletto springs forward with a cry of "No, old man! You shall be avenged! Vengeance, direst vengeance, is all I live for now! Heaven's thunderbolt shall strike through me!":

No. 15

Allegro vivo ♩=138

Si,   ven — det—ta, tre-men-da ven~ det— ta

In vain does Gilda implore him to spare the wrongdoer for whom she already feels love; there is no room in Rigoletto's heart now for any thought but that of revenge. He hurries away, taking his daughter with him, and the curtain falls.

8

The third act shows us the fulfilment of Monterone's curse on the buffoon who had jibed at him in his moment of misery.

No information is vouchsafed to the spectator of what may have happened in the interval between the second and third acts, and for a little while no hint is afforded him why any of the characters should be just where they are when the curtain rises again. The scene is a deserted spot on the Mincio, a glimpse of whose waters we catch over a ruined parapet in the background. On the left of the stage stands a dilapidated two-storeyed house, the front of which has to be non-existent for operatic purposes, so that we see that the ground floor is a sort of inn, from which a rickety staircase leads up to a loft in which is a rough couch. This is evidently the secluded lair to which, Sparafucile had told Rigoletto in the first act, his sister was in the habit of decoying the men of whom the hired assassin had to dispose. When the curtain rises Sparafucile is seen sitting at a table in the lower room, polishing his belt. It is night.

To the accompaniment of some sombre preludial phrases in the subdued strings Rigoletto and Gilda come into sight on the road that runs by the side of the building. Their conversation (in recitative) runs thus:

Rigoletto: And you love him!
Gilda: Always.
Rigoletto: But I have given you time enough to cure yourself of that.
Gilda: I love him.
Rigoletto: Poor woman's heart! Ah, the base villain! But you shall be revenged on him, my Gilda.
Gilda: Have pity, father.

Rigoletto: But if you had proof that he is false to you, would you love him still?
Gilda: I do not know; but he adores me.
Rigoletto: He!
Gilda: Yes.
Rigoletto: Well then, observe.
  Leading her to the house he bids her look through a fissure in the wall.
Gilda: I see a man.
Rigoletto: Wait a while.
  The Duke appears in the inn, disguised as a cavalry officer.
Gilda: Oh, my father!

The spectator may reasonably feel that he is entitled to a little more explanation than this. Verdi and his librettist, however, scorn detailed elucidation; their sole concern is to get to grips at once with the main tragic action.[1]

Addressing Sparafucile, the Duke orders two things—a room and some wine. Sparafucile, scenting profitable business of the kind he likes, goes out, while Rigoletto remarks cynically to Gilda, "This is the way with him!" Left alone, the Duke sings his famous canzone, "La donna è mobile"—"Woman is as variable as a feather in the wind, false to the marrow, yet the man who does not love does not know what felicity is"; it is an expanded version of the famous dictum—"Souvent femme varie"—of King François the First of France, who has obviously sat as a model for the Duke of Mantua:

> *Souvent femme varie,*
> *Bien fol est qui s'y fie.*
> *Une femme souvent*
> *N'est qu'une plume au vent!*

9

At this point we must digress for a moment to throw a little more light on the situation than, as has been remarked above, Verdi and his librettist have done. In the opera no information is vouchsafed us as to anything that may have happened between acts two and three: and it is only after the third act has been running for a little time that we begin to understand just why

[1] On this point see *infra.*

Rigoletto and Gilda happen to be outside Sparafucile's inn when the curtain rises. For elucidation of it all we have to turn to the fourth act of Victor Hugo's play. There we discover, from the opening colloquy between the father (Triboulet) and the daughter (Blanche), that some time has elapsed and much has happened between the end of the third act and the beginning of the fourth. It appears that Blanche had settled down quite comfortably in the palace as the mistress of the King, with whom she had fallen deeply in love: only yesterday, we learn from her own lips, he had assured her once more that he adored her, and her present considered opinion of him is that he is an excellent King, brilliant and handsome. Triboulet had given her ample time to think it over and change her mind, but she had seen no reason to do so; and latterly she had thought that he too was now kindly disposed towards the King. She assures Triboulet, however, that her love for him is as great as ever, and that in fact she would be ready to lay down her life for either her father or her lover—a remark that becomes of considerable dramatic significance later.

Triboulet, however, declares that if he had seemed to have forgiven the King he had only been feigning: he is as resolved as ever on revenge. What would she say if she were to discover that her lover is deceiving her? he asks tentatively. She refuses to believe that this is possible. What would you say, he continues, if before your own eyes you had evidence of his perfidy? He bids her look through a crevice in the wall of the inn; and she sees the King, in the costume of a simple officer, entering from an inner room. It now becomes clear to us that Triboulet had already worked out with Saltabadil (Sparafucile) a plan for the murder of the King in the hut, the assassin's sister Maguelonne (Maddalena) being used as a decoy. A week ago, we and Blanche soon learn, Triboulet had taken the King to some hostelry or other where he had been introduced to Maguelonne; he had fallen in love with her at first sight, and agreed to an assignation with her at the miserable inn kept by her brother; and there he intends to spend the night with her.

While the scene of amorous ardour on the one side and coy refusal on the other is being played out inside the inn, Saltabadil has a brief conversation with Triboulet outside. "Your man is inside there," he says: "is he to live or die?" "Come back in a little while," replies Triboulet, and sends him away. Blanche, as in the opera, becomes the horrified witness of the long scene between the King and Maguelonne. When her father rejoins her she bids him, in a moment of bitter revulsion, to proceed with his plan for revenge. This rejoices him, but he will not disclose to her yet what his plan is; he merely tells her to hasten back to their house, dress herself as a man, take money and a horse,[1] and make with all speed to Évreux, where he will rejoin her the day after to-morrow: on no account is she to return to the inn, "for here something terrible is about to happen."

10

We can now return to the opera, from which, for clarity's sake, we had to digress at the point where, having dismissed Sparafucile with orders to prepare a room and bring him wine, the Duke launches his nonchalant "La donna è mobile." Sparafucile, adopting no doubt what is his regular technique on these occasions, returns with a flask of wine and a couple of glasses, then knocks at the ceiling twice with the hilt of his great sword, whereupon a handsome, smiling girl of gipsy aspect comes down the staircase. The Duke tries to embrace her, but she makes a coy pretence of eluding him. Sparafucile slips out of the house for a quick dialogue with Rigoletto: "Your man is inside there. Is he to live or die?" to which the hunchback replies, "I will return later, and the job can be finished then."

Verdi now gets fairly into his musical stride. In a gay conversational strain the Duke assures Maddalena that he has loved her ever since he first met her, and, having learned that it is here she lives, he has made bold to follow her. She fences with him dexterously—no doubt, she says, he has told the same tale already to many another woman. He goes so far as to promise to marry her, but she still declines to take him seriously. Their dialogue is heard by Gilda and Rigoletto outside, who comment on the situation each according to character. All is now set for the great quartet,

---

[1] The costume, he tells her, he has already had made expressly for her; she will find it in the chest near the portrait of her mother. The horse stands ready saddled. Triboulet, we see, has thought of everything; the plan for the murder of the King and the disposal of his body has evidently been worked out in careful detail with Saltabadil.

one of the marvels of the Italian opera stage. The core of it is a splendid continuous melody for the tenor—a declaration of his love for Maddalena—upon which each of the other three characters embroiders his or her reactions, Maddalena laughing it all off ironically, Gilda bemoaning her lover's perfidy and her own sad lot, and Rigoletto assuring her with grim persistence that she shall soon be avenged. Victor Hugo, when he heard the opera, commented wistfully on the advantages music sometimes has over poetry or prose, opera over spoken drama: what would the ordinary dramatist not give, he asked, to be able to make four people animated by different sentiments speak all at the same time, each in character, and each fully intelligible to the audience!

The superb ensemble over, Rigoletto bids the protesting Gilda return to their house, dress herself as a boy, and make for Verona, where he will rejoin her on the morrow. Inside the house the Duke and Maddalena are still laughing and drinking. Sparafucile returns, and in a scene of sinister orchestral suggestion Rigoletto pays the bravo, as arranged, half his money in advance, the remainder to follow when the deed is done. He will return, he says, at midnight. Sparafucile assures him that there is no need for that—he himself will throw the body into the river; but Rigoletto insists on having that pleasure himself. "Who is the victim?" Sparafucile asks. "His name," replies the buffoon, "is Crime, and mine, Punishment." With that he leaves his confederate, going off in the night alone. Within the house the ardent Duke would press matters to their logical conclusion with Maddalena, but she fends the prospective victim off with the warning that her brother is coming.

11

She remarks to him that a storm is brewing; thunder and lightning, indeed, roar and flash in the orchestra, while the soughing of the wind is suggested by a chorus of tenors and basses behind the scenes, singing with closed lips a phrase:

No. 16

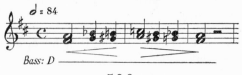

which will be employed frequently later to convey the sense of storm in the air all the while the human tragedy is working itself out. As the moment for the murder approaches, Maddalena feels a pang of pity for this handsome young gallant and—quite unprofessional conduct on her part—urges him to leave. He refuses to do so in such a torrent of rain as is now falling, whereupon Sparafucile obligingly places the upper room at his disposal until the storm shall have died down. The Duke, who is very tired, accepts the ominous offer, and soon we see him in the upper room divesting himself of his hat and sword and singing a phrase or two of his "La donna è mobile" before sleep overcomes him. Thither Maddalena goes and contemplates him pityingly, a brief colloquy with her brother having convinced her that the ruffian is inexorably bent on earning the money he has been promised for the murder.

Gilda's love and pity for the Duke have made her disobey, in part, her father's orders. Instead of going to Verona she has returned, now in male costume, booted and spurred, and once more, as the storm rages in the orchestra and in the choral figure, with closed lips, seen in example No. 16, we see her again peering through the fissure. She sees Sparafucile seated drinking, and Maddalena returning to the lower floor and placing the Duke's sword on the table: Gilda also hears her pleading with her brother for the life of this agreeable young man, handsome, as she says, as Apollo, who apparently loves her and with whom she is now in love. Sparafucile's only reply to this is to throw a sack at her and bid her mend it; it will do excellently, he says, for her Apollo, who, after he has had his throat cut, will find his grave in the river.

Maddalena continues her pleadings and suggests an alternative plan. Her brother, she reminds him, has already received ten pieces of silver; why not kill the hunchback, then, and so secure the remaining ten while sparing the life of the stranger? This kindles Sparafucile's anger; his professional pride is hurt, his professional honour impugned. Does she take him for a thief, he asks her reproachfully, a mere bandit? When has she known him to betray a client's trust? The hunchback is paying him, and it is the job entrusted to him by the hunchback that he means to do. Maddalena makes to run up the stairs to warn the victim, an act

591

which draws an approving comment from the listening Gilda outside. Sparafucile begins to weaken; while still reluctant not to keep the money he already has and earn the remainder in a way of which his conscience can approve, he now consents to a compromise—if someone else happens to come to the inn before midnight he shall die for the young Apollo, and his body be palmed off on the hunchback:

No. 17

Se pria ch'ab-bia il mez-zo la not-te toc-ca-to

But who is likely to come on such a night as this? Maddalena asks distractedly; and the voices unite in a short tense trio, with Gilda's voice soaring above the other two in a wild appeal to heaven for pity:

No. 18

ff Oh —— cie — lo! pie ——tà!

Maddalena, now in tears, is not consoled by her brother's reminder that they have only half an hour before them. With No. 16 still wailing in the orchestra a clock strikes: the sands are running out. Gilda's resolution has already been half-taken. Touched by the pity that even this woman in the inn seems to feel for the destined victim—for Maddalena has again implored her brother piteously to wait a little longer—she decides to offer herself up as a sacrifice.

As the storm rises to its height she knocks twice at the door of the inn, to the great astonishment of the couple inside. In answer to Sparafucile's cry of "Who's there?" she declares herself to be a beggar seeking shelter for the night. Another trio follows, launched by Maddalena to the strain of No. 17: feverishly she exhorts her brother to do at once the deed that shall spare the life of the gallant, while Gilda once more appeals frantically to heaven as in our No. 18. The storm in the orchestra rises to its height as Gilda, in response to Sparafucile's invitation, enters the hut, where he is waiting for her behind the door with a raised dagger. Darkness closes in as the bravo shuts the door, and the rest is left to our imagination.

12

For a little while after, the storm continues to rage in the orchestra, but it begins to abate as Rigoletto appears outside the inn, closely wrapped in a cloak. The gateway, he sees, is still fastened, so presumably the murder has not yet been done. But he can wait, he says, and he savours voluptuously the completeness of his coming revenge on his master and on the world that has so long misused him. He knocks at the door, and Sparafucile appears, dragging a sack. A hurried colloquy ensues: Rigoletto, having discharged the remainder of his debt, will not allow the assassin to throw the body into the river; that last exquisite satisfaction he reserves for himself. Sparafucile directs him to a spot where the river is deeper, bids him good night, and re-enters the inn.

Rigoletto places his foot on the sack and revels in his triumph; it is the Duke, without a doubt, for he can feel his spurs! He invokes the courtiers to behold the victory of the poor buffoon over the powerful prince who had lorded it over him so long. And now for the river! But just as he is about to drag the sack away the voice of the Duke is heard, singing once again his "La donna è mobile" as he crosses the stage at the back.[1] As the song dies away in the distance Rigoletto realises that the Fates have played their last and cruellest trick on him. But whose, then, is the body before him? Frenziedly he tears the sack open and discovers the still-

---

[1] Some producers show him accompanied by Maddalena. This is quite nonsensical. In Hugo everything is perfectly lucid. Some time has elapsed between the murder of Blanche and the scene of Triboulet with the body, and at the climactic moment, just as the buffoon is about to throw it into the Seine, we get the following stage directions; "just as he places the sack on the parapet the lower door of the inn is cautiously opened. Maguelonne comes out, looks anxiously round her, makes a gesture signifying that there is no one about, goes into the inn again, and returns in a moment with the King, to whom she explains by signs that the coast is clear for his departure. She re-enters the inn and closes the door, while the King makes his way across the strand in the direction she has indicated." Triboulet is about to tip the sack into the Seine when he hears the King, at the back of the stage, singing his "Souvent femme varie."

living Gilda, who has only just strength enough to tell her broken-hearted father how she had deceived him and died to save the man she loved too much. She is going to rejoin her mother in heaven, she says:

No. 19

where they will pray for him together and wait for him. She dies, and Rigoletto throws himself in grief and despair upon her body, with a wild cry of "Gilda! Gilda! Dead! The Curse is fulfilled!"

Il Trovatore

VERDI [1813–1901]

PRINCIPAL CHARACTERS

MANRICO (THE TROUBADOR)	*Tenor*
LEONORA	*Soprano*
AZUCENA	*Mezzo-soprano*
COUNT DI LUNA	*Baritone*
INES	*Soprano*
FERRANDO	*Baritone*
RUIZ	*Tenor*

1

VERDI's appetite for dramatic gloom had been far from sated in *Rigoletto*. Even before he decided to concentrate on that work, indeed, early in 1850, he had spoken of the fancy he had taken to a romantic play by a Spanish dramatist, Antonio García Gutiérrez (1813–1884), *El Trovador*, which had been highly popular in its own country since its first production in Madrid in 1836. (García Gutiérrez recast it in 1851.) It made an irresistible appeal to Verdi by reason of its abundance in "powerful" situations of the kind his sombre genius loved, and above all by the character of the gipsy woman Azucena, with the perpetual conflict raging in her bosom between, as he put it, maternal and filial love. His first idea was to name the opera after her; Leonora, in his view, was a secondary figure.

In April 1851 the poet Cammarano sent him a draft of a proposed scenario for an opera on the subject, in which Verdi made many changes. In September of that year we find him telling his librettist that for some time he had been unable to do any serious thinking about the new work because of an accumulation of misfortunes and griefs, chief among them being the death of his mother on the preceding 30th June. Rome and Venice, it appears, were both anxious to give the first performance of *Il Trovatore*, and of the two casts likely to be at his disposal Verdi perferred on the whole that of Rome, though just then he could not see his ideal Azucena in any mezzo-soprano there. A few weeks later, his health and spirits having returned, he was pressing his collaborator to finish the text with all possible speed; but apparently there was still some work to be done at it when Cammarano died in July 1852, and one Leone Emanuele Bardare had to be called in to add the final touches. The legend, for what it is worth, is that the music was "composed" between the 1st and 29th November 1852, but obviously Verdi must have done a good deal of preliminary work at it long before then. The orchestration was finished by the 14th December. The first performance—very successful in spite of the headshaking of the critics over some features of the opera—took place in the Apollo Theatre, Rome, on the 19th January 1853.

2

The course of events in the opera is not easy to understand at a first acquaintance, largely because Cammarano copied too closely at times the layout of the García Gutiérrez drama, in which stage narrative plays rather too large a part. The action takes place in Aragon, and García Gutiérrez specifies the fifteenth century as the period. There is no overture, twenty-seven bars of orchestral flourish serving as introduction to the first scene, which shows us the hall of the Queen's palace of Aliaferia. The hall is occupied by soldiers, for the loyalists live in constant danger of attack from insurgents led by the Count Urgel. There is also a bevy of servants, and all are awaiting the return of their master the Count di Luna, who, we learn, is at his usual nocturnal occupation of watching before the window of a lady of the palace, Leonora, on the trail of a rival—a troubadour who is in the habit of serenading her. As the company are finding it difficult to keep awake they entreat Ferrando, the Count's trusty retainer, to tell them a story which, one would imagine, must have been familiar enough by that time to the whole countryside—that of the tragedy of the Count's brother. However, we in the audience have to be made acquainted with it, so Ferrando tells it at considerable length.

It seems that the old Count, now gathered to his fathers, had two sons, one of whom had been confided when an infant to the care of a nurse, who, waking up early one morning, was startled to see a repulsive gipsy woman gazing intently at the child. The nurse's shrieks brought the servants to the spot; they drove away the intruder, who made the excuse that she had merely come to cast the child's horoscope. But from that day he fell into a decline; so the witch was pursued, captured, and burned at the stake. She left behind her, however, a daughter bent on vengeance. The sickly child disappeared, and later some still smoking remains, obviously of an infant, were found on the very spot where the gipsy's mother had been burned. The company listen to Ferrando's harrowing story with occasional interjections of horror.

His narrative is based on a phrase:

No. 1

which typifies the manner of much of Verdi's writing in his middle period. The Italian audiences of that day required of a composer that no one of his melodies should remind them of any other; at a much later date, indeed, we find them abusing Puccini for his use of reminiscent motifs, which they took to be an indication of his inability to invent new melodies. Verdi had consequently to make it clear from the outset of a given "number" that it was based musically on a melody not to be met with elsewhere. To do this he had to give it an individuality of physiognomy and of gesture, as it were, that easily degenerated into an automatic *tic* of which he sometimes became the servant instead of the master. In our No. 1, for example, and its sequel:

No. 2

we see him almost hypnotically constrained to repeat again and again the semiquaver figure that is the outstanding feature of it: this figure recurs no less than twenty times in the forty-odd bars of Ferrando's narrative, and the final effect, as elsewhere when Verdi became the victim of an obsession of this kind, is un-designedly comic—in some cases, indeed, downright ludicrous.

Ferrando goes on to inform his listeners (and us) that the old Count had to the last been reluctant to believe that his child was dead, and had laid on his surviving son the injunction to look for him unceasingly; but not only has the search been in vain but the spirit of the witch is said to haunt the scene of her crime. (Here we find Verdi employing in the orchestra, for the expression of horror, the wailing thirds of which he had already made such good use in the final scene of *Rigoletto*: see Ex. No. 16 in our analysis of that work.) The scene ends with the whole company calling down curses on the sorceress.

3

The necessity for narrative elucidation of the plot being over for the moment (though only for a moment), Verdi can now look forward to a spell of more lyrical writing. The scene changes to the garden of the palace, on the right of which a marble flight of steps is visible. It is night, with the moon trying fitfully to pierce the heavy clouds. We see the lady Leonora expressing to her confidante Ines her perturbation at the non-appearance lately of a knight who had been in the habit of serenading her. Once more Verdi is reduced for a while to narrative, though now it takes the loftier form that befits the heroine of the opera. Leonora tells Ines how she had first met this knight at a tournament where she had bestowed on him the meed of valour and victory: then she had seen him no more for a time, and she had eaten her heart out in silent grief, till one night she had heard beneath her window a song of love and devotion and the calling of her name:

No. 3

mf Ta—cea la not-te pla-ci—da e bel-la in ciel se—re——no;

and looking out she had recognised in the singer the gallant
knight of long ago, and her soul had dissolved in ecstasy. Ines'
advice to her is to forget this disturbing stranger whose name,
even, she does not know; but this merely provokes her to a declaration of undying love for him:

No. 4

the melodic outline, as was usual with Verdi at that period, becoming more and more exuberantly florid as it evolves:

No. 5

Come life, come death, she swears, she is the Troubadour's alone.

As she and Ines make their exit to the palace by way of the
steps, the Count di Luna enters; he too, at this witching hour of
night, has come to commune with Leonora while everyone else
in the palace is deep in slumber. As he makes to ascend the steps
he hears the strumming of a lute, and ejaculates angrily "The
Troubadour!" It is indeed Manrico, singing softly:

No. 6

of his lonely desolate heart and his one consolation in life—his
love for his lady. Leonora comes out of the palace, sees a figure
wrapped in a cloak, and, under the combined influences of her
agitation and the darkness, mistakenly assumes it to be that of her
Troubadour and rushes towards the Count with a rapturous cry;
to the great annoyance of the Troubadour, who, hiding among the
trees, naturally assumes her to be unfaithful to his memory. As
the moon shines out, revealing a knight with closed visor,
Leonora realises her mistake, and, running to the Troubadour

and throwing herself at his feet, assures him of her devotion. Raising his visor, he declares himself to be the knight Manrico, whom the furious Count at once denounces as the partisan, proscribed and condemned to death, of the rebel Urgel, whose blood he means to have:

No. 7

Upon this theme a vigorous trio is constructed, the jealous Count vowing vengeance, Manrico replying in kind, and Leonora trying in vain to pour oil on the troubled waters of love and jealousy. As Manrico and the Count go off with drawn swords to fight their quarrel out in a more convenient spot, Leonora falls senseless and the curtain descends on the first act.

4

When it rises again we see an encampment of gipsies in a wild spot in the Biscayan mountains. Day is dawning. Azucena is seated by a camp fire, with Manrico, wrapped in his cloak, reclining on a couch at her side, his helmet at his feet and his sword in his hand. A piquant orchestral introduction leads into a chorus in which the gipsies—the men striking their anvils with their hammers—sing the praises of the nomad life with its agreeable combination of work, drinking and love-making; it is the second of the two main phrases of the chorus:

No. 8

that makes the strongest impression on us and is of most importance in what follows.

Into this atmosphere of gaiety the brooding Azucena suddenly breaks with a sombre canzone that gathers the gipsies round her in rapt attention. Her mind is running reminiscently on the burning of her mother, which she describes in graphic detail—the crowd crazy with blood lust, the indignities heaped on the victim, the binding to the stake, the lighting of the fire:

No. 9

Stri-de la vam——pa, la——fol-la-in- do——mi—ta

But she has a further story to tell, for the ears of Manrico alone; so the gipsies obligingly replace their tools in their bags, and, to the melody of No. 8, go off nonchalantly to seek the day's provisions in the neighbourhood.

Left alone with Manrico, Azucena tells him what apparently his long absence at the wars has prevented him from learning until now—how her mother, accused by the old Count of magic arts, had been burned at the stake on the very spot on which Manrico now stands. (He recoils in horror.) Azucena, her son in her arms, had watched the whole terrible scene, and heard her mother's dying injunction to her to avenge her. Then Azucena had stolen the Count's child and brought him to the still burning pyre. For a moment she had been moved to pity by its crying; then, as the vision of her mother in her death agony stole over her again, reason deserted her; she had thrown, as she thought, the Count's child into the flames, only to discover later that it was her own son she had sacrificed. As she recalls it all, her hair stands on end in horror, she assures Manrico, in a sombre phrase:

No. 10

Sul ca—po mi—o le chio-me son-to driz-zar— si an—corl

in which Verdi makes effective use of the darkest tones of the mezzo-soprano voice. The character of Azucena obviously made a profound appeal to Verdi; he generally finds for her a musical idiom less conventional than the one that comes almost too readily to his pen for the others.

Manrico is quite understandably puzzled by Azucena's revelation. "So I am not your son," he says; "who then am I?" She assures him that she is indeed his mother, and, apparently realising now that she has said more than was discreet, she puts an end to his questioning by saying that when her ancient wrongs take possession of her mind she is apt to wander. Has she not always been the tenderest of mothers to him? Was it not she who had nursed him back to life when he had been wounded in the battle at Pelilla? In a long lyrical outburst he recalls that combat with the forces of Count di Luna, and his own gallantry in it; he had had the Count himself at his mercy, but had spared him. And in return for his clemency, says Azucena bitterly, the Count has ever since pursued him with unrelenting venom; what had moved him to grant the man his life? Manrico does not know. He had beaten down his enemy's puny resistance, it appears:

No. 11

and was about to deliver the death blow, when an irresistible, incomprehensible power within him had stayed his hand. Ferociously she implores him, should the Count ever be in his power again, to slay him without mercy; and this he promises to do.

Off-stage a horn call is heard, and soon a messenger from Manrico's henchman Ruiz enters with the tidings that the fortress of Castellor has been taken. For its defence, however, the Prince orders the immediate return of Manrico. Ruiz too bids him lose no time, for the Lady Leonora, having received false news of her lover's death, is about to enter a convent. The distressed Azucena implores him not to leave her, but he wildly declares that nothing will shake his resolution to fly to the rescue of the woman he loves:

No. 12

5

The scene changes to a convent garden; it appears that Count di Luna also has heard of Leonora's decision to take the veil, and he has come with Ferrando and others of his men at dead of night to abduct her before she can take the fatal step. An aria being by this time no more than the leading baritone's due, Verdi decides to indulge him in it here: the result is the famous "Il balen" ("The light of her smilè dims the radiance of the stars"):

No. 13

that had an almost unparalleled vogue in the concert room and on the barrel organ during the second half of the nineteenth century.

From inside the convent comes the solemn tolling of a bell announcing that the moment for the rite has come.· Sending his retainers out of sight, the Count, taking up the momentarily dropped thread of his aria, gives excited expression to his resolve that Leonora shall be his or no one's:

No. 14

and notwithstanding the urgent need for immediate action Ferrando and the others repeat his sentiment at leisurely length. Di Luna and his crew are never anything more than stock figures of melodrama, but musically this is melodrama in Verdi's most vigorous middle period style.

The overlong episode ends with the Count taking cover with his retainers to await the moment for decisive action. From inside the convent a chorus of nuns is heard exhorting the postulant Leonora to renounce the world and find enduring peace in the bosom of the Church; the incident would be mightily impressive were it not for the unfortunately comic turn Verdi has given to it by the ejaculations of the hidden Count, Ferrando and the retainers, calling on gods and men to witness that these things shall not be. Our gravity returns when Leonora enters, accompanied by Ines, to the accompaniment of a series of those volleying chords in the orchestra that were a favourite device of Verdi's to establish an atmosphere of tragic presage. Leonora, in accents of sincere feeling, bids her confidante not to weep for her, for her soul will soon be at peace. As she turns away to go to the altar the Count rushes forward, crying that the only altar deserving of her is that of Hymen, and that he has come to make her his. But just then the Troubadour appears, and the stage is now set for the big ensemble that is to end the act. Leonora expresses her amazement at this unexpected turn of events in a melody:

No. 15

("Can I believe I see you once more? Is it a dream, some marvellous enchantment?"), that does not ring quite true; but it gives Verdi the material for the launching of a fine ensemble, in which the Troubadour and the Count hurl vigorous defiance at each other, Leonora pours out her joy in an exuberant repetition and expansion of No. 15, Ferrando and the retainers warn the Count that the hand of heaven is manifest in all this, and even the nuns congratulate Leonora on having escaped the convent through this providential reappearance of the lover she had supposed to be dead. When the furious Count draws his sword to attack his rival he is overpowered by Manrico's followers, headed by Ruiz. Again a big ensemble is built up, and it looks as if this is to be the end of the act; but Verdi has a more telling effect in reserve for us. He suddenly checks the choral flood in full torrent and lets us hear for a moment or two the voice of Leonora alone, singing of the ectasy of reunion with her lover: then the other principals and the chorus join in a final four bars of fortissimo comment, and the curtain falls.

6

The third act brings us, as the penultimate act of all plays should do, to the vital turning-point in the action. Azucena is now the centre of interest.[1]

Manrico has gone to Castellor, taking Leonora with him. The towers of the fortress are visible in the distance; the foreground of the stage is occupied by the camp of the loyalists, the tent of the commander, Count di Luna, being distinguishable by the banner that floats above it. A vigorous orchestral and choral introduction shows us some of di Luna's soldiers preparing for the imminent battle by playing dice, while others, more professionally minded, are bracing themselves at the bidding of Ferrando for the assault on Castellor that has been ordered: "grandioso" is Verdi's marking for the martial chorus in which they declare their eagerness to fight and their confidence of victory:

No. 16

Laurels and loot, they are convinced, await them in abundance. The *entrain* of this marching-song is irresistible even today.

Di Luna is about to indulge himself in dreams of the recovery

---

[1] For the first scene of this act Verdi wrote a series of ballet numbers for the Paris production of the opera. These do not appear in any of the scores except the French, and the spectator is not likely to meet with them in any ordinary performance.

of Leonora and victory over his rival when Ferrando brings him the news that some of the soldiers have captured a gipsy woman whom they suspect to be one of the enemy's spies. (It is, of course, Azucena, on the last stage of her journey in search of Manrico.) She is brought in with her hands tied, and is interrogated by di Luna. She is a gipsy, she tells him, wandering as is the way of her race, trying to find, if she can, a son who had left her. When she discloses that she has come from the Biscayan mountains dim suspicions arise in the minds of the Count and Ferrando. These suspicions are confirmed when, in an unguarded moment—not knowing to whom she is speaking—she half admits knowledge of the burning, years ago, of a child whom the Count now declares to have been his brother. Ferrando thereupon denounces her as the daughter of the sorceress of that old story. Her bonds are strengthened, and when, in her despair, she calls on heaven to send her "son Manrico" to her aid the Count exults in the prospect of a double vengeance on his hated rival. The voices are built up into an impressive ensemble, the whole scene, indeed, being musically one of the finest in the opera. It ends with Azucena being taken away by the guards, and with the withdrawal of the Count to his tent, followed by Ferrando.

The next scene shows us Manrico and Leonora in colloquy in a hall in Castellor, with Ruiz in attendance; the latter is soon sent away to prepare the garrison for the assault on the fortress. Leonora sees nothing but gloom in the omens for her marriage to Manrico, and he tries to inspirit her with an aria, in Verdi's most serious vein, in which he assures her that, if it should be his fate to fall in the coming battle, his last thoughts shall be with Leonora, for whom he will wait in heaven. The soft pealing of an organ in an adjoining chapel recalls them to the realities of the moment; and they are about to enter the chapel to be wedded when Ruiz rushes in with the news that Azucena has been seized by the enemy and is now being led in chains to a pyre already lighted. It is his mother, Manrico informs the astonished Leonora; and frenziedly he orders Ruiz to prepare for an immediate sortie in the hope of rescuing her. His first duty, he tells Leonora, is to this most affectionate of mothers; the pyre his enemy has kindled has lit a fire in him that cries aloud for vengeance:

No. 17

This rousing episode has always been a favourite with operatic tenors, particularly those who feel sufficiently sure of themselves to finish on a high C. Ruiz having returned with a number of soldiers, Manrico bids a final farewell to Leonora and makes an imposing exit to trumpet tones in the orchestra.

7

The spectator of the opera has now to assume, in the absence of any direct information on the matter, that Manrico had failed in his sortie from Castellor, and that he and Azucena have been brought back prisoners to Aliaferia, where they are both in a dungeon in a tower of the palace. The fourth act opens with an expressive orchestral introduction, appropriately elegiac in tone. Ruiz and Leonora, both heavily cloaked, steal in; here, says Ruiz in a whisper, is the tower in which prisoners are confined, and where Manrico now is. He leaves her to her meditations. She has come to save her lover if she can; for herself she has no fear, she says—glancing at a ring on her right hand which we presume to contain a poison for use in case of need. In an expressive adagio she sighs out her soul to the night and to the captive Manrico; for modern ears the self-conscious coloratura with which the aria is larded takes some of the sincerity out of it.

But Verdi now launches into one of the greatest scenes of the older Italian opera. The death bell tolls, and from within we hear a choir of tenors and basses chanting in broad harmonies and in solemn rhythm the Miserere, the prayer for mercy on the souls of those about to set out on the journey from which there is no return. This is followed by the supreme example of those "volley-ing" chords in the orchestra to which, as has already been pointed out, Verdi instinctively resorted for the suggestion of an atmosphere charged with doom:

No. 18

The persistent rhythm serves as the basis for a moving cry from Leonora, "What solemn sounds are these, sounds of darkness and terror, that halt my breath and make my heart stand still?":

No. 19

Her cry ends in a series of broken sobs in a descending scale:

No. 20

From the tower is now heard the voice of Manrico bemoaning his unhappy lot and thinking of his lost Leonora—"Ah, how slow is the coming of Death to him who longs to die; farewell, Leonora, farewell!":

No. 21

The inner choir breaks in again with its solemn Miserere; and the whole expressive episode is repeated and expanded, with Manrico vowing that he will wait for Leonora in heaven, she promising that she will never forget him, the choir of monks intoning their sombre elegy, and underneath it all the orchestra hammering away with the persistent rhythm shown in our No. 18. These pages of the score have never been surpassed in Italian opera.

As the choral and orchestral mass thins out the voice of Leonora is heard singing once more of a love that Death itself cannot end:

No. 22

All this rings rather less true for us of a later day because of its unnecessary repetitions and the coloratura of some of the writing. It is too obviously the prima donna's showpiece.

Her aria over, Leonora stands aside as the Count enters with a number of attendants to whom he gives the order that at dawn the son is to be beheaded and the mother burned at the stake. They go into the tower, leaving the Count to indulge in a short soliloquy: if he is exceeding the powers entrusted to him by the Prince, he says, his excuse is Leonora's fatal fascination for him. But where is she now? he asks; in vain he has sought for her. Hearing this, Leonora comes forward. In a long duet she pleads for mercy for Manrico:

No. 23

or, alternatively, that he will take her life too. He rejects her appeal; so blind is his hate for Manrico that simple death alone cannot slake his desire for vengeance. As a last resort the desperate Leonora offers herself as the price for the Troubadour's pardon. Having extracted an oath from her to that effect di Luna gives a whispered order to the guard. While his back is turned she takes the poison from the ring and swallows it, muttering "The bride you shall have will be a lifeless one!", and then bursts into a song of joy, welcoming death for herself if only she succeeds in saving her lover's life:

No. 24

while di Luna congratulates himself on his unexpected good fortune. The over-long and too conventionally treated episode ends with them going into the tower together.

8

The final scene takes place in Manrico's dungeon, a gloomy cell half lit by a lamp hanging from the ceiling. Azucena is lying on a rough pallet, exhausted; Manrico sits by her side. The rank air of the dungeon has brought the gipsy, accustomed to life in the open air, near death's door. Verdi is at his convincing best in the opening dialogue between the pair, with Azucena racked with fear of the fire and her son unable to offer her any consolation. To the accompaniment in the orchestra of No. 9 she once more sees, in imagination, her mother being dragged to the stake and burned. This hysterical access is succeeded by a mood of exhausted resignation. In a state between waking and sleeping she indulges herself in a nostalgic dream of a return with Manrico to their beloved mountains:

No. 25

never to leave them again. He endeavours to soothe her, and the tender, quiet-toned duet is one of the finest episodes in the score; Verdi has once again shown a genius for rising to the full musical and dramatic height of his subject after a complacent lapse into much that was merely conventional.

As Azucena drops into a sleep and Manrico is still on his knees beside her Leonora enters with the news that he is free. His suspicions aroused, he gathers that his liberty has been purchased by Leonora at a price, and he refuses to accept a life bought by the passing of Leonora into the possession of his rival. In vain she implores him feverishly to fly without delay; and Azucena, waking from her sleep, breaks into the musical tissue with a poignant repetition of the nostalgic No. 25.

Once more Leonora begs him to fly to freedom, and once more he rejects the suggestion with bitter scorn. His resolution breaks down only when she falls at his feet with a confession that she has taken poison for his sake and already feels the death agony coming upon her. As she is bidding him a last farewell the Count enters and, standing silently on the threshold, realises from what he overhears that Leonora has cheated him. As she falls dead he calls to the guards to seize Manrico and take him to the scaffold. As a last refinement of cruelty he drags the half-awake Azucena to the window to witness the execution. As the axe falls she gives a wild cry of "This man was your brother; now, oh my mother, you have been avenged!"; and the last thing we hear is an agonised cry from the Count, "And I still live!"

Aïda

VERDI [1813–1901]

PRINCIPAL CHARACTERS

AÏDA	*Soprano*
AMNERIS	*Mezzo-soprano*
RADAMES	*Tenor*
THE KING OF EGYPT	Bass
RAMPHIS, THE HIGH PRIEST	Bass
AMONASRO	*Baritone*

1

N November 1869 a new Italian opera house had been opened in Cairo, and Verdi had been invited by the Khedive, Ismail Pasha, to write an opera for it, to be performed in connection with the opening of the Suez Canal. Verdi had refused. In the early part of 1870, when he happened to be in Paris, the offer was renewed and again declined. But a little later his Paris friend Camille du Locle sent him a brief outline of a possible opera subject that at once took his fancy. The sketch, which ran to no more than four pages, was the work of a famous French Egyptologist, Mariette, who had lived and worked for some years in Egypt, where he had been made Inspector-General of Monuments and given the title of Bey. Verdi and du Locle having between them developed the scenario in French prose, the composer's friend Ghislanzoni was called in as librettist. It was planned to produce the new work in Cairo in January 1871. But in July 1870 the Franco-Prussian war broke out and Mariette was immured in Paris during the siege of the city. With him were the designs and costumes and some of the properties for *Aïda*, without which no progress could be made in Cairo. Verdi now felt himself justified in negotiating with the Scala for a first production in Milan, as the terms of his contract with Draneth Bey, the director of the Cairo theatre, authorised him to do; but when the causes of the hold-up were explained to him he waived that right, and *Aïda* after all received its first performance in Cairo, on the 14th December 1871, under Giovanni Bottesini. Verdi had taken advantage of the enforced delay to revise some portions of his work, especially in the second act.

2

He had been even more critical of his librettist than usual during the construction of the text of *Aïda*, not only suggesting a recasting of the words at many points but occasionally demanding lines to fit in to music already composed or sketched. After the opera had been produced he was angered by the frequent criticism that much of the work was "Wagnerian." We know him to have had a profound respect for Wagner as an artist, and there can be no doubt that he had given intensive study to the German master's scores. His letters of this period show him doing some new thinking about the problems of form and texture in opera. He was no longer content with the four-square melodic structures he had inherited from his Italian predecessors and so effectively manipulated himself in earlier works. "Melody," he told one of his correspondents, was not in itself everything: "Beethoven was not a 'melodist,' nor was Palestrina," i.e. "in our Italian acceptation of that term." He no longer thought it necessary for melody to be on all occasions constructed on a pattern of balanced symmetrical phrases; there were times, he held, when asymmetry was called for. Further, more care should now be taken than of old in the fusion of the recitatives with the cantilenas; the musical disparity between the two should be diminished, and the joins not be too obvious. All this, of course, was "Wagnerian," in the sense that Wagner had long been practising it in his "endless melody." But the charge against Verdi of having succumbed to the Wagnerian "influence" was ridiculous: in the new operatic style of which *Aïda* was the first foreshadowing he was simply following the natural, inevitable bent of his own maturing genius. By 1870 he had developed enormously as a musician; he had a wider and richer sense of harmony, of rhythm and of orchestral colour, and was master of a new craftsmanship of musical development." It is true that there is still a fair amount in *Aïda* of the earlier Verdi, content with the traditional formulae. But for the most part it is a new Verdi that we see. His musical imagination takes charge of things in a way that it had rarely managed to do before then: the melodic structure—to consider that feature alone—was no longer the outcome of a simple addition of limb to limb, but at its best flowed on unbrokenly, evolving not by way of imposed patterns but of inner proliferation. It is for this reason, among others, that quotations from the mature Verdi is so difficult. The "melody" is no longer in the parts, or even—by simple addition—in the sum of the parts, but in the whole; and we have often to think to the end of a long melodic line before we can appreciate the subtle interconnection of bar with bar within it. The "Wagnerism" of the Verdi of· *Aïda*, the Requiem, *Otello* and *Falstaff* is a myth. He had undoubtedly assimilated certain new procedures which by that time—largely, of course, through Wagner's use of them—were in the European musical air. But the ability to make these procedures his own, to incorporate them organically into his own artistic individuality, was the result of a long process of silent, subconscious development in the depths of his own musical being. There is not a page in his later works that derives, either imaginatively or in the technical handling, from Wagner; everything bears the unmistakable dual stamp of "Verdi" and "Italy."

3

The brief orchestral prelude to the first act introduces us at once to the slave girl Aïda:

No. 1

and in these seventeen bars we see at once the ability of the new Verdi both to invent an individual melodic line and to "develop" and inflect and nuance it not in accordance with any stylised formula of melody but in terms of psychological characterisation; for anyone who knows the opera as a whole can see in these few bars the essential Aïda, at once sensitive and timorous. This motif is followed by one associated in the opera with priesthood—one uses that word advisedly instead of "priests" of the temple of Isis, for they are more than conventional stage figures called in now and then to help the action along:

No. 2

Verdi, as his letters show, visualised them as a kind of inflexible massed power, against which Radames and the gentle Aïda are flung and shattered. Conquerors, he remarks ironically in one of his letters, always attribute their success to the co-operation of the deity, so he wants Ghislanzoni to model the priests' words at one point on the famous announcement of the virtuous King of Prussia after Sedan—"By the help of Divine Providence we have conquered. The enemy has been delivered into our hands. May God be with us also in the future!" [1]

The remainder of the short prelude is devoted to a dramatic opposition of these two motifs; it ends with the Aïda theme dying out in the highest regions of the orchestra.[2]

The curtain rises on a hall in the palace of the King of Egypt in Memphis; it is flanked by imposing colonnades. Through a great gate in the background we see the temples and palaces of the town, with the Pyramids in the distance. Radames, a young

---

[1] Or, as an English humorist paraphrased the pious sentiment:
God be praised, my dear Augusta:
The French have come another buster.

[2] At one time Verdi thought of beginning the opera with a more formal "overture," the manuscript of which is now in the Verdi archives. We may congratulate ourselves that he finally decided to leave the brief prelude as we now have it.

Egyptian soldier, and Ramphis, the High Priest of Isis, whose characteristic motif runs thus:

No. 3

are seen in conference. Egypt, it appears, is once more threatened by the Ethiopians, whose hordes have advanced far into the Nile valley. The goddess Isis, says Ramphis, looking meaningly at the officer, has already declared who is to lead the homeland army—one young in years but great in valour; and the High Priest is now on his way to make the announcement to the King. "Oh happy chosen one!", sighs Radames.

The High Priest having departed, Radames, against a background of rousing brass fanfares, lets his imagination play on the thought of himself being placed in command of the army, winning a glorious victory over the invaders, and returning to lay his laurels at Aïda's feet and restore her in triumph to her native land. This is the theme of his famous aria "Celeste Aïda," which is externally like many of the arias of Verdi's early and middle periods, but far above most of these in the sweep of its melody and the varied expression of the orchestral accompaniment.

4

On the conclusion of the aria Amneris, the daughter of the Pharaoh, enters, heralded by one of the main motifs that will henceforth characterise her:

No. 4

It shows her in her gentler aspect. She is secretly in love with Radames. He confesses to her that he has been indulging himself in the ambitious dream of being the goddess's choice as com-

mander-in-chief of the army, whereupon she asks him insinuatingly whether there is not also room in his breast for a tenderer
emotion and even bolder hopes. He wonders anxiously whether
it is possible that she has divined his love for her handmaiden
Aïda, while Amneris begins to harbour a suspicion that there is
a rival to herself in the field: perhaps it is this Aïda, she surmises
as the slave girl enters and the sudden light in Radames' eyes
betrays his feelings towards her. This episode is dominated by an
agitated orchestral motif expressive of Amneris' jealousy:

No. 5

a passion which bodes ill for them all. She dissembles her real
feelings, however, under a mask of sisterly affection for this
Ethiopian servant of hers. Why is the girl so distressed? she enquires. Because war has been declared and the country will now
be plunged in woe, Aïda replies. Is that all? asks Amneris; is not
her heart ill at ease because of some tenderer, more personal
emotion? The voices unite in an admirably dramatic trio, during
which, to the dismay of Radames and Aïda, Amneris shows more
and more clearly her jealous suspicion of them.

With the entry, to a rousing brass fanfare, of the King, Ramphis,
the other priests, the ministers of the Court, captains of the
guard and others, we embark on one of those spectacular concerted pieces that play so large a part in the opera. At the bidding of the King a Messenger gives the assembly the news that
the Ethiopian army, led by its ferocious, indomitable king, Amonasro, is marching on Thebes, and a great battle is imminent. The
goddess Isis has named as leader of the Egyptian forces Radames
—an announcement that draws an "I tremble!" from the fretted
Aïda, who knows something which none of the others know as yet
—that this Amonasro is her father; henceforth her soul is to be
divided between two loyalties, to her lover and to her father and
her native land. Verdi lapses for a while into his older idiom in
the bouncing melody:

No. 6

Su! del Ni-lo al sa—cro   li-do ac-cor-re-te, E-gi—zü e—roi,

to which the King bids them all do or die in defence of their country and its gods. Radames and the others take up the martial strain, while Aïda laments the burden the Fates have imposed on her, and the proud Amneris places the royal standard in Radames' hands. "Return as conqueror!" are her final words to him; and with the others echoing the words in a thundering unison the massive ensemble ends.

All leave the stage except Aïda, who repeats, with sad irony, this "Return as conqueror!" Should that come true, she muses in a recitative, it means that her lover will return to her red with the blood of her kith and kin, in his triumphal chariot the King, her father, in chains. In a more lyrical vein she implores the gods to give the victory not to the Egyptians but to her own people; then, as the sensitive No. 1 sings out quietly in the orchestra, she reminds herself of Radames, asking how it will be possible for her to reconcile these two affections; and she ends with a prayer for help and pity, to music that already foreshadows the appealing pathos of Verdi's Desdemona: "have pity on my sufferings, ye gods; let me die":

No. 7

Nu-mi, pie—tà   del mio sof-frir! Spe—me non v'ha pel mio do-lor

As she leaves the stage the curtain falls.

5

The scene changes to the interior of the temple of Vulcan at Memphis. A series of columns, receding in a far perspective, is bathed in a mysterious light. Statues of the gods are scattered about, and sacred emblems surmount the great altar in the centre of the stage; below this is a carpet-covered platform. Incense is

burning in golden tripods. This is the imposing setting for the
ceremony of the consecration of Radames.

A chorus of priestesses invokes "mighty Phtha, the spirit that
animates the universe":

No. 8

the sombre tones of Ramphis and the priests striking in at intervals in solemn chords. Here, and in the final flourish of the
priestesses' prayer:

No. 9

we see Verdi in full possession of new melodic and harmonic
resources, creating and maintaining convincingly an exotic atmosphere without a suspicion of pseudo-"oriental" pastiche.

The priestesses perform a sinuous sacred dance in which the
exotic colouring is maintained by new scalic and harmonic devices.
Radames now enters and goes up to the altar, where a silver veil
is placed on his head, and Ramphis hails him as the chosen of the
goddess for the task of defending Egypt. The High Priest invokes
the blessing and protection of the great god of the land on him,
to a strain:

No. 10

that shows Verdi still fluctuating uncertainly at times between his
older idiom and his new. On this theme, entrusted to the High
Priest, the other priests and Radames, with occasional interpola-

tions, admirably managed, of No. 8 by the priestesses, a great ensemble is built up: it ends with a combined cry of "Mighty Phtha!", and the curtain falls on the first act.

6

In the second act we are first of all taken into a luxurious hall in the apartments of Amneris, where female slaves are engaged some in waving feather fans over her, others in attiring her for the coming triumphal festival. Their song is one of felicitations to Amneris and to the conqueror who is soon to return to them: the refrain of their melody:

No. 11

Vie-ni, sul crin ti pio-va-no, vie-ni, sul crin ti pio-va-no,

and the clinching cadence of Amneris, in which she sighs out the longing of her heart for the return of Radames:

No. 12

Ah! vie——ni, vie-ni a-mor mio, m'i— neb-bria,

are particularly captivating.

A repetition of the charming vocal vignette is followed by a dance of Moorish slaves, and this by yet another repetition of Nos. 11 and 12.

Aïda enters, to a timid voicing of her motif (No. 1) in the orchestra. Amneris is filled with pity for her in the disaster that has befallen the Ethiopian forces, but at the same time the sight of her awakens the old jealous suspicions in her, and she determines to wrest the slave girl's secret, if there be a secret, from her. She begins with a suave expression of sympathy with her in her sorrow:

No. 13

but when Aïda, deeply moved, speaks ecstatically of the joy and the torment of love Amneris becomes more and more watchful of her. In smooth, friendly tones, but with her eyes fixed on the trembling girl, she professes great solicitude and affection for her, and by a casual hint at the possibility of the dauntless leader of the Egyptian army having met his death in battle she betrays Aïda into an impulsive expression of grief that leaves no doubt as to her love for Radames. Changing her tactics, Amneris declares that "Radames lives," whereupon Aïda falls on her knees with a rapturous cry of gratitude to the gods. Throwing off the mask now, Amneris discloses herself as Aïda's rival—she, a daughter of the Pharaohs. For a moment Aïda is on the point of revealing that she too is of royal birth, but manages to check herself in time. Humbly, at Amneris' feet, she confesses her love and implores her powerful and fortunate rival's pity:

No. 14

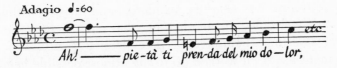

Amneris, almost beside herself, pours out her scorn and hatred on the presumptuous slave.

The duet is broken in upon for a moment by martial fanfares and a chorus of triumph from without, to the melody of No. 6; then it is resumed, Aïda wailing her grief and despair to the gods, and the exultant Amneris heaping on her contumely and threats. The scene ends with a repetition of Aïda's piteous appeal to the gods in the first act (No. 7).

7

The remainder of the second act is devoted to the grand pageant of the return of the victorious Egyptian army. The scene is an avenue leading to the entrance gate to Thebes; on one side is the temple of Ammon, on the other a throne with a gorgeous purple canopy. At the back is a triumphal arch. To rousing martial music the King enters with officers, priests, standard bearers and others, and takes his seat on the throne; Amneris, who has entered after him with a bevy of slaves, among them Aïda, seats herself at his left.

In a succession of vigorous tunes the assembly gives thanks to Isis for the triumph of the Egyptian arms, and the priests are prominent with a four-part chorus based on the motif shown in our No. 2—"Lift up your eyes to the supreme arbiters of victory, and return thanks to the gods for this happy day." Then, to the strains of a stately march:

No. 15

the Egyptian troops pour in and pass before the King: they are followed by dancing girls carrying the spoils of battle, and these by more troops, war chariots, standards, and images of the gods. They are welcomed in another massive chorus, the priests, as before, asserting themselves as a collective entity. When the excitement has been worked up to the utmost possible height the hero Radames enters under a canopy carried by twelve of his officers. The King comes down from his throne to greet and embrace him and hail him as the saviour of his country; and at his bidding Amneris, to the strain of No. 4, comes forward and places on his head the garland of victory. The King having promised to grant the hero anything he desires, Radames asks that first of all the captives shall be brought in: this is done to a renewed professional muttering of thanksgiving to the gods of victory by Ramphis and the priests, to a variant of the motif shown in our No. 2. The dusky prisoners file in under the surveillance of the guards, the last of them being the Ethiopian king Amonasro, in the accoutrement of an officer. At the sight of him Aïda rushes towards him with a cry of "My father!" The multitude cries out in astonishment "Her father!", to which Amneris adds the significant comment "And in our power!"

Amonasro has only time to whisper to Aïda "Do not disclose my rank!" before the King orders him to come forward. "So you are her father?" he says, to which Amonasro replies in tones of quiet dignity, "Yes, her father. I fought like the others: we were conquered: death I sought in vain. My uniform will show you that I defended my country and my king. Fortune was not on our side: at my feet in the dust lay my king, pierced by many wounds. If love for one's country is a crime, all we here are guilty, and we are ready to die. But, oh mighty King," he continues, "show us clemency; today it is we who are at the bottom of fortune's wheel, but tomorrow it may be your turn to lie there":

No. 16

Ma tu, Re, tu si-gno-re pos-sen-te,

Aïda and the captives repeat this appeal; but the priests, true to their character throughout the drama, urge the King to harden his heart and exterminate this rabble. A great choral ensemble is built up on these rival psychological themes, with Aïda joining in the appeal for mercy, Amneris noting jealously the glances of love and compassion that Radames is turning on the Ethiopian girl, Amonasro repeating his warning that fortune's wheel will one day turn against the conquerors, the priests, as usual, clamouring for a comprehensive sentence of death, and the people urging them to show humanity towards the captives. Nothing comparable in dramatic drive and technical craftsmanship to this masterly ensemble, with its fusion of so many conflicting psychological elements into a single musical whole, had ever been seen before in Italian opera.

But even yet Verdi has not exhausted his resources; indeed, so far he has exploited only half of them. A temporary lull occurs as Radames, reminding the King of his promise, asks that the prisoners shall be released. The priests protest against this act of clemency, Ramphis urging that as soon as they are free the vanquished will begin a new war of revenge on their conquerors. To this Radames replies that with Amonasro dead they have no hope of rallying. Then the High Priest stipulates that for greater security they shall at least keep Aïda's father in their hands. With this counsel of prudence the King agrees; and as a further pledge of enduring peace he will bestow on the gallant saviour of the country the hand of his daughter, with whom, in course of time, he will share the government of Egypt. This announcement is greeted with joy by Amneris: "now let the slave, if she can," she cries, "rob me of my love—if she dares!" There follows a fresh chorus of general rejoicing, in which even the priests join. Only Radames and Aïda are dismayed. "What remains to me?" Aïda asks despairingly; "he will ascend the throne, while I can only weep, forgotten!" But Amonasro, drawing near to her unnoticed, quietly urges her to take heart and hope on, for the day of vengeance for Ethiopia will come. Amneris, of course, exults in her triumph, while Radames, in an aside, laments his miserable fate: he has won a kingdom but lost Aïda. Once more a massive ensemble is built up, the act closing in almost universal jubilation.

8

The third act is set on the banks of the Nile. It is night, with a bright moon and many stars. On the summit of some granite rocks, studded with palm trees, stands a temple dedicated to Isis. It is the eve of Amneris' wedding day.

After a brief orchestral introduction that suggests curiously the mysterious silence of the night and the place, we hear from within the temple tenors and basses (in quiet unison), reinforced at the cadences by the soprano voice of a Grand Priestess, praying to the benign goddess who is at once mother and spouse of Osiris, mother also of love, invoking her grace for those who are coming to seek her protection. A boat is seen approaching the shore, from which descend Amneris, Ramphis, some veiled women and a few guards. The High Priest bids Amneris enter the fane and implore the favour, on this her wedding eve, of the goddess who knows all the secrets and the mysteries of the heart of man. She will pray until the dawn, she replies, that Radames will give her all his heart, as hers is now and always will be his. They all enter the temple, to the strains of the chorus of inside worshippers with which the scene had opened.

As the prayers die away into silence the stage remains empty for a few moments, till No. 1 in the orchestra—now presented in such a guise that it blends subtly with the scene, the occasion and the hour—announces that Aïda is somewhere near. When at last she makes her appearance we learn from her lips that she has come there at the wish of Radames. What will he have to say to her? she asks: if a last farewell, then she will seek eternal peace in the dark waters of the Nile. This is the prelude to one of the finest sections of the score, a romanza in which she gazes, in imagination, for the last time on the serene sky, the green fields and the scented shores of her native land, which she will never see again. This romanza alone would suffice to show how far Verdi had travelled as a musician since the days of *Rigoletto* and *Il Trovatore*: the melodic lines are now more delicately drawn, the harmony freer, the orchestral colour more subtly appropriate at once to the psychology of the character and to the milieu; and even when, as he does at one or two points, he makes a little concession, as of old, to the desire of the singer for an opportunity to demonstrate her quality, the vocal difficulties are made so organically part and parcel of the whole melodic line that they never kindle any suspicion of having been put there for simple display's sake, as had been the case again and again in the arias of his earlier days.

9

Amonasro, it appears, has evaded his captors, and now he approaches the astonished Aïda from the cover of the palm trees. He knows that she is here awaiting Radames, on whose love for her he intends to play for his ends and hers. She has the opportunity, he tells her, to avenge herself on her powerful rival the Pharaoh's daughter, and at the same time to restore Ethiopia's fortunes. Eagerly he speaks of the joy of seeing their beloved country again, its odorous forests, its verdant valleys, its golden temples:

No. 17

Ri-ve-drai le fo-re-ste im-bal-sa-ma-te

a theme which she takes up with him with even greater ardour.
He reminds her of what their land has suffered from the ravages
of war, and Aïda's imagination plays ardently on the hope of
liberty and peace. The Ethiopians have rallied and are armed, he
tells her, and the moment has come to strike the decisive blow.
One thing only is lacking to Amonasro's plans—he must know
by what route the enemy will march against him. It is certainly
known already to Radames, and from him she must worm the
secret, playing upon his love for her. She recoils from the suggestion in horror, but he renews the attack still more vehemently,
painting a moving picture of the desolation that threatens her
land from the Egyptian invaders; and as she still refuses his
demands he casts her off from him, calling her no longer his
daughter but the Pharaohs' slave.

This brings us to the great climax of the scene. Aïda throws
herself at her father's feet, and, to music of a unique poignancy,
declares that she is no slave but her father's true daughter, worthy
of him and of her country. "Remind yourself," he urges her, in
one of the greatest phrases Verdi ever wrote, "that a nation conquered and oppressed can find its salvation in you alone":

No. 18

Pen—sa che un po——po—lo vin-to, stra-ʒia-to

per te sol-tan-to, per te sol-tan-to ri-sor-ger può.

The long melodic line here is one of the most signal evidences of
Verdi's growth as a musician during the years that immediately
preceded *Aïda*. His imagination had already sought an expression
of the same basic kind in the concluding phrase of Leonora's aria

"Madre, pietosa Vergine" in the second act of *La Forza del Destino* (1862);

No. 19

Non m'ab-ban-do-nar, pie-tà, pie-tà di me, Si-gno-re, deh!

non m'ab-ban-do-nar, ah! —————— pie-tà, pie-tà di me, Si-gnor.

("Forsake me not, oh Lord; have pity on me.") The melodic intention and design are essentially the same in both cases. But the earlier line becomes somewhat embarrassed in the fourth bar, while in the critical seventh it dives helplessly down on a broken wing; whereas in the *Aïda* example it first of all soars to successively greater heights in its first half, and in its second descends in complete possession of its vital powers. One can speak here, unfortunately, of the melodic line alone: in harmonic resource, and especially in the management of an accompanying orchestral figure, sharply rhythmed, that takes twenty-eight bars to ascend slowly to a climax as Aïda sings "Oh my country, what a price I am paying for you!", the long episode is the best proof conceivable of the arrival of a new Verdi on the operatic scene.

Seeing Radames approaching, Amonasro takes cover among the palms. Aïda checks Radames' protestations of devotion; she does not doubt his love, she says, but what hope can he have against a combination of the wiles of Amneris, the power of the King, the devotion of the people, and the wrath of the priests? He replies that the two countries will soon be at war again; he will be in command of the Egyptian forces, and when he returns victorious, as he assuredly will, he will confess to the King his love for Aïda and claim her hand as his reward. Aïda's reply is that she has a surer plan to realise their dream of happy union—flight together to a happier land, on the tone-painting of the charm of which Verdi once more lavishes some of the best of his new art.

When the soldier and the patriot in him revolt against her suggestion she turns on him in anger, professed or real, declaring that he no longer loves her, and bidding him enter the temple where Amneris is awaiting him; "and then let the axe fall on me and my father," she concludes. On this his resolution fails him; and in a passionate duet—not in Verdi's best vein—they both revel in the thought of the new happiness that lies before them, and are already about to take flight when Aïda asks by what route they can evade the troops already marshalled for the invasion of Ethiopia. "By the route already chosen for us to march upon the enemy," he replies; "till tomorrow it will be deserted." "And where is that?" asks Aïda. "The mountain gorges of Napata," is the answer; whereupon Amonasro emerges from his hiding-place with a cry of "And there I will post my men—I, Aïda's father and Ethiopia's King!" In the depths of bewilderment and despair Radames cries out again and again that he is dishonoured and lost; Aïda and Amonasro endeavour to calm him; and the latter is on the point of dragging him away when Amneris, crying "Traitor!", rushes out from the temple, followed by Ramphis, the priests and the guards. "My rival!", Aïda exclaims. Amonasro draws his dagger and rushes at Amneris, but as the guards advance on him Radames bids him and Aïda take to flight, and then surrenders himself to the High Priest.

10

The first part of the fourth act is staged in a hall in the King's palace: on the left is a great door leading to the subterranean chamber of justice, on the right a passage leading to a prison in which Radames is confined. When the curtain rises Amneris is crouched, in an attitude of despair, before the door on the left; and writhing in and out of the orchestra we hear the motif of her jealousy (No. 5). She is a complex character, this Amneris, more complex, indeed, than any other in the opera. Her detested rival, she muses, has escaped her, while Radames is awaiting the sentence of the priests on him as traitor. But a traitor he is not, she continues, for though he had revealed the high secret of the war his intentions were to fly—with Aïda. Then, in an access of fury, she cries out that they are traitors all, deserving of death.

But once again her mood changes, and with No. 4 breathing softly in the orchestra we see the gentler side of her nature reasserting itself. She loves Radames, she declares, and if only he could love her in return she would try to save him. At an order from her the guards bring him in. She addresses him in measured, mournful tones:

No. 20

The priests, she tells him, are now assembled to pass judgment on him; yet it is not too late for him to clear himself, and she herself is willing to plead with the King for his pardon. To the melody of No. 20 he rejoins that he has been guilty of no treachery: his incautious lips had betrayed him, but there had been no thought of evil in his heart, and his honour is unstained: he is ready to die, for life without happiness and hope would be abhorrent to him.

Passionately she appeals to him to live:

No. 21

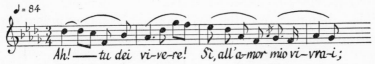

To save him she, who has suffered so much through him, will give up throne and country and life itself. He rejects her offer with scorn. With a reversion to the melody of No. 20 he reproaches her for having separated him from Aïda, whom no doubt she has already slain. She assures him, however, that Aïda still lives, though her father had died in the fighting; but where Aïda now is she does not know. If she saves Radames, will he promise to renounce the girl for ever? This he refuses; whereupon the desperate Amneris declares that he has changed her love for him into enmity, and calls on the gods to avenge her. Death for him, he tells her, has no terrors: gladly will he die for Aïda; and he heaps scorn upon Amneris and her pity for him. As she falls back exhausted the guards enter and take Radames away.

Left alone, Amneris reproaches herself bitterly for having delivered him, in her blind jealousy, into the power of the priests, whose sinister motif (No. 2) accompanies her brief monologue. Soon the white-robed ministers of death, as she calls them in her despair, are seen crossing the stage on their way to the subterranean hall of justice, to the unceasing accompaniment in the orchestra of the inexorable No. 2. "He is in their power!" Amneris moans, "and I it was who delivered him up to them!" From below there comes now a unison canticle of Ramphis and the priests, praying to their gods for their blessing on what they are about to do; and interspersed with their pious phrases are wild laments from Amneris.

From the crypt Ramphis is heard denouncing Radames as a traitor and bidding him defend himself against the charge. To the long and impressive indictment he makes no reply; only the wailings of Amneris punctuate the solemn monotones. Then judgment of death is passed on him—slow death by immurement under the altar he has profaned. As the priests, still to the unwavering tread of No. 2, emerge from the crypt, Amneris turns on them in fury, denouncing them as blood-lusting tigers and heaping curses on them for sending to his death an innocent man; to which their only reply is a reiterated "He is a traitor and must die!" As they disappear from the scene Amneris launches a final curse on them, and rushes out madly as the curtain falls.

11

The final scene occupies two floors. The upper one shows us the splendid interior of the temple of Vulcan; the lower one is a gloomy crypt with long receding arcades, and colossal statues of Osiris, with crossed hands, supporting the pillars of the crypt. Radames is on the steps leading down to the vault; above him are two priests lowering the great stone that is to seal it off. He laments the ending of his days in this dark dungeon, and his separation from Aïda: wherever she is, may she know nothing of the fate that has befallen him! But he hears a groan, and searching the gloom he sees a human form which he soon identifies as Aïda. Sadly she tells him that, anticipating his fate, she had crept unseen into the crypt, there to die in his arms.

From now to the end of the opera Verdi is at the summit of his powers. In passionate but mournful tones Radames laments the extinction, for love of him, of so much beauty and sweetness;

while she, for her part, has an ecstatic vision of their reunion in a world free from all sorrow. From the temple above floats down a chorus of priests and priestesses solemnly invoking, to the strains of No. 8 and No. 9, the mighty Phtha, the informing principle of the universe.

Vainly Radames makes an effort to dislodge the stone that closes the crypt, and the lovers resign themselves to their fate. They sing their Liebestod, a sad farewell to life, Aïda leading off with "Farewell, ye vale of tears, dreams of a joy that faded out in sorrow":

No. 22

Radames echoes the resigned lament. The chorus break in again with their solemn ritual song, and on the upper level we see a desperate Amneris throwing herself on the stone, imploring, in choked accents, peace for the soul of her beloved Radames. The lovers continue with No. 22, the final cadence of which:

No. 23

constitutes their last farewell to life. Aïda falls dying into the arms of Radames, Amneris numbly stammers again her prayer for eternal peace, the chorus inside the temple invoke Phtha for the last time, and the curtain falls with the mystical Nos. 22 and 23 slowly fading into silence in the highest reaches of the orchestra.

Otello

VERDI [1813–1901]

PRINCIPAL CHARACTERS

OTELLO	*Tenor*
DESDEMONA	*Soprano*
IAGO	*Baritone*
CASSIO	*Tenor*
RODERIGO	*Tenor*
LODOVICO	*Bass*
MONTANO	*Bass*
EMILIA	*Mezzo-soprano*

1

T is probable that the idea of an opera based on Shakespeare's *Othello* had occurred to Verdi in the 1860's, though for a long time *King Lear* interested him more. It was not until 1879, however, that the Othello idea was taken up seriously, when the young poet and musician Arrigo Boïto (1842–1918), the cultured son of an Italian father and a Polish mother, came into friendly relations with Verdi after a longish period of mutual misunderstanding. The first-fruit of their collaboration was the *Otello* of 1887, the second the *Falstaff* of 1893. Boïto was enough of a poet to see a great subject imaginatively and to be scrupulous about style, and enough of a practical musician to understand from the inside the many problems involved in the co-operation of words and music in opera; and it is fairly safe to say that without his generous servicing of Verdi we should never have had an *Otello* at all. He skillfully condensed the five acts of the Shakespeare play into four, retaining practically everything that was vital to the action and inserting little that was not, and making a remarkable success of the rendering of many of Shakespeare's best-known lines into Italian.

The poet in him made him at times, of course, more poetical than was necessary for the composer's purposes. He gave himself a great deal of needless trouble to preserve a particular rhyming scheme intact even when the lines in question were divided between different characters. The mature Verdi had no use for these technical verbal refinements, and ruthlessly scrapped them whenever they conflicted with his musical purpose. He would make mincemeat of Boïto's carefully concocted rhyme-patterns, shaping his melodic line to convey the simple sense of the words, so that sometimes an end-rhyme on which the poet had evidently plumed himself finds itself lost, unnoticed, in the middle of a musical line. Verdi, in fact, had outgrown the age-old notion that it was the first duty of a composer to cut and trim each limb of a melody to the measured inches and the neat rhyme-click of the lines of poetry: his new dramatic sense and his great growth as a musical craftsman both urged him on to the creation of long melodic sentences that took the shape not of pre-dictated symmetrical patterns but of a continuous run-on of the notes from the beginning to the end of a given dramatic idea. If in this process the poet's rhymes were swamped, so much the worse for the poet and his rhymes. Verdi was wholly bent now on what he called "la parola scenica"—the diction of the musical stage, which is often quite a different thing from the diction of a poem intended primarily to be read.

It seems to have been Iago who first captured his imagination in *Otello,* and for a time he proposed to call his opera after that character. He probably began formal work at the score about 1884, though there must have been a good deal of quiet sketching before then. The music was completed on the 1st November 1886, and the first performance took place at the Scala, Milan, on the 5th February 1887, under Franco Faccio, with Tamagno as Otello and Maurel as Iago.

2

Providentially, as it happened, certain psychological defects of the Shakespeare drama played right into the hands of the opera composer. A modern reader of Shakespeare sometimes finds it hard to understand how any man of ordinary intelligence could be so blindly credulous of what he was told about his wife as Othello was. Old Thomas Rymer, in a famous passage in his book *Tragedies of the Last Age,*[1] did not mince his words where the bard was concerned. He wrote Othello off as "a tedious drawling tame goose, gaping after any paultry insinuation, labouring to be jealous, and catching at every blown surmize." "Testy Rymer" has been described by at least one Shakespearean scholar as the worst critic who ever lived. Maybe, though there are many other claimants to that distinction. Even a bad critic, however, cannot help being right sometimes; and today we find so acute a psychologist as Mr. T. S. Eliot confessing that no convincing refutation of Rymer's views on the jealousy of Othello has yet come his way.

The problem of Othello's "gullibility" has been dealt with in masterly fashion by the American professor, Elmer Edgar Stoll,[2] who demonstrates in the first place that this—to us—amazing credulity figures again and again in the plays of Shakespeare and his contemporaries, the "motif" evidently being one that the public of that day was prepared to swallow whole,[3] and in the second place that Elizabethan audiences did not look for quite the same things in drama as we do. They laid less stress on "dramatic psychology" and its slow consistent developments than the modern world does, and, as Dr. Stoll puts it, "from beginning to end the Elizabethan dramatic method was founded on speech and outcry." We cease to jib at Othello's endless capacity for credulity when we realise that Shakespeare was less concerned with making the man wholly credible than with making him the excuse for the pouring out of a vast amount of great poetry. Music, in its turn, asks primarily for opportunities to spread its own wings in its own way. And not only does Shakespeare's play of itself provide a composer abundantly with these opportunities for rhetorical expansion, but Boïto artfully provided Verdi with another entirely of his own invention—the "Credo" which he puts into the mouth of Iago in the second act. Here he boldly out-Shake-

[1] 1692; Vol. II, p. 120.

[2] In his *Othello; an Historical and Comparative Study* (1915).

[3] It was older than the Elizabethan age, and it makes its appearance in more than one later drama.

speares Shakespeare. "Iago's don't exist," says Dr. Obispo in Mr. Aldous Huxley's *After Many a Summer*. "People will do everything that Iago did; but they'll never say they're villains. They'll construct a beautiful verbal world in which their villainies are right and reasonable." That may be so; Boïto's Iago perhaps paints himself in colours too uncompromisingly black. But as in doing so he gave Verdi an opportunity and a pretext for writing the "Credo" music, we turn an indulgent eye on his offence against normal human psychology. On this point, however, there will be more to be said when we arrive at the "Credo."

3

Otello does not lend itself well to point-to-point exposition and fragmentary quotation, because so much of it is taken up by big scenes into which Verdi crams a vast amount of musical detail of which no idea can be given by citation of a bit of a theme here and a bit there.

In the opera the whole action takes place in "a seaport in the island of Cyprus"; the period is the end of the fifteenth century. The curtain rises on a quay, on which stands a tavern with an arbour. It is night, and a hurricane, accompanied by thunder and lightning, is sweeping the sea. The quay is crowded with Cyprian citizens and Venetian soldiers, anxiously awaiting the arrival of the commander of the Venetian forces, Otello; among them are Cassio, Otello's lieutenant, Iago, his ensign, a Venetian gentleman, Roderigo, and Montano, Otello's predecessor in the government of Cyprus.

There is no overture, Verdi plunging at once into a lurid orchestral description of the storm at sea, where Otello's ship is fighting for its life, and the inferno in the sky. Boïto indulges himself in a good deal of rich poetic imagery on these subjects, but his labour is mostly in vain, for it is only the general musical effect, not the actual words of the chorus, that counts in performance. At last there comes a great choral cry of "She's safe!", and in a few moments Otello appears on the steps leading up to the quay from the shore. In stentorian tones—the brief passage of eleven bars is perhaps the most difficult tenor "entrance" in all opera; it at once reduces many an otherwise good Otello to something like ineffectualness—he announces complete victory in the recent battle; the Turkish fleet lies at the bottom of the sea. The storm now abates, enabling us to overhear a conversation between Iago and Roderigo. The latter simple-minded gentleman has come from Venice filled with a hopeless passion for the fair Desdemona, and the master villain, confessing his own hatred for Otello, who has passed him over and made Cassio his lieutenant, promises Roderigo full success in his pursuit. Already at the words (in Shakespeare),

> *He [Cassio] in good time, must his lieutenant be,*
> *And I—God bless the mark!—his Moorship's ancient,*

we see Verdi limning the false, plausible Iago in the serpent turns and twists of the melody he puts into his mouth:

No. 1

Ed io ri-man-go di suo Mo-re-sca Si-gno-ria— l'al-fie——re!

Note the sardonic shake on the final "alfiere" ("ensign," "ancient"). The two go out at the back, still talking.

There comes now a lapse into "opera" of the more conventional type. Boïto and Verdi could have gone on quite easily and naturally from here to the big scene in which Iago gradually envelops Cassio in his coils; but apparently before then the audience must be granted a little "relief." So they show the stage gradually lighting up with festal bonfires, coloured lanterns, and so on, and start the chorus off on an elaborate set piece in praise of fire and flame and the similarity of these natural phenomena to the ardours of love.

This unnecessary interpolation out of the way, and the storm having by now died down completely, we can concentrate our attention on a group standing and sitting near a tavern table, among them Iago, Roderigo and Cassio. The action now follows Shakespeare closely. Employing a musical conversation tone of admirable directness and speed, Verdi shows us Iago drawing both Cassio and Roderigo deeper and deeper into his net. He forces Cassio, against his better judgment, to drink with him: his

drinking song—"And let me the canikin clink"—fulfils all the functions of an old-style aria yet is wholly one in substance with the
course of the action, not interrupting it at any point but carrying
it easily on: its vigorous pendant:

No. 2

Chi al–l'e–sca ha mor–so —— del di — ti — ram — bo

has an *entrain* that Cassio and the others find irresistible. There
is a foretaste here, not only in the solo parts but in the choral
ensemble, of the light and easy musical speech of *Falstaff*; and
what is most remarkable of all, while ensembles of this kind in
Otello run to a length rare in the earlier Verdi they do not immo-
bilise the drama but keep it moving steadily forward.

4

As the serpent's coils weave themselves closer and closer about
Cassio, Iago gives Roderigo his instructions; when the lieutenant
is thoroughly and pugnaciously drunk and obviously incapable
of fulfilling the commission brought to him by Montano from
Otello to guard the bastion, Roderigo is to inveigle him into a
brawl. This ends in Montano, who has tried to make peace between them, being sorely wounded for his pains, with Iago hypocritically professing to be anxious to end the fray, and sending
Roderigo off to rouse the town by spreading a rumour of mutiny.
Soon the alarm bell is heard ringing, and the tumult brings
Otello on the scene, hot with anger. He demands to be informed
of what has happened. The wounded Montano, and Cassio, now
sobered, can tell him nothing; Iago also hypocritically professes
to lack all understanding of how the insane quarrel had begun.
By now the turmoil has brought Desdemona from her bed; and
at the sight of her Otello's Moorish blood boils over. To Cassio
he turns with a curt "Thou art no longer my lieutenant." Cassio
lets fall his sword, which Iago picks up and hands to one of the
soldiers, muttering "I triumph!"
Otello having dismissed them all, bidding them see that peace
is kept in the town, everything is now set for the great duet be-

tween him and Desdemona that is to end the act. This begins in exquisite soft orchestral colours as Otello sings of the calm of love that has at last succeeded the dangers and tumults of the day:[1]

No. 3

His later development of the ecstatic strain is to a skilful adaptation on Boïto's part of a famous section of Othello's speech to the Senate in Shakespeare's first act—

> *She loved me for the dangers I had passed,*
> *And I loved her that she did pity them:*

No. 4

The long and lovely episode was obviously intended to suggest the extreme of quiet happiness under a starlit sky of peace; it should not be bawled at us in the way it too often is by singers who no longer have a mellifluous pianissimo left in them.

The duet ends with a rapturous cry of "A kiss, and again a kiss!", to a motif that will make a poignant reappearance at the end of the drama:

[1] Verdi's dynamic indications are very quiet almost throughout the duet, ranging mostly between *ppp* and *pppppp*. But these must not be taken too literally: as Toscanini has reminded us, the average Italian orchestra of that period was so prodigal of tone on almost all occasions that in order to get a real *pp* Verdi had to write *ppppp* or even, as in one case in the present duet, *pppppp* in a score. One is reminded of Berlioz's story of the singer who always pronounced "poisson" as "poison." The conductor managed to get something like the *ss* out of her only by assuring her that the word was spelt with three s's.

No. 5

and with a last happy glance at the Pleiades and an invocation to
Venus the pair go out arm in arm towards the castle, to a final
soft breathing of No. 3 by the orchestra.

5

Boïto has thus dexterously condensed Shakespeare's first two
acts into a single act of the opera, and now, having disposed of
the preliminaries, he can get down in good earnest to the core of
the drama—the gradual bringing by Iago of the other main characters into his toils.

The second act shows us a hall on the ground floor of the castle,
with two spacious galleries at the sides, and at the back a door
opening upon a garden. The serpentine twists and coilings of the
brief orchestral introduction:

No. 6

show us Iago's evil mind at work; and when the curtain rises we
see him entering and engaging Cassio in conversation.

Verdi's conception of Iago is already suggested in our musical
examples No. 1 and No. 6; always the stress is on the smooth-
moving, snake-like element in the man's intellectual and moral
make-up. If he were an actor, Verdi told one of his correspondents
in September 1881—the painter Domenico Morelli, who had sent
him a sketch in which Iago figured as a small man in a black costume [1]—and were called upon to play Iago, he would present him
as a tall, lean man with thin lips, small eyes set near the nose like

[1] Verdi did not object to this: "that Iago should be dressed in black," he
told Morelli, "nothing better, seeing that his soul is black. . . ."

a monkey's, his forehead high and receding, the back of the head markedly developed; in manner he would be *distrait, nonchalant*, indifferent to everything, cutting, lightly throwing off remarks good and evil with an air of not attaching the least importance himself to what he was saying, so that if anyone were to accuse him of having said something infamous he would reply "Really? I didn't think it so; but don't let us say any more about it." A man of this type, Verdi continued, could deceive anyone, even, to a certain extent, his own wife, whereas a small, malignant man makes everybody suspicious of him and so deceives no one. That was the Iago, basically evil-minded, unscrupulous, plausible, self-contained, self-controlled, that Verdi set himself the task of portraying in music. He succeeded admirably.

When the curtain rises we see Iago, always to the accompaniment of the twisting No. 6 in one form or another, giving the disconsolate Cassio some advice—he is to work on Otello's feelings through Desdemona. It is the latter's habit to rest at mid-day in the garden with Emilia, Iago's wife; there, then, let Cassio await her. Having dismissed his dupe, Iago, still to the accompaniment of No. 6, embarks upon a soliloquy in which he expounds his own philosophy of life—the famous Credo. A tremendous unison in the orchestra, ending with a sinister shake:

No. 7

prefaces his confession—"I believe in a cruel God who has created me in his own image . . . From some vile germ, some atom, was I generated. Because I am human I am evil . . . Whatever I do or think that is vile was decreed for me by Fate. The honest man is merely a poor actor, whose tears and kisses and glances and professions of honour are only lies. Man is the sport of the evil Fates, from the germ in which his being began to the grave and the worm." At this point No. 7 reappears in a weightier and darker harmonic form:

No. 8

which is repeated as Iago resumes his brooding: "At the end of this farce comes death. And after that? Nothing! heaven is but an ancient idle tale!"

6

The musical idiom changes as Desdemona and Emilia appear in the garden: Iago hurries to the colonnade into which Cassio had retreated, and bids him hasten to Desdemona. This he does, and we see them strolling up and down together, in close conversation, with Desdemona smiling in friendly fashion on the suppliant. Now is the time, says Iago to himself, to bring Otello here; but before he can move to do so he already sees him on his way thither. Taking up a position by one of the columns on the left, he gazes fixedly at the pair in the garden, and, pretending to be talking to himself, mutters, "That I like not!" Otello, having overheard the remark, as it was intended that he should, comes forward and asks him what he means. To the smoothest of music Iago begins to stir up Otello's suspicions—for he has observed that at the precise moment he had appeared, Cassio had taken leave of Desdemona. The episode that follows is modelled closely on Shakespeare's handling of the intrigue. In oily tones Iago asks Otello whether, when he was wooing Desdemona, she was acquainted with Cassio, and if that young man had enjoyed his confidence at the time:

No. 9

Cas-sio, nei pri-mi dì del vos-tro a-mor, De-
sde-mo-na non co-no-sce-va?

Otello's suspicions are soon at boiling point, while the crafty Iago remains cool, feeding the flames with sly insinuations and warn-ings—"Beware, my lord, of jealousy!":

No. 10

Bass: B♮ C♮ C♯   D   C♯ B♯ C♯   G♯   C♯

It is the green-eyed monster, which doth mock
The meat it feeds on.

With hypocritical professions of love and loyalty Iago advises the now maddened Otello to delay action until he has proof: let him observe Desdemona well with Cassio, for a single unpremeditated word of hers may either dispel Otello's suspicions or finally con-firm them.

Their talk is broken in upon by a chorus in the distance singing the praises of Desdemona, who now re-enters the garden through the great door at the back of the scene: she is accompanied by women and children of the island and Cypriot and Albanian mariners, who come forward offering her flowers and other gifts. Some of them break into song, accompanying themselves on the guzla (which Verdi is careful to describe as "a sort of guitar") and small harps slung across their shoulders; children strew lilies on the ground; some of the sailors present Desdemona with necklaces of corals and pearls. This overlong and dramatically superfluous episode is a blot on the construction of the drama, a sad lapse on both Boïto's part and Verdi's into operatic convention; and what makes it worse is that Verdi's music for it all is in anything but his best vein.

When the chorus has ended, Desdemona graciously kisses some of the children and bestows a purse on the mariners, while some of the women kiss the hem of her gown. The crowd departs, leaving only Desdemona and Emilia at the back of the stage. Des-demona comes forward to the hall and greets Otello—who, with Iago, has been watching the preceding scene—and poet and composer take up again the temporarily severed threads of the dramatic action. We get back to Shakespeare once more. Desdemona pleads for the restoration of Cassio to Otello's favour. Her innocent importunities end in exasperating him, and when she offers to bind her handkerchief round his throbbing temples he throws it down angrily. It is picked up by Emilia. There follows a masterly quartet, in which Desdemona humbly and affectionately begs forgiveness if she has unwittingly offended, and Otello bewails his lost illusions, while in the background Iago wrenches the handkerchief from Emilia's reluctant hand; "now," he ejaculates, "I have them in my meshes, to work upon as I will!"

7

At a sign from Otello, Desdemona and Emilia leave the stage, Iago launching a veiled threat at his wife as she goes out—"Say nothing. Do you understand?" "Desdemona false!", moans Otello, while Iago, glancing at the handkerchief before placing it in his doublet, mutters the equivalent of Shakespeare's:

> *I will in Cassio's lodging lose this napkin,*
> *And let him find it. Trifles light as air*
> *Are to the jealous confirmations strong*
> *As proofs of holy writ.*

Otello turns on him furiously, reproaching him for having placed him on the rack as he has done by making him doubt Desdemona. The text now follows closely the superb rhetoric in which Shakespeare (Act III, scene 3) makes Othello bid farewell to everything he has done and been:

> *Farewell the neighing steed and the shrill trump,*
> *The spirit-stirring drum, the ear-splitting fife,*
> *The royal banner and all quality,*
> *Pride, pomp and circumstance of glorious war!* . . .
> *Farewell! Othello's occupation's gone!*

His recollection of the glorious warlike past to which he must now bid adieu is accompanied by military fanfares and by a march-like figure in the orchestra:

643

No. 11

a presumable variant of which will appear later. He threatens Iago with dire punishment if he fails to prove to him that Desdemona is guilty. In reply Iago tells him, in smooth, insinuating tones, how, sleeping in the company of Cassio lately, he had heard the young lieutenant murmuring endearments in his sleep to Desdemona and crying "Cursed fate that gave thee to the Moor!" This crazy babbling, of course, Iago points out hypocritically, was only in a dream; but what if a simple fact should confirm it? Did not Desdemona once possess "a handkerchief spotted with strawberries?" he asks. "I gave her such a one," replies Otello; " 'twas my first gift." That handkerchief, says Iago, he had seen for certain yesterday in Cassio's hand. For Otello this is the last faggot on the flames. Calling insanely for blood he falls on his knees and summons heaven to witness that his hatred for the guilty pair will never end until he has been avenged by his own hand. This superb piece of musical rhetoric is based on a figure:

No. 12

which certainly seems to derive from our No. 11, though one has to confess that one can give no valid reason for the affiliation.

Before Otello can rise, Iago too sinks to his knees and, taking up the strain, vows that until the sun shall cease to shine he will give himself up, body and soul, to Otello's service. Then the two voices blend in a duet that ends with a great united appeal to an avenging God. And so the second act ends, with a credulous Otello caught beyond hope of liberation in Iago's snare.

8

The setting of the third act is in the great hall of the castle. On the left is a large colonnade, which joins on to a smaller hall; at the back is an open gallery. After a short orchestral introduction, which becomes more and more agitated as it proceeds, the curtain rises, showing Otello and Iago. To them comes a Herald, with the news that the watch at the port has signalled the arrival of a galley bringing the Venetian ambassadors to Cyprus. The Herald having been dismissed, Iago begins a fresh assault on the credulity of Otello. He has arranged for Cassio to call on Desdemona again: and Otello, in hiding, is to observe the pair closely. Iago would speak of the handkerchief, but Otello sends him away with a curt "Go; I would forget that!"

Desdemona having entered by a door on the left, a conversation ensues between her and Otello that is one of Verdi's masterpieces of dramatic characterisation. Desdemona is all affection; Otello treats her with all imaginable courtesy, in which, however, we detect a sinister sub-ironic note. Desdemona, in her kindhearted innocence, at once broaches the subject of the discarded Cassio. Otello asks for her handkerchief, but the one she offers him is not the one he wants to see—one given to him, he tells her, by his mother, who had it from an Egyptian charmer; while in his mother's possession it would secure her the love of her husband, but

> To los't or give't away were such perdition
> As nothing else could match.

The tension of the music increases as Desdemona protests that though she has it not with her at the moment it is not lost, and tries to turn the conversation once more to the subject of the forgiveness of Cassio. Losing control of himself Otello imperiously demands the handkerchief again and again, each time more angrily, and ends by damning her for a strumpet. Wrenched out of her obsession now, she protests her loyalty in accents of the deepest feeling, while Otello, torn between anger and love, raves madly against her.

Suddenly he regains command of himself, and, as Verdi's stage directions put it, his tone changes for a moment from that of rage to one of an ironic calm that is even more terrifying. Reverting to the smooth melody with which their conversation had begun he takes her by the hand and conducts her ceremoniously to the door by which she had entered. There he dismisses her with a

645

final brutal insult; then he returns to the centre of the stage in deep dejection. There follows the great soliloquy that is Verdi's supreme achievement in serious opera. The words are a masterly Italian paraphrase of the words Shakespeare puts into Othello's mouth at a later stage of the drama:

> *Had it pleased heaven*
> *To try me with affliction; had they rain'd*
> *All kinds of sores and shames on my bare head,*
> *Steeped me in poverty to the very lips,*
>
> .   .   .   .
>
> *I should have found in some place of my soul*
> *A drop of patience;*   .   .   .   .
>
> .   .   .   .
>
> *But there, where I have garner'd up my heart,*
> *Where either I must live or bear no life,*
> *The fountain from the which my current runs,*
> *Or else dries up; to be discarded thence!*
> *Or keep it as a cistern for foul toads*
> *To knot and gender in! Turn thy complexion there,*
> *Patience, thou young and rose-lipp'd cherubin,*
> *Ay, there, look grim as hell!*

9

The first part of the long soliloquy is based on a tiny orchestral figure:

No. 13

that twists and turns, in one astonishing mutation after another, through more than twenty bars of the score. Here, if anywhere, we see how marvellously Verdi had developed as a musical crafts-man in this final phase of his career. Basically his procedure here is the one to which attention has been more than once drawn in our analyses of *Rigoletto*, *Il Trovatore* and *La Traviata*—he fastens upon a small melodic turn which he pursues with dogged persistence through bar after bar. But in his middle period he had confided the turn to the vocal part, and his unchanged repetitions of it were often so mechanical as to make it in the end ludicrous. But here he allots the figure not to the voice but to the orchestra, and by means of one harmonic and contrapuntal change after another he gives it a new psychological significance each time it recurs, for there seems to be no limit to his resources of deducing B from A, and C from B, and so forth in a single organic process. Nowhere else is Verdi so "Wagnerian" as in these remarkable pages; yet nowhere else is he so completely, so loftily and profoundly, just Verdi.

The procedure, as we have seen, is one in which the main burden of expression is laid on the "symphonic" developments in the orchestra, the voice part being confined throughout to what is virtually a brooding monotone. Nothing could have suggested better than this monotone the numbness of the man's spirit. But with consummate tact Verdi breaks off the procedure at just the right moment, and launches Otello on a great lyrical flight on his own account at the point indicated by the line

But there, where I have garner'd up my heart,

a flight that finds its culmination in a great soaring and then drooping phrase:

No. 14

Spen-to è quel sol, quel sor-ri-so, quel rag—gio che mi fa

vi —— vo, che mi fa lie ———— to.

as he speaks with infinite regret of the extinguishing of the sun, the smile, that had been his life and his joy.

This melting mood soon vanishes: frenzy takes possession of

him, and as he cries "Damnation! She shall confess, then die!" Iago enters with the news that Cassio has arrived. He places Otello in the colonnade, where he can see without being seen, then runs to usher in his dupe. His speech is once more deceptively smooth; he ends his first sentence—"Come; the hall is deserted; step within, Captain"—with one of his customary sardonic shakes on the third syllable of "Capitano." Well he knows that he is now complete master of the game.

Cassio is in poor condition; his only hope, he says, is in Desdemona, whom he had hoped to find there; and at that name Otello pricks up his ears. Iago leads Cassio up within earshot of Otello, and, affecting a friendly gaiety, as of one man of the world to another, decoys him into speaking of his mistress Bianca. This puts the lieutenant for a moment in merry mood, and he begins to tell of his finding a handkerchief in his room, placed there by some unknown hand. Iago's strategy is to keep Otello on tenterhooks by moving the lieutenant now and then out of Otello's range and bidding him speak softly, so that his words are now and then lost; but when he shows Iago the handkerchief Otello has no further doubts. The conversation is carried on to light-hearted music, so that the episode has something of the effect of a musical scherzo, in an idiom that is an anticipation of some portions of *Falstaff*. Knowing that Otello has seen what he intended him to see and that, as he puts it, the fly is now caught in the web, Iago launches a fast-moving trio, in which we see Cassio lost in admiration of the workmanship of the handkerchief he innocently holds in his hand, while Otello, bemoaning his own tragedy, manages to conform to the rhythm and pace of the other two without any sacrifice of his own musical individuality.

10

Suddenly, as Otello conceals himself again, trumpets sound without and the great gun of the castle booms out, announcing that the Venetian ship has dropped anchor. Iago hustles Cassio away; and Otello, emerging from his hiding-place, asks him the sinister question, "How shall I murder her, Iago?" The crafty villain plays on his frenzy, reminding him of Cassio's brazen display of the handkerchief, and Otello bids him get him some poison, for Desdemona shall die that very night—only to decide a moment later that she shall die not by poison but by suffocation in her bed. As for Cassio, Iago promises to see to him, and Otello makes him his lieutenant from that hour.

Otello now prepares to greet the ambassadors, and sends Iago off to find Desdemona, whose presence he desires in order to avert any possible suspicion. The fanfares ring out once more, and the stage gradually fills with a great crowd, among them the dignitaries of the Venetian republic, the still lovelorn Roderigo, the ambassador Lodovico, noblemen and ladies and soldiers, while Iago has returned with Desdemona.[1] Otello, ostensibly reading a document handed him by Lodovico, watches Desdemona suspiciously, and is goaded to fury when he hears her tell Iago that she hopes to see Cassio soon returned to her husband's favour. Maddened beyond endurance he strikes her, to the general horror —can this be the noble Moor, Lodovico asks, who is the pride and glory of the Senate?

At Otello's command Cassio is brought in, and Otello discloses the contents of the document the ambassador has brought—the Doge has recalled him to Venice, and his lieutenant Cassio is to succeed him in the command of Cyprus; he himself will set sail for Venice on the morrow. He lays a violent hand on Desdemona, who falls to the ground. Helped to her feet by the pitying Emilia and Lodovico, she sings a sorrowful lament for the love she has plainly lost. Her song rises to ecstatic heights as she recalls the days when she was all in all to Otello:

No. 15

dolcissimo E un di sul mio sor—ri—so fio—ri—va la spe—me e il ba—cio

Round this strain is built up a massive ensemble, in which not only the chorus but Emilia, Roderigo, Cassio and Lodovico comment, each according to character, on the horror of the situation, while Iago urges Otello to act quickly, before his wrath dies down; he himself will deal with Cassio before the evening is out. Roderigo he counsels to be of good heart: as things stand now,

---

[1] At this stage of the action Verdi later added a ballet for a production in Paris. This is dramatically superfluous.

Otello will depart on the morrow—and with him Desdemona, whereas if some "accident" should befall Cassio, then perforce Otello would have to remain in Cyprus. For the "accident" to Cassio—at the point of Roderigo's sword—Iago himself will provide.

The huge ensemble ends with Otello being seized by one of his Moorish brain storms. In terrible tones he bids them all leave him. Desdemona gives an appealing cry of "My husband!", but he repulses her with a curse. She is led away, half-fainting, by Emilia and Lodovico, and the crowd breaks up in dismay. Left alone with Iago, Otello is seized by a convulsion as he recalls the episode of the handkerchief, and falls to the ground in a swoon. "My poison works!" ejaculates Iago; and as shouts of "Long live Otello! Glory to the Lion of Venice!" resound without, accompanied by rousing orchestral fanfares, he makes a horrible gesture of triumph over the inanimate body, and, as the curtain falls, cries "Behold the Lion!", with his usual ironic shake on the second syllable of the last word ("Leone").

11

The scene of the short fourth act is Desdemona's bedroom, with a bed, a prie-Dieu, a looking-glass and some chairs. Over the prie-Dieu is a statue of the Madonna, before which a light is burning. On the table is a candle. It is night. As the curtain rises the orchestra gives out softly a plaintive theme:

No. 16

that anticipates the melody of Desdemona's "Willow" song. When this brief prelude has run its course we find Desdemona and Emilia in conversation. The maid would persuade her mistress that Otello seemed calmer when last she saw him. He had bidden Desdemona go to bed and there await him; and now, with a premonition of evil, she is asking Emilia to lay on the bed the white sheets that had been on it on her wedding night, adding

If I do die before thee, prithee, shroud me
In one of those same sheets.

Sad and weary, she seats herself before the looking-glass and sings, to the melody of No. 16, of a poor maid of her mother's, one Barbara, who had died of love, and who used to sing a ditty with a refrain of "Willow, willow, willow." That mournful song Desdemona cannot get out of her mind tonight—

Sing all a green willow must be my garland.

She starts as she imagines she hears a knock at the door, but it is only the wind. Voice and orchestra are hushed as she bids Emilia good night; but in an instant there comes from her a passionate cry, as of a frightened child, of "Ah! Emilia, addio, Emilia, addio!":

No. 17

This cry is one of Verdi's masterstrokes of dramatic timing and expression.

When Emilia has left her, Desdemona kneels before the image of the Madonna and prays for herself and for all souls in affliction, for the sinner and the innocent, for those oppressed and for their oppressors—"Pray for us now and in the hour of dying":

No. 18

As her tones die away and she lies down on the bed Otello becomes visible on the threshold of a secret door; he is accompanied by an ominous theme in the depths of the double basses which develops into a kind of long recitative. For some time not a word is spoken. Otello places a scimitar on the table, then halts and stands before the candle, as if in doubt whether to extinguish it or not. His glance falls on the sleeping Desdemona, and he puts the candle out. With a furious gesture he approaches the bed, pauses, raises the curtain, and, to the accompaniment of phrases in the orchestra that are like sobs, looks down for a long time on the quiet figure, and kisses it three times, the orchestra giving out a poignant reminiscence of the "Kiss" motif from the first act (No. 5).

She awakes. He asks her if she has said her prayers, and in sombre tones exhorts her, if she has any unredeemed sin on her conscience, to pray heaven's forgiveness for it now, for he would not kill her soul. She protests that her only sin is that of love for him, and for that she is now to die! He charges her with having loved Cassio, and bids her confess it; he would not have her die perjured. Passionately she demands that Cassio be sent for; but he tells her that Cassio is dead. Despairingly she pleads for life, but now he is beside himself with grief and rage, and he suffocates her.

As he stands motionless, gazing down at her, he is startled by a knocking at the door and the voice of Emilia crying out to him to admit her. When he does so she brings the news that Cassio has killed Roderigo, but—a bitter blow, this, for Otello!—"Cassio lives." From the bed comes the pitiful small voice of Desdemona, declaring "I have been unjustly done to death; I die innocent!" She has died by her own hand, she continues as Emilia hastens to her in terror: "Commend me to my Lord; I die innocent! Addio!" Emilia turns furiously on Otello, whose only reply is the equivalent of Shakespeare's

> *She's like a liar gone to burning hell:*
> *'Twas I that killed her,*

for she had been Cassio's strumpet; that he had had on the word of Iago. "And you, oh fool, believed him?" cries Emilia. She runs to the door, crying despairingly "Help! Help! the Moor has killed Desdemona!"

Lodovico, Cassio and Iago come in, followed by Montano and some soldiers. The raging Emilia turns on Otello, denouncing him as the murderer of his innocent wife. "Not innocent," he says, for he had seen in Cassio's hand a handkerchief he had once given her as the pledge of his love. Disregarding Iago's angry attempt to silence her, Emilia discloses that the fateful handkerchief had been taken from her by force by her husband. "And I found it in my chamber," says Cassio; to which Montano adds, "Roderigo, before he died, revealed to me the infamous wiles of this villain." Otello, sword in hand, turns furiously on Iago, who takes to flight, pursued by some of the soldiers. Lodovico orders Otello to surrender his sword. The wounded Lion answers him with a strange gentleness: "Let no one fear me, armed though I be. This is the end of my journey. Of Otello nothing remains." He turns a pitying gaze on Desdemona, with a heart-breaking cry of "Desdemona! Desdemona! Dead! Dead! Dead!" He has let fall his sword; but now he draws a stiletto from his doublet and stabs himself. His last words, as he falls on the body, are virtually Shakespeare's

> *I kissed thee ere I kill'd thee; no way but this,*
> *Killing myself, to die upon a kiss;*

and the orchestra closes it all with a last poignant reminiscence of No. 5.

The Magic Flute

MOZART [1756–1791]

PRINCIPAL CHARACTERS

TAMINO	*Tenor*
PAMINA	*Soprano*
PAPAGENO	*Baritone*
PAPAGENA	*Soprano*
THE QUEEN OF NIGHT	*Soprano*
SARASTRO	*Bass*
THE SPEAKER OF THE TEMPLE	*Bass*
TWO PRIESTS	*Tenor and Bass*
TWO MEN IN ARMOUR	*Tenor and Bass*
THREE GENII OF THE TEMPLE	*Soprano, Mezzo-soprano and Contralto*
THREE LADIES OF THE QUEEN OF NIGHT	*Two Sopranos and Mezzo-soprano*
MONOSTATOS	*Tenor*

1

s Hermann Abert remarks in his monumental work on Mozart, the text of *The Magic Flute* has come in for more disparagement than all the rest of Mozart's libretti put together. It has frequently been described as the silliest of all opera libretti. On the other hand Goethe—who, by the way, began, without finishing, a continuation of the theme—declared that "it takes more culture to perceive the virtues of *The Magic Flute* text than to point out its defects," and laid it down that while for the generality the stage spectacle was the great thing, it was the "higher meaning" of the work that would be fastened on by "initiates." Writing in much the same vein in 1849, Joseph Cornet—the Hamburg impresario to whom reference has been made in our chapter on *Don Giovanni*—laid it down that *"The Magic Flute* is the central point of German opera, towards which for centuries to come the eyes of all will turn who want to study the basic elements of the German opera style."

When opinions upon a work are as sharply contradictory as this, the inference is that neither camp is talking at the same time about quite the same thing; each is seeing only what it wants to see in order to establish a thesis of its own and turning a blind eye on the remainder. It can hardly be denied that if by some accident or other nothing of Mozart's score had survived to be published beyond the first of the two acts, the eulogies of Goethe and Cornet and many others in the first half of the nineteenth century would seem very wide of the mark today. If later the second act had come to light, it would have been evident that the enthusiasm of all these people had been evoked only by that act, to the discreet ignoring of the first; while the upholders of the thesis that nothing so inane as the plot of *The Magic Flute* had ever been seen or ever will be seen again on the operatic stage would obviously be judged to have underrated the second act out of sheer exasperation with the first. Mozart's opera is manifestly not one work, but two. How then did a musical dramatist of his quality manage to persuade himself that the two halves constituted a single valid whole? To that century-old question no satisfactory answer has yet been given.

2

The circumstances of the origin of the opera are too familiar to every student of musical history for it to be necessary to do more than outline them here. About 1790 the old yearning to write a "German" opera seems to have taken possession of Mozart once more. The decisive moment came when, about that time, he renewed an old acquaintance with Emanuel Schikaneder (1748–1812)—a remarkable character in many ways. He had been in turns or simultaneously actor, singer, stage manager, impresario and heaven knows what else. In our time he would have drifted as a matter of course to Hollywood, where he would soon have become the leading purveyor of easy amusement for the simple-minded populace. He specialised in gorgeous and expensive stage and open-air spectacles—and generally made them pay. By 1791 he had established himself in Vienna, in a theatre of his own "auf der Wieden." At that time perhaps the most popular of all stage genres in Vienna was that of the fairy play or fairy opera, which gave the crowd its fill of marvellous happenings and romantic sentiments. The leading literary figure in this development had been Wieland, upon whose fantastic stories the playwrights and opera poets drew liberally. The most successful provider of this kind of theatrical fare in Vienna just then was one Marinelli, with whom Schikaneder boldly entered into competition.

It was Schikaneder, apparently, who first thought of the concoction that was ultimately to become the plot of *The Magic Flute*. He succeeded in interesting Mozart in it, though the composer, significantly enough, seems not to have been over enthusiastic about it at first, judging from his remark to Schikaneder in March 1791, which was in effect this—"All right! but if we come a cropper over it don't blame me, for I have never written a *Zauberoper* [magic opera] before." However, each needed the other at that time, Schikaneder because he was in one of his usual economic fixes, Mozart because he was desperately anxious, for both artistic and financial reasons, to get into the German theatre again. The fact that both the musician and the impresario were freemasons seems also to have influenced him to some extent, for he took his masonic obligations very seriously.

3

In the text book and on the theatre bills Schikaneder was named as the author of the libretto. In 1849 Cornet, in his book *Die Oper in Deutschland*, described how, some thirty years before then, he had met in Vienna a middle-aged gentleman, of the name (it was an assumed one) of Giesecke, who declared that *he* was the main author of *The Magic Flute* text, Schikaneder having contributed only "the figures of Papageno and his wife." The Mozart biographers have wrangled over this statement ever since. This Giesecke was a delver into mineralogy, geology and some kindred sciences who, after many years of capable work, ended his days, in 1833, as the much respected Professor of Mineralogy in Dublin.

Too much ink has perhaps been expended on the subject of this claim of his to the authorship of the libretto of *The Magic Flute*, but there seems to be no valid reason for disputing it. He had been on Schikaneder's staff in Vienna in various capacities round about 1790, and he is known to have written the whole or part text of more than one "fairy opera" or "magic opera." (He was a student in Vienna at that time, and possibly eked out a slender living, as Berlioz and others were to do later, by singing in the chorus and doing odd jobs about the theatre.) We need not assume that he was the author of every line of the *Magic Flute* text; things of that sort are usually pies in which more than one chef or scullion can have a finger. But on the main point there is no reason for doubting his veracity and Cornet's.

Mozart made good progress with the music of the opera in June and July 1791, and in the latter month began the orchestration of the first act; in that month too, apparently, although the work was far from finished, he entered it, in a handwriting that betrays haste, in his Catalogue—the *Verzeichnis aller meiner Werke*.[1] For some time after that he was occupied with other plans, in particular the Requiem Mass that had been so mysteriously commissioned from him, and the opera *La Clemenza di Tito*, for the production of which—on the 6th September—he had to spend some time in Prague. On his return to Vienna he took up *The Magic Flute* again, and on the 28th September completed the work with the composition of the March of the Priests (No. 9 of the printed score), and the overture. Both of these he entered in the *Verzeichnis*, together with the customary quotation of the opening bars of each. Two days later the opera was produced, with Mozart conducting, in Schikaneder's Theater auf de Wieden: Schikaneder was the Papageno, Schack the Tamino, Nannina Gottlieb (the Barbarina of *Figaro*) the Pamina, Josepha Hofer the Queen of Night, Gerl the Sarastro, and Nouseul the Monostatos. The opera soon became enormously popular, and remained so for many years, to Schikaneder's great profit. Its success, however, mattered little to poor Mozart, who died in poverty and misery

[1] As usual, he jotted down in the *Verzeichnis* the opening bars of the work —in this case the first four bars of the orchestral introduction to the aria of Tamino, "Zu Hülfe! Zu Hülfe! sonst bin ich verloren," with which the stage action opens.

ten weeks after the first performance of the work—on the 5th December 1791.

4

Let us now glance at the curious farrago that was *The Magic Flute* as first conceived. The overture does not concern us in the least at this point of our study, for it lacks the smallest relevance to the action that is now to be put before us. The setting is one of trees and rocks plus a circular temple—where, we are not told. There enters what is described as a Japanese (why Japanese?) Prince, Tamino, carrying a bow. He is in a state of abject terror, as well he may be, for he is being pursued by a great serpent, and he has run out of arrows. He gives anguished expression to his fears and calls desperately for help in a short quasi-aria, whereupon the doors of the temple most opportunely fly open and three veiled Ladies appear, each armed with a silver spear, who proceed to slay the serpent, congratulating themselves volubly on having arrived in the nick of time to rescue the young man by what they call their "heroic deed." It is their duty now, they continue, to carry the news to their Queen; perhaps this handsome youth will bring back her lost peace of mind. But each has been favourably impressed by the comeliness of the youth who still lies unconscious before them, and coquettishly each of them tries to persuade the others to leave *her* to attend to him while *they* go off to take the good tidings to the Queen. At last they depart in company, each swearing fidelity to the young stranger until they and he shall meet again. Their repetitive chatter occupies some ten pages of the score. It is difficult to believe that Mozart could have taken much interest in them; but his sound craftsmanship enabled him to spin out their talk plausibly enough in the accepted musical formulae of the period.

When they have left the stage, Tamino, having regained consciousness, is greatly astonished to find the terrible serpent dead at his feet. Hearing sounds in the distance, he takes cover among the trees as he perceives a man approaching across the valley. It is the bird-catcher Papageno, a simple child of nature, for whom Mozart, who dearly loved a character of this type, has written a quantity of enchanting music. He is heralded by a light-hearted

658

strain, in the purest folk vein, in the strings, the horns joining in with gravely comical effect at the end of each line:

No. 1

Strapped to his back is a large bird-cage, containing several little captives, and every now and then he puts a Pan's pipe to his mouth on which he blows an artless half-scale:

No. 2

In a delicious little ditty to the tune of No. 1 he informs the universe that he is the care-free bird-catcher, known to young and old throughout the land; if he could only capture pretty girls by the same means and in the same numbers his happiness would be complete!

5

He and Tamino converse for a time in spoken dialogue. Tamino tells him he is a prince with large possessions. This astonishes Papageno, who did not know that there were any lands or people beyond the mountains. About himself he can tell Tamino little except that he was born some time or other, has a little hut of his own, exists, like other people, by eating and drinking, and makes a living by providing the Queen of Night and her maidens with captured birds. "Have you been so happy, then," asks Tamino, "as to have seen the Queen of Night?" No mortal has had that good fortune, Papageno replies. "Surely," Tamino muses, "this must be the great Queen of whom my father has so often told me." His brooding air rather frightens Papageno, who warns him to stand back, for when he fights, he boasts tremulously, he has a giant's strength. Then no doubt it was he, the Prince surmises, who had fought the serpent. Papageno, having first made sure that the monster is dead, modestly admits that his was the great deed, accomplished, too, without a weapon of any kind.

Thereupon the Ladies re-enter; he recognises them as the three who give him his daily bread, figs and wine in payment for his birds. Being the servants of the virtuous Queen of Night they are naturally all for truth; so they censure him for his fibs and teach him a lesson. Today he gets from them, instead of wine, cold water, instead of bread, a stone, and instead of sweet figs a golden padlock on his mouth. Then the Ladies inform Tamino that it was they, not the mendacious bird-catcher, who had killed the serpent, and hand him a medallion that is a gift from the great Queen herself; it contains the likeness of her daughter.

With an "Auf Wiedersehen" they leave the astonished young man to contemplate the portrait with wonder and delight, and to sing, in an expressive aria, of his love at first sight for the beautiful original, whom he longs to make his.

The Three Ladies return to assure him that that felicity shall be his, the Queen having promised that if the youth turns out to have as much courage as, according to them, he has tenderness of heart, he will be able to rescue her daughter, who has been stolen from her by an evil magician. Tamino has time only to ejaculate "Lead me to her!" when there is a sound of thunder in the distance; the rocks divide and the Queen herself appears. In a dignified recitative and aria, laid out on the grandest scale, she confides to him the task of "bringing solace to her sorely tried mother's heart"; for with the loss of her daughter—abducted by a miscreant—all joy in life had left her. But if the Prince can rescue the maiden then her hand shall be his reward; and to leave him in no doubt that she means what she says she performs the most wonderful feats of vocal agility through fourteen bars (60 notes in all) on the single word "then" ("Dann"), ending up with a staggering F *in alt*. ("Dann" was no doubt selected for this purpose because its vowel is the easiest of all on which to sing coloratura).

She leaves the stage with the Three Ladies, and Tamino is about to follow them when he is intercepted by Papageno, who, because of his padlock, is now incapable of articulate speech; in reply to Tamino's expressions of sympathy all he can do is to mumble "Hm!", mocked at the unison by a humorous bassoon:

No. 3

The Three Ladies, however, soon come to his rescue; the Queen has relented, it appears, and the padlock is removed. The real business of the Ladies, however, is with Tamino. They hand him a magic flute, a gift from the Queen, which will protect him in danger and give him power to subdue human passions and increase the sum of happiness on earth. As for Papageno, he is horrified to learn that he must now, by order of the Queen, accompany the Prince to the castle of the terrible Sarastro; but to hearten him the Ladies give him a chime of silver bells. The music of this scene has so far been, on the whole, of only average quality; but we get a touch of the greater Mozart in a trio in which the Ladies promise Tamino that three young genii shall attend him on his quest; to their counsel alone must he give any heed. And so, after a charming quintet, the Prince and the bird-catcher set out on their mission.

6

The scene changes to a splendidly furnished room. We see the Moor Monostatos dragging Pamina in, who declares that she has no fear of death but is concerned about her mother, who must be dying of grief on her account. Breathing fire and slaughter, Monostatos summons his fellow-minions, who put fetters on her hands; whereupon she falls senseless on a couch. The slaves having been sent away, Monostatos, left alone with the unconscious Pamina, seems to be contemplating some further villainy when Papageno enters, after having observed the beautiful damsel admiringly from the window. There follows a humorous scene between him and Monostatos: each takes the other for the devil and is mightily afraid; and the comical situation ends with them running off in opposite directions, having meanwhile drawn from Mozart some naïvely diverting music.

Papageno soon returns, and Pamina having awakened and called piteously for her mother, the two have an explanation scene in recitative. He tells her who he is, and of the noble young Prince whom her mother, having given him Pamina's portrait, has sent out to rescue her. There is not a moment to be lost, she replies, for the sun is high in the heavens, and at noon Sarastro will return as usual from the chase. The conversation somehow turns upon love, and Papageno regrets that he himself, poor simple soul, is without a sweetheart; whereupon, regardless of the fact that time is now of the essence, the pair indulge themselves in a delicious duet on the theme of love as the greatest blessing mankind can know:

No. 4

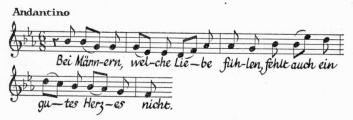

7

They depart in company, and the scene changes for the finale to the first act. The setting shows a grove, with a temple at the back, over the portal of which are inscribed the words "Temple of Wisdom." Rows of pillars lead to two other temples at the side, one the "Temple of Reason," the other the "Temple of Nature." And with this change of scene comes a great change in the spirit of the drama and in the mood and quality and colour of the music; three trombones and muted trumpets lend solemnity to the texture, while the strings are without double-basses. To a solemn melody three Genii, each carrying a silver palm branch, lead Tamino in. They inform him that he is at last near the goal appointed him, but if he is to win through to the end he must be "steadfast, obedient and silent." He asks them if it will fall to him to rescue Pamina, but they reply that it is beyond their powers to tell him that.

When they have left him he muses on his present condition. The words of his mysterious conductors seem to him to have been words of wisdom, and the place in which he finds himself appears to be the seat of the gods, for the very gates and pillars bear witness that here are the fruits of "industry and art." He will save Pamina from the tyrant, he vows, or die. He approaches the temple gates on the right and the left in turn, and from each is bidden sternly to "Stand back!" by a voice within. But his knock on the gate of the third temple brings out an aged Priest to whose question "What would you here?" he replies that he seeks the reward of love and virtue. How can he hope for that, answers the Priest, when he has been driven thither not by virtue and love but by the mere craving for revenge and death? Told that the ruler of the holy place is Sarastro he bursts into a denunciation of the evil magician, as he believes him to be on the strength of the word of an unhappy woman, crushed by a great wrong done her— the abduction of her daughter. The old Priest, calmly advising him never to pay too much attention to the chatter of women, assures him that while Sarastro had indeed conveyed the daughter away it was for no wicked end, though what his purpose was the Priest cannot at the moment disclose, for duty and his oath bind his tongue.

8

To a grave strain in the orchestra:

No. 5

he tells Tamino that he shall learn the full truth when, led by friendship's hand, he is made one of the eternal brotherhood. A chorus of priests within assures him, however, to the music of the solemn No. 5, that Pamina still lives; and in wild enthusiasm he thanks the almighty ones in the medium that seems to him the most appropriate. He plays a charming melody on his flute, whereupon wild animals come forward and listen entranced, subdued. To the same melody he sings a song of praise to his flute, the giver of a joy that even the savage creation shares. But Pamina he has not yet found, and, still accompanied by gracious phrases in the magic flute, he pours out his anxious heart to her. Where shall he find her? he asks despairingly.

A cheery, companionable sound falls on his ear; it is that of Papageno blowing the only melody possible to him on his pipes (No. 2). The Prince has no sooner gone off in search of his birdcatching friend than Papageno himself enters with Pamina, both in quest of the promised rescuer. Papageno again essays his little melody (No. 2) and is answered from afar by the same figure on Tamino's flute. After a simple little duet they are both of them about to set off on the Prince's tracks when they are intercepted by Monostatos and a number of slaves, who are about to put fetters on them when Papageno opportunely bethinks him of his magic chime of bells; their pretty tinkle has an astonishing effect on the Moor and his minions, all of whom dance off singing a delightfully naïve little chorus, to which Pamina and Papageno add a comment in the same simple vein: "Would that every good man could find some such chimes; then would enmity disappear and he would live in the harmony of friendship, which alone can lift from him his load of care and give him happiness on earth."

From within comes a choral cry of "Long live Sarastro!" The name strikes terror into the hearts of Pamina and Papageno; the latter wishes he were a mouse or a snail that could creep away and hide. "What shall we say?" he asks. "The truth!" cries Pamina ecstatically; "the truth, even if it were judged a crime!" Just then, to solemn music, Sarastro enters in a splendid triumphal chariot drawn by lions (a genuine Schikaneder touch, this!), followed by a train of priests and attendants, all singing his praises as the giver of peace and joy and wisdom. Pamina throws herself at his feet and confesses her fault in trying to escape, to which she had been driven by the unwelcome attentions of the Moor. With dignity and gentleness he bids her rise; he knows her heart is given up to love:

No. 6

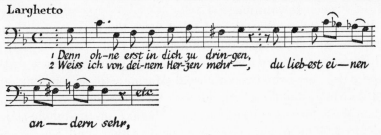

Larghetto

1 *Denn oh—ne erst in dich zu drin-gen,*
2 *Weiss ich von dei-nem Her-zen mehr—, du lieb-est ei—nen*

an — dern sehr,

but as yet he cannot set her free. She speaks of the mother she loves; but he tells her that her only hope of salvation lies in escape from her mother's power: "Proud is she. A *man* must guide your heart, for without the guidance of a man a woman steps out of her proper sphere."

Monostatos enters, bringing with him the captured Tamino, and the Prince and Pamina recognise each other as predestined rescuer and rescued. Monostatos claims Sarastro's favour for having frustrated their plan for flight, and is very sorry for himself when his master sends him off to be bastinadoed. At Sarastro's command the Priests veil the heads of Tamino and Pamina and lead them away to the temple, there to undergo the necessary spiritual probation, and the act ends with a chorus in praise of Sarastro: "When Virtue and Justice hold sway, then earth will become heaven, and mortals the equals of the gods."

9

As the reader will have observed, in this last scene of the first act (No. 8 of the score), the whole dramatic scheme has suddenly been turned upside down. The virtuous Queen of Night, filled with a most sincere mother love, has in the twinkling of an eye become an evil principle from which her daughter must somehow be saved, while the wicked magician is transformed into the best and wisest of beings, the analogue of that Zoroaster from whom his operatic name seems to have been derived. In general terms, the work is no longer a naïve *Zauberoper* but an exposition of freemasonry, the supposed Egyptian mysteries of long ago, and the noble sentiments of "freedom," "truth," "human brotherhood" and all the rest of it that had long been circulating more or less underground among men of intelligence and goodwill and had recently come into the full light of day as the first result of the French Revolution of 1789.

What was the occasion and what were the real causes of this sudden right-about-face on Schikaneder's and Mozart's part? It has been conjectured that it came about primarily through the production by Schikaneder's rival Marinelli of a Singspiel entitled *Kaspar der Fagottist, oder die Zauberzither*, which ran on much the same general lines as *The Magic Flute* had done so far, the hero being endowed with a magic zither, and Kaspar, the simple child of nature, with a bassoon, an instrument capable of a good deal of rough rustic humour. This may have been a contributory cause of the Schikaneder-Mozart right-about-face, but surely not the whole cause, or perhaps not even the vital one. Granted that a change of direction now seemed advisable, why should the new course have been set with full sail for freemasonry and humanitarianism and all the attendant solemnities?

Schikaneder, Mozart and Giesecke were all masons, and it is probably the last-named, as the only literate of the triumvirate, who must be credited with an acquaintance with the Abbé Terrasson's novel *Sethos*, in which the ancient "Egyptian mysteries" and the mode of initiation into them were ostensibly set forth; this work was undoubtedly drawn upon for the business of recasting the opera. But when all the external facts are sorted out and put together again, so far as that is possible today, we are still no nearer a satisfactory answer to the question why the new *Magic Flute* should have taken so decidedly the line that it did.

There are, of course, traces even in the original scheme of a leaning in that direction from the beginning. Insufficient attention, perhaps, has been paid to the masonic and humanitarian slogans in the text *before* the change of course was decided upon. It is the Queen of Night whom we find, in No. 4 of the opera, spouting, through the medium of her Ladies, the best Sarastrian sentiments: the magic flute, the Ladies inform Tamino, will not only protect him in his wanderings but enable him to purify the passions of mankind, to turn tears into joy, to move even the unmarried man to submit to the bonds of love: "Such a flute is worth more than gold and crowns, for it will increase the sum of human happiness and content." Neither Sarastro nor his Priests could have phrased the aspirations of the epoch in general and of freemasonry in particular more precisely; yet it is the Queen of Night who is speaking! In the later duet between Pamina and Papageno—"Bei Mannërn, welche Liebe fühlen, fehlt auch ein gutes Herze nicht" (No. 7 of the score)—the praises are sung of pure love, through which beneficent nature subdues all the creatures of earth. Once more we seem to hear the all-good and all-wise Sarastro and his Priests declaiming.

10

What with one thing and another we have the feeling that it was the basic intention of Schikaneder and Mozart from the first to make the drama one of humanitarianism and ethics (with comic and romantic elements liberally thrown in), the centre of which should be the virtuous Queen of Night, and that all the later change amounted to, in fact, was the substitution of a newly-conceived Sarastro for the Queen as the mouthpiece of the most enlightened views of the period on the ideals of brotherhood, industry and art towards which humanity should now strive. To give full value to this conception a Sarastro would obviously be more serviceable than a Queen—a man rather than a woman, and a man surrounded by a grave ritual, ostensibly derived from the "Egyptian mysteries," from which woman, by the very misfortune of her sex, was excluded.

The new "pull," in fact, seems to have been towards freemasonry in one guise or another. But how did that pull come to be so strong and so decisive as it was? Shall we be wrong in ascribing it primarily to Mozart? Had there been something in him, between his first work at the text in July 1791 and his return to Vienna in September, that was calling out more and more imperiously for expression and for which *The Magic Flute*, as it had originally been, provided only an imperfect outlet? Though he did not know it, he was already a doomed man, and something in the very depths of him was calling, as it did also in the Requiem, for realisation in music—a sense of the seriousness of life and the gravity of death. In the second act of *The Magic Flute* there is manifestly a great *approfondissement* of the spirit, resulting in what we should now be calling an elderly man's music had Mozart been one who had lived out the normal span of humanity—his *Parsifal*, his *Lied von der Erde*. He attained to ethical

667

illumination in his art so much earlier than most men because he was doomed to die so early. Now freemasonry was a channel to which his spirit had instinctively turned for a long time for the outpouring of his profounder broodings. His masonic music, in particular the impressive *Maurerische Trauermusik* ("Masonic Funeral Music," K. 477),[1] has a peculiar gravity not found anywhere else in his work except in *The Magic Flute*.[2]

11

Is the suggestion too far-fetched, then, that it was from Mozart himself that the idea emanated to change the action of the opera and from the end of the first act onward to make its central motive the exposition of certain "mysteries" and "initiations"? He had perhaps already become a little weary of the dramatically thin fantastic element in the work, and doubted whether he could sustain his interest in it much further. He clearly had no desire to turn back on what he had already written, no intention of scrapping this and beginning afresh on a completely rewritten text. Into what he had composed between Nos. 1 to 7 and No. 8 he had put much of the best of himself as he then was; and he saw no reason to sacrifice this music. Overall dramatic consistency mattered little to him so long as he could now throw himself heart and soul into masonic and other "mysteries."

It would help us a good deal in our enquiry if we could discover the dates of composition of the various numbers (9 to 21) of the second act. Mozart had returned to Vienna from Prague, deeply disappointed by the failure of *La Clemenza di Tito*, about the middle of September 1791. The first performance of *The Magic Flute* took place on the 30th. On the 28th of that month he noted in his *Verzeichnis* the composition of two pieces "for the opera *Die Zauberflöte*," a March of the Priests and the overture.

[1] It was written in September 1785 on the occasion of the death of two "brothers" the Duke of Mecklenburg and Count Esterhazy.

[2] It is noteworthy, too, that the last work of his to be entered in the *Verzeichnis*, the last of his completed works, indeed, was a masonic cantata (K. 623) to words by Schikaneder. This he wrote on the 15th November 1791, for the inauguration of the second temple of the lodge *Zur neugekrönten Hoffnung*; and he himself conducted the performance of it on the 18th. Two days later he took to his bed for the last time; on the 5th December he died.

Plainly these were the last to be written, yet it is in these two that for the first time the work becomes frankly "masonic" by the insertion at the end of the March of the three solemn long-held chords, given out with the full weight of the orchestra, that are so prominent a feature of the overture. It would be interesting to know when this motif was first decided upon, for presumably Mozart must have had it in his mind, in some form or other, for a little time before committing it to paper. But we know that it was his general practice to write his overture last of all, some-times on the eve of the first performance, and the coupling in the *Verzeichnis* of the Priests' March with the overture seems to suggest that the former also was definitely decided upon at almost the last moment. Did the second act, one wonders, begin originally with the spoken dialogue between Sarastro and the Priests that follows the March in the score, the March itself being a later thought? That is a possibility, and it might account for the March not having come into being till practically the last moment. But let us now look at the second act in more detail.

12

It opens with this "March of the Priests"—so designated in the score—a strain of the utmost dignity and solemnity:

No. 7

Then Sarastro informs the assembly of "servers of the temple of Wisdom of the great gods Isis and Osiris" that it has been called together to take part in the initiation of a royal youth, Tamino, who "desires to rend his veil of darkness and see into the sanctuary of the great light." Sarastro assures them that the Prince is virtuous, silent and well-wishing, whereupon they signify their approval of the proposed initiation by sounding the three solemn B flat chords referred to above. Sarastro, having thanked them "in the name of humanity," now tells them that for this worthy youth the gods have destined a virtuous maiden, for which reason he had taken her away from her haughty mother, who, in her

669

pride, "hopes to destroy our mighty temple." In this she will not be allowed to succeed; for Tamino shall join with them in strengthening it, and, as an initiate of it, become the upholder of virtue and the scourge of evildoers. He orders the pair to be brought in, and bids the Speaker instruct them, out of his wisdom, in their duty to mankind and to the gods. After that he sings his great invocation to Isis and Osiris, commending the pair to their divine protection:

No. 8

Adagio

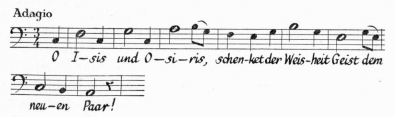

O I-sis und O-si-ris, schen-ket der Weis-heit Geist dem

neu-en Paar!

then he and the Priests depart.

13

Tamino and Papageno are now led to the porch of the temple by some of the Priests, Papageno providing an expected humorous touch by his craven fears. He is no hero, and has no desire to become one; to the Speaker he confesses that his modest desires run to nothing beyond food, drink and sleep, with a nice little wife thrown in if possible. Wisdom he can perfectly well do without; he is the Natural Man pure and simple. The Speaker half-promises him a pretty maiden named Papagena, on the condition that he exercises sufficient control of himself not to speak to her. Henceforth Tamino's manly virtues and Papageno's little human weaknesses will be shown in humorous apposition.

On Tamino, too, the Speaker lays the injunction that when he sees Pamina he shall not speak to her: this is to be the first stage of his probation, the first injunction of Wisdom, for, as two of the Priests assure him in duet, the basic law of the brotherhood is that man shall see through women's falsity and escape the ruin that invariably befalls those who trust in them. As if precisely to give point to this sage masculine advice the Three Ladies now enter to warn the young pair that they are doomed if they do not fly from this evil place at once; and Mozart builds up an admirable quintet, in easy conversational style, in which the Ladies repeat their warning, Papageno would fain back out of the adventure, and Tamino has to remind him of the virtues of silence.

As the Ladies turn to depart they are consigned to Hades by a chorus of Priests within the temple, and they sink into the earth, to the great terror of poor Papageno. Tamino, however, is congratulated by the Speaker on his steadfastness; now, he is told, he can continue his pilgrimage. The Speaker throws a veil over the Prince's head and leads him out; Papageno too is veiled and taken away, much against his will, by some of the Priests.

14

We now lose sight of the pair for a time, for Mozart has at the moment two pressing operatic tasks on his hands—to provide first Monostatos and then the Queen with an aria. The occasion for the first of these is given by a change of scene to a garden, where the Moor finds Pamina sleeping and is overcome by passion for her, the passion, he explains in a lively aria:

No. 9

that holds the whole world in its sway. Is he not also of flesh and blood? he asks; why then should he be condemned to go unloved? But if so it must be, he continues, still to the comically naïve strain of No. 9, he himself will love and bill and coo all the harder while life is in him; and he begs the moon to deny her light to the universe for a moment while he kisses the captive Pamina.

But before he can accomplish his fell design the Queen of Night appears, accompanied by a clap of thunder, and he makes an ignominious exit. Naturally the thunder has awakened Pamina. In reply to her mother's questions she discloses that the young Prince has become a devotee of the temple. "Then you have lost him forever!" cries the Queen, "for with your father's death my power came to an end; he gave of his own free will the sevenfold shield of the sun to the brotherhood, and Sarastro now wears it on his breast. But there is still a way out for us. Take this dagger—I had it specially sharpened for Sarastro—slay him, and the mighty shield is ours." Pamina is too shocked to do more than ejaculate "But, my dear mother!"; and brushing her aside the Queen launches the mighty aria of hatred and revenge that is to this day the mingled delight and terror of dramatic sopranos who pride themselves on their coloratura, or, to put it in another way, of coloratura sopranos who imagine they can be dramatic. The number of singers, however, who can reel off the difficult coloratura and at the same time convey a sense of the tornado of anger and hatred that rages at the core of it is very small.

The exit of the Queen brings Monostatos once more on the scene, and we are back for a moment to the simple humours of the first act again. The Moor would persuade Pamina that there is only one way out of her difficulties—to love him; and when she refuses he tries to stab her with the dagger left behind by her mother. In this nefarious design he is frustrated by the opportune reappearance of Sarastro, who, telling him that his soul is as black as his face, bids him depart. Monostatos' philosophical line as he goes out is one of the surest laughter-makers in the opera—"Well, if I can't have the daughter I must see what I can do with the mother."

15

It is time now for an aria for Sarastro. He speaks comfortingly to Pamina, telling her that he is well aware how her mother haunts the subterranean vaults of the temple, breathing fire and slaughter against him and all mankind. In due course he will take the right revenge on her; but for the present the great thing is to endow the Prince with courage and steadfastness in his pious purpose. For that the Prince, it appears, has come to the right place, for, as he explains in a noble aria:

No. 10

Larghetto

In die-sen heil'-gen Hal—len kennt man die Ra-che nicht,

within these hallowed halls revenge has no place;[1] if a man has fallen, he must be raised up again by friendship and love.

They both go off, and with another change of scene we find ourselves in a large hall, into which the Speaker and the Priests conduct Tamino and Papageno, leaving them to themselves immediately, however, with the injunction that they are to maintain silence or be punished by the gods with thunder and lightning. The Prince obeys this command as well as Papageno will allow him to do, for soon there enters an old woman who brings Papageno a welcome cup of water, declares that she is only eighteen years and two minutes old, and tells him that she has a lover ten years older—whose name happens to be Papageno. But when he asks her own name there comes a clap of thunder, the old woman disappears, and Three Genii enter with a table (spread with food), Tamino's flute and Papageno's chime of bells. In a pleasant little trio they speak some words of comfort to the two men, exhorting the one to have courage, the other to keep silence; then they disappear. No sooner have they gone, and Papageno is beginning to compliment his absent host Sarastro on the quality of his viands and his wine, than Pamina comes in. Mortified to find that Tamino will not respond to anything she says, and seems indeed, anxious to get rid of her, she pours out her grief over a lost illusion in an expressive air in G minor:

No. 11

Ach, ich fühl's, es ist ver—schwun-den, e—wig hin der Lie-be
Glück!

If he no longer loves her she will be content to die.

[1] At first sight this may seem inconsistent with what he has said a moment before about "revenge" on the Queen; but there is really no contradiction. His "revenge" on her will be to nullify her attempt to "revenge herself" on Sarastro and all mankind, by rescuing the young Prince from her coils and making him an instrument for the highest good.

As she leaves them a peal of trumpets is heard—evidently the summons to the tribunal—and the two go out after the usual little witticisms from Papageno, for Schikaneder has taken good care that whatever may happen to the drama of noble sentiments, *he* will always be within call to get an easy laugh. With another change of scene we are transported to a vault beneath the temple, where Sarastro and the Priests are assembled. In a chorus of grave beauty the Priests commend the noble youth on trial to the favour of Isis and Osiris, for his heart is pure, his soul is brave, and he will prove himself worthy of admittance to their company. First Tamino is brought in, then Pamina—to receive, so Sarastro informs her, Tamino's last farewell. This leads to an expressive trio in which Pamina laments her sad lot, Tamino protests his undying love, and Sarastro exhorts them both to be brave and bow to the decree of the brotherhood, for the separation will not last forever.

The three go out, leaving Papageno alone, and it is now Schikaneder's turn once more. The Speaker enters to tell Papageno that owing to the incurable earthiness of his nature he can never be admitted to the company of the blessed, but that the gratification of such common appetites as his will not be denied him. He asks for a cup of wine, and one rises from the ground. But that is not enough for him; accompanying himself with his chime of bells he sings, in his simple, charming fashion, of his desire for a nice little wife after his own heart:

No. 12

Andante

Ein Mäd-chen o-der Weib —chen wünscht Pa-pa-ge-no—sich,

The song over, the old woman presents herself again, transforms herself into a young girl, tells him her name is Papagena, and gives him her hand. But just as he is about to embrace her the spoil-sport of a Speaker enters, tells the maiden that Papageno is not worthy of her yet, and sends them both away.

16

We now meet again with the Three Genii, who sing a dignified little trio in praise of the rising sun, before which superstition shall vanish from the earth and Wisdom and Peace come into their own. We have now entered on the finale. This is by far the most extended and the most unified of all the "numbers" of the work: at last Mozart is free to develop his musical-dramatic plan organically according to his heart's desire, with only a few irrelevances from outside.

Pamina enters, half-crazed and carrying a dagger; soon, she declares, she will be united with her loved and lost Tamino in death. As she raises the dagger the Three Genii stay her arm, assuring her that what Tamino is doing is all for love for her, though the secret meaning of his apparent indifference they cannot as yet disclose.

With a change of tempo to adagio, and with trombones lending a solemnity of their own to the situation, the music now attains its profoundest depth of feeling. Wailing figures of this type:

No. 13

repeat themselves in one mutation after another in the orchestra, while through the texture Two Men in Armour steadily intone an old German chorale: the whole episode is a masterly reversion to the chorale prelude form in which Bach achieved such wonders.

From within comes the sound of Pamina's voice calling to Tamino, and now the Two Men in Armour grant him permission to speak to her. The temple gates open, Pamina appears, and the lovers greet each other ecstatically. She bids him place his trust in the flute, which, we now learn, had been carved by her father in a magic hour out of a centuries-old oak tree; and their voices and those of the Two Men in Armour unite in a quartet in praise of the marvellous instrument. With Tamino playing a long melody on it the lovers survive the ordeal of passing first through fire, then through water: then the gates of the temple are thrown open, the scene is flooded with light, and a chorus within hails the triumph of the virtuous pair and bids them enter the shrine of Isis.

But there is still the irrepressible Schikaneder to be reckoned with. The scene changes to a garden, in which Papageno, playing on his pipes (No. 2), calls piteously on his Papagena to appear and make him happy. He is on the point of hanging himself, with much comic by-play, when the Three Genii arrive in the nick of time to frustrate that dire intent. On their advice he sets his chimes pealing; and soon Papagena appears, and the two children of nature express their joy in a duet that is one of Mozart's most delightful creations.

Even after this the road is not quite open to Mozart to end the drama. There comes a short serio-comic episode in which Monostatos ushers in the Queen and her Three Ladies: they have come to destroy the temple, the hand of Pamina being Monostatos' reward for his participation in the scheme. But a great upheaval of the elements—thunder, lightning and tempest—fills them with terror, and they sink impotently into the depths. The stage is flooded with light, and we see Sarastro in all his glory with Tamino, Pamina and the Priests. Sarastro hails the victory of moral light over darkness, and the chorus gives thanks to Isis and Osiris, who have brought the steadfast pair of lovers to the successful end of their trials. "Beauty and Wisdom and Strength and Constancy of spirit have triumphed over the forces of evil," they continue; and the opera ends in general jubilation.

17

The score of *The Magic Flute* is of great importance in the history of the development of German opera; but in the foregoing pages we have had to confine ourselves mainly to exposition pure and simple of the course of the action. The work has perhaps been rather over-written during the last century and a half, especially in Germany, where undue stress has been laid on its "ethical" virtues—its laudation of Virtue, Justice, Humanity, Universal Brotherhood, and all the rest of it. These academic expressions seem a little fly-blown today, and we have got past the stage when we can take a work of art to our bosoms merely because it spouts lofty sentiments: in a work of art it is only the art that finally matters. Still, these sentiments played a large part in making the music of such works as *The Magic Flute* and the choral finale of the Ninth Symphony what it is, and so we must be content, for the time being, and for purely artistic reasons, to accept them at the valuation Mozart and Beethoven placed on them, just as when watching *Hamlet* we do not admit that ghosts exist, but merely suspend temporarily, for the sole purpose of playing the game along the lines laid down by the poet, our disbelief in them.

The familiar overture hardly calls for detailed analysis. It opens:

No. 14

with the threefold "masonic" chords (now in the key of E flat major instead of in B flat as in the opera) which, as we have seen, had played so impressive a part in the action after the March of the Priests at the beginning of the second act. The grave adagio introduction to the overture (lasting only fifteen bars) leads into an allegro section based on a subject:

No. 15

that looks at first as if it were going to be the basis of a fugue, but is actually treated later in a free sonata style, with a great deal of contrapuntal device. Half-way through this development of it the three *tutti* chords strike in again with arresting effect. Much has been written, especially in Germany, of the profoundly "symbolic" nature of the overture. Without being able to subscribe to all this, we are at any rate conscious that in some strange way Mozart's imagination was playing strongly on the dramatic and psychological framework of the action, without even as much thematic quotation from the opera itself as he had permitted himself in the *Don Giovanni* overture.

Index

i